HUSBANDS & WIVES

HUSBANDS & WIVES

**Howard & Jeanne Hendricks, General Editors
with LaVonne Neff**

VICTOR BOOKS ®

A DIVISION OF SCRIPTURE PRESS PUBLICATIONS INC.
USA CANADA ENGLAND

Recommended Dewey Decimal Classification: 155.645
Suggested Subject Heading: MARRIAGE

Library of Congress Catalog Card Number: 88-60209
ISBN: 0-89693-302-4

CONTENTS

CHAPTER 15 • Divorce

CHAPTER 16 • Where to Find Help

CONTRIBUTORS

Mr. Robert Arnold
Executive Director
Metro Maryland Youth for Christ
Baltimore, Maryland

Dr. & Mrs. Bruce Barton (Mitzie)
Vice President/Ministry Services
Youth for Christ/USA
Wheaton, Illinois

Dr. & Mrs. V. Gilbert Beers (Arlisle)
Gil—Author, Editor
Arlie—Homemaker
Elgin, Illinois

Mr. Gary D. Bennett
Administrative Staff
Delta-Thumb Youth for Christ
Marlette, Michigan

Jo Berry
Author, Speaker
Granada Hills, California

Mr. & Mrs. Ronald W. Blue (Judith)
Ron—Managing Partner/Ronald Blue & Co.
Judy—Speaker, Teacher
Atlanta, Georgia

Mr. & Mrs. Pat Boone (Shirley)
Entertainers, Speakers, Authors
Burbank, California

Dale Hanson Bourke
President
Publishing Directions
Washington, D.C.

Dr. D. Stuart Briscoe
Senior Pastor/Elmbrook Church, Author
Waukesha, Wisconsin

Mr. & Mrs. Andre Bustanoby (Fay)
Andre—Marriage and Family Therapist
Fay—Homemaker
Bowie, Maryland

Margaret Davidson Campolo
Writer, Editor
St. Davids, Pennsylvania

Dr. Gary D. Chapman
Director of Adult Ministries
Calvary Baptist Church
Winston-Salem, North Carolina

Evelyn Christenson
Founder and Chairman of the Board
United Prayer Ministries
Minneapolis, Minnesota

Mr. & Mrs. Larry Christenson (Nordis)
Director
International Lutheran Renewal Center
St. Paul, Minnesota

Mr. & Mrs. Randall Cirner (Therese)
Marriage and Family Life Seminar Speakers
Ann Arbor, Michigan

Dr. & Mrs. John J. Colligan (Kathleen)
Codirectors
Pastoral and Matrimonial Renewal Center
Endwell, New York

Dr. & Mrs. Gary R. Collins (Julie)
Gary—Professor of Psychology, Trinity
Evangelical Divinity School
Julie—Registered Nurse, Diet Center
Counselor
Kildeer, Illinois

Dr. & Mrs. Jim Conway (Sally)
Directors
Mid-Life Dimensions
Fullerton, California

Win Couchman
Special Representative
International Teams Mission
Menomonee Falls, Wisconsin

Mr. Howard L. Dayton, Jr.
Founder
Crown Ministries
Longwood, Florida

Dr. Arthur H. DeKruyter
Founding Pastor
Christ Church of Oak Brook
Oak Brook, Illinois

Mr. & Mrs. Byron Emmert (Linda)
Special Representative
Youth for Christ
Mountain Lake, Minnesota

Dr. Ted W. Engstrom
President Emeritus
World Vision
Pasadena, California

Mr. George Fooshee, Jr.
Business Consultant
Associated Credit Services
Wichita, Kansas

Mr. David Foster
Freelance Writer
Jackson, Mississippi

Dr. Garry Friesen
Author, Professor
Portland, Oregon

Mr. & Mrs. Bob Fryling (Alice)
Bob—Vice President / InterVarsity Christian
Fellowship
Alice—Freelance Writer, Homemaker
Madison, Wisconsin

Dr. & Mrs. James C. Galvin (Kathe)
Training Director
Youth for Christ/USA
Wheaton, Illinois

Dr. & Mrs. Kenneth O. Gangel (Elizabeth)
Kenn—Chairman/Christian Education De-
partment, Dallas Seminary
Betty—Author, Seminar Leader
Rockwall, Texas

Mr. John Gillies
Director of Communication
Presbyterian Children's Home and Service
Agency
Austin, Texas

Patricia Gundry
Freelance Writer, Speaker
Grand Rapids, Michigan

Dr. & Mrs. Howard Hendricks (Jeanne)
Howard—Professor/Department of Christian
Education, Dallas Seminary
Jeanne—Author, Speaker
Dallas, Texas

Dr. & Mrs. Robert Hicks (Cynthia)
Minister of Family Life Development
Church of the Saviour
Berwyn, Pennsylvania

Mr. & Mrs. William Hochstettler (Jeannie)
Executive Director
Palm Beach County Youth for Christ
West Palm Beach, Florida

Mr. & Mrs. J.D. Holt (Christy)
Conference and Production Coordinator
Youth for Christ/USA
Wheaton, Illinois

Dr. & Mrs. R. Kent Hughes (Barbara)
Pastor
College Church in Wheaton
Wheaton, Illinois

Mr. & Mrs. Keith Hunt (Gladys)
Keith—Special Assistant to the President of
InterVarsity
Gladys—Freelance Writer, Historian for
InterVarsity
Ann Arbor, Michigan

Dr. & Mrs. Joel Hunter (Becky)
Senior Pastor
Northland Community Church
Longwood, Florida

Mr. & Mrs. Dave Jackson (Neta)
Self-employed Writers/Editors
Evanston, Illinois

Mr. & Mrs. Mark Jevert (Debbie)
Executive Director
Youth for Christ of the Kalamazoo Area
Kalamazoo, Michigan

Dr. & Mrs. Donald Joy (Robbie)
Don—Professor of Human Development
and Christian Education / Asbury Seminary
Robbie—Reading Specialist and Curriculum
Writer
Wilmore, Kentucky

Dr. Jay Kesler
President
Taylor University
Upland, Indiana

Mr. Earnie Larsen
E. Larsen Enterprises, Inc.
Brooklyn Park, Minnesota

Dr. Judith C. Lechman
Freelance Writer, Workshop Leader and
Lecturer
Williamston, North Carolina

Dr. Kevin Leman
Psychologist, Consultant and Speaker,
Author, Family Seminar Leader
Tucson, Arizona

Mr. & Mrs. David Mace (Vera)
Directors/Founders of the Association of
Couples for Marriage Enrichment
Black Mountain, North Carolina

Dr. & Mrs. David Mains (Karen)
Director/Cohosts of Chapel of the Air
West Chicago, Illinois

Mr. Mike Mason
Author
Hope, British Columbia

Mr. & Mrs. Jack Mayhall (Carole)
Marriage and Family Discipleship
Department
The Navigators
Colorado Springs, Colorado

Mr. Josh McDowell
Josh McDowell Ministry
Campus Crusade for Christ
Richardson, Texas

Dr. Richard A. Meier
Marriage and Family Counselor
Minirth-Meier Clinic, P.A.
Richardson, Texas

Mr. Dean Merrill
Editor
Christian Herald magazine
Danbury, Connecticut

Dr. Calvin Miller
Senior Pastor
Westside Baptist Church
Omaha, Nebraska

LaVonne Neff
Editorial Consultant
Wheaton, Illinois

Dr. Wayne E. Oates
Professor of Psychology and Behavioral
Sciences
University of Louisville
Louisville, Kentucky

Janette Oke
Author
Didsbury, Alberta

Dr. James H. Olthuis
Senior Member in Theology and Ethics
Institute for Christian Studies
Toronto, Ontario

Dr. Luis Palau
President
Luis Palau Evangelistic Association
Portland, Oregon

Mr. & Mrs. Dennis Rainey (Barbara)
National Director/Family Ministry
Campus Crusade for Christ
Roland, Arkansas

Dr. George A. Rekers
Professor of Neuropsychiatry and Behavior-
al Science
University of South Carolina School of
Medicine
Columbia, South Carolina

Mr. & Mrs. Rolly Richert (Sandy)
Vice President/Communications
Youth for Christ/USA
Wheaton, Illinois

Mr. Jeff Ringenberg
Campus Life Staff
Youth for Christ of Dane County
Madison, Wisconsin

Mr. & Mrs. David Roper (Carolyn)
David—Senior Pastor/Cole Community
Church
Carolyn—Director of Cole Women's
Ministries
Boise, Idaho

Dr. Charles M. Sell
Professor/Christian Education
Trinity Evangelical Divinity School
Vernon Hills, Illinois

Luci Shaw
President
Harold Shaw Publishers
Wheaton, Illinois

Judith Allen Shelly
Eastern Area Director
Nurses Christian Fellowship
Frederick, Pennsylvania

Dr. Dwight Hervey Small
Professor Emeritus/Marriage Studies
Westmont College
Santa Barbara, California

Mr. Gary Smalley
President
Today's Family
Phoenix, Arizona

Mr. Jim Smith
Executive Director
Family Life Counseling Center
Dallas, Texas

Lynda Rutledge Stephenson
Author, Writer
Downers Grove, Illinois

Dr. Judson Swihart
Director
International Family Center
Manhattan, Kansas

Joni Eareckson Tada
President
Joni and Friends
Agoura Hills, California

Mr. & Mrs. Thomas Taylor (Linda)
Writers, Editors
Youth for Christ/USA
Wheaton, Illinois

Dr. John K. Testerman, M.D.
Family Doctor
Glendale Family Practice
Glendale Heights, Illinois

Rev. John Robert Throop
Executive Director
Episcopalians United
Shaker Heights, Ohio

Kristine Tomasik
Author, Editor, Educator
Oak Park, Illinois

Dr. John Trent
Associate Director
Today's Family
Phoenix, Arizona

Ingrid Trobisch
Author
Springfield, Missouri

Mr. & Mrs. David Veerman (Gail)
Author, Speaker, Veteran Youth Minister
Naperville, Illinois

Mr. & Mrs. Norm Wakefield (Winnie)
Marriage and Family Life Consultant
Phoenix, Arizona

Dr. Ed Wheat, M.D.
Family Physician, Certified Sex Therapist,
Marriage Counselor
Springdale, Arkansas

Dr. & Mrs. Jerry White (Mary)
President
The Navigators
Colorado Springs, Colorado

Mr. Pat Williams
President, General Manager
Orlando Magic Basketball Club
Orlando, Florida

Dr. & Mrs. Wesley R. Willis (Elaine)
Senior Vice President
Scripture Press Publications, Inc.
Wheaton, Illinois

Dr. & Mrs. Earl Wilson (Sandy)
Earl—Lake Psychological Counseling
Center
Sandy—Lay Counseling Program
Lake Oswego, Oregon

Mary Jane Worden
Homemaker
Austin, Texas

Dr. H. Norman Wright
Founder, Director
Christian Marriage Enrichment
Long Beach, California

Mr. Zig Ziglar
Chairman of the Board
The Zig Ziglar Corporation
Carrollton, Texas

General Editors
Howard & Jeanne Hendricks
LaVonne Neff

Managing Editors
Ronald A. Beers
Greg D. Clouse
Linda Chaffee Taylor

Special Consultants
Bruce Barton
Jim Galvin
David Veerman

PREFACE

Christian marriage is the ultimate merger. It calls two different persons to blend into a unique mixture without losing their identities. No forcing a square peg into a round hole, pinching one and pulling another. Rather, God planted a magnet inside His creatures. One shares another without losing oneness. Two bond into a unit without two-ness. The Bible calls it a mystery. We may describe some of its parts; we can only experience its fullness.

To snatch the wisps of feeling and longing, of conviction and regret that swirl over us, and to commandeer them into a disciplined task force of words is a formidable job. To hold with rational enclosure the divine plan for marriage and to suggest a blueprint for a contemporary quake-proof husband/wife team requires meticulous work. Each heart beats personally; each head perceives a private idea. Each couple shares a private linkage like no other.

Our own confidence grows out of 40 years of faithfulness in the God who brought together these two green shoots, a couple of kids from Philadelphia who really had only two donations to bring to the wedding party: wildly enthusiastic commitment to each other, and deep dedication to our Lord and Saviour Jesus Christ. It was enough. He has held us firmly and walked us through the swamps and the deserts as well as the green meadows and quiet woods. His presence has held us together and nourished our spirits. It's not just marriage, but Christian marriage that really works.

Howard & Jeanne Hendricks
Dallas, Texas 1988

INTRODUCTION *DISCUSSION STARTER*

Answer these questions with your spouse, or answer them separately and then discuss them together.

1. What is marriage? Check all the words that apply to yours:
   - companionship
   - contract
   - economic unit
   - lifetime commitment
   - sacred union
   - sexual relationship
   - team
   - _____
   - _____

2. What can you give to your marriage partner?
   - affirmation
   - affection
   - companionship
   - emotional support
   - enabling
   - encouragement
   - excitement
   - faithfulness
   - friendship
   - handyman skills
   - hard work
   - help
   - housekeeping skills
   - insights
   - listening skills
   - loyalty
   - material support
   - openness to change
   - organization
   - physical love
   - responsibility
   - roots
   - steadiness
   - understanding
   - unselfishness
   - willingness to spend time
   - wings
   - _____
   - _____
   - _____

WHAT GOD HAS JOINED TOGETHER

Marriage: A Vehicle of God's Love

ARTHUR H. DeKRUYTER

We Christians know that marriage is not an accident of history. Marriage is God's gift. He instituted it and means it to be a source of happiness and fulfillment. In His wisdom and creative power, He gave us the capacity for a relationship as intimate and permanent as anything on earth can be. Because of its depth, it is the source of the greatest joy—but it also carries with it the possibility of the greatest heartache.

It is a unique and wonderful experience to love and be loved so profoundly that both body and soul are surrendered to one another in a lifetime covenant. It is even better to know that such a relationship is not an accident, but that God wants you to love and enjoy each other. To recognize Him as the direct cause of your marriage is to respond with gratitude. He uses each partner to minister to the other. He loved you enough to give your spouse to you, and He uses you together as a vehicle of His love.

Because God's love for you is unconditional, it provides a great sense of security. You do not have to be good enough to represent Him to your spouse. His love is unfailing and will, on every occasion, enable you to minister to every need. You do not have to be perfect to receive your spouse's love. God's love tells you that all your disappointments, losses, and heartaches are shared by Him. Sin and evil are not sent by Him, but through it all, He provides and sends His enabling Spirit. Ultimately, God will triumph through you as you claim His love and open your heart to Him.

Does this sound idealistic? Nonsense! This is the most practical aspect of the Christian faith. God's love is the cement of marriage. Without it, there is nothing transcendent to inspire us. Let me share with you the way in which God's love has given my wife and me the liberty to love each other.

Our courtship began while I was in seminary. We both knew we were headed for the ministry and shared a deep sense of calling and commitment. My wife had many talents that complemented my own, and together we made a team with interests in music as well as the ministry of the Word.

Soon after our marriage, 38 years ago, I discovered that my wife was blessed not only with a great faith and a heart of love for God's people, but also with a capacity for work that exceeded my own. She could work longer hours and endure more tedium in the routine tasks that demanded perseverance. She

17

loved to share in the work of the church, and nothing was ever too much to ask of her.

Two years after our marriage, our daughter was born. Six months later my wife had her first heart attack. Imagine our shock when we learned from a specialist that she would eventually become unable to function and would need heart surgery, which in those days was extremely dangerous. We postponed the procedure as long as we could, but after five years of misery, we had to go through with it.

My wife survived the initial surgery as well as a subsequent surgery for valve replacement, but she has spent the last 35 years in and out of hospitals. Her physical vitality is limited, and for her this has been extremely frustrating. All the things she had dreamed of doing have been curtailed, and some of them have been totally suspended. During the last few years she has been especially limited.

I suppose we could have found many reasons to feel sorry for ourselves. But both of us are convinced that God loves us. He has called and guided us, and He will support us regardless of our worth. He has not made any mistakes in our lives. Just because we do not understand does not mean He has abdicated. Rather, we have found that through our trials He has opened up to us many new and enlarged areas of ministry.

We cannot imagine that we needed this kind of burden. But we know that God's love is anchored in His wisdom and grace, and this provides a stable basis for our faith. God's presence is a source of strength to us, just as it was to Joseph in prison or Isaiah in the temple when the king died.

Marriage is not built on convenience, success, health, or prosperity. It is a covenant between two people who are loved by God. When we understand this, we are prepared to live with life's difficulties and disappointments. If the intrusion of sin in this world results in personal suffering, God's grace is always sufficient. I know He loves my wife, and therefore He ministers to her through me. His love gives me a capacity to love, and it gives her a capacity to receive His love through me. My wife and I put no conditions on our loving service to each other and ask no questions regarding a trade-off of responsibilities, burdens, or duties.

Deeper than that, because all that we are we owe to God, we willingly use our abilities to serve as He directs. Life is therefore never a burden. We treasure each other because God loved us enough to give us an intimate covenant—marriage, the closest relationship this side of heaven.

I hope you have the same experience in your trials and losses. Keep your eyes upon Jesus, live in His love, and you will enjoy a married life that exceeds your fondest dreams.

Related Articles

Is Christian Marriage Any Different?

RANDY & THERESE CIRNER

Several New Testament passages refer directly to Christian marriage. Many Christians fail to understand that while the rest is not specifically speaking to husbands and wives, the same scriptural principles apply in the marriage relationship as in the rest of our relationships. One of the most important New Testament principles is the Lord's teaching on love.

The love God has for us, called *agape* in the Greek, is a love that wants nothing but the highest good for the other person. To love our husbands, to love our wives as God Himself loves us—that's pretty overwhelming, isn't it? In fact, it would be totally impossible to achieve this kind of Christian love without the power of the Holy Spirit and the grace of God.

What does *agape* love look like in practice? It is not based on emotions. Instead it is the commitment we have to one another. When we marry we declare that we will love and care for and serve our spouse, and we are supposed to live in accordance with that declaration—regardless of how we're feeling at any given moment. It is *agape* love that makes Christian marriage different from secular marriage. Look at the differences that should be evident, as illustrated in the accompanying chart (p. 20).

In a Christian marriage, as the chart shows, each individual and the couple together have committed themselves and their marriage to Jesus Christ. He is their firm foundation, the rock mentioned in Matthew 7:24-27. Unless a marriage is grounded and rooted in Jesus Christ, the waves and wind of stress, temptation, and trial—the everyday ins and outs that we all experience—are likely to destroy it. And every marriage will experience stresses, whether financial, sexual, or relational; every marriage will have problems with fatigue, with children, with relatives. The marriages that last are the ones founded on Jesus Christ.

If you are not a Christian, we encourage you to get down on your knees right now and give your life to Jesus Christ. He is reaching out to you; He wants to touch your life and save you and your marriage. If you are already a Christian but have not committed your marriage to be ruled by the Lord Jesus Christ and His scriptural principles, we invite you now to get down on your knees together and commit your marriage to Him. Ask Him to be Lord of your marriage. Welcome Him in. Study Scripture together, and then ask God for the wisdom He desires to give you so you can have a victorious Christian marriage.

In the words of the Apostle Paul: "I urge you to live a life worthy of the calling you have received. Be completely humble and gentle; be patient, bearing with one another in love. Make every effort to keep the unity of the Spirit through the bond of peace" (Eph. 4:1-3).

Related Articles
Chapter 3: Making the Right Choice
Chapter 5: Husbands and Wives
    With Jesus as Lord

AREA OF LIFE	CHRISTIAN	SECULAR
individual	committed to Jesus Christ	committed to self-fulfillment and personal rights
couple	centered on Jesus	centered on personal happiness
goal	unity—one mind/heart/life	individual satisfaction, success
power source	the Holy Spirit	personal motivation, personality strength
marriage vows	life commitment, sexual fidelity, loyalty	as long as it works and allows me to be a "full person"
love	*agape* love rules	erotic love, attraction, circumstances, and feelings rule
ideal	a family that knows, loves, and serves God	personal happiness
children	an integral part of the union, whether biological, foster, or adopted	none or few, at convenience of career or personal pleasure
home	a place of refreshment for family and others, a place from which to serve others	a refuge from the world and responsibilities; a place for a woman to express her individuality through her home decorating taste and skill
end result	unity, peace, and joy in serving Christ and His kingdom	marriage often partially or totally unsatisfying; high rate of divorce

The Invasion of Intimacy

MIKE MASON

Marriage is the closest bond that is possible between two human beings. That, at least, was the original idea behind it. It was to be something unique, without parallel or precedent. In the sheer sweep and radical abandon of its commitment, it was to transcend every other form of human union on earth, every other covenant that could possibly be made between two people. Friendship, parent-child, master-pupil—marriage would surpass all these other bonds in a whole constellation of remarkable ways, including equality of the partners, permanent commitment, cohabitation, sexual relations, and the spontaneous creation of blood ties through simple spoken promises. As it was originally designed, marriage was a union to end all unions, the very last word, and the first, in human intimacy. Socially, legally, physically, emotionally, every which way, there is just no other means of getting closer to another human being, and never has been, than in marriage.

Such extraordinary closeness is bought at a cost, and the cost is nothing more nor less than one's own self. No one has ever been married without being shocked at the enormity of this price and at the monstrous inconvenience of this thing called intimacy which suddenly invades their life. At the wedding a bride and groom may have gone through the motions of the candle-lighting ceremony, each blowing out their own flame and lighting one central candle in place of the two, but the touching simplicity of this ritual has little in common with the actual day-to-day pressures involved as two persons are merged into one. It is a different matter when the flame that must be extinguished is no lambent flicker of a candle, but the blistering inferno of self-will and independence. There is really nothing else like this lifelong cauterization of the ego that must take place in marriage. All of life is, in one way or another, humbling. But there is nothing like the experience of being humbled by another person, and by the same person day in and day out. It can be exhausting, unnerving, infuriating, disintegrating. There is no suffering like the suffering involved in being close to another person. But neither is there any joy nor any real comfort at all outside of intimacy, outside the joy and the comfort that are wrung out like wine from the crush and ferment of two lives being pressed together.

What happens to a couple when they fall in love, when they pitch headlong into this winepress of intimacy, is not simply that they are swept off their feet: more than that, it is the very ground they are standing on, the whole world and ground of their own separate selves, that is swept away. A person in love cannot help becoming, in some sense, a new person. . . . The very next step in human closeness, beyond marriage, would be just to scrap the original man and woman and create one new human being out of the two. . . .

Everywhere else, throughout society, there are fences, walls, burglar alarms, unlisted numbers, the most elaborate precautions for keeping people at a safe distance. But in marriage all of that is reversed. In marriage the walls are down, and not only do the man and woman live under the same roof, but they sleep under the same covers. Their lives are wide open, and as each studies the life of the other and attempts to make some response to it, there are no set procedures to follow, no formalities to stand on. A man and woman face each other across the breakfast table, and somehow through a haze of crumbs and curlers and mortgage payments they must encounter one another. That is the whole purpose and mandate of marriage. All sorts of other purposes have been dreamed up and millions of excuses invented for avoiding this central and indispensable task. But the fact is that marriage is grounded in nothing else but the pure wild grappling of soul with soul, no holds barred. . . .

Good marriages are the foundation of society. They are seeds, or cell groups, pointing the way to man's great dream of Utopia, which is fundamentally his urgent longing for the kingdom of God. It is the church, of course, which is the true harbinger of the kingdom. But not even in the church does the dedication of one particular human being to another turn out in practical terms to be so all-embracing, so fleshly, so deep and searing and permanent as it is in the lifelong eating-sleeping-thinking-together bond of marriage.

[Excerpted from *The Mystery of Marriage*, Multnomah Press, 1985, pp. 71-76. Used by permission.]

Related Articles
Chapter 1: Love Always Hurts
Chapter 2: Stages of Intimacy
     in Marriage
Chapter 4: Identity and Intimacy

Three Essentials for a Successful Marriage

DAVID & VERA MACE

We live near Mount Mitchell, North Carolina, the highest peak east of the Rockies. One late afternoon the man for whom the mountain was named, after climbing the peak, took a shortcut, hoping to get down quickly. Unhappily, he missed his footing and fell to his death.

Something like that is happening to half of all new marriages in the USA today. Couples seeking happiness take shortcuts, get in trouble, and end the relationship in divorce.

Imagine John and Mary standing at the altar, taking their marriage vows. How well do they understand the task that lies before them? In many cases, hardly at all. They expect lifelong happiness as a free gift.

Would they expect lifelong success in their careers without learning what is required, practicing new skills, and doing plenty of hard work? Of course not. But they expect marriage to succeed without learning, without practicing, without working. No wonder many marriages fail.

Let's look at the essentials for a suc-

cessful marriage. There are three of them.

1. *You've got to work at it.* We once lived on a street containing a vacant lot. Somebody bought it, planning to put a house there. One day a huge truck drove up, unloaded a three-story house, and dumped it on the lot. Next day the family moved in and settled down.

You know that isn't true. What really happened was that many trucks brought many loads of bricks, sand, lumber, and a lot more. Then, over time, the house was gradually put together by skilled workers. The house is still standing there today.

A marriage is built in the same way. John and Mary each bring a big pile of materials—the habits, attitudes, and values they have learned in their earlier years. Slowly, these all have to be fitted together and adjusted to each other—not by expert builders, but by John and Mary themselves. If they want lasting happiness, they had better do the necessary work.

So the first essential for a good mar-

SONNET 116 (17TH CENTURY)

Let me not to the marriage of true minds
Admit impediments. Love is not love
Which alters when it alteration finds,
Or bends with the remover to remove.
O, no! it is an ever-fixed mark,
That looks on tempests and is never shaken;
It is the star to every wandering bark,
Whose worth's unknown, although his height be taken.
Love's not Time's fool, though rosy lips and cheeks
Within his bending sickle's compass come;
Love alters not with his brief hours and weeks,
But bears it out even to the edge of doom.
 If this be error and upon me proved,
 I never writ, nor no man ever loved.

William Shakespeare

riage is *commitment*—readiness to work, long and hard, at the task of building a marriage. Nobody else can do this for you. The vows you take on your wedding day mean, "In the presence of God, we promise to work long and hard together till we have built a good marriage which will last a lifetime."

2. *You must do it together.* There's no way *one* of you can build the marriage alone, while the other sits back and watches. It's a joint task. And the first requirement is that you must develop an effective system of communication, so that each always knows what the other is feeling, thinking, and planning.

In the last 20 years we have learned a great deal about couple communication. Each member of the couple must be aware of what is going on in the mind of the other. You don't do that with most people in your life. You don't need to— many personal things you just keep to yourself. But in a relationship as close as marriage, you are living a shared life; and if you don't know what the other person is feeling, thinking, and planning, you'll soon be in trouble. In our marriage we have learned every day to have a

"sharing time" when we really open up to each other, so there can be no possibility of misunderstanding. That way we can keep in tune as the days go by.

It is essential in marriage always to speak "the truth, the whole truth, and nothing but the truth." Only by doing that can you achieve a close relationship that you can completely trust.

3. *You must learn to manage anger.* This is the hardest of the three essentials, because many people just don't understand it. So let us explain.

As Christians, we sometimes think it is sinful to feel angry. But that is not so. Anger is an emotion that always first develops below the level of the conscious mind. You never make yourself angry; but once you *are* angry, you are responsible for what you do about it. While defending yourself is sometimes necessary, that should never be necessary with someone with whom you are sharing a love relationship.

So what do you do when you become angry with each other? This is something that often happens in a close relationship, and married couples do often fight. But that is unfortunate and only alienates them from each other. What else is possible?

There is an answer to that question, and we hope that someday all couples will learn it. In marriage, behind your anger there is always a feeling of being *hurt*. In other words, anger is always a signal that the close relationship between husband and wife isn't working properly. You have to learn how to *use* the anger by getting behind it to the hurt feeling deeper down, working diligently till you clear it up, and then renewing the love relationship.

We admit that this is hard work, and it takes some skill. But until the husband and wife learn this vital lesson, they are in danger of drifting apart and putting protective distance between them. That is tragic, because it ends their chance of building a really close relationship. How much better to work through all the anger situations, one by one, until love and trust prevail. Then, and only then, can they enjoy a truly happy relationship.

Marriage is a lifelong task. We have tried to explain the three essentials for a successful marriage. Please understand that you can't get by without them. Without commitment, you just won't be able to do the necessary work. Without open communication, you just won't stay in touch with each other or understand what is happening to the relationship. Without healing the hurts that can happen to each of you, you can't reach the trustful closeness that makes a marriage truly fulfilling and enduring.

It's up to you. Marriages don't just happen. They have to be built, like houses, and then lived in. A really good marriage is the best gift life can offer, and so it is worth every effort to achieve it.

Marriage Is a Relationship

PATRICIA GUNDRY

What is marriage anyway? This question came up for me years ago when I was doing research for a book on marriage. It occurred to me that unless I defined marriage, which no one else had seemed to think necessary, I wouldn't really have a basis for talking about it.

Researching the history of marriage, I discovered that it has been different things in different times and places, and among people with differing backgrounds and from different social strata. So how was *I* going to define marriage?

The Bible reflects the culture of the time. It talks about marriage as it was for those people in their own places and times, much as it talks about shepherding, parenting, soldiering, and selling. The Bible uses marriage sometimes as an illustration, taking what people knew about marriage from experience to expand their understanding of something else. Because the Bible was written over a considerable span of time and in different cultural environments, it presents several kinds of marriage experiences. So you can't really point to the Bible for a definition of marriage.

But what is marriage, in its basic essence? What is it now that has some connection with what it has always been? I found only one constant: *mar-*

riage is a relationship.

Of course, you may say, "I knew that, everyone knows that." Well, maybe—and maybe not. Because if marriage is basically and above all a relationship, then it cannot be viewed primarily as a legal obligation or a religious bond or a state of existence or a family responsibility or what one does to be accepted in society. If it is first and foremost a relationship, then it can be studied in the light of what we know about relationships. And that has important implications.

We know that relationships can ebb and flow, that they can grow uncomfortable and unfair, that they must be treated with respect if they are to continue, that they must be invested in if they are to be satisfying. Most of all, we know that relationships are the business and concern of the people involved in them.

For many years now, the church has been intimately involved in the relationships of people who choose to marry. This has not always been so. In fact, it may not have been an altogether good idea for the church to get involved in the marriage ceremony, because the church's involvement has tended to obscure the reasons for marriage and to separate the relationship from its reasonable and necessary roots. Because of the church, getting married has become a *religious* experience rather than an *interpersonal* one, and that has made it harder for the participants to understand the basic relational nature of their union and to give it the care it needs. The marriage too often gets to be God's problem, not the couple's.

"If we follow the rules and have a proper wedding and are the right kind of people, we will have a happy marriage," some people think. This is a simplistic kind of trust. Somehow, we feel, God has promised that marriage will be satisfying if we get married in church to a fellow Christian and do all the right Christian things—go to services regu-larly, pray, work in the church, give to missions, and so on.

If we married as the ancients did—as a reasonable way to continue families, protect the vulnerable, and make alliances among likeminded people—then we wouldn't be so puzzled by our differences and the stresses they create.

And perhaps we would more carefully and diligently search out and put into practice practical ways to live together comfortably and satisfyingly in spite of those differences. But as it is, too often we expect God to give us some special information that will magically lead us into happiness. We may expect it to come through a fellow believer or some authority figure such as a pastor, teacher, author, or conference speaker; or we may expect it will just miraculously happen if we "commit ourselves to God" (although we aren't always too sure what that means).

So I suggest, encourage, and urge you to begin looking at marriage—yours in particular—as a relationship.

GENESIS 2:18, 21-24

The Lord God said, "It is not good for the man to be alone. I will make a helper suitable for him." . . . So the Lord God caused the man to fall into a deep sleep; and while he was sleeping, He took one of the man's ribs and closed up the place with flesh. Then the Lord God made a woman from the rib He had taken out of the man, and He brought her to the man. The man said, "This is now bone of my bones and flesh of my flesh; she shall be called 'woman,' for she was taken out of man." For this reason a man will leave his father and mother and be united to his wife, and they will become one flesh.

Let the statement *Marriage is a relationship* sit in your mind for a few days or weeks or months, coming up to conscious awareness from time to time. Turn it over in your mind, imagining what it might mean.

What does a relationship require for satisfaction? For success? What do other relationships of yours require? How does this affect the way you approach your differences with the one you are in relationship with?

To change your perspective on marriage from God's problem to your relationship is not giving God less place in your life. It is putting the relationship in focus. God relates to us one by one. He is interested in our relationships, but they are ours. We are responsible for selecting them, maintaining them, and making them more satisfying. He provides guidance in many forms. But the relationship and the responsibility are ours.

Related Articles
Chapter 4: Never Take Your
  Mate for Granted
Chapter 4: Making Your Spouse
  Your Best Friend

The Demise of an Expert

DAVID VEERMAN

I used to be an expert on marriage and family. I say "used to be," because over the past few years certain personal events have eroded the foundations of my expertise.

I'm not exactly sure how I came to such self-confidence. Perhaps it was my birth order—as the oldest, I directed my younger brothers and sister and sent a steady stream of advice toward Mom and Dad. Maybe it was the dogmatic church of my youth—in my earliest sermon recollections, I hear the pastor exhorting the faithful to "stand for the truth" (our doctrine). Or perhaps it was my profession—as a minister to youth and their families, challenging talks to kids on sex and dating, counseling sessions for soon-to-be-weds on marriage, and seminars for parents on raising children were my stock in trade. Whatever the reason, I became an expert who willingly dispensed counsel, advice, solutions, and exhortations.

During those years, I built my own set of marriage ideals. My wife would be beautiful, talented, fun, charming, intensely spiritual, and submissive—and, of course, she would love me totally. Our wedded bliss would be unending. We would love each other unselfishly; we would communicate effectively; and we would have children who would mirror our talents and temperaments and would cause very few behavioral problems.

I had watched and heard couples arguing in the mall, babies screaming in church, and toddlers spilling and wailing in restaurants. I knew that the children created by my wife and me would be different. When the need arose, we would discipline them just right; like a heavenly thermostat we would set a positive spiritual climate in the house; and our children would respond and grow to be wonderful young adults. After all, I was the expert.

The erosion of my expertise began just before the marital bliss began. It was just a hint, a clue, at the wedding rehearsal. When the minister asked my bride-to-be if she'd take me "for better or worse, for richer or poorer, in sickness or in health," Gail quickly said, "I'll take *better, healthy,* and *rich.*" I chuckled with the others and thought, "What a woman! What a great sense of humor!" Of course I fully expected to be all of these and more. The seed-hint fell on a closed mind. But a few days later came the second one.

Honeymooning in serene northern Michigan, we had decided not to look like typical newlyweds, giggling, wide-eyed, and glued to each other. Instead, we would register at the hotel, order meals, and stroll arm in arm like any normal young couple on vacation. But on the grocery store checkout counter, right in the midst of our purchases, I saw something alarming—Crest toothpaste. "But I use Colgate!" I blurted loudly. Our newness and communication lapse brought knowing smiles from the cashier and the dozen or so others in line.

During the weeks, months, and years that followed, the clues mounted—perhaps I was not an expert after all. Living together in close and often gross quarters brought out all sorts of personal rough edges that we would bump and rub against and often work around. Our marriage ideals—impossible pictures of perfection—fell like overripe tomatoes in a storm. No matter how much I had lectured on marriage or how much Gail and I knew, we were rank amateurs, and we struggled together to make our marriage work. I found my premarriage and marriage counseling changing to more practical realism.

Children, however, were another story. I could hardly wait to father those beautiful, God-given blessings, and my eagerness was heightened by our seeming inability to conceive. But finally there she was—tiny, heaven-sent, and precious. With wrinkled yawns and profound gurgles, Kara epitomized innocence. When she first cried in Gail's arms in the hospital, tears fell from Mommy's eyes too.

Once home, however, we had many rude awakenings! Darling Kara cried for a month, usually at night. The doctor said it was colic; I thought I was losing my mind. "Why did I ever want a child?" I wondered. Another ideal bit the dust as I immersed myself in the real world of parenting—incredibly soiled diapers, pablum pools, bruises, weeping and wailings and even gnashing of teeth (mine). Believe me, I now empathize and sympathize with parents and unruly kids *wherever* I see them.

Now our oldest is in junior high school. Other "experts" say this is the age for wide swings in emotions. I'm sure they're talking about the parents. One moment we are so proud of our little lady, who is growing, maturing, thinking, being polite and thoughtful. And then suddenly we are convinced she is demon possessed. Alas, the last bastion of my expertise has fallen. I've spent 25 years working with teenagers, and yet I'm an amateur with my own.

The expert is gone, but through these experiences I have discovered invaluable lessons that I'd like to pass on:
- Gail and I are two *imperfect* (fallible and finite) human beings; but committed to Christ and each other, we can weather any personal storm.
- Gail and I are two *amateurs* at love, sex, parenting, and life. We didn't get a set of instructions for each child or for each other, and we had no chance to practice. All we can do is depend on God, accept each other, and work together.

And so, by God's grace, we've survived—by trusting, praying, laughing, working, confessing, and forgiving.

Related Articles

Two Shall Become One

LUIS PALAU

Some marriages may be made in heaven, but many of the details have to be worked out here on earth. Unfortunately, many couples enter into this most intimate of all relationships with little or no thought about how such a relationship is designed to work.

"I married only to get away from home, to get a house of my own, and to be independent," admitted a young woman named Jane. "My parents tried to talk me out of it, but you always think you know better."

Jane thought she was breaking away from her parents. In reality, her marriage was only a contest to prove she knew best. She failed to develop a close bond with her husband, however. "After six months I knew it was a mistake," she said, "even before my baby was born." Shortly afterward her marriage dissolved.

The names change, the circumstances vary, but the tragedy remains the same: about half the new marriages in America eventually end in divorce. Why? One Christian leader states, "All my counseling in marriage and family problems can be categorized on the basis of one of these three problems: (1) failure to truly leave the parents, (2) failure to cleave to the partner, or (3) failure to develop a unified relationship."

Leave. Cleave. Unify. The Prophet Moses, the Lord Jesus Christ, and the Apostle Paul all used these concepts to describe how God designed marriage to work. Marriage involves leaving our parents and clinging to our spouse. It is an intimate, exclusive union between a man and his wife.

First, the Bible teaches that marriage is an *intimate* union. "For this reason a man will leave his father and mother and be united to his wife, and they will become one flesh" (Gen. 2:24). When you marry, you leave your parents and bond with your spouse. A totally new, intimate union is formed; this union between one man and one woman is meant to last a lifetime.

Unity in marriage should exist on every level. It starts on the spiritual plane: a couple is united in their love for Christ and each other. It also brings a couple together intellectually, volitionally, emotionally, socially, and physically.

Second, the Bible teaches that Christian marriage is an *exclusive* union. It is unmixed, pure. Husband and wife are no longer two, but one. No one else can be part of them the way they are part of each other. The Bible says, "What God has joined together, let man not separate" (Mark 10:9).

When you get married, you take a tremendous step in God's eyes. You join your whole life—body, soul, and spirit—to that one person. This excludes all third parties. The Bible clearly states, "You shall not commit adultery" (Ex. 20:14).

In God's eyes, marriage is absolutely exclusive. Once you are married, your affections belong to your spouse. There is no room for sexual looseness, no room for playing games or even flirting with someone else's spouse. Why? Because it destroys everything marriage was meant to be.

Third, the Bible also teaches that marriage is a *symbolic* union, a beautiful metaphor of Christ and the church. Just as a husband and wife are one flesh, so

Jesus Christ is one spirit with His church. As the church is to respond to Christ, so a woman is to respond to her husband. As Christ loved the church, so I am to love my wife. This symbolism elevates marriage to its highest dimension.

Christian marriage is really a triangle: a man, a woman, and Christ. My wife, Pat, committed her life to Christ at the age of eight. I was 12 when I made the same decision. When we joined our lives, we did so in the presence of the Lord. He is the third party to our marriage. He is the one who keeps us together and draws us closer to each other as we seek to draw closer to Him. He will do the same for you.

MARRIAGE TEACHES ABOUT GOD

To understand the biblical ideal of marriage, one has to start in Genesis 1:26-27 where the Bible records that God made man in His own image; male and female He created them. *Man* here means "mankind"; the male and female attributes taken together reflect God's own image.

When a man and woman become one in marriage, their marriage becomes a symbol of the unity of the Godhead. Their relationship enables them to understand more of the nature of God's personality than either one would be able to understand alone. This is not to say, of course, that an insensitive, brutish married person knows more of God than a sensitive, thoughtful unmarried person. In fact, thoughtful, obedient single people can learn infinitely more about God vicariously than can casual, careless married people. But from a biblical viewpoint, when two become one in marriage, the door is opened that allows them to refine human relationships to the degree that they can begin to understand more of God's nature, because the Godhead includes both male and female attributes.

I believe the marriage relationship is intended, at its most foundational level, to open to human beings the opportunity of knowing God at a glorified, deeper level—and also to grow in knowledge of one another.

Jay Kesler

Is Marriage More Chancy These Days?

DEAN MERRILL

I am always wary of the Good Old Days Syndrome—the assumption that everything used to be wonderful and clean and virtuous and upright, but now we're all going to the dogs. Grandpa and Grandma did it right ("it" being anything from earning a living to raising kids to serving God), but their modern offspring are a disaster rolling toward the gulch.

Most generations have said the same thing. The 19th century praised the 18th while worrying about themselves, and so on back down the line. A Babylonian clay tablet dating from 2000 B.C. complains that things are not the same anymore: the young no longer respect their elders, public truthfulness has eroded, old values are seeping away. . . .

Certain facts about the present, however, are hard to sweep under the historical rug. Certain attitude shifts and technological changes have definitely transpired, with the result that marriage today is *not* the same as it was in 1960 or 1945. It's hard to deny that a number of the old allies have fled—the traditions and forces that used to prop up marriage as an institution. Our generation is in greater need of distinctly Christian reasons to stay married and work at it than others in the recent past.

Here's what's different about today:

1. *The consensus about marriage has faded.* Not everybody agrees anymore that normal adult behavior is to get married and stick together for the duration. Pollster Daniel Yankelovich in his book *New Rules* even goes so far as to say, "In sharp contrast with the past, it has become normal to think of marriage as not being permanent. When an NBC/Associated Press poll asked Americans in 1978 whether they thought 'most couples getting married today expect to remain married for the rest of their lives,' a 60 percent majority said no. As Sheila M. Rothman writes in *Woman's Proper Place:* 'In the 1950s as in the 1920s, diamonds were "forever." In the 1970s diamonds were for "now." ' "

The days are gone when a frustrated husband or wife would hesitate to file for divorce because "that's never been done in our family." It *has* been done in virtually every family in the nation, and subsequent breakups seem to come a little easier.

A *New Yorker* cartoon once showed a wedding scene in which the minister says, "Do you, Jane, and you, Jonathan, jointly vow to split the royalties, paperback rights, book-club proceeds, and movie options with each other in the event that the marriage dissolves and results in a work of fiction or nonfiction based on this union?" That's the way it is in the late 20th century.

2. *Premarital sex (aided by modern contraception) starts off a lot of marriages with "baggage."* Yes, there's always been premarital sex—but not nearly as much of it as today. Only in our century have young lovers been given the means to find seclusion (the automobile, plus a society that has stopped paying attention or asking nosy questions) and the means for the

woman to prevent pregnancy ("the pill"). The risks, both culturally and personally, seem to have been greatly reduced.

Accordingly, people have adjusted their beliefs to match what feels good. The percentage of Americans branding premarital sex "morally wrong" plunged from 83 percent to 37 percent *in only 12 years.* This means millions of brides and grooms are coming into marriage with memories of partners past. Comparisons are inevitable. It's tougher to build a rock-solid commitment under such conditions.

3. *Current media (TV, movies, and modern novels) have, for whatever reasons, decided to major on irregular relationships and minor on the standard ones.* In 1982 *TV Guide* ran a brave article called, "Looking for a Happy Marriage on TV? Forget It." The author searched almost in vain among the legions of shows featuring single, divorced, and unfaithfully married people for an honest-to-goodness happy husband and wife. Well, there *was* "Little House on the Prairie," but that was all.

Things have gotten a little better since then, but the fact remains that popular writers still have trouble finding an exciting story line in the territory called Good Marriage. They instinctively run to the troubled side. Meanwhile, Hollywood and New York actors not only play the parts realistically on screen, they go back to their penthouses and estates to continue the same roles in real life.

With millions of Americans watching all this in the afternoons, evenings, and on weekends, is it any wonder that marital discontent is on the rise?

4. *Meanwhile, husband-wife communication is ebbing away.* Every hour spent watching TV is an hour lost to the possibility of talking together. Evenings are no longer available to work out

problems, hear about each other's day, plan together for the future. The box with the canned laughter and alluring characters takes precedence.

"The danger of TV," says noted Cornell University psychologist Urie Bronfenbrenner, "lies not so much in the behavior it produces as in the behavior it prevents." That is true for children who watch; it is also true for married couples.

5. *Quick gratification is in; sacrifice is out.* Our consumer-oriented society, bent on the business of selling things and experiences, has done a pretty thorough job of convincing us that if we're not happy at the moment, we should *do something about it.* Don't just sit there. Get a Pepsi or a Bud Light. Call your travel agent. Head for the mall. You deserve better than this.

The same mentality is being applied to marriage. Does it feel good? Are you happy? Is your spouse enhancing your self-fulfillment? If not, then find somebody who will. Don't just put up with a bad situation. Add up the pluses and minuses, and if you'd be ahead to move on to other things, why not? It would be hard to find views less biblical than these—but these are the views our culture promotes.

All of these cultural questions and suggestions have rebuttals that are good, biblical, and reliable. God has infinitely superior reasons for us to commit ourselves to our marriage, whether others do so or not. But we have to listen to Him, not the boisterous voices of the times. We can no longer expect to have a good marriage if we simply drift with the current.

Related Articles

Marriage Isn't Always Easy

MARGARET DAVIDSON CAMPOLO

Some of us who are veterans of long marriages have erred in not allowing the younger generation, and especially our own children, to know of the hills and valleys we have traveled together. Most of us have "war stories," but it is not the fashion to tell them. We want the world, including our children, to believe myths about marriage, myths like, "Our love is so great that we never have had any problems," or, "Because we let the Lord choose us for each other, it has all been smooth sailing." While this approach may elicit admiration and even envy, in most cases it isn't the truth.

Tony and I want our son and daughter to know about those times when one or both of us felt like bailing out—when we did not feel all warm and good inside. That we have a marriage that has not only endured, but has brought both of us real satisfaction and happiness, does not change the fact that it has been created through self-sacrifice and the doing of what ought to be done, rather than what either of us felt like doing at a given time.

I used to think how pleased I would be if our son and daughter perceived our marriage as one so blessed by God that it had had few problems. Now I pray that they will see how hard Tony and I have worked, and that we have tried to allow a sense of *oughtness* that comes directly from the Bible govern our marriage. Someday one of them, at a difficult time in marriage, may remember how Mom and Dad hung in there through some tough times and know that he or she can do the same.

That those who seek to save their lives will lose them is never more true than when applied to marriage. In a marriage, as in so much of life, those who do what they ought to do are rewarded. It is one of God's ironies that when happiness becomes an end in itself, it is never realized. Happiness is a by-product of living out one's obligations.

One of the reasons Tony and I were able to work so very hard at finding the way to be happily married in our early years together is that each of us knew there was no getting out of it. The choice was to be happy in it or to be miserable in it. A marriage is not something to be shed like an ill-fitting shoe. I do not deny that there are marriages that must be ended, but I believe they are few and far between. Ending a marriage should be considered only at the end of a struggle to which one has given one's all.

A good marriage is not a gift bestowed by anyone, not even by God. What God has given us are the rules for a good marriage, and applying His rules takes precedence over our own happiness. Christian newlyweds want to create a good marriage, but so do people of this world. The difference is that Christians have been given rules to live by, and only those rules make the difficult possible.

Most people realize that how a person feels influences what that person does. But we sometimes do not realize that the way we choose to act can determine how we feel. When a wife acts lovingly toward her husband, she will come to feel loving even if she did not feel that way to begin with. Love can be created.

If this were not so, the Bible would not have commanded us to love. It may not always be easy, but love is a decision, not a happening.

To young people starting out in marriage I say: enjoy the easy parts, but be prepared to dig in your heels and fight the urge to quit during the hard parts. Study your mate and use all your heart and mind to figure out how to love him or her. It is sad but true that many people spend more time practicing their tennis game or learning how to refinish furniture than they do studying the art of creating their own marriage. Your mate isn't like anyone else, and neither are you. You are pioneers exploring new territory.

And to those who, like Tony and me, have older marriages that work well, don't make the mistake of making it look too easy. Find ways to share the hard times you have had as well as the easy ones. That will give you the opportunity to share God's book of rules, without which Christian marriage is not possible.

WHERE TO BEGIN

The place to start saving marriages is with your own marriage. You might not be able to save the marriage of your next-door neighbor, but you can concentrate on not only saving, but improving, your own. If everyone would work objectively and consistently on his or her own marriage, just think what it would do to the statistics—and to the homes.

Janette Oke

Related Articles
Introduction: Three Essentials
for a Successful Marriage
Chapter 2: Characteristics of a
Mature Marriage
Chapter 11: Let Your Children
See You Love Your Mate

What's Right With Families

JUDSON SWIHART

For a number of years many popular books on families have dealt with what's wrong with them. Perhaps it's time to begin looking at the other side of the coin—what's right with families. If we could look at a large group of strong families and see what characteristics they have in common, we might encourage other families to develop those same specific qualities.

By looking at a cross-section of studies and observations by professional authors, I have developed a list of nine characteristics that seem to be shared by strong, healthy families:

1. *Ability to communicate.* Communication begins with self-awareness. Good communicators are able to look inward, to understand what they are thinking and feeling, and to express their thoughts and feelings verbally. Developing the ability to communicate needs to go hand-in-hand with developing good character. If people learn to express themselves better but neglect character development, they can become even more destructive to each other. For example, a person who learns how to ex-

press anger but does not grow in his ability to love is likely to create more problems, not fewer.

2. *Willingness to encourage individual identity.* Strong families appreciate one another and promote each other's happiness. They show respect for each other's individual gifts and are sensitive to each other's needs. Strong families allow their members to be unique individuals; they don't expect each member to be a copy of everyone else in the family.

3. *Commitment to each other.* In the late '80s commitment has come back in vogue. Committed families have a strong sense of family identity. They enjoy frequent activities together and often keep some kind of family history, perhaps a picture album. Each individual is concerned for the well-being of the entire family.

4. *Religious orientation.* Strong families usually have a high level of commitment to their faith. They have a spiritual lifestyle that senses a higher purpose beyond the daily activities. Biblical virtues such as love, commitment, honesty, and forgiveness all tend to promote family well-being.

5. *Links to a wider society.* Strong families do not fit the rugged, independent frontier family model. Rather, they tend to participate in activities with other families. They are not isolated but tend to get involved in different kinds of support networks.

6. *Willingness to affirm one another.* Strong families frequently express appreciation. They often comment on the things they value in one another or express gratitude for what another family member has done. Affirmation tends to build cohesion and self-esteem. It encourages family harmony, which is an environment in which people can thrive.

7. *Sense of structure.* In strong families, roles, expectations, and boundaries are clear. Within the family it is understood that certain subgroups are special, particularly the husband-and-wife relationship. The roles and expected behavior of family members are consistent and clearly defined.

8. *Adaptability and flexibility.* Our world is becoming increasingly oriented toward change, and a healthy family is able to adapt to change as it comes along. Some theorists note that a family can err in either direction: it can be too rigid and thus fragment itself, or it can be too flexible and thus have no stability. Strong families have a good balance: they have structure and yet can adapt to transitions and unexpected changes.

9. *Commitment to spend time together.* The way people spend their time says something about their value system. We've heard arguments about the importance of quality time versus quantity time. Probably both ingredients are necessary in order for time together to be effective. Family time may be very simple, however: playing table games, going sledding, a trip to the beach.

These nine characteristics are not the only ones needed for family strength, but they make a good starting point for reflection. Is your family strong? How is it doing on each of the nine points?

Related Articles
Chapter 1: Love as Togetherness
Chapter 9: Communication That Energizes
Chapter 9: The Language of Appreciation

God's Blueprint for Happy Homes

LUIS PALAU

Newspapers, magazines, and movies frequently publicize and sometimes glamorize infidelity, family breakups, and divorce. We've almost become used to it all. It doesn't shock us anymore. What's surprising to some today is to find a happily married couple! Yet that should be the norm, the standard, the expected.

We don't have to settle for unhappiness, however. God has left us with a blueprint for enjoying marriage and building happy homes. It's the Bible, the Word of God. If we follow its instructions, we can enjoy marriage to the full.

God designed marriage, like everything else He created, to be "very good" (Gen. 1:31). But let's face it—many couples struggle with their marriages. What's the problem? Not marriage itself. We've simply failed to follow God's blueprint as found in Scripture. The Bible is not simply another book on marriage; it is the first and best book on how to have a happy home. That is because it is not a collection of man's best ideas; it is the very Word of God.

The Bible teaches that there are three divinely appointed institutions in the world—the government, the church, and the family. It also teaches how each can be successful. We expect the Bible to tell us how to run the church. We also may expect it to have words of wisdom for government leaders. But it has just as much to say about the family as it does about either of the other institutions.

In fact, if families are unhappy, if homes are breaking up, neither the church nor the government can do a good job.

In the Bible God tells us His plan for marriage (Matt. 19:4-6) and describes the joys of a loving union (Prov. 5:18-19; the Song of Solomon). He gives specific commands to husbands and wives (Eph. 5:21-33), and He gives general instructions that can make marriage partners easier to live with (Phil. 2:3-11). One of the Bible's most famous chapters tells how true love behaves (1 Cor. 13).

Perhaps you're experiencing boredom or tensions in your marriage. Perhaps you've given up your dreams for a happy home. Perhaps you and your spouse are already contemplating separation or divorce.

If you and your spouse face problems, don't run *from* God—run *to* Him. Lay your problems at His feet. Acknowledge your struggles in prayer to God, and ask Him to speak to you through His Word. Read one of the biblical passages I have mentioned with your spouse tonight. Commit yourselves to shared Bible study from now on. As you read God's Word, share your feelings with each other and together pray about your mutual needs and concerns.

Admit your need for God's wisdom and strength, and trust Him to work mightily in your marriage for His glory. And prepare for your marriage to become more loving, more satisfying, than ever before.

Related Articles
Introduction: Marriage: A Vehicle of God's Love
Chapter   1: Love Is the Gift of a Caring Self
Chapter   4: The Love Exchange

Love has many faces. Your way of expressing love may not be identical to your spouse's way. Here is a list of some of love's different faces. How important is each of these aspects of love to you? Give a 1 to qualities that are very important, a 2 to those that are somewhat important, and a 3 to those that don't matter to you. Then ask your spouse to mark the list without reading your answers. When you compare notes, you may be surprised at the different ways you see love!

For me, love is . . .

	HIS	HERS
adventure	___	___
bliss	___	___
caring	___	___
comfort	___	___
commitment	___	___
contentment	___	___
duty	___	___
faithfulness	___	___
forgiveness	___	___
friendship	___	___
harmony	___	___
honor	___	___
hugging	___	___
intimacy	___	___
mercy	___	___
pleasure	___	___
providing	___	___
respect	___	___
responsibility	___	___
romance	___	___
sacrifice	___	___
service	___	___
sex	___	___
sharing	___	___
suffering	___	___
work	___	___
unity	___	___
_____	___	___
_____	___	___
_____	___	___

1

LOVE

When Jesus Christ was asked, "What is the greatest commandment?" He replied: "To love the Lord. . . . To love your neighbor. . . ." The vertical relationship of love for God is vital before the horizontal connections of life and love can work. And yet, in our world:

- Love has become a tag term with nonstick backing, slapped on everything from a new convertible to a wild hairdo.
- Love is an illusion. Our credo: "Please release me, let me go; I don't love you anymore." The dream died, the bubble burst.
- Love is confused with lust. In a society that can't distinguish perfume from sewer gas, problems are paramount.

The Apostle Paul prayed that our love may abound in knowledge and discernment so we may approve things that are excellent and be sincere and blameless until Christ returns (see Phil. 1:9-10). Love is a dynamic, discerning, and redeeming quality of life. Jesus Christ taught that love is a two-way process, where equal partners respect, need, and value each other.

To have a chapter on love may seem a bit redundant—after all, isn't that the easy part? But in reality, love is work—love for better or worse, richer or poorer, in sickness and in health. This chapter is about the meaning of love and how to keep it alive in a world that has lost the understanding of God-given love.

Howard & Jeanne Hendricks

Love Is Something We Learn

DWIGHT HERVEY SMALL

What is this elusive something we call "romantic love"? A quality of enduring married love? A short-lived emotional at-tachment that may or may not lead to love?

Romantic love usually begins with infatuation. In the words of the late American writer Dorothy Parker, infatuation is "the gun you didn't know was loaded." It starts with an initial fascination, usually with someone relatively little known. An aura of mystery surrounds this newly discovered person. Initial encounters involve a degree of romantic play. This leads to fantasies of an exciting relationship ahead.

Early on, the passion to possess the other takes over. Almost from the start, a powerful emotional bonding takes place. Carried along by strong passions, two people believe they are made for each other. If asked about their relationship, they would describe it in romantic terms.

Unrecognized personal needs may propel infatuation further. A person may have a need to be loved or just to find affirmation as someone of worth. But love is more than meeting one's own needs, more than emotional attachment. A person is deceived who thinks that the enraptured moments of a romantic relationship are a sure sign of love.

There is little doubt that romantic love serves a self-enhancing purpose. Young and old alike find in the adoring eyes of another a magic mirror reflecting back an image of what they wish themselves to be. It is exhilarating to one's sense of self to see in someone else's eyes the reflection of a wished-for self. How easy it is to fall in love with your magic mirror! We're blinded to the fact that romantic attachment is not really love at all. Instead it is an idealized emotional relationship, a deceptive illusion. It is little more than an ego trip, little more than being in love with love.

Romantic love idealizes people by projecting imagined attributes that may not exist. Whenever an idealized image is superimposed upon another person, a mystique is created. One falls in love with the mystique, not the person. But consider the danger of seeing only what one wishes to see, only what one has created in imagination. Think of the likely results if romantic love blinds one to the real person, and yet chooses that very person as a life-mate!

It is true that people reveal the part of their personalities they want to reveal, not wanting others to observe their less-than-ideal qualities. People also create impressions that are not authentic. For short periods and in planned circumstances, playing the role one believes the other expects is relatively easy. But under the light of continual association, such illusions cannot continue. An idealized image cannot forever take the place of the real person. Time and familiarity scale down romantic dreams. It takes honest self-disclosure and the willingness to share life with its problems and struggles for people to see each other as they are.

Another feature distinguishes romantic love: it thrives on captured attention. It is exciting to discover an attractive person who responds to a show of attention. From there on, the newly discovered object of attraction is never out of mind. The adventure of imagining what he or she is really like becomes an all-consuming passion. Right from the start of the relationship, the illusion of instant intimacy inclines people to say, "We really understand each other perfectly! This must be love!" But is it? Is captured attention an adequate foundation for a future life together?

We must recognize that emotions are ambivalent, marked by peaks and valleys, sometimes turning from positive to negative for little or no reason. Romantic love is ambivalent because it is unable to cope with changing circumstances. When negative emotions come into play, they tend to cause anxiety about the whole relationship. Lovers become confused, hurt, then disenchanted. Often they blame each other for feelings they cannot understand.

Romantic love has been guilty of promoting the deceptive notion that peak emotional experiences are the norm. But for genuine love to develop, more is required than merely sharing love passions and romantic myths. Love is built on a commitment to care for another person. What is needed, then, is a more stable, more predictable, less exciting, less self-centered love. The love that lasts is described in 1 Corinthians 13.

Romantic passion intensifies when threatened with obstacles, and soon it overestimates its own power. It thinks it is strong enough to overcome any roadblock. Nothing is greater than this great love, so it believes. But when it is slighted ever so little, it can turn into destructive passion with remarkable suddenness. If the obstacle happens to be an intruding third party, jealous passion may rise to the point of violence. Jealousy—the desperate fear of losing what is considered one's own—can destroy romantic love in the shortest of time.

Romantic passion is subject to the law of diminishing returns. It must be continually intensified just to sustain a level of response. But there is a limit to which any passion can be intensified, and when intensification slacks off, a swift letdown usually follows. Romantic love can end with the same suddenness with which it began.

Invariably, the history of romantic love is the drama of its fight against time. Time and familiarity scale down idealized images and destroy romantic

myths. It doesn't take long for flaws and failings to appear. While married love is realistic about the imperfect human creatures we are and loves accordingly, romantic love cannot handle imperfections in the beloved.

Love is not something we fall into, but something we learn. It matures over time and through many shared experiences. Love isn't something that happens to us, but something at which we work hard to keep happening. Essentially, it is a commitment to care, to give oneself to the other's needs, to work through problems with patience and understanding. For Christian couples, it is letting Jesus' love shape their love until it is like His—centered on others, relinquishing independent self-will for the sake of the beloved, and determined to assist the other to become all that he or she is meant to be.

Related Articles
Chapter 1: Dimensions of Married Love
Chapter 3: Friendship: Foundation for Marriage

Troth: The Love Connection in Marriage

JAMES H. OLTHUIS

Marriage is the ultimate human connection in which two people commit themselves to each other in a lifelong communion of sharing and caring. In a phrase, the partners exchange pledges of *troth*. *Troth* is an Old English word for fidelity, truth, trust, love, and commitment. In a single word, it captures the special flavor and nuances of the love connection between husband and wife.

"Therefore a man leaves his father and his mother and cleaves to his wife, and they become one flesh" (Gen. 2:24,

RSV). To *cleave* is to keep the troth, holding on to each other in a joining of spirits, a wedding of bodies. Keeping the troth is counting on each other, giving the utmost, sharing inner selves, and sticking together through thick and thin, in good times and bad. Husbands and wives are open and vulnerable together, not closed and defended. "And the man and his wife were both naked, and were not ashamed" (v. 25, RSV).

Troth is the glue that holds the one-flesh union together, the mutual bond

SONNET 43 (19TH CENTURY)

How do I love thee? Let me count the ways.
I love thee to the depth and breadth and height
My soul can reach, when feeling out of sight
For the ends of Being and ideal Grace.
I love thee to the level of everyday's
Most quiet need, by sun and candlelight.
I love thee freely, as men strive for Right;
I love thee purely, as they turn from Praise.
I love thee with the passion put to use
In my old griefs, and with my childhood's faith.
I love thee with a love I seemed to lose
With my lost saints,—I love thee with the breath,
Smiles, tears, of all my life!—and, if God choose,
I shall but love thee better after death.

Elizabeth Barrett Browning

that makes a marriage a marriage. To pledge troth is to commit oneself to another person; to promise trust, care, devotion, openness, and respect. Marriage is the conjoining of two people who embark on a shared journey of expanding troth, growing wholeness, ongoing encouragement, and deepening intimacy. Sexual intercourse and romantic involvement are indispensable ingredients of being one flesh, but troth is the key. Troth without sexual passion and emotional connection is thin, uninspiring, and cold. But sex and romance without troth is capricious, fleeting, and unfulfilling. Troth with sex and romance can mean compassion, connection, and fulfillment.

Troth is commitment. Husbands and wives promise to stand by each other. They count on each other. When our commitment is clear and unreserved, we are encouraged freely and openly to share our inner struggles and fears as well as our joys and triumphs. Without commitment, every unpleasantness, problem, or disagreement easily escalates into yet another "discussion" about whether we really belong together. Fear

of such crises often leads partners to hide what is really going on in their lives. The danger is boredom and loss of inner contact. With commitment, on the other hand, comes the freedom to face our problems honestly together.

Troth is mutuality. There is no room for superiority or inferiority. Husbands and wives are called to a copartnership of equality in difference. Neither may lord it over the other. Genesis 3:16 is a curse on human sin, not a command to be obeyed. Troth flourishes in a mutual relationship of belonging in which partners, secure in their own identities, commit themselves to sharing life together.

Troth is mutual presence and acceptance. Partners promise to be there with and for each other. When we reach out and are accepted, when we feel seen and heard, our hearts leap with joy and our spirits are enlarged. And we begin to risk more and more of ourselves from deeper and deeper places within ourselves. When our partners are not really "home," when we don't feel welcomed and encouraged, our spirits sag and our hearts grow heavy. We hold back parts of ourselves, dry up inside, and retreat.

Acceptance makes all the difference between ecstasy and the terror of rejection and loneliness.

Troth is being vulnerable. Slowly together we are able to let down, take off our masks, expose our fears, and become vulnerable. We reach out from open hearts, meeting in the middle—face to face and soul to soul. Intimacy!

Troth takes time. Instant trust and instant openness are suspect and shallow. Troth is a tree of slow growth; two people edging out on the limb inch by careful inch. Troth needs attention, patience, understanding, and gentleness.

Every couple develops its own cycle of troth. When, as so often happens in our age of alienation, we get caught in negative cycles and our souls begin to wither, we need to seek help from friends and professional counselors.

Shared troth is not a treasure we can take out on occasion and admire. It is not a big stick to force our partners into line. Shared troth is an ever-changing gift we freely and continually give and receive.

Related Articles
Chapter 1: Love as Honoring Each Other
Chapter 1: Love as Faithfulness

Love as Friendship

JERRY & MARY WHITE

When most couples marry they assume they will be best friends for life, but we know from the sad statistics in the divorce courts that this simply is not the case. A marriage friendship needs development, care, and feeding like any other friendship—indeed, more than other friendships.

How disheartening it would be to endure years together without real friendship as an expression of love! The friendship we experience in marriage should be the strongest, most fulfilling friendship of a lifetime. It should sustain us through difficult times and give mutual joy in life's happy experiences. The closer and deeper the friendship grows, the more carefully we must guard it from destructive influences.

Many people enter marriage without giving a thought to being friends with their partners. Hormones are flowing, and the physical emphasis of the relationship is so strong that building a true friendship is neglected.

At Creation God said, "It is not good for the man to be alone. I will make a helper suitable for him" (Gen. 2:18). Then God made woman to be man's partner—and friend. The purpose of their union far superseded procreation. They were coworkers in God's kingdom, totally tuned in to one another's needs.

The teaching of Ephesians 5:21-33 becomes reality and joy only in the fertile ground of friendship. Love and submission present no barriers to husbands and wives who are deep friends. In the love song of Solomon, the bride says with conviction, "His mouth is sweetness itself; he is altogether lovely. This is my lover, this is my friend" (Song 5:16).

But when that friendship is not present, what can be done to remedy the situation?

Make a commitment to friendship with your spouse. At whatever point you are now in your marriage, 5 months or 50 years, determine together to continue developing your friendship.

In a 1979 ABC television production, "Summer Solstice," an aging couple reflect on their life together. They review their wedding in flashbacks. They disagree over the phrasing of the vows, and after a lengthy discussion they agree to take one another "as is." Not a bad beginning for a marriage friendship. Later they discuss why he returned to her after marital difficulty. He thinks for a long time and then says quietly, "Because of our vow."

If both partners feel secure in the commitment, the friendship will deepen faster and encounter fewer roadblocks. But commitment of this nature must be preceded by a recognition of need.

Plan communication and activities that will foster the friendship. Look for areas of mutual interest and pleasure. Experiment with new activities. Accept responsibility for suggesting ideas, but refuse to feel rejected if some ideas aren't accepted by your partner.

Keep notes of thoughts, ideas, and happenings when you are apart in order to share your life more fully with your spouse. What made you feel happy? Laugh? Cry? Get angry? How did you respond to the news of the day? What are your goals and aspirations? We should all feel free to share the ridiculous and the sublime of life with our mates, knowing we will receive a sympathetic, understanding, and interested response.

A caution here. Keep complaints and criticisms to a minimum. They are occasionally legitimate, but a steady diet of complaints does little to enhance a friendship.

Communication requires both speaking and listening. Sometimes people who have been married for a long time tend not to bother with conversation because they think they already know what their partner is going to say. But we must never assume our spouse has nothing new to say. We all change in outlook and thinking, and our conversa-

tions should reflect that.

If you spend much of your time together watching television, turn it off for a couple of evenings and test your capacity to talk. The silence may be deafening! It will force better communication. Your conversational interests should increase with your years of marriage. The desire for communion grows in direct proportion to the love relationship and to the experience of good past conversations.

Protect the friendship from excessive outside activity and interference. If one marriage partner is highly active, it is imperative to guard against filling time with extraneous activities that exclude the mate. We have friends that are particularly sensitive to this. If their schedules become so crowded that they have no time for one another, they simply "cancel a weekend" and devote the time exclusively to their own relationship.

Practice courtesy and kindness toward one another. Any friendship will break under the burden of rudeness, anger, and unkindness. In marriage, we need more kindness and consideration because of the closeness of the relationship.

Place the highest priority on your marriage friendship. Praise and commend each other publicly and privately. Voice aloud your appreciation and thanks. A couple we know well are particularly adept at this kind of verbal praise. Stan lavishly commends Lois' cooking, child care, tennis skills, Bible studies, or anything else that comes to mind. Lois usually smiles tolerantly; it's obvious that she is used to hearing such comments often in private as well as in public.

If this habit is missing from your marriage, start today to verbalize, at least once a day, a quality you esteem in your partner.

The Apostle Paul's practical definition of love in 1 Corinthians 13 can help us foster the best of marriage friendships.

By substituting *a friend* for *love* in verses 4-7 we gain a clearer perspective on the attitudes and behavior that marriage friends should have: "A friend is patient, a friend is kind. A friend does not envy, a friend does not boast, a friend is not proud. A friend is not rude, a friend is not self-seeking, a friend is not easily angered, a friend keeps no record of wrongs. A friend does not delight in evil but rejoices with the truth. A friend always protects, always trusts, always hopes, always perseveres."

Paul's timeless suggestions for exhibiting love can help marriage partners emphasize the loving actions that will allow their friendship to flourish and increase.

Related Articles
Chapter 4: Making Your Spouse Your Best Friend
Chapter 4: My Husband, My Best Friend

Love as Togetherness

JANETTE OKE

Probably no other era in the history of the world has been harder on marriage than the present one. Society demands that our attention be given to other things. First priorities are often the house and its condition rather than the home. The standard of living insists that two paychecks are needed in order for a family to be respected in the neighborhood. Everything, including children, is costly.

Even the church compounds the problem. There is so much to be done and so few workers to do it. Those who are willing find that their time is quickly gobbled up by good things.

Perhaps, with all that fights against the home, we should be surprised at the large number of marriages that manage to survive, rather than shocked over the number that succumb to the pressures.

We need survivors. We must have solid Christian homes if our society, with its Christian principles and teachings, is to continue. What can we do about it? How can we help?

It is impossible to build a home in isolation. Home means *togetherness* in attitude and spirit as well as in proximity.

To help love grow in togetherness, a husband and wife must capitalize on the things they hold in common. It is important to build the feeling of family. We are all individuals with personal likes and dislikes, fears and favorites, but we need to find those things that draw us together and use them as building stones in our relationship.

Family is such an important word. It should give a feeling of warmth, of care, of safety, and of love and acceptance. It should give us each a sense of uniqueness. Our family is a unit that is not shared by everyone. It is ours by design, by tradition, by growth. We love and protect it in our own special way.

Even though the family is a unit, each person within that unit is an individual with rights and privileges that are allowed and encouraged as long as they do not damage or bring harm to another. Individuality, if it is kept within the proper framework, can only strengthen the family unit.

Togetherness can be fostered in many ways. We learn to enjoy new experiences when we share something new with someone we love. Because I love

43

my husband, I have learned to feel excitement at the discovery of a hard-to-obtain stamp. Because I love my sons, I have learned to enjoy basketball and soccer. Because I love my daughter, I have learned a new appreciation for crafts I do not have time to pursue myself.

Togetherness can be fostered by sharing tasks around the home. Raking fall leaves or trimming the hedge can turn into fun if the work is shared. Pride in the appearance of "our place" can be family pride if it is shared with family members.

We should learn to compliment one another on a job well done. I love freshly painted walls, but I am a klutz with a paintbrush. My husband has a steady hand. So who does our painting? I have learned that the task can be shared, not by picking up a paintbrush and messing up his otherwise perfect job, but by checking in every now and then to see how the job is progressing. By showing appreciation for his work, I too can be involved in the process.

Togetherness can be greatly enhanced by discussion. Not stilted, fixed discussion but free and easy comradeship that lends itself to conversation about many things. Whether it is work, children, new neighbors, faith, church affairs, politics, feelings—discuss it. If you find it hard to discuss things with one another, practice. Begin with things that are of little importance, things you are quite sure you will agree on. Talk about them, and then go on to other things. Eventually you will be able to talk about those things you might see differently. In discussing them, try hard to understand the other person's view. Be tolerant, thoughtful, caring. It is hard to feel togetherness if you cannot be totally honest and open with one another.

The Christian home has a powerhouse to draw upon that should never be ignored—prayer. We should employ it at every turn. Pray in thankfulness for the good times. Ask for help with the difficult times. Pray together for patience in the trying times. Ask God for understanding in the troublesome times. Seek for wisdom when it is needed. Thank God for health, love, jobs, opportunities—all that He gives us. Teach your children to pray. Teach them early, and make it a family habit. You may be amazed at how quickly it becomes an important part of them.

Remember that you are a team. You are not working independently but for one another. What affects one will affect the other; what hurts one will bring pain to the other; what lifts one will promote the other; what brings happiness to one will bring joy to the other.

God the Creator said, "The two shall become one." This is God's ideal. We can help it happen, or we can fight and hinder the process. In hindering it, however, we are the losers. God knows us, and He knows what is for our good. It was not good for man to be alone.

To make the most of our life together, we must work on fostering togetherness without stifling each other's individuality. Be more than a spouse; be a helpmeet. You will gain as much as you give, and you will feel secure and contented in your togetherness.

Related Articles

Love as Teamwork

V. GILBERT & ARLISLE BEERS

We confess that our situation is unique: we have spent more than 20 years together in the same house 24 hours a day. If you were to follow our daily routines you would often find Gil washing dishes, helping Arlie make the bed, and participating in various housekeeping chores. But then you would also find Arlie working with Gil in the study to handle many of the business chores.

Some men would think Gil's housekeeping chores are out of sync with the macho image men should prize. We have a number of happily married male friends who would not be caught dead doing "women's work." It would be out of keeping with their upbringing and their views of the division of labor in the home.

We do not suggest that every couple should divide their work the way we do. Our way is not the only right way, although it has been right for us. Our system, for example, would be unfair for a husband who works hard at his job while his wife has little to do during the day but read and socialize. It would be equally unfair for a wife who has a stressful job while the husband sits around the house. Every situation is unique and thus requires a unique concept of teamwork. But we think every husband-and-wife team should have some form of teamwork, a form both agree is best for them.

Actually every husband and wife already have a form of teamwork, even if they have not consciously planned it. The way they divide the work and work together is their system of teamwork, no matter how good or how bad it is. The way you team up with each other re-

flects the way you love each other. It shows how sensitive you are to each other's needs and problems. Teamwork is love, and love is teamwork. In marriage, they are inseparable and mutually dependent.

Love includes the "warm fuzzies" and romantic feelings, but it goes beyond them. It is first and foremost the way we think about each other, the value we each place on the other's personhood.

Placing a high value on each other's personhood sensitizes us to those things which threaten the other—pressure points, times when things are too much, times when we feel inadequate to deal with problems. It's fun to move onto the scene and shoulder part of the other person's burden, thus relieving some of the threat. Teamwork, to us, is this kind of leveling process, where one partner absorbs pressure points for the other.

A husband may not like to wash dishes, but his desire to equalize his wife's pressure point overrules his dislike of dishwashing. A wife may not like to wash clothes, cook, or vacuum the house, but she gladly does these things because she values a clean, well-run household, one that provides her husband with a sense of peacefulness after a hectic day. If we did only those things we like, some of us wouldn't be very busy!

Like any other form of giving, however, teamwork done grudgingly as a chore is not loving teamwork. It misses the mark. True teamwork is a sacrifice of love, a gift of self, not because we have to bail our mate out of difficulty, but because we value him or her so much as a person that we want to celebrate that personhood—build it, enhance it, confirm it, and reveal our devotion to it.

But the team process is not merely helping one another with pressure. It is also equalizing life's delights. Watch this happen when a member of a pro football team makes a touchdown. These grown men hug each other, dance around, pat each other on the back, and show that the hero's delight is the team's delight. Think what it would do for our marriages if we did that when our mates "scored a touchdown" in the game of life.

As we said earlier, we don't expect others to practice the kind of teamwork which has worked so well for us. But you will discover a unique delight in practicing the teamwork that works best for you. All good teamwork in marriage begins with a sincere desire to enhance, build, or celebrate the other's personhood. Then, as you live and work as a team, you divide your sorrows and multiply your joys.

LOVE IS A DIRTY DIAPER

A while ago, my wife and I talked about things we could do for each other around the house. I volunteered to change the baby's diaper—cloth diapers!—whenever I was home. I admit this isn't one of my first choices on a list of fun things to do, but it expresses my love in a way that my wife appreciates. We both share the chores as well as the pleasures of our children and of our relationship.

Jeff Ringenberg

Related Articles
Chapter 1: Love Is Meeting Each Other's Needs
Chapter 6: Respecting Each Other's Gifts
Chapter 12: Learning to Be Supportive of a Working Wife

Love as Respect

JUDITH C. LECHMAN

When we consider the qualities of a healthy Christian marriage, *respect* is a word that automatically comes to mind. Yet rarely do we bother to define it; we think we know what is meant by respecting our marriage partner.

Over the years I thought I had grasped the dynamics of respect. I saw it as the Christlike recognition of my husband's dignity. I knew it implied freedom from all stereotyping—role, race, or sex—in relating to him. I knew that to act with respect toward him, I must begin by having wide-open communion with God. If I didn't, disrespect to my hus-

band would appear in my heart at the time of prayer, blocking my communication with God as it earlier had blocked my communication with my husband.

As with most spiritual lessons, however, I am learning this one over and over again on ever deeper levels of understanding and practice. So it was no surprise to me that on a recent trip to the interior of Mexico, I realized that the Spirit was instructing me still further on the meaning of respect.

Staying away from the resorts usually frequented by Americans, I visited an assortment of relatives and friends, out-of-the-way shrines, and open-air markets. I had difficulty understanding the rapid flow of Spanish. After a while I found I had begun to listen with an invisible ear, one that bypassed words and "heard" facial expressions and other communication of emotions.

With wondrous clarity I understood the devoutness of the humble pilgrim at the shrine of Father Kino, the love and pride of the young Magdalena mother of two healthy babies, and the remarkable resiliency of the ancient woman who offered us hospitality, goat's milk cheese, and tortillas at her roadside home. These people included me, a stranger, in the circle of their warmth, and I learned anew how respect could remove barriers of language, custom, and class and replace them with a spirit of harmony grounded in sensitive communication with one another and God.

This experience of communication grounded in respect helped me realize the importance of respect in marital communication. Respecting my husband means ministering to him with a truly listening ear, a warm word of support, a loving embrace, a flexible mind, and a generous spirit. Respect means looking past our differences to the basis of our similarities. It means not staying aloof, but sharing his concerns, accepting the necessity of becoming involved with others' lives as Christ did.

To live a Christian life, I must continue to develop this quality of respect, making it an essential part of who I am and all that my marriage can become.

When I returned home, I developed the following personal queries to help me practice respect in my marriage:

☐ In a highly charged situation, do I cut off my partner when he holds views contrary to mine?

☐ Do I resent him or feel threatened when he opposes me?

☐ When my husband challenges me or when I think his opinion or attitude is wrong, is my manner curt and my language harsh?

☐ Do I make exacting and inflexible demands of my spouse?

☐ In my daily communication and actions with him, am I more abrupt than caring?

☐ When discussing my faith and beliefs, am I dogmatic and opinionated rather than gently persuasive?

☐ Am I so driven by the need to be right that I try to intimidate or coerce him into believing as I do?

☐ Do I judge his weaknesses and correct his faults without making allowances for his shortcomings?

☐ Am I rigid, like the Pharisees, in my relationship with him?

☐ Is my spouse afraid to express himself honestly in my presence?

In answering these questions honestly, we take the first steps toward change. Having pinpointed when we act with disrespect, we now can turn our previously unrecognized faults into virtues rooted in respect. We begin by learning to practice careful listening rather than threatened opposition, honest expression rather than resentment, flexibility rather than rigidity, loving censure rather than harsh coercion, encouragement rather than intimidation.

In a respectful marriage, we take responsibility for creating an atmosphere in which genuine openness, trust, and vulnerability can flourish. Seeking to understand one another better, we stand before our marriage partners as we are, not as we wish ourselves or others to be. In such an environment, we make no room for masks or game playing. As children of God, we are striving to remove the destructive barriers that exist between us and to replace them with the freedom, dignity, and harmony of respect.

Related Articles

Love as Honoring Each Other .

GARY SMALLEY & JOHN TRENT

Sprinkled throughout Scripture is a concept we feel is at the heart of all truly loving relationships. In fact, the biblical concept of *honor* is one of the most powerful tools a husband or wife can use to carve out a lasting and intimate marriage.

In Scripture, wives are told to give honor to their husbands (Eph. 5:33) and husbands, to give honor to their wives (1 Peter 3:7). What do we mean by *honor?* Perhaps the best way to illustrate what the word means is to look at its opposite.

In the Old Testament, the word *dishonor* literally means "to give something little or no weight or value." Dishonoring people, then, means treating them as if who they are or what they have to share has little value. Dishonoring actions in a marriage may start with a critical word, an angry glance, or a statement that devalues a person's feelings or opinions. This may not provoke a major problem at first. Dishonor may settle like a mist over the relationship, so light that neither partner notices the change in climate. But if left unchecked, one day that mist of devaluing words and actions may build up and turn into a blanket of fog. It may then create physical, emotional, and spiritual problems and even jeopardize the marriage.

How can we avoid dishonoring our loved ones and begin to honor them instead? We can get a handle on honoring our spouses by looking at an important aspect of the word *honor*.

Throughout Scripture, giving people honor involves recognizing that they have great worth and then treating them like a valuable treasure. The word itself denotes placing a great price, weight, or significance on something. How does my treating my spouse like a valuable treasure draw us together?

One of our favorite verses reads, "Where your treasure is, there your heart will be also" (Matt. 6:21). In other words, what we treasure is what we have feelings for. The more we treasure God, the greater our desire to spend time in His Word and in prayer. The more we treasure our spouses and treat them like valuable gifts from God, the greater our positive feelings toward them will be.

We can picture it this way. If you had a priceless vase that had been in the family for years, you would go to great lengths to protect and care for it. You'd put it in a prominent place in your home and set up indirect lighting to highlight its beauty. You wouldn't think of picking up a priceless vase and shaking it or throwing it around like a Frisbee. Instead, you would treat it with tenderness and gentleness because it was so valuable to you.

Now stop and ask yourself a few important questions. On a scale of 1 to 10, where 1 is of little value and 10 equals highest value, how highly do you value your spouse? Do you treat him or her like a special treasure God has entrusted to you? Other than your relationship with the Lord, are there things in your life or home that you consider more valuable than your spouse—your job, a ski boat, or even TV? If your spouse were asked to stand up in front of your closest

DO I TRULY CARE FOR MY SPOUSE?

Whether you are a husband or a wife, or planning to become one, test your love against these questions:

1. *Am I willing to order my marriage values around the discipline of caring, so that caring is primary and all else is secondary?* Amazingly, you'll find life less complex when caring determines decisions and actions. Caring harmonizes life, integrates and simplifies it. Things seemingly important fade in importance; insignificant things take on meaning in the light of caring. More than that, you will find that caring brings its own rewards in unexpected ways!

2. *Am I willing to accept new demands and disciplines that caring will require of me?* This means continual reassessment of time, interests, leisure pursuits, social relationships, use of money—everything that affects a marital partnership. Not that you must give up all self-interest, but self-interest must not get in the way of caring. The hardest tasks will be caring enough to make a difficult decision, to confront when necessary, and to say no should the other's good require it.

3. *Am I willing to let my mate into all my life, to be open and self-disclosing, vulnerable to any revelation of flaws and faults?* Caring is not one-sided. You must let your mate minister to you as well, developing his or her own ability to express caring love.

Dwight Hervey Small

friends and share how highly he or she felt valued by you, what rating would he or she mention?

In any relationship, there will be times when we are tempted to lower our spouses' value below where it should be. Times such as when they forget to tell us about an important call, when they've dented the car for the second time this month, when they've used bubble bath to clean the kids' turtle bowl and accidentally killed the turtle as a result, and so on. However, when we make a decision to grant honor to our spouses—to recognize them as people of great value and then treat them like priceless treasures—we go a long way toward strengthening our marriages so that they can survive such times.

Do you need practical examples of what it means to honor your spouse? Here are just a few ideas to get you started:

Be interested in her friends. Ask his opinion frequently. Be gentle and tender in your tone of voice and touch. Avoid sudden changes without discussion or giving the other person time to adjust. Follow through on promises. Set and keep specific family goals for each year. Go on a romantic outing. Surprise her with a card or flowers. Defend him to others. Keep your spiritual life in shape. Don't ever say in anger, "You're just like your mother!"

You can waste hours on a hundred different things, but you'll never waste one minute putting honor into practice in your most important relationships. Do yourself and your spouse a favor. Give him or her a gift that can continue to bless both of you for a lifetime—the gift of honor.

Related Articles
Chapter 4: Never Take Your Mate for Granted
Chapter 4: Learning to Be Considerate
Chapter 9: How to Affirm Your Spouse

Love as Faithfulness

JAY KESLER

Much of the recent Christian literature about marriage has been a reaction to changing lifestyles. In contrast to secular books that assume their readers have many sexual partners, Christian writers stress that marriage partners should be sexually faithful. A man should have one wife and be faithful to her until death. This is certainly the biblical ideal, and it is the only kind of sexual relationship sanctioned in Scripture.

Lately, however, I find myself feeling that when we emphasize only sexual conduct or behavior, we miss something of what the Bible is actually talking about.

Once in a counseling session a wife told me she would rather find out that her husband was involved in a short-term sexual fling, where the motive was confused male desire and animal lust, than that he was involved in a long-term, caring, emotional relationship with another woman, even without sex. This wife did not want her husband turning to someone else for friendship, sharing, confidence, and trust. She did not want him to find his intimate intellectual and emotional support outside the marriage union, even if no sex was involved.

At first I was surprised by this woman's comments, but the longer I have thought about them, the more I understand the depth of what she was saying. Sexual faithfulness is important, to be sure, but faithfulness goes beyond the physical. It is based on trust, confidence, intimacy, and sharing in all areas.

The goal in marriage should be intimacy. According to Scripture, man was not made to live alone. He is a social being, and ideally he will live in an intimate relationship with a marriage partner. Biblical marriage should lead toward the total harmony and unity of two persons: body, mind, and spirit.

In the same way that Abraham knew God and was His friend (Isa. 41:8), a married couple—through all aspects of living together in a concerned, caring, unselfish manner—begin to learn about one another until their devotion ultimately can turn into *agape* love, that is, the willingness to give oneself for the benefit of the other.

Love in the biblical sense is not something we feel; it is something we do. It is responsible behavior, commitment to another person. Love is demonstrated by the Golden Rule: "Do to others as you would have them do to you" (Luke 6:31).

This kind of love, of course, was most dramatically demonstrated in Christ's death on the cross for us. "Greater love has no one than this, that one lay down his life for his friends" (John 15:13). When a man and woman have an intimate marriage based on biblical principles, they will develop this kind of sacrificial love for each other.

God's love is unconditional. He never fails us; He is totally faithful. Ultimately our goal in marriage is that our love will have those same qualities, so just as we can feel totally secure before God, we can also feel totally secure with our mates.

Christians often quote Romans 8:38-39: "I am convinced that neither death nor life, neither angels nor demons, neither the present nor the future, nor any powers, neither height nor depth, nor anything else in all creation, will be able to separate us from the love of God that is in Christ Jesus our Lord." Ideally a Christian marriage should have that same sense of certitude: nothing should be able to separate us; our faithfulness to each other should be total.

Related Articles
Chapter 4: Three Important Choices
Chapter 8: Mental Fidelity

Love as Mercy

JUDITH C. LECHMAN

Shortly after moving to New Mexico, I visited a Navajo weaver on a nearby reservation. Like many Eastern transplants, I soon grew to love the intricately designed weavings. Before long I wanted to learn more about their history and symbolism as well as about the mathematical precision of the techniques that transform random strands of sheep wool into stunning works of art.

Over the years I've been fortunate enough to indulge this interest with books and firsthand experience. Time and again, when I see my clumsy attempts at weaving or look at the truly masterful productions of native American weavers, I think of the gift of mercy in marriage. Let me explain.

To casual observers, these Indian weavings appear beautiful, eye-catching, or at least interesting in their harmony, color, balance, and design. We may notice size, shape, or texture; we may appreciate the overall artistic effect or sense the ancient roots of this craft. But the weaver, and the careful observer, can see the work with a different eye, one that considers each strand individually and understands why its placement, color, shape, and thickness are true to the pattern being created.

When we look at mercy in marriage, we tend to be like casual observers. We see mercy as a whole, without bothering to examine the individual strands that together create it. We see that mercy is showing practical compassion to our spouses when they are needy. We know that joy can come from doing unexpected deeds of loving-kindness, and that suffering can be alleviated when our caring turns into genuine acts of sharing. Yet to find out what mercy truly consists of, we need to look at its various intertwining strands and seek to understand what they are and why they are needed in a Christian marriage.

Forgiveness is the most important strand woven into the fabric of mercy. In fact, without forgiveness, mercy can't exist. Before we are able to feel compassion or alleviate suffering, we have to recognize God's unconditional forgiveness of our sins and adopt that same attitude toward our spouses when they have wronged us. We must be willing to forgive others as we wish to be forgiven.

Forgiveness also demands that we probe the painful bitterness, animosity, and antagonism of our daily encounters and let go of them. Yet we'll never be able to let go and turn to our spouses in a spirit of loving forgiveness until we cut out the remnants of self-pride that prevent us from forgiving them. For it is pride that makes us remember the hurts and scorn we've received, that allows the insults and undeserved rebukes we've allowed to fester within.

Forbearance is the second crucial

51

strand found in our weaving of mercy in marriage. While forgiveness implies a heartfelt pardoning of those who have wronged us, forbearance suggests something more far-reaching. Looking beyond forgiving our spouses, we now need to learn how to accept and tolerate our loved ones complete with their failings, annoying habits, and irritating mannerisms. With forbearance, we rise above finding fault with our marriage partners and bear with these faults in a spirit of loving acceptance.

Silence, the third strand in our weaving of mercy, is a natural outgrowth of forbearance. In learning to tolerate our spouses, we refrain from commenting on their behavior in a negative and destructive manner. Yet silence in mercy means more than stilling our tongues whenever we feel like speaking evil of husband or wife. We must silence our judgmental thoughts as well. Each time we think of our spouses critically, we need to consciously isolate that thought and replace it with one that is imbued with gracious tolerance for their faults. And through the use of silence, we not only drive out our desire to dominate and control; we also learn to listen to one another. When, in the respectful silence of our hearts, we truly hear what our partners are saying to us, we can begin to serve them with mercy, for now we know what they need from us and we can respond accordingly.

Confrontation, the fourth strand, appears an odd choice to include in the fabric of mercy. Yet it adds a necessary and vibrant color to our weaving. Forgiving others, tolerating their faults, and silencing our judgmental tongues and hearts are merciful responses to make in certain situations. But there are also times when we show mercy best by confronting our spouses about a bad habit, a slight or hurt, a hidden resentment or failing.

Mercy in marriage needs the cutting edge of confrontation, for it brings about

---

1 CORINTHIANS 13:4-8

Love is patient, love is kind. It does not envy, it does not boast, it is not proud. It is not rude, it is not self-seeking, it is not easily angered, it keeps no record of wrongs. Love does not delight in evil but rejoices with the truth. It always protects, always trusts, always hopes, always perseveres. Love never fails.

---

change in a most effective manner. Without confrontation, mercy is merely a patient, forgiving, tolerant reaction to others' shortcomings. With confrontation, it is something more. We, through the Holy Spirit, are capable of creating change in the person we confront, leading him or her closer to God by our attitude during the confrontation. But a word of warning—confrontation is likely to be ineffective unless it is practiced together with the other strands of mercy.

Any examination of mercy in marriage would be incomplete without considering the practical role played by discipline. We need to practice forgiveness, forbearance, silence, and confrontation whenever the proper occasion arises. The more frequently we exercise these four aspects of mercy, the easier it becomes to feel compassion and to do something constructive with it. Disciplined mercy, with the four strands of forgiveness, forbearance, silence, and confrontation woven through it, moves our marriage deeper into the realm of service to others. And this is where we rightly belong.

Related Articles
Chapter 10: Gentle Anger
Chapter 10: Tender Acceptance and
   Total Forgiveness

Love as Grace

NORM WAKEFIELD

For many years I had the haunting sense that all our talk about the biblical view of marriage lacked a vital element. I heard many messages based on the Bible. I participated in sermons and seminars on commitment, headship, submission, roles, and communication. Yet the element that held everything together seemed to be missing.

Marriage is the union of two imperfect individuals. Each brings to the relationship a host of habits, failures, and prejudices. No matter how good one's intentions, these forces undermine marriage, always threatening to weaken or destroy it. Some powerful ingredient is required which will bind a man and woman together when their imperfection pulls them apart.

Grace is this vital link. It provides the cohesion that holds two individuals together. It allows love to develop. Commitment says, "I'll stay with you." Grace says, "I'll accept you, and treat you with dignity and love, even if you fail me." Grace is the spiritual quality that undergirds all healthy relationships.

Christians should be experts on grace. We have discovered an incredible God who in His rich mercy made us alive with Christ when we were dead in our sins (Eph. 2:1-9). He was kind to us when we cared nothing about Him. Even after coming to know God through Jesus Christ, we are painfully aware of our inability to live lives worthy of Him. Yet He is patient and kind. If anyone should be motivated to be gracious to others, we should be.

I confess that when I married my wife, Winnie, 24 years ago, I knew little about grace in marriage. I discovered that I had many expectations for her. I planned to change her to fit my mold. I became impatient with her refusal to cooperate with my plans for her. After all, I was assigned by God to be in charge, and she should appreciate my commitment to be God's agent to refine her! In essence, that was what I had been taught.

Then I discovered the principle of grace. The Lord began to show me that when a relationship is based on unconditional acceptance, we say the following things by word and action:

"I will never condemn you." When we speak by grace, we say those things that build up our partner. We affirm his or her strengths. Our words are couched in patience, forgiveness, and compassion. We are committed never to tear down or destroy. We do not speak words of criticism, attack, or ridicule. Grace gives life; it never kills (Eph. 4:29).

"You are free from my rules, demands, or 'laws' of marriage." In unhealthy marriages each person is trying to establish control of the relationship for his own gains. Sometimes the person tries to manipulate the other out of the belief that "I know what is best for you." Ultimately this makes the marriage confining, restrictive, and destructive.

But in a marriage based on grace both individuals are free from the need to perform to gain the other's love, acceptance, or favor. This creates an environment of freedom and growth. We have no need to fear each other and to establish a defensive posture to protect ourselves.

"I accept you as an equal partner. I am an heir with you of the gracious

SONNET 14 (19TH CENTURY)

If thou must love me, let it be for naught
Except for love's sake only. Do not say
"I love her for her smile—her look—her way
Of speaking gently—for a trick of thought
That falls in well with mine, and certes brought
A sense of pleasant ease on such a day"—
For these things in themselves, Beloved, may
Be changed, or change for thee—and love, so wrought,
May be unwrought so. Neither love me for
Thine own dear pity's wiping my cheeks dry—
A creature might forget to weep, who bore
Thy comfort long, and lose thy love thereby!
But love me for love's sake, that evermore
Thou mayst love on, through love's eternity.

Elizabeth Barrett Browning

gift of life." When the spirit of grace rules our marriage, we are freed from the obsession to master each other. We become genuine partners in our pursuit after God. We have no need for hierarchies. Both husband and wife are secure living under the Lord's leadership, and they feel no need to manipulate, control, or dominate each other.

"I invite you to share your deepest hurts and fears, as well as your dreams and yearnings. Never fear that I will make fun of them or ridicule you." A relationship founded on grace opens the door to our inner life. In such a relationship, I discover a friend who will accept me, warts and all. I find a person who is generous in compassion and kindness. I discover a partner who laughs with me, but not at me. What a wonderful basis for a wholesome, affirming relationship!

A marriage based on grace is a gift from God. He enables us to understand and show grace, because He has dem-onstrated it in every action toward us. Unfortunately, many individuals have never comprehended God's gracious nature. They still see Him as a harsh, demanding taskmaster. Thus they cannot understand how to relate to their marriage partner with freedom, generosity, and mature love.

Grace is your warm, inviting smile.

Grace is giving me freedom to do it my way, not yours.

Grace is saying, "I admire how you. . . ."

Grace is not letting my bad habit ruin our evening.

Grace is being patient when I'm irritable.

Grace is telling others about my strengths, not my weaknesses.

Related Articles

Chapter 2: Characteristics of a
    Mature Marriage
Chapter 4: Building Your Mate's Self-esteem

Love as Romance

EARL & SANDY WILSON

"**M**y husband is about as romantic as a cold baked potato," Nancy said. "I can't even remember the last time he did something special for me. I think he still loves me because he comes home at night, but sometimes I wonder. He has changed so much since our courtship days. Then, he seemed to know how to do all the right things to make me feel like a queen. I feel so starved for his attention."

When we talked to Nancy's husband, Bill, he too expressed dissatisfaction. "It seems I can never do the right thing," he said. "I try to show her how much I love her, but she just doesn't hear. Even when I am affectionate she acts like I'm trying to rape her. When we were going together she used to snuggle up to me and even pat my knee in public. Now she rarely moves in my direction, and she seems to have lost all her playfulness. I don't know how long we can go on this way."

Nancy and Bill's marriage was hanging on the cord of commitment, but the cord was beginning to fray. Their relationship needed the strengthening of romance. Neither Bill nor Nancy could figure out how a relationship that started out so spicy could end up so bland. We discovered several things that had taken away the pizzazz.

First, Bill and Nancy had started taking each other for granted. Instead of continuing to work to impress each other, they had each gotten involved in other areas of priority. Nancy devoted her best creative efforts to the children and her teaching at church, while Bill threw himself into his job. They were missing the mark because they had stopped looking at the target.

This switch in priorities had led to another problem—spitefulness. Spitefulness usually takes this form: "If he doesn't, then I'm sure not going to." If you don't try to make me feel special, I'm not going to do anything special for you. If you won't scratch my back, I certainly won't rub yours. This type of thinking is a deadly trap.

In addition, Bill and Nancy seemed to be frozen by lack of excitement. When you are not being romantically stimulated by your spouse, it is easy to become less and less creative yourself. You can't think of anything new to do together. You always approach lovemaking in the same old way. Television takes the place of talking. These are the elements of romantic disaster.

Bill and Nancy both knew they didn't want to live the rest of their lives together without romance. They came up with a plan. Their ideas worked for them, and they will probably work for you.

First, they agreed to forgive each other and to stop focusing on the negative. "He couldn't be as bad as I have been thinking of him," Nancy said. "I'm too smart to marry someone like that!" Bill in turn began to look for the little ways Nancy was trying to be romantic.

They began to date regularly, and they started to really look forward to time together. Bill learned to say, "I would like to take you to dinner Friday evening. Let's dress up and make an evening of it." This was in contrast to what he used to say: "I don't suppose you would like to do anything, would you?" He recognized the definite romantic difference in

INTIMACY

The intimate is Adam and his rib.
Does the metaphor make Adam
   seem
To be the source and Eve his
Subjugated consort?
No . . . both have one source.
Please let's not ask
For a theology
Of love and loving.
You and I are;
We touch, it is enough.
We wake sometimes in Eden,
Grateful for our gift.
Our need for all five senses
Dwindles in the night to one . . .
We touch!
The lie so often told in cinemas is
   cheap.
Real intimacy is not
R-rated, exhibitionist—
Photographs in half-light—
Show-off eros picking at our
   appetites
Without regard to real
Or long-term needs.
Have I told you lately that
On certain heavy nights
I've come
Home to find you sleeping
And touched you as you slept,
And was assured that I could make it,
Rather, we could make it!
Our world, strong as Kepler's
   Cosmos,
Will survive.
You were there
Waiting in the darkness
That forbade my eyes
But welcomed me to draw upon
That odd security that speaks
From heart to heart and from
   inwardness to
Inwardness—never traveling
In those open spaces that
We-at-touch forbid to be.
Intimacy is a giver

Whose gift is strong security.
I once learned the proverb,
"Given a good home life,
A man can stand anything."
How beautiful the fountain
Of our strength
Should reside
In this one simple sense: touch.
Touch is the giver.
A powerful miracle
Of skin confronting skin.
When my arm but brushes yours
My survival
Is made sure.
So tell me not that intimacy
Is mere sexual encounter.
To be sure, sex is touching
At its ultimate . . .
Touching at the center of our
   passion.
But it carries too much fire.
Burning before it really warms,
It is too much incendiary storm
And leaves us like Lear in lightning,
Still befuddled over who we are.
I must confess
I've been afraid
Like other men,
I never said it
Quite aloud.
But when I touched you,
Intimacy gave rise to steel
Too strong to be diminished
By life's dragons
Who always lay their demon eggs
Before I quite dispatch
Their parent woes.
Greatness comes in touching you.
My universe,
So microscopic,
Then grows large
And, dwarfing Sagan's quasars,
Celebrates its right to be.

Calvin Miller

the two statements! Nancy responded by sitting close to Bill during the date and at other times. Their feelings for each other began to change.

Bill and Nancy also began to communicate more romantically on a day-to-day basis. They talked more, cuddled more, played more, and began to enjoy their sex life again. Bill said, "I sure think the next 10 years are going to be more fun than the last." Nancy commented, "I feel married again, and it really feels good."

Bill and Nancy had to continue to work to protect their newly established romance, but each time they agreed to give more time and attention to each other, they grew closer. Maybe that's what romance is: love plus time and attention.

Developing and Nourishing Love

RICHARD A. MEIER

When we talk about love, we are talking about something with many components. The Bible identifies three of these: *eros, phileo,* and *agape.* Married love requires us to know how to love all three ways.

Eros is the *emotional* and physical aspect of love. It is best described by emotional words such as those in Proverbs 5:18-19, which describes a man's sexual excitement about his wife.

Eros includes, but is not limited to, romantic sex in marriage. According to the Apostle Paul, romantic sex is so important that the pattern should not be disrupted except by mutual consent, and then only for a little while as the couple gives itself to prayer (1 Cor. 7:5).

This kind of love is nurtured by hugging and touching in nonsexual contexts. Practice hugging and touching your spouse often—when you leave the house and come home again, during the course of the evening, as you walk together. Those tender touches communicate, "I care for you."

Phileo love, mentioned in Titus 2:4, is the *relational* aspect of love. A reciprocal kind of love, it is nurtured by open communication and common interests. A man and woman who love this way delight in each other's presence. They enjoy being together to work on common hobbies, to talk and pray, to go to church, to go on dates.

Phileo love provides the incentive to reinvest affection—to recreate the conditions that were present when the couple first fell in love, which was probably in a relaxed setting with abundant relational opportunities.

Do you and your spouse have fun times together? Do you make time for each other just to fellowship and share? Do you delight in being together? Can you hardly wait to see each other? Sit down together and talk about ways you could nourish this type of love. Make a list of things you would like to do together, things you both would enjoy. And then do them!

Agape love, mentioned many times in

Scripture (i.e., Eph. 5:25), is *mental* in the sense that it is not necessarily connected to the emotions or the strength of the relationship. It is the commitment side of love—a choice, not a feeling.

Agape love means taking the initiative to meet your spouse's real needs, thus fostering his or her growth. It can be unilateral: one person can do it even if the other will not.

The agape aspect of love energizes the other two aspects. If a need exists in the eros area, it is the commitment of agape love that motivates the individual to try to understand the spouse's needs and take the steps necessary to meet them. If a need exists in the phileo area, agape love motivates the spouse to make more time to relate, to share, to do things together, to communicate, to learn how to be best friends.

The commitment of agape love motivates the partners to solve the problems within their marriage without giving up. It is nurtured by the spiritual life of each person in the marriage. As the husband and wife put Christ first, feed on His Word, and share their lives in praise and prayer, their commitment to God strengthens their commitment to each other. Their relationship is enhanced by God's grace, which is always available to those who are obedient to His will.

Related Articles
Chapter 4: Never Take Your Mate for Granted
Chapter 4: Cultivating Romance

Dimensions of Married Love

GARY D. BENNETT

There are distinct dimensions of married love that every couple experiences, endures, and encompasses in the marriage relationship. Couples who recognize and utilize each of these dimensions to its fullest enjoy a genuinely satisfying relationship. What are these dimensions of married love, and how can you experience them in your own marriage?

Romantic love is characterized by intense emotions, excitement, anticipation, hoping, and dreaming. It's the sparkle in the fireworks of love.

Romantic love is good: it draws us together, gives us strength, helps us transcend the ordinary and mundane aspects of day-to-day living.

But romantic love is also unreal. It causes us to view ourselves and our mates through rose-colored glasses. We cannot live on romantic love alone, even though romantic love can and should play an important role throughout marriage. The best romance includes the unexpected and spontaneous, the impractical, and the dating and wooing of one another.

Disenchanted love is romantic love shattered. It is part of every love relationship. Disenchanted love sees the hard realities, the ordinary, the negative. It often keeps a record of wrongs. It's the explosive in the fireworks of love.

Disenchanted love can, if ignored, become a stumbling block—or you can use it as a stepping-stone toward each other. When handled properly, with forgiveness and acceptance, disenchanted love is a tremendous catalyst for growth. Honesty and open communication, of course, are prerequisites.

When we learn to forgive and overlook one another's faults, we learn more about God's love and acceptance of us. And when we cope with disenchanted

THE TROUBLE WITH WARM FUZZIES

The value we place on each other's personhood determines how we treat each other, and that in turn determines how we feel. Too often our society teaches just the opposite: feelings are made the basis for behavior and for valuing the other person.

The trouble with "fuzzies first" is that we all face temperature changes in our marriage relationships. We don't heat up the marital temperature to 100 degrees on our honeymoon and leave it there consistently until the day we die. That is an unrealistic view of human relationships, especially one as intimate as marriage. If we let our feelings alone determine our conduct with each other, we are ready to get divorced as soon as the temperature cools. As soon as "we ain't got the feeling," as a popular song describes it, "we ain't got the marriage."

But the value we place on each other's personhood is the foundation stone for love and marriage. Since we determined long ago the value we each place on the other, we are not looking for a way out as soon as the temperature drops. And we have discovered that since we each place such a high value on the other as a person, the temperature doesn't drop as often or as much as we might expect.

Gil & Arlie Beers

love, we learn how to rise above frustration and disappointments. Living through disillusionment, we strengthen the hope that our marriage can and will survive any difficulty.

Mature love is a decision, a choice, a conscious commitment of the will to love in spite of circumstances and without conditions. It allows us to accept uncertainty with the conviction that we will make our love endure. It's what gives beauty to the fireworks of love.

Mature love goes beyond the notion of having a "meaningful relationship" until things get tough. There are no veneers in mature love. Faced with trials and difficulties, mature love actually deepens and gives us strength of character.

Ask yourself and then discuss with your spouse the following questions:

1. How is our love romantic? As time goes on, what part of our romantic love do I want to see continue? What part does my spouse need and enjoy?

2. Has disenchantment affected my love? How? When?

3. Mature love is a conscious commitment of the will. Have we experienced this in our love relationship? In what ways?

4. Have we faced problems together? When? Which ones have strengthened my love? How?

5. Am I confident of my spouse's love for me?

Related Articles

Introduction: Marriage: A Vehicle of God's Love
Chapter 4: Three Important Choices

Love Is the Gift of a Caring Self

DWIGHT HERVEY SMALL

What pattern of love serves to guide Christian husbands and wives? In the New Testament the model is that of God who so loved the world that He gave His Son to redeem the undeserving, and that of Jesus sacrificing Himself for us. Here is a God who cares, loving us in spite of our sin and rebellion. *Love is His gift of a caring Self.*

As we experience God's love, we may say with John, "We love because He first loved us" (1 John 4:19). His is creative love. Since in our humanness we cannot love as God Himself loves, He gives the power of His transforming love to create in our hearts a responding love. Even more, His loving us makes possible His loving others through us. His design is that this divinely implanted love reach out first of all to those closest to us: our husbands and wives.

How is this possible? "God has given us the Holy Spirit to fill our hearts with His love" (Rom. 5:5, TLB). He Himself *teaches us how* to love, then by His Spirit *enables us* to love. The lesson is plain: we cannot give what we haven't first received, nor can we love unconditionally unless He loves through us.

God's love is unearned, freely given with no expectation of return for our welfare and blessing. Though we disappoint Him and sin against Him, His is an ever faithful, never diminished love. What a model for husbands and wives! Covenant love in marriage, like Jesus' love, is described in 1 Corinthians 13. Think of your marriage as you read and apply each quality described there.

When God's love rules our hearts, we can say to our spouse, "I love you for who you are in yourself, who you are as God's special gift to me, who you are meant to be in His purpose, and yes, for all you can be within my caring love."

Love within marriage makes three demands:

1. *Humble yourself that you may affirm and elevate your partner.* Since marriage involves compromise, accommodation, and relinquishment of our self-indulgent spirits, a humbleness is required that God alone can give. Husbands need to know that a humble spirit is not unmanly, but takes strength, courage, and faith. Humble love revels in the joy of servanthood.

2. *Acknowledge your own offenses, take rightful blame, and seek reconciliation through forgiveness.* A caring spirit doesn't deny its share of blame, make excuses, or ask for leniency. It is quick to confess and seek healing, concerned more for the health of the marriage than for self-justification.

3. *When you are the offended partner, reach out with forgiveness.* Sure, you can pout, sulk, give in to hurt pride, make demands, and refuse to forgive. There's a better way, however—the way of caring. Let pride give way to humility and forgiveness as part of the gift of a caring self.

God's forgiving love is merciful, full of grace and hope. It is not concerned with who deserves what, only with how love might forgive, heal, and restore. Forgiving love is creative within marriage, bringing new dimensions of conflict resolution, deeper trust, and unity.

While married love may sometimes dry up, God's implanted love can transform weakened human love, renewing it and making it like His own. As He cares for us through our failures, so we must care for our mates when they fail us or disappoint us. This is the work of His Spirit, and it is ours for the taking.

Shortly before his death, world-renowned cellist Pablo Casals remarked, "I feel the capacity to care is the thing that gives life its deepest significance." Modern American philosopher Milton Mayeroff writes, "The highest claims of love are represented in the call to care for one another." Far better than ambivalent feelings as the foundation of marriage is the higher call to care for one's partner, to practice the real discipline of love.

In the last analysis, love is the caring interaction between two people who embody mutual esteem for each other. The quality of their loving derives from their commitment to caring. This is what we as husbands and wives should cherish for ourselves, commit ourselves to, and work continually to actualize.

The creative power of caring love is beyond estimation. It can replace negative attitudes and actions with positive ones. But caring runs counter to a self-seeking nature. We cannot care for someone and at the same time manipulate him or her for our own ends. By caring, we help our partner become all that he or she can be. This takes time, thought, and creative action. As husband and wife try to decide how best to divide tasks at home, spend their money, use their time, or plan their leisure, the underlying principle must be their commitment to caring.

Larry Christenson reminds us that a genuine, caring love is like a mature tree. It doesn't get uprooted by every wind of change. It develops a strong root structure and sends out sturdy branches. It can survive dry spells. It can produce healthy fruit. Love builds a marriage on commitment to caring, not directed by feelings but only enhanced by them.

As you seek God's enablement as husband or wife, commit yourself to caring. Let your love be the mutual exchange of the gift of a caring self.

Related Articles
Introduction: Marriage: A Vehicle of God's Love
Chapter   1: Love as Grace

Love Always Hurts

DAVID VEERMAN

She sparkles in white as she walks slowly toward her beloved, standing tuxedoed, tall, and confident at aisle's end. For this day they have dreamed and planned. Even as children, they each knew that someday they would meet just the right person, fall in love and be married, and live "happily ever after." And then, after repeating sincere vows to love and cherish each other forever, they rush headlong through honeymoon and ideals into life together and reality.

Most soon-to-be-marrieds are wildly idealistic, never dreaming that "in sickness or health, richer or poorer, and better or worse" could mean sick, poor, and worse. In fact, I have found these to be the most difficult counselees. When I explain that life (and marriage) can be tough, they smile sweetly and say, "Yes, we know that there will be problems, but our love can take it." Unfortunately, however, the sweet taste of being newlyweds

61

soon turns bitter to many as their idealism hits real life.

Of course this unrealistic view of life and love is intensified by our culture. Songs, ads, and TV sitcoms picture unending romance and pleasure with that "special person." The truth is that in a fallen world, life is difficult—pain is the rule and not the exception. No one is perfect, neither you nor that person who will stand (or who stood) beside you in church and whose commitment to each other you share. Far from offering a life free from discomfort, *love always hurts*. When you commit yourself in love to someone, you are opening yourself to pain.

Love Hurts Because . . .

True love involves sacrifice. "God is love" (1 John 4:8), and His perfect love for us cost Him His Son, Jesus (John 3:16) who suffered and died for us on the cross (1 John 4:9-10). When we truly love someone, we will do anything we can for him or her—often this will mean sacrifice and suffering. Our firstborn had trouble sleeping at night. Gail and I would take turns at 2 or 3 A.M. trying to rock little Kara to sleep. We could have ignored her painful cries, but our love sent us into her room, regardless of the cost in sleepy days to follow. And I think of the sacrifice my parents made to raise five children, including this stubborn and self-centered boy. Because they loved, they gave.

True love means feeling the other person's pain. Because I love Gail, I hurt when she hurts. To do otherwise would mean that I didn't care or that I was insensitive to her needs. Recently Dana, our youngest child, broke a finger. We held her, cried with her, and felt her pain as the finger was set. There are also the pains of failure, sin, and discipline. When we love people, we feel with them.

True love means being vulnerable. When you live with someone, they soon learn everything about you—your strengths and weaknesses, likes and dislikes, habits, idiosyncrasies, and pressure points. That's why arguments can be so painful—a hateful spouse has a quiver full of hateful arrows to shoot, which usually hit their mark. In his book, *Why Am I Afraid to Tell You Who I Am?* Father John Powell says, "I am afraid to tell you who I am because you may not like who I am, and that's all I have." Many men and women, afraid to open themselves to the possibility of rejection and pain, shut themselves off and refuse to love. But true love means being honest and therefore wide open to hurtful attacks. This is why it is so important to "fight fair" in marriage and to protect each other.

True love means feeling deeply any separation. Quite naturally, when you love someone, you want to be with him or her. And if you are separated for any length of time, you feel your loss—of companionship, personality, support, and love. When a man and a woman marry, the two "become one flesh" (Gen. 2:24). When this bond is severed, the pain is deep and the loneliness overwhelming. It is impossible, of course, to be with another person 24 hours a day (and this would cause other kinds of pain), and with certain jobs, trips away from home are a way of life. Separation is inevitable and with it pain.

And then there is the ultimate separation, death. In our vows we say, "until death parts us." Only in rare circumstances do husband and wife die together. This means that one will be left to live alone. When you truly love someone, you miss him deeply when he's gone.

I write this, not to cause depression or second thoughts about marriage, but to provide a balance, a realistic perspective on life and love. Because love involves vulnerability, handle each other with care. Because life involves struggles and problems, encourage and support each other. Because love involves giving, express your deep gratitude to each other for sacrifices big and small. And because life involves separation, make each moment together count for each other and for God's glory.

Love Is Meeting Each Other's Needs

LUIS PALAU

My wife, Pat, and I have been married for more than 25 years, and every day I thank God that I married *her!* We're different in many ways, but we complement each other. Pat is a levelheaded thinker, while I tend to be a more impulsive decision-maker. I appreciate her strengths and have learned to rely on them regularly. In marriage, God wants us to learn to rest in each other's strengths.

It's exciting to have a wife who complements you, and if you marry in Christ, that's what happens. Your weaknesses she supplies; her weaknesses you supply. God built this concept of complementing one another into marriage at the very beginning. After creating Adam, God said, "I will make a helper suitable for him" (Gen. 2:18), and then He formed Eve. Why? Because without her, Adam was incomplete.

Interestingly, that word *helper* is used throughout the Old Testament to describe someone of strength. Obviously Eve had a lot going for her. She supplied what Adam lacked. But Adam could receive what she had to offer, and she could receive what Adam had for her, only by submitting to each other.

The Apostle Paul had a lot to say about how husbands and wives should relate to each other, but before saying any of it he commanded, "Submit to one another out of reverence for Christ" (Eph. 5:21). Fact number one in God's blueprint for happy homes, then, is that the husband is to submit to his wife, and the wife is to submit to her husband.

I can't insist on having my own way all the time, and neither can Pat. Our marriage relationship immediately begins deteriorating when either of us wants our own opinion to dominate. That's why the Bible teaches that we are to submit to one another.

The concept of submission is found throughout Scripture. In 1 Corinthians 16:16, we're told to "submit to . . . everyone who joins in the work" of serving others. Hebrews 13:17 says, "Obey your leaders and submit to their authority." First Peter 2:13 says, "Submit yourselves for the Lord's sake to every authority instituted among man." First Peter 5:5 says, "Be submissive to those who are older."

In the home, as we see in Ephesians 5:21–6:4, the wife submits to her husband by respecting and obeying him, the husband submits to his wife by sacrificially loving her, the children submit to their parents by obeying and honoring them, and the parents submit to their children by spiritually nurturing them. The Apostle Paul goes on to say that even slaves and masters are to submit to one another, because we all serve

63

God.

Submission is necessary for order and stability. Without it, each person does his own thing. One popular song says, "I did it my way." Go ahead—and see how many people you hurt, including yourself. Lack of submission leads to disaster.

To husbands: Too often, we men insist on having our own way in a futile attempt to mask our insecurities. Listen, your wife knows your weak points! The Bible encourages you to rely on her, just as she is to rely on you.

Notice that God doesn't tell us, "Make your wives submit. Assert your authority as head of the house. Show who's boss." Instead, Ephesians 5:25 tells us men, "Love your wives, just as Christ loved the church and gave Himself up for her." To do that, we must die to self.

By dying to self, I can enjoy my wife's specialness. I can let her meet my needs—even needs I might rather not recognize. As I honor Pat, my relationship with her—and with God—is blessed (1 Peter 3:7).

To wives: Remember that your husband is the head of the home, not because he is superior but because God has given him this responsibility. Frequently, husbands try to shirk their duties as leaders of the home. When we get married, some of us men secretly hope our wives will be tough-minded

---

SIGNS OF MATURE LOVE

Where these qualities are present, love is mature:

Confidence
Fidelity
Trust
Contentment
Unity
Camaraderie
Peace of mind
Sacrifice
Sense of humor

Gary Bennett

---

and good decision-makers. You may have to help your husband be the spiritual leader in your home. How?

Early in our marriage Pat told me, "The Bible teaches that you are the head of the home. I will help you make decisions, but I will not make them for you." This encouraged me to be a better husband and a better Christian. Encourage your husband to do the same.

Related Articles
Chapter 7: Marriage as Mutual Servanthood
Chapter 7: God's Plan for the Husband-Wife Relationship

Love Without Fear

JOHN & KATHLEEN COLLIGAN

It is not uncommon in our society for a person to sincerely have love in his heart for another family member, and yet be unable to show it. Sometimes we hesitate to say "I love you" because it hasn't been part of our family custom or because we don't want to look foolish. We fear being vulnerable. We don't want to be laughed at or rejected. We don't want to be used. If you tell someone you love him, he may feel free to make demands on you. Some of us worry what will happen to us if we love too much. Some of us feel a strong sense of guilt and sadness because our beloved died without our having said "I love you."

When Kathy spoke to a group of women about making their husbands their first priority, the question came from the audience, "What will happen to me if I love my husband the way you're describing? If I center my life on my husband, what will my life be like when I'm a widow?" Men frequently comment, "I don't have time to make my wife that important to me. I have too many other things to do and too many demands on me already."

Both concerns are real, but they are basically self-centered. The husband worries about overextending himself, so he shuts his wife out of his life so he can do what's important to him. The wife worries about a future that might never happen. She lives many long years of a guarded relationship in marriage, preparing for widowhood. She's afraid to love too much because it will hurt too much to lose him. Sometimes both mates hold back in their love because they fear being hurt in a divorce—thus making divorce more attractive because they have so little to lose.

If we're going to have a love relationship with anyone—a brother or sister, son or daughter, father or mother—we will always run the risk of grief and separation. Love and suffering seem to go hand-in-hand, just as they did for Jesus. We have the incredible delight in our beloved, warm smiles, affectionate hugs, companionship, and sharing. But we also have pain and sorrow when we part—whether temporarily or permanently.

Is the reward of loving totally, and being loved totally, worth the risk of the grief and suffering which come with death? Speaking personally, the answer is definitely yes. We have just marked the anniversary of our son's death. Johnny was the only son to whom we gave birth and he was, quite literally, a beloved son. He was murdered when he was 21 years old. A month before he died, we spent a weekend together in a mountain cabin. Before we parted, we gave him our blessing and a letter in which we told him once again of all the good qualities we saw in him and of how blessed we were to have such a wonderful son. He had that letter with him when he was killed. As we look back, we thank God that it is common in our family to say "I love you" to each other every day in both words and actions.

A friend whose husband died a few years ago spoke at our church and said, "I miss Mike immensely; my life will never be the same. But I have the satisfaction of knowing I loved him as well as I could every day of our marriage. And he knew it too because I told him often. We had no unfinished business."

That's how we loved Johnny—there was no unfinished business between us. That's all God asks of us—to simply love those whom He sends into our lives, and especially our family. The loneliness we feel four years after Johnny's death is alive and catches us by surprise sometimes with its intensity. The desire to see him again is very real. The intense grief is over, but there is a permanent place in our hearts where our son lives, and always will.

Through Scripture, God calls us to forget our fears, risk everything, and love one another totally. The death of our son showed us that none of us have until tomorrow to do that.

Related Articles
Chapter 1: Love Always Hurts
Chapter 4: My Husband, My Best Friend

Marriages, like the people in them, pass through stages of growth and development. How much do you know about these stages? Take this quiz and see. Mark these statements true (T) or false (F):

_____ 1. A happy honeymoon means a happy marriage.

_____ 2. You have to have children to be a family.

_____ 3. Children tend to make a marriage happier.

_____ 4. You'll have more time for your family later on.

_____ 5. Once you've been married for 20 years, you're safe.

_____ 6. Real Christians don't have midlife crises.

_____ 7. Most couples find that the "empty nest" is an especially painful time.

_____ 8. Older couples don't usually enjoy sex.

_____ 9. It's better not to think about the possibility of your mate's dying.

_____ 10. A good marriage gets better as the years go by.

ANSWERS: Questions 1-9 are false. Only question 10 is true.

2

SEASONS
OF MARRIAGE

Each marriage is unique and yet each one follows prescribed patterns of growth—seasons—as each spouse masters the art of togetherness, gains insights, faces crises, acts upon decisions, makes adjustments, solves problems. Solomon states simply: "There is a time for everything and a season for every activity under heaven. . . . [God] has made everything beautiful in its time" (Ecc. 3:1, 11).

In marriage, two soloists become a wedded duet; together they pick up the pace of parenting and move into the booming momentum of midlife. With the measured cadence of grandparenthood a sweet wisdom of old age rounds out the cycle of husband-and-wife love. Such is the intended rhythm of the Creator. Yet human nature stumbles; we tend to balk at our challenges and to fear the future.

To ignore the inevitable and to refuse to anticipate change thwarts harmony. Marriage is smoothed out when we:

● See the whole of marriage in perspective
● Understand how problems tend to cluster at certain places
● Face our own unique cycles, those personal tasks God gives only to us

Seasons provide stability and orientation. They help us to appreciate yesterday, to enjoy the moment, and to prepare for tomorrow.

Howard & Jeanne Hendricks

The First Years

JIM & SALLY CONWAY

The early years of marriage are the time to form life dreams and set those dreams in motion. Each of the mates had an identity as a single, and now both adjust to having an identity as a couple. When they have children, they will be identified as a family. During these early years they establish their patterns of relating to each other and generally choose their career direction, where they will live, their friends, and what lifestyle fits them as a married couple. The choices made at this time set the foundation for the rest of their married years.

The first year of marriage is the most dangerous, with the highest potential for divorce. Several factors can tip the scales toward success during the first year and the years that follow. Applying some practical insights will not only help a marriage to survive, but will also make it more satisfying and fulfilling.

1. *Personal maturity.* If both mates have sufficiently matured, they will bring strength to the marriage. Areas of immaturity—"carryover baggage"—are likely to cause stress in the relationship as each person continues his or her own personal growing.

We've observed that a major area of immaturity causing marital stress in the early years is a poor self-image. Because people with low self-esteem are essentially uncomfortable with themselves, they tend to keep looking outside themselves for approval. They believe they're unworthy; therefore, they are suspicious of approval when it does come. These people are prone to please other people and are afraid to speak their own opinions. They may become very destructive, trying to bolster their own ego by cutting other people down.

People with a poor self-image frequently are perfectionists, which only reinforces their feelings of inadequacy. They plan too much in a day and never enjoy the accomplishments they achieve. "Enough" is never enough.

People with a low self-image frequently are embarrassed because they feel inadequate. They may be very secretive. It's hard for them to be vulnerable or to receive advice and counsel from others. They often procrastinate. "I'll put it off until tomorrow because I'll probably do a better job then." They are so afraid of producing something inferior that they produce little or finish it late.

Obviously, people who know and feel comfortable with themselves will be better marriage partners. They can continue their personal growth and encourage their mate's growth.

2. *Individual identity.* A second concern for couples in their early years is independence and separation from their parents. An inappropriate attachment to parents may exist because one or both feels incapable of living married life without the parents' support and guidance.

Sometimes dominant parents have so controlled their children that, even as young adults, they aren't able to think for themselves or act on their own. In a sense, the umbilical cord has never been cut.

Some Christian parents have misunderstood the biblical instruction to "train up a child." They feel that the child should think and respond to life as the parent thinks and responds. However, that verse goes on to say, "Train up a child in the way *he* should go." The biblical meaning is that God has a unique direction for each person, and the role of the parent is to help the child discover that uniqueness. The child should not be a clone of the parent.

The young adult who comes into marriage having established his or her own identity will be like a bird on the wing, free to fly, instead of like a kite on a string. Once a person has an individual identity, he or she is ready to be an interdependent marriage partner, able to be independent but also able to share and contribute to his or her mate.

3. *Realistic expectations.* Another tendency in the early married years is to expect that marriage should solve all of life's problems and bring ultimate happiness. Happiness actually is related to our adjustment to God, the people around us, and our environment. Happiness is our internal response and our personal determination to be happy, not something that comes from the outside. In other words, if we don't know how to be happy on our own before marriage, we're not likely to be happy in marriage. Marriage is a voluntary sharing of our happiness and experiences. It is expecting too much to ask that our mates make us happy.

4. *Down-to-earth image.* Another important task of people in the first years of marriage is facing the reality that they have married a real person rather than an ideal one. They have not married a "vision," but they may try to

superimpose that vision on the human being they've married. They either ignore the weaknesses of the human being or expect that, with a little bit of help and encouragement, their mates can be changed to become the ideal. Reality may strike like a giant wrecking ball. The mate is not perfect, is not ideal, and never will become like the fantasy.

We hope that the reality of who this person is has been faced before the couple married. If not, it must be faced in the early years so that the necessary adjustments can be made to have a long-term successful marriage.

5. *Healthy adjustments.* Another hurdle in the early years of marriage is adjustment to each other. The most mature, well-balanced couple with a deep understanding of themselves, of marriage, and of the realities of their future together will still have many adjustments that will cause some degree of stress.

One couple came to us in tears after one month of marriage. They were so sure that God had called them together, yet now they were having arguments and misunderstandings. Had they misunderstood God? Was it wrong for them to be married? Whatever happened to the romance, the magic, the wonder of it all? It disappeared as they started the adjustment process. They hadn't misinterpreted God's leading in their lives. They had, however, missed the point that *all* marriages must adjust in several major areas during that first year.

Following is a list of the issues that need time and energy for adjustment. We suggest that you read the sections of this book that cover these concerns in detail.

☐ Money—how do we earn it, who manages it, and who spends it?

☐ Work—who works, how much, and how is that integrated with the rest of our life?

☐ Decision-making and leadership—how are each one's gifts and abilities utilized; how is mutuality achieved?

☐ Sexual adjustment—is each one being fully satisfied?

☐ In-laws—is there a true interdependence as peers?

☐ Leisure—are our emotional batteries being recharged?

☐ Roles—who does what in each part of life?

☐ Children—will we have them, when, how many?

☐ Friends—do we have couple *and* individual friends?

☐ Spiritual life—are we growing individually and as a couple?

6. *Intimacy foundation.* An overriding cause for much of the marital stress of the first years is the preoccupation with living life, resulting in a failure to build intimacy in the marriage relationship. Before marriage, much of your time and personal energy was spent in getting to know each other. Many couples assume that after marriage they don't need to keep at this process of developing intimacy; however, the adjustment process will tend to drive you apart unless intimacy continues to be cultivated.

Intimacy demands time together, effective communication, a willingness to know and be known by each other, and a desire to meet each other's needs. As a couple in the early years of marriage, you need a commitment to build an intimacy base. Then at each of the later stages of marriage, you will be held together because of intimacy, not just because of obligations such as the mortgage or children. Any investment in each other now will be enjoyed all during your married years. If you invest now, in the midst of being very busy, you'll receive the reward of a strong marriage for the rest of your lives!

Related Articles
Chapter 3: Before You Say, "I Do"
Chapter 4: Identity and Intimacy

The Surprises Marriage Brings

TOM & LINDA TAYLOR

Marriage, as glowingly wonderful as it seems before the wedding day, often brings with it many unanticipated changes and surprises. Before the wedding day, couples often feel that their marriage will be the best—there will be few arguments or disagreements, love will conquer all, sex will always take care of everything, life will be so much easier. And even if a realistic couple doesn't hold these notions, they will still be in for a few surprises. The reality is that two people won't live together without at least a few disagreements, love doesn't conquer all, if there are problems you won't even want to have sex, and life is easier in some ways and more difficult in others. But every marriage can anticipate and weather the surprises, and be stronger because of them.

For us, the surprises began as we planned our wedding. Tom didn't want a long engagement, so we gave ourselves three months. It couldn't be that big a deal, could it? Just some organization is needed, right? Not when you both have completely different ideas of how a wedding should be. Not when one wants a big Greek-style reception and the other wants cake and punch in the church basement. Not when you have six attendants on each side. Not when you need to get a photographer, a church, and wedding and bridesmaids' gowns. We quickly learned the art of compromise and jokingly decided that couples are required to plan weddings as a mutual exercise in how to handle their future decisions of day-to-day living.

After we got married, we discovered that our friendships changed. Most of our friends were single, career people—we were in our late 20s when we got married—and when we went from being "eligible" to married, many of those friendships dwindled, not without some sorrow on our part. Whether it is because your interests have changed or your focus has shifted, you may find that some of your friendships won't stay the same. But many will—and it is both healthy and valuable to keep your individual friendships. Obviously, you should be careful about opposite sex friendships, making sure that they are mutually shared and don't become a threat (either real or imagined) to your marriage.

You may be surprised to find that wedlock is not the bed of roses you thought it would be. Linda always thought that she'd never mind picking up after Tom because she loves him so much (never mind what all the books on marriage said). But she soon discovered that love doesn't conquer all. Tom knew Linda was a worrier, but neither of us realized what a strain that can put on a marriage. We've both had to do some changing.

You also may be surprised to find that your spouse isn't going to change. Many people go into marriage thinking they'll transform their spouse—get rid of this or that habit, make him or her more outgoing or quiet, give him or her more confidence, whatever. Though your love for each other will help you grow and change, neither of you is going to become the ideal for the other person. Don't expect the impossible.

As two lives merge, so do two sets of goals, plans, ideas, and desires. You have each other to think of as you con-

LOVE IN THE RUINS

We are not sure we would ever want to take our first honeymoon again. Much of it was spent in garages getting our old car pasted together again and again, draining off the cash wedding gifts. When we came home, we had only a few dollars left to set up housekeeping.

Nor would we want to repeat what we came home to—our first year in a grubby basement apartment on the south side of Chicago, with one window looking onto an alley. Our last month there was a race to see if the rat gnawing on our wall would get in before we got out. But it was the best we could do to give us a year of earning money to go to seminary.

That first year, including the honeymoon, taught us something important—we can love each other and enjoy being together even under adverse circumstances. That's an important lesson for any young married couple to learn, the earlier the better. If you are truly together, not merely living in the same home, adverse circumstances are transcended by a persistent honeymoon mentality.

Gil & Arlie Beers

sider the future. Nothing is yours or mine anymore; it's ours. Together you share the joys and the problems. You both have to share the decisions—even when you've had to come to a compromise or when one of you still disagrees but is willing to concede. You have become a part of another person. And it is selfish to refuse to consider that other part of your life in your decisions and plans.

When you get married, you're truly not alone anymore. You can't be in a bad mood and be alone; you can't even cry alone. Linda has difficulty expressing deep feelings, so Tom's caring concern is intimidating and sometimes irritating. But that concern shows his love and gradually there has been easier communication of feelings and thoughts—which is vital to a healthy marriage.

Marriage is also a merger of gifts. Two people come to the marriage with skills and talents that can be shared to benefit their relationship. In our family, Tom is the creative idea person; Linda is the administrative detail person. Tom helps set the budget, but Linda pays the bills and keeps the checkbook. Tom can plan for the future a year or more from now, but Linda keeps the day-to-day details together. Tom can mastermind blueprints for fixing up the house; Linda helps him see how those plans can or can't happen according to the budget. As frustrating as our differences can sometimes be, we know we need each other's viewpoint in order to get anything done well and safely! You may be surprised to find talents that you never knew your spouse had; or you may be surprised how you can use your differences to an advantage you didn't have alone.

Perhaps the most wonderful thing you'll discover in your marriage is that you love and are truly loved "for better or worse." Even when you've made a mistake, blown it, shown your ugly side, or said something you're sorry for, you can look into the eyes of your spouse and know that you'll never be unloved. When you have discovered that, you have discovered the essence of godly marriage, and it truly is a blessing.

No matter how well you know each other, marriage will bring a few surprises. You can allow these to make you bitter and angry, or you can have a few good laughs and some interesting talks. Let those very surprises bring spice to your marriage and work together to make your marriage strong. Then it can weather any other changes and surprises your future years together will bring.

When the Honeymoon Is Over

DENNIS & BARBARA RAINEY

DENNIS: When Barbara and I were first married, we each thought the other person had life pretty well wired together. We looked at one another and thought, "This is a solid Christian person with a good track record of obedience to Christ."

It wasn't long though—within the first 12 to 18 months—before we both began to realize that appearances could be deceiving.

Behind my self-confident front lived a guy who was not nearly as secure as he projected himself to be. Barbara also showed signs of insecurity. She was shy and reserved and often avoided speaking up in a group of people or at a party.

Our insecurities began to come out in different ways in our relationship. They showed up as we made day-to-day decisions and as we related to our friends. They especially became evident as we related to each other.

Eventually our growing awareness of each other led our marriage to a real fork in the road. Both of us had to decide whether to accept each other just as we were. Now that Barbara could clearly see my inadequacies, would she continue to accept me? And now that I could clearly see hers, would I accept her?

I knew I had to choose either to believe that Barbara was God's woman for me, to accept her as she was at each moment, to give up hoping she would change, and to expect God to use her greatly and do mighty things through her—or to reject her and settle for a mediocre marriage like those of so many of our friends. I decided to accept her just as she was.

BARBARA: At the time when we were first married, there were a lot of things about Dennis that I also didn't know. Still, though, I believed God had brought us together. I believed Dennis had great potential before the Lord, even though I had no idea what he would end up doing. But it didn't matter to me what we did or became. The fact that God chose us to be together was my basis for believing in Dennis.

Believing in each other was not so hard during dating, engagement, or even early marriage, but it became more difficult as the months progressed and we saw more weaknesses that were previously hidden or overlooked. And yet if marriage partners do not believe in each other, then neither individual can easily believe in himself or herself.

DENNIS: Our decision to believe in each other—regardless—became the bedrock on which both of us began to build up each other's lives, to edify one another. I was 25 when we were married, but in many ways I was still a boy. Like most young men, I desperately needed a woman to believe in me as I moved from boyhood to manhood, ultimately becoming a husband and father. I believe it was through Barbara's belief in me that that process occurred.

72

When a man starts doubting himself, as we all do from time to time, it's imperative that his wife not join him in his unbelief. She should never say, "You know, you're right—you are a turkey." Sometimes when I've been feeling like a failure, Barbara will remind me of how God has used me in the past, and she'll encourage me with hope for the future. This puts whatever doubts I'm feeling in context and helps me respond to the truth rather than being emotionally sucked down the drain by temporary setbacks.

BARBARA: It is essential not only to continue to accept your mate, but also to regularly and effectively communicate your acceptance to him or her. Acceptance can be given many ways, but verbal acceptance is critical. Despite whatever may arise in your relationship, state over and over that you still accept each other totally, just as you are.

Related Articles

The Late 20s/Early 30s Era

JIM & SALLY CONWAY

A major life reevaluation often takes place in a person's late 20s or early 30s. At this time he or she asks, "Am I on course? Am I going to be able to fulfill the dreams and visions for my life that God helped me form in my late teens and early 20s?"

This life reassessment considers personal development, marriage, family, and career. A strong urge is now present to correct anything that doesn't seem to be in line with the overall life direction.

During most of the 20s a person goes about life responsibilities and relationships using the dreams formed in the late teens and early 20s as guideposts. The goals might have been to: get stabilized in a job, get married, launch a family, and get integrated into the church and the community. Goals that aren't materializing by a person's late 20s can create a crisis.

Bill and Karen were married just as Bill began studying for his doctoral degree. It was supposed to be a three-year process. Karen was willing to forgo completing her own education and starting a family so that she could work to provide the funds for Bill's schooling.

Near the end of the three-year period, Bill told Karen it looked as if his education would take another year. She was now 26 and he was 28. She willingly accepted the year's extension, realizing they had probably been overly optimistic in their original projections.

At the end of that year, Bill announced that it would take another year. This produced a great amount of conflict. Karen resented continually putting her life goals on hold while Bill pursued his dreams. She also began to nag him about his inefficiency on the Ph.D. project.

At the end of the fifth year, Bill very sheepishly told Karen it was going to take another year. She didn't say anything. She could tell by his lack of progress during the past year that he was not going to be done at the end of a sixth or even a seventh year.

About 10 days after his announcement, Bill came home to find Karen's closet empty. She had moved out without saying a word. He was devastated. He came to us, wanting help. It was only then, in counseling, that he discovered he was an extreme perfectionist and was not completing his projects because he was afraid to present what he thought to be inferior work. In reality, because of his perfectionism, he probably never would have completed his degree.

Some weeks later, we learned that Karen had relocated in the most distant point in the United States that she could. She had no intention of returning. She was not willing to delay her own life agenda any longer. She had wanted to complete college and have two children by age 30. These pieces of the puzzle had not come together for her.

The anxiety of unfulfilled dreams broke Bill and Karen's marriage. Bill did not understand Karen's agenda, and neither of them understood Bill's personal inadequacies that caused him to procrastinate.

After a few years of marriage, a couple may be so preoccupied with career, raising children, paying bills, meeting mortgage payments, and the overall busyness of life that they fail to focus on each other. They neglect to check if their life and marriage are progressing according to God's vision for them.

This focusing on outward activities frequently causes a couple to be surprised by the late 20s/early 30s life reassessment. A husband or wife may become depressed, moody, and irritable. Neither of them may understand what is happening.

Frequently mates blame each other for the turmoil, but the real cause may be a normal developmental reassessment. One partner may be preoccupied with an evaluation of his or her present life situation, wanting to bring it into closer alignment with earlier dreams.

Think of space travel to the moon. Imagine that you're launched into orbit and your trajectory, or path, is preset. Partway out, you recalculate and find

---

AN ANNUAL REMINDER

A survey conducted by a commission on the family under former President Carter concluded that 70 percent of the married couples in the United States would not marry each other if given another chance. While our marriage isn't perfect, I could never imagine being married to anyone but my wife, Debbie. One thing we have done every anniversary (we just celebrated our eighth) is repeat our wedding vows to each other. I used to think this was kind of corny, and it was uncomfortable at first, but it has developed into an intimate tradition we enjoy together.

We also have an audio tape of the wedding ceremony, and we listen to it together, laughing as we remember the funny incidents involved in making that special day.

To relive our wedding day and reaffirm our words of promise and commitment helps us remember our dedication to each other, and together to God. And that helps keep us firmly in the 30 percent of married couples who would happily marry each other all over again.

Mark Jevert

---

you need to make a slight course correction in order to actually arrive at the moon. It's this type of redirection that can happen in the late 20s/early 30s reassessment.

Sometimes the course correction is so severe that the marriage itself is threatened. A person may conclude that his or her mate is the cause for being off target. Unfortunately, that person may decide to dump the mate in order to achieve his or her goals.

Solutions for some of the stresses of the late 20s/early 30s are to be found in several areas:

1. Take a yearly assessment of your personal life development and your marriage.

2. Try to establish a more balanced life which includes personal development, leisure, and relationships with people, along with the busy activities of a career and family.

3. Refocus on your original life dreams. Work together so that both of you are becoming all that God intended you to be and doing what He intended you to accomplish.

4. Concentrate on your marriage relationship. It is extremely easy for the obligations and responsibilities of life to cause each of you to spend all your energy on those concerns rather than on the continuing need to build intimacy. Reflect on your earlier married years. How did you develop intimacy and closeness in those days? What did you do then to give you a deeper understanding of each other and a greater ability to meet each other's needs?

Use some of your energy, time, and money now as an investment in each other and your marriage relationship instead of all the good but peripheral concerns such as work, mortgage, children, and church or community activities. This reassessment time can actually enrich your marriage so that it will be strong for years to come.

Related Articles
Chapter 3: What If I Don't Marry Until I'm 30?
Chapter 6: Respecting Each Other's Gifts

Stages of Intimacy in Marriage

JAMES H. OLTHUIS

Intimacy in marriage develops and deepens in a sequence of stages, each with its own calling, opportunity, and danger. That is God's intention. Every marriage, of course, develops its own rhythms and routines reflecting the individual styles of husband and wife. But every marital craft sets sail on the same Sea of Marriage, seeking passage through the same dark waters with their hidden rocks, shimmering sandbars, strong gales, and gentle breezes. A chart of the stages of marriage can help couples avoid the dangerous shoals. It can help them locate where they have been, where they are, and where they need to go in their search for deepened intimacy.

The journey of intimacy in marriage can be described in five stages:

STAGE	CALLING	DANGER
1. ROMANCE	grounding in reality	ungrounding
2. POWER STRUGGLE	adjusting to differences	competing, projecting
3. SHIFTING GEARS	renegotiating	retrenching
4. MUTUALITY	connecting	retreating, idling
5. CO-CREATIVITY	interconnecting	scattering

The names chosen to describe each stage attempt to focus on its strongest feature. That *romance,* for example, is the name for stage one does not mean romance is limited to that stage. Romance will show up renewed and re-worked in later stages. In similar fashion, co-creativity will have some place in all the earlier stages. It is also important to note that movement from stage to stage is more like an advancing spiral than simple linear progression. We first circle back to deal with an unresolved issue or hurt before we advance.

Romance is the only appropriate name for the initial dreams-and-roses, prince-and-princess stage of marriage. We are beside ourselves with love, caught up by a passion bigger than ourselves. Romance is the total delight and abandon I experience with another person. Bewitched and enchanted, a man and woman pledge troth and are married. They become one flesh, momentarily forgetting that they are unique persons with separate identities and histories.

In our epidemic of broken marriages, romance is often singled out as the culprit. It is seen as the irrational frenzy that raises unrealistic expectations. But romance is not the problem. Without romance, a marriage lacks the emotional connection that brings it zest and vibrancy. The problem is not romance, but rather the lack of a settled identity that makes us unable to cope with the power of romance. Romance then becomes romanticism—escaping from ourselves into fantasy worlds where two people remain strangers because they are estranged from themselves.

Power struggle is the second shake-down stage of marriage, in which husbands and wives are impressed with the reality of their individual differences. How can we do justice to each other as persons in our shared life? This period of mutual adjustment with its inevitable struggle and tension is unavoidable. It

becomes extremely frightening when we get lost in our needs and fears, because we feel powerless and unlovable inside. Then, driven by fears, we put up defenses, trying to control our partners and remake them according to our needs and desires.

Control, games of domination/submission, and masks hiding our anger and despair undermine genuine intimacy. But if we are at all in touch with our need for such deep connection, a deep unrest begins to smolder in our breasts. Somewhere in the course of the power struggle, most of us seek a way out and strike a truce of sorts. We resolve to back off and may attempt to reduce the pressure by beginning a family or turning to careers, church, or friends.

But cessation of hostilities is not intimacy. And sooner or later, slowly or abruptly, the pain of disconnection finds voice in a renewed cry for affirmation and acceptance. Sometimes we are unable to work through the truth of the situation and the cry goes unheeded. We may retreat and agree to settle for less; we may dissolve the relationship; or we may lose ourselves in affairs. But there is another way: when we turn inward, face ourselves, and own our fears and projections, a deeper connecting and sharing of selves begins to take place. This marks a breakthrough in genuine intimacy.

Shifting gears is the stage in which we put aside our competing and projecting and begin to look at ourselves, our fears, and our masks. When we face our own fears and own our own patterns, they no longer control us. We begin to control them, and we find we can let them go. This journey is not without pain and struggle. But it is the way to deeper healing and wholeness. Learning to accept ourselves more fully, with our gifts and our limits, we are able more fully to accept our partner and receive him or her in intimacy. Feeling heard and accepted as the person I am,

I am empowered in turn to hear and accept you as the person you are.

Shifting gears to a new way of being together is a three-stage process. We take off our masks, owning our fear, anger, and despair. Then we disentangle ourselves by giving each other the necessary space. Finally we reach out with open hearts to each other and meet in the middle.

Mutuality is the fourth stage. In this stage, giving and sharing rather than taking and demanding become the settled and easy pattern. My deepest intimacy needs are met even as my deepest identity needs are honored. The "letting be" of compassion and love replaces the need to defend and control. We are able to be close without fear of engulfment, and we are able to be apart without fear of devastation.

Co-creativity is the stage when the joy of mutuality flows over into caring and sharing for all of God's creatures. We become cocreators of newness in ourselves, in our children, with friends, and in the world at large. At every stage of life and marriage we are, of course, called to be copartners with God in the ministry of healing and justice. But especially when we are nourished through mutuality and love, our intimacy opens up creatively into a deeper intimacy with God, our neighbors, and all of God's creatures.

Related Articles
Chapter 1: Dimensions of Married Love
Chapter 4: Identity and Intimacy
Chapter 15: Bringing Love Back to Life

The Couple With Small Children

JAY KESLER

From that first breakfast meeting when husband put down his newspaper and said, "You're *what*?" the marriage changes. No longer can the couple focus solely on each other; no longer are they a twosome. Their energies have to turn outward to other people, and this changes their lifestyle in every way.

In most cases, when the first child is born, the couple's discretionary income goes down. They quickly find they have much less time to devote to romance and to enjoying each other. Someone is always watching them—even if that someone is very small—and this changes the way they relate to each other both verbally and physically.

Children, by their very nature, are demanding and selfish. Most idyllic mythology about young children misses this point, but children demonstrate our fallen nature in the most pointed ways. One of the saints of old said it's a good thing children are so small and uncoordinated; otherwise, most infants would strangle their parents in a fit of selfish rage.

By definition, to be childish is to be overly preoccupied with oneself. Children demand cookies; they demand drinks; they demand to go out and play; they demand toys—and someone has to meet or at least respond to their demands. That someone is usually their mother, who as a result suffers from a great deal of physical fatigue.

Many women live with what is almost like a low-grade fever for the 8 or 10 years that the children are small. First their bodies are depleted from giving birth; then they lose sleep, must meet daily frustrations, and forget how to relax.

It is this commitment to others that turns a young mother into the kind of person we praise on Mother's Day. A selfish young single woman does not just naturally turn into a selfless, caring, loving, revered grandmother. It happens through the incessant demands of small children and her decision to lose her life for their sake. The end result of losing herself is the beauty of saintly womanhood, but the process can be extremely painful and is often traumatic to marriage.

Part of the task of parenting, of course, is to teach children how to meet their own needs and how to postpone various kinds of gratification. But those lessons take a long time to learn, and meanwhile the children's selfishness and demanding spirit break the couple's concentration and attention span.

When our children were small I often said, "When you have one child, it slows you down. When you have two, you are brought almost to a stop. With three, you simply give up and quit doing certain things and going certain places because it's just too complicated. You have to stop a lot of activities and simply concentrate on the task at hand."

For many couples this moratorium on outside interests begins with the birth of the first child and continues until the last one leaves the nest. Virtually all their energy—personal, intellectual, and economic—is aimed toward the well-being of the children. It's wiser, of course, for the parents to carve out time for each other and for other interests, but in more cases than not, they give in to immediate pressures and gradually grow apart from each other. But unless a couple, during the child-rearing years, spends a good deal of energy on developing, maintaining, and refining their two-becoming-one relationship, they will hit a crisis of rediscovery at midlife.

Related Articles
Chapter 11: How Children Affect a Marriage
Chapter 11: Parenting as a Team Activity

Family of Two

LYNDA RUTLEDGE STEPHENSON

Today, married couples come in four varieties—those newly married, those raising children, those whose children have left home, and those who do not have children.

Which of the above constitute a family?

Because we're living longer than ever before, a couple married in their 20s can now look forward to the very real possibility of 50 years together—the golden wedding anniversary. Of those 50 years, probably fewer than half will be spent in the company of children and adolescents.

Do we quit calling ourselves a family when the kids leave home? Do we ever start calling ourselves a family if we never have kids? And what are we before we decide to be fruitful and multiply?

The real question is this—"What is a family?"

The idea that two is a marriage and three or more is a family seems to be the consensus definition. "When are you going to have a *family?*" we've all been asked. Yet to buy into the idea that "family" is not created in a marriage until a third person is introduced is to cheat ourselves, to put ourselves in a sort of holding pattern not of our making.

Family is a warm, intimate term that conjures up images of devotion, love, mutual trust, and acceptance. We all would like to have such feelings in our extended families—the sisters, mothers, and cousins in our lives. But where do we most want those qualities? First and foremost, we want them with the person we've chosen to spend the rest of our lives with.

To the newlywed, the experience of spending days and nights, fun and work, dreams and schemes with a brand new person is so enthralling that a feeling of family easily courses through the relationship. But it becomes harder, not easier, as the years go by to keep this family-of-two feeling alive and healthy.

The couple raising children may allow the minute-by-minute urgencies of those little people underfoot to erode that special feeling. Living out society's definition of family, even for a short span of years, may make this couple forget how special it can be to belong to each other and each other alone.

If that happens, then the period known as the empty nest will not only shock this husband and wife, it may throw their marriage for a loop. Sadly, divorces happen often at this stage. Nourishing that family-of-two feeling all through those child-rearing years is one of the most essential preventives of such a crisis.

But the family-of-two feeling may be most important for the couple without children. "Sometimes I wish I could borrow a friend's child so my husband and I would have a good excuse to fly a kite or see *Bambi*," one woman said. Social pressure in almost every area is extreme for a couple without children. Redefining the way they see themselves—rediscovering the freedom, the specialness of being "two" that they felt as newlyweds—will give them that essential family feeling to build on for all those years ahead.

No matter what period of marriage you and your spouse are experiencing, your marriage will only be strengthened, enriched in amazing ways, if you discover the power of viewing yourselves as a family of two. It's a conviction upon which to build a life view.

How do you feel about your spouse? Do you love him? Do you respect her? Do you share your most intimate details, most important and most trivial thoughts and feelings with that unique individual? Are you planning to spend the rest of your days in that friend-and-lover's company?

Then you are a family. A family in and of yourselves—a family consisting of two.

Related Articles
Chapter 4: Making Your Spouse Your Best Friend
Chapter 11: Childless By Choice

THE ANNIVERSARY

Do we undercelebrate the years?
Do seasons blaze past us because
we do not willfully rebuke the
    clock?
Can the quiet moments of our
    special past
be summoned back and ordered
to give full account of all their
hurried negligence?
Is there no way to call again the
    flying years?
Yes, for anniversaries come like
    late rains
Refreshing old, first promises.
Anniversaries are the markers of
    years—
Prodding our reveries,
Saying again and again,
    remember . . .
Love was once new,
The naive nexus of our unstudied,
    untried dreams.
Love was fervent, even fiery!
And anniversaries recall the fire.
Sure, they are melodramatic,
Overcontriving the contrivances—
    flowers and dinner—
The chicken kiev once a year,
Even though we don't much like it;
It is one recipe not in the church's
Self-published, heavy-with-
    casserole cookbook.
Chicken kiev—we heard the
Czars once ate it and it
Conjures up the mood of that
    faraway day.
We eat, forget the czars and
Remember the church decked out
    in white,
And that on that very day
We sat down to a candlelight
    dinner for two

Between the over-rehearsed
    formalities
And the forces we couldn't
    rehearse
Before even Christian books spoke
    their cautious "how to,"
That called our highest wonder
    and deepest fear.
In anniversaries old covenants visit
    us anew,
Reminding—but shouting the
    aged, black-crepe warning
That sits beside our long-ago white
    day!
These anniversaries fly by so fast.
How well we know that
One day—some anniversary
    distant—the table will
No longer be set for two. There will
    be a single plate,
A cup of tasteless coffee
    . . . tasteless because
Coffee always should be drunk
    from two cups by
Two who understand each other.
And when the lonely season
    comes, should I be the one
Who sits alone—I promise to
    remember you as long
As memory can manage.
But it may happen
That in the reverie of silence,
The counselor of years will meet
    with me
And our love, bright-washed with
    grief,
Will even then be the subject of
My solitude.

Calvin Miller

The Second Decade of Marriage

LaVONNE NEFF

Soon my husband and I will celebrate our 20th wedding anniversary. After 20 years, there have been a few changes:
- We are now a family of four, with two daughters in high school.
- We have lived in four states in four apartments, five houses, and a motel.
- We have owned nine cars, six bikes, and a mo-ped.
- We have had eight dogs (if you count the one that stayed only two hours), two cats, and innumerable hamsters and guinea pigs.
- We have worked at five careers between us.
- We have added several hundred gray hairs and numerous expressive facial lines.

The second 10 years look pretty stable for most couples. If they were going to divorce, they would have done so during their first decade—or will do so during their third. During the second decade, most couples are just too busy with children and careers.

When we had been married 10 years, we were getting ready to send our younger daughter to kindergarten. Approaching the 20-year mark, we are preparing to send our older daughter to college. For us, this was the decade of braces, books, and puppy love.

Other couples wait until the second decade of marriage to have their first child. First they establish their careers and buy a home; then they decorate the nursery. Diapers and day care may occupy their thoughts for most of the decade until their youngest child begins school.

In either case, the second 10 years becomes a time of almost impossible demands. Children, whether infants or adolescents, want and need hours of their parents' time every day. At work, supervisors discover your increasing ability to handle responsibility and give you correspondingly more, which you hesitate to turn down because of your mortgage and the specter of college tuition ahead. The church asks you to serve on this committee and teach that class, and charitable organizations hope you'll solicit for them in your neighborhood.

And if you bought major appliances when you first married, you can be sure they all will break down during this decade.

Some couples choose not to have children or discover, usually near the beginning of the second decade, that they cannot. For them, these 10 years look quite different. The career pressures are similar, but at home, different questions surface: Are we sure we don't want children? Can we deal with parental pressure to reproduce? Can we handle our grief over infertility? Should we adopt? If these couples remain childless through the decade, they will not have to deal with the pressure of combining child rearing and working. However, with less to take their focus off work, they risk becoming slaves to their careers.

In short, whether couples have young children, older children, or no children at all, the second decade of marriage is often a time of relentless demands and unremitting busyness. Married 10 years,

81

a couple may still be best friends who enjoy doing things and talking together. The same couple 10 years later may be virtual strangers, too exhausted at the end of the day to discuss more than the logistics of buying groceries and going to the orthodontist and taking the second car in to have its brakes checked.

Oddly enough, though, many an older couple looks back on that second decade with fond remembrance. How can a couple enjoy it while it's happening? How can a husband and wife manage to have a happier, more solid marriage at 20 years than at 10?

1. *Accept the fact that you are going to be busy.* If you have children at home, a growing career, or both, these will be the busiest years of your life. If both of you work outside the home, you will never have enough time. If only one of you does, you will never have enough money. In either case, you will face stress.

2. *Give thanks for your blessings.* So far you've survived—that means you probably have good *health* and at least some of your youthful *energy*. Take a good, long look at your *children*. It's hard to believe, but those older people who say, "You won't have them for long," are right. How old will they be on your 20th anniversary? When will your nest be empty? Look at your *possessions* too. Do you have a comfortable house, an adequate car, good food? Then you're more fortunate than most of this world's inhabitants.

3. *Consider making unthinkable changes.* Many American couples have to work harder than they like in order to maintain a lifestyle they don't need. What would you give up in order to have 10 free hours a week? Your second car? Your video equipment? Your summer vacation trip? Could you be comfortable in a smaller home? Some couples bring sanity back into their lives by cutting back both their income and their expenses.

4. *Insist on regular time together.* To assure a successful second decade of marriage, this is the most important step you can take. Couples who let daily pressures crowd out their time together turn into strangers. Some of these married strangers fall in love again in their 40s and 50s; many do not. It's not a risk you want to take. Besides, your children will be happier if you are friends while they're growing up.

Some couples keep in touch by working together: they go to the same office or they spend weekends weeding and wallpapering together. Others remain friends by playing together, whether tennis or Scrabble. Some learn together. They take the same classes or read the same books. Most couples need to spend time talking together about what really matters to them individually.

How do you find this together time during the busiest decade of your marriage? You don't. It isn't there—unless you make it. Write it on your calendar, in pen. Refuse to let other demands crowd it off. Let other duties go, when necessary, in order to keep your time with your spouse.

5. *Look ahead.* It's easy to get so mired in the present that one forgets to look down the road. No matter what you do, you *will* be too busy during this second decade. But you will not be racing from crisis to crisis forever. The time will come when you can take leisurely weekends again, when you can plan an evening out without feeling guilty about the mountain of undone tasks at home, when you and your spouse can actually hear each other across the dinner table. Build a few dream castles now. Imagine together what you will do when you have more time and money. Strangely enough, dreaming about the future can help you enjoy the present.

As we approach our 20th anniversary, my husband and I are tired a good deal of the time. Still, we know these have been good years. Much as we look forward to a return to civilized adult evenings at home, we can get a little misty-eyed as our daughters head off to examine distant universities.

I hope we never say these were the best years of our lives—I would rather think that the present is always the best.

But I know we will say this second decade of marriage, though hectic, was very, very good.

Related Articles
Chapter 11: How Teenagers Affect a Marriage
Chapter 12: How Much Time Should We Spend Together?

Marriage and Midlife

JAY KESLER

After 20 years of working and bringing up children, many husbands and wives discover that they have become wholly different people from the ones who exchanged marriage vows so long ago. For their marriage to survive and thrive, they have to rediscover each other, to begin almost from scratch to develop the romantic and personal side of their relationship.

People face this midlife discovery in different ways. Some have crises; some do not. But if someone in your family is going through a midlife crisis, you are probably looking for help.

Dozens of books about the midlife crisis have been written. In many ways they are very different books, and yet they are all true. Each person faces midlife in a different way; each responds with different levels of competence.

Most discussion of midlife crisis has to do with adjusting expectations. One day it dawns on people that their youthful dreams are not going to be achieved. Life is going to take on a certain tedium. They are not going to be great in any human sense. Rather than being president of the United States or CEO of the company, they fear they are more likely to join those lackluster senior citizens who parade in polyester through retirement centers and cafeteria-style restaurants.

One definition of maturity is the ability to accept life as it is, but not everyone is able to do this immediately. People flail against these losses—loss of dreams, youth, sexuality; the need to adjust to ordinariness. Many fight back with pathetic gestures of defiance. They purchase sports cars. They unbutton their shirts to expose macho chests. They buy a gold necklace and a hairpiece. Or, sadly, they trade in their wives for younger women who are willing to admire their strength and adore their sex appeal.

When a mate, usually a husband, begins to go through this stage, the marriage partner is best advised to be patient and realize that accepting inevitability may take a certain amount of percolation time. The process cannot usually be speeded up. It has to take its natural path.

Usually people come through a midlife crisis feeling a little silly but without serious damage. If the partner has been supportive so there are no bridges to mend, and if the person in crisis expresses his or her feelings in socially acceptable terms, life can go on in a relatively smooth manner.

But while it's one thing to buy a boat or a sports car or bizarre clothing, it's another to have an affair. And of course there's no comparison in the way this affects the marriage partner—or the individual in crisis. Why do people turn from their spouses at this time?

In my over 30 years of working with people in these relationships, I have almost never felt that the problem had anything to do with sexuality. It almost always has to do with impotence—not sexual impotence, but life impotence. The person feels unable to cope with life as it now appears, stalled in his or her career, cut loose from aspirations and dreams. He or she is strongly tempted to do anything that will restore feelings of power and adequacy, and infidelity seems a convenient shortcut to fulfilling at least some dying dreams.

The long-term effect of infidelity, of course, is not renewed youth and power but rather heartbreak and tragedy.

How can such tragedy be prevented? Sometimes it can't. One partner cannot control the other partner's life. But here is some helpful preventive medicine:

1. Take the temperature of your marriage. Have years of married life cooled you off? Are you relative strangers to each other? Or have you grown as friends, partners, and lovers?

2. If your marriage has gotten stale or boring, do something to liven it up. It's time to turn some of your attention away from your children and toward each other again.

3. If your partner is beginning to act like a teenager again, don't make fun, ridicule, or shame him or her. Be thankful the midlife crisis is hitting in this fashion and not taking a more dangerous form. In fact, why not join your partner in

---

THE "EMPTY NEST"

Surprisingly, some researchers have found that most couples do not suffer greatly when their nest empties out.

Yes, the house is unnaturally quiet. It's hard to remember how to cook only two portions again. And certain songs, sights, and memories can bring a painful lump to the throat.

On the other hand, the house almost never gets dirty. Groceries seem to last forever. Best of all, husband and wife have the freedom and privacy to fall in love all over again.

In fact, most mothers positively enjoy the empty-nest period. The parents with the most regrets are those fathers who realize too late that they were always too busy to spend time with their children.

YFC Editors

---

a few silly activities? It might be fun.

4. If you fear that your partner is involved in adultery, get help immediately. Talk to a pastor or a counselor, not a close friend or relative. You may still be able to save your marriage.

Related Articles

Chapter 4: Building Your Mate's Self-esteem
Chapter 14: The Affair: An Empty Promise
Chapter 15: Overcoming Five Underlying Reasons for Divorce

Characteristics of a Mature Marriage

WESLEY & ELAINE WILLIS

Recently we puzzled over a particular feature of our house. We wanted to do some minor remodeling but needed information on how our house was designed. Nine years ago our contractor had given us two copies of the architect's drawings, but where were they now?

Naturally the first thing Wes did was ask Elaine if she could remember where they were. We both seemed to recall one of our boys taking a set to school for a speech prop. But what did we do with them after that? Had they ever been returned? Finally we settled on the entry hall closet. Sure enough, at the back of the top shelf behind assorted gloves (some matched and some didn't), winter hats and scarves, an umbrella, and the detachable sleeves of a quilted vest, we found the plans.

Once we had the plans in hand, we were able to locate the needed information and to complete the project. The task was easier because we knew how the house was planned originally. Any task, in fact, is easier if we have the original plans.

If we want to evaluate the health of a marriage, we need something against which to measure it. What is a normal, healthy marriage? How can we tell if a level of maturity has been achieved? We can tell by reviewing the original plans. But they're not in the back of a closet somewhere. They are in plain view in Genesis 2:18-25.

This passage can easily be divided into three sections: the problem (vv. 18-20), the solution (vv. 21-23), and God's commentary (vv. 24-25). Let's consider each of these sections and then draw some conclusions about how a healthy, mature marriage should look.

The problem. The first chapter of Genesis describes God's activity in creating the world. Chapter 2 presents a more detailed explanation of various aspects of that creation, particularly the creation of man. After each step of creation, God declared that all He had created was good. But when He observed man, He saw something that was not so good: Adam's aloneness (v. 18). He needed another person, one with whom he could communicate, one with whom he could share. The Authorized Version uses the word *help-meet,* while other translations indicate that God intended to provide a "helper suitable for him."

A literal translation could be "one who could face him as an equal and communicate with him." This had to be someone who shared the same longings and desires—a person who could understand. So, according to verses 19-20, Adam viewed all of God's other creatures. He observed, evaluated, and named all of them; but none was a suitable helper for him.

The solution. So a new creation was in order: specifically, the kind of person who could relate on Adam's own level. Rather than start from nothing, God chose to begin with a rib from Adam. Around that rib, God fashioned a woman. And when Adam encountered Eve, his response was one of great joy. With unprecedented enthusiasm he exclaimed, "Finally, at last, this time, she is of the very same essence as I; she shall be called Woman" (author's translation).

God's commentary. After God revealed how He created Adam and then Eve, He explained some key elements in the institution of marriage. By combining God's explanation with certain observations that we can make about the passage, we can identify many characteristics of a mature marriage relationship. This passage serves as a blueprint to help us understand the way God intends a marriage relationship to function.

1. *Marriage is a new relationship.* It is important that both spouses recognize that this relationship takes priority over previous family ties. The husband is to initiate in breaking with parents, and instead should cling to his wife.

2. *Marriage is permanent.* God described husband and wife as one flesh, a divinely ordained union not to be broken. When we, Wes and Elaine, made our marriage vows, both of us committed ourselves to this permanency. We entered marriage with total conviction that we were marrying for life. Under no circumstances would either of us consider a divorce. With such a presupposition, marriage partners determine to resolve differences that arise, and both are committed to working through life's difficult circumstances together. Trying to duck out the back door is not an option.

3. *Each one respects the other.* In a healthy marriage there is mutual respect and encouragement. God did not provide a beautiful but stupid partner for Adam. Rather He created a help-meet, one who could meet Adam as an equal and communicate with him. It is amazing to observe the number of couples who seem to compete with each other. Instead of encouraging and building up the other, rejoicing in the other's successes, such partners mock, demean, and poke fun at each other. Such competitive attitudes contradict God's plan for mutual respect in marriage.

4. *Partners communicate and share.* The obvious lack in Adam's idyllic environment was someone with whom he could communicate. During dating and courtship, couples usually spend hours talking, dreaming, and sharing together.

A PROMISE OF LASTING LOVE (16TH CENTURY)

I wot full well that beauty cannot last;
No rose that springs but lightly doth decay,
And feature like a lily leaf doth waste,
Or as the cowslip in the midst of May;
I know that tract of time doth conquer all,
And beauty's buds like fading flowers do fall.

No force for that, I price your beauty light
If so I find you steadfast in good will.
Though few there are that do in age delight,
I was your friend, and so do purpose still;
No change of looks shall breed my change of love,
Nor beauty's want my first good will remove.

George Turberville

And yet after those same people get married, they often ignore each other. A healthy, mature marriage is one where both partners work at communication. This means sharing more than just ideas. It means sharing feelings, values, aspirations. It means communicating honestly and consistently. And since all of us are growing and changing, this means that partners grow and mature together, not apart.

5. *Sharing is open and natural.* A marriage relationship should include a natural enthusiasm and transparency. Adam was delighted when he met Eve. God related that their physical relationship was open and natural—without embarrassment.

In the final analysis, a healthy, mature marriage is one in which an easy, natural relationship exists. This relationship develops as two mature, growing persons commit themselves to each other, with a mutual goal to support, promote, encourage, and share. And the end result is that both receive, while the marriage grows and matures to the glory of God. This is the kind of marriage that reflects the qualities of relationship that God described in Genesis 2.

Related Articles

Making the Later Years Even Better

JANETTE OKE

There is nothing quite like young love. You see it glow in the cheeks of the blushing bride, in the eyes of the adoring groom. It makes even the observer's heart beat a little more rapidly. Young love! There is nothing more beautiful— unless it's old love.

Old love? Yes. Love that has stood the test of time and come out triumphant, love that has grown with each of the marriage's trials and joys. Love that overlooks wrinkles and gray hair and stooped shoulders, sagging muscles and diminished strength, and still sees in the beloved the person who was at the altar so many years before.

I remember as a teen visiting the home of an elderly couple. He was so thoughtful, checking with his wife for ways to lend assistance—in fact, seeming to know before he was called on how to ease her load as a hostess. She was so sweet, thanking him for the help he was giving. Their smiling, touching, and chuckling over shared jokes was beautiful to see.

I also have been in homes quite different from theirs. Tension wafted through the air even though the host and hostess were courteous and correct with their guests. Sad to say, even Christian homes can seem this way, the husband and wife doing little more than determining to weather the rough years of marriage by gritting their teeth and enduring. After all, one would not want to dishonor the Saviour by breaking up the home.

I knew from the moment I said "I do" that divorce was not an option for me. I had promised before God to remain faithful to the man I took to be my husband. I knew also that even though I loved him, he was not perfect. I knew I was not perfect either. Very plainly, that meant our marriage would have some difficult times as we sorted and adjusted and worked things out. Nor would we get everything worked out in the first few years. Marriages, like everything else in life, have a habit of changing. We as individuals change. This means we must keep working on our relationship.

I determined, as I observed other marriages, that I didn't want to be caught in a marriage in name only. "What a sad, sad thing to spend all one's life with a person and only endure it," I remember thinking. "What a way to waste so much of what life has to offer!"

No one can hand me a good marriage. If I wish to have one, I must work for it myself.

I have designed a few rules to help me make my marriage grow better through the years. I am happy to share them with you.

1. *Remember that it was you who selected your spouse.* Something drew you to him or her. Keep concentrating on what made you love in the first place. True, you will find a few things you don't love as much, but minimize those. Allow your partner to have some imperfections. Remember that you also have some characteristics that others must endure. We don't have, and we don't need, perfect mates. If we did, could we really stretch and grow by living with them? Isn't life a lesson in give and take? Can't we find strength in complementing the shortcomings of another? Doesn't teamwork mean something special?

2. *Will to love.* Yes, I really mean that. You fell in love with someone because of pretty eyes, broad shoulders, a sense of humor, a sweet disposition. Now, *will* to continue loving that same person. Study your mate. Seek ways of bolstering the ego, strengthening the self-esteem, encouraging talents, expressing thanks for thoughtfulness. Look for strong, good character traits. Emphasize them. Point them out to others. *Will* to love and to build love.

3. *Learn to forgive.* When the Lord's Prayer talks about forgiving others, it includes your spouse. When Christ spoke of the need to forgive 70 x 7, He also included your spouse. If you truly forgive, you will push the incident out of your mind and not dredge it up at convenient times. Forgive. Really forgive.

4. *Develop your sense of humor.* It is fun to share laughs with someone. A marriage provides an excellent opportunity to share many little jokes that no one else knows anything about. Laugh with one another. Laugh at yourself with your spouse. Don't be afraid to let him or her see the real person you are. A sense of humor is a must in a marriage. And don't be afraid to let each other know just where the boundaries are— where laughing should stop to prevent hurt or humiliation. Be sensitive and caring. Protect one another.

5. *Find common things to enjoy and share.* Rosebushes. Scenic pictures. Wildflowers. Barbecues. Recipes. Walks. Anything you can find pleasure in sharing. Take time to enjoy these things together.

6. *Look for little ways to say, "I love*

PROVERBS 5:19

May your fountain be blessed, and may you rejoice in the wife of your youth. A loving doe, a graceful deer—may her breasts satisfy you always, may you ever be captivated by her love.

you." It might be as simple as a smile across a crowded room. It might be the touch of a hand in passing. It might be a sincere compliment paid in the presence of others. Keep the feeling of caring constant, and keep it sincere. It will not wear well if at other times you are cutting and careless.

7. *Touch each other.* This is one of the biggest ways to keep old love fresh and blooming. Touch is a way of communicating that we should not ignore. You do not touch something that repulses you; you touch what you find appeal-ing. There are many opportunities every day to reach out and touch your spouse. It needn't be maudlin or showy. It can be simple and unobtrusive. Others might not even notice—but your spouse will. For with the touch comes the message, "I care." Use it often.

Practice these simple rules of caring and watch your love season with age, getting better and better as the years pass by.

Related Articles
Chapter 2: Characteristics of a Mature Marriage
Chapter 4: Never Take Your Mate for Granted

If It Were Our Last Day Together

INGRID TROBISCH

When a wife complains to me about her husband, I listen; but then I gently shake her awake by asking, "And if you knew this would be your last day together?"

I wish I could live it over again—our last day together on this earth. I would not have repeated to Walter that criticism I had heard about one of his talks. He was tired from a long walk and vulnerable. Several times I heard a heart nudge to give him a foot massage ("body ministry" we called it) as we sat together in the evening, but I didn't do it. Instead I busily wrapped little gifts for our youngest daughter for her birthday celebration the next day.

I would have looked for just the right record when he suggested that we listen to music—Mozart's orchestra concert in C Major for flute and harp instead of the Debussy tape, which he said was "too melancholic."

I would have understood what he meant when we went for a walk that af-ternoon in the beautiful Alpine meadows surrounding our little home and he said, "Ingrid, I'm homesick—but for what?" I didn't recognize the signs of the calling for his heavenly home that afternoon.

I felt him reaching out to me that last evening of his life. He wondered why our friends hadn't called us, now that we were safely home after a three-month teaching trip which had taken us around the world together. "Does anyone still love me?" he asked.

His question took me by surprise, for I thought of all the quiet acclaim and affirmation he had received in his ministry of soul-counseling. Not until later did I understand. This was the call of the child who is hurting and wants to be comforted, the call of the wounded soldier, the call of the mature man longing for love and understanding.

One of America's foremost marriage counselors, Dr. Paul Popenoe, once said, "Men are hard, but brittle. Women are soft, but tough." In his unfinished manuscript that he had laughingly enti- tled *The Pain of Being a Man* (as op- posed to my book *The Joy of Being a Woman*) Walter had written:

"I believe that a man can be more easily hurt inwardly and mortally wound- ed in his heart than can a woman. Sui- cide rates for men are higher than for women. I have no doubt that the ego of a man is more fragile than that of a woman. . . . The role which we men cannot play comfortably is that of being the strong sex. We strain and strain at it and still our performance is not very credible. We may have illusions about ourselves in our early years, but later on in our marriages we find that we cannot earn much applause for our efforts. The real woman sees through the preten- sions and would like to ask her husband to be just a kind human being and not some sort of superman. . . .

"Love means that I can let myself be seen by my partner and be accepted that way. Because of our vanity this may seem impossible, but it would be a way of healing the vulnerability of the man if he would deliver himself up just the way he is to the love of his wife."

This was just what Walter was doing, but I did not hear. Now the wax would be out of my ears and I could under- stand better one of Walter's favorite Scripture passages: "Like a man whom his mother comforts, so will I comfort you, and you will be comforted in Jeru- salem" (Isa. 66:13, BECK).

One young widow said after the too- soon death of her teacher-husband, "Did we have a good marriage, Pete?" and then answered her own question: "Yes, only we didn't discover it until it was too late."

I'm glad, though, that Walter and I did take time to celebrate that last day together, that we prayed together, that I cooked his favorite meal, that we went for two walks together and still had time for him to take care of the urgent mail on his desk, some of it life-changing. I'm glad he told me he loved me, so I could hang on to that spoken word in the shock-filled weeks ahead of me.

Later my oldest son said, "Mother, that which you have had no one can take away from you."

Related Articles
Chapter 4: Never Take Your Mate for Granted
Chapter 4: My Husband, My Best Friend

Be Prepared to Say Good-bye

MARY JANE WORDEN

What kind of information is needed in an obituary? Where do you keep your marriage license? Your spouse's birth certificate? Your insurance policies? If you had to decide in the middle of the night, which funeral home would you choose?

These were only a few of the ques- tions and decisions I had to face when my husband died unexpectedly. The ag- ony of losing a spouse is great enough without the added stress of having to make decisions for which you are un- prepared. Every married couple should sit down together on a regular basis and discuss the kinds of decisions and de- tails which one of them will someday have to face.

An annual "review" on some fixed date—perhaps the day after Thanksgiv- ing or the first Sunday of the new year— can help prepare us for the unexpected.

It can also be an opportunity to express our appreciation and affection for one another by reminding us in a very real way how often we take for granted the ones we love.

Death is not easy for any of us to face, but better decisions are usually made when one's health and judgment are sound. Don't wait. Choose a time (preferably when you're both rested and well-fed) and a place (relatively quiet and unendangered by interruptions). Plan to spend several hours on this, particularly the first time you do it; the annual review, in which you evaluate and revise your decisions, may take less time.

1. *Wills.* Yes, you need one, particularly if you have children. Find a lawyer to help you with this, and go prepared to provide the following information:

—the name of an executor, that is, a person who will carry out the provisions of the will.

—the name of a guardian for minor children, in the unlikely event that you and your spouse die at the same time.

—any bequests, that is, items you would like to give to a certain person. With your lawyer's advice you can make decisions about setting up a trust, naming trustees, the age at which your children would inherit, and other necessary details.

2. *Insurance.* This field changes rapidly, so I won't presume to make specific recommendations. In most cases, both spouses should be covered during the child-raising years. The house, mortgage, and car should also be adequately covered. Find a competent professional who has your best interests at heart, and be sure both spouses know *what* policies are in force and *where* they are kept.

3. *Informing friends.* Together make a list of those people you want to be informed of your death: family and relatives, close friends, clergy, business associates. Decide whether letters or telephone calls are more appropriate. You

DOUBLE BED

Now every night I dig a grave
　　and still as death I lie
and resurrect by morning light
　　to live, again to die

Though smooth my sheeted grave-
　　　　　　　　　　clothes
　　and pillowed soft my head
my dearest dear will sleep no more
　　beside me in this bed

Luci Shaw

might ask yourself, "If I were to hear of that person's death, would it be important to me to be able to get to his or her funeral?" Names and telephone numbers of your children's schools or caregivers can be useful to others who wish to assist you in that stressful time.

The hardest thing I ever had to do was tell my three children that their daddy had been killed by a drunk driver and was never coming home again. What did I want them to know of my faith? What did I want to remind them about God? I didn't think they would remember my prefacing statements, but I was wrong. It might be a useful exercise to attempt to distill into a single sentence the essence of your beliefs about God.

4. *Funeral arrangements.* Which funeral home? Embalming? What kind of casket (the price range is enormous)? Open or closed casket for the services? Or cremation? Will you scatter the ashes, bury them, or put them in a permanent storage site? Place of burial? What kind of grave marker, and what will it say? Flowers or memorial fund? What do you want to have included in the obituary notice? Most funeral homes will willingly discuss with you all these details in advance. Call one, arrange an appointment, and go prepared to resist their possible sales pitch but with the

clear intent of gathering as much information as possible. Your resistance to overspending in this area will be much greater now than when you are in the stressful situation of coping with a loved one's death.

5. *Funeral service.* Discuss together and make lists of some of your favorite hymns and passages of Scripture. You might find it useful to look at the liturgy for funerals and burials in the *Book of Common Prayer* or something similar; ask your pastor for a suggested format. Whom would you like to have participate? How do you feel about a reception following the service? In some respects a Christian funeral is a celebration—of the joy of our past life together and the new life promised us as God's children. It is a time for friends and family to gather to mourn their loss and comfort one another, and a reception at the church or at someone's home can facilitate that process.

6. *Personal decisions.* Some decisions concerning the death of a spouse can't be made in advance, but the questions may still be worth asking: when one of you dies, will the other move to be nearer family? (A major move during the first year of grieving is advised only under unusual circumstances.) What kind of support system do you have in an emergency? How do you each feel about the possible remarriage of the other?

As difficult as these issues are to face, an annual planning-and-review time can be invaluable for every couple. The most important work you do will not necessarily be in the decisions made, but in the reminder that life and love must never be taken for granted. Are you ready to say good-bye? Are you up-to-date in the forgiveness department? Would there be major regrets or "if onlys"? We can never say too many times or in too many ways, "I love you."

Related Articles

Do you know how your future partner would answer these questions? Imagine his or her responses. Then ask the questions directly, and see how well you know your intended spouse! (It might be a good idea to take only a few questions at a time. You may want to answer them by groups.)

Getting Married
Why do you want to get married?
What do your parents think about our marriage?
What is an ideal wedding like?

Family Planning
How many children do you want?
How do you plan to space children?
How important is a good sex life to a good marriage?
What would you do if we had sexual problems?

Work and Money
What do you expect to be doing 10 years from now?
In a family with children, should both partners work outside
    the home?
Are you in debt? If so, by how much?
When will you be debt-free?

Likes and Dislikes
What do you most like about me?
What do you think I most like about you?
What irritates you about me?
What do you think irritates me about you?
What is your pet peeve about the person
    or people you're living with now?

Beliefs and Traditions
What does your religion mean to you?
How does it affect your actions?
What is an ideal Christmas celebration like?
Should the man be the head of the house?

3

PLANNING
TO MARRY

The idea of marriage has always been both fascinating and frustrating. At first sight it appears like a garden of roses—beautiful, fragrant, inviting. Our desire pushes us; our friends urge us to "go for it!"

Then comes a slightly chill wind of warning, a shiver of indecision. Some vague memory of caution builds toward a quaver of doubt. The mass media make it sound too easy; people don't seem to take marriage seriously. The more we ask advice, the more confusing our plight. How much can we trust feelings? What if it doesn't turn out? What if we make a mistake?

Listen closely. The God who made marriage also made the people He puts in them. Start with Him; His routing is clearly marked: Master, Mission, Mate. The order is critical. First, who is in charge of your life? Then, what is He calling you to do with your life? Finally, with whom should you share your life? He wants to guide and show you as much as you want to know His answers.

Underlying marriage is this principle: it may be made in heaven, but the maintenance work is done on earth. Utopian systems have one fundamental flaw—they fail to understand that marriage begins in infancy. Marriage preparation is not a new program, but a lifetime process. It's never too early to begin.

Howard & Jeanne Hendricks

Making the Right Choice

ZIG ZIGLAR

Outside of the decision to choose Christ as Lord, surely the right choice of a mate is the most important decision you will ever make. The right mate will add immeasurably to your joy, happiness, excitement, contentment, peace of mind, and success. The wrong mate will add immeasurably to misery, contributing to mental as well as physical disorders, addictions of one kind or another, failure in the business community, and a host of other things. Despite this fact, untold millions of people plan the wedding more carefully than they plan the marriage.

First, let's explore from a secular point of view why a good marriage is important. A recent study on millionaires contained some intriguing data. These millionaires were people who had been working hard for 20 to 30 years. They were conservative in their spending habits and earned their money by meeting basic human needs. Most significant, they were still married to their high-school or college sweethearts, who, in virtually every case, did not work outside the home. Instead they provided a "haven of rest," a wall of protection, and a comforting, helping, encouraging hand. In short, these millionaires and their wives were a team.

Another study involved over a thousand executives who were being groomed for the CEO's chair. Of these, 87 percent were still married to their one-and-only wife. Incidentally, less than 1 percent of these senior executives had never been married. These and countless other studies clearly establish the point that your choice of a mate is extremely important.

From personal experience, I can say without any reservation that the comfort, meaning, encouragement, support, counsel, and enjoyment of life that my wife has brought me has played the major role in whatever success I have enjoyed.

So the obvious question is, "How do you go about choosing the right mate?"

Obviously when you go "mate hunting," *you invite God, through prayer, to participate in the search.* I do not necessarily believe there is only *one* possible person out there for you, but I do believe there is *a* person who as a mate will be the helper God wants you to have.

Then *you shop for your mate in the right place.* Yes, I know that occasionally you can find a good biscuit in a garbage can, but the odds are against it. Likewise, any place that is basically destructive of mankind and contrary to biblical principles is going to be frequented by people who are looking for playmates and not lifemates. I'm speaking of night-clubs, casinos, bars, racetracks, and other places where destructive morals are the order of the day instead of the exception to the rule.

You are far more likely to find a good lifetime partner in a place where ambitious, morally sound people congregate for mental or spiritual growth. A Bible-teaching church is the most likely place to find a mate with whom you will not be "unequally yoked," though it is not a guarantee. You might also consider university classes, personal-growth seminars, and training schools where serious people who are ambitiously dissatisfied with their current situation are inclined to gather for growth and stimulation. Other possibilities include lectures, musical presentations of a high order, community events, charitable organizations, and volunteer service.

Some basics in searching for a mate must absolutely not be violated. *You must not be unequally yoked*—the Bible is crystal clear on this. Those who marry in the hope that they can win their mate to their way of believing are more often than not going to be disillusioned, disappointed, and embittered. For a maximum marriage, being equally yoked is a must. Remember, if being happy and healthy, having lots of friends, and enjoying peace of mind is important to you, then being single is infinitely better than compromising and marrying the wrong person.

The next consideration in choosing a mate is to *find someone with the same general philosophy of life.* For example, if you are very close with your spending (yes, I mean tightwad) and your mate wants to buy everything in sight, some serious difficulties will arise. If one mate believes in controlled corporal punishment while the other feels there should never be a hand laid on the child, you could have problems. If one person prefers staying home with a book, music, or a TV show, while the other wants to go out to a show or to

WHY DO MARRIAGES FAIL?

Marriage today is like flies on a windowpane: those out want in, those in want out. Marriage has never been more popular, and never more perverted. Why are marriages failing at an alarming rate? Dr. James Peterson, professor at the University of Southern California, cites three reasons:

1. *Improper choices.* Most couples marry too soon with only limited exposure based on limited knowledge. The result? A lethal form of Russian roulette.

2. *Unrealistic expectations.* Most couples are expecting marriage to do what only God can do. Marriage is not a matter of finding the right partner, but of becoming the right person. The only options: tear up the picture of the ideal mate or tear up your partner.

3. *Inadequate preparation.* Sadly, we spend more time, money, and energy preparing for the wedding than for the marriage itself. It's easier to get married than to get a driver's license.

Someone has observed, "The trouble with American marriage is American courtship." Our society is shot through with the romantic complex. Love is an hypnotic/ ecstatic condition that will hit one like the chicken pox with its characteristic markings. The care and feeding of romantic love has lifelong implications. Marriages may be made in heaven, but the maintenance work is done on earth.

Howard & Jeanne Hendricks

visit friends several nights a week, your lifestyle difference may cause conflict. If one person comes from a family of huggers while the other does not express affection easily or often, again you have a difference that will affect the relationship.

All this sounds as if I'm advocating total agreement in all these areas. Ideally that would be nice, but often reasonable compromises can be—and are—made. However, *work out your compromises in advance, before you marry.* You can rest assured that if your beloved resists changing before you are married (when he is seeking the prize—you), the odds are prohibitive that he will change after the wedding (when the prize is his). Specifically, a person with a slight drinking problem during the courtship may have a serious problem after the wedding. Likewise, a person who is overly aggressive and rough before marriage may turn into a spouse- or child-abuser afterward, especially if he or she was once a victim of abuse. A note to the ladies: if your father had a drinking problem and/or abused you and/or your mother, watch out. Incredibly enough, you will probably be attracted to a man with the same problems. *Don't marry him.*

The family of the one you marry is extremely important. Many people contend you do not marry the family, but nothing could be further from the truth. If you are embarrassed by your future in-laws or are unduly uncomfortable around them, you have a potentially serious trouble spot. *Spend a considerable amount of time with both families before marriage.* Men, watch the way your wife-to-be treats her father, and you will get a good idea of how she's going to treat you. Ladies, watch the way your husband-to-be treats his mother, and you'll get a pretty clear picture of how he's going to treat you.

Some sound advice was given me by a Christian psychiatrist when we appeared on a talk show together. He pointed out that the serious courtship process that precedes a mature person's decision to marry should last from one to three years. He says, however, that regardless of how mature you might be, you should *never marry anyone until you have courted at least one year.* In a year's time, with all the changes that take place during the four seasons, you will be able to learn a great deal about how your mate-to-be handles the various "seasons" in life. In short-term courtships, virtually all of us can put our best foot forward, keep our halos firmly in place, and come across as saints who've already arrived. What a rude awakening when the marriage vows are exchanged, you become husband and wife, and your partner discovers who you really are!

You may be wondering where love fits into the picture. It *is* important—very important—but I'm convinced that if you've sought God's will, have been faithful to His Word, and seek your prospective mate by following the principles and procedures outlined here, you will avoid the infatuation trap. Instead, you will find someone you appreciate and admire so much that your love for that person will turn into an unbreakable bond. You truly will become one.

Even with the wisest and most careful of courtships, however, there's no guarantee you're going to marry the "right" person. Your beloved has no guarantee about you either. Now, if you will just remember that *being* the right mate is infinitely more important than *finding* the right mate, your chances of a successful, happy marriage will be dramatically improved.

God's Will and Your Choice of a Mate

GARRY FRIESEN

Many Christians believe and study those Bible passages that provide direction for selecting a spouse. In fact, in many circles, it is the traditional view that has been held for years. But is it entirely accurate?

Proponents of this view often refer to two beautiful stories in Genesis to support their approach. In both instances, God chose the bride.

The first story is found in Genesis 2:20-23: "So the man gave names to all the livestock, the birds of the air and all the beasts of the field. But for Adam no suitable helper was found. So the Lord God caused the man to fall into a deep sleep; and while he was sleeping, He took one of the man's ribs and closed up the place with flesh. Then the Lord God made a woman from the rib He had taken out of the man, and He brought her to the man. The man said, 'This is now bone of my bones and flesh of my flesh; she shall be called "woman," for she was taken out of man.'"

Some Christians take this passage to indicate that for each man, God has prepared one woman who is perfectly suited to be his wife. However, nothing whatever is said here about mate selection. No promise is made, or implied, that God will prepare and introduce men and women that He has chosen to be joined in marriage as He prepared and introduced Adam and Eve. The whole scenario is an extraordinary event never again repeated in biblical history. There could be only one first man and one first woman. That's what it took to start the human race.

Perhaps the safest deduction one could make from this passage concerning mate selection is this: if you ever discover that you are the only surviving representative of your sex in the world, and you come across your only existing counterpart, the two of you should consider marriage.

The second story—and without question the most frequently cited in favor of the concept of a divinely chosen spouse—is found in Genesis 24. The account is well known. Abraham sends his trusted servant to seek out a wife for his son Isaac from among Abraham's relatives. Upon arrival at his destination, the servant stops by a well and makes this request of God: "O Lord, God of my master Abraham, give me success today, and show kindness to my master Abraham. See, I am standing beside this spring, and the daughters of the townspeople are coming out to draw water. May it be that when I say to a girl, 'Please let down your jar that I may have a drink,' and she says, 'Drink, and I'll water your camels too'—let her be the one you have chosen for Your servant Isaac. By this I will know that You have shown kindness to my master" (Gen. 24:12-14).

Soon thereafter, Rebekah came to the well and fulfilled the sign completely. The servant visited her family; Rebekah

---

COMMITMENT

When I was in high school, I'd daydream of what it would be like to be married someday. When I went to college, I thought I had a better idea of what marriage would be like because I dated more. I had friends who got married and when we got together, they'd describe marriage and share personally about their experiences. It made me feel like maybe I had a good idea of what marriage was all about. But I really didn't.

Finally, I found my one-and-only. I fell in love with her and began to imagine what marriage with her would be like. I figured that when we got engaged I'd really begin to "understand" marriage. The engagement was special all right, but I still didn't know what it was like to be married.

In fact, not until March 12, 1977, did I really know what it was like to be married. As I look back, I realize that prior to our wedding, Linda and I could have lived together, made love to each other, spent 24 hours a day telling each other that we believed in each other, but we still would not have been married. These are things that married people do, but they don't make unmarried people married, or even show them what marriage is like.

It was our definite commitment to each other that united us in marriage. Now, because of that commitment, our marriage keeps getting better.

Commitment isn't just valuable. It's priceless. Commitment isn't just a part of marriage. It's what marriage is all about.

Byron Emmert

agreed to become Isaac's wife; and the servant was able to take her back to Canaan.

This passage seems to provide support for the idea that God's will includes the specific mate that is best for each person. It also seems to support the idea that God's will in this matter can be discovered through using a circumstantial "fleece." But is that what the story means?

The problem with arguing these points from Genesis 24 is that the experience of Abraham's servant is not normative. In other words, it tells what happened to particular people in a particular situation, but it does not tell what should or will happen in other situations. And actually, though I know many people who believe God leads mates to each other, I don't know anyone who would be willing to send out a servant to seek a wife for a son and then accept that servant's choice on the basis of a drink of water for man and beasts.

This is not to say it could not be done. Making allowances for differences in time and culture, a man could hire a representative from a Christian dating agency. He could send that agent on a search to find a wife for his son. The agent could drive into a service station, offer a prayer, and sign up the first woman who meets his request for a drink by bringing him a Coke and checking his radiator. The idea sounds preposterous, but if Genesis 24 is normative, it would be a legitimate approach to mate selection.

But Genesis 24 is not an example of how God customarily works in the lives of His people. And that is so for several good reasons. First, the Bible does not promise that every believer will marry, even though Isaac had to marry in order to fulfill God's promise to Abraham of innumerable descendants (Gen. 15:5; 24:7).

Second, God does not always promise us special guidance to guarantee the success of our ventures, though in the case of Abraham's servant, He promised that an angel would go ahead of the servant to help him find Isaac's wife (Gen. 24:7, 40).

Third, the servant's method of finding God's will was not normative even then. Having no idea how to proceed, yet being fully assured of God's guidance, the servant asked God to give the needed guidance through an arbitrary method. He did not know for sure that the Lord would do what he asked; he simply asked and then watched to see what would happen. Even when the sign was quickly fulfilled, he still was not sure God was using it. To confirm his choice, he watched the woman carefully (v. 21), checked into her background (vv. 23-24), asked for her family's consent (vv. 49-51), and waited for the woman to indicate a willingness to return with him (v. 58). By following all these precautions, the servant showed an awareness that his procedure was not to be fully trusted until all other conditions were met.

Genesis 24, then, is the story of specific guidance in a particular situation so that God could be faithful to His covenant with Abraham. It does not say or imply that God will guide marriage partners to each other by similar methods today. In some cases He may; in more cases He will not. There is no record of extraordinary divine guidance in most biblical marriages—Abraham and Sarah, Ruth and Boaz, even Joseph and Mary seem to have found each other by normal methods. Yet God blessed these marriages and used them, as He used Isaac and Rebekah's marriage, to fulfill His covenant with His people.

[Excerpted from Decision Making and the Will of God, by Garry Friesen with J. Robin Maxson, Multnomah Press, 1980. Used by permission.]

What the Bible Says About Choosing a Mate

GARRY FRIESEN

When a believer begins to think about getting married, the first question he or she should ask is this: are there any scriptural commands that relate to this decision?

The answer is yes: believers may marry only other believers.

This has been repeated by countless pastors, teachers, counselors, and writers. Everyone seems to believe it. And yet when push comes to shove, a remarkable number of Christians disregard the command and marry unbelievers. After falling in love with non-Christians, they find supposed loopholes in the biblical statements, and they rationalize that in their situation the rules do not apply. Then they blatantly disobey God's revealed will.

A Christian principle is not established simply by force of repetition. It needs a firm biblical foundation. And in my judgment one of the most transparent teachings of Scripture is that believers may marry only other believers.

Throughout 1 Corinthians 7, Paul assumes this principle, especially in verses 12-16 dealing with marriages in which one partner has become a Christian after the marriage. But the imperative is clearly stated in verse 39: "A woman is bound to her husband as long as he lives. But if her husband dies, she is free to marry anyone she wishes, but he must belong to the Lord."

Looking at this issue from its negative side, Paul in 2 Corinthians 6:14-15 commands: "Do not be yoked together with unbelievers. For what do righteousness and wickedness have in common? Or

what fellowship can light have with darkness? What harmony is there between Christ and Belial? What does a believer have in common with an unbeliever?"

The opening statement calls up a mental image of an ox and a donkey being harnessed together in a double yoke (see Deut. 22:10). No believer is to be so mismated with an unbeliever. Not only are the believer's values, goals, standards, and motivations incompatible with those of an unbeliever; they are diametrically opposed! A Christian and a non-Christian are serving two different lords who are archenemies of one another.

If this passage does not apply to marriage, then it doesn't apply to anything. Marriage is much more than a "double yoke." It is a joining together of two individuals into a relationship that can only be described as "one flesh" (Gen. 2:24; Matt. 19:5; Eph. 5:31). Marriage is more than a contract; it's a covenant—the most intimate human relationship into which two human beings can enter. For a Christian to marry a non-Christian is to rule out the possibility of that marriage's fully accomplishing its design; it is to sow seeds of conflict. For a believer and an unbeliever are fundamentally different, not on the surface, but at the very core of their lives.

But there is an issue that is even more important than the eventual success or failure of the marriage—the issue of obedience. Christians are not left on earth to promote their own success; they are on assignment for the kingdom of God. To disobey a direct order from the

King is to capitulate to the authority of the other side. Alice Fryling puts it well: "Words cannot express the tragedy of this situation. The Christian is mocking God by reneging on his or her commitment to Him. A Christian is committing idolatry by falling down before someone other than God. And he or she is blatantly disobeying God, who said we are to marry only within the faith" (*An Unequal Yoke in Dating and Marriage*,

InterVarsity Press, 1979, p. 14).

I totally agree: the only acceptable mate for a believer is another believer.

[Excerpted from *Decision Making and the Will of God*, by Garry Friesen with J. Robin Maxson, Multnomah Press, 1980. Used by permission.]

Related Articles

Chapter 3: Making the Right Choice
Chapter 3: God's Will and Your Choice of a Mate

Friendship: Foundation for Marriage

NORM WAKEFIELD

Ann Landers invited her readers to respond to the following question: "Would you be content to be held close and treated tenderly, and forget about 'the act'?" Of the more than 90,000 women who responded, 72 percent answered yes. Landers observed that 40 percent of those who replied yes were under 40 years old.

I believe those women said something we all know at heart. Deep within we all agree that a satisfying marriage is more than good sex. Yet our society seduces us by saying that the key to happy marriage is romantic attachment, expressed through intense sensual feelings. Media messages cry loudly, "Be romantic and you'll get your woman!" "Be sexy and you'll have a great marriage!"

Alan Loy McGinnis says, "In research at our clinic, my colleagues and I have discovered that friendship is the springboard to every other love. Friendships spill over onto the other relationships of life" (*The Friendship Factor,* Augsburg, 1979, p. 9). It follows naturally that friendship between husband and wife is vital to a healthy, satisfying marriage.

When I meet with a couple contemplating marriage I work hard to show them how essential friendship is to the success of their relationship. If I can get them to commit themselves to a growing friendship, I believe I have given them a golden key to unlock the riches of their marriage.

You may be saying, "What makes friendship so critical? What does it do for the marriage?"

First, true friendship implies mutual respect, and respect is crucial to a healthy marriage. A friend treats me with dignity. He listens to my ideas with interest and shares his openly with me. Friendship suggests that we trust each other and are able to reveal hidden aspects of our lives. If we are friends, I know you will not reject me, ridicule me, or make fun of me.

Romance, by contrast, can exist without respect. Romance may thrive on the other person's attractiveness, charm, or sensuality. My romantic feelings may feed off what I like about the person, but never move to a deeper level of commitment to enrich the other person's life.

Romance apart from friendship is more likely to take from the other person than to add to him.

Second, friends support and strengthen each other. They have a genuine interest in the other's well-being. They find joy in contributing to each other's growth. Sharing time and resources for the other person's benefit is a pleasure, because we want to encourage each other to become all we can be. My friend weeps when I weep; she is full of joy when I am joyful (Rom. 12:15).

My wife, Winnie, is my best friend. Whenever I am thinking through a new idea, dream, or issue, she is the first person I share it with. She will be the first to read this article, for example, because I value her opinion and want her input. I am confident that her intention is to see me succeed in this writing project. If she is troubled about how something sounds or finds an idea confusing, I trust her perception.

Friends have the other person's interest at heart. They experience joy when the other person is promoted. If they can do something to improve the other person's chances, they gladly undertake it. Friends don't tear us down; they build us up. Marriage partners who are friends are blessed with a person who stands with them and enriches them for a lifetime.

Third, friendship is the doorway to intimacy, and an intimate marriage is a solid marriage. Intimacy suggests closeness, confidence, and affection. Deep within, all of us crave it, but many people have experienced rejection in some form and thus are afraid of the very thing they desire. A friend cherishes intimacy and holds it sacred.

There are healthy and unhealthy forms of intimacy. Romance *as an outgrowth of genuine friendship* is healthy and will add richness to the relationship. Apart from friendship, however, romance is dangerous because it lacks the nonemotional elements vital to a healthy marriage. Typically, couples approach marriage from a romantic orientation. Since romance cannot sustain a marriage, a relationship is in jeopardy unless genuine friendship emerges. Thus it is vital to build the relationship on the foundation of friendship. When intimacy and affection then emerge, they are rooted in and sustained by the friendship.

Fourth, friendship is the natural context for cultivating communication. It lays the foundation for the positive attitudes essential to communication in marriage. If we are true friends and not merely acquaintances, we like each other, respect each other, have each other's interests at heart, want to understand each other. These elements encourage and nurture a healthy communication process.

Many couples who enter marriage from a romantic orientation quickly find they have little of substance to talk about. Their relationship has been built around the romantic experience, and this is unable to sustain the demands of marriage.

Over the years I have observed that husbands and wives who are friends not only stay married, but their marriages usually grow richer, stronger, and more satisfying. Though physical beauty deteriorates over the years, intimacy and affection thrive. Friendship draws out the hidden beauty of the inner life and bonds the couple together even more. They grow stronger in admiration, respect, and support for each other. Genuine friendship builds a strong, fruitful marriage.

Robert Bolton illustrates this point

CAN YOU WORK TOGETHER
ON A PROJECT?

Walter often counseled young people not to just have dates where they go out and hold hands and see a movie. They need to go shopping together, plan a picnic or a meal, or go to the laundromat. It's important for a young couple to know if they can work together cooperatively on a project.

One of my sons was in love with a beautiful American girl, and he spent his savings to buy her a ticket to visit our home in Austria. One day they decided to lay the carpet in the hallway for me. The two of them could not agree on how it should be done. There seemed to be no way they could work together without getting into each other's hair. Their relationship deteriorated over the three weeks until it was time for her to return home. In a sense, her visit was a disaster. Yet my son felt it was worth every penny because they found out they could not even do a small project together.

By contrast, it has been a great joy for me to watch another of my sons and his fiancée working together in our home, getting meals, writing papers. He would help her with certain things and she would help him with others. It was so harmonious that it made you happy just to be near them.

My sister took the young people from her church on a week-long camping trip where they carried their knapsacks and hiked 20 miles a day. She said you could soon tell which young couples were compatible and which weren't. I suggest that a rigorous expedition is another excellent way to find out if a couple can work together!

Ingrid Trobisch

---

well. He dedicates his book *People Skills* to his wife, Dot. Here is what he says:

To Dot

My best friend, closest companion, fun playmate.

Enabler of my various selves, nurturer of my dreams.

Marvelous wife—sensitive, loving and genuine with me, our children, parents, and friends.

Effective in tasks that sustain our common life—colleague, teacher, partner.

I love it that when I am with you I most often discover, choose, disclose the selves I really am.

I love my experience of you as a lifeful, love-ful, value-ful person.

Imperfect, changing, growing, becoming, yet rooted, consistent—a friend for all seasons.

You are "something else."

[Prentice-Hall, 1979, p. V]

Related Articles
Chapter 4: Making Your Spouse Your Best Friend
Chapter 4: My Husband, My Best Friend

104

Before You Say, "I Do"

ZIG ZIGLAR

To give your marriage an honest chance at succeeding, you need to bring several attitudes into marriage with you. Most important, you need to *view marriage as a lifetime commitment.* Unless you commit yourselves to each other for life, your chances of a successful, happy marriage are greatly diminished. Commitment makes the difference.

Not long ago a close friend of mine was suddenly taken ill and soon died, leaving a wife and two children. He and his wife were both outstanding people, but I believe their marriage was one of the stormiest I have ever witnessed. They had serious problems for a number of years, but to their everlasting credit they persisted. They kept working at it. They had made a commitment; they were determined that somehow, some way, with God's help they would work it out.

One of the most pleasant experiences of my life was a visit with my friend's widow about 16 months after his death. She said, "I will never forget those last few months with my husband. I am so grateful we had that time together. They were absolutely beautiful, and so meaningful that it made all the problems for all those years more than worthwhile. I'm convinced that those happy months are what the kids will remember." I know they are what the widow is remembering. I believe she was able to make that statement because early on, she and her husband had made a commitment to their marriage. They were determined to make it work.

The second attitude you need to bring to your marriage is to *be willing to wait.* In this day of instant gratification, far too many people rush pell-mell to the altar and later realize they were not mentally, spiritually, or financially prepared for the big event.

In their hurry to get married, many couples temporarily put their brains on hold, throw caution to the wind, and invite their emotions to take over. They use the "ready, fire, aim" approach. Sometimes this is motivated by fear that the one who means everything to them might change his or her mind. If that's the basis on which a marriage is started, that's the basis on which it will probably end. If the decision to marry is based on the feelings of the moment, you can rest assured those feelings will change.

Some people rush into marriage because they're of sound moral character and they know a sexual relationship outside marriage is a sin. They feel they cannot wait, and therefore they think it is better to marry quickly rather than to commit a sinful act that they will later regret. At least part of their thinking is sound: my Christian counselor friends tell me that their number-one problem is dealing with Christians who were sexually active before marriage and who now are consumed with guilt.

But a marriage that is rushed into, no matter what the reason, is going to experience some rough sledding. It might survive, and it might not. Much depends on the strength, character, and commitment of both individuals. It is far better to do the necessary preparation *before* marriage rather than trying to do it after the vows have been said. Let's look at some of the preparations you need to make:

1. *Make financial plans.* Marriage

counselors agree that finances cause more arguments than virtually any other single factor. That is why the bride- and groom-to-be need to sit down and, with the aid of parents or a counselor, seriously plan a budget.

The most important item in that budget will be labeled "unexpected," because in addition to food, shelter, clothing, transportation, insurance, tithe, savings, recreation, and medical bills, there will be an incredible number of expenses that will shock someone who's been living at home with Mom and Dad and paying only a few bucks in rent or board money, if even that.

As you work out your budget, find the place you're going to live. Decide on the type of furniture and car you're going to buy. Be ultraconservative as to what you're willing to pay for rent, car payments, and the absolute necessities of life. Include, from day one, 10 percent of your earnings as tithe and 10 percent to go into a savings account so that you can start building financial security.

Construct your budget so that if a baby should arrive earlier than planned, you could survive on just the husband's income. In short, a fancy apartment or home with a lot of expensive, heavily mortgaged furniture, along with a car payment, is not exactly a good way to start a successful marriage.

2. *Practice discipline and common sense.* In our affluent society, young people often spend an incredible amount of money during their courtship days. A dozen roses are romantic, and what young girl is not impressed when she receives them? Candlelight dinners in sophisticated restaurants are beautiful, and a gift of expensive perfume or a cashmere sweater says, "You're important to me, and I love you." However, when you start preparing for marriage, you need to realize that a lot of financial self-discipline is necessary for most couples.

Don't fall for the old idea that "two can live as cheaply as one." Some couples think that with one rental payment instead of two, they will be rich. They throw financial caution to the wind and buy anything they want—and then discover how expensive maintaining a household really is. Once again, when you start preparing for marriage, you need to make a budget and stick to it. If you cannot discipline yourselves to handle money wisely, you will quickly be carrying a real burden.

3. *Get acquainted with each other.* One way to do this is to get acquainted with each other's families. Spend time with them; get to know their thoughts and feelings. In most cases they'll be delighted to have you around for visits and family dinners—they want to get to know you too!

Attend church together. It costs nothing to go, and the benefits are enormous. Besides growing spiritually yourself, you will have increased opportunities to discuss spiritual matters with the person you want to marry. Being "equally yoked," spiritually in tune with each other, is vital.

Long walks, where you can really talk, are a marvelous way to get acquainted. Conversation is critically important. It enables you to find out just how much you have in common and helps ensure that in coming years you will be even more in love, even more excited about each other.

4. *Go for serious counseling.* Spend time with an experienced minister who has a strong commitment to serving Jesus Christ and who fervently believes marriage is a lifetime commitment. He can bring out things in open discussion that two people in love may forget or refuse to face.

Marriage is truly a give-and-take situation. Romance fades and the couple has to face hard reality—sick babies, overdue house payments, a car that won't run, a husband who has just lost his job. It takes a tremendous amount of pure love for a marriage to survive such setbacks. Proper planning will enable a couple to mentally and emotionally adjust to them and be strengthened by them when they occur.

In the sports world, it is often said that spectacular performance is preceded by unspectacular preparation. That is also true of marriage. First, a couple must be totally committed to one another. Then they must be willing to wait while they do the necessary preparation. I'm convinced that spectacular performance and happiness in marriage are preceded by careful, prayerful preparation.

PREMARITAL SEX

My son, who is dating a very special young lady, recently said to me, "You know, Dad, when you get to know a person before you start dating, it certainly gives you lots of advantages."

You become emotionally involved after you start dating, but you can talk about what you believe—your social, spiritual, and moral values—in an unemotional way when you are still just friends. If you make your values clear in general conversation before dating, he pointed out, this starts the courtship in an emotionally healthy way and helps avoid some of the problems that arise in most extended courtships.

Yes, I'm talking about a premarital sexual relationship, which is an absolute no-no.

For one thing, it is possible for a couple to be sexually compatible but have nothing else in common. Mistaking a biological urge for love, they end up married—but become bitterly disillusioned in a matter of months.

Or a couple may feel that since they broke God's law by engaging in premarital sex, they are now obligated to get married. But guilt is no foundation on which to build a marriage, and their chances of happiness are reduced.

Those are just two reasons God so clearly says *any sexual relationship other than that between a husband and wife is either adultery, fornication, or perversion. In short, it is sin.* Period.

Zig Ziglar

Sex Before Marriage: Why Say No?

KEVIN LEMAN

Recently I was invited to speak at Washington State University to 750 fraternity and sorority leaders on the subject of sex. My wife thought I was absolutely nuts to accept the invitation, but I thought I had something to say. So I got up in front of these university students and gave them a number of reasons they should say no to premarital sex. And amazingly, when I concluded my remarks, they got on their feet and gave me a raucous standing ovation. Not only did that feel good, I could hardly wait to tell my wife.

Here's what I told the students:

1. *Pregnancy* is still a good reason to avoid sex outside marriage. No method of contraception is foolproof, and a lot of premarital sex takes place without contraceptives anyway. Every year thousands of unmarried girls and women unintentionally become mothers.

2. *Abortion* is the answer some women choose—but it is not a good one. It is much better to avoid premarital sex in the first place than to kill the child that results from it.

3. Other women decide to keep the baby and marry its father, but many of these women and men soon feel *trapped in an unwanted marriage.* The momentary excitement of premarital sex is not worth the agony of a bad marriage or a divorce.

4. Sex outside marriage spreads *disease.* Some sexually transmitted diseases can be cured, but some cannot. Is sex worth having Herpes Simplex II for life? Is it worth dying of AIDS?

5. Another good reason to avoid premarital sex is to avoid *flashbacks.* A person who has taken a hallucinogenic drug may be off the drug for a year or two and then all of a sudden have a flashback. Something similar can happen with sex. Here's a husband and wife who are deeply in love. They're in the bedroom making love, and suddenly into one of their minds comes a flashback of a previous lover. That can do nothing but interfere with their sexual relationship, and good sex is important in a good marriage.

6. Finally, a very important reason that people often don't realize—*sex precludes intimacy.* This goes back to a basic difference between men and women: once a relationship becomes sexual, in many men the need to communicate and share decreases, but in many women the need increases. Men try to solve emotional problems sexually, while women must first have an intimate relationship before they enjoy sex. Typically, once the couple starts having sex, the man wins out—intimacy is put on hold indefinitely. If I had a nickel for every woman who has told me she felt like nothing more than a sexual receptacle, I'd be a wealthy man.

When I gave this talk at Washington State University, I mentioned God only in passing. "For those of you who believe in God," I said, "there's another reason that's more important than any of the others. Don't have sex before marriage because God tells you not to."

I gave this reason last because this was a secular group, but really this should be the first reason. God tells us to say no to premarital sex because He wants the very best for us. He knows that in the long run, sex outside marriage will not make us happy.

Related Articles
Chapter 8: How Premarital Sex Can Affect Your Marriage
Chapter 8: What to Do When You've Already Messed Things Up

IT WOULD MAKE AN HONEST COUPLE OF US

Bill and Diane had sex on their third date—in spite of the fact that for both of them, this behavior was just plain, old-fashioned wrong. Nevertheless, they continued to have sex regularly from then on. They tried to quit dozens of times, but when they were together the chemistry was overpowering, and they ended up in bed.

Because of their sexual relationship, they both felt extremely guilty. Since giving up sex seemed impossible, they decided to make things right by getting married as soon as possible. The wedding was just before Christmas during their junior year in college.

Unfortunately, the only thing Bill and Diane mutually enjoyed was a great physical relationship. She loved classical music, the arts, and photography. His idea of a perfect weekend was going to the rodeo, watching big-time wrestling on TV, and making fun of classical music, the arts, and photography.

After 18 months of marriage, just before they were graduated—Diane from the Conservatory and Bill with a degree in physical education—Diane decided she had fallen out of love. Her physical attraction for Bill had played its final chord.

The reason for marriage between Bill and Diane was guilt. They expected, of course, that marriage would bring relief. This did not happen for two reasons: first, release from guilt can be given only by the offended party. They were not offending each other. They assumed they were offending God, but marriage does not cure this kind of offense. If two people are sinning, forgiveness comes through repentance and confession, not through marriage.

Second, even after marriage, if guilt is not confronted and erased the proper way, it will continue to stain the relationship. People who are suffering from guilt will not be able to accept love freely until the guilt is gone. The good news for believers is that God is eager to forgive. If forgiveness can be accepted, the relationship can be made new.

Guilt should never be the reason for getting married. Take care of your guilt first. Only then will you be able to build your marriage on a secure foundation.

Joel & Becky Hunter

CAN A RELATIONSHIP START OVER?

Genital contact changes a relationship: it is virtually impossible for a couple who have reached genital intimacy to return to non-genital friendship and start over. Those who try to sustain the benefits of sexual contact without incurring responsibilities may move into secrecy. Others, fearing obligations or feelings of attachment, may abandon their partners at this stage and look for someone new.

People who rush into new social involvement before working through their grief usually begin new relationships at the same intimate point at which the old relationship ended. This explodes the new relationship, ending its innocent form almost before it begins. Two or three of these quick relationships in series sets a pattern of compulsive promiscuity that is extremely hard to break.

People who are involved in premarital sexual experience have only two possibly healthy choices: either get married and maintain the sexual intimacy under the protection of public, legal sanctions, or end the relationship and go through a two- or three-year grieving process before continuing the search for a lifelong, monogamous partner.

Donald & Robbie Joy

Cultural Differences and Their Effects on Marriage

INGRID TROBISCH

Every marriage is difficult. As Ann Landers puts it, "You have to work like a dog at it to succeed." Marrying outside your culture means you have even more problems and adjustments to face. A cross-cultural marriage includes the same adjustments as any other marriage—plus many more.

A marriage is obviously cross-cultural when it involves people of different nationalities. My husband, Walter, was born in East Germany; I was born in Tanzania of Swedish-American parents. Racial differences, even when both partners are from the same country, make the marriage cross-cultural. Social and educational levels can also cause problematic cultural differences. The hardest kind of marriage, I think, would be one with large religious differences, such as between a Muslim and a Christian.

But just because a marriage is cross-cultural does not mean it is doomed. I have known many such marriages to be exceptionally strong and loving. The greatest secret of success is for the partners to have an equal exposure to each other's culture.

A wise German pastor told me before we were engaged, "Ingrid, if you love

Walter and are going to marry him, you must learn German." There's no way around it—you can't completely understand a person if you don't understand his language. You won't appreciate his humor, and you will certainly have a hard time understanding his family.

I think of a Malaysian graduate student who married a Dutch missionary nurse he met while she was working in Singapore. She had learned his language—Chinese—in her work, and he took the trouble to learn hers. Such willingness shows respect for each other's family and background, and respect is the basis for a successful marriage.

Ideally, this mutual respect goes beyond the couple to their extended families. I asked the Malaysian student, "How did your Dutch wife get along with your mother?" He said, "I told her just to love my mother as she loves her own, and she succeeded in doing that." For example, she gave his mother equal time—if she wrote to her own mother, she also wrote to his.

Christa, an Austrian woman married to a man from the Bahamas, said the same thing—"The key to making peace with my husband's family is to honor his mother and give her equal time with my own mother." If this is not done, a great deal of difficulty can arise in any marriage, but especially in a cross-cultural marriage.

It helps, of course, if both partners gain their families' support before the marriage takes place. My Dutch friend asked her parents, "What would you think if I married an Asian?" They replied, "We trust you. We will evaluate him on the basis of his character and not his race."

Such understanding, however, is not always forthcoming. While doing a workshop in Indonesia, I met a troubled Indonesian mother. Her son, academically brilliant and educated for an important governmental post, was about to marry a European girl. Bitterly opposed to the marriage, the woman had refused to accept her son's fiancée in her home. "She's just not worthy of him," she wept.

Happily, during the course of our family life seminars she was convicted that her attitude was wrong. She stood up in front of the whole group and confessed her prejudice, vowing, "From now on, when my son wants to bring his fiancée home, I will accept her as my daughter."

A couple who cannot gain their parents' blessing can plan to marry anyway, especially if they are Christians and have commonness in Christ. If they do this, though, they must both be assured that the husband will henceforth take his wife's point of view and not his mother's. If he cannot cut the cord with his mother, then it's usually too bad for the marriage.

If I, an American, had married a typical German son of a typical German mother, I most likely would have faced this problem. But my mother-in-law told me how much she had suffered as a daughter-in-law. Her husband's mother constantly put down her cooking and housekeeping skills. My mother-in-law said, "My husband always took my side, and because of that we made a success of our marriage. I have made the resolve in my heart that I will never give any daughter-in-law of mine a hard time." She stuck to her resolve, and I felt a closeness to her that was as great as the closeness I felt with my own mother.

Cross-cultural marriages can bring great richness to a family. For example, my Malaysian friend comes from a gentle, nonaggressive background; his wife comes from a family of hard-working and competitive Dutch businessmen. She is used to the confrontation style of the West, while he is used to discussion and reconciliation. Through their good marriage, she has learned a certain politeness in personal relationships. She has also learned to relax and not be so time-conscious.

By contrast, he has learned the impor-

good Chinese food, and she knows how to cook good Dutch food. So we just take turns."

Child raising was another area of difference. She was brought up with a strong disciplinary hand, which she has carried over into her approach to their children. He is more likely to spoil the children. Again, the two of them had to learn from each other how to strike a balance.

According to her husband, she has the better head for money, budgeting, and financial planning. So he has entrusted the financial planning to her.

Attitudes toward time, sex, food, child raising, and money—these can cause problems in any marriage. In a cross-cultural marriage, the differences are all the greater. Such a marriage is not for the fainthearted. As Christa observed, "It takes hard work if you're going to make it."

Still, a cross-cultural marriage can bring great dividends. The couple learns new ways of seeing life, new ways of doing things. The children may have a double heritage in music, literature, history, and language. The family is likely to travel widely and have many kinds of friends.

If the partners worship the same God, deeply respect each other's backgrounds and cultures, and maintain their sense of humor, a cross-cultural marriage can be a gift from God.

Related Articles
Chapter 3: Making the Right Choice
Chapter 6: Making the Most of Your
Differences

tance of working toward goals. "I'm very thankful for her time-consciousness now," he says, "because it complements me." He has also learned from his wife the importance of family activities with the children.

In sexual matters, he was much more puritanical than was she. Their honeymoon was rather embarrassing, especially for him, but they have learned to communicate and now have a beautiful relationship.

I asked about food, because I've seen marriages go to pieces over that. He said, "As a bachelor, I learned to cook

Quality Time Together for Engaged Couples

BOB & ALICE FRYLING

We learned early in our engagement that there was one thing we could give each other that no one else could give: *time.* Time to talk, time to share dreams, time to revel in our special sense of oneness. We also learned that quality time together did not and would not come easily. We found we could depend only on ourselves to carve out our times alone. People, obligations, and opportunities all conspired against us.

We were engaged on July 17. In September we both attended a training session for the student workers of Inter-Varsity Christian Fellowship. We were soon immersed in meetings, conversations, and planning sessions. It took only a few days for this to affect our relationship. Alice felt it first. Little hurts from a sense of being ignored began to accumulate. Loneliness replaced the joy of being loved. Then a dryness crept into our relationship.

Finally one night we stood on the large porch at the conference center. Swatting the bugs playing around the light, we fought back tears. "I'm just so alone," Alice confessed. "I feel like I need a long drink of love."

We didn't think of it at the time, but this longing to drink in love reflects the psalmist's words, "As the deer pants for streams of water, so my soul pants for you, O God" (Ps. 42:1). We are the bride of Christ. The marriage relationship is intended to reflect our relationship with God. It is appropriate that a man and a woman long for time to be together.

But certainly engaged couples, of all people, spend a lot of time together!

Yes, most couples we know spend a lot of time socializing, shopping, going to movies, and—to be honest—kissing. While these activities are not wrong, they are not the most effective means to build the relationship. It is often these ordinary experiences that rob couples of the extraordinariness of a relationship designed in heaven.

Perhaps because marriage is so important, the enemy of our souls has many effective ways of stealing the special times of communion that nurture the love relationship. One of the greatest thieves of quality time together during engagement is the wedding itself. How many times have we heard couples bemoan the fact that with so much to do to prepare for the wedding, they cannot enjoy each other!

Another thief of quality time together is the blindness of love. "He knows all about me! He knows without my even telling him!" "I love her so much I know what she is going to say before she says it!" "Our love overflows without words!" Human love is wonderful, but it is not omniscient. Even God communicates His love through words (John 1:1). We cannot expect to do less.

A third thief of quality time together during engagement is the illusion that there will be more time to talk after marriage. Rarely is this true. If you do not carve out time to be together, to talk, to plan, to enjoy each other during engagement, you almost certainly will not do so after marriage. The time thieves will still hover in the corners of your lives.

Some couples are willing to resist the

WHAT ABOUT A TEEN MARRIAGE?

All marriages are complicated and difficult. For two to become one is mathematically impossible, but it is the mandate for marriage. Blending two personalities into one that reflects the unity of God's nature is not simple even for the most mature people, however. For teenagers who bring a high level of immaturity to their marriage, it is even more difficult—but it is not impossible.

A frequent complicating factor in teenage marriages is the teenagers' parents. They may choose to focus on their own loss and broken dreams, not on the potentially happy future the young people might create. When parents set themselves up as critics or even enemies of the marriage, the young people have to defiantly assert that they're going to make it in spite of everybody else, and this lonely commitment is hard to carry out.

If the teenage marriage is surrounded by patient, caring parents and other adults who are willing to allow the young people certain immaturities and give them opportunities to grow, then it can often develop into a very happy union.

Jay Kesler

time thieves, but they don't know how to spend quality time together. There is nothing mysterious about it; it is really very simple. First of all, pick times and places where both of you are comfortable talking. We like to talk in restaurants. We also like to talk in our living room, in the dark, with just one candle lit. We have friends who talk best while they are walking outside. Other friends talk better if they are working on a project together. Pick your own time and place. Vary it enough to be interesting, and keep it the same enough to make it predictable and secure.

When you talk, ask each other questions. How was your day? What was most satisfying? Did you read anything interesting? Did you have any good conversations? Did you learn anything new about yourself? About God?

Listen to each other with eagerness and curiosity. Don't make judgments unless your advice is welcomed. The idea here is not so much to solve problems as to commune. Get to know each other. Learn to value what the other values. Learn to enjoy what the other enjoys. Dream together. Enjoy each other. Weep together. Talk together.

We started doing this the very night we discovered we were "thirsty" for each other. That was 17 years ago, and we have been setting aside special times to talk ever since. We haven't run out of things to talk about yet! That is because we are both learning and growing all the time. We are not the same people we were the day we were engaged. Every day is a new experience, and we keep on sharing those experiences.

Because we share our experiences day by day, we have built a mutual values system. We certainly feel free to disagree with each other, and we occasionally misunderstand and hurt each other. But over the years, our times of sharing have given us accumulated information that helps us resolve conflict and make mutually satisfying decisions.

The tears we cried 17 years ago because we needed each other have brought forth "songs of joy" (Ps. 126:5). We expect to be singing for a long time!

Related Articles
Chapter 4: Never Take Your Mate for Granted
Chapter 9: Perspective: Seeing What Your Spouse Sees

Leaving Home to Marry

JOHN TRENT

Jim and Susan sat in my office at opposite ends of the couch. Filled with anger, hurt, and resentment after only three years of marriage, they were ready to bail out of their pain-wracked relationship. As I began talking with this couple, I discovered that like many other husbands and wives they had ignored a fundamental biblical principle. While they wanted desperately to do what Scripture says and "cleave" to each other, they had never taken the time to learn how to leave home in an emotionally healthy way.

In God's first instructions concerning the marriage relationship, He details in stairstep fashion the road to genuine intimacy. "For this reason a man will leave his father and mother and be united to his wife, and they will become one flesh" (Gen. 2:24).

What many people don't realize is that failing to leave home properly is like climbing onto a ladder with the first rung missing. Instead of leading to greater heights of intimacy, such an approach can cause a marriage—like Jim and Susan's—to crash to the ground before the climb ever begins.

Isn't leaving simply a matter of physically moving out of the parents' house? While physically moving away from one's parents can help a person become more independent, the biblical concept of leaving has always involved much more than that. There is also an important emotional side to leaving home that can't be ignored. Many people today physically live thousands of miles from their parents, but emotionally they have never moved an inch.

Gary Smalley and I have found that those couples who have left home in a positive way are the ones who have come to grips with at least three important questions. By facing and answering these questions, husbands and wives can provide their marriages with this crucial first step toward intimacy.

1. *Did I receive my family's blessing?* Esau was a man in the Old Testament who waited for years to receive his father's blessing. Tricked by his brother, however, he missed out on his one chance to hear these words of love and acceptance. In desperation he cried out, "Bless me—me too, my father!" (Gen. 27:34) That same cry is echoed today by men and women who have missed out on their family's blessing—people who have never heard words of love and acceptance from their parents. What does this have to do with leaving home?

Very often, people who have missed out on their parents' blessing have difficulty emotionally leaving home. Such people often have a deep longing for love and acceptance, yet they find it hard to feel genuinely loved by a spouse or even by God. In marriage in particular, they may struggle with knowing how to communicate warmth and love to a spouse, because they never felt these things themselves.

If you did receive a blessing from your family—affirming actions like being meaningfully touched, hearing words of praise and acceptance, and having your parents believe in you and picture for you a special future—it is much easier to accept a spouse's love and to put your love into action with a marriage partner. If you did not receive the blessing from your parents (and some of us dishonor them by treating them as if they had little value, you are actually lowering your own value at the same time. And the lower your own value goes, the more likely you will act out your negative feelings with others—especially your spouse. People with low value often get their spouses to treat them with as little worth as they feel inside. Not only are such people often hard to live with, they are actually shortening their lives and darkening their days. Ask any family doctor what holding anger and resentment inside does to a person physically and emotionally.

The damage you do by leaving home with anger and bitterness can chain you to the past and keep you from intimate relationships in the present. Even if there were problems in the past, wise husbands and wives can make the decision to honor their parents—a decision that not only benefits their parents, but blesses and protects their own marriage as well.

3. *Where do my ultimate loyalties lie?* Family loyalties are powerful. They can stretch across thousands of miles and decades of time. They are the patterns you saw in your parents' marriage that shout at you with the force of years of habit and modeling. They often tempt you to say, "Now that I'm married, right or wrong we're going to do things the right way—the way they were done in *my* family."

In most cases, family loyalties are positive. Be sure to repeat those positive things in your parents' marriage that strengthened their relationship. Be aware, however, that you will be just as tempted to loyally repeat negative patterns you may have seen over and over while growing up.

An important part of leaving home in a healthy way is to talk about and recognize family patterns from the past. Whether it's discussing family traditions (like whether to open presents on Christmas Eve or Christmas morning) or rec-

never will), you don't have to despair. You can still find, experience, and model the blessing you missed out on, through your relationship with the Heavenly Father and the spiritual family He has provided (1 Tim. 5:1-2).

Coming to grips with whether or not you received your family's blessing is an important first step in leaving home. A second is to make sure you leave home in obedience to the first commandment God gives us with a promise attached.

2. *As I leave home, am I honoring or dishonoring my mother and father?* Husbands and wives who leave home in a healthy way make sure they practice honoring their parents. Why is honoring them important?

Like it or not, all of us are very much like our parents. Each cell in your body bears their mark on your life. When you

ognizing a family pattern of angry yelling, sift through the negatives and positives in light of God's Word. Those couples who take a long look at their family backgrounds go a long way toward leaving home in an emotionally healthy way.

Physically moving away from home can happen overnight, but for most couples, emotionally leaving home takes time. Husbands and wives who take leaving home seriously protect themselves from missing the first rung of the ladder leading to intimacy.

Related Articles
Introduction: Two Shall Become One
Chapter 3: Before You Say, "I Do"

Your Wedding:
The Longest Day of Your Life

MARK & DEBBIE JEVERT

You are engaged to be married. Now what? Should you have a simple ceremony or an elaborate one? Lots of guests or a few close friends?

There are more resources today than ever before to help you plan your wedding. Under the heading "Wedding Supplies and Services," the Yellow Pages of your telephone book list bakers, balloonists, calligraphers, engravers, florists, musicians, photographers, video recorder experts, sellers of bridal gowns, renters of formal attire, and even wedding consultants to help you make sense of all the other services. Books and magazines offer checklists and timelines, and usually at least one mother or sister is full of suggestions!

We're not going to offer yet another outline for a perfect wedding. Rather, from our experience with our own wedding and with the weddings of several other couples, we offer several important principles to keep in mind as you make your plans.

The earlier you can get it done, the better you will feel. There is no such thing as getting it done too early! Things always seem to snowball as the wedding day approaches, and the unprepared couple will suffer unneeded stress. Make a list of everything you need to accomplish, and check items off as far in advance as possible.

Learn from others' experience. Ask married couples what were the three best things they did at their wedding. Attend friends' weddings together if you can, and discuss together what you liked and disliked about the ceremonies. Ask if you can attend a wedding in the church you have chosen to be married in. Pay attention to the lighting, the sound, the arrangement of people, the decorations. Borrow ideas you like, and improve on the things you don't care for.

It's your day—be sure it reflects you. Think of the different ways your wedding can reflect your interests and personality. The music, the decorations, the wedding vows, the program, the reception—all can and should incorporate your tastes and beliefs.

Use a wedding coordinator. This might be a paid consultant, but it doesn't have to be. A close friend, a family member, or the person who helps with weddings in your church can help you immensely. When the ceremony is about to begin, you will not be available to make sure the attendants have their flowers, to supervise the ushers, to keep the program moving according to schedule, and to tend to all the other minor details. Your wedding coordinator can relieve you of this burden and help you avoid last-minute tension and confusion.

Remember your parents. Keep in mind that parents can have mixed feelings about their child's wedding, which for them means letting go of someone they love very dearly. At the end of our ceremony, we presented our mothers with gifts. This added a touch of sentiment and reassured them that even as we were beginning our own family, we were not going to forget their love.

Keep your wedding plans in perspective. As you plan, remember that your wedding is not your marriage. A wedding is a historical event that takes place at a specific place and time. It is only one day in your lifetime. Details that seem monumental the day before the wedding may not even be remembered a month or a year later. Enjoy this special day, and cherish the memories the rest of your life.

Related Article
Chapter 2: The Surprises Marriage Brings

What If I Don't Marry Until I'm 30?

JUDITH ALLEN SHELLY

When I was 25, my mother gave me the silver tea set she was saving for my wedding present. She simply got tired of waiting and assumed I would remain single forever.

Pressure to marry by the early 20s comes from many directions in our culture—despite the flashy image of "swinging singles." To a great extent, marriage is the final rite of passage into adulthood and the formal establishment of independence from parents. Parents usually have difficulty emotionally letting go of their children until they are safely married. They also face the peer pressure of their friends who have lovely pictures of weddings and grandchildren to show off.

Most people do marry soon after high school or college graduation, and the world suddenly seems like a couples-only club to the working person who is still single. Few churches know how to incorporate singles into congregational life. Doomsayers make the problem worse by quoting research statistics about the increasingly bleak possibilities of marriage as age creeps upon us. However, for the Christian single, the prospects are not as gloomy as they seem.

The Prophet Jeremiah reminds us of God's promise, " 'I know the plans I have for you,' declares the Lord, 'plans to prosper you and not to harm you, plans to give you hope and a future' " (Jer. 29:11). Constantly remembering that promise can make a major difference in the years between graduation and marriage.

My husband, Jim, and I were 31 when we married, and I can honestly say I'm glad I waited. Those 10 years between college graduation and marriage were

MAKE YOUR WEDDING GO SMOOTHLY

1. *Choose a photographer you can work with.* Don't expect your photographer to read your mind: make a list of the photographs you want, and then ask him or her for further suggestions. You may wish to ask a friend to complement the official shots by taking several rolls of candids during the rehearsal, ceremony, and reception.

2. *Consider having your formal portraits taken before the ceremony.* This was the best thing we did in our wedding. By having pictures taken a couple of hours beforehand, the wedding party was able to relax, have fun, and enjoy the ceremony. In addition, the wedding party was able to proceed directly to the reception, so the guests didn't have to wait a long time for it to begin.

3. *Draft written instructions for your ushers.* Ushers can make or break a wedding. Tell them how to greet your guests, how to seat family members, how to clear the lobby if it is still congested when it is time to begin the ceremony. If you put your guidelines in writing, the men will not have to second-guess your wishes.

4. *Consider spending a few minutes alone with your spouse-to-be before the ceremony.* We spent 10 minutes together sharing how we felt and exchanging special gifts. This brief time is a warm memory. It allowed us to really know how the other was feeling, and it relieved some of the pre-wedding anxiety.

Mark & Debbie Jevert

not always easy, but they definitely contributed to making our marriage satisfying and solid.

First of all, by age 30 I knew where I was headed in life and was able to find a husband who shared my goals. I'm not sure I could have done that when I was 21.

Second, the life experiences of those years taught me basic skills that made marriage easier. Living with 16 different roommates in households of up to 7 people certainly helped me develop flexibility and taught me how to get along with people. One of the great joys of marriage was knowing I wouldn't have to switch roommates the next year.

Third, I had the freedom to pour myself into my work, to travel, to go to graduate school, to set my own schedule, to try out different churches and fellowship groups without worrying about what anyone else thought. When I finally married, I was confident that I was in the right job and the right church and could share that with my husband. I had also had enough of the transient lifestyle and was ready to settle down and be accountable to someone else on a daily basis.

Marriage after age 30 does have its drawbacks. Some of the very factors that make it so satisfying can also make it frustrating. After 10 years of independence, interdependence can take awhile to get used to. I'll never forget the time during our first month of marriage when I went shopping and said I'd be back in about an hour. I got involved in talking with some people and came home two hours later, only to find my frantic husband driving around looking for me, fearing something terrible had happened. Other seemingly minor adjustments like sharing a car and a checkbook were also difficult for me.

Another drawback of later marriage is that fertility decreases with age. Jim and I both wanted children deeply. Only after six years of frustration and disappointment were we able to adopt our first child. But there are also joys in delayed parenthood. With two active preschoolers in the family now, we certainly haven't had time for a midlife crisis. Our children are probably more precious to us than they would have been had they come easily.

In the overall balance, I would recommend later marriage if you are not totally convinced that a prospective spouse is the person with whom you want to spend the rest of your life. I have seen too many young marriages dissolve as the partners discover they have grown in separate directions or feel trapped or cheated out of life experiences. Waiting a few years provides time to grow, explore, and develop a clear picture of what you want to be and do.

The Lord's promise through Jeremiah provides the key to whether the waiting period will be a constructive time of growth or a desperate time of searching. If you believe God, you do not have to despair. Granted, marriage may not be in His plans, but if it is not, He has something better for you. If marriage *is* in His plans, He will provide the *right* spouse at the *right* time.

What can you do as you wait? First, avoid the extremes of either concentrating all your energy on finding a spouse or retreating entirely from social contacts in mixed groups of singles. The desperate spouse-hunter will scare off most eligible mates right away. However, avoiding contact with people of the opposite sex limits possibilities of meeting the right person.

The best plan is to do those things you enjoy most, work toward accomplishing your dreams, and get involved in a ministry to which you believe God is calling you. Find social settings where you can make friends with both men and women without the pressure of dating. Continuing education courses, church committees and fellowship groups, ethnic and cultural societies,

ASSUMPTIONS AND EXPECTATIONS

It is amazing what assumptions and expectations each individual brings to a marriage. Whatever we lived with in our family is the "right" way to do things—and the jolt of marriage and opposite ideas can cause some real struggles for couples.

Before getting married, and even as your lifestyle changes over the years, together discuss the roles that need to be taken care of in your home and who can best do them. Consider time, desires, physical ability, and responsibilities for the children. Areas that need to be examined include: paying the bills, doing the laundry, cooking, mowing the lawn, cleaning the house, shoveling snow, and taking out the garbage. Just remember there is no eternal law about which spouse pays the bills and which cooks dinner. Put aside your own assumptions and expectations, and as a couple decide a system that works for you.

YFC Editors

and community action groups can provide opportunities for meeting people with similar interests.

Jim and I met in seminary. Within the first week of classes we became good friends, realizing we shared many goals and interests. We started a campus prayer group together, gravitated toward the same friends and activities, and spent hours talking about ideas and dreams. Neither of us was actively looking for a spouse, but after a year of being "just friends" we knew we were headed toward marriage. By then we knew we could work together as a ministry team, and that our ministries would be enhanced, not threatened, by our marriage.

I would not recommend going to seminary to meet a mate, but for us it provided an ideal environment to get to know one another without feeling like we were courting. It was also a turning point in both of our lives, so that we were ready for marriage—at last—by age 31. Yes, I'm glad I waited.

Related Articles
Chapter 2: The Late 20s/Early 30s Era
Chapter 3: Before You Say, "I Do"

Second Marriages: Two Important Issues

ANDRE & FAY BUSTANOBY

Whether widowed or divorced, those who marry a second time face two issues they didn't have to cope with the first time around: dealing with children, and handling money fairly. It is good to look at these issues before remarrying, since solutions may be much more difficult to work out afterward.

Whether your children are dependent and still living at home or grown and living in homes of their own, when you remarry you must establish a new family system where two family systems already exist.

You already have a family system with your children, as does your mate. Each of you has developed patterns that are not easily changed. When their parents remarry, children are expected to change loyalties and rules of relating that they have known all their lives, and this makes their adjustment to the new family difficult. The children's failure to adjust often makes the stepparent feel like an outsider. Sometimes a parent unconsciously favors his own child over the stepchild, further complicating adjustment to a new family system.

Family therapists talk about establishing *blended* families that give up old loyalties and establish new ones with a new spouse, his children, her children, and sometimes their children. This blending is not easily achieved. We don't easily change our ways of relating to our own children and accept new ones, nor do we easily give stepchildren the consideration and rights we give our own.

We most easily solve the problem of loyalties when we observe a foundational principle of family relations: primary loyalty goes to the spouse, not to the children. Husbands and wives should be strengthening their ties to each other throughout their marriage, with a view to spending the rest of their lives together. Parents, on the other hand, must gradually loosen their ties to their children, with a view to making them independent, with new loyalties to marriage partners of their own.

Though the Creation story tells of children separating from parents, the separation works both ways. The "one flesh" relationship in marriage requires that boundaries be set between parents and children. Loyalty between parent and child is superseded by loyalty between husband and wife. If forced to choose between them, the spouse comes first— an especially difficult decision if the child is still dependent. But loyalties are an

121

issue even with older couples who have no dependent children at home if one partner shows more concern or gives more attention to an adult child than to his or her own spouse.

If you have not already remarried, give careful attention to how your prospective mate relates to you and his or her children. Do you feel the children are more important than you? Then think twice before marrying. Likewise, ask yourself if you would be willing to put this man or woman ahead of your own children. If not, you too should be hearing warning bells.

Children are not the only touchy issue in second marriages. How money is spent and what it's spent for can become a real battleground, particularly when your spouse seems more concerned with his or her children's comfort and financial security than with yours. Money can raise the question of primary loyalty once again. If the children's well-being appears more important than the spouse's, this suggests that the primary loyalty is with them.

The older woman who remarries will feel financially insecure if her husband does not make adequate provision for her in his will, and especially if he ties up his assets with a prenuptial agreement so as to retain sole ownership. This is a difficult problem to solve. On the one hand, his primary loyalty should be to his wife, and he should make her feel secure. On the other hand, he also has loyalties to his children, and he should not disinherit them.

The problem can be solved by making the wife the beneficiary of a substantial life insurance policy and the inheritor of their home. The rest of the estate that he brings into the marriage, such as other real estate and investments, should be left intact for the children. Buying a substantial term insurance policy can be expensive, especially if the husband is older. But it is a worthwhile investment of his resources to make his

JUST LIKE MOM AND DAD

One day Gail and I were talking about how we were reared and about our parents. I don't know why I thought to ask this, but I said, "What if your mom had married my dad? What would *their* marriage have been like?"

We laughed as we imagined the potential conflicts between that unusual pairing of two very strong-willed and outspoken individuals.

Suddenly we stopped laughing as we realized the truth. Each of the problems we imagined would be theirs, *we* were now facing. And we knew why. The truth is that in many ways, Gail is like her mother and I am like my father.

This is normal, of course, because they were our main role models for being a woman and a man. And so we shouldn't be surprised that we have caught personal traits, reactions, temperament, ways of communicating, ways of expressing love and anger, and ways of dealing with conflict.

Do you want to know what your potential spouse will be like? If he or she has lived with that person for any length of time, look at his father or her mother.

Dave Veerman

wife feel secure.

With respect to the home, when a couple marries for the second time they *must not* move into either his or her home. Though it may not be financially sound to pool their resources and buy a new house together, it is psychologically a good choice to begin the marriage in a new home. It will help them break with

122

the past and establish some financial security for the wife in the event of the husband's death.

Second marriages bring unique complications, but they may also bring increased maturity and willingness to work out differences. The two biggest issues you are likely to face concern children and money. Look at these carefully and clearly before you marry, and your marriage will start out on the right foot.

Ogden Nash once observed that marriage is an alliance of a person who can't sleep with the window open with a person who can't sleep with it shut. How do you and your spouse react to the following statements? Take the quiz separately and compare notes. Circle the A if you agree; the D if you disagree.

HIS	HERS	
A D	A D	Toothpaste tubes should be squeezed from the bottom up.
A D	A D	It's pleasant to have lots of people in the house.
A D	A D	My spouse is my best friend.
A D	A D	Dinner should be at 7.
A D	A D	Having fun is more important than being neat and clean.
A D	A D	My spouse accepts me the way I am.
A D	A D	A house should usually be spotless.
A D	A D	Never throw anything out you might need later.
A D	A D	Watching TV is a good way to relax after work.
A D	A D	A family isn't complete without a dog.
A D	A D	It's important to be on time or early for appointments.
A D	A D	The man should take out the garbage.
A D	A D	Toilet paper should unroll clockwise.
A D	A D	I can't stand to be criticized in front of others.
A D	A D	Husbands should keep the house in good repair.
A D	A D	Wives should serve meals on time.
A D	A D	My spouse's relatives are good company.
A D	A D	I do my best work early in the morning.
A D	A D	I can't sleep unless the room is dark and quiet.
A D	A D	I'd rather eat in restaurants than at home.
A D	A D	The toilet seat lid should be put down.
A D	A D	Middle-aged people should not gain weight.
A D	A D	Giving presents is a sign of affection.
A D	A D	Having sex is a good way to apologize after a quarrel.
A D	A D	I like my spouse's old friends.
A D	A D	Dogs should not be allowed to sleep with people.
A D	A D	I need at least eight hours of sleep a night.
A D	A D	I like to go to church once a week or more.
A D	A D	I enjoy playing table games.
A D	A D	A really good vacation involves lots of active sports.

LOOKING AT YOUR ANSWERS: No couple will agree in all these areas. The important thing is not agreement, but constructively working out ways to live together happily in spite of difficulties. What compromises have helped you in your life together? In what areas do you still need to compromise?

LIFE TOGETHER

In our world where marriage quackery is commonly practiced, it is little wonder that weddings are often a waste of time. Like some back-street bookbindery we stand two people side-by-side, require each to say "I do" without knowing why, and then apply the glue of an official stamp to bind them together. Strong and lasting kinship may or may not take place.

A lifestyle in concert with a spouse requires tailoring which tends at times to tax partners to the point of uncertainty. "In rock climbing there is a technical term called a 'commitment move,'" says Tim Hansel in his book *Holy Sweat*. "Often it's the crux move of the climb. Handholds seem scarce and footholds appear nonexistent. The tendency is to 'bogart'—to freeze, to panic, to wait until exhaustion causes you, the climber, to quit the climb." The inevitable "bogarts" of wedlock need not destroy the union; success lies in discovering the crevice where a connection can be formed, where attachment will begin to secure mutual harmony.

Marriage often seems to take more than it gives. In *Mystery of Marriage*, Mike Mason describes the relationship as "a lifelong encounter . . . much more rigorous and demanding than anything human beings could ever have chosen, dreamed of, desired, or invented on their own."

The concept of "together" in Christian marriage is like the Old Testament drink offering poured over the grain as a symbol of joy, two lives flowing together in a blended gift to God. The art of fusion—its discipline delves deeply into sharing self and embracing another. Stability and strength sprout from gentle care of each other in a duet of daily duty.

Howard & Jeanne Hendricks

Never Take Your Mate for Granted

V. GILBERT & ARLISLE BEERS

Marriage has an all-too-familiar cycle. It goes like this. We fall in love, cultivate the romance leading up to the wedding, put on a great display of affection and excitement on that special day, then put the icing on the cake on our honeymoon. We have stars in our eyes and love in our hearts. But for many, it's all downhill after that.

Returning from their honeymoon, the star-struck young couple now faces the reality of settling down to work, adjusting to one another, coping with budgets and meals, repairing cars and buying insurance policies, perhaps paying off college loans or continuing in school.

For some this is a delightful experience, a challenge. For others it is a drag. But in either case it is of necessity a time of building settled routines so creative energies can be spent on those things that do not fit easily into routines.

The routines of life are both life-saving and life-threatening. We must have routines so we don't reinvent the wheel every morning. No couple or individual can deal with all facets of life fresh every morning without something being settled and repeated. Routines spare us from pointlessly wasting our creativity on secondary matters. We don't care if there are six different kinds of knots we could use to tie our shoes. We are content to use the same old knot morning after morning. There must be many creative approaches we could use to brush our teeth or put on deodorant. Who cares? Let's get the job done and move on to more important matters.

But if routines spread too far over our lifestyles, they can also become life-threatening. It's OK to tie your shoes and brush your teeth routinely, but don't start kissing your mate or expressing your thanks as a routine. If you do, you are starting to take your mate for granted, and your marriage is growing stale.

Developing routines for the little tasks helps you get comfortable with the process of living. But developing routines for the more important tasks that affect your husband-wife relationship makes you too comfortable. When you become too comfortable with each other, you may easily take one another for granted. You assume, "I've got you, so I don't have to be romantic anymore." When you don't have to be romantic anymore, even if your mate "understands," you are taking your mate for granted.

Somewhere along the marriage path, children enter the picture, and children don't take a backseat to anything else. When a diaper needs changing, someone has to do it, *now*. When a baby is hungry, someone has to feed it, *now*. When a thousand other demands arise, either mother or father has to attend to them. (Guess who gets the job most often!) Many of these demands must be met *now*.

It takes commitment from both husband and wife to get through these everyday demands. Commitment says, "I will remain with you no matter what happens." It is a wonderful, essential glue that binds us together in marriage. Without it, we would all chase after pretty rainbows.

But it would be easy for a scoundrel to take advantage of his mate's commitment. If he knows his wife will stay with him no matter what, why should he work hard to keep her? It's easy to abuse a mate's commitment and feel assured that he or she will not leave you when the going gets dull. No one with a decent character would consciously do that, of course. But either mate or both can drift into that trap. You or your mate may be acting that way without even being aware of it. If you have, you are taking each other for granted.

Are you so comfortable with each other that you know your mate understands that you love him or her without your saying it today? When was the last time you showed your mate the kind of attention you both enjoyed before you were married? When was the last time your mate said to you, "You're really fun to live with"?

At the heart of this problem is the basic question, "What do you think of me as a person?" How much do you really value your mate? What are you willing to do for your mate to show that value? What are you willing to give up to show your mate that you love him or her?

We have tried to keep romance alive, but it's easy to drift. You who have been married a long time know that. Here are some things we have found helpful to keep romance in bloom:

1. We have traveled extensively to-

gether, long trips and short, holidays and business travel. Whether it's primarily work or play, we always try to find some time to play.

2. Holidays are a big deal in our house, and we try to show some special touches to one another.

3. Birthdays never go by without cakes and candles, gifts and singing. Though Arlie is usually the cake baker, she is sometimes given a special decorated cake from the bakery.

4. We make appointments for lunch, breakfast, or dinner out. We feel it is as important to make appointments with one another as with business associates.

5. Flowers and candy come to Arlie several times during the year—Valentine's Day, her birthday, and often for special occasions. Sometimes they come for no good reason except to say, "Surprise, I love you."

6. We both like to take little breaks during the day (this is easy for us since we both work in the home) and go hiking for an hour or browsing through an-

tique shops for an afternoon or playing a game for a few minutes or a dozen other things.

7. We hardly let a day go by without saying, "I love you" or, "You are special."

Be sure to say thank you to your mate for the little things, such as a good meal, ironing your clothes, taking out the garbage, shoveling the snow from the sidewalk, building a fire in the fireplace, or a dozen other "small" favors. "Thank you" says "I noticed what you did, and I don't take you for granted."

Are you taking your mate for granted? If so, it's time to reread this article and then get busy rekindling the fires of romance. You don't have to be a die-hard romantic to say "I love you" or "thank you" occasionally, and that's a wonderful place to start.

Related Articles
Introduction: What's Right With Families
Chapter 2: Characteristics of a Mature Marriage

Three Important Choices

DAVID VEERMAN

The choices began the moment they met—he, choosing to ask her out; she, choosing to accept. They were moved by mysterious feelings of love and passion, to be sure, but they had to make choices nonetheless—to be honest with each other, to share real feelings, to risk being hurt, to ask and say yes to marriage, to set the date, to walk the aisle.

The wedding came at the end of a long series of choices—but more choices would follow. Too often, however, a new husband and wife settle into a dull routine of reacting and floating through life, and soon they wonder what

went wrong in their marriage.

The problem is, they stopped choosing. But to decide not to choose is to choose—to choose to be swept into the wide American stream of mediocre marriages.

The best choices are conscious acts of the will. I will highlight three important ones that each married person can take, whether better or worse, sick or healthy, rich or poor.

1. *Choose to act in love.* In our culture, *love* is used primarily as a noun. It is something we possess, feel, fall into or out of, find, and make. But the primary

IDIOSYNCRASIES

They may seem insignificant, but over time habits and idiosyncrasies can grind away at a relationship.

For example, he throws his socks in the corner; she throws the newspaper out before it's read. He prefers the toilet paper to unroll from the bottom; she prefers it to unroll from the top. She likes clothes folded in a certain way; he's the only one who can "properly" wash the car. And on and on goes the list of habits and idiosyncrasies which, if left unchecked, can simply drive us nuts! Frequently they are unconscious, which makes them even more difficult to deal with effectively. But deal with them we must.

It's important to bring irritating habits to our spouse's attention before major problems occur. This can best be done with honesty and a willingness to bear with one another patiently while working out reasonable compromises. It also helps to discuss how each of your family backgrounds may be influencing your present behaviors.

Gary Bennett

---

use of this magical word is as a *verb*. Love is something we do, an action we take.

Everyone wants to feel love—chills, goose bumps, warm fuzzies. But even when feelings are absent, we can still love and be loved. In fact, this is what true love is all about—loving someone, whether my enemy or my spouse, when I don't feel like it. People flock to divorce court because they "fell out of love." In truth, they chose not to love anymore, not to do loving acts. Strong marriages are based not on feelings but on commitment.

I realize that nearly all relationships begin selfishly—we don't really believe in "mercy dating"—but they must progress to unselfish, giving love if they are to last. This means choosing to meet the other person's needs.

Every day with your spouse, you have countless opportunities to choose to act in love. Ask yourself, "What would be the loving response?" and then do it!

2. *Choose to listen to each other.* Communication is the key to relationships, and effective communication involves more listening than talking. Have you ever had "conversations" where you were sure the other person didn't hear a word you said, but was only waiting for his chance to talk? It was frustrating and discouraging and did nothing to enhance the relationship. You wanted someone to hear what you were saying and feeling, but you got a speech instead.

On the other hand, genuine, honest listening acts like glue in a relationship. You want to be near people who care enough to take time to listen, to really hear you.

Effective listening means concentrating on what the person is saying, refusing to interrupt or to let your mind wander. And it means watching for silent clues—furrowed brows, clenched fists, agitated feet, tears.

Like loving, listening is an act of the will, a conscious choice. Instead of defending yourself, listen. Instead of hurling a put-down or using another verbal weapon, listen. Instead of dogmatically stating your "correct" position, listen.

3. *Give first place to God.* The final choice is the key to marital happiness: choose to give God first place, to put Him at the center of your relationship.

Sometimes a person will say to his lover or spouse, "You are the most important thing in my life," or "I can't live without you." This puts tremendous pressure on the other person. The speaker, thinking to be romantic, is actually saying, "All my happiness, security, fulfillment, and dreams depend on you. Don't let me down!" No one can bear that burden for long.

In the best marriages Christ, not the other person, is at the center. Choosing to put Christ at the center means depending on Him for happiness and fulfillment. It means asking for His direction and guidance and then doing what He says. When husband and wife place Christ at the core of their marriage, centering their lives around Him, He draws them closer together.

A relationship with God also releases power to make other important choices. As Paul states in Philippians 2:13, "It is God who works in you to will and to act according to His good purpose."

Solid, sound, unbreakable marriages are built and nurtured by the right choices. Choose now to act in love, to listen, and to give first place to God.

Related Articles
Chapter 1: Developing and Nourishing Love
Chapter 5: Husbands and Wives With Jesus as Lord
Chapter 9: The Art of Listening

Making Your Spouse Your Best Friend

ANDRE & FAY BUSTANOBY

How do you make your spouse your best friend? Answer these three questions:
☐ What is friendship?
☐ How do you know when your spouse is your best friend?
☐ How do you improve friendship in marriage?

To understand friendship, it's helpful to contrast it with intimacy.

Friendship centers on something besides each other. It involves mutual interest and joy in sharing activities such as sports, nature, music, or even dominoes. Intimacy centers on each other. This is an important dimension in marriage. But if marriage is to survive, a couple must be friends as well as intimates. They must have common interests outside of each other.

Friendship loves with an appreciative love, whereas intimacy loves with a need love. Though a friend is appreciated, he is not needed, and therefore he has the freedom to function as an individual apart from the friendship without spoiling it. Friendship is liberating. Obviously, marriage includes both kinds of love. We always should need and be needed by each other. But over the years, as spouses feel secure with each other and know that their needs will be met, they are able to function as individuals apart from each other without jeopardizing their relationship. They sometimes can opt for solitude rather than activity with the friend-spouse and not hurt the friendship.

Unlike intimacy, friendship is not exclusive. Though your spouse is your best friend, both of you should enlarge your worlds by enjoying the company of other like-minded people. By sharing your friend with other friends, you don't have less of him but more. Others are able to draw from your spouse ideas and responses you are incapable of eliciting, and you are the richer for it.

THE FRIENDSHIP INVENTORY

Are you and your spouse best friends? Take this quiz and find out. When you have finished, read "Making Your Spouse Your Best Friend" on page 129.

_ YES	_ NO	I respect my spouse.
_ YES	_ NO	I like him/her as he/she is.
_ YES	_ NO	I could live without him/her, but my life would be poorer for it.
_ YES	_ NO	I enjoy sharing what we have in common with others of like mind.
_ YES	_ NO	If we were not married, we would still share many of the same ideas, ideals, and activities.
_ YES	_ NO	I respect him/her even when he/she does things that upset or annoy me.
_ YES	_ NO	I know him/her well enough that I can anticipate what his/her words or behavior will be in most circumstances.
_ YES	_ NO	It's easy to turn a blind eye to his/her faults.
_ YES	_ NO	I want what is best for him/her.
_ YES	_ NO	I care enough to let him/her go or even give him/her up.
_ YES	_ NO	My respect for him/her is not based on his/her accomplishments.
_ YES	_ NO	I know he/she is a kindred spirit even though I may not be assured of this frequently.
_ YES	_ NO	He/she brings out the best in me.
_ YES	_ NO	I feel we can stand together against the views of outsiders.
_ YES	_ NO	I can be both strong and weak with him/her.
_ YES	_ NO	My giving to him/her is characterized by freedom and willingness and not grudging sacrifice.
_ YES	_ NO	My relationship with him/her is characterized by trust.

Rate your friendship level by giving one point for each "yes" answer:

15-17	Very good
12-14	Good
9-11	Needs work
6- 8	Poor
0- 5	Very poor

[The Friendship Inventory is adapted from Andre Bustanoby, *Can Men and Women Be Just Friends?* Zondervan, 1985, pp. 112-116.]

Andre & Fay Bustanoby

You know your spouse is your best friend when you respect him or her, treat him or her as an equal, enjoy many things in common, and prefer activities and interests with your spouse above those with other people. The friendship inventory on page 130 will help you determine how strong friendship is in your marriage. Take a minute to fill it out.

How did you rate your spouse? Have him or her do an inventory on you, and compare notes. Now comes the tough part, particularly if you gave or got a low friendship rating. Go over each item that did not receive an unqualified yes. *In as loving a way as you can state it,* tell your spouse why you rated the item as you did. For help in doing this, you will want to read our article on page 285,

"Making Your Communication Work."

Be prepared for your spouse to express lots of feelings, but don't find fault with them. Acknowledge those feelings and let your spouse know you care how he or she feels.

Once you have thoroughly discussed your feelings about friendship in marriage, decide what you want to do to rectify the weaknesses you have spotted. Be patient with yourself and your spouse. It may take weeks or even months before you see change. Actually, the process takes a lifetime—but that's what the commitment of marriage is all about!

Related Articles
Chapter 1: Love as Friendship
Chapter 4: My Husband, My Best Friend

My Husband, My Best Friend

LUCI SHAW

Though we have left the Victorian age long behind, a common rumor persists—that the word *spouse* suggests love, romance, marriage, procreation; whereas *friend* stands for companionship and same-sex camaraderie. For most of us, marriage and friendship connote two mutually exclusive categories.

For 33 years my husband and I proved that belief false. We not only were lovers (with 5 children), we not only built and maintained a warm home for our family, we not only were committed and loyal to each other in fulfillment of our marriage vows, but we *liked* each other. We were happiest in each other's company. We shared just about everything.

Even business. In 1967 we started a publishing company together in response to what we believed was God's call. We pooled our experience and gifts, beginning in our home, but later expanding into our own office and warehouse building. Because of our team approach to book publishing, many of our daily work hours as well as our home times were spent together. We would often drive to work together. We consulted often during the day about ideas and decisions. We went home for lunch together when one of us wasn't entertaining a client or an author. We'd wake and talk in the middle of the night about an ongoing publishing or personnel problem, and still we didn't tire of each other's company!

C.S. Lewis distinguishes between four kinds of love: "*Storge* means affection, the sort of love there ought to be between relations. *Philia* means friendship. *Eros* is, of course, the love between the sexes. And *agape* is love in the Christian

131

sense, God's love for man and the Christian love for the brethren." It seems like a large claim, a tall order, but Harold and I attempted, and to a large extent succeeded, in joining all four kinds of love in our marriage.

Well before his marriage, Lewis—a confirmed bachelor—wrote: "The decay of *friendship,* owing to the endless presence of women everywhere, is a thing I'm rather afraid of." Then he married Joy Davidman. Because of her cancer, their marriage was brief and full of the ups and downs of terminal illness. Yet after her death his opinions about friendship and women (one in particular) had changed so radically that he could say of her: "She was my daughter and my mother, my pupil and my teacher, my subject and my sovereign; and always, holding all these in solution, my trusty comrade, friend, shipmate, fellow-soldier. My mistress, but at the same time all that any man friend (and I have good ones) has ever been to me. Perhaps more." Once again, a large claim.

How, in the current vortex of damaged family relationships and personal emotions, can such a satisfying married friendship be built, and sustained? All I have to go on is personal experience which developed as we lived together, by trial and lots of error, and with many false starts, disappointments, and struggles. But I think I can identify some values that proved vital for us.

One was finding joy in ordinariness—in discovering common interests and doing simple things together. Putting in a garden every spring, visiting flea markets, shopping for antiques and restoring them, listening to good music. Picnics with our kids, summer vacations at Cape Cod, long walks together in early morning or twilight. These things were part of our lives' pattern, and the fun was more than doubled because we did them together.

But there was divergence too. My love for reading and art and the life of the mind was balanced by Harold's active *doing* and sense of Christian ministry. My impulsiveness was matched by his caution in decision-making. (It would take him months to research the purchase of a new car!) In our joining there was a happy blend of mutuality and individuality. In a poem I have described this as being "seamed, not grafted." While being one flesh, we were still two people, with strong personal convictions, likes, and dislikes; and we valued and guarded the freedom to express them. Harold encouraged me in my writing and expressed reservations about my demanding speaking schedule only when he thought *I* was the one who was overburdened.

Harold and I were both strong-willed people. We often disagreed forcefully. When we fought it was intensely, but we tried to be fair, not to exaggerate, not to generalize ("You *always* . . ." / "I *never* . . ."). Harold's tendency after a disagreement was to let the issue fade away gradually and hope it wouldn't reappear. I always held out for resolution. I can remember fiercely whispered conversations at midnight—

HAROLD: Can't we go to sleep? I can't think straight anymore.

LUCI: How can we go to sleep when you still don't understand what I'm trying to tell you?

Inevitably we shaped each other. He helped stabilize the very emotional, immature young woman he married straight out of college. I think I taught him the value of flexibility and openmindedness. He respected my logic. I respected his integrity. We both ended up better and happier people than we were when we first married.

Much as two pianists can play duets on the same piano with an infinite number of variations, so two partners can make music together as friends within the context of marriage. But the instrumentalists must cooperate, each listening to the other's melodic line, sometimes the treble and sometimes the bass voice dominating in a counterpoint that is like a conversation. The relationship is antiphonal. The listening, the working of two together is essential to perform an integrated, satisfying duet.

"Greater love has no one than this, that one lay down his life for his friends" (John 15:13). Harold didn't die for me, but at the age of 69 he made a large and significant life change for my sake. One day he resigned his eldership in the Christian group in which we had both been raised and had worshiped all our lives, where the public ministry was limited to men. He said to me, "Let's look for a new church." And we did.

Two years later, just months before he died, when we were well established in the new church to which God led us, I asked Harold, "Why did you do it? Give up your leadership and make that move?" He told me, "All my life I've been able to participate in worship and use my communication gifts in the church, while you have had to sit silent. I know you have a good mind and a will-ing spirit. I want you to have the opportunities that have been denied you. I want your gifts to find creative expression in the church." I thank God for that gift from my husband, my friend, and if people in heaven can be pleased about what's going on here below, I think Harold must be pleased when he sees how much I love my church, how much they love me, the ways I am part of that family of God.

It's funny, but even now, two years after Harold's death, I still ask his opinion in my mind: "Do you like this poem?" "How would you feel about publishing this book?" "Wasn't that a marvelous sermon?" "Am I doing a good job clipping the bushes?" "Isn't this a gorgeous day?" "Should I go on that trip to Israel?" I still want to share my life with him; it's hard to forsake the friendship habits of a lifetime. Perhaps I shouldn't try to.

Related Articles

Building Trust

KENT & BARBARA HUGHES

John and Mary were concerned about building trust in their marriage. Recently they had seen the tragic effects of its absence in the lives of some of their acquaintances—suspicion, defensiveness, distancing, withdrawal, and, in one instance, divorce. Though their own marriage was good, they had had some unsettling moments when they experienced similar signs of mistrust. So they wisely sought out their pastor and his wife for advice. This is what they learned:

If there is to be trust between spouses, *each must be trustworthy.* Each marriage partner must be *generally trustworthy:* that is, entirely dependable in speech and action. This is not always simple, because our culture fosters deception. Exaggeration, hyperbole, half-truths, and even lying are common in the media, especially in advertising. And many Christian husbands and wives are infected with untruthful habits of speech that promote conscious and unconscious lying to each other. Stories are colored. White lies (incredible term!) are told without the slightest twinge of conscience. Moreover, many share a related

133

weakness: they cannot be depended on to follow through on their word.

The bottom line for those who want trust in marriage is this: regardless of where your spouse is, *you* must begin by being trustworthy yourself! Though this truth is self-evident, it is often overlooked by those who long for trust in their marriage. Their focus is on reforming their partner; nevertheless, it is with oneself that trust must begin.

How can you become more trustworthy? Begin with an honest assessment before God of your trustworthiness. In prayer ask Him to help you see yourself clearly. Hold yourself up to the mirror of God's Word regarding trust and truth (Ps. 51:6; Matt. 5:33-37; Eph. 4:25). Discipline yourself to godliness (1 Tim. 4:7) in all you say and do. Enlist your spouse's help in holding you accountable in truth telling and keeping your word. Free your spouse to privately call you up short if need be. It is said that the 18th-century English author Samuel Johnson used to do this for his children by insisting that even unwitting misstatements of the truth be immediately corrected, so that the habit of truth telling would be instilled.

By commiting yourself to general trustworthiness, you have taken a major step in building trust in your marriage. This prepares the way for the challenge of building *marital trustworthiness*—assurance that each of you will always be faithful to the other. This is certainly one of the greatest felt needs in marriages today, as Christians observe with dismay the crumbling relationships around them. Here we suggest four ways to enhance marital trust:

1. *Be candid with one another.* Begin with spiritual candor with God and each other about your humanity. You are sexual beings, and the fact that you are Christians does not make you impervious to infidelity. As with all sexual beings, you will be tempted, and if you think your Christian commitment frees you to be overly familiar with members of the opposite sex, you are putting yourself in harm's way. In fact, being a caring, empathetic believer may make you even more vulnerable to seduction. Thus, to safeguard marital fidelity and build trust, be honest about your humanity and realize together that you must live wisely in relation to people of the opposite sex.

2. *Pray.* Candor and prayer make a powerful combination. At times you should pray together for your intimacy and fidelity. Pray regularly, perhaps daily, in detail for each other. Prayer will steel and seal your trust.

3. *Discipline yourselves.* The quality of self-discipline is indispensable to marital trust. Both spouses must refuse to allow stimuli encouraging sensuality and unfaithfulness to touch their lives—namely lewd and suggestive TV shows, movies, and literature. Job spoke of this discipline when he said, "I have made a covenant with my eyes not to look lustfully at a girl" (Job 31:1). Husbands and wives need to make a mutual covenant with their eyes. In a culture increasingly shot through with sensuality, where many Christians have become cable-TV voyeurs, this may require radical action like tossing the TV! Jesus said, "If your right eye causes you to sin, gouge it out and throw it away" (Matt. 5:29)—and the principle still stands. Discriminate about where and with whom you spend your time. Fill your mind with "whatever is true, whatever is noble, whatever is right, whatever is pure, whatever is lovely, whatever is admirable" (Phil. 4:8). Such discipline, especially if it is mutual, will go a long way in developing marital trust.

4. *Cultivate intimacy.* A good way to cultivate marital trust is to invest thoughtful care in providing for growth in intimacy. Couples must plan for time alone—nights out or weekends away—where there is plenty of opportunity for conversation, dreaming, and romance.

Communication must always be high on each other's list. Sexual intimacy is an ultimate expression of communication. In it, as the Bible says, husband and wife "know" each other. How much richer it is when the knowing is a physical expression of a deep knowledge and love of one another's being! Couples who take time to build intimacy will grow to treasure each other, and this will inevitably build marital trust.

There is a second element in building trust between spouses. Not only must each be trustworthy, *each must also be trusting*. Simply put: suspicion is perversely self-fulfilling. Husbands and wives who distrust their spouses (with no adequate reason) may sometimes find that their suspicion drives the other toward the feared sin. "He's been accusing me of it for years anyway—so why not?" goes the twisted reasoning.

Scripture calls us to be trusting. Love "always trusts," says Paul (1 Cor. 13:7). And trust is self-fulfilling: a trusting spirit promotes trustworthiness. Moreover, in regard to marital intimacy, trust is indispensable, because it is the key to giving oneself body and soul. Are you irrationally distrustful? If so, ask God for help to trust, and see your pastor if necessary.

Finally, *there must be a mutual commitment to building trust.* We suggest that you do what John and Mary did:

Officially covenant with each other to be trustworthy. Take each other's hands and promise out loud to help the other to be generally trustworthy, speaking the truth always and following through on one's word. Also promise to build marital trustworthiness through candor, prayer, and self-discipline.

Then, in prayer, officially call God as the witness to your covenant, humbly asking for His grace to fulfill your promise.

Related Articles

Encouragement: That Vital Element

EARL WILSON

It is better to be encouraged than to become a starved duck. I don't know if I have ever heard anyone make this statement, but it must be true. The world is filled with people starving for encouragement.

Scripture tells us over and over again to encourage one another. Take Hebrews 10:24-25, for example: "Let us consider how we may spur one another on toward love and good deeds. Let us not give up meeting together, as some are in the habit of doing, but let us encourage one another—and all the more as you see the Day approaching."

Encouragement seems to be a vital element in all human relationships. There are plenty of people and events to keep us humble, but there seems to be a serious lack of people who encourage. Show me a marriage where encouragement is missing, and I will show you a marriage that may end up in divorce court.

Some time ago on one of my overly busy days, my receptionist said, "Your wife is on the telephone." My first thoughts were, "Oh, no! Now what's wrong? I don't have time for this." I answered the telephone sternly (that's one way to keep control).

Sandy said, "Hi, Sweetie! I know your day is busy, but I just wanted to say I love you. I'll be praying for you, and I can hardly wait until you get home tonight."

Quizzically I said, "Anything else?"

"No," she said. "Good-bye."

As I hung up, my whole attitude began to change. "That was nice," I said to myself. "I really needed that. I don't feel nearly so weighed down."

Later I realized I hadn't even thanked her for the call. "I'll be sure to do that this evening," I said to myself. "I think I'll stop by Rancho Flowers and get a rose also."

Encouragement isn't a very expensive gift to give your spouse. It takes only a touch, a wink, a telephone call, a card, or a few words. Sometimes it is just being there.

Encouragement is what lovers do that helps them stay in love. Sometimes encouragement is asking your wife to talk instead of talking for her. Sometimes it is thanking your husband for the time he did put his dirty clothes in the hamper instead of reminding him of the numerous times he failed.

To be a successful encourager, you need to begin to see the world from your spouse's perspective. Psychologists call this *empathy*. When Sandy is struggling to finish a paper for graduate school or needs time to study for a test, I can encourage her by making or buying dinner, running the Wilson "shuttle bus" so she won't have to, or choosing not to turn the sound up on "Monday Night Football." Any of these things may say "I understand, and I want to help. I care that your life is a little frantic right now."

In marriage, encouragement tends to beget encouragement just as bitterness begets bitterness. When I take the time to consider Sandy's needs and see life from her perspective, I often find her do-

1 THESSALONIANS 5:11

Encourage one another and build each other up, just as in fact you are doing.

ing the same thing for me. For example, she didn't call me on the telephone because she lacked something to do. She herself was very busy with school that day. She called because she was sensitive to my need for encouragement and was unselfish enough to reach out. This is called building up one another.

Mutual encouragement enables a couple to accomplish more than they ever imagined possible. When you are encouraged you feel better about yourself. You feel less burdened, and I daresay you even find it easier to trust God. In one way or another the encourager is saying,
- I know.
- I care.
- I'm with you.
- I can help.
- God loves you, and so do I.

In case you have struggled lately to find ways to encourage your mate, here are some ideas you might try:
- Write a note.
- Give a back rub.
- Call to say what time you will be home.
- Pass up an opportunity to criticize.
- Remind your spouse of something you like about him or her.
- Whisper a prayer.
- Share lots of pats, hugs, and kisses.
- Take out the garbage.
- Wear something sexy to bed.
- Look for opportunities to compliment.

Too often mates try to please each other in the obvious ways—by how they look and what they do. Encouragement reaches into a deeper level which is vitally important in marriage. It includes telling your mate how proud you are of him as you see him struggle to grow or change. It is listening to her when she needs to tell you hard things. It is extending love and forgiveness even before he asks.

You may find that as you encourage, your mate will be transformed from what appeared to be a starved duck into a lovely swan.

Related Articles
Chapter 9: Communication That Energizes
Chapter 9: How to Affirm Your Spouse
Chapter 9: The Language of Appreciation

Learning to Be Considerate

WAYNE E. OATES

Scripture tells us to "be considerate" as we live with our partners (1 Peter 3:7). This ability is not an inborn skill. We learn it through patient practice. It means studying each other closely enough to know what helps and what hurts the other. It means taking time to accumulate the wisdom we need so that we can have empathy for each other.

Let me suggest some ways to be considerate of our mates:

1. *Be exceptionally careful in all your responses to your partner when you are in a hurry, are extremely tired, or have just had an accident of some kind.* These are times when husbands and wives tend to "blow their tops" with each other in a way that, upon later reflection, proves foolish and unwise.

2. *Do not make big decisions without careful consultation with your partner.* Unilateral (one-sided) decisions at home, at work, or at church are inconsiderate of the people who have to help carry the burden of putting the decision into action. Decisions such as quitting your job, buying a car, taking a long trip, or making commitments to friends and relatives that involve your partner all call for prior consultation together.

3. *Make careful note of the things that delight and please your partner.* If he likes to settle down and cool off in the evening before talking, give him some space. If she likes to eat at a particular restaurant, suggest that one first. If he does not like teas, receptions, and large parties, check with him before committing him to go with you. If either partner is terribly upset about a particular kind of sexual activity, search for a kind he or she is more comfortable with. Considerateness requires a steadfast commitment to your partner's comfort and happiness.

4. *Keep your promises quickly.* Many married people complain of nagging spouses, but few confess their own procrastination, which can be a kind of passive hostility. Most often it is preoccupation with whatever you are doing that causes you to forget your partner's request. Thus it is a good practice, insofar as possible, to do what your partner asks in the hour that he or she asks it. Do it now and forget about it; don't forget about it, have to be reminded of it repeatedly, and finally do it in a rage. This is the essence of being thoughtful.

5. *Clean up your own messes as soon as you have made them.* Nobody, man or woman, likes cleaning up other people's messes. Clothes left on the

137

floor, dishes left on a counter, tools left on the stairs are all enormous irritants to the spouse who has to walk around them, stumble over them, push them aside, or pick them up. Instead of leaving a mess, clean it up—this is a quiet way of showing your considerateness. Studies of people living together in small communes show that these experiments in human living tend to succeed or fail depending on the level of the members' willingness to do their share of the menial tasks—that is, their willingness to be considerate of others. Husbands and wives are the same way. Messes may seem trivial, but they can shatter marital happiness.

6. *Challenge your own perceptions of your partner's words or behavior before you fly off the handle.* Is there something he or she knows about the situation that you don't know? Situation comedies are often built around pieces of information that one person has which the other does not. Could there be another interpretation of your partner's intentions? Before responding inconsiderately or withdrawing to pout, ask your mate: "When you said this (or did that), what did you mean by it? It puzzled me." It is far more considerate to be puzzled than to throw a tantrum.

7. *Live the self-emptying life in relation to each other.* Take the other person's form and spirit into yourself and practice seeing, feeling, and experiencing the world as he or she does. Ask God's strength to love your partner as he or she is. Ask that your love for each other will increase as your understanding increases, and that you will be united in Christ's love for both of you.

Related Articles
Chapter 1: Love as Honoring Each Other
Chapter 4: Never Take Your Mate for Granted
Chapter 9: Perspective: Seeing What Your Spouse Sees

Cultivating Romance

CHARLES M. SELL

It *is* possible to keep romance alive in marriage. In fact, the Bible urges couples to cultivate an intense feeling between them. For example, husbands are commanded, "Rejoice in the wife of your youth, a lovely hind, a graceful doe. Let her affection fill you at all times with delight, be infatuated always with her love" (Prov. 5:18-19, RSV). One Old Testament scholar describes this exhilaration as "an intensity of love connected with the feeling of superabundant happiness—'to be wholly captivated by her.'" The key to being romantic is knowing what romance is. It consists of many things.

Idealism. People madly in love also love madly; that is, they are somewhat out of touch with reality. The biblical man Jacob proves this. He served seven years to earn the right to marry Rachel (her father's price), but "they seemed like only a few days to him because of his love for her" (Gen. 29:20). Being a little bit crazy is OK if you are in love.

Therefore, it helps if you and your spouse can do things that keep such idealism in your lives. Dream, play, enjoy, plan, relax. Here are a few ideas: Collect travel brochures to plan for that special vacation the two of you can take someday. Take your spouse away for a week on a houseboat. Prepare a basket of fruit and a thermos of coffee and go out together to watch the sunrise.

Preoccupation. Lovers are so preoccupied that they just can't get enough of each other. "Arise, come, my darling; my beautiful one, come with me" are the words of a lover (Song 2:13). After marriage the intensity of the need to be together may fade a bit, but you can nurture the feeling: Write a note on the bedroom mirror telling your spouse how much you'll be thinking about him/her while you're separated for the day. Take her walking in the rain. Go late-night window shopping and end up in a coffee shop holding hands. Buy her a charm bracelet and add charms that symbolize great moments you have had together.

Intimacy. Lovers slowly get closer and closer. Romance flourishes as deeply held feelings and secrets are shared. Married couples need to continue to discover each other; there is always more to learn. If the discovery goes out of a marriage, so will the excitement. Write long notes to tell how you are feeling and thinking; read love poems that express your feelings; watch an emotional TV program together, and then talk about it over a cup of hot chocolate; give her a shampoo; each write a daily journal and allow your partner to read it periodically.

Pampering. Lovers pamper each other, not because they have to, but because they are inwardly compelled to. These unusual sacrificial acts confirm to your spouse that you still feel very much in love. Try drawing a bath for her and putting bath oil and flower blossoms in the water; give her the evening off and do the dishes and watch the children; serve your spouse breakfast in bed and put wildflowers on the tray; give your spouse a back rub. Buy tickets to a sporting event; watch football with him. Buy her a long-stemmed rose.

Affirming. By falling in love with her, the boy confirms the teenage girl as a woman, and by returning his love, she confirms his maleness. These first ro-

mantic episodes make us feel positive about ourselves. In the Song of Songs, both lovers sing songs describing each other's masculine and feminine charms (4:1-7; 5:10-16). There are many ways to affirm: tell him what his lovemaking means to you; tell her how the sight of her body delights you; write down things you really like about your spouse and then take one item per day and mention it repeatedly to him or her.

Surprising. Because a person never knows when he or she will fall in love, romance is connected with spontaneity. Because of this, it might be supposed that we can't plan to be romantic, since spontaneity by definition excludes planning. But we can plan experiences that might generate some surprises: a weekend at a motel, a walk by the lake or in the woods, a dinner in a dimly lit restaurant. And one of us can plan things that will be a surprise for the other: placing a bunch of violets on a pillow, giving a gift when it's not expected, throwing a surprise party with decorations and all, just for the two of you. Or try phoning on Wednesday and asking for a date on Saturday without telling where you're going.

Being suggestive. Romantic acts may express love or sensuality. They don't always lead to the bedroom, however, and when they are sensual, they are usually not too intense, direct, or explicit. Words are suggestive: "How I ache to be beside you." Comparing her feminine charms to a garden, the woman in the Song of Songs invites: "Let my lover come into his garden and taste its choice fruits" (4:16). Be subtle. Whisper into his or her ear what you are feeling. Buy her a negligee for her birthday; buy yourself a negligee for his birthday and model it for him; give a back rub; stroke her arm with a featherlike touch.

Being romantic is like painting a picture. Each of you is an artist who has a different idea of what romance is like. Your job is to discover what romance is in your partner's eye and then artistically to create together your own painting.

Related Articles
  Chapter 1: Love as Romance
  Chapter 8: Rekindling the Flame of Romantic Sex

Building Your Mate's Self-esteem

DENNIS & BARBARA RAINEY

Many women today are insecure. The women's movement has redefined the traditional roles until many women no longer know what's right for them, especially if they are wives and mothers.

Many men are equally or even more insecure. They are not confident in their manhood. They don't know who they are or how to behave. They don't know how to be the family's spiritual leader.

That is why it is important for husbands and wives to build up each other's self-esteem. This is what Scripture calls *edifying* one another (see Rom. 14:19; 1 Thes. 5:11). The stronger each marriage partner becomes, the stronger the marriage becomes.

In our book, *Building Your Mate's Self-Esteem*, we offer 10 building blocks for people who want to develop their partners' self-esteem.

1. *Accept your mate unconditionally.* Many marriages start on an emotional base and try to build from there. But because emotions change as a husband and wife get to know each other, this is like building on sand. Acceptance is the bedrock that helps people move out of the quicksand of emotions. When your mate knows you accept him or her totally, he or she has enough self-confidence to go on even when the way seems difficult.

2. *Put the past in perspective.* No one has a perfect past. An increasing number of people come to marriage with a history of moral failures. Many also bring a history of poor family life. One powerful way to build up your mate is to understand why he or she behaves in certain ways. This does not mean dwelling on the past, but rather using it to gain perspective from which to see a hopeful future. Help your mate realize that the Gospel redeems us from the past, because God's healing hand offers forgiveness and restoration.

3. *Plant positive words in your mate.* Words have the power either to contaminate another's self-image or to plant the seeds of a growing, positive self-image. If you appreciate your mate's fine qualities, he or she will begin to believe in himself or herself; if you systematically chip away at him or her, you will bring your mate down. Words of praise, affirmation, encouragement, and acceptance help the image of Christ begin to make its way through all the debris that is in your mate's life. It is hollow to say you accept your mate if you do not back this up with affirming words.

4. *Encourage your mate during difficult times.* A time of suffering can be

140

critical to the health of a marriage. It is important to go through suffering *together,* not rejecting or turning on each other but turning toward each other, expressing need for each other, and aggressively building up each other's lives. When you express your need of another person, that person feels valued and worthwhile.

5. *Give your mate freedom to fail.* A lot of people are terrified of failure. They are afraid that if they let their guard down, the other person will reject them. There's no joy in that kind of life. It's a legalistic bondage where relationships can't flourish. But a person can fail without being a failure. If a husband and wife give each other the freedom to fail without withdrawing their acceptance, their belief, and their unconditional commitment, then they will have an atmosphere in which they can both grow and develop freely. They will have released each other from self-imprisonment to performance.

6. *Please your mate.* Let your mate know he or she is valued by doing the things that please him or her. Too often we let marriage rob us of our sense of romance. We stop cherishing each other. Don't give up the sense of adventure, the thrill, the intrigue that marriage once had. Continue doing the things you did when you first dated, the things that let your beloved know he or she was of great value in your eyes.

7. *Help your mate do what is right.* Obviously you cannot obey God for another person. But you can create a family environment that enhances obedience. Rather than condemning disobedience or trying to make your mate change, model obedience and encourage your mate when he or she does what is right. Don't take right choices for granted; affirm your mate for making them.

8. *Help your mate develop friendships.* It's important to have friends outside your marriage—both friends as couples and friends individually. If the husband and wife depend only on each other for encouragement, they may begin to wonder about the other one's genuineness. When close friends who know you well accept you, believe in you, and encourage you, that bolsters the self-image of each marriage partner.

9. *Help your mate keep life manageable.* When you are constantly overextended, always reacting to crises, always running to and fro, you can't enjoy peace and contentment. A great way to help each other is to protect each other from the schedule monster. Clear your responsibilities through your partner. Encourage your mate to say no when necessary to keep life on the manageable side. Take time to prayerfully contemplate how God's Word applies to your life. A reasonable schedule can help both of you keep your perspective of who you are in Christ.

10. *Help your mate discover a sense of destiny.* Far too many people today think of themselves as just one of the 5-plus billion people in the world rather than as one of God's elect with a chosen path to follow. We need to have a sense of Ephesians 2:10: "We are God's workmanship, created in Christ Jesus to do good works, which God prepared in advance for us to do." Your mate is the person who knows you best—your gifts, the pattern of your life, where you seem to click best, what brings you satisfaction. Likewise, you know your mate better than anyone else. Thus marriage partners are uniquely qualified to help each other discover their mutual destiny. Helping each other find that sense of purpose is one of the most important things you can do for each other.

Related Articles
Chapter 1: Love as Grace
Chapter 9: Communication That Energizes
Chapter 9: How to Affirm Your Spouse

Making Home a Safe Place for Your Spouse

KEITH & GLADYS HUNT

"**H**ome is a safe place"—this is a favorite definition in our family. The word *home* is one of the most emotionally effective words in our language. It conjures up all sorts of warm feelings of security and affirmation for those who truly have a home, not just a house or an apartment.

Everyone wants a safe place; everyone needs a safe place. Remember when you used to play tag and arrived breathless at what we called "home" without being tagged? Remember how good it felt to be "safe"? But not everyone has a safe place. Some people are always running, trying to avoid being "it."

Safe places are made by safe people. When people are not safe to be with, they can make life miserable for their mates. At first it may seem like a game of who can best put the other one down. But the fun of that game is short-lived. Wounds are sustained, often reopened by the next verbal jab. Competition between spouses is one of the quickest ways to make home seem unsafe. We don't mean competition on the tennis court; we mean competition of personhood—a desire to be better than the other person or to demonstrate one-upsmanship in any way.

Sometimes a man does this to his wife. He makes her feel inadequate every time he gets a chance, especially if others are present. Any mistake she makes is exaggerated and becomes a major topic of the day. If we were to ask him about this he'd say he was only joking, but the sting is still there. He is looking for a chance to destroy any feeling of

well-being she might have. The bottom line is this: unsafe.

He wants her to be affectionate. He accuses her of not being romantic enough, of not setting things up for the two of them. He is annoyed when she acts hurt or misunderstood and finds a way to blame her for being so "touchy." In a seminar on marriage he accuses her of these things in front of others. When she confronts him about this or any other subject, he rearranges the facts so that, in the end, she is the one who is wrong.

Another person comes home from work with all the frustrations of unmet goals and the boss' unrealistic expectations. His world out there isn't safe. He's heard nothing but complaints all day long. He desperately needs a safe place, but whatever safety existed in his home he quickly destroys by venting his pent-up emotions on his wife.

It can just as easily be the wife who makes things unsafe. It's a cruel world out there. She's overworked and underpaid, and now she has to get dinner. She dislikes the people she works with, but her husband thinks she dislikes him. She's not safe to be around. Tension can be cut with a knife, it is so tough and thick. Nothing he says seems right. He says, "Excuse me for living," and this makes her madder than ever.

And of course there are the children. They are his kids too, but she gets stuck with all the trouble, especially when stuffing toilets with toys or dumping water in window wells has been the excitement of the day. He finds himself wish-

TRUE LOVE
(19TH CENTURY)

True love is but a humble, low-born thing,
And hath its food served up in earthenware;
It is a thing to walk with, hand in hand,
Through the everydayness of this work-day world,
Baring its tender feet to every roughness,
Yet letting not one heart-beat go astray
From beauty's law of plainness and content—
A simple, fireside thing, whose quiet smile
Can warm earth's poorest hovel to a home.

James Russell Lowell

ing there was a safe place to go as he listens to her litany. Nothing wrong with her reporting all the difficulty, but it's the angry voice that blames *him* somehow, as if he should have done something. He feels attacked the minute he walks in the door.

You get the idea about safety? You can't have a safe place unless the people are safe to be with. That's the place to begin.

Somewhere in the loving confines of marriage we need space to find out who we are, to have someone be glad we are who we are and say so by words and actions. We need to set up for each other the climate where each can become all God had in mind for each person to be. We'll love each other more as we become that. It's an investment in which we can't lose.

We need to get outside of *me* and begin to think *we*. Better still, each of us needs to stand emotionally in the other person's shoes and feel what the other feels. All of us want the closeness of intimacy—being known for who we are, and feeling safe as we express who we

are. It's the real person of the one meeting the real person of the other. You don't do that any other way but by making an effort to understand and feel and communicate until you do understand. Everything in married life is better when understanding exists—your prayer life, your sex life, your family life, your budget, and anything else that could be a stumbling block in your relationship.

The biggest hindrance to reaching out and meeting each other's needs is our own insecurity or self-centeredness. We need to take the risk of being who we are and give the other person the freedom to be who he or she is. Then we need to enter into the life of our mates with understanding and compassion. That's not always easy. It may take a large amount of talking and praying and even guessing—sometimes years. But it is worth it, and it will be *you* reaching outside yourself to make a safe place for the person you love.

Related Articles
Chapter 1: Love as Honoring Each Other
Chapter 9: Reflecting Each Other

The Love Exchange

KAREN MAINS

The game of Pit is based on the grain exchange at a board of trade. Just as in real life, the commodities bartered are barley, corn, wheat, oats, flax, hay, and rye. The object of the game is to be the first player to capture the market by holding nine cards of one commodity.

To accomplish this, Pit players trade aggressively and noisily. If I am holding six corns and three ryes, I will put my ryes face down on the table and shout "three, three, three" until somebody trades me, sight unseen, three of whatever he wants to dispose of. Most likely I will not receive corns on the first try; the other player's medium of exchange may just as well be oats or hay.

Through the years I've discovered that one reason I've experienced difficulty in loving certain people is because I've not understood the exchange by which they measure love. The way we humans give and measure love is a lot like the transactions that occur in Pit. One person holds out his "cards," hoping that birthdays and anniversaries will be remembered. He may discover that his wife, however, does not offer holidays as her "love exchange." Instead, she offers a listening ear—but he doesn't feel like talking.

Each of us, because of patterns established by our own families or because of deprivation we experienced when love was not given, has an exchange by which we measure love. These love exchanges are personal and often unidentified, but they are absolutely influential in the way we give love and measure the love that is given to us.

If we do not understand the individual love exchanges of the people with whom we are working out love relationships, it can be disastrous. In fact, it is one of the major reasons we humans fail so often in this matter of loving.

The greatest mistake we can make is to assume that our spouse's love exchange is the same as our own. We'd be much safer assuming that it is different.

My spouse may measure love by the way I stop everything I'm doing, look him directly in the eye, and listen completely to each word he says. His exchange may even require that I repeat back to him key phrases which indicate that I have heard and understood what has just been said. He may interpret my washing dishes while we talk as a sign of disinterest, and he may mistakenly conclude that I don't really love him. This conclusion may be reached without any words, without any discussion between us as to the nature of my love.

Thus it is extremely important to determine the love exchange out of which my spouse functions. I have to ask continually, "In what terms, in what exchange, does he measure the giving of love?"

Misunderstanding about the love exchange is a major reason our loving is much like the floor of the Board of Trade when the market is open—a mass of confusion, a pit, with some people making fortunes while others face financial ruin. We humans have difficulty with love, because we trade in different commodities.

But with God, there is only one commodity to trade—"This is how God showed His love among us: He sent His one and only Son into the world that we might live through Him" (1 John 4:9).

The emphasis is repeated in the next verse: "This is love: not that we loved God, but that He loved us and sent His Son as an atoning sacrifice for our sins."

Christ Himself explained God's love exchange. According to John 15:13, "Greater love has no one than this, that one lay down his life for his friends." God's love exchange was the giving of His Son for the sake of the world. Christ's love exchange is the laying down of one's life for a friend.

We cannot love one another adequately until we experience on a daily basis God's total love for us, which began with Christ coming into the world, and which will continue into eternity. "Whoever does not love does not know God, because God is love," says the apostle (1 John 4:8). One reason we do not know God is because we try to measure His love according to our human love exchange. "I'll know You love me," we cry to Him, "when You change my husband," or "I'll know You love me when we're out of debt."

The beautiful thing about God is that He often does accommodate our human love exchanges by trading three corns to complete our hand of six corns. But there comes a time for each of us when God insists that we begin trading with one commodity alone, *His* commodity of totality.

It's only when we begin to understand that God's love exchange was totality, a total offering of the life of His Son, with an expectation of totality on our part in return, that we will begin to know Him. Only then will His love be made complete in us, and only out of this dynamic will we begin to love each other.

Related Articles
Chapter 1: Developing and Nourishing Love
Chapter 9: Speak Your Partner's Language

Identity and Intimacy

JAMES H. OLTHUIS

Most of us marry, confident that we are reaching out to meet our deepest needs for *intimacy* with another. In fact, we are more often reaching out to meet our deepest unmet needs for *identity*.

Paradoxical as it may seem, the best preparation for intimacy is a clear and robust sense of self-identity on the part of both husband and wife. Genuine intimacy between two lovers requires intimacy-with-self (identity) on the part of each person. This point needs to be emphasized again and again, because underneath the boredom, affairs, or incompatibilities which erode and destroy marriage, the root of trouble is often a profound lack of self-knowledge and self-identity.

Identity and intimacy belong together. That is the way God made us. Every "I" is part of "we." That is the meaning of Jesus' command that we love our neighbor as we love ourselves. If we do not love ourselves, we cannot truly love our neighbors. And unless we love our neighbors, we do not really love ourselves.

Marriage is a special gift of God for the sharing and caring of intimacy. But marital intimacy is endangered when we are not in touch with ourselves. For if we are not in touch with ourselves, how can we be in touch with another person? How can another person be deeply connected with me when I am at loose ends with myself? If I have little sense of myself, can I really commit myself to another person in marriage? Do I really have a self to give and share with another person?

The conclusion is disturbing: if we lack a solid self-identity, when we reach out for intimacy we are really attempting to find a base for our own identity. We are not *giving* ourselves so much as trying to *gain* ourselves. We use the other person to fill up our emptiness, to shore up our insecurities, to give us confidence, to help us fight off feelings of abandonment, or to meet any number of other personal needs. We are not able to see the other as a unique person with whom to share ourselves, but rather as a way to meet our unmet needs.

Too little identity, rather than too much, is the greatest threat to intimacy. For when we are insecure in ourselves, we selfishly try to take and demand rather than give and share. Intimate sharing is replaced by the entanglement of needs. Wedlock becomes deadlock.

The consequences of such enmeshed relationships are vast and often frightening, especially because most of us are blissfully unaware of the underlying dynamics. If Peter doesn't really have an adequate sense of his own power, if he doesn't accept himself, if he doesn't feel adequate and lovable, he will retreat from intimacy when approached. Because he doesn't feel good about himself, Peter cannot believe that Mary feels good about him. So, frightened, he puts up walls, pretends to be who he is not, and hides his true self from Mary (and himself), all the while desperate for intimacy. His outer self and his inner self are in conflict.

Mary is soon confused as she picks up the mixed messages he is sending. Peter pretends to have it all together. He exudes strength, yet Mary tunes in on an underlying sense of powerlessness. And Mary is most likely doing the same

ROUGH EDGES

We all have our rough edges. We all have our little habits that could drive another person crazy—especially the spouse who lives with us day and night. We may not see those rough edges before marriage, but day-to-day living acts as a magnifying glass that brings them into sharp focus. And marriage itself is a multiplying factor—certain problems arise just because you live together.

Realize that the very qualities that made you fall in love with that person may very well drive you crazy a few years into the marriage. You may have loved your boyfriend's spontaneity; you may eventually wish your husband would plan ahead at least once! You may have loved the fact that your girlfriend was constantly the life of the party; you may wish your wife wouldn't always draw attention to herself. You may have loved how your boyfriend showered you with gifts; you may wish your husband would be more careful with the money.

These qualities need not ruin your marriage. The rough edges can be smoothed out with a little communication and compromise. But let the rough edges add a little spice to your marriage—after all, would you want to be married to a person just like you?

YFC Editors

thing—putting on masks and playing games.

The stronger our sense of identity, the more freely and fully we are able to reach out to others, giving of ourselves. The more tenuous our sense of identity, the more we retreat from intimacy. Lacking self-identity, we tend to over- or underinvest in our marriages. Either we withhold ourselves in fear of being discovered, or we are overly submissive in hope of discovering ourselves. Usually under- and overinvesters gravitate toward each other. It's a safe, but ultimately dangerous, dovetailing. The withholder receives care without having to commit himself or herself; the submitter gains a sense of belonging without really having to face his or her inner emptiness.

In our culture it is especially difficult to experience intimacy because the behaviors we are taught undermine rather than nourish intimacy. Women are taught that their identity comes through connectedness with and caring for others. Men are taught that their identity is in separateness, power, and accomplishments. The result is tragic.

Men and women both fear deep intimacy even as they intensely long for it. Women often lack a separate sense of self and fear invasion of the fragile sense of self they do have. Men often lack the ability for inner connection and fear engulfment of a self that is not very strong. The intimacy of marriage becomes most difficult to achieve. Women suffer because they don't receive the connection they need for their identity; men suffer because they fear losing their separateness.

Identity-in-intimacy and intimacy-with-identity is the rhythm of the dance of life. The two belong together. When we have a good feeling about ourselves, we do not fear connection with another. We can be present with the other person without needing to use him or her for our own neurotic ends. I can let you be, because I am learning to let myself be. "Letting be" is what love is all about— and it is to love that we are called.

Intimacy is difficult, and husbands and wives often remain strangers to each other in our broken world. But God created us for each other, and showed us in Jesus Christ that intimacy, not alienation, is the fundamental truth of the universe. In that confidence we may set out on the Sea of Marriage and learn to negotiate the passages to intimacy. God is with us; we are not alone.

Related Articles
   Introduction: The Invasion of Intimacy
   Chapter   1: Troth: The Love Connection in
      Marriage

That's Where We're Headed

BILL & JEANNIE HOCHSTETTLER

Management and planning seminars are the rage today. People flock to them. Unfortunately, hearing isn't doing, and many of us simply respond to the daily pressure, becoming mired in the "tyranny of the urgent."

Many couples, however, discover that because of differing expectations, personality conflicts, and changing circumstances, this lack of direction can cause a marriage to flounder very quickly.

A stabilizing force in our marriage has been our yearly goal setting. Through the years, we have refined this annual procedure to a predictable agenda.

First we review the previous year. We make notations by the goals we have not met so we can change them, drop them, or incorporate them in the next year's plan.

Next we list our individual goals under four headings: physical, mental, social, and spiritual. We share these goals with each other to help keep us accountable.

Then we proceed to mutual goals: family, financial, recreational, and vocational. We assign a time period to each one, projecting as much as five years ahead. We find that long-term goals stretch us by giving us something to reach for.

Our family goals include our desires for our children. We wanted to be sure we were teaching good characteristics in a thoughtful and planned, not haphazard, manner. So we listed the characteristics we wanted to cover, and each year we choose two that are appropriate for our children's age levels.

Finally, we review our discussion. We check to be sure that each area of our lives has been searched, and each of us responds to what the other has said. We are very specific and personal. For example, at first I was angered when my husband set a goal of spending quality time with me. I wanted him to want that time and spend it spontaneously! As we discussed my feelings, I began to see that if he listed this goal on a sheet of paper and put my name on his calendar, we were much more likely to have time together than if we relied on his spontaneous but "just-can't-make-it" desires.

When we have set our goals, we write them down and keep them in a place of constant but private use. Good places are the Bible, an appointment calendar, a prayer journal, and so on. When the year is over, we file the old goal sheets. It's great fun to review the past years and see how much we have accomplished, how much we have grown and changed.

The setting for our discussion is very important. The time and place need to be agreed on well enough in advance so that both partners have time to pray, be rested, and prepare mentally. We have found that a long trip in the car is a great time for this. It puts otherwise wasted time to good use, and it keeps both of us in one place, forced to talk out whatever differences may arise.

We set our goals early in the calendar year. Then, usually during our summer vacation, we review the first six months and make any needed modifications. We rejoice together over fulfilled goals and renew our pledge to fulfill the rest.

If you decide to take time with your spouse to set goals, remember to be honest but sensitive, to dream but be realistic, to share but not be greedy. Just setting goals can be a wonderful exercise. Putting them to use can give direction to your marriage.

Related Article

Chapter 16: Making Your Dreams Come True

Ministering as a Couple

JERRY & MARY WHITE

"Glorify the Lord with me; let us exalt His name together" (Ps. 34:3). Marriage offers many rewards. One of the most significant is the privilege of seeking ways to glorify God together. In a marriage relationship that honors God, power for God's service is unleashed as husband and wife join forces to reach out and minister together.

All around us we see splintered lives.

Complex schedules. Diverse goals and dreams. Frenzied activity. Emotional tensions that cry for communication and closeness. These phrases describe the weekly traumas of so many people—even Christians. The growing demand for two incomes, the consuming activity schedule of so many serious Christians, and the demands of growing families increase the pressure on the most committed marriages.

We so easily slip into separate lives, passing each other like ships in the night as we serve God. But wait. Let's back up to an even more fundamental issue.

Life, and especially marriage, is more than a 168-hour week punctuated by restless sleep to restore strength to keep going. Daily time of Scripture reading and prayer, applying God's Word to life situations, and surrendering daily to His lordship provide the only foundation on which to build a ministry.

Then comes the urge from God to develop a ministry. The word *ministry* scares many people, but to minister is simply to serve. That is the root meaning of the word. A ministry is a service to others—in this case, a spiritual service. It has nothing to do with being a full-time pastor, missionary, or Christian worker. Ministry is the task of every believer, just as the Great Commission, the Ten Commandments, and the spiritual gifts apply to every believer.

When we speak of the ministry of a lay person, we mean focusing one's spiritual life and gifts on people—both believers and nonbelievers.

We have observed that when some couples get serious about their walk with God, they do so individually. They are not convicted at the same time, and many husbands or wives have awakened to find themselves next to a newly fanatic spouse. This may strain rather than strengthen the marriage for a period of time. In this situation, ministry together is impossible to imagine, because only

RELATIONS WITH FRIENDS

Marriage can change the nature of friendships you may have formed as a single. After marriage, these friendships may suffer due to less frequent contact or fewer common interests. Often the result is a realignment of friendships: the couple sees old friends less and less as they form new friendships with other couples.

When you are able to maintain old friendships, however, you should keep two things in mind. First, carefully work out any possible difficulties regarding friends of the opposite sex. Establish clear lines of understanding for the sake of both your spouse and these friends. Maintaining a strong allegiance to a friend of the opposite sex is not worth jeopardizing your marriage.

Second, keep a closed-mouth policy with your friends, male or female, regarding your spouse. Most aspects of your marriage should be held confidentially between you and your spouse. No third parties—not even good friends—should intrude. Make and keep your spouse your very best friend!

Gary Bennett

one wants to minister.

Later the other spouse may also repond to God's urgings to reach out to others. Then the husband and wife may find themselves in separate ministries. This is not always a negative situation. We need men ministering to men and women to women, as well as many other individual contributions.

Yet there is a special bond and blessing in working together, sharing the same vision, praying about the same people, planning ministry together. Even with radically different gifts, husband and wife can work together as a team. Who needs two first basemen? A team implies different functions.

We have done many things separately through the years, but we are learning more and more to collaborate and work together in several kinds of ministries—writing, speaking, couple's Bible studies, and even counseling.

Early in our marriage we attempted some Bible studies with couples. The Lord probably used our attempts, but we felt ill-prepared and awkward. Then God led us to a discipling ministry with young and single Air Force Academy cadets. Later still, God allowed us again to lead Bible studies with couples, this time with more confidence in Him and more visible growth and fellowship among the couples. Even now, as we frequently travel, we are committed to work together as a couple.

What things can you do together?
- Teach a Sunday School class.
- Use your home for reaching teen-agers.
- Start a Bible study for young couples.
- Serve on the same committee or work group.
- Help a widow or single mother.
- Visit and pray with the elderly.

The opportunities are limitless, because there is always room for servants to meet the needs in God's kingdom. The only perplexing part of ministry is finding God's niche for each of us as couples.

Most important, develop your vision together. When one of you is the prime mover, make a point of being together in vision. "Can two walk together, except they be agreed?" (Amos 3:3, KJV) Take turns being in the support role. When one of you reaches out "solo," pray together and share the vision.

Join forces. In your shared ministry, you will sense new meaning in your lives and marriage.

Related Articles
Chapter 5: Church Involvement
Chapter 5: How to Have a Team Ministry

How to Survive a Move

BOB & CINNY HICKS

It all started with Adam and Eve—the first couple to pack up and leave their comfortable home and face the uncertainties of the next day in a new place (Gen. 3:24). From Abram and Sarai leaving Ur (Gen. 12:1) to Priscilla and Aquila leaving Rome (Acts 18:1-2), couples have been on the move ever since. Today more than ever we are a nation of nomads. In our 20 years of marriage, we have moved 11 times. Some have been good moves; others, disasters. But somehow we have survived them all.

Moving is a very stressful experience. Dr. Thomas Holmes, creator of a widely used scale for measuring the effects of stress, lists *change of residence* as number 32 on his list of stressful life events. However, moving brings other stresses with it—work readjustments; change in daily habits; changing schools, church, or social activities; taking out a mortgage. When all these circumstances associated with a move are rated on Holmes' scale, the stress points easily approach 450. And any score over

300, according to Holmes, gives a person an 80 percent chance of major health breakdown!

Some experts believe it takes as much as two years to readjust after a move, even if you just moved down the street. What then are some helpful insights that can help couples survive this mobility malaise?

1. *Expect and accept emotional highs and lows.* When our network of friends and relationships are taken away, our emotions are greatly affected. They play games on us: in five minutes we can go from sheer excitement about the new situation to utter despair for what was lost. After one of our moves, Bob was set to begin his new job when the reality of the 3,000-mile move hit him. He put his head down on his desk and wept uncontrollably for what was lost—old friends, familiar scenery, feelings of security.

Feelings of estrangement, loneliness, or just a vague uncomfortableness often set in after a move. These are natural readjustment responses. Even Naomi, after moving from Moab back to familiar Bethlehem, confessed her bitterness toward God for what had happened (Ruth 1:20-21).

2. *Don't compare.* The grocery stores are not as clean; the people are less friendly; it's harder to get your utilities hooked up; your new driver's license exam is more difficult—and on it goes. The new place isn't quite like the one you left. Before, all you saw were the quaint colonial homes; now all you see are the enormous energy bills.

Comparison is natural, but it is also lethal. No two places are going to be the same, and it is unreasonable to expect them to be. We can appreciate good things about the place we left while at the same time realizing our new home has good points also. Perhaps Paul's word about being "content whatever the circumstances" (Phil. 4:11) is appropriate here.

3. *Get back into your old routines.* A move breaks our stride. Schedules change, driving time changes, houses change, the scenery changes—all is changed. Our continuity is lost. During the settling-in time, we need to bring back some sense of our former habits. Whether it is playing tennis, going out to eat, or unpacking a favorite family game, sometimes a simple thing can bring back family continuity. So even before all the boxes are unpacked or the walls repainted, start the old routines.

Whenever the Apostle Paul went to a new city, he immediately went to the synagogue. He knew the Jewish mind and culture, and here was one place he felt comfortable—at least until they started throwing stones! Finding a church home brings back the familiar feeling of belonging to God's family. Adults and children alike need to belong to some caring group for support, encouragement, affirmation, and love. The Spirit of God is the same around the world.

4. *Deal with unrealistic expectations.* No one in his right mind freely chooses to move to a place he expects to be difficult, unsatisfying, and frightening. Most of us expect the new situation to be better than the one we left, or why else would we leave? Of course we believe God leads us, and most of us are willing to sacrifice for Christ's sake, but still most moves are made in anticipation of more money, more opportunity, more freedom, or more responsibility. In short, we move with gigantic expectations.

These expectations can be real killers in marriage and family relationships. Our Lord was very realistic when He sent His disciples on their first move without Him: "I am sending you out like sheep among wolves," He said (Matt. 10:16). We trust our moves will not throw us into the midst of wolves, but we need to at least prepare for the possibility that the new situation may not fulfill all our dreams.

We have moved great distances thinking God was leading us to new and exciting ministries, only to find that the person who hired us had just left the organization. We have also faced misunderstandings about job descriptions, staff changes, and a host of other things that have made us realize no situation is perfect. We now move with our eyes open.

5. *Get people back into your life.* The right people make the difference between a good move and a bad one. When all our friends are far away, we tend to withdraw. Doing this, however, cuts us off from some of the best free therapy in the West—new friends! Jump in by faith even though your emotions say "wait," and show the new neighborhood or other employees that you are ready to be a friend. Quickly look for a church, or introduce yourself to your neighbors, or invite your work associates over for a painting-and-pizza party. If you advertise that you want friends, you will probably find them.

After our move from Honolulu to Dallas, we immediately began going to a couple's home Bible study. When several members of the study showed up the day we moved into our newly purchased house, we knew the adjustment to our move was going to be much easier. A few friends make a big difference, but we must reach out and make ourselves friendly to begin the process.

6. *Give your kids some developmental rope.* If a move affects adults certain ways, it stands to reason it will affect children as well. Kids, however, have a more difficult time verbalizing how they feel. In some cases they act out their feelings through temper tantrums, bad grades, or other extreme behaviors. From the beginning it is helpful to make the children a part of the moving process. Throw open the discussion about the possibility of moving, and involve them in the decision if possible. Once you have moved, allow them a few long-distance calls to their old friends. The phone cost is a small price to pay for their adjustment.

Some parents fear that a move will hurt their children. Most researchers, however, would confirm that there is no evidence that a move, in and of itself, is harmful. What is important is how the parents handle the adjustment. A child's attitude is closely linked to the parents' attitude. A good suggestion is to give your kids some long developmental rope for about the first six months after a move, enough time to work through their feelings.

Moving is a time of adjustment and change for the whole family. Thus it is an important time to immerse yourself in the constancy of God's unchanging character and grace. We have an eternal home in Him (Ps. 90:1). Even when we have been dislodged and feel more like aliens than fellow-citizens with the saints, His steadfast love can be our security. In reality, we are all aliens living in tents, "looking forward to the city with foundations, whose architect and builder is God" (Heb. 11:9-10).

Related Article
Chapter 1: Love as Teamwork

The Battle of the Bulge

JOHN ROBERT THROOP

Chances are that sometime during your marriage you will hear the anguished cry from the bathroom at about 7 A.M., "Oh, no! I've *got* to go on a diet!" In our home, we call it "scale shock." Somehow the scale's calibration is way off, because it's showing me to be 15 pounds heavier than I really am. But then the trousers don't clasp as easily as they once did, either, and my wife is complaining that I approximate the shape of a Bosc pear. It's time for a diet. Mercifully, my wife says she needs to lose about 10 pounds too. "Let's diet together," she says. For someone like me who likes to eat, that's tantamount to saying, "Let's take our winter vacation in the Northwest Territories this year!"

Dieting is a national pastime. It is estimated that three out of every four people in this country are or have been on a specialized eating program or diet, and diet books are the hottest selling items in most bookstores. Sometimes the urge to diet comes from within, as we see the spread without. Sometimes it comes from a concerned mate, who threatens to kidnap the leftover cake and hold it for ransom.

In fact, we're all on diets—our eating patterns are diets, whether those patterns are good or bad. A good diet can give strength and energy to do the work God has given us to do. It can make us more likely to live out the full life span God intended for us. It can even help us maintain better relationships with family and friends.

A bad diet, by contrast, can result in poor health even early in life. In my pastoral ministry, I have seen innumerable people whose heart and circulatory problems, strokes, diabetic comas, and even asthma are related to poor eating habits. Obesity, which afflicts 4 out of every 10 Americans, is a contributing factor to many chronic illnesses, and much obesity is due to bad eating habits.

So being overweight is serious business. Paul says, "Glorify God in your body," for the body is the temple of the Holy Spirit (1 Cor. 6:19-20, KJV). God wants us to treat our bodies right, for we are His creation and we reflect His glory physically as well as spiritually.

I've tried a couple of diets, one of which I would stand by and one I'd never try again. To be truly effective, a diet must teach you a sensible way of eating over the long term. It should not disrupt the normal pattern of family eating, either: it's inconvenient to fix separate meals for different family members, and inconvenience quickly leads to abandoned resolutions.

If both partners do not need to lose weight, it will still help the dieter if the partner will follow the pattern too, even if he or she does not watch the quantity eaten so closely. Perhaps both partners could vow to abstain from certain foods for a while. Husband and wife could work together in deciding which diet to follow, and each could pledge to be accountable to the other regarding what is eaten.

Dieting together can be a fertile ground for prayer. A diet can be a spiritual discipline not unlike fasting, and anyone who has dieted prayerfully knows that it is a spiritual as well as physical battle. For many people the basic problem goes deeper than merely

BATTLING OVERWEIGHT TOGETHER

How can husbands and wives support each other in battling overweight and being out of shape? Some ideas might include the following:

1. Support one another's exercise program. Give your spouse time to exercise during the day, and encourage each other to take the time. This is hard to do with busy schedules, but it is essential to good health.

2. Exercise together when possible.

3. Have an exercise date instead of a dinner date. Taking a long, brisk walk on a regular basis is a great date!

4. Plan family times around fitness activities. This will encourage both of you and will set a good example for your children.

5. Keep a food diary. Record what you eat, and show it to your spouse daily.

6. Learn to cook light, calorie-reduced meals. Take a course together at the local park district or community college, or do it yourself with cookbooks.

7. Get regular physical checkups from a doctor who will be frank with you about your physical condition and will give you practical advice about what to do to get into shape.

8. Weigh in daily! Share the true figure with each other.

John Throop

eating too much; they need a significant healing in the area of appetite.

Here are some tips on dieting:

1. Make a mutual and prayerful decision to diet, even if you aren't going to diet together.

2. Keep a food diary, recording *everything* you put into your mouth. Show it to your spouse every day.

3. Before going on a diet, research the matter. Be sure your diet supplies required nutrients in balanced proportions and is easy to follow.

4. Prepare foods at home whenever possible. Foods in the grocery freezer labeled "lite" or "lean" are not necessarily low in calories or even healthful.

5. Weigh in every day, and post a chart of the results. If both partners are dieting, put the charts side by side.

6. When you've reached your goal, pause to celebrate—sensibly.

7. Remember that the only way to keep weight off is to adhere to sensible eating and exercise habits. If you go back to your old way of eating, you will go back to your old weight.

Rarely is food merely food. It often has spiritual or sacramental meaning: our central act of worship, Communion, is centered around eating. Food also has emotional meanings: think of Thanksgiving without turkey or a birthday without cake. What we eat, then, affects more than our belt size. It affects our relationships with God and with others, especially with our family members. The Apostle Paul in 1 Corinthians 10:31 gives good advice: "Whether you eat or drink or whatever you do, do it all for the glory of God."

Related Article
Chapter 5: The Spiritual Side of Looking Our Best

You and your spouse did not grow up in spiritually identical homes, and you did not come to the Lord in exactly the same way. As you work together to build a God-honoring family life, you need to understand each other's spiritual beliefs and needs. Take this quiz, and then discuss your answers. (Circle A if you agree with the statement; D if you disagree.) Where you find areas of disagreement, take time to talk them through. Both of you may grow spiritually, and that can only be good for you individually, as a couple, and as parents.

HIS	HERS	Spouses should . . .
A D	A D	pray together every day
A D	A D	study the Bible together regularly
A D	A D	discuss spiritual issues
A D	A D	go to the same church
A D	A D	lead out in family devotions
A D	A D	agree on theology
A D	A D	pay tithe (at least 10 percent of income)
A D	A D	attend church at least once a week
A D	A D	go together to Sunday night or midweek church meetings
A D	A D	pray for each other
A D	A D	minister as a couple
A D	A D	minister individually
A D	A D	have the same level of spiritual maturity
A D	A D	confront each other in areas of sin and weakness
A D	A D	take responsibility for each other's spiritual growth
A D	A D	leave each other's spiritual life up to God
A D	A D	require the children to attend church
A D	A D	consider mission service
A D	A D	be willing to change denominations for each other
A D	A D	look to the Bible for directions for family life
A D	A D	witness to their neighbors

CHAPTER
5

SPIRITUAL LIFE

The Christian life is the life of Christ reproduced in the believer by the power of the Holy Spirit in obedient response to the Word of God. It is the incredible blend of supernatural power transfused into an ordinary life.

What is the best laboratory in which to develop this remarkable life? Perhaps the most realistic test site is marriage. The highest highs and the lowest lows are likely to happen there.

We easily recognize the physical, intellectual, emotional, and social components of life, but often overlook the spiritual dimension. However, we err in trying to make spirituality an add-on. Instead, it is the presence of a third Person, God, who produces a profound harmony in the husband/wife relationship. His stability transforms the benefits of human togetherness into a team which ultimately advances the entire community.

Howard & Jeanne Hendricks

Husbands and Wives With Jesus as Lord

WAYNE E. OATES

When a husband and wife commit themselves to Jesus Christ as Lord of their lives, they order, transform, and bring peace to their life together. Such a commitment does several things to enhance and enrich a marriage:

1. *Jesus as Lord of your marriage relieves each of you of the burden of "lording it over" the other.* Jesus said to His disciples: "You know that those who are regarded as rulers of the Gentiles lord it over them, and their high officials exercise authority over them. Not so with you. Instead, whoever wants to become great among you must be your servant" (Mark 10:42-43).

It is part of our fallen nature to want to control each other rather than sacrificially to serve one another as an act of love. Competition for first place, the right to rule the roost, threatens the health of any marriage. When we submit ourselves to the Lord Jesus Christ, however, competition turns into loving empathy. As the Apostle Paul puts it, we "outdo one another in showing honor" to each other (Rom. 12:10, RSV).

2. *Enrolling ourselves under the lordship of Jesus Christ turns each of us into both the student and the teacher of the other.* Jesus opens our hearts to each other and enables us to learn

from each other. This does not mean we are not going to disagree with each other. When we have disagreements, however, we will work hard at getting each to listen to the other, to understand the other's point of view, and to face up to whatever we stubbornly refuse to change. If we cannot hear each other and we come to an impasse, Jesus instructs us to find a third person who can help us listen to each other. Today this often becomes marriage counseling.

Once we break through to each other and cease to harden our hearts stubbornly against each other, then we realize what Jesus meant when He said, "Where two or three come together in My name, there am I with them" (Matt. 18:20). This can happen when two people, married to each other, crucify their self-centeredness in obedience to Jesus Christ. It can happen when a husband and wife, in fellowship with a trusted, competent, committed Christian counselor, commit themselves to Jesus as Lord.

3. *A husband and wife with Jesus as Lord have in Him a higher authority than themselves, and thus they do not insist on "playing God" in the lives of their children.* When we feel we are the final authority over our children, we lose our capacity to learn from them. We become know-it-alls who cannot listen to our sons' and daughters' deepest needs. If we keep them in servility throughout their infancy, childhood, and youth, they will be ill-prepared to face life without us. The time soon comes when they have to stand on their own. To keep them forever dependent on us rather than committing them to Christ's lordship and care causes them to lean dependently on our "arm of flesh," which will sooner or later fail them for lack of strength or life.

4. *Husbands and wives with Jesus as Lord have in Him a leader in times of major decision-making.* We can gather all the facts needed in making a decision. We can thresh out our differ-ences as to the shape and direction our decision should take. We can put off the decision while we allow the relevant information to simmer in our minds. Even then, however, we may be uneasy: we still don't know what is best to do, and the right decision just won't come.

When we turn to the Lord Jesus Christ and open our consciences to His Spirit's leading, some new events, re-membrances, and forgotten facts will come to us. A whole new pattern will emerge. We can then move with aban-don in a whole new direction which we had not previously considered. Looking back, we may conclude that God's prov-idence delivered us from what would have been the worst possible decision. Jesus as Lord made the difference be-tween deliverance and destruction.

5. *When Jesus is Lord of our mar-riages, He keeps us from idolizing each other and expecting each other to be perfect.* He enables us to affirm each other's humanness, to be patient with each other's limitations, and to bear the burdens of each other's faults, thus ful-filling the law of Christ. When we over-take each other in a fault, having Jesus as Lord of our lives enables us to restore each other gently, watching ourselves lest we also be tempted (see Gal. 6:1-2). What a deliverance from idolatry!

Sooner or later one of us will die and leave the other alone. If we worship each other rather than Jesus as Lord, the one who faces that loss will feel entirely abandoned. But if we rely on the resur-rected Lord Jesus Christ, we are not alone. He is with us.

Let us pray as husbands and wives that "the God who gives endurance and encouragement" will give us such a spirit of unity as we follow Christ Jesus that together with one voice we "may glorify the God and Father of our Lord Jesus Christ" (Rom. 15:5-6).

Related Articles
Introduction: Marriage: A Vehicle of God's Love
Chapter 3: Making the Right Choice

Devotional Life Together

WIN COUCHMAN

Designing and building a satisfactory devotional life took us the first 20 years of our marriage.

Bob is an engineer and I am a people-oriented Bible teacher. He came from a non-Christian home and put his faith in Christ as an adult. I grew up with believing parents and accepted Christ as a toddler. Bob is competent and at ease with technical concepts. My bookish taste runs to relational and philosophical concepts, especially those in the Bible.

Now, as we look back over all our struggles, we are gleeful to see the fruit God produced in us during those years. We can see how our failures caused us to lean more and more on Him. And it is clear to us that our mutual devotional life is a key element in our growing understanding and acceptance of each other.

Bob and I were best friends. We respected each other and found ourselves really in love after years of being married. Yet when we committed ourselves to a regular time of prayer and Bible study together, it was out of the conviction that this ought to be the heart of our relationship.

As we put energy into each aspect of designing a devotional pattern, we began with *time*. We had tried praying together just before we went to sleep and the moment we woke up in the morning, but we didn't pray—we slept. So we began to get up an hour early, have our showers, and eat breakfast first. We found we were alert; the caffeine helped. We stayed wide awake for both prayer and Bible study. This was a good plan for us because we are both morning people, and our children left for school an hour before Bob had to leave for work.

Time design has to be customized for each couple, but the second-best time we know of is immediately after a meal. Send the children off, put the milk back in the refrigerator, shove the dishes to one side, pull your chairs close together, hold hands, and go at it. And of course, start small, with 5 minutes of prayer and 10 minutes of Bible study, so you do not get discouraged.

The second thing we worked on was the *design* of our devotional life itself. How should we pray? What kind of Bible study would be right for us? As we prayed about these things, God gave us ideas that were marvelous for us—"user friendly."

Because I have good verbal skills and enjoy talking, I enjoyed talking to God. I enjoyed talking to God for such a long time that Bob got bored stiff.

For Bob, talking to people is not the easiest part of his life. He had come to know God rather late. He couldn't see this Person. Yet he needed to talk to Him. How difficult! So his prayers were brief and general. I was really bored with his prayers.

But when we started taking time to *interview* each other, our prayers were transformed. I would ask Bob what he wanted me to pray for him that day. Usually he would mention something that was going on at work. I limited my prayer to what he asked me to pray. Then he would interview me. My requests would be about my personal growth, about relationships and ministry. It was not threatening for him to pray specifically for what I had just men-

INDIVIDUAL SPIRITUAL GROWTH

Don't expect your spouse to be at the same place as you spiritually. Each Christian must be encouraged to grow in his or her relationship with God, but people grow at different rates, in different ways, at different times in their lives.

Some people grow best through relationships. They may learn the most in small-group Bible studies and may profit spiritually by talking something over with someone. Some people need concepts to learn and grow. They need a quiet place to sit and read, and personal study time. Some people grow best through experiences—doing things in order to learn more about God.

Encourage your spouse in his/her own personal devotional life and service, but realize that this may take a very different direction than what works best for you.

YFC Editors

tioned. We both relaxed. Our prayers for each other helped us to know much more about each other's lives and what each of us was really concerned about.

Afterward, of course, we prayed for our families, friends, church, and so on. But first we interviewed and prayed for one another.

The Bible-study aspect of our spiritual partnership was in trouble too. It needed a healing, freshening idea to make it a blessing to us rather than a source of tension.

We found that a Bible-study guide, the sort that asks good questions (What does it say? What does it mean? What do I need to do about it?) was right for us. We also needed a Bible-study guide that didn't give us answers to the questions but left us with the freedom to answer as well as we could and then go on. The study guide was our private tutor.

One of us would read the Bible material and the questions, and then we took turns trying to answer and apply them. I disciplined myself to be quiet while Bob pondered. As I listened, I learned new insights from his perceptions, so different from mine. He began to go beyond grasping the facts of what he was reading to grappling with their meanings, and to understanding how these truths might be applied to his life to change his viewpoints and behavior.

As we praise God, study the Bible, and bring our failures and worries to Him, we are lifting our souls to Him as David says he did (Ps. 25). But we are also doing this in front of each other and for each other. Our devotional partnership has become the freshest, most intimate part of our lives. Because it keeps us honest and open to God and each other, we are able to begin each day with a clean sheet. Every morning we get to start all over again.

Related Article
Chapter 5: Prayer in the Husband-Wife Relationship

The Fruit of the Spirit in the Marriage Relationship

GEORGE A. REKERS

Several years ago while I was presenting a workshop on family relationships, a physician asked me an interesting question. He happened to turn on the hotel TV during a Billy Graham sermon on marriage. Graham was saying that in an ideal marriage there are three people, not two—the husband, the wife, and God. If God is not part of your marriage, it is not everything it could be.

"You're a Christian and a marriage counselor," the physician said to me. "Just what do you think Billy Graham meant by that?"

As part of my answer, I turned to Galatians 5:16, 19-23: "Live by the Spirit, and you will not gratify the desires of the sinful nature. . . . The acts of the sinful nature are obvious: sexual immorality, impurity and debauchery; idolatry and witchcraft; hatred, discord, jealousy, fits of rage, selfish ambition, dissensions, factions and envy; drunkenness, orgies, and the like. . . . But the fruit of the Spirit is love, joy, peace, patience, kindness, goodness, faithfulness, gentleness and self-control."

Looking at this list of "acts of the sinful nature," any marriage counselor would immediately see that these are the very behaviors that most often cause problems in marriage relationships. By contrast, the description of the "fruit of the Spirit" includes the characteristics that make marriages strong. When God's Spirit is indwelling both the husband and the wife, each spouse is developing the qualities necessary to establishing a much closer, more intimate, and more effective marital relationship.

Let's take a brief look at the nine qualities known as the fruit of the Spirit:

Love. God is love and the source of true love (1 John 4:7-21). If both husband and wife are believers, they are able to tap that source and experience true love in their relationship. Love involves affection, but it goes beyond that. It also means desiring the other person's welfare. Married love requires a commitment to act sacrificially on the partner's behalf. God loved us to that extent, and because of His love we can love one another.

Joy. True joy is an antidote to depression. John 16:19-24 and James 1:2-4 show how joy triumphs over grief and trials. A couple who has this fruit of the Spirit is able to transcend the frustrating and difficult times that are part of every marriage. Seeing their trials from God's perspective, they are able to experience joy even in rough times.

Peace. Peace is an important quality with several aspects. First there is the *upward* aspect in terms of our relationship to God. Through Christ He created peace between us and Him. Next there is the *inward* aspect of freedom from anxiety (1 Peter 5:7). And finally there is the *outward* aspect of peace between individuals (Heb. 12:14; 1 Thes. 5:13; Rom. 14:19). Because of their upward peace with God and the inward peace in their hearts, a Christian couple has the resources to resolve outward conflict and experience true peace with one another.

Patience. I once saw a sign that said, "Lord, give me patience, and give it to

161

A MEDITATION FOR COUPLES

Relax. Get as comfortable as you can. Take some deep breaths and roll your head around. Close your eyes. Using all five senses, put yourself and your partner in the most peaceful, beautiful setting you know.

If you are by an ocean, hear the waves, taste the salt in the air, and feel the sand beneath your feet. Watch the birds soaring overhead.

If you are in a forest, look up at the small blue circle of sky overhead. Feel the pine needles in your path. Breathe in the scent of the trees and hear the breeze whispering far above you.

Now, in a quiet place in your spirit, hold the person you love the most. Look deeply and quietly into [his] face. Tell [him] how much you love [him]. Lovingly wish [him] all good things. What do you say to your beloved?

Slowly become aware of a great pair of hands, larger than the both of you, holding you. God is telling you that you are two holy bodies, and that He loves you. He tells you that everything you desire is wished for you. God wills your happiness. What does your God say to you?

Take your partner's hand. Through touch, tell [him] that you know what it means to be lonely and afraid. Tell [him] [he] isn't alone. Tell [him] that despite the fear and hurt and pain, you believe in the power of God to bring life out of death.

Tell your partner you love [him].

Earnie Larsen

me right now." But patience is a quality the Holy Spirit develops in us over time through our experiences. In relationships, forgiveness is the basis for patience. That's why Jesus told Peter to forgive his brother 70 times 7 and then told the Parable of the Unmerciful Servant (Matt. 18:21-35). If you understand that God has forgiven you, then forgiveness will flow from you and you will be patient with others, especially your marriage partner.

Kindness. This fruit of the Spirit, like patience, is based on forgiveness (Eph. 4:32). Paul says in Colossians 3:12, "Clothe yourselves with . . . kindness." If you have experienced God's kindness toward you, you will be kind to your spouse. Matthew 10:8 says, "Freely you have received, freely give." One way to implement kindness in marriage is to express appreciation to your mate for what he or she does and for who he or she is.

Goodness. Goodness is one of God's character qualities. Psalm 107:1 says, "Give thanks to the Lord, for He is good," and in John 10:11, Jesus says He is "the good shepherd." But we learn from Scripture that none of us is good in himself or herself (Ps. 14:1; Rom. 3:12). For a husband and wife to express goodness, they must be indwelt by God's Spirit. Goodness is never "holier than thou." It does not call attention to itself, but works quietly to help others. There are many opportunities in marriage to be good to one's spouse.

Faithfulness. Marital fidelity, is basic to the marriage relationship. Faithfulness includes more than this, however. It means being reliable and responsible—doing what we say we are going to do. Without faithfulness, there can be no trust. Fear and anxiety then characterize the relationship. "Great is Your faithfulness," says the prophet to God (Lam. 3:23). The Spirit works in believers to give them God's great faithfulness, which is so vital for a strong marriage.

162

APPLY THE BIBLE AT HOME

Too often when we read the Bible or hear a sermon, we think, "This would be great for So-and-so to hear." We can find terrific applications for everyone but ourselves.

But application must begin with us in our homes. Application is finding the timeless truth in the passage we're reading and taking action to make it true in our own lives. In order to apply God's Word to our lives, we need to: (1) bring the Bible's words into the present; (2) discover the timeless truth; (3) consider how that truth applies to our lives; and (4) develop an action plan to implement it in our lives— "What should I/we do now?"

Bruce Barton

Gentleness. Also translated "meekness," gentleness is the humility of submitting to one another. This fruit of the Spirit is not for weaklings. You have to be very strong and secure in yourself to submit to your spouse. Recognizing that God is in control of circumstances, a Christian husband doesn't have to try to control or manipulate his wife, and a Christian wife doesn't have to try to control or manipulate her husband. In Matthew 5:5 Jesus says the meek are "blessed" (see Titus 3:2 and 1 Peter 3:4 for more counsel on gentleness). And Christ Himself is described as meek and gentle (2 Cor. 10:1).

Self-control. We Christians are not just puppets of the Holy Spirit. This last fruit of the Spirit is the ability to control ourselves. The Spirit gives us the power to discipline ourselves as an athlete in strict training would do (1 Cor. 9:24-27). The Apostle Peter also lists self-control as a virtue (2 Peter 1:5-7). Self-control makes it possible for us to practice all the other Spirit-given qualities regularly and dependably.

Why, then, is marriage less than it could be when God is not part of the relationship? Without God, the couple is likely to fall victim to the marriage-destroying acts of the sinful nature. They will probably relate as two selfish people trying to obtain their rights.

By contrast, if husband and wife have truly yielded themselves to the Holy Spirit, the fruit of the Spirit will be evident in their lives and in their relationship. And the fruit of the Spirit includes the very qualities that make a marriage strong and rewarding.

Related Articles
Chapter 1: Love as Honoring Each Other
Chapter 5: Husbands and Wives With Jesus as Lord

Prayer in the
Husband-Wife Relationship

WAYNE E. OATES

Married couples report uneven results in their efforts to blend their personal prayer lives into a genuine and meaningful prayer life together. Some share prayer just before going to bed in the evening. Others say the morning or evening mealtimes provide their best opportunity for common prayer, though couples with children often find themselves delegating table prayers to children, especially very young ones. For many couples, prayer is an intensely personal experience. Each partner prays privately and often silently, but each is aware of the power of the other's prayers.

To say the least, there seem to be few set patterns of prayer in the husband-wife relationship. With the majority of couples where both husband and wife work outside the home, often eating their main meal in a restaurant or at different times from each other and even having different sleep schedules, prayer becomes a casualty along with other forms of intimate sharing. In all the confusion, we need some guidelines to help us sustain a shared prayer life as a couple. Let me, with abundant aid from Scripture, suggest a few.

1. *Prayer is effective only when you are treating each other considerately.* If your prayers together are hindered—that is, if you can't bear the idea of prayer with each other—examine closely the way you treat one another. Peter urges, "Husbands . . . be considerate as you live with your wives . . . so that nothing will hinder your prayers" (1 Peter 3:7). In this day of concern for women's equali-

ty, we can extend Peter's counsel to women: "Wives, be considerate as you live with your husbands." Inconsiderateness is not unique to either sex: both engage in it. When you have searched your own heart and have identified ways in which you have been thoughtless and devoid of grace in relation to your spouse, confess this to him or her. Pray that you may learn the grace of considerateness for each other. Then begin to practice thoughtfulness—a form of prayer in action.

2. *Prayer does not have to be verbal.* When a severe crisis strikes, we are often rendered speechless with shock. One of us loses his or her job. We narrowly escape death in an automobile accident. We discover that our child is addicted to drugs. We learn that a loved one has a chronic or terminal disease. These are just a few of the dozens of severe crises that can leave us with nothing to say. As the Apostle Paul says, "We do not know what we ought to pray" (Rom. 8:26). Paul goes on to say that when we are in this speechless condition, "the Spirit Himself intercedes for us with groans that words cannot express." As husbands and wives, we can simply hold each other in our arms and be silent as we count on the Holy Spirit to pray for us. This is the silent prayer of the heart, and it can be used whenever a couple has no words to express their deep feelings.

3. *Prayer does not have to concern "religious" subjects.* A healthy sexual union between husband and wife, for example, is cause for thanksgiving to each

other and to God. In 1 Timothy 4:1-5 Paul calls teachers "hypocritical liars" when they "forbid people to marry," since "everything God created is good, and nothing is to be rejected if it is received with thanksgiving, because it is consecrated by the Word of God and prayer." Thanksgiving for your sexual relationship will help you set aside the old, un-Christian taboos that make us feel ashamed of the sexual union. It will help you achieve the communion of souls and bodies that sex should facilitate. Such thanksgiving does not have to be formal. It can begin with expression of gratitude and adoration for each other, and it can continue as a silent prayer of the heart as you hold each other tenderly.

4. *Pray when you are separated even more than when you are together.* Every marriage has unavoidable times of separation because of work, childbearing, the care of sick parents in distant cities, military service, and so on. More serious are the times of separation when a husband and wife cannot stand to be in each other's presence, when the threat of divorce hangs like a cloud over their relationship.

Any time of separation is a time for some heavy-duty praying. The Apostle Paul, in 1 Corinthians 7:5, speaks candidly about this. He urges a couple not to refuse each other sexual access, so that Satan will not tempt them. When a husband and wife must discontinue sexual relations for whatever reason, this can be the beginning of serious division between them. Paul says this should be done only for a short time, and then only

PRAY FOR YOUR SPOUSE

Do you ever pray for your spouse? It's easy to pray for him or her to overcome shortcomings, change his or her ways, or wise up. But do you think about what he or she is going to go through today and pray about it? Do you pray for blessing and spiritual growth?

Who knows? Such prayers could draw you closer together—not to mention closer to God.

YFC Editors

to devote themselves to prayer. If a couple feels the need for a time of separation, they should keep the separation brief and they should pray earnestly while they are apart, because the tempter is at work providing opportunities for sin at the same time the Holy Spirit is at work creating tenderness of heart and reconciliation.

5. *Talk about your prayer life in light of Scripture.* Rarely do we think of Scripture as being this concrete and specific about prayer between husbands and wives. Nevertheless, it is clear, specific, and helpful. Lay aside all shyness with your partner, and dare to discuss your prayer life and your love life as frankly as Scripture does.

Related Articles
Chapter 4: Building Trust
Chapter 5: Devotional Life Together

Church Involvement

DEAN MERRILL

If anyone can take a realistic view of church life, it's married couples. That's because being married and being part of a congregation spring from the same idea. Paul said so in Ephesians 5:25: "Husbands, love your wives, just as Christ loved the church and gave Himself up for her." More than once the Bible pictures the church as Christ's wife.

So if anyone can appreciate the need for closeness and fellowship, it's we who are married. We can also understand that some sermons are better than others, just like some suppers. We can understand tensions over money, both at home and at church. We can understand when hurtful words fly. We can appreciate the hard work of nurturing the young. That's how it goes in family life, whether our own or the Family of God.

So how do we settle into a congregation and make the most of our time there?

1. *Always remember that there's no perfect church.* Even the spectacularly successful Jerusalem church in the Book of Acts had occasional problems (lying, disorganization), and yours won't do better than that. Young congregations have certain kinds of weaknesses that older, more established groups don't—and vice versa.

There's no point wasting a decade or two looking for perfection. Better to use that time contributing to, helping, and improving an imperfect church. However—

2. *Distinguish the important flaws from the casual ones.* The previous point is not meant to say that anything goes. The Apostle Jude felt strongly that

he should "write and urge you to contend for the faith that was once for all entrusted to the saints" (v. 3). If a church is not solidly based on the Bible, it really is a hopeless case. Human beings simply aren't wise enough to concoct their own answers in the spiritual realm. God's written Word must be embraced as the authority.

On the other hand, you can afford to be flexible about musical style, size of Sunday School classes, form of government, and age mix. Just because a church isn't like "back home" doesn't mean it's wrong.

3. *Settle your allegiance early, especially before your children start to wonder.* Don't "shop" indefinitely. Some shopping is necessary every time you move, of course. But get the matter settled as quickly as you can, in order to stop analyzing and start participating.

By the time children reach third or fourth grade, they really need the security of being able to say "*my* church." It's especially dangerous to be floundering from place to place during their teenage years, when friendships with Christian peers are so important and larger questions about the Christian walk are sprouting.

4. *Stick with the rhythm: go to give as well as receive.* The household that has a weekly debate over "Shall we go or not?" is asking for trouble. Church is, in one sense, a family meal. As at home, some menus are more popular than others. But most parents insist that kids come to the table whether they're thrilled about asparagus or not. The same holds true for weekly worship.

5. *Try to find at least one opportuni-*

CHURCH TIME, FAMILY TIME

Church involvement is important for your family's spiritual development, but, depending on the size of your church, you may feel undue pressure to participate in any number of activities. That's why all families must remember to balance church involvement with family time, job responsibilities, personal health, and recreation.

Realize that there is *active involvement* and *supportive involvement.* Active involvement includes the obvious (teaching Sunday School, helping in the nursery, singing in the choir, hosting the youth group in your home, etc.), and is essential to any healthy, growing congregation. But you don't necessarily need to make a lifetime commitment. You also can take on a duty (notice we said a duty) and set a time limit—one year, one quarter, whatever. Then learn to say no. Don't get into the trap of volunteering inordinate amounts of time. If you have undertaken a heavy responsibility, get an assistant to help you and delegate various jobs.

Between times of active involvement, you can give supportive involvement. You are just as involved in the church when you call or write another member to offer words of encouragement, participate on a prayer chain, or write to missionaries, as when you do more visible ministry.

Look for creative, less time-consuming ways to minister to people in the church. Some of these activities can be enjoyed by the whole family—giving you family time as well.

YFC Editors

---

ty where you can serve together. Too many Christian couples arrive at church and head in separate directions while still in the parking lot—she to teach the five-year-olds, he to check on the heating or air conditioning; later on she sings in the choir while he ushers. This pattern continues throughout the week and the year. How much better to team-teach a class, sing together in the choir, or codirect a nursing-home outreach! With a little planning, it's possible to be drawn closer together at church rather than separated.

6. *Don't bad-mouth your church, or anyone else's.* As we already said, the church is not perfect and never will be. You don't need to announce the fact. You don't even need to point out all the flaws to one another. The flat sopranos who ruined the morning anthem for you may have gone unnoticed by your spouse. If so, why spoil a good thing?

Make it a standard practice to discuss problems only with those who can make a difference, and even then to speak kindly and lovingly. Assume your fellow members and leaders are well meaning, if not always well prepared. Along with your pinpointing of weaknesses, be sure to include what you'd be willing to do to help improve the situation.

And remember: it's Christ's church, not yours, or your spouse's, or the pastor's, or the denomination's. If Christ can stand it and love it, so can you.

Related Articles
Chapter 4: Ministering as a Couple
Chapter 5: How to Have a Team Ministry

How to Have a Team Ministry

BOB & CINNY HICKS

To many married couples, ministry is a task done during working hours. Marriage is separate from ministry; in fact, the two often conflict. Many years ago Dr. Howard Hendricks jolted us into a different perspective on marriage and ministry. Speaking to Campus Crusade staff members, he said, "Your marriage *is* your ministry."

This was our introduction to the concept that one's ministry is a natural outgrowth and extension of one's marriage, not a task performed outside it or in spite of it. We decided to found our marriage and ministry on this idea, and we looked to an intriguing New Testament couple as our model for team ministry. They were not ordained, apparently had no formal Bible training, and yet had one of the most significant ministries in the early church. The couple—Aquila and Priscilla.

Four essential commitments are apparent in this couple. Throughout our years of marriage and ministry we have seen these commitments to be crucial to our success and survival also. These four joint commitments are the necessary components for a team ministry.

1. *A commitment to God's Word.* Priscilla and Aquila sat under Paul's teaching for a year and a half (Acts 18:11) and became so knowledgeable of the Scriptures that they were able to correct Apollos, one of the most dynamic teachers of the early church (Acts 18:24-26). Some of our most enjoyable experiences as a couple have been studying the Word of God together, often through seminars, conferences, and couples Bible studies. The best part of these is always the drive home! We talk about what we learned, what we think God was saying to us, or even how boring and irrelevant the speaker was. The important point is that we are communicating about God's Word. One of the best ways to study together is to volunteer to team-teach a Sunday School class. At least one evening a week or very early Sunday morning you will be in the Word together!

2. *A commitment to God's work.* Everywhere Priscilla and Aquila went, a ministry happened. When we meet them in Corinth they are inviting Paul into their home. Paul then takes them with him to Ephesus and leaves them there to initiate the ministry (Acts 18:19). Later they have a church in their home (1 Cor. 16:19). In fact, wherever we find them they are ministering through their home. They obviously viewed their marriage as their ministry; though their profession was tentmaking, their vocation (calling) was church-making.

When a husband and wife open their hearts to God, the doors of their home usually follow. As a team they open themselves to people, allowing who they are and what they have in their marriage to minister to others. Our guest book is simply a list of names, but behind each name is a story of ministry. A stressed-out pastor's wife who needed to get away for a few days. Friends out of work and in need of housing. A dear Christian brother with multiple sclerosis. A live-in seminary student. Our home is simple, but it is our place of ministry. In the context of phone calls, barking dogs, and small children, we hope the love of Christ shines forth through all the meals served, miles driven, and linens

was born in Pontus (Acts 18:2), but he saw himself not as a Pontian but as a pilgrim. They went wherever they were needed for the cause of Christ. They knew God's work was not only local but global.

It is easy for couples to get so bogged down in jobs, activities, and even ministries that they begin to think the whole world is where they are. A husband and wife can increase their world concern by adopting missionaries, using vacation time to have a cross-cultural experience, or even volunteering for short-term missionary service. Together we have climbed most of the mountains in Israel, ridden a pre-World War II train through the outback of Australia, and stayed with a Bermudian family while doing "beach evangelism" on that lovely British island. These shared experiences not only built our marriage but also enlarged our vision. Seeing the world increases the likelihood of serving the world, and serving the world is one of the main elements of a team ministry.

4. *A commitment to God's workmen.* On whom did Priscilla and Aquila, a lay couple, have an impact? On some of the greatest names in 1st-century Christianity: Apollos, Timothy, and Paul. Paul, author of almost half the New Testament books, was especially close to them and went out of his way to make contact with them.

Ministers are often neglected as they do their ministry. They need understanding lay couples who can provide an environment of love and acceptance where they can dash, crash, and hash. Pastors and their wives need friends. Many are lonely and isolated. They don't feel a part of normal community life, and they are asked out only to speak, pray, or put in an expected appearance. Over the years God has blessed us with a few Pauls and Timothys to whom we have tried to give the greatest of gifts—friendship. Over coffee in our kitchen, or fixing broken appliances, or learning to

changed. Add to these the hours of debate, discussion, and counsel, and you have the essence of Christian ministry, whether 1st- or 20th-century.

3. *A concern for God's world.* The world God made is much larger than our neighborhood or our local church. Priscilla and Aquila were surprisingly mobile; every time we meet them they are in a different city. This enabled them to be available to many kinds of people when they were most needed. Aquila

play tennis together, we listened to their fears, frustrations, dreams, and wants. We talked of children, money, sex, and God. We weren't pastor and layman; we were friends.

Priscilla and Aquila, one of the few couples mentioned in the New Testament, show that marriage and ministry go hand in hand. A team ministry begins with the Word, works through the home in natural ways, invades the world, and ministers to God's workmen along the way. Whether you are a clergy couple or laypersons, you have a ministry. Your marriage is your ministry.

Related Articles
Chapter 4: Ministering as a Couple
Chapter 5: Church Involvement

The Dangers of Hospitality

KAREN MAINS

Hospitality is a beautiful ministry, ideally suited to husbands and wives. The church as a whole has neglected it, and that may be why some families find their own ministry of caring for others growing out of control. You may be in one of those families.

You have more than an open door; you have a rotating front door, and it never stops turning. You feel overworked, exhausted, desperate—all for the love of God.

Perhaps you have taken an aging parent into your home. You never dreamed there would be intergenerational conflicts.

Maybe company's coming for dinner (the third night in a row) and your back is aching already.

Maybe you love crowds, but your wife is protesting. She's had enough.

Or perhaps your teens' friends love to make themselves at home. They raid your refrigerator and gab for hours, and you know this is because their own parents don't give them the time of day. But this daily open house is becoming expensive.

Maybe you've taken a foster child, or you baby-sit for the mother down the block whose infant was born with birth defects, just to give her some time away.

Perhaps you're the one who always entertains half the church.

Maybe a missionary's child is living with you, or an unwed mother, or you've just opened your home to someone recovering from drug abuse or years of street life.

And the truth of it is, you're depleted and on edge, wondering in your heart if sometime, somewhere, it isn't all right to close the door and lock it.

Yes, it is all right. You need time to be quiet, to renew, to become strong again.

In her book *What Is a Family?* Edith Schaeffer says that a family must have a lock on its door as well as a hinge. She's right. *Need does not constitute a ministry;* that is, just because someone out there needs help does not necessarily mean you have been called to give it. Obedience to the Holy Spirit is what determines our ministry, and right now He may be saying to you, "Take a rest."

One summer I discovered again the dangers of hospitality. A young woman had come to live with us, and when we brought her into our home we had no idea of the spiritual warfare we would have to conduct on her behalf. I was filled with God's incredible, unexplainable love for His damaged, rejected, lost children—but that love went out from

170

PROTHALAMION

How like an arch your marriage! Framed
in living stone, its gothic arrow aimed
at heaven, with Christ (its Capstone and
its Arrowhead) locking your coupled
weakness into one, the leaning
of two lives into a strength.
Thus He defines your joining's length
and width, its archetypal shape. Its meaning
is another thing: a letting in of light,
an opening to a varied landscape, planned
but yet to be explored. A paradox, for you
who doubly frame His arch may now step through
its entrance into His promised land!

Luci Shaw

From *The Sighting*. Used by permission.

me in one massive energy drain.

When our young woman friend left, she was more ready to face the world and to follow the One who had become her Lord. I had a week to change rooms and get out summer clothes. Then some relatives moved in with us for a month. I loved having them with us, but let's face it, the nuts and bolts of living together, cooking meals, doing laundry, meshing schedules, and finding play room for everyone was another energy drain.

Soon they too were gone—except for one child who stayed on with us and, with our daughter, held two massive bake sales to make money for college. Baked goods were on the dining room tables, in the garage, and on the Ping-Pong table, and flour was in every corner.

Toward the end of the summer I began to have mood swings. When I found myself overreacting to minor, unimportant incidents, I reminded myself that fatigue is a danger of hospitality. I thought of all the women I had wisely told: "You must learn to take care of yourself as well as others."

I decided to stay home from a family vacation in my quiet house all by myself. Later David and I went away together for a week. I began to feel strong again, to feel emotionally rested. At this point the Lord spoke to me in a new and fresh way regarding hospitality.

During a quiet time with the Lord, I turned to Isaiah 58 and read, "Bring right into your own homes those who are helpless, poor, and destitute" (v. 7, TLB). Then suddenly I saw the promises—17 of them in that hospitality chapter: "If you do these things, God will shed His own glorious light upon you. . . . When you call, the Lord will answer. 'Yes, I am here,' He will quickly reply" (vv. 8-9, TLB).

Have you experienced the dangers of hospitality? Are you overworked in the cause of the Lord? Are you just plain worn out? Find an hour of quiet and pray, "Lord, speak." Then open your Bible to Isaiah 58 and listen to what He has in store for those who have been obedient in His service.

Related Articles
Chapter 6: Living With Differing Capacities
Chapter 12: Beware of Overscheduling!

Resisting Satan's Attacks on Your Family

PAT & SHIRLEY BOONE

I read recently where Jimmy Carter admitted that he and Rosalyn nearly came to blows trying to write their new book together. Each remember the same events, through which they had both lived, differently—and wanted to tell the story differently too. Shirley and I had the same experience when we wrote our book *The Honeymoon is Over.*

I mention this to illustrate my premise: pain, disappointment, and disagreement enter into the best of marriages. This is partly because God intended it that way. And there's a corollary premise—the devil intends it that way too.

The pattern was established in the Garden of Eden with the very first marriage. Adam and Eve were a perfect couple in a perfect environment. But in the midst of perfection, God had allowed for choice and disobedience, the possibility that Adam and Eve would get out of harmony with each other and even with God's plan. Satan was allowed to tempt, corrupt, and destroy, and he did just that.

Don't get me wrong. God didn't want Adam and Even to disobey. He wanted them to obey—not because they had no choice or alternative, but because they believed Him and trusted His guidance and provision. Unfortunately, Adam and Eve failed the test, and you and I have been paying a penalty for that ever since.

And the pattern continues, in a suspiciously similar way. Our pastor, Jack Hayford, is one of many, many ministers who have confided that Sunday morning can be the most trying time for a minis-

ter's family. Arguments arise; the kids scrap with each other; husband and wife flare up over seemingly nothing; dishes break; the car won't start. When the pastor arrives to lead his flock on Sunday morning, he may be seething inwardly and feeling definitely unspiritual. Jack told me he finally recognized the source of this kind of trial and harassment. Now he starts his Sunday morning rebuking Satan and ordering him to leave the Hayford family alone. The results have been remarkable.

It's hard to know whether the Lord or the devil is the source of your current trial. In the magnificent Book of Job we find out it was both, in a curious way. Satan asked permission to afflict that good man, and he's the one who brought the disasters, the boils, and the accusations. But God permitted it!

Remember, the Apostle Paul promised us, "No temptation [or test] has overtaken you but such as is common to man; and God is faithful, who will not allow you to be tempted beyond what you are able, but with the temptation will provide a way of escape also, that you may be able to endure it [pass the test]" (1 Cor. 10:13, NASB).

And James actually proposes, "Consider it all joy, my brethren, when you encounter various trials, knowing that the testing of your faith produces endurance. And let endurance have its perfect result, that you may be perfect and complete, lacking in nothing" (James 1:2-4, NASB).

Maybe you hadn't applied these Scriptures to family life before, but Shirley

172

and I have had to, and gratefully. Family problems are often the result of tension, but tension itself is an evidence of being out of harmony with God's will. The Bible says, "Be anxious for nothing, but in everything by prayer and supplication with thanksgiving let your requests be made known to God. And the peace of God, which surpasses all comprehension, shall guard your hearts and your minds in Christ Jesus" (Phil. 4:6-7, NASB). I think it goes deeper than tension.

Why does the Lord says God's peace "shall guard your hearts and your minds"? In a family situation, in the security of your own home, is there something to guard against? You bet there is!

Especially in your own home you have to be on guard against Satan, the accuser of the brethren, the one who comes to rob, kill, and destroy. He is the enticer who uses our fleshly appetites to corrupt us, the insidious conniver who turns even our good motives and loving concern for each other into dangerous traps (Matt. 16:22-23).

As wonderful an institution as the family is, it can also be the place where people are everlastingly warped and doomed. Psychologists tell us that our personalities and characters are shaped very early. Our attitude toward God can be shaped or twisted by our attitude toward our parents. I talk to people all the time who have no concept of a Father God at all, because their own fathers provided such a poor example.

God intended the family to be the workshop, the school of life. Once we "graduate" from the family, we should be ready to be good, productive citizens; children of God; enemies of Satan. Do you really think Satan is gentleman enough to wait until we have "graduated" to go to work on us?

Remember, Satan was audacious and desperate enough to meet Jesus face to face, after He had been baptized by John and received the Holy Spirit in a

---

PERSONAL DEVOTIONS

A personal devotional time is vital to your marriage. You alone are responsible for your personal relationship with God and, even in marriage, you need to continue to nurture that relationship.

We find that our own personal devotions continue to be very important to us. Setting aside that time alone with God not only refreshes us for the tasks and challenges ahead, but it gives us better perspective on life and on each other. It gives us time to grow closer to God, a relationship that needs to be in tune if our marriage is going to be strong. We grow closer to each other because we pray for each other. We are more at peace about our lives and the future because we have entrusted each other to God.

Tom & Linda Taylor

---

special dimension. Later he entered into the heart of Judas right during the Last Supper! And don't forget that Jesus told His disciples that they would be betrayed even by their parents, brothers, relatives, and friends. Another sobering example: Ananias and Sapphira, an early Christian couple, though they were making a large charitable donation to the church, lied to the Holy Spirit about it and were struck dead on the spot! (Acts 5:1-10)

My heart breaks when I read these stories, because I feel that most husbands and wives are in the same danger. We all try to do good for our families and other people, but if we deny the Holy Spirit's working and prompting in our lives, we're doomed to failure or, at best, only partial success.

The Lord will put up with our blunders and mistakes and ignorance, but when we deliberately resist the work of the Holy Spirit, we're in for real trouble. There is a kingdom to be entered into, full of miracles and the very presence and power of Jesus, the refreshing of the Holy Spirit, and the mighty working of God's plan through each member of the family. But woe to that family which tests God, refusing to enter into that kingdom. They may seem to get away with it for a while, but then the roof will cave in as the family is attacked by the temptations of the world and the ravages of demonic enemies.

So many church leaders today are seeing their own homes and marriages break up. Dear friend, think about it. If we agree that the family today is the target of a powerful supernatural enemy—one armed with drugs, sexual promiscuity, diseases, homosexuality, occult religions, suicide, and so many other vicious weapons—how can we possibly expect our families to survive if we don't call on our supernatural and more powerful friend, the Holy Spirit? Let's face it,

there's a war going on, and our homes are not some kind of spiritual Switzerland. They're the battleground!

Then what's the answer? How can we win this crucial, elemental struggle taking place right in our own homes? Sincere prayer and skillful use of God's Word are proven weapons against harmful intrusions into our homes. Allow the Holy Spirit to use them for the spiritual security of your family. Memorize and meditate on these key verses:

1. "So, as the Holy Spirit says, 'Today, if you hear His voice, do not harden your hearts'" (Heb. 3:7-8a).

2. "Learn how to walk in the Lord and in the comfort of the Holy Spirit" (Acts 9:31, TLB).

3. And we can again and again turn to Ephesians 5:21–6:4 for a picture of God's rule for family life, a rule only made reality through the power of the Holy Spirit.

———

Related Article
Introduction: Marriage Isn't Always Easy

Living With an Unbelieving Spouse

JO BERRY

Amy and Tim Jordan had been happily married for eight years when they were faced with a series of crises. Their only child almost died when she was struck by a car. The company Tim worked for went bankrupt, and he was without a job for months. And Amy's father had a heart attack.

Amy's neighbor Sue, who had been praying for the Jordans for years, invited them to church. Tim wouldn't go, but Amy did. She was so comforted and encouraged when she heard about how

she could appropriate God's love and power that within a few weeks she made a personal commitment to Christ. At that moment she became one of thousands, if not millions, of Christians faced with learning how to live with an unbelieving spouse.

The Apostle Paul warned, "Do not be bound together with unbelievers" (2 Cor. 6:14, NASB). Does this mean that Amy, who is now a Christian, should end her marriage?

The Corinthians, many of whom were

in similar situations, asked that same question of Paul, to which he replied, "If any brother has a wife who is an unbeliever, and she consents to live with him, let him not send her away. And a woman who has an unbelieving husband, and he consents to live with her, let her not send her husband away" (1 Cor. 7:12-13, NASB). In other words, God does not want any Christians to end their marriages because of this "unequal yoking." Rather, the Lord wants to use the believing mate to woo his or her spouse into the faith.

But how does one do this without preaching, acting pridefully pious, or seeming spiritually superior or judgmental? Let's explore some practical ways to live in loving harmony with an unbelieving spouse:

1. *Believe that your faith will be an asset, not a detriment, to your marriage.* You have something wonderful and marvelously constructive to contribute to your union that you never had before: the unconditional love of God! Your relationship with Christ should make you easier to live with, kinder, more patient and understanding.

2. *Cultivate quality communication with your mate.* All good marriages are grounded in open, honest communication, regardless of a person's religious beliefs. Many times the Christian spouse has a tendency to stop sharing with his or her unbelieving partner. Carol confessed that she felt as if her husband would never understand her once she became a Christian. "My respect level for him dropped because I was a Christian and he wasn't, so I shut him out and confided in my friends at church instead. This caused serious problems, which I initially blamed on Don's unregenerate heart. Actually, the breakdown in intimacy was my fault. Don hadn't changed; I had."

3. *Concentrate on what your mate is—all of his or her good points—rather than dwelling on the fact that he or*

SPIRITUAL KEEPERS?

Are you your spouse's spiritual keeper? No. Each person is accountable to God for his or her own spiritual life and growth. The secret of spiritual life in marriage is to deliver your spouse into God's care. This frees you from nagging, criticism, and undue guilt over your spouse's spiritual condition.

But you *can* do some things. You can pray, encourage, assume the best, not be a stumbling block, be a good example, be concerned, and share your own spiritual insights and victories.

The spiritual growth of both spouses is vital to them personally and together. But one spouse is not responsible for the other's relationship with God.

YFC Editors

---

she isn't a Christian. Thank God for the many positive attributes your life partner possesses. Be generous with praise and compliments. Speak well of him or her to others.

4. *Accept that God can and will use your unbelieving mate to guide you and to help you grow.* When the Lord instituted marriage, He meant for husbands and wives to encourage, uphold, and affirm one another. Loving support is a necessary ingredient in any marriage. Never discount your mate because he or she isn't a believer.

5. *Do not compare your marriage to what you perceive as ideal Christian marriages.* Too many unequally yoked believers play a deadly, destructive game I call "If only my mate were a Christian." They mistakenly believe that if their mates became Christians, all of life's problems would miraculously disappear

and their marriages would be perfect. That simply is not true! *All* marriages have problems. *All* husbands and wives have disagreements (even fights) and differences of opinion. Don't blame your spouse's unbelief for problems that are common to all marriages.

6. *Have fun!* Don't turn into a holier-than-thou bore who imposes "thou shalt nots" on his or her mate. Let the joy of the Lord overflow in your life. Cultivate a sense of humor. Zealously enjoy your marriage and the pleasure of being with the man or woman you love.

7. *Finally, leave the future in God's hands.* Don't devise spiritual plots to try to force your mate into the faith. Regeneration is the work of the Holy Spirit.

Setting a godly example is your job. Be such a good Christian that your husband or wife will want what you have. Pray faithfully and expectantly for your spouse. Claim promises from God's Word. Remember, God wants your unbelieving mate to become a believer as much as you do. "The Lord is not slow about His promise, as some count slowness, but is patient toward you, not wishing for any to perish but for all to come to repentance" (2 Peter 3:9, NASB).

Related Articles
    Chapter 1: Love as Respect
    Chapter 1: Love Is the Gift of a Caring Self

Can I Trust God for My Spouse?

JUDITH ALLEN SHELLY

Susan, a nurse and the wife of a first-year seminarian, shared her deep concern with me. "John has no concept of human suffering. I don't see how he will be able to empathize with sick people when he becomes a pastor. He has had no experience with illness. I'm trying to see if I can get him a part-time job as a hospital orderly. That would give him the experience he needs."

My heart went out to Susan. She wanted to spare John from failing as a pastor. Her motives were good, but she may have been blind to what God was already doing in John. Working as an orderly may be a good learning experience for him. With the right timing and a recognition on John's part that he needs more experience with sick people, it would be entirely appropriate for Susan

to suggest the possibility of the orderly job. However, God may have another plan.

Learning to trust God for another person is always difficult. In a marriage it can be doubly hard, because your own future and identity are tied to your spouse's responses to God. There is always a temptation to take matters into your own hands, to nag or manipulate rather than believe that God is at work in your spouse, shaping him to His own image.

Early in our marriage my inability to trust God came out in subtle ways. My husband, Jim, was still in seminary. His pre-seminary education and experience were in electrical engineering. I had four years of campus ministry experience. Often, as Jim began in ministry, I would see better ways of doing things based on my own experience. It was hard to see him make the same mistakes I had made or neglect areas I felt were important. So I usually told him about it, trying to be tactful. But it wasn't long before Jim made it quite clear he did not appreciate my "wise teacher" attitude. I learned to keep quiet, to pray when I felt like instructing.

The difference was amazing. I began to see God at work in my husband in a new way. As Jim struggled with the challenges of ministry, he would spend time in prayer and Bible study, then come to the same conclusions I would have preached to him—or he would come up with a totally different, and much better, plan. At other times he would strike out on his own, fail, and learn lessons that can be learned only by experience. His faith grew stronger and more mature in the process.

It is normal to want to protect those we love from pain and failure, but God often uses the hard things to teach us important lessons. It took awhile to realize that my eagerness to spare Jim the hard knocks of ministry was actually rooted in my lack of faith—faith that the Lord would speak to Jim, and faith that Jim would hear His voice. We have both learned to trust God for one another over the years, and that has drawn us closer to each other and to the Lord.

That trust does not mean that we do not express our opinions to each other, or that we blindly accept whatever the other is thinking as from the Lord. For instance, when Jim comes home from a particularly stressful council meeting at church and announces that he wants to change careers, I no longer panic. My human reaction is to want to jump in and fix things, but I am learning I can trust God to reaffirm His call to Jim or give us oneness of mind on the subject after talking it through—or, more accurately, *listening* it through. Usually the process of coming to agreement is

PSALM 127:1

Unless the Lord builds the house, its builders labor in vain. Unless the Lord watches over the city, the watchmen stand guard in vain.

more important than the final decision, because through that process we get to know one another better.

During the course of a marriage, couples are faced with numerous minor annoyances and a few major crossroads where one spouse is convinced that God is making His will quite clear while the other is moving in the opposite direction. The minor annoyances can become major problems if spouses cannot learn to trust God for one another. A nagging belief that your spouse is preventing you from doing God's will can hammer a tremendous wedge into your marriage.

The mission field is one area that has periodically arisen in our marriage to try our faith that God is at work in one another. As a college student I was convinced God was calling me to India. I checked with a mission board and was amazed at the long list of qualifications required, but I set out to meet them. During the course of preparation, I became satisfied that I was already on the mission field where God wanted me. When Jim and I married, India was far from my mind. Then we went to an Urbana missionary convention.

When the time came to fill out missionary decision cards, I tucked mine quietly in my Bible, feeling complacently secure that I was where I belonged. My heart skipped a beat as I saw Jim sign his and put it in the collection box. We did a lot of talking over the next months. Jim's decision was to be open to whatever God called him to do, whether or not that might entail going overseas.

Essentially, what God called him to do

177

was to begin a new missions emphasis in our own church. We worked together to educate the congregation and plant a new vision for missions. I became chairperson of a new missions committee, and we served as cochairpersons of our denominational synod missions committee. Eventually the vision took hold on our members, and we saw a new vitality and desire to reach-out developing in the church. But then out of the blue came a phone call from a church in another country asking Jim to consider becoming their pastor.

We alternated believing that God was or was not calling us to go overseas. When I thought He was, Jim was hesitant. When Jim was sure, I wasn't. Finally we were both convinced that since only the Holy Spirit could orchestrate so many affirming coincidences, God must be calling us. But then a letter arrived from overseas saying the church had called another pastor. Jim and I amazed each other by both sighing in relief at the news.

The six-month process of waiting and planning left us exhausted. Why all the eerie coincidences to convince of God's leading, only to be let down? Why all the months of struggle? I think God was at work in a deeper way than we imagined. He was teaching us to trust Him to be at work in one another.

Whenever Jim and I differed about the direction to take, we spent time in prayer and Scripture study, together and individually. We learned to differentiate between our emotional responses and what God expected from us. We grew to respect one another's motives and desire to do God's will.

SPIRITUAL STORIES

Each person brings to a marriage his/her own spiritual story. One may have grown up in a Christian home learning Bible verses, going to Sunday School, and studying in a Christian college. The other may have never gone to church while growing up, became a Christian in college, and is just becoming grounded in the faith.

Spouses need to respect each other's spiritual story and not try to force their own growth pattern and maturity on the other. One may want to teach; the other may be best at personal encouragement. One may see fresh insights in God's Word that the other has heard in sermons many times.

Be sensitive to your spouse's spiritual story and be thankful for the very unique way God brought him or her to salvation.

YFC Editors

We realize we can't tell each other, "We have to do this, because it is obviously God's will." If something is unquestionably God's will, He will convince both of us. We do not have to nag or manipulate each other. Yes, we *can* trust God for one another.

Related Articles
Chapter 5: Husbands and Wives With Jesus as Lord
Chapter 13: Faith, Finances, and Vocation

The Spiritual Side of Looking Our Best

JOHN ROBERT THROOP

The other day my wife and I were gazing at our honeymoon picture. The same question occurred to both of us at once: who are those two thin people? After two children and in the midst of hectic careers of ministry and writing, we are still in pretty good shape, but we are widening a little here and sagging a little there. We certainly aren't the same as we were when we married just a few years ago.

We are blessed that our relationship has a deep emotional component. We find each other stimulating intellectually and socially. We enjoy each other's friendship. But our relationship is not strictly spiritual. We share more than a living relationship with the Lord. We share a relationship through our bodies.

Christians often have appeared not to care much about their physical life in marriage. After all, what really matters is that we have a common relationship in the Lord, and that is spiritual. To attend to the physical seems nothing more than vanity, a worldly diversion. So we live with the illusion that if our mate is obese or not physically attractive to us any longer, we can still focus on the spiritual side of the relationship where all is well.

But the fact is that our spiritual, intellectual, and emotional lives are mediated through the flesh, through our physical bodies. We are not incorporeal spirits drifting in some platonic atmosphere without regard to the physical nature. If we believed that, we would be denying one of the fundamental doctrines of the Christian faith—the Incarnation. The salvation of humankind was not simply a spiritual transaction within the Godhead. No, God became flesh, our flesh, to redeem us. "The Word was made flesh, and dwelt among us . . . full of grace and truth," says John (1:14, KJV). Our faith teaches us that the physical matters in the spiritual life. According to the biblical view, the whole human being is flesh and spirit combined. Who we are as physical human beings matters to the relationship we have together.

Some couples I have seen in counseling report that when they do not attend to their bodily shape and condition, they are less attracted to one another and find themselves less attractive. One of the most magnificent expressions of love for a mate in marriage is a healthy and vital sexual relationship. When our imperfect bodies get in the way, when we become less appealing, our sexual relationship may be deeply affected, and an important aspect of communication and expression of love and care can be cut off.

Remember the days when you were courting. You tried to look your best to each other. When I met my wife, I had just lost a tremendous amount of weight and had just returned tanned and fit from a vacation in Bermuda. She says I looked like a knockout. She looked very attractive to me in a sharp, trim business suit. Is your story the same?

Many creatures besides human beings seek to look their best to attract a mate, engage in sexual activity, and procreate. We are infinitely more complex than the other animals, however. We

179

hunger to establish a relationship in which sex helps to establish a spiritual and emotional bond. When we neglect the condition of our bodies, we alter the course of our marriage.

Now it is true that human bodies age. Bones deteriorate, flesh wrinkles, hair grays, and the middle thickens. I've come to call that last phenomenon the Midriff Crisis. It happens when the "sansabelt" can't lie about your waistline any longer. But far more than the cult of youth and fitness is at work here. We care for ourselves, making the best of what God has given us physically, not only to honor Him but also to show love for one another. Paul declares that neither husband nor wife rules over the body he or she possesses; we share our bodies with our mate (1 Cor. 7:3-5). So we are accountable to one another for the use or misuse, the shape or misshape of our bodies, insofar as we have control over our condition. And often we do.

The shape our mate is in is often a difficult subject to address in a conversation, for the self-image is usually fragile. I remember one conversation my wife and I had as I began to put on some weight after writing a popular book on weight loss. There was my reputation, of course, my responsibility to be true to my story. But there was also her very real concern for me, my self-image, my health, and our mutual pleasure as lovers and as Christians. My wife was so hesitant, and I was so defensive! She finally got up her nerve to say, "Honey, you really need to take off some weight. And I need to do the same. Let's do it together!" Shortly thereafter, we began.

Her concern—not nagging, but concern—touched me deeply. I wanted to be back in shape for her, and she wanted to be back in shape for me. As we stare at those strangers in the honeymoon photo, we realize we want to be in the best shape for each other so we can enjoy each other fully, just as God intended, for the rest of our lives.

Related Articles

180

What kind of person are you? What is your spouse like? How alike or different are you? This exercise can help you find out.

1. Use a black or dark blue pen.

2. Look at the first pair of characteristics on the graph. Are you extremely reserved? Put an X on the line near the left-hand 3. Are you very outgoing? Put an X near the right-hand 3. Are you right in the middle? A little of one or the other? Put the X wherever you think it belongs. Fill out the entire graph the same way.

3. Give your partner a red or bright green pen. Ask him or her to do the same exercise.

RESULTS: When you have both filled out the graph, you will clearly see where you feel alike and where you feel different. You may be surprised at some of your perceived similarities and differences. Talk about them. Where you are both the same, how do you keep balance in your marriage? Where you are different, how do you achieve harmony?

reserved	__3__ 2__ 1__ 0__ 1__ 2__ 3__	outgoing
aggressive	__3__ 2__ 1__ 0__ 1__ 2__ 3__	passive
emotional	__3__ 2__ 1__ 0__ 1__ 2__ 3__	rational
casual	__3__ 2__ 1__ 0__ 1__ 2__ 3__	formal
pessimistic	__3__ 2__ 1__ 0__ 1__ 2__ 3__	optimistic
spontaneous	__3__ 2__ 1__ 0__ 1__ 2__ 3__	planned
humorous	__3__ 2__ 1__ 0__ 1__ 2__ 3__	serious
organized	__3__ 2__ 1__ 0__ 1__ 2__ 3__	disorganized
cautious	__3__ 2__ 1__ 0__ 1__ 2__ 3__	daring
restless	__3__ 2__ 1__ 0__ 1__ 2__ 3__	contented
easygoing	__3__ 2__ 1__ 0__ 1__ 2__ 3__	driven
relaxed	__3__ 2__ 1__ 0__ 1__ 2__ 3__	tense
observant	__3__ 2__ 1__ 0__ 1__ 2__ 3__	absentminded
cool	__3__ 2__ 1__ 0__ 1__ 2__ 3__	warm
compliant	__3__ 2__ 1__ 0__ 1__ 2__ 3__	rebellious
sensitive	__3__ 2__ 1__ 0__ 1__ 2__ 3__	tough
quiet	__3__ 2__ 1__ 0__ 1__ 2__ 3__	talkative
conforming	__3__ 2__ 1__ 0__ 1__ 2__ 3__	original
scheduled	__3__ 2__ 1__ 0__ 1__ 2__ 3__	impulsive
loud	__3__ 2__ 1__ 0__ 1__ 2__ 3__	quiet

PERSONALITY TYPES

Personality prints, like those of fingers and voices, are unique. No two are alike, but certain pairs in marriage blend better than others. Few irritations frustrate more than the chafing of a marriage partner. Yet what we call conflicts and incompatibility are often a good match slightly out of adjustment.

If marriage is a true twosome (and it is!), it wins or loses as a team. Each person brings assets, advantages, and pluses to strengthen the relationship, as well as weaknesses to be sustained. The basic rule is: build your marriage on the basis of your strengths, not your weaknesses.

Strong marriages have two universal characteristics: (1) the partners know each other very well, and (2) the partners accept each other unconditionally. Nothing embalms a marriage faster than compelling your partner to conform to your own personality. Differences are dynamic. In courtships differences attract; don't allow them to repel during the long haul. Differences tend to irritate, but like the irritant of sand inside the oyster's shell, a pearl may result.

Howard & Jeanne Hendricks

How Can We Turn Our Differences Into Strengths?

PATRICIA GUNDRY

Many people are threatened by difference and do everthing they can to stamp it out. They subscribe to the identical-twin model of marriage. They do everything together—have the same friends, interests, and hobbies; eat the same food, and eventually dress alike and think the same thoughts.

The problem is that people who aren't identical twins by birth *are different* from each other. (Even identical twins are not exactly the same.) If they have to become the same, it means that one or both must give up larger and larger pieces of who they are to become clones of the other. So marriage is dehumanizing for these people. They feel they must give up themselves for the sake of the relationship.

That is a crime that should not be committed in the name of love, peace, order, or whatever excuse one gives for it. God did not create us in order to rob us of who we are. He created us with a tremendous individual potential, and I believe He intended us to nourish and develop and joyfully use that potential in order to become all we can be. It is God's gift to us, not to be given away or allowed to be stolen from us.

Actually, difference can be an advantage to marriage partners. Differences are fascinating to discover, to understand, and to use.

A few years ago I became interested in research on how the mind processes information, and I have read extensively in the field. Wanting to use what I was learning, I began to apply the information to people in my family to discover how their minds worked. One of the first things I discovered was that my husband was more different from me in the way he used his brain than I had thought.

Everyone receives, processes, and stores information through sensory channels. That is, we see, hear, feel, smell, and taste the world. If you could look (or listen, feel, smell, taste) into our mental filing cabinets you would find a full-spectrum printout that is sensory specific for all that is there. Though everyone stores information in all senses, each person seems to have a favorite channel.

I might prefer a visual way of storing experience, so when I want to retrieve information, I see it again. Or I might have an auditory tape of the information, hearing again conversations, thinking to myself verbally when I sort out ideas and come to conclusions. Or I might principally feel the world, remembering touch and sensation and bodily feeling.

I discovered that when my husband and I had conversations, I was thinking primarily visually and auditorially, while he was thinking kinesthetically (the feeling mode). He would talk slowly, give me time to feel the same thing he was feeling during long pauses, and wait for my response. But I was making pictures and quickly going on to further ideas. The visual thinker talks faster and leaps around like a rabbit with his or her ideas, while the kinesthetic thinker takes time, savoring the feeling.

They aren't speaking the same language either. I might use auditory or visual terms like "that sounds right to me" or "I see what you mean." For kinesthetic thinkers, on the other hand, it has to "feel right." They have to "get a handle on it." Some experiences might be *smooth* for them but *bright* for visually oriented people.

If you want to enjoy the differences between the two of you, first learn to detect them. Listen for words that are visual, auditory, or feeling oriented in the other person's conversation. Then translate what you say into his or her language. Match what you want to communicate to your partner's preferred mode of storage and retrieval.

Your spouse is like a tremendous reference work or research service. By approaching his or her differences from you as another way of operating in the world, you can have access to his or her perspective, skills, and information. If we can learn to respect difference in each other, then we can turn difference into an asset rather than a source of conflict.

The key, I am convinced, is respect. We must respect the right of the other person to be different from us. At the same time, we must respect our own differences too. For it must go both ways. If you do not respect your own uniqueness, you will allow it to be sacrificed to the other person. And that is not fair to either of you, nor does it respect God's gift to you of yourself.

Does this mean you should never change anything or never request a change from your partner? No, not at all. It means you must be respectful when making requests or when seeking to change yourself. Is the difference something that needs to be changed, or does only the way the difference is manifested need changing? Is a change needed to prevent harm to yourself or your partner, or is the proposed change only a preference or whim?

I've talked about only one kind of difference. There are many others: life experiences, parents, backgrounds, genetically determined traits, abilities. These differences can be a treasure house or a minefield. It all depends on whether we seek the disadvantages or the advantages of our differences.

Related Articles

Valuing the Differences Between Men and Women

GARY SMALLEY

Several years ago, after going through the section in Ephesians on husband-wife relationships, I decided I was going to wholeheartedly commit myself to my wife, to "become one flesh" with her as it says in Scripture (Eph. 5:31, KJV). But how could I demonstrate to her my willingness to spend more time with her and to build an intimate relationship?

Suddenly the idea hit me—shopping! Of course! My wife loves to shop, and even though I had never volunteered to go with her before, I could show her how much I care for her by getting a babysitter and going with her to the mall.

That evening as we walked around the shopping center, I got a real-life lesson in some of the common differences between men and women. What I learned that night began to change the way I related to my wife, and it's continued to be one of the most enriching concepts we've ever applied to our marriage.

As we walked into the mall, Norma told me she needed to look for a new summer blouse. After walking into the nearest women's clothing store, she held up a blouse and asked, "What do you think of this one?"

"Great," I said, "let's get it."

Then she picked up another blouse and said, "What do you think about this one?"

"It's great too," I said. "Get either one of them." But after looking at a number of other blouses, we walked out of the store without getting *any* of them!

Then we went into another store where she did the same thing, and then into another and another. All the time we were going into and out of all those shops, I was getting more and more anxious. Then, after looking at what seemed like hundreds of blouses, she held up a dress that was our daughter's size and said, "What do you think about this dress for Kari?"

I couldn't take it any longer. I blurted out, "What do you mean, a dress for Kari? We're here shopping for blouses for you, not dresses for Kari!" And if that wasn't bad enough, after we left that store without buying anything, she asked if we could stop, sit down and talk, and have coffee!

Do you know what I learned that night? I wasn't at the mall shopping for blouses with my wife. I was *hunting* for blouses. I wanted to conquer the blouse and then get back into the car and head home. My wife, however, looked at shopping from a very different angle. For her

185

it meant more than simply buying a blouse. It was a way to spend time communicating and sharing together as we enjoyed an evening away from the children.

Over the next several days, as I thought back to our shopping trip, I realized that for years I had heard about unisex haircutters, unisex clothing, and coed dorms. But in all the rush for equality of the sexes, I hadn't heard much about a major aspect of a healthy marriage—recognizing and valuing the differences between men and women. What are some of those differences, and why is it important to be aware of them?

Doctors and physiologists tell us that there are many differences between men and women. Some of the more obvious ones we all know about, but there are others that are less obvious. For example, many women have already recognized that men's skulls are thicker and their skin is thicker as well.

Men have at least 20 percent more red blood cells and muscle tissue in their body than women, which translates into greater brute strength. However, even though women don't seem to have the bursts of energy men do, they tend to be more resistant to heat and cold and to outlive men by several years. Yet

ARE YOU SAYING WHAT I THINK YOU'RE SAYING?

When I have a decision to make or a problem to solve, I like to think through the possibilities out loud.

My husband, by contrast, prefers to go off to some quiet place with a pen and paper and work out the pros and cons by himself.

For years, this personality difference led us to misunderstandings. I would make a statement ("Let's move to southern France"). David would assume I had thought it through, had decided this was what I wanted to do, and was expecting him to fall in. His reaction? Panic!

Or David would make a statement ("We need a new car"). Assuming he was opening a discussion, I would eagerly jump in. "We could do that," I'd say, "or with the same money we could take a family vacation in Tibet, or perhaps we could add a wing to the back of the house." David would sigh and go back to his quiet corner where he would begin listing the relative advantages of automatic and manual transmissions.

It took years, but we finally figured out what was going on. I am not unusually frivolous. He is not unusually stodgy. We simply enter conversations at different points.

I knew we were over the hump the day I brightly announced, "I'd like to adopt a child."

"Tell me," said David, "do you mean you have thought this through carefully and concluded that you would like to do this, or do you mean you would like to talk about this idea?"

"I'd like to talk," I said.

And we did. No panic, no accusations of impracticality or heartlessness. No child either—but then we haven't stopped talking yet.

LaVonne Neff

of all the differences between men and women, the area of communication is the one that is most crucially important to a healthy marriage.

Many experts now believe that from the time a baby is in the womb, the factors that help make that child distinctively male or female also affect the child's approach to communication later in life. From the first moments after birth, little girl babies have more lip and mouth movements than little boys. Girls usually talk earlier and are more expressive than boys.

In a Harvard study of several hundred preschoolers, the researchers discovered an interesting phenomenon. As they taped the children's playground conversation, they realized that 100 percent of the sounds coming from little girls' mouths were recognizable words used in conversation either with another child or with themselves. However, only 60 percent of the sounds coming from little preschool boys were recognizable words. The other 40 percent were yells and sound effects like "Vrrrooooom!" "Aaaaaaagh!" and, "Toot, toot!"

This difference persists into adulthood. Communication experts say that the average woman speaks over 25,000 words a day while the average man speaks only a little over 10,000. What does this mean in marital terms? Very often a man has already used up his 10,000 words at work by the time he gets home, while his wife is just warming up!

As I travel all across the country, I have asked several thousand women how much time they need to spend with their husbands in meaningful conversation. On average, a wife will say 45 min-utes to an hour *each day*. What do their husbands sitting next to them say is enough time for meaningful conversation? Fifteen to 20 minutes—*once or twice a week!*

If we are truly committed to valuing our life partners, one thing we need to do is understand and learn to appreciate their differences—particularly in the area of meaningful communication.

Because I'm committed to valuing my wife, ever since our shopping trip I have made a decision to look at shopping and other shared activities as opportunities to communicate, not to conquer. I can truthfully say that while shopping still isn't my favorite thing to do, today I can actually share how I feel about certain items she'll hold up in a store. I can even sit down and have coffee and talk!

When God created man, He designed within him the need for a helper, a completer (see Gen. 2:18). One area where most men need help is in sharing their emotions, feelings, dreams, and needs with their wives. In response, God seems to have given woman more of a natural bent toward meaningful communication. While many a man doesn't realize it, right under his roof is a built-in communication manual—his wife.

It took a shopping trip for me to realize I needed to slow down and start learning how to communicate. However, as I made a decision to value my wife's natural differences and even learn from them, we took a giant step toward building the kind of "one flesh" relationship Paul pictures for us in Ephesians 5.

Related Articles
Chapter 6: Making the Most of Your Differences
Chapter 9: Why Men and Women Have Trouble Communicating With Each Other

Making the Most of Your Differences

CHARLES M. SELL

Things that go together are often very different: peaches and cream or a violin and a bow. Some of these have been used to illustrate marriage: a lock and a key, for example. Biblical marriage results from the union of opposites. Two halves become one whole. When God created the woman for Adam, she had to be somewhat like him: "bone of my bones and flesh of my flesh" (Gen. 2:23). But she also qualified because she was different: "a helper suitable for him" (v. 18). The word *suitable* means that she was opposite to him and therefore complementary. Being his sexual opposite, female, she could couple with him, the male.

There are differences besides our being male and female that attract a man and a woman to each other. We tend to marry people who have different traits. For example, a man who struggles with depression may fall for a lighthearted woman. Lighthearted Lisa keeps depressive Dan's spirits up, and he loves her for it. A poorly organized woman may be drawn to a highly disciplined man, and the well-disciplined person brings some order into his partner's otherwise chaotic life.

After marriage, the very things that brought two people together often drive them apart. Lisa gets tired of always pulling Dan out of the emotional pits. The poorly organized wife wishes her husband could be more spontaneous. Or else her husband begins to pressure her to be more neat and orderly. Each tends to blame the other for the conflict that erupts. Instead of criticizing each

other for the differences, however, couples need to learn how to capitalize on them.

First, they need to recognize that some of the diversity is due to being male and female. Physically, men and women differ in every cell of their bodies. They differ in skeletal structure, and the woman has a shorter head and broader face. Woman's blood contains fewer red cells, making her tire more easily than man and more prone to faint than he. Woman has a larger stomach, kidneys, liver, and appendix, but smaller lungs. Woman has several very important functions totally lacking in man— menstruation, pregnancy, and lactation. There are scores of other differences, all of which may influence the way each sex feels and behaves. For instance, the reproductive organs are inside the woman's body, but outside the man's. This may be partly why a woman views sex in a more personal way than a man does.

Either because of the way they were brought up or because of actual distinctions between male and female brains, the sexes may even think differently. A wife may think in broader terms, being more aware of what is happening around her, while her husband tends to see things separately, concentrating on one thing at a time. A woman may think about her husband all during the day and not be able to understand why he says his mind was too occupied to include thoughts of her. Brain differences may also explain why a woman wants sex and romance together, while a man can be ready to make love without much personal contact beforehand.

Above all, husbands and wives need to accept each other with their differences. They should not pressure each other to change. This is one of the joys of marriage: learning to receive and know fully a person unlike oneself. Accepting the differences can enable the partners to capitalize on them instead of allowing them to conflict. Suppose one of them decides things logically while the other depends on feelings. No doubt these two approaches will create frequent clashes. But if they accept each other, the couple will see that they have two ways of looking at every issue instead of just one.

A couple should also avoid competing with one another. Ever hear a man and wife argue over who has the best memory for detail? "It happened on Thursday," she says. "No," he retorts. "It was Friday." Instead of arguing, they should allow the differences to work for them. Not long after our marriage, I learned that my wife's memory for details was far superior to mine. Through frequent arguments with her, I soon discovered she was right 98 percent of the time. I finally developed a genuine appreciation for her memory. Whenever we have to move a sofa out of the house, for example, I can go to her for help. She usually remembers which door we brought it in and even how we turned it to get it through the doorway.

Like a lock and a key or a violin and a bow, two married persons are more than the sum of the two of them. "One plus one equals three" is the way one person put it. Each person brings strengths to the marriage that often complement the other's weaknesses. When each permits the other to be what he or she was meant to be, nearly total oneness is possible. But if you stifle each other or fail to assert yourself, you prevent your marriage from being all it could be.

Of course, not all differences are handled easily. Sometimes differences make it hard to adjust, such as when an introvert marries an extrovert. One always wants to be out with people, and the other is content to stay home and read. Besides demanding a good dose of tolerance, such cases make it necessary for a couple to deal positively with conflict. Many differences, however, lead to needless strife because we tend to want to change our mates into our image instead of fully appreciating them as they are.

Related Articles
   Chapter 1: Love as Honoring Each Other
   Chapter 6: Valuing the Differences Between
      Men and Women

To Study Each Other Is to Understand

CAROLE MAYHALL

She raised her eyes skyward in a look of hopelessness and frustration. "I'm so upset!" she rasped. "Every night he comes home, plops himself on the davenport, tunes out all four kids, and reads the paper. Meanwhile I'm trying to get supper on the table, and the kids are all over me in the kitchen. And he just *sits* there. Finally I get so mad I go over to him and yell, 'Pick a kid—any kid!' "

I suppressed a smile and said, "What does he do then?"

"Oh, he gets angry."

"What would he do if, when he came home after you've had an exhausting day, you asked him gently to help with the children?"

"Why, he'd do it."

"Then what is the reason you don't ask him right away?" I queried.

She grimaced and said what dozens of wives have said to me over the years, "Well, he should *know* how I feel!"

Even after being married to me for 37 years, Jack still looks at me at times and says with a grin, "Honey, I can't read your mind."

And after 37 years, I still think sometimes, "But you should be able to by now." However, my next thought is this: "That's right. And I shouldn't have expected you to."

Jack and Carole Mayhall. Color them different. Very different.

Jack is nearsighted. I am farsighted.

When Jack is nervous, he gets quiet. When I get nervous, I talk faster.

Jack is objective, logical, and fact-oriented. I am subjective, emotional, and people-oriented. He tends to be an introvert; I tend to be an extrovert. Jack wants tapes organized, suitcases in the car arranged just so, and his life well-ordered. I throw Christmas cards in a basket; only *I* can find anything on my desk; and who has time to organize tapes anyhow?

For many years these differences were a source of irritation. Now they are a source of learning how to complete each other, to change, to let God put the principle of "as iron sharpens iron, so one man sharpens another" (Prov. 27:17) to work in our lives and fashion us to be more like Jesus.

The difference? We began to *study* each other. We did this by first praying for God's wisdom (He alone really knows that spouse and will give us the insight we need to understand).

We grew through hours, days, and weeks of talking and being vulnerable to each other.

We studied each other by analyzing happenings, even conflicts, to see why we responded so differently.

Both of us had to study ourselves in order to explain ourselves to the other. Jack needed to work harder at this because he wasn't able to express his feelings as easily as I.

Avid readers, we made use of temperament tests, personality profiles, and the zillions of helps available in articles and books today. We learned from them about ourselves and each other. And then we talked some more, comparing notes, exploring the reasons behind our individualistic behaviors.

As we studied, we learned that Jack responds to situations as a choleric/melancholic and I as a sanguine/phlegmatic. We realized that Jack tends to draw strength from being alone and I sometimes draw strength from being with people, though I need my alone times too. We found that Jack's capacity for relationships works best with a smaller group of people than mine; that his habits are more disciplined; that he wants lots of tender, loving care when he is sick and I want to hole up in a shaded room with no one talking. We discovered that celebrations are more important to me, active sports to him. In learning these differences and many others, we have worked hard to change, to grow, and to expand our perspectives of each other, which in turn enables us to help, adapt to, and adjust to each other.

The study of one's partner is a lifetime occupation. We as individuals are always changing, so we'll never have another person totally figured out. But part of the wonderful adventure of marriage is to study one's partner until you actually know that person as well as you know yourself. Now that's a challenge!

Related Articles
Chapter 1: Love as Friendship
Chapter 6: Making the Most of Your Differences

Who Is That Person I Married?

DALE HANSON BOURKE

Television interviewers have the uncanny ability of getting celebrities to spill secrets to the world that they wouldn't tell their own mothers. That's because professional interviewers look interested, take time, and ask questions about what the celebrities know most about—themselves.

If after years of marriage we still don't know much about our spouses, maybe it's because we haven't asked the right questions.

Here are some questions a talk-show host might ask. Try them on your spouse. Ask your spouse to try them on you. Try them on yourself.

Don't answer the way you think you should: be honest. The point of this exercise is to help your spouse learn who you are, to learn who your spouse is, and maybe even to learn about yourself.

And don't limit yourself to two-word answers. Feel free to explain your answer, to give examples, to tell a story it reminds you of. Keep in mind that this is a talk-show game, not an oral examination!

1. What kinds of books do you like to read (suspense, romance, biography, self-help, etc.)?
2. What magazines do you like to read?
3. What are your favorite TV shows?
4. What movies have you enjoyed most?
5. What leisure activities do you enjoy?
6. In what type of clothing are you most comfortable (business suit, blue jeans, jogging suit, etc.)?
7. What type of music do you enjoy?
8. What is your favorite sport?
9. What type of work do you enjoy?
10. What relaxes you?
11. Whom do you admire?

GIFTS AND BEHAVIOR

I am beginning to realize how our gifts affect our behavior and reactions. For instance, I have learned that some women whose husbands have the gift of mercy misinterpret that gift. They feel their husbands are not the spiritual head of the home. Why? Because a man with the gift of mercy may have a hard time confronting the workman who does a sloppy job, disciplining the children, and even facing conflict with his wife.

A husband, on the other hand, may not recognize his wife's gift of administration. She may be able to handle finances (and the checkbook) far better than he, but because he views her gift not as a gift but as an attempt to take over the leadership, he muddles through their financial affairs instead of delegating this task to his wife and using and appreciating the gift God has given her.

To study our partner's gift or gifts is vital in relating to one another in a loving, understanding way and in *completing* each other as God would desire.

Carole Mayhall

12. What famous people would you like to meet?

13. What is your favorite time of day?

14. Who are your favorite people?

15. What do you like most about yourself?

Take a minute to review your answers. What have you learned about your spouse? What have you learned about yourself?

I've reminded myself to appreciate some of my favorite people, places, and things a little more. My husband and our children are my favorite people in the whole world. It's a good feeling to put them in that perspective. And I think I'll get up early tomorrow and watch the sun rise. After all, early morning is my favorite time of day, and lately I've forgotten to simply enjoy it.

Related Articles

Chapter 1: Love as Togetherness
Chapter 6: To Study Each Other Is to Understand

Respecting Each Other's Gifts

DAVID & GAIL VEERMAN

Each Christian has a unique gift-mix—a blend of God-given desires, abilities, and spiritual gifts. Often, however, we do not respect the other person's uniqueness, expecting him or her to be exactly like us. If, for example, I have the gift of teaching, I might expect others to have this same gift and become impatient with their lack of skill or effectiveness. C. Peter Wagner calls this "gift projection."

There is also the distinction between "spiritual gifts" and Christian responsibilities. All Christians have the responsibility to tithe, but not everyone has the gift of "giving." All Christians have the responsibility to tell others about Christ, but not all have the gift of "evangelism."

Both of these factors affect marriage. It is easy for one person to project his or her gifts on the spouse, causing tension and dissension. And it may lead to feelings of guilt because a person doesn't think he or she is being "spiritual enough." If, for example, John has the gift of evangelism, he may expect Sue to become involved in the church's evangelism program and to join the calling team. Because it is difficult to argue against someone who is quoting Scripture, Sue may feel pressured and guilty. Or Joanne may have the gift of giving and can't understand why Peter isn't more generous.

A common area of tension is in how each spouse views the home. Every Christian has the responsibility to be hospitable, but not everyone has the gift of "hospitality." Reared in a home that featured a steady stream of students, missionaries, and needy folks passing through the doors, sitting at the dinner table, and sleeping in the beds, Frank couldn't understand why Jackie was reluctant to have anyone over, even for dessert. He even accused her of being materialistic and, in weaker moments, would say that she loved her furniture more than people. This was a real struggle for Jackie. She liked nice things, and her home was her place to decorate and to live in. She wondered about the truth of Frank's accusations, but she also knew that if she left it up to him, the place would be a wreck. He could live, sleep, and eat anywhere.

Of course there is the constant tension between "stewardship" and "owner-

192

ship" that each of us must resolve. Everything we have belongs to God—He merely has given us temporary use of them. It is our responsibility to use them well. But the conflict between Frank and Jackie centered more around their understanding of Christian responsibilities and gifts. Eventually, through much prayer and discussion, Jackie began to loosen her hold on the home, and Frank found an outlet for his gift of hospitality at the monthly church socials and by taking people to lunch.

In your home and marriage, watch out for "gift projection." Your marriage should be a team effort of glorifying God with your life together, not a battlefield of competing gifts.

Related Articles
Chapter 1: Love as Teamwork
Chapter 6: Living With Differing Capacities

Living With Differing Capacities

JERRY & MARY WHITE

JERRY: We sat side by side on our bed, the only private place available in our home that evening as people crowded in for a potluck dinner and Bible study. I had just suggested another activity for the following evening, making eight nights in a row that our home would be used for social or ministry functions. Tears rolled down Mary's cheeks. She said, "I can't keep up this pace. I want to, but I'm not superwoman. The schedule is just too heavy. Can't you understand how I feel?" There was desperation in her voice.

MARY: I felt guilty. We both wanted to serve God. But with four young children, an active ministry to people, and supporting Jerry in his career, I just didn't have the energy. I thought I should. Jerry tried to understand, but he seemed to have so much more energy than I had.

JERRY: For years I didn't really understand. After Mary and I had been married for about 8 or 10 years, I began to understand her limitations, strengths, capabilities, and mindset. Finally I began to see that my drives, capacity, and pace could not be Mary's. And God worked in both our lives. Looking at her schedule and responsibilities, I began to realize that she had great capacity for certain things and I for others. I also saw that my frantic pace and schedule were not always focused. Mary would ask, "Why?" and I often would only say, "Because I think we should." Hardly a good enough reason.

MARY: I think the breakthrough came in a discussion one Saturday. I was trying to explain to Jerry that our schedule was so crowded with activities, *good* activities, that we had little or no time to spend with each other. "All you have to do is ask for time with me," Jerry said. Through tears I told him, "I shouldn't have to *ask*." Jerry looked stunned for a moment and finally said, "You're right."

A simple fact stands out. Few husbands and wives possess the same *capacity*—a term we define as "the amount of activity, relationships, emotional stress, and physical stress a person can handle over a long period of time without wearing out."

Capacity relates intricately to natural and spiritual gifts, personality traits, age, current and past physical health, and family circumstances. People differ greatly. No one can expect another to be able to do the same things he or she does. In marriage these differences surface and result in periods of conflict, often lasting years before they are identified. Often, still more years are needed to reach agreement and understanding.

We cannot generalize one pattern for men and another for women. However, circumstances often affect men's and women's capacities in predictable ways.

For instance, a wife often feels the brunt of the physical load of raising small children as well as the emotional load of raising teenagers. She also does most of the physical work around the house (we are not saying this is the way it *should* be). And men wonder why their wives don't have the physical energy they think they ought to have!

Men traditionally have borne the family's financial burdens. Now, however, with more women in the work force, both husbands and wives are often drained by their jobs.

Let's examine some specific differences in capacity which can cause stress and conflict:

1. *Relationships.* One spouse thrives on many relationships, usually of limited depth. Another wants fewer, but deeper, relationships. One person handles social events and fleeting acquaintances with ease, while another dreads a social event where many of the people are strangers. One person likes to share openly and bluntly; another values privacy and caution in direct personal dialogue. Some are more comfortable with their own sex than with the opposite sex, or vice versa. One spouse loves to invite several people into the home, while the other wants only one or two people—or none at all.

2. *Schedule.* One person packs as much in the schedule as any day, week, or month will bear, leaving no free space at all. Another person needs flexibility and open space. One likes to work hard on one thing, while the other thrives on many varied activities in a day. One schedules so heavily that it becomes totally impossible to do all that is planned.

The other finds that kind of schedule physically and emotionally draining. One prefers a day or a week carefully lined out, and reacts badly to changes or surprises. The other likes to set a general list and flex with the tempo of the day.

3. *Physical stamina.* Some people seem to never wear out. They go hard and long and refresh themselves with a few hours of sleep. Others must get additional rest or they simply wear down faster. Some have excellent health and recuperative ability. Others are prone to illness or weakness. One person tires from physical exertion, another from emotional exertion. Physically, we are *not* created equal. We each tire from different activities at different rates.

4. *Emotional capacity.* People vary a great deal in their ability to handle conflict, to meet children's incessant questions and demands, to adjust to a new location, job, or home. Some need to talk extensively about their feelings, while others internalize their feelings. Some people are adventurous and unafraid of new experiences, while others value the familiar. Some rise to emergencies, while others panic.

People have different expectations of their spouses regarding communication, expressions of love, orderliness. A person's family background can make him or her emotionally sensitive to particular issues such as disagreement, financial security, and sex.

These preferences are not right or wrong. They just *are*. But when the differences occur in a marriage we each need to grow, change, and compromise within limits. What limits? Only you can determine that.

Knowing is the first step to understanding. We suggest that you talk about the preceding items that fit each of you. Pray over your differences and thank God for the way He made you.

Then ask your mate, "Which of these areas do you want me to change and grow in?" Then discuss *how* you can grow—but with great understanding and sensitivity. We believe you can increase and change your capacity, but only by a moderate amount. Each of you, however, can curb your personal tendencies that push your spouse past his or her endurance.

You are unique, both as individuals and as a couple. You have different capacities in many areas, sometimes varying greatly. It is God's plan that we understand and adjust to one another for the greatest contribution to His kingdom, as well as for our personal happiness and joy.

Don't make life miserable by constantly pushing one another past the brink of personal capacity. Let your uniqueness as a couple be forged as you blend your capacities. Allow each other to use capacities independently when it does not hinder the relationship. Be sensitive to one another. Give preference to one another. Honor one another. Live with each other in an understanding way (1 Peter 3:7).

Related Articles
Chapter 6: Respecting Each Other's Gifts
Chapter 6: To Study Each Other Is to Understand

STRENGTHS AND WEAKNESSES

They sat across from me in our living room, a bit nervous, holding hands, and occasionally glancing at each other as they spoke. "What attracted you to Don?" I asked.

Ginnie responded quickly. "Oh, that's easy. He's so strong, quiet, and self-assured—and I'm so flighty. I really love his steady, quiet confidence!"

"And what about you, Don," I said, turning to the husband-to-be. "What attracted you to Ginnie?"

"I guess it was her outgoing personality. She's so enthusiastic and effervescent—and I'm so conservative and boring."

I then had to reveal the uncomfortable truth that "strong, quiet, and steady" is often very "boring," and that "enthusiastic and effervescent" can bear a striking resemblance to "flighty." The truth is that every attribute has a flip side; every strength *is* a weakness. And the very qualities that attract one person to another before marriage tend to drive him or her crazy during marriage.

There's not a whole lot you can do about this except be prepared. No one is perfect, not even that one to whom you have pledged your undying devotion and at whom you now look with eyes of love. Before the wedding, you see only the strengths and are blind to the weaknesses. Afterward, you often see only the glaring weaknesses and forget about the strengths.

Try reversing that tendency. Before you marry, prepare yourself for the weaknesses. Then, after the wedding, focus on your partner's strengths.

Dave Veerman

Birth Order and Marriage

KEVIN LEMAN

Swiss psychologist Alfred Adler is credited in most circles with being the first to recognize the importance of one's family position to one's personality. The first-born child, for example, tends to have some personality traits like those of other first-born children. Likewise, middle children, only children, and the baby of the family have traits in common.

Specifically, first borns are achievers and perfectionists—no doubt because they get a lot of concentrated attention from their parents during their earliest years. They get high SAT scores and become good readers. If there is an accountant or engineer or dentist or airline pilot on the horizon, chances are it's going to be a first-born child. First borns are goal-oriented, structured, and reliable. They make a lot of lists. In fact, some have lists of their lists!

Middle children, squeezed on all sides, learn to negotiate and compromise as a way of life. Maybe that's why they tend to be the best adjusted of all the birth orders. When in doubt, marry a middle child—they tend to be most monogamous. George Burns and Bob Hope are middle children, and few Hollywood marriages could rival the longevity of their marriages.

"Babies" learn to be good attention getters at a very young age. Because they tend to be written off, they often develop a fierce sense of competition. Often they are late bloomers, and many of them feel nobody ever gives them credit for growing up. Babies are charmers and manipulators who could sell a dead rat if they had to.

And only children are like first borns, only more so.

When I first heard this theory, it made a lot of sense to me. My own family was a perfect example of it. My oldest sister, the first born, never got anything less than an A, and she still irons the davenport in her spare time. My brother was a rough-and-tumble middle child, and I— the baby of the family—graduated near the bottom of my high-school class but was very good at entertaining people. Seeing my own children unfold further convinced me of the truth of the theory.

What effect does birth order have on marriage?

When we start talking about matching up people in marriage according to birth order, it sounds a little strange. You meet someone, say "Hi, how are you— and by the way, where were you in your family?" Still, knowing how birth order affected your spouse may help you understand him or her.

One researcher, for example, found that the best bet in a husband is the youngest male in a family with older sisters, and the best bet in a wife is the youngest female in a family with older brothers. Why? Because both of these people are going to be very sensitive to members of the opposite sex. They have to be in order to survive!

In my opinion, the first born and the baby are natural friends and make a good combination in marriage. Any time you go outside your own birth order, in fact, you are on safe ground. When people marry outside their birth order, they set up a natural check-and-balance system. The fun-loving baby loosens up the structured first born; the diplomatic middle child helps the only child look at other people's feelings as well as at the unbending rules.

Put two people in the same birth order together, and you're likely to have problems. The most disastrous relationships that walk through the door of my office are certainly two first borns. That doesn't mean two first borns can't make it—my older sister is married to another first born, and they've been happily married for over 30 years. But when you put two perfectionists together, they tend to blame each other for every imperfection they find. They butt heads like two mountain sheep fighting for territorial rights. And they often try to control each other. First borns need to develop the courage to be imperfect, to accept the fact that things aren't always going to go just the way they want them to.

Two middle children may be so diplomatic that they refuse to face up to real problems in their marriage until it's too late. They avoid confrontation, and so their relationship cannot grow. They squirrel away their feelings, and before long their communication has broken down. Middle children need to learn to verbalize their feelings, to let some air out of the balloon before it pops.

Two babies sit around waiting for the other to take the lead. In the meantime they're having lots of fun, but they also may be going deeply in debt. Since babies tend to think of themselves too often and not often enough of others, they need to focus on doing something really unselfish for each other or for someone in their community.

Of course, even when you marry outside your birth order you can have problems. The first born is naturally a good caregiver, and the baby is naturally a taker. This can lead to a neurotic relationship.

My wife is a first born and I'm a baby. When we first married, I remember praying, "Lord, thank You for giving me this wonderful woman to take care of me—to pick up my socks, to fix me canned

ROMANS 12:3-8

Do not think of yourself more highly than you ought, but rather think of yourself with sober judgment in accordance with the measure of faith God has given you. Just as each of us has one body with many members, and these members do not all have the same function, so in Christ we who are many form one body, and each member belongs to all the others. We have different gifts, according to the grace given us. If a man's gift is prophesying, let him use it in proportion to his faith. If it is serving, let him serve; if it is teaching, let him teach; if it is encouraging, let him encourage; if it is contributing to the needs of others, let him give generously; if it is leadership, let him govern diligently; if it is showing mercy, let him do it cheerfully.

peas but not frozen, to treat me just like Mom did." Fortunately, about two years into our marriage, she very gently but firmly told me I was going to have to grow up. First borns and babies are a good match, but not if they take their natural tendencies to extremes. Balance is the key to a good marriage.

You don't marry someone because of his place in his family, of course, but understanding why he acts the way he does can be a big help in living with him after the wedding. Birth order also helps you understand why you act the way you do, and can give you ideas for where you both need to grow.

Related Articles
Chapter 6: Making the Most of Your Differences
Chapter 6: To Study Each Other Is to Understand

The MBTI

LaVONNE NEFF

Over 50 years ago, a reserved, imaginative, sensitive, and curious young woman named Isabel Briggs married a quiet, matter-of-fact, logical, and decisive young man named Clarence Myers. It was a good match that lasted a lifetime. But Isabel and Clarence were different from each other in almost every respect, and their differences fueled Isabel's interest in work her mother, Katharine Briggs, had already begun—studying and cataloguing personality types.

Today the Myers-Briggs Type Indicator (MBTI), a questionnaire based on the theories of Carl Jung as well as the observations of Katharine and Isabel, is the most widely used evaluator of personality type in the United States. Often used in businesses, churches, and marital and personal counseling, it has helped many people say, "Now I know why he acts that way—and how I should relate to him."

On the MBTI, there are no good or bad answers. Isabel Myers was committed to Paul's idea in Romans 12 that we all have different gifts, and that each gift is valuable in God's service. Thus the questionnaire does not analyze whether people are normal or abnormal, bright or slow, strong or weak. Instead, it helps them discover ways they are most comfortable conducting their lives in four different areas.

One of the most obvious of personality differences is between those who focus on the outer world and those who turn inward to do their best work. *Extroverts* prefer to operate in the outer world of people, places, things, events, and situations; while *introverts* are far more at ease in the inner world of sense impressions, ideas, dreams, and private thoughts.

Another key difference is in the way people perceive the world: how they take in information about it. *Sensers* are practical, present-oriented, matter-of-fact realists who rely on the evidence of their five senses. *Intuiters* are more interested in possibilities than actualities, more in tune with the future than the present. Information comes to them in the form of flashes of insight, hunches, and sudden understanding.

People not only perceive the world, they also make decisions and act on what they see. *Thinkers* prefer to use logical analysis in their decision-making; *feelers* are more comfortable with human-oriented value judgments.

Finally, people tend to deal with the world around them either with their favorite judging function (that is, thinking or feeling) or with their favorite perceiving function (sensing or intuiting). *Perceivers,* who like to gather information, are often adaptable and spontaneous; *judgers,* who like to act on what they know, are likely to be well-organized and decisive.

These 4 pairs of characteristics can be combined in 16 ways, giving 16 different personality types. In marriage, opposites often attract—but they may have trouble understanding each other.

For example, imagine an extroverted woman who is home with three preschoolers all day. When her introverted husband comes home from work, he wants to burrow into the nearest cave; she wants to go out or invite friends in. Suppose she is a sensing type, and having a beautiful home is extremely important to her. When her husband walks in the door, he could see daffodils on the table, smell bread in the oven, and hear Mozart on the CD player. He doesn't, however; he is an intuiting type, and his mind is filled with plans for reorganizing his office that will revolutionize his department's output.

Imagine that she is a thinker and he is a feeler. The children have been bickering, and she has punished them by isolating them in their rooms, where even now they are audibly sobbing. She is not disturbed; she believes they will profit from the separation and will behave more reasonably all evening. Her husband, however, is a feeler who can't stand sadness and disharmony. He sneaks up to each little criminal's room to offer a warm hug and a cookie.

Finally, suppose he is a judger and she is a perceiver. She has prevailed; they are going out. He suggests the movie at the corner theater. She says, "Yes, that would be nice, but let's see what's showing at Cinema 8. Or maybe we should go out to eat. Unless you'd rather go bowling. Or what about visiting the O'Briens?"

In MBTI terminology, she's an ESTP; he's an INFJ. Most couples are not such complete opposites, but few couples are alike in all four areas. And each couple's differences have great potential for good or for ill.

If personality differences lead to fights, accusations, and unwillingness to work together, they can bring down a marriage. But if they lead to variety and richness and balance, they can strengthen it. As Isabel Myers observed about her own marriage, "We realized our differences could be either annoying or amusing. I decided to be amused."

Opposites can be extremely helpful to each other. Extroverts married to introverts can help their spouses and themselves find a good balance between the inner world and the outer world. Sensers can help intuitives pay attention to reality, and intuitives can help sensers see possibilities. Thinkers can help feelers analyze a situation; feelers can help thinkers see what's really important. Perceivers can help judgers slow down and look at the evidence; judgers can help perceivers quit gathering information and make a decision.

Now that my husband and I understand each other's personality types, we are more likely to appreciate each other's strengths. What's more, our communication with each other has improved.

For example, as an introvert, he carefully thinks through his ideas before announcing or proposing them. As an extrovert, I find it hard to think anything through without talking about it. The other day I threw down this conversation starter: "Let's adopt a child."

In years past, my husband would have turned pale, assuming he was hearing what I really wanted to do. He then would have marshaled all available evidence to persuade me that I was mistaken, and I would have taken the defensive. This time, enlightened by personality type theory, he tried a different approach.

"Are you telling me you want to adopt a child," he said, "or are you in extrovert fashion suggesting that this would be an interesting subject to talk about?"

"Let's talk," I said. We did. Our conversation was friendly. He actually got interested in adoption, even as I began to back away from the idea. The final decision isn't in, but at least we've been understanding each other at every step of the way.

From this brief description you may already recognize your own or your spouse's personality type. If you want to learn more about what type differences mean, how to use a knowledge of them to strengthen relationships, or where you can take the MBTI, contact the Center for Applications of Psychological Type,

2720 N.W. Sixth Street, Gainesville, Florida 32609.

Related Articles
Chapter 6: Making the Most of Your Differences
Chapter 6: To Study Each Other Is to Understand

WHEN EXTROVERTS MARRY INTROVERTS

According to some researchers, most couples whose personalities differ widely get along with each other no better and no worse than couples whose personalities are closer together. The ultra-logical and the highly subjective, the tightly structured and the laid-back—such "mixed" couples make happy marriages as often as anyone else. One difference, however, seems associated with problems: when an introverted man marries an extroverted woman.

Why should this be a problem? No one knows for sure. Introverts tend to think things through before acting, while extroverts often jump into new projects and reflect later. Perhaps extroverted wives tend to take the lead more often than their introverted husbands like.

Extroverts and introverts may see their home differently. If the man sees it as a refuge from all the people pressures at work, and the woman sees it as an entertainment center, conflict could ensue.

In fact, traditional work patterns could make this type of marriage uncomfortable. If the man works around people all day and the woman stays home, by 5 P.M. they may both be ready to bang their heads against the wall—or against each other.

Does this mean extroverted women and introverted men should never marry? Of course not. (My husband and I have been happily married for 20 years!) It means instead that such couples should allow themselves plenty of time—for the introvert—and conversation—for the extrovert—to explore their differences and find ways of turning them into assets.

LaVonne Neff

When a group of people live together, certain tasks just have to get done. How do you divide up the chores in your family? Circle the letter or symbol representing how you assign each task:

H = husband does it
W = wife does it
C = child or other family member does it
$ = you pay someone outside the family to do it
0 = nobody does it

You may circle more than one responsible party for each a task.
SUGGESTION: It can be very revealing to duplicate this list and ask each family member to fill it out. You may discover that someone in the family is doing far more or far less than his or her share. Or you may learn that everyone thinks someone else is going to do a particular job!

H W C $ 0	prepare breakfast		H W C $ 0	discipline children
H W C $ 0	clean up after breakfast		H W C $ 0	go to children's activities
H W C $ 0	prepare lunch			
H W C $ 0	clean up after lunch		H W C $ 0	chauffeur children
H W C $ 0	prepare dinner		H W C $ 0	care for sick children
H W C $ 0	clean up after dinner		H W C $ 0	launder clothing
H W C $ 0	cook for company		H W C $ 0	iron clothing
H W C $ 0	invite guests		H W C $ 0	take clothing to dry cleaner
H W C $ 0	arrange evenings out			
H W C $ 0	call the baby-sitter		H W C $ 0	mend clothing
H W C $ 0	chauffeur the baby-sitter		H W C $ 0	shop for clothing
H W C $ 0	clean the bathroom(s)		H W C $ 0	do home repairs
H W C $ 0	vacuum		H W C $ 0	wait for repairmen
H W C $ 0	dust		H W C $ 0	work full time
H W C $ 0	mop		H W C $ 0	work part time
H W C $ 0	sweep		H W C $ 0	plan vacations
H W C $ 0	empty wastebaskets		H W C $ 0	write thank-you letters
H W C $ 0	take out the garbage		H W C $ 0	keep in touch with relatives
H W C $ 0	wash windows			
H W C $ 0	pick up things that are left lying around		H W C $ 0	plan holidays
			H W C $ 0	schedule family activities
H W C $ 0	put gas in the car			
H W C $ 0	arrange for or do car repairs		H W C $ 0	answer phone
			H W C $ 0	set the table
H W C $ 0	mow the lawn		H W C $ 0	wait on the table
H W C $ 0	do other yard work		H W C $ 0	paint or wallpaper
H W C $ 0	pay bills		H W C $ 0	shovel snow
H W C $ 0	do taxes		H W C $ 0	plan menus
H W C $ 0	care for pets		H W C $ 0	shop for groceries
H W C $ 0	supervise children		H W C $ 0	lead family devotions
H W C $ 0	play with children		H W C $ 0	buy presents

7

ROLES AND EXPECTATIONS

"Because I am a woman does not make me a different Christian, but because I am a Christian it does make me a different woman." So spoke Elisabeth Elliot in explaining that relationships determine roles and roles create responsibility.

Confusion about men and women in our world is the result of ignorance and cultural seepage. We do not understand Scripture and what we understand is not Scripture. If we do not know what God expects, we do either the wrong thing or nothing at all.

The ancient wisdom of the Book of Proverbs pictures the husband valuing and praising the wife; she desires to be his most highly esteemed asset. "He who finds a wife finds what is good and receives favor from the Lord" (18:22). "A wife of noble character who can find? She is worth far more than rubies. Her husband has full confidence in her and lacks nothing of value. She brings him good, not harm, all the days of her life" (31:10-12).

Paul wrote of marriage as a mystery; a concept inaccessible to the unaided human mind. It is, he said, a structure for family functioning, a love relationship not locked into unrealistic expectations but performed with deep mutual caring for a lifetime. "Husbands, love your wives, just as Christ loved the church and gave Himself up for her. . . . Each one of you also must love his wife as he loves himself, and the wife must respect her husband" (Eph. 5:25, 33).

The love-submission interchange is God's theft-proof combination for lasting and satisfying marriage.

Howard & Jeanne Hendricks

Marriage as Mutual Servanthood

DWIGHT HERVEY SMALL

Is the notion of equal partnership in marriage compatible with what Ephesians 5:21-32 teaches about headship and submission? What genuine equality can there be when a husband is the head and his wife is subject to him? If the husband is head of the wife, won't this incline him to be a domineering partner? If he stands above her in some "chain of command," won't he be disposed to rule by the dictates of his own will?

God appointed separate roles for husbands and wives as the means by which an equal partnership can function. At first glance this seems strange. Doesn't

203

headship make husbands "more equal" than wives? And why only wives in subjection, never husbands? Scripture nowhere rescinds or reverses these roles—does this mean that wives, poor things, must knuckle under, play doormat, just obey the "commander"? In short, does God play sexual favorites in marriage? It doesn't seem fair!

Worse still, verse 22 says, "Wives, submit to your husbands as to the Lord." Verse 24 adds that she is to submit "in everything." It sounds as if husbands call all the shots, are in charge of everything—are, in fact, boss.

A beautiful paradox puts in balance this seeming inequality. Our first clue is in verse 21: "Submit to one another out of reverence for Christ." This means that each partner is subject to the other in ways that involve self-giving service.

This is no chain of command. What the husband gains as the head is a unique responsibility for the welfare and functioning of the marriage. He is accountable to God. Together with headship, God gives him the necessary authority to carry out his responsibility. He himself, however, exercises his headship under Christ's authority. Thus headship has no independent, self-assertive function. Nor is the husband's God-given authority *over* his wife, as some might suppose, but *on her behalf.* It is for her welfare, not his.

Headship functions as the love of Christ flows through the husband to his wife. Submission, likewise, functions as Christ's love flows through the wife to her husband. This reciprocal action is possible as both partners are committed to the Lord Jesus Christ, to each other, and to the mandate for marriage as presented in Ephesians.

A Christian couple has as their model Christ, the governing head of the church (Eph. 1:22). Ephesians 5:23-24 provides the analogy which helps us understand this model. The husband stands in the same relation to his wife as Christ does to the church: he is head. The wife stands in the same relation to her husband as the church does to Christ: she is subject to his headship.

Wives, don't bristle! This isn't the injustice it seems at first glance. Fully understood, headship doesn't give a husband an advantage but a responsibility. He isn't appointed to be lord and master, the resident autocrat, the heavy-handed boss. Nor is he privileged to make demands on his wife or assume personal rights over her. Neither does he have the prerogative to make all the important decisions, arbitrate all questions, initiate all plans, control all funds, and so forth. He cannot say, "See, the Bible says I'm in charge here—obey me!" How completely contrary that would be to the whole biblical concept.

Headship is for the purpose of maximizing a wife's potential for personal growth and fulfillment. Husbands are under the headship of Christ for the purpose of carrying out God's will in this respect, not their own. The husband is to relate to his wife in ways that enable her to fully utilize the gifts God has given her, to the end that their marriage might be all that God intends it to be. The key to headship is found in verse 25: "Husbands, love your wives, just as Christ loved the church and gave Himself up for her." What an incredible demand! The motivating force of headship is Christlike, self-giving love. Is there a wife anywhere who would not gladly submit to a love like that?

There is no room here for a husband to be manipulative, intimidating, or self-centered. No room for his taking advantage, getting back, putting down, or placing his own interests before his wife's. Instead, love builds her up; defers to her tastes, opinions, and feelings; brings out her gifts; and in every way encourages her personal development.

Christlike love results in a clearer vision of a wife's capabilities, such as being the better financial or home manager, the more capable leader, or perhaps the more competent adviser in various matters. In other words, wherever a wife has superior abilities, headship love encourages her to take the lead. Wherever she has similar abilities, partners may mutually agree to share responsibilities. This is headship working as it is intended to work.

While the wife's submission, according to this view, in no way diminishes her person or place, the question remains: is submission required only of wives? Or is there a sense in which husbands are subject to their wives? This is the paradox of headship which lies at the very heart of Ephesians 5:21-32.

Christ the head is also Christ the servant. Philippians 2:8 records how He, taking the nature of a servant, came in submission to His Father to give Himself for His bride, the church. This shows that love is always subject to the other person's needs and potential. When a husband and wife are obedient to the mandate in Ephesians, the Lord transforms a wife's submission into loving servanthood, at the same time transforming a husband's headship so that he becomes willingly subject to his wife in the same Christlike, loving servanthood.

To love one's wife as Christ loved the church is possible when one has surrendered any existing spirit of domination, any notion that one is top person in a chain of command. Only then can couples create a truly loving, equal, and mutually serving relationship.

Apart from Christ's model of headship as servanthood, headship would be insufferable. But with this God-appointed model, headship for husbands and submission for wives is transformed into something both workable and beautiful. In obedience to the model, Christian couples can be sure that God's mandate for marital roles carries an unimpeachable warranty for successful marriage.

Related Articles

Submission, Servanthood, and the Chain of Command

DONALD & ROBBIE JOY

The vertical structure of marriage—"the chain of command"—is a universal pattern in marriages, including Christian ones. It is not difficult to locate biblical foundations for the hierarchical power model. Here are a few:

"Your desire will be for your husband, and he will rule over you" (Gen. 3:16), spoken of the first marriage.

"Adam [re]named his wife Eve, because she would become the mother of all the living" (Gen. 3:20).

"Every man should be ruler over his own household" (Es. 1:22).

"Wives, submit to your husbands as to the Lord" (Eph. 5:22).

"Wives . . . be submissive to your husbands" (1 Peter 3:1).

The pattern of male dominance would appear to be the hallmark of God's order for marriage. But these biblical statements are all organized around the Fall, tragedy, and exploitation. Take a closer look at them:

The Genesis quotations are taken from the context of the curse and its consequences. They must be regarded as reflections of original sin, not of God's intention or will. God's intention was quite different. He created the man and woman as co-regents. Together they were to rule: "God blessed them and said to them, 'Be fruitful and increase in number; fill the earth and subdue it'" (Gen. 1:28).

The statement from Esther is the edict drafted by King Xerxes when he needed to save face with the men of his empire. Xerxes and his guests had been partying for 180 days when Queen Vashti refused to obey him. The word of her insubordination got out, and the king's guests were afraid to return home to their wives without a law to reinforce their patriarchal authority. It should be kept in mind that Xerxes was the immoral ruler of a heathen nation, and that Vashti may have refused to submit to him on moral grounds.

The Ephesians and 1 Peter passages must be wrested out of context to build any doctrine of hierarchy. In both passages the pattern of submission is intended to be bilateral. "Submit to one another out of reverence for Christ," the Ephesians passage begins, defying all justification of a vertical power structure (5:21). Peter starts by telling wives how to deal with painful relationships with unconverted husbands (3:1-6), and he closes his long discourse with a similar word to the men: "Husbands, *in the same way* . . ." (3:7). In short, he cautions that if men forget that their wives are "heirs with you of the gracious gift of life," their prayers will be hindered.

The Bible does not advocate a rigid power structure; it commands *servanthood*—Jesus' word for Paul's idea of submission. When we take Jesus seriously, this is the first and final command. It sets the stage for us to listen instead of to give orders. Active servanthood, rooted in self-respect and respect

EPHESIANS 5:24-33

Submit to one another out of reverence for Christ. Wives, submit to your husbands as to the Lord. For the husband is the head of the wife as Christ is the head of the church, His body, of which He is the Saviour. Now as the church submits to Christ, so also wives should submit to their husbands in everything. Husbands, love your wives, just as Christ loved the church and gave Himself up for her to make her holy, cleansing her by the washing with water through the word, and to present her to Himself as a radiant church, without stain or wrinkle or any other blemish, but holy and blameless. In this same way, husbands ought to love their wives as their own bodies. He who loves his wife loves himself. After all, no one ever hated his own body, but he feeds and cares for it, just as Christ does the church—for we are members of His body. "For this reason a man will leave his father and mother and be united to his wife, and the two will become one flesh." This is a profound mystery—but I am talking about Christ and the church. However, each one of you also must love his wife as he loves himself, and the wife must respect her husband.

for all other people, leads to mutual appreciation and harmony.

The chain-of-command advocates, by contrast, assume an adversarial relationship between husband and wife. "Do you know why a husband and a wife cannot have equal authority in a home?" runs their classic question. "It is because 'no man can serve two masters.'" Such a position betrays complete ignorance of God's order for marriage where two become one.

Where two become one, consensus orders decisions and active dialogue establishes policy. The mutual-respect marriage is characterized by servanthood and mutual submission. Two healthy people form a unit that combines differing gifts. Their sexual and personality differences guarantee a combined "full deck."

Two people enter into such a marriage noncompetitively and with reverence. They participate in their relationship spontaneously. Both of them listen and speak, receive and give. They can debate without name-calling or cutting down the other person.

And when the best they have has been offered all around, they consolidate, sift, and sort until they reach consensus. Then they can both own their eventual joint decision. No one has to cling to an individualistic, peevish, personal perspective. If they cannot arrive at consensus, their mutual respect is so deep that they agree not to make this decision at this time.

Any power structure that claims "somebody has to make the final decision" is guaranteed to start up feelings of inferiority, and to plant seeds of resentment that may someday grow and choke the marriage. It is far better to say, "If we cannot arrive at a consensus on this issue, then we have a deeper problem than the issue itself. Let's spend some energy on renewing our basic bond and increasing our respect for each other."

Related Articles
Chapter 1: Love as Honoring Each Other
Chapter 7: All

Handling Disagreement About Submission

PATRICIA GUNDRY

Some Christians earnestly believe that wives should submit to their husbands, while others just as sincerely believe that marriage partners should share equally in decision-making. What should you do if you, the wife, want an egalitarian marriage, while your husband expects you to submit to him?

First, make sure you understand what you want. I believe what all of us really want is to be treated as fully human. We do not want to be denied or put down or treated in any way that diminishes our full humanity. We want to be able to live before God as individuals, responsible directly to Him. We want the doctrine of the priesthood of the believer to apply to us as well as to anyone else in God's family. And I believe this is a right we have, given us by God.

Next, proceed wisely and respectfully. If you want to be regarded as fully human, you have to respect the full humanity of your husband as well. This means you give him the option of not changing. All men should have the right to *not* agree on this issue and still be respected as persons—even if they never change at all. Give your husband the option not to agree with you at all, ever. I don't see how you can do less if you want respect for your own individual choices.

Now that I've said that (and I think

such a stance is imperative to be fair), I'll share some ways to make it easier for your husband to change if he should ever want to.

1. *Don't bring up the subject.* I know this sounds frustrating and unreasonable, but it is usually unproductive to do so. Wait for the subject to arise naturally.

2. *Ask respectful questions.* If he says, "You have to do this because I am your husband and the Bible commands you to submit," get more information. Ask, "Where?" I am assuming here that you know enough about the biblical evidences to know that, in the original Greek, Ephesians 5:22 does not command wives to submit, and you can show him evidence of that. If you don't have such information, then your first task is to find it and understand it.

If he doesn't accept that evidence, ask, "Do you believe I must live by my own conscience before God?" In other words, find out more about what he honestly thinks.

3. *Find areas of agreement between you.* Even if it's difficult, keep looking until you do. For example, you both believe the Bible and want to know what it says and means. That's a good basis for studying the subject together, examining both sides of the issue.

4. *Share from your own experience.* Don't tell him what he needs to know in order to agree with you, or set him straight, or talk down to him, or otherwise try to convince him. Simply tell him from your own perspective what has happened to you. One cannot logically reject another person's experience.

5. *When it is asked for, share information from an observer-searcher position.* "I wondered about that, so I looked for an answer. This is what I found." Be prepared that your answer probably will not convince him, nor should you expect it to. He is coming from a different life experience and has different beliefs based on different foundations. But by telling him only your

own experiential knowledge, you are giving him room to think about what you have said rather than having to accept or reject an argument. Any disagreements then are with the source of information, not with you. In this way the issue is defused and taken from the personal (between the two of you) to the impersonal (between him and the source of the information).

6. *Give him room to change.* Beliefs are entwined with other beliefs and reinforced by many different experiences. Thus they do not usually change immediately. Your husband must have time and space to think about the information he is discovering and sort through his beliefs.

Women often do not understand that they were ready to change their minds on this subject because of many sensitizing and enlightening experiences they have had. Your husband has not had those experiences. Give him time and space to make changes at his own speed.

7. *In the meantime, remember what you share.* Your understanding of submission is not the only important thing in your life and relationship. Enjoy what there is to enjoy. You must have areas of mutual interest that give you pleasure. Focus on them while giving him time and space. I'm not saying to ignore the issue; just don't focus on it. Allow it its proper place in your relationship, but no more than that.

8. *Put concerns and requests in a positive frame. How* you approach a subject is an important part of bringing about change. It is mentally more difficult to process a negative request. Experiment with putting everything in a positive frame and make it easier for others to give you what you want from them. Instead of saying what you don't want, say what you do want.

There is one extremely important condition to all this kindness and consideration and patience on your part: through it all you must be true to yourself 24 hours a day. Do not give away your full personhood. Do not allow yourself less than full respect from yourself. Others do not have to regard you as fully human, but you must. So even if you and your husband continue to disagree, live responsibly before God as an individual. Love and respect all of who you are, not allowing yourself to be demeaned or harmed in any way that it is in your power to prevent. Grant yourself the full personhood you desire as a matter of course; it will guide you in making many small choices daily.

And I must add this: make sure you understand the difference between a disagreement between the two of you about submission, and oppression by someone who wants to control and dominate you or hurt you. If you are in danger emotionally or physically, protect and care for yourself. Meet your needs for wholeness and health.

But if you merely disagree, don't interpret it as oppression. Make changes wisely and respectfully. Give your husband what you want for yourself—allow him to be fully responsible for his own behavior and beliefs while you are fully responsible for yours.

Related Articles
Chapter 7: All
Chapter 10: Handling Conflict—Good Ways and Bad

Who's Really the Boss?

JANETTE OKE

The issue of who has the right to be in charge of the home has been bandied about a fair bit in the last decade. Many people much more qualified than I have gone to great lengths to present their case. I am not going to attempt to defend my position, only to share with you my experience. And as I am a woman, it will be from a woman's perspective.

I was brought up to believe that the man was the head of the household. I had no argument with that. We children recognized our dad as the final authority, and he wore his authority well. He did not use it to get his way, to dominate, or to bully. As a child, I would not have thought of challenging him. I feared him.

Since growing up, I have wondered why. I never had one spanking from him. He rarely even raised his voice. The fear was all wrapped up in love—I just did not want to displease him. He is gone now, but his memory is one of my cherished treasures. He made it so easy for me to understand a Heavenly Father who gives love unsparingly and yet demands high standards.

When I married, it was easy for me to accept the role of helpmate, with my husband having the final authority and responsibility. I did not particularly want the responsibility, so I was happy to give it over to my husband. That meant I also needed to give him the authority. I did not want a wishy-washy man for a husband. I wanted someone with backbone.

It sounded like such a good arrangement. I had forgotten only one thing— my will. For some reason our ideas, goals, and desires did not always quite mesh. There was a bit of iron in my own backbone; I had ideas too. It was not always easy to give in. But I tried to follow the scriptural pattern and yield to my husband.

209

For many of the years of our marriage I considered myself an obedient, submissive wife. Then we had some special meetings in our church and I suddenly saw clearly that I was not submissive at all. I merely gave in with reluctance and feelings of "OK, do it your way—but you'll be sorry." Then I proceeded to put the heat on in a number of sly little ways. I did not rant and rave; silence is more my style.

When I realized that submission is more an attitude than an act, I decided I'd best do something about the attitude I had carried for so many years.

I managed, with God's help, to *choose* to be in submission to my husband, not because it was decreed, but because of my love for him. My whole feeling about our marriage relationship changed. It was easier to bend, to compromise. Yet, strangely enough, it was not as necessary as the days went by. He was yielding on issues too.

I suppose I have heard all the arguments, pro and con, concerning male authority in the home. The arguments are often presented with a great deal of feeling, and accompanying the discussion is much tension and unhappiness. It is apparent that giving another person, any person, authority over us is a difficult thing to do.

I guess I have heard all the reasons why a more workable arrangement is 50-50 sharing. Some reasons sound so logical, so workable; and for some couples, the arrangement has worked. They have managed to hit a fairly good balance in shifting the authority back and forth. There are some problems with this solution, however, and I would like to state a few.

1. *All couples are not created equal.* People interact differently. If one of the parties is just a little more assertive or self-oriented, the balance will shift. And what couple is perfectly matched?

2. *Where is the dividing line?* It is not easy to keep a 50-50 arrangement

consistent. Do we go by turns? Do we decide what is your area and what is mine? Do we balance one decision or task against another? How do we determine? I remember asking a class of young marrieds if they felt that marriage was 50-50. One young husband answered, "No way. It's more like 90-90." He was right. We both need to be willing to give more than our share in everything.

3. *If no one has the final authority, who has the final responsibility?* When there is a stalemate, who decides? There are times when we can't just sit and wait for a matter to resolve itself or go away. Faced with a deadline, we must answer yes or no. Two final authorities is a solution that just doesn't work. Government and business know that. The buck has to stop somewhere. Someone has to have the final say.

4. *Continually trying to hold a marriage on track is a constant tension.* It is difficult for both husband and wife. Submitting to my husband—in attitude—was the nicest thing I have ever done for myself. It brought a new freedom, a new love, a new happiness, and a new meaning to life, as nothing else could have done. I fully recommend it.

I can see many women cringing at my words. They are thinking, "Not me. I can't do that. Do you know what he'd demand? I can't trust my husband to desire my good. He'd trod roughshod all over me if I didn't stand up for myself."

I suppose that trust is one of the most needed elements in a marriage. For a good, workable, mutually satisfying marriage, we must have trust. Yet many of us feel we can't really trust any other person with our life, our emotions, our needs. "I need to look out for number one. No one else will meet my needs or understand my desires quite like I do."

But someone needs to lead the way in establishing a trust relationship. As a follower of Christ, why don't you choose to be that someone? When your husband sees that you are really putting his interests ahead of your own, he will—perhaps slowly and gradually—respond by considering you. The trust between you will build and grow, and more and more you will seek to please and support one another. It is such a wonderful feeling to be a team, braving the world together rather than competing for leadership.

Look around you. Pick out what you consider to be good marriages. Find the happiest, most joyous people. Are they the contenders, the 50-50s? Likely they are the 90-90s, those who, in love and trust, submit to one another out of love.

I love what Scripture says in Ephesians 5:21: "Submit to one another out of reverence for Christ." If we could understand and obey that verse, there would be no quibbling over who has the final decision.

Of course we are imperfect. We are still striving to become. To me, the ideal marriage arrangement is mutual submission, with the man, as head of the home, making the final decision on matters that need a final decision maker. With the decision comes responsibility, so the decision should be made, after much prayer and discussion, with love and consideration for the total household. The woman, in love for her mate, should respect that decision, knowing fully that he has her best interests at heart as well as his own.

This is submission! This is freedom! This is trust! And it is also, in my thinking, the makings of a good and happy marriage relationship.

Related Articles
Chapter 1: Love as Respect
Chapter 7: All

THE HEAD AND THE BODY

Most interpretations of the biblical metaphor of *headship* have been done by men, about the role of men, and with an obvious bias suggesting a superior role, status, or privilege for males. Occasionally an interpreter stresses the enormous responsibility of a "head of household," but most often the stress is on authority, power, and status.

Whatever Paul may have meant by his "head and body" metaphor of marriage, it must somehow be consistent with his other images: the equal worth of male and female described in Galatians 3:28, the complete interdependence of male and female mentioned in 1 Corinthians 11:11, the mutual submission of husband and wife enjoined in Ephesians 5:21.

Paul explicitly links head and body. Thus it is not easy to understand some men's preoccupation with using the "head" texts to speak of men's power and authority. One could conclude they think the head might thrive by putting down the body, which furnishes all the signals and all the muscle and skill for executing its missions.

"He shall rule over her"—part of the original curse—suggests a marriage in which imperfect and contradictory messages race between head and body. In the physical world this is not the ideal state—it is spastic.

We wonder when we will begin to hear sermons on marriage which exalt the symphonic union of man and woman, their creative co-parenthood, their dynamic dialogic vocations, their healthy celebration of life together without competition or envy.

Donald & Robbie Joy

Equal Persons, Unique Roles

V. GILBERT & ARLISLE BEERS

Long before women's lib was popular, we practiced the theology of equality of personhood and uniqueness of roles. Since the day we were married 37 years ago, we assumed that each was equal to the other and that therefore neither was inferior to the other. That has been the basis of our entire marriage relationship, which may suggest one reason we have remained happily married for 37 years!

The theology of equality works its way out in little things, such as helping a wife with dishes when she is under pressure, or not expecting the husband to help out when he is under pressure. Equality reaches out to help the other when help is needed, whether the work is considered "man's work" or "woman's work." If the husband is under special pressure, the wife is glad to take out the garbage. If the wife has three children crying for attention, the husband is happy to help her with them. If the husband has an important presentation to make the next day, the wife gets up in the middle of the night to respond to a crying child. If the wife has gotten up the last two or three nights, the husband relieves her.

Equality says, "You are as important as I am."

Somehow we should know these things if we have been reading our Bibles. The theology of equality is mingled with the theology of servanthood. If I think I am better than you, I may be tempted to make you my servant or even my slave. If I think you are equal to me, I should not hesitate to serve you in the name of Christ.

Jesus told us about this when He said, "Among the heathen, kings are tyrants and each minor official lords it over those beneath him. But among you it is quite different. Anyone wanting to be a leader among you must be your servant" (Matt. 20:25-26, TLB). The theology of equality does not let me demand service from you; it requires instead that I render service to you.

Christlikeness is wrapped intimately in this kind of thinking. The Bible says, "Your attitude should be the same as that of Christ Jesus: who, being in very nature God, did not consider equality with God something to be grasped, but made Himself nothing, taking the very nature of a servant, [and] . . . humbled Himself and became obedient to death —even death on a cross!" (Phil. 2:5-8) Is it beneath our dignity to serve those we love? Christ didn't think so. Is it Christlike to enjoy serving each other in love? We think it is.

But equality of personhood does not mean identity of roles. In our household, Arlie likes to cook and take care of the house. Gil prefers to write and edit. Perhaps we prefer to do those particular things because they are in line with our capabilities. Gil recognizes that he can't cook or sew or manage the household as well as Arlie, and she recognizes that she can't write or edit or speak as well as he. That simplifies the division of responsibilities.

But it does not prevent Gil from helping Arlie with the housework when the going gets rough, nor does it prevent Arlie from helping Gil with his work when he gets in a bind. It simply helps us assign certain roles, or functions, to each other and rest assured that that person is more content to serve in them.

If you believe in equality of personhood, then it naturally follows that you will believe in the equal value of the work each person does. We think this is what Christ was talking about in Matthew 20:25-26. Are the "kings of the earth" more important than the servants? Perhaps that can best be answered by another question, "Is Mikhail Gorbachev more important than Mother Teresa?" That depends on whether you are building *a* kingdom or *the* kingdom.

Is the breadwinner more important than the home manager? We don't think so. Is it more important to win a contract than to diaper a baby? Not really, because you wouldn't trade your baby for a hundred contracts, and you wouldn't exchange your baby's eternal future for all the financial futures in the world. This is a problem of perspective, for when we start thinking money is more important than God, or business is more important than family, or careers are more important than eternal futures, we have lost our sense of Christian values and begin to do strange things to our families.

We have no desire to be "kings of the earth," because they come and go on the tides of public opinion. The most secure job on earth is to be a servant, first to one another, and then to those about us. Servants are always assured of work, for one can't be fired from this kind of servanthood. The pay is excellent, for we are rewarded with the sure knowledge that we are also serving Christ. The retirement program is fantastic, for it is eternal.

The role of servant to each other is a natural outcome of the theology of equality. But this servanthood is not hard to take. It gives us each the freedom to fulfill those special roles for which we feel we are most capable and therefore most likely to enjoy.

Related Articles
Chapter 1: Love as Teamwork
Chapter 1: Love Is Meeting Each Other's Needs

God's Plan for the Husband-Wife Relationship

LARRY & NORDIS CHRISTENSON

In 1963 a few frustrated families in Southern California went on a retreat together. What frustrated us was our family relationships.

Most of us had tried an assortment of popular prescriptions for improving our marriages, but with few noticeable results. We went off to the mountains together with what we thought was a rather novel idea: we would see what the Bible said about marriage and family life.

We went at it in a pragmatic way. We read the parts of the Bible that deal most directly with family life and relationships, primarily the New Testament passages in Ephesians, Colossians, and 1 Peter. Then we said, "Let's make an experiment of this, the way a scientist would. Our families will be the laboratory. Let's see whether the hypothesis proves true in experience."

In the months that followed, we put the biblical hypothesis to a variety of excruciatingly practical tests. The results were dramatic. In some cases, the atmosphere in a family changed almost overnight. In other situations change came

213

more slowly. What none of us could escape, however, was the overwhelming evidence that a straightforward application of biblical teaching on family life *works.*

This experiment in family living spread to a wider circle of people and went on for a number of years. It involved us in a thorough treatment of the three basic questions relevant to our theme: (1) What does the Bible *say* about the husband-wife relationship? (2) What does the Bible *mean?* (3) What should we *do?*

1. *What does the Bible say?* How are we to understand the language of the Bible in any given passage? How were the biblical writers understood in their own time and setting? Whether this makes sense to us, whether it is relevant to our own situation, whether we can or should apply it to our own lives—these are subsequent questions.

First we must pay attention to what Luther called "the plain sense of the Scripture." The plain sense of Scripture in regard to the husband-wife relationship is not terribly complicated: "Wives, submit to your husbands as to the Lord. Husbands, love your wives, just as Christ loved the church and gave Himself up for her" (Eph. 5:22, 25).

It is both accurate and adequate to state that, according to the New Testament, wives are to be submissive to their husbands, and husbands are to love their wives. That is what the New Testament writers wrote; that is how they meant their words to be understood in their own time. A more nuanced answer to our first question would not add anything of significance for our consideration.

2. *What does the Bible mean?* The biblical use of *submission, head(ship),* and *love* to characterize the husband-wife relationship is not the same as the common use of these terms today. The same words may be used, but they carry different meanings. In popular usage today, the idea of subordination is commonly linked with the idea of inferiority, particularly with reference to the marriage relationship. One writer says, "If woman must of necessity be subordinate, she must of necessity be inferior."

The Bible, however, makes no distinction between men and women with regard to their standing before God. "There is neither . . . male nor female, for you are all one in Christ Jesus" (Gal. 3:28). Men and women are "heirs together of the grace of life" (1 Peter 3:7, KJV). They participate in the same baptism.

The Bible spells out the issue of status most clearly by comparing the husband-wife relationship with the relationship between God the Father and God the Son: "The head of every man is Christ, and the head of the woman is man, and the head of Christ is God" (1 Cor. 11:3). The Son is subject to the Father but not inferior to Him. Jesus said, "I and the Father are one" (John 10:30). The Sanhedrin condemned Jesus precisely because He claimed equality with God. He did not think it "robbery" to be equal with God (Phil. 2:6). The teaching of the church through the centuries has been that the Son is equal to the Father in dignity, honor, and status: "God of God, Light of Light, Very God of Very God." The implication for the husband-wife relationship could not be clearer. The stigma of inferiority is as inappropriate for the wife as it would be for Christ.

Status and subordination are two separate issues in Scripture. The Bible does not draw any necessary connection between them. It is possible to be subject to one who is *superior:* Israel was subject to the Lord; believers are subject to Christ; Abraham submitted to the priesthood of Melchizedek, who is described as his superior (Heb. 7:7). There also can be subordination among *equals:* Christ is equal to God, yet subject to Him; believers who are equal to one another—"fellow citizens with God's people"—are admonished to "submit to one another" (Eph. 2:19; 5:21). One can even be called to submit to someone who is *inferior*, as Christ submitted to Pontius Pilate.

The fact that wives are told to be subject to their husbands tells us nothing about their status. If we had that statement only, we wouldn't know whether they were inferior, equal, or superior to their husbands in status. In comparing the husband-wife relationship to the Father-Son relationship, however, the question of status is settled decisively.

The headship of the husband and the submission of the wife is assumed throughout Scripture as the normal and proper order of things. The first chapter of the Bible describes the creation of mankind as "male and female," bestowing equal dignity on man and woman (Gen. 1:27). The second chapter, going into greater detail, shows God creating woman to be "a helper suitable for him [man]" (2:18). She is brought to the man and he names her, an act expressive of headship.

In the third chapter we see the Fall: the man and the woman disobey God and begin to reap the consequences of their sin. God says to the woman, "I will greatly increase your pains in childbearing; with pain you will give birth to children. Your desire will be for your husband, and he will rule over you" (3:16).

Some have interpreted this to mean that the woman's subjection to her husband came as a result of the Fall and that in Christ this burden is lifted. But then we should also expect pain in childbirth to be lifted, which is not the case. Even more to the point, if one argues that in Christ the husband's rule is set aside, then one would think that the parallel condition, a woman's sexual desire in marriage, should also be set aside. No one seems to be making a case for that.

A more natural interpretation is that God speaks a word of mercy along with the punishment (pain in childbirth),

something He often does when pronouncing judgment. The woman's relationship with her husband, which existed before the Fall, will carry over and be a comfort and strength to her. This relationship has two essential characteristics: sexual union and headship.

The argument that submission implies inferiority does not stand up under scrutiny. The Bible, without contradiction, sees the wife as fully equal to her husband and fully subject to him.

Jesus said, "You know that those who are regarded as rulers of the Gentiles lord it over them, and their high officials exercise authority over them. Not so with you. Instead, whoever wants to become great among you must be your servant, and whoever wants to be first must be slave of all" (Mark 10:42-44).

Headship is a means of loving and serving others. That is its essential function. One who exercises headship must understand it first of all as an expression of love, a position from which to serve. This does not mean that one in headship is under the authority of those he serves. He does not take orders from them. On the contrary, the particular kind of service he gives them is the *service of leadership*.

Ephesians 5:21 says, "Submit to one another out of reverence for Christ." Some have taken this to mean that the Bible teaches mutual submission between husband and wife: in some situations the wife is in submission to her husband, while in others she exercises headship over him. The Bible certainly teaches a high degree of mutuality in marriage, but this is not the same as mutual submission.

The word translated *submit* means "to put oneself under authority." The idea of mutual submission flies in the face both of the context and of common sense. We would have to go on and say that parents on occasion are under the authority of their children. Masters are to submit to their servants. And, ultimately, the church may on occasion be lord over Christ. When we look at the context, the meaning is simple and clear. Verses 22-33 explain what Paul means in verse 21. Having said "Submit to one another," Paul goes on to mention some of the most important relationships to which this applies: wives/husbands, servants/masters, children/parents. His point is not that submission is reciprocal, but that it applies to a variety of relationships.

As head, a husband serves his family by giving them loving, intelligent, sensitive leadership. His headship is not given for domineering and stifling his wife and children, but for leading, protecting, and providing for them. It is a service of love, probably best characterized by the word *care*.

3. *What shall we do?* A straightforward reading of Scripture would probably lead most people generally to agree with us up to this point: yes, that is what the Bible *says,* and that is what is *means.* The critical question is, "So what?" Are the New Testament Scriptures that deal with family life authoritative for us as Christians today?

Some Christians say these Scriptures are *descriptive* of family life in the first century, not necessarily *prescriptive* for us today. This principle, as such, is certainly valid. Nobody assigns equal weight or applicability to every part of Scripture. Yet all of us recognize some parts of Scripture as having universal, transcultural authority and application. The question is, what weight do we assign to these particular Scriptures?

When we went on that family retreat in 1963, we took a pragmatic approach to the Scriptures dealing with family life. We did not put them into practice because they were authoritative, but in order to see whether they would work. The end result was that they became authoritative for us.

In the light of its own self-understanding, the New Testament deals with these questions in universal rather than particular terms. It delineates the roles of men and women in two contexts, both of which transcend any particular culture. First, it treats them in terms of "first principles" or as belonging to "orders of creation" (1 Cor. 11:3, 14; 1 Tim. 2:13-14); second, it patterns them after the model of Christ and the church, a culture-transcending figure of the highest order.

Certainly the weight of history is on the side of interpreting these New Testament Scriptures on family order as having universal validity. The fact that men and women in every culture, or even whole cultures, have made messes out of marriage is not an argument to abandon biblical norms. The cure for abuse is not disuse but proper use.

In our day, the issue of a wife's submission to her husband seems to be particularly nettlesome. In the context of Ephesians, however, the husband's love for his wife is of a piece with her submission to his headship. Those who would set aside the wife's submission in marriage must allow that others can, with as much justification, set aside the husband's love. And what then becomes of marriage?

The model for marriage that is given to us in the New Testament is not a simply human possibility. Far from being a pattern of a bygone culture, the model of a husband who loves his wife as Christ loves the church, and a wife who is subject to her husband as the church is subject to Christ, is a standard that no man or woman in any culture has lived or can live, apart from the power of the Holy Spirit.

Related Articles
Chapter 7: All

216

SEX ROLES IN THE BIBLE

Scripture says that men and women are equal before God (Gal. 3:28), but it also differentiates between men and women in terms of certain behaviors. Take this quiz and see if your view of sex roles matches that of the *King James Version*.

1. God commands (the bride, the groom) to leave family behind at marriage. [Gen. 2:24]
2. The nursing parent mentioned in Numbers 11:12 is a (father, mother).
3. Joshua expected the (fathers, mothers) to be responsible for educating the children. [Josh. 4:4-7]
4. When the evil captain Sisera, longtime oppressor of Israel, was slain, Israel's ruler was a (man, woman); the head of the army was a (man, woman); and the person who stabbed Sisera was a (man, woman). [Jud. 4:4, 6, 21]
5. The only mention of dishwashing in Scripture depicts a (man, woman) drying dishes. [2 Kings 21:13]
6. The Book of Proverbs personifies wisdom as a (man, woman). [4:5-11]
7. The venture capitalist of Proverbs 31 is a (man, woman). [v. 16]
8. In Solomon's Song, the lover whose "neck is like the tower of David builded for an armory" is the (man, woman); the lover whose "cheeks are as . . . sweet flowers" is the (man, woman). [Song 4:4; 5:13]
9. Paul's first European convert was a wealthy business (man, woman). [Acts 16:14]
10. Philip had four children who were all prophets. These children were (sons, daughters). [Acts 21:9]

LaVonne Neff

Submission and Culture

LARRY & NORDIS CHRISTENSON

Some people interpret the Bible's words about the man's headship in marriage as a cultural phenomenon. The New Testament writers, they say, simply reflect the customs of their own age and culture. When we examine the matter closely, however, it is not that simple.

In Greek culture, except for Macedonia and Asia Minor, women were generally considered inferior to men and were kept in seclusion in the family. Roman women enjoyed greater practical, if not legal, freedom; women participated more freely in religious activities, and this aided the spread of Christianity.

In Macedonia, after the time of Alexander the Great, women began to have a relatively greater measure of freedom. Women played a large part in civic affairs: they received envoys, built temples, founded cities, engaged mercenaries, commanded armies, held fortresses,

217

and acted on occasion as regents or co-rulers.

In Asia Minor (the western part of modern Turkey, where Ephesus and Colossae were located), women enjoyed unusual privileges and status. A practical equality between the sexes had emerged in considerable measure before the Christian era. This was especially evident in religion, where women played an important part.

In Jewish culture the position of women was somewhat paradoxical. On the one hand there is the well-known prayer in the synagogue service, "Blessed art Thou, O Lord our God, King of the universe, who has not made me . . . a woman." On the other hand, there are the lofty words concerning womanhood in Proverbs 31. The paradox makes sense only if we recognize the high value Jewish culture placed on women in her proper sphere of service, the home. Legally she had few rights, but in the home she held a place of unparalleled dignity.

The "emancipation movement" in Asia Minor may have had some effect on Jewish culture. According to one inscription there may have even been a female synagogue ruler. On the whole, however, women's place in Jewish culture would accord with the form of family life outlined in Paul's writings, and could be seen as a source for it.

Given the background of a changing role for women in Asia Minor, Paul's teaching would seem to be somewhat at variance with the prevailing culture, a corrective rather than an accommodation. This becomes more apparent when we examine the context of the Scripture texts themselves. Ephesians 5:22-23 is set in a larger section dealing with practices the apostle wants to correct. The context suggests he is advocating a structure of family life that was not generally being followed or was in danger of being eroded away. It may be that he saw certain cultural forces, such as a women's emancipation movement, carrying things to extremes, and therefore introduced a word of correction.

In his letter to the Ephesians the apostle addresses words not only to husbands and wives, but also to slaves, and this has raised another kind of question. True enough, Paul says, "Wives, submit to your husbands." But he also says, "Slaves, obey your earthly masters." Therefore, some argue, to say that 20th-century women should continue to be subject to their husbands is as foolish as to make a case for the continuance of slavery.

This, however, misses Paul's point. He is not discussing the relative merits of slavery and freedom; as, indeed, he is not discussing the relative merits of marriage and celibacy (he discusses both of these questions in other places). Instead he is telling people who *are* married or who *are* slaves how they should conduct themselves.

Paul is not making parallel statements about slavery and the husband's headship, but about slavery and marriage. To draw a comparison between slavery and marriage in this context does not make a case against headship and submission in marriage, but against marriage itself.

Paul does not make a case for slavery. He says, "If you can gain your freedom, do so" (1 Cor. 7:21). He treats the institution of marriage in an altogether different way. It is divinely instituted and structured. The relationship of husband and wife is modeled on the relationship of Christ and the church. Nothing could make the case for headship and submission more clear: "As the church submits to Christ, so also wives should submit to their husbands in everything" (Eph. 5:24). In other words, wives can set aside the headship of their husbands as little as the church can set aside the headship of Christ. This is not a mere cultural accretion. It has its source and model in an eternal reality, the love of Christ for His bride, the church.

The argument that headship is only a

cultural phenomenon, to be modified or discarded as cultures change, does not stand up under scrutiny.

Related Articles
Chapter 7: All

What Is a Wife's Primary Responsibility to Her Husband?

KENN & BETTY GANGEL

Our wedding plans were complete, and September 1, 1956, finally arrived. We were so much in love that we were sure love could carry us through any problem. As we grew in our marriage relationship as well as our knowledge of the Word, however, we discovered that love was not enough. Indeed, it was not even the primary element that was to hold us together for over 30 years.

Please accept our invitation to pull up a chair, grab a cup of coffee, and listen in as we dialogue about this very important question: what is a wife's primary responsibility to her husband?

KENN: Dearie, as you look back over our years together, what do you think has been your most important contribution to me and to our relationship?

BETTY: I believe it has been my effort to be your best friend, your companion, the person you can talk to about anything, confident that I will listen in confidentiality. My understanding of the Bible elevates this role and makes it a priority.

KENN: Yes, it certainly does. In fact, when God created Adam and saw he was incomplete, He created a woman who would be a fitting companion for the man. Listen to Genesis 2:18 from *The Amplified Bible:* "Now the Lord God said, 'It is not good [sufficient, satisfactory] that the man should be alone; I will make him a helper meet (suitable, adapted, completing) for him.' "

BETTY: That's a beautiful verse, Honey; I think of it often. And closely linked to this whole idea of fitting into the husband's plans is the command for a wife to be submissive. It seems that every time I read a passage of Scripture which talks about responsibilities and relationships within the family, wives are commanded to submit.

Ephesians 5:22 says, "Wives, submit to your husbands as to the Lord." Colossians 3:18 says, "Wives, submit to your husbands, as is fitting in the Lord." And again in 1 Peter 3:1 we read, "Wives . . . be submissive to your husbands."

KENN: Have you found these commands comfortable, easy to live out?

BETTY: No, this has not always been an area of quick or easy obedience. However, I'm confident we have worked hard on balancing love, submission, discussion, decisions, openness, and patience. Your leadership style has certainly not been dictatorial, but rather you have encouraged each family member to share in the decision-making process.

KENN: Yes—even though our children are now married, they helped just recently as we discussed the pros and cons of an important decision. I understand that God has given me the responsibility to be the final decision maker, and yet it was great to have the entire family concerned enough to speak to the issues.

219

TAKING LEADERSHIP

What can a wife do when her husband refuses to take leadership? Is it leadership in disciplining the kids? Spiritual leadership? Financial leadership? In whatever area she discovers, she must then be committed to not taking over the leadership by default.

Think about it: perhaps you're upset because when the kids misbehave, you always have to do the punishing. But if you step back and refuse to take the leadership in that area, chances are your husband will be forced into it.

What about financial leadership? Maybe you wanted a new refrigerator. You did the shopping, decided the best price and/or financing, and made your choice. You went to your husband, gave him all the information with your decision, and he said, "Well, whatever you say." What else could he say? You already did everything. You have already taken the leadership role.

Both husband and wife, by virtue of their gifts and abilities, will take leadership roles in different areas in the home, a subject which is valuable to discuss before marriage. But generally speaking, unless the husband is just plain irresponsible, when a wife is upset over his leadership or lack thereof, she has either taken the leadership already, or she wants him to lead in a different direction. The two of them need to discuss the issue openly and work together to maintain harmony and accountability.

YFC Editors

While considering the responsibilities of the wife, we certainly cannot ignore Proverbs 31. Many say this woman is too perfect to be real. However, whether or not this woman actually lived, certainly God was giving us an ideal for which to strive.

BETTY: Let's look at that passage to find another approach to our question. If a wife tries to be like the Proverbs 31 woman, how will it affect her relationship with her husband?

Verse 11—She is trustworthy.

Verse 12—She brings her husband "good, not harm, all the days of her life."

Verse 13—She "works with eager hands."

Verse 15—She "provides food for her family."

Verse 18—She is careful with money.

Verse 20—She "opens her arms to the poor."

Verse 26—She "speaks with wisdom."

Verse 30—She "fears the Lord."

KENN: There is one other important responsibility a wife needs to be attentive to, and that is to always be beautiful. Oh, it would be great if you would always have that slim figure and long brown hair I flipped for in college. But in 1 Peter 3:4 we read that even more important than outer beauty is "the unfading beauty of a gentle and quiet spirit, which is of great worth in God's sight."

BETTY: God's plan for us is so wise. He knew that as the years begin to give us gray hairs, wrinkles, and some extra bulges, the Holy Spirit would be maturing and bringing the inner self more and more into the image of Christ. Now we can praise God that our relationship is deeper, our love more enduring, and our commitment even greater than it was on September 1, 1956.

Thank you for joining us as we reminisced and looked again at the biblical ingredients that have gone into our marriage.

It doesn't matter if you are newly married or have been together for 50 years;

God's commands to the Christian wife do not change. She should be a real companion to her husband, submit to his leadership, respect him, encourage him, and grow in the mature beauty of a gentle and quiet spirit.

What Is A Husband's Primary Responsibility to His Wife?

KENN & BETTY GANGEL

Recently a newspaper columnist in a major city suggested that the number-one cause of poverty in America is absent fathers. Particularly among minority groups, but increasingly in middle-class society, fathers either leave their families entirely or devote so much of their time and energy to work that nothing is left for the wife and kids.

After reading the article, we began to wonder whether *spiritually* absent fathers may be the greatest cause of spiritual poverty in Christian families. You know the kind—fathers who leave Bible teaching and spiritual instruction to Mom; fathers who spend four hours on the golf course on Sunday but can't find time for two hours at church; and un-saved fathers who impede every effort as Christian moms struggle to pull together the fragments of the family.

Backing up a step, we need to look at husbands. Most fathers become husbands first, and inadequate husbands almost always turn into inadequate fathers. To put it another way, effective parenting is based on effective partnership. A man who can't relate biblically to his wife will not relate biblically to his children.

A responsibility is not the same as a role, but in family life there is a great deal of overlap between the two. The Bible lays out important roles for men, and each role carries appropriate responsibilities. The husband as *provider,* for example (1 Tim. 5:8), bears the responsibility for procuring life's necessities for his wife and family. Might the massive surge of mothers into the workplace during the past two decades be, in part, a result of inadequate providing—even by some Christian fathers? The husband/father as *teacher* (Eph. 4) is responsible to learn a great deal in order to teach both children and wife (1 Cor. 14:35). As *leader* or *head* (1 Peter 3:6; 1 Cor. 11:3-10), the husband is responsible to set the stage so that the wife can fulfill her biblical responsibility of submission.

The Bible, then, identifies clear and specific roles, and each role carries fairly defined responsibilities. God holds husbands accountable for doing what He has asked of them in Scripture. It's like the third-grade boy who came to his teacher one morning and said, "Mrs. Adams, I don't want to scare you, but last night my dad said if my grades don't pick up soon, somebody's going to get a spanking." The corollary threat in the Christian family might read, "Wife, I don't want to scare you, but God said if we don't function more biblically in this family, somebody's going to have to

221

take the blame."

But do husbands have a *primary* responsibility—one that is basic to all the others? Does the Bible lift one function above the others, one task beyond everything else a husband does for a wife? Without question it does, and that responsibility is *loving* with the same sacrificial self-denial Christ demonstrated when He died for the world. Scripture uses the same Greek word to describe husband-love in Ephesians 5:25 and Colossians 3:19 and the Saviour's love in John 3:16. The same word describes the essence of love itself in 1 Corinthians 13. A husband's love for his wife forms the very foundation upon which the family structure is built.

Can we justify selecting one responsibility as more important than the rest? We can, *because God Himself chose love for heavy emphasis in the Bible.* In the Colossians passage, for example, when He prioritizes one task for each family member, He says, "Husbands love—wives submit—children obey."

A second reason we can isolate loving as most important is *because it is most closely related to the key purpose of marriage*—fellowship between a man and a woman (Gen. 2). How many times folks approach us in a family-life conference to ask questions about some facet of family living such as discipline or worship, and how many times the core of their problem is neither discipline nor worship but the husband-wife relationship! As we do in our other activities, we must learn in the family to put first things first, and a husband's first responsibility is to love his wife.

Third, it's appropriate to emphasize loving *because of what it means in the lives of our children.* Psychologists repeatedly tell us that children benefit more from seeing that their daddy loves their mommy than even that their daddy loves them.

Finally, the role model of a loving husband serves as the very present and constant figure of the relationship of Christ to His church. To the extent that a Christian husband fails to love his wife, he is unlike Jesus Christ in his attitudes and lifestyle. By contrast, to the extent that a Christian husband loves his wife, he is living out a powerful witness of God's persistent love for His human family.

Related Articles

Husbands, Beautify Your Wives

LUIS PALAU

Scripture says that a Christian husband is to love his wife "just as Christ loved the church and gave Himself up for her to make her holy, cleansing her by the washing with water through the word, and to present her to Himself as a radiant church, without stain or wrinkle or any other blemish, but holy and blameless. In this same way, husbands ought to love their wives as their own bodies. He who loves his wife loves himself" (Eph. 5:25-28).

What happens when you love your wife? Look at what the Bible says: a husband who loves his wife transforms her. Just as Christ makes the church beautiful by His love, so we men can make our wives beautiful. Our self-sacrificing love

MACHO OR MASCULINE?

Some men feel that if they want their boys to be masculine, they must be standoffish. They will not express tender emotions in the boys' presence. They don't want the boys ever to see them with tears in their eyes. They might even avoid physical contact with their sons. Psychological research shows, however, that little boys become much more secure in their male identity and much better adjusted psychologically if they have a warm affectionate father who expresses emotion to them, hugs them, pats them on the back, and is affectionately involved with them. Our culture's phony macho image of masculinity is neither psychologically nor biblically sound.

George Rekers

directly affects our wives' sense of self-worth and dignity, our wives' attitudes, actions, and words.

The Bible challenges us to love our wives as our own selves. In reality, we men tend to do quite well looking out for our own interests. We spend vast amounts of time and energy taking care of ourselves—seeing that we have the food, material goods, recreation, and accomplishments that we think we need. God calls us to lavish even more attention and devotion on our wives.

Is your wife your best friend? Can she tell that you value her? Women at our counseling center have said, "My husband must love me—after all, he's still around after 20 years of marriage. But he never shows it." Husband, your wife longs to hear you say that you love her.

We are to love our wives as Christ loved the church. This love, according to the Bible, is more than an emotional feeling. It means giving yourself for another person. Love is what Christ did on the cross: He died for our good, for our salvation. A man who loves his wife is willing to do anything for her joy, happiness, and good.

The Scripture says, "Husbands, love your wives." This love is a commitment, a decision a man makes day after day. Sometimes he feels loving; sometimes he doesn't. But no matter how his feelings fluctuate, he continues to love his wife steadfastly.

And the results of such love? A happy home, a solid marriage, and an increasingly lovely—and loving—wife.

Related Articles
Chapter 4: Making Your Spouse Your Best Friend
Chapter 7: What Is a Husband's Primary Responsibility to His Wife?

What Would You Do If You Loved Her?

WESLEY & ELAINE WILLIS

Recently a friend of Wes' described the total absence of love he had once felt for his wife. And yet as a Christian he knew he was wrong. So he asked himself what he would do if he *did* love her. He made a list of the things he would do, and he started doing one of them each day. He later told Wes how amazed he felt when all of a sudden one day he realized he was beginning to love her a little. Today they have a deep and genuine love for each other because he did the things to build that love.

Why not determine to start doing some things that will increase your love for your wife? The suggestions that follow are divided into four categories. Start with any category and try any suggestions within that category. Better yet, try some of your own suggestions. They'll probably be even better!

1. *Share activities with your wife.* It goes without saying that it is important to worship and study the Word together with your wife. But it might be a novel idea for you to sit next to her in the worship service. Seat the children on your other side for a change, not between you and your wife.

Ask your wife out for a date. No, you don't need to blow a bundle. Try a bike ride, a picnic, or a walk in the park. Or get together with another couple and plan something the four of you can do.

Try planning joint activities around the house. Plant and care for a garden together. Take on a landscaping project or some redecorating. Maybe your wife has been wanting some remodeling done. You could make it a shared project.

Many men assume certain things are the wife's job: attending PTA or the children's Christmas program at school, for example. Suggest that the two of you attend together.

One very meaningful activity my wife and I are sharing is a Tuesday night Bible study with several other couples. This helps us learn the Word together, but we also get to talk about biblical concepts and their implications with the group and as a couple.

2. *Do things for your wife.* How long has it been since you brought a surprise present for your wife (when you haven't been out of town)? She probably doesn't need candy, but what about something most men see as worthless—flowers? Try not to choose a gift she would have bought anyway, like a new mop!

Surprise your wife with an invitation to dinner in a restaurant. You may have to cut out doughnuts at coffee break to swing it, but it's worthwhile because it says to your wife that you think she's important.

Encourage her to develop her own skills and interests. Generate an interest in the things she likes. Look for ways to encourage and support her in these activities. For example, you could assume responsibility for the children and cleaning up after supper one or two evenings a week so she could take an adult evening class at the local high school.

Offer to put your children to bed—regularly, not just once! Not only does this relieve your wife, but it's a great time for you to share with your children.

Try looking for ways to express genuine compliments to your wife in public. Many men put down their wives in public, but few actively compliment them. Read and reread Proverbs 31 and then try talking about your wife that way to your friends, even if she isn't there. She'll hear about it before long.

Thank her for things she does that both of you take for granted: the thought and energy that goes into planning and preparing meals, her willingness to hold down a job and still care for the home. Think of the special things she does that you often overlook.

3. *Assume responsibility.* You probably have a list of things that need to be done around the house that could take from now until the Rapture. Undoubtedly you procrastinate about the most unpleasant ones—but these may mean a great deal to your wife. Suggest that every other project will be done on her priority schedule. You pick one off the list and do it. Then it's her turn to choose.

Share with your wife in child rearing. The children are not her responsibility alone; they are yours together. Look for ways to do your part. Be sure to support her authority by backing up her expectations for the children, just as you expect her to support you.

Help with entertaining. Many men act as if this is the wife's job. The husband sits watching a football game on TV while his wife frantically scurries about doing all the last-minute things before company arrives. Offer to help, perhaps by vacuuming or setting the table.

When you come home from work, look for ways to be helpful instead of retreating with the newspaper and asking when supper will be ready. Why not offer to call the children and urge them to wash up? We know you've had a hard day, but she has too. And she still has other responsibilities before her day is finished.

Start viewing your day off not as your (singular) day off but as your (plural) day

off. Look at those days as a resource that you and your wife can share, and take the opportunity to minister to your wife with that day. Incidentally, which day is *her* day off?

4. *Talk with your wife.* How long since you've sat down to talk with your wife when there were no pressing problems and the children weren't there? Think back to your endless conversations when you were courting. Remember how love grew and blossomed? A big part of that was the time you spent talking and sharing together. Believe it or not, the same thing can happen after marriage too.

Regularly schedule time to talk with you wife. It could be in the evening with the TV off and the children in bed, or maybe a Saturday morning or Sunday afternoon. Several weeks ago in a local restaurant on Saturday morning, Wes saw a friend having breakfast with his wife. That's a great time just to be together and talk.

If your wife is home caring for young children, it is all the more important to talk with her. Diapers, dishes, and drains will dull the keenest mind and discourage even the optimist. Talk to her. Share what has happened during the day. Even if it seems dull and commonplace to you, it will be a change of pace for her.

Greet your wife when you come home. Elaine hates it when our boys walk through the door after school and, without even a "Hello," demand, "Where's my snack?" We've noticed that many husbands never get over that habit. They treat their wives like household appliances, not like real people. Try giving your wife a genuine kiss when you first walk in the door. And then some genuine conversation (that includes listening) can follow.

When you talk to your wife, tell her how you feel. Don't be objective and analytical all the time. Express yourself. Share your joys and frustrations. Let her know what you feel as well as think.

How long since you've written your wife a note? Even if don't leave town, drop her a note and tell her you love her or send her a well-chosen card. This gives her something tangible to refer to periodically.

Commit yourself to telling your wife at least once a day that you love her. Periodically repledge yourself to her. Reaffirm that she is the only woman you care for, and promise her your faithfulness.

Talk to your wife about spiritual things. Discuss together the Sunday morning sermon or the Sunday School class. Listen to tapes together and talk about what you should do. Attend a seminar and then talk about the implications for your Christian life. Pray together about the things that concern you.

The Apostle Paul commands husbands to love their wives (Eph. 5:25). You may not always *feel* loving, but it is your responsibility to *act* loving. Try some of these suggestions, or find other ways to treat your wife as if you love her. We guarantee that before long, you will!

──────────

Related Articles
Chapter 1: Love Is Something We Learn
Chapter 15: Bringing Love Back to Life
Chapter 16: Restoring a Broken Marriage

How Much Is a Woman Worth?

DAVID & CAROLYN ROPER

There's a bumper sticker around town that reads, "On the sixth day God created man and rested. Then He created woman and no one has rested ever since." You read the sticker and weep for the woman or women in that man's life. Somewhere along the way the poor guy bought Archie Bunker's notion that "men are worth more than women! Everybody knows that." But it's not the way a real man ought to think about a woman.

Some men do think that way. Tragically, even Christian men are duped into believing that God puts a premium on being a man. This shows up in the way they treat their women. We hear a lot nowadays about emotionally and physically battered wives, and more and more women are feeling deprived and oppressed.

We wonder at times if the church isn't partly to blame for this: it has often taught women to submit to their husbands in a way our Lord never intended.

Please understand we believe in the headship of husbands, an idea clearly taught in Scripture, but we also believe that sometimes even well-meaning expositors turn headship into nothing more than male dominance. Because of this, a thorough rethinking of woman's worth is in order.

First of all, the Bible teaches that God deems every woman worthwhile, fully equal in value to a man. Genesis puts it this way: "God created man in His own image, in the image of God He created him; male and female He created them" (Gen. 1:27).

It's very clear that *man* is made in God's image, that is, like Him. And *man* in this passage means "mankind"—"in the image of God He created *him;* male and female He created *them.*" One aspect of Hebrew poetry is parallelism in which each successive line intensifies the meaning of the preceding line. Thus, according to the Creation story, man as male and female is made in God's image. The two sexes have equal dignity.

Furthermore, according to the text, man and woman both rule over creation: "God blessed *them* and said to *them*, 'Be fruitful and increase in number; fill the earth and subdue it. Rule over the fish of the sea and the birds of the air and over every living creature that moves on the ground'" (v. 28). It is sometimes said that the mandate to subdue the earth was given only to the male, but the text can't be read that way; the female also has a mandate to rule. She's a reigning monarch, co-regent with the male. They have equal authority.

More light on the worth of woman comes from Genesis 2:18, a text that is sometimes abused: "It is not good for the man to be alone. I will make a helper suitable for him." From this text come our words *helpmeet* and *helpmate,* often seen as a mere servile assistant. But the Hebrew text actually says that God provided "a helper according to his need," and the man's need was for companionship, not housekeeping. He was alone, which, as God Himself observed, was not good. So God provided him with a *helper*—a word often used of God Himself, who is our "help." Man's helper is not one who runs and fetches for him—a "gofer"—but rather one who saves him from loneliness, his best friend.

All this leads us to believe that women have special worth and must be treated with respect and honor. Men who treat their women like children, monitoring their activities, curbing their creativity, doling out money like an allowance, restricting their freedoms, using them as their servants, are not leading; they're dominating. That's why we believe that much of so-called Christian headship is sexist and mere male domination. No wonder women are disaffected; no wonder the feminists rage!

When men in the church or in our culture treat women with disdain or be-

MY HUSBAND DOESN'T WANT TO BE A LEADER!

For every wife who is unhappy because her husband bosses her around, there is another wife equally unhappy because her husband refuses to lead.

If she asks his opinion he says, "That's up to you, Dear." If a child asks permission to do something he says, "Ask your mother." If a salesman calls, he passes the phone to his wife. What can a wife do to encourage her husband to take leadership?

First, she'd better be sure she really wants him to do so. If two spouses get along well, make decisions easily, and are generally happy with their relationship, why rock the boat?

But maybe he isn't egalitarian—he's just lazy. He's letting her take responsibility that ought to be his. If that is the case, there's only one solution. The wife obviously can't order her husband to lead. All she can do is refuse to do his work or make his decisions for him.

A lot of wives, however, can't bear to sit back and wait for their spouses to act. They remind. They nag. They eventually do whatever needs doing. And then they wonder why the men refuse to lead.

A word of warning: if you turn a decision over to your husband, you must be willing to let go of it completely. Whatever he does, whatever he decides, you must support him. If you want a say in the outcome, don't tell him it's his decision. Make the decision together.

YFC Editors

227

little them; or when they think that women, merely because they are women, are troublesome or shallow, fold under pressure, gossip, and are unreliable and frivolous, then they have missed what's being said in Scripture, and they have missed the spirit of our Lord.

About 40 years ago Dorothy Sayers wrote a remarkable essay entitled, "Are Women Human?" in which she observed that "it is no wonder that women were first at the Cradle and last at the Cross. They had never known a man like this Man—there has never been such another. A prophet and teacher who never nagged at them, never flattered or coaxed or patronized; who never made arch jokes about them, never treated them either as 'The women, God help us!' or 'The ladies, God bless them!'; who rebuked without querulousness and praised without condescension; who took their questions and arguments seriously; who never mapped out their sphere for them, never urged them to be feminine or jeered at them for being female; who had no axe to grind and no uneasy male dignity to defend; who took them as He found them and was completely unself-conscious. There is no act, no sermon, no parable in the whole Gospel that borrows its pungency from female perversity; nobody could possibly guess from the words and deeds of Jesus that there was anything 'funny' about woman's nature" (Eerdmans, 1984, pp. 47-48).

If Jesus took women seriously, so should we. They are not subsets of Christian men, nor are they disciplettes of Christ. They can be grown-up believers, fully man's equal in their capacity to know God, learn from Him, and grow in grace. Paul declares that in terms of Christ's call to discipleship there is "neither . . . male nor female" (Gal. 3:28). And Peter refers to men and women as "heirs together of the grace of life" (1 Peter 3:7, KJV). The differences between the sexes ultimately make no difference at all. To think any less of a person because she is a woman is both unmanly and ungodly.

Related Articles
Chapter 1: Love Is Meeting Each Other's Needs
Chapter 7: Equal Persons, Unique Roles

Do Parents' Roles Affect Their Children?

GEORGE A. REKERS

From a biblical perspective, the two-parent family does more than simply provide two adults to bring up the children. There are certain distinctive roles of the husband and father that are different from those of the wife and mother. In the Bible, fathers and mothers are not totally interchangeable.

A lot of child-development research bears out the importance of the roles we see in Scripture. For example, research shows that to promote children's optimal well-being, the father should do three things. First, he should *show affection* toward his wife and their children. Second, he should *be actively involved* in family relationships. Third, he should *assume a leadership role.* Where the father has these qualities, the children are better adjusted by all kinds of psychological measures; where these features are absent, the children—particularly boys—have much higher rates of emotional disorders, academic problems, drug abuse, and a number of other significant problems.

These conclusions are in harmony with the Scripture's admonitions. An *affectionate* father loves his wife as he loves himself (Eph. 5:28-29; Col. 3:19) and does not embitter his children (Col. 3:21). An *involved* father brings up his children "in the training and instruction of the Lord" (Eph. 6:4). A *dominant* father manages his own family well (1 Tim. 3:4).

It is important for the father's role to include all three of these qualities, and not just one or two of them.

Some fathers are dominant and involved but not affectionate. Like dictators, such fathers order their wives and children around. You can picture them coming home from work, flopping down in an easy chair, picking up the paper, and barking orders: "Bring me my slippers; bring me the TV control; get me something to drink!" These fathers generally have uneasy marriage relationships and poorly adjusted children.

Other fathers, though dominant and affectionate, are not involved. They think caring for children is the wife's duty. They are willing to do something special with the children from time to time, but this is not the kind of involvement that is important in child development. The involvement that makes a difference is day-to-day contact: wiping little Johnny's runny nose, tying his shoe, helping him zip up his coat. Uninvolved fathers usually do not know their children well enough to have a strong influence on them.

Nowadays it is popular for fathers to be affectionate and involved, but not dominant. Research shows that this too causes problems for their children. If Mom runs 95 percent of what goes on at home, her sons are more likely to have identity problems than the sons of fathers who are in charge. Some studies were done in which children were asked whether they would rather be male or female when they grew up. More sons of dominant mothers chose female than did sons of dominant fathers. In addition, the children were asked which of their classmates they would rather play with. Children of dominant mothers

229

were more likely to dislike and be disliked by children of the opposite sex than were children of dominant fathers. Thus in families where Dad has at least some leadership, children are likely to be more secure in their own identities and have better relationships with their peers.

Our culture sometimes gives us phony stereotypes of masculinity and femininity. Sometimes these define certain tasks as masculine and others as feminine, when in reality men and women can perform the tasks equally well. At other times, the masculine stereotype emphasizes dominance over everything else. This is a distortion of the biblical picture of leadership. The godly husband and father does not order his wife and children to submit. He does not make demands. His love and involvement draw a boundary line around his dominance and make him a gentle shepherd, not a dictator.

Again, the important thing to remember is this: an effective father shows all three qualities simultaneously. He is affectionate, involved, *and* dominant in his relationship with his wife and children.

Related Articles
Chapter 11: Let Your Children See You Love Your Mate
Chapter 11: The Most Important Thing You Can Do for Your Child

SEPARATE CAREERS

In contemporary marriage, the question of careers increasingly presents problems. Should both spouses work outside the home? Can both pursue careers and find fulfillment without harming the kids? If parenting is a career in itself, why do some homemakers feel inferior or worthless in social groups that include working mothers? If two paychecks are necessary to the family's comfort, why do some working mothers feel guilty? These are tough issues facing today's couples, sometimes because of economic necessity.

No matter what you and your spouse decide about this issue, you must keep two things in mind. First, *recognize the inherent difficulty of pursuing two separate careers.* Balancing conflicting schedules, dividing household responsibilities, arranging for child care, maintaining a sense of family life—these tasks can strain even the best marriages. And with increased taxes and increased expenses for transportation and wardrobes, the financial returns from two careers may not be worth the drain on your marriage.

The second important concept for both husband and wife to keep in mind is this: *never put your career before your marriage.* Careers and jobs can change, but your mate should be with you for life. Keep the proper perspective and make your marriage more important than your career. Doing so will enable you to enjoy married life now and long after you are finished with your career.

Gary Bennett

If only because one of them is a man and the other a woman, married couples usually have quite different attitudes and approaches to sex. In addition, in an age when sexual values are being attacked and revised, people may come to marriage with varying beliefs and expectations. Clifford and Joyce Penner devised this attitude assessment tool to open up discussion about these differences. Take it with your partner and see what you can learn about each other.

Agree Disagree Uncertain

——— ——— ——— Sex is one of the most beautiful aspects of life.

——— ——— ——— It is more enjoyable to give than to receive.

——— ——— ——— Bodily pleasure is fleshly and not of God.

——— ——— ——— Sexual intercourse is primarily for physical release.

——— ——— ——— Our religious beliefs have the greatest influence on our attitudes toward sexual behaviors.

——— ——— ——— Men and women have equal right to sexual pleasure.

——— ——— ——— There are sexual activities that I would consider wrong for a married couple to practice. If you agree, list these: _____

_____

_____

——— ——— ——— To be satisfying, intercourse must lead to simultaneous orgasm.

——— ——— ——— Sexual fantasies are normal.

——— ——— ——— Masturbation (self-stimulation) is an acceptable means for sexual pleasuring and release.

——— ——— ——— The male should be the aggressor in sexual activity.

——— ——— ——— In general, women don't enjoy sex as much as men.

——— ——— ——— Men should be allowed more freedom in sexual behavior than women.

——— ——— ——— The quality of a sexual relationship is more than just physical release.

[Excerpted from *Sexual Fulfillment in Marriage: A Multimedia Learning Kit,* by Clifford and Joyce Penner, Family Concern, Inc., 1977. Used by permission. Available through the Penners at 2 N. Lake Avenue, Suite 610, Pasadena, California 91101.]

8

SEX

Why should we be ashamed to discuss what God was not ashamed to create? Sexuality was created before sin entered the human race; yet it has become a current topic of buffoonery and obscenity. Our world suggests that experience should precede explanation, and a general consensus of confusion and guilt leaves us ill-informed and overexposed.

When parents relate affectionately and appropriately, they teach their children the divine intent for sex in several basic principles:

1. Sex is a gift from God and designed for people's good. Like all His gifts, it can be perverted or enjoyed. It was meant to be the greatest form of intimacy known to people, producing deep fulfillment, but it is also capable of devastating frustration.

2. Sex has a variety of purposes. We cannot use anything properly unless we understand its intended function: procreation (Gen. 1:27-28); prevention (1 Cor. 7:1-2); pleasure (Deut. 24:5).

3. Sexual prohibitions in Scripture always protect (1 Cor. 6:13). "You shall not commit adultery" (Ex. 20:14) is not an attempt to ruin, but to preserve sex life. All prohibitions are given for outside, not within, marriage.

4. Sex involves much more than physical union. It embraces all the feelings of love, intimacy, yearning, and respect.

5. Biblical sex is always other-centered (1 Cor. 7:3-4). One's only right is the right to satisfy his/her partner.

The Song of Songs stands as a classic monument to enduring married love. The words of the lover capsulize the essence of married intimacy: "Place me like a seal over your heart . . . love is as strong as death" (8:6).

Howard & Jeanne Hendricks

How to Obtain and Maintain Sexual Intimacy

BOB & CINNY HICKS

Someone once said, "God gave us sex to enrich our lives, but a funny thing happened to it on the way to the 20th century." En route, attitudes toward sex have ranged from those of pleasure-denying ascetics to those of the pleasure-deifying Playboy profiteers. Today Christians often wonder where to place themselves between the two extremes of "nothing goes" and "anything goes." To add to this confusion, the church has frequently ignored sexual intimacy altogether, regarding sexual functioning solely for the purpose of procreation.

Scripture, however, recognizes marital sexual intimacy as a normal human experience that fulfills three purposes: to produce children (Gen. 1:28; 9:1), to prevent immorality (Prov. 5:15-23; 1 Cor. 7:1-5), and to give pleasure (Gen. 18:1-12; 26:8). One entire book of the Bible is devoted to the passion of marital lovemaking—the Song of Songs, or Song of Solomon. Although some interpreters, uncomfortable with its unabashed sexuality, have tried to make it a spiritual allegory, it is more natural to understand the book literally: King Solomon describes his courtship and marriage with a girl he calls the Shulammite. In this book we find four principles of sexual intimacy.

1. *Sexual intimacy takes time.* In the opening chapter of his book, Solomon gives the first description of the Shulammite (1:10, 15). It is short and simple: all he describes are her eyes, cheeks, and neck. In ancient Near Eastern culture women's entire bodies were covered except for their faces, so Solomon describes the only part of his beloved he can see.

His second description of her is on their wedding night (4:1-7). Here he has obviously explored his wife to a greater extent. Beginning with her eyes, he proceeds to her teeth, lips, neck, and breasts.

The final description (7:1-9) takes place after the couple has been married for some time and encountered some conflict. This description is by far the most intimate. Solomon covers his wife's features from the bottom of her feet to the top of her head. Their sexual intimacy has grown as they have spent time together.

Couples in marriage counseling often confess that their sexual expectations were much higher than their actual performance. Many people have bought the Hollywood picture that any two individuals passing in the night can jump into bed together and experience mutual cli-

INTIMACY BEGINS IN THE MORNING

If you start the day with a growl, ignore your spouse at breakfast and after work, and treat him or her rudely, you can't expect an amorous response the minute you get into bed at night. Sex isn't something you put on your "to do" list; it's part of the ongoing intimate relationship you have with your spouse. Intimacy begins in the morning and continues all day long as you show your spouse love through your attitudes and actions. Then sex becomes a fitting climax to that constantly intimate relationship.

YFC Editors

max at will. In reality, a good sexual relationship takes time—time to explore, to get to know each other, and to experiment gradually. Every couple's timetable is unique, and no one else's experience or process should be taken as normative for any other couple.

2. *Sexual intimacy requires good timing.* Solomon knocks on the door of the Shulammite's sleeping chambers very early one morning (5:2). He has become sexually aroused, but as he advances, she makes excuses (v. 3). The traditional headache has biblical precedent! Since she is not interested, Solomon, in typical male fashion, leaves. But as she thinks about her man, she in turn is aroused.

This passage is describing what happens in households all over the world every evening. It's a problem of timing. Solomon forgot to look at the sundial in the courtyard, and the Shulammite forgot for whom she made her nightly preparations. To enjoy sexual intimacy, couples must think through their schedules and find the best time to enjoy each other.

It is important to evaluate whose need is greatest at the moment. The Apostle Paul tells couples that each one's main concern should be what pleases the other (1 Cor. 7:3-4; 32-35). Therefore, if the greater need is sleep, then the other accepts this reality. If the greater need is a moment of sexual pleasure, then this as well is accepted and acted upon. In both cases the couple's goal is for each to please the other, and this takes appropriate timing.

3. *Sexual intimacy requires communication.* Our English word *intercourse* has to be prefaced by an adjective in order for us to understand its meaning. In sexual intimacy, *verbal* intercourse is a basic prerequisite to *sexual* intercourse.

In the Song of Solomon, the partners communicate what is pleasing about the other. They praise each other's physical attractiveness, verbalize their desires, and even communicate during their lovemaking. This verbal communication creates the romantic atmosphere in which sexual intimacy can blossom.

4. *Sexual intimacy requires time away.* Our technological society has created an abundance of time-saving devices, but too often these push us ever faster into the laser lanes of life. If we want to maintain sexual intimacy, we have to learn to slow down and take a break.

When the Shulammite is caught up in her love for Solomon, she initiates some time away with him (7:10-12). She says in effect, "Let's go out in the country, find a cute place to stay, see if the leaves have turned, and make love." She knows that time away from the kids, from responsibilities, and even from friends is essential to a growing intimate relationship.

Such time away needs to be budgeted for, planned, and written in ink on the calendar. It may seem impractical, selfish, or even unspiritual, but in our pressure-cooker society it is essential. Couples need time away to devote themselves to their own marital and sexual enrichment. Whether they go to an inexpensive motel down the street or to a friend's cabin in the mountains, they must find or create the time to seek out a relaxed environment in which sex can again be refreshing, spontaneous, and inventive.

God offers the world the Good News of Christ. He also offers good news on the subject of sex. Couples can celebrate their sexual desires knowing that God has placed His personal blessing upon their marital sexual intimacy. He did not give this gift to be used selfishly or manipulatively. He does not want sex to become stale and boring. God gave it so each married couple could deepen their intimacy and create a mutually satisfying relationship that brings glory to Him.

Related Articles
Chapter 8: Learning to Be Lovers
Chapter 8: Sexual Stages in Marriage

Rekindling the Flame of Romantic Sex

RICHARD A. MEIER

God tells husbands: "Rejoice in the wife of your youth. A loving doe, a graceful deer—may her breasts satisfy you always, may you ever be captivated by her love" (Prov. 5:18-19). God is not referring only to occasional acts of procreation; rather He commands us as married believers to develop a healthy, exhilarating sex life with our mate.

Sadly, Christian counselors see scores of Christian couples who are going through life missing out on the most pleasurable experience created by a loving and imaginative God. Throughout a married couple's life the flame of romantic sex should continue to burn. The key word is *romantic*. Without romance, the total sexual experience loses its sparkle and becomes tedious when it was meant to be funloving, vivacious, exciting, exhilarating, and totally fulfilling.

What is romance? Romance is the fun of sexuality. Marriage should be one continuous love affair. A romantic sex life may be inhibited by any of the following factors: poor attitudes toward sex because of an absence of positive input from our parents or the church, physical or mental sickness, fear of failure, overeating or excessive drinking, boredom, preoccupation with work or economic difficulties, mental or physical fatigue, inability to let oneself go completely, unresolved feelings of resentment, or a lack of concern for the spouse's satisfaction during sexual intercourse. Getting older can also inhibit the flame of love, but it doesn't need to. Even though the sex drive declines slightly with age, unhurried sex play can still lead to a romantic

sexual experience for an older couple.

Let me suggest some ideas for turning on the romantic flame again. Remember that romance means relating to each other emotionally and affectionately and not just physically. Romance expresses tenderness and caring throughout the day, not just at bedtime. It includes respect and kindness along with signals of sensuality. A romantic couple enjoys cuddling whether or not it leads to intercourse. In short, romantic sex focuses on the joining of two souls, not just the connection between two bodies.

Romance includes surprising each other with creative gifts and calling each other from work. A woman needs to get in the mood for sex, and a man needs to become a specialist in what makes his wife want to make love. Preparation for sex can include candlelight dinners, flowers, soft music, gently taking off each other's clothes, and kissing and touching each other.

Women often feel romantic about special times together—dinner in a quiet restaurant; walking in a park, along a lake, or even through a shopping mall. These are good times for communicating, caring, and sharing intimacy.

Romance includes mutual gratification. Most husbands want to receive love as well as give it. A man likes his wife to take the initiative some of the time.

Communication during romantic sex is important, especially to the wife. A man can tell her what he likes about her and what feels good to him. He can give her encouragement (but never make demands), he can express pleasure, and he can give gentle instruction. He can ask her what kind of foreplay she would enjoy or how she wants him to help her reach orgasm. Positive communication during lovemaking gives each partner a feeling of acceptance with intimacy and caring.

The flame of romance is fueled by creativity. Sleep together in the nude on occasion. Develop new positions and variations in intercourse. Move out of the bedroom for sex. Play seductive games with each other. Meditate on selected passages from the Song of Solomon. These things can develop an intensely passionate time together or can produce a light and relaxing atmosphere. Good lovers avoid boredom.

A couple needs to be enthusiastic about each other, excited about life and about their relationship. A good sense of humor helps. Each partner should be dedicated to staying physically fit and well groomed.

Making time instead of just finding time is also important for romantic love. Many people are so chronically bogged down with commitments that their romantic love life is squeezed out into the unimportant category. But it is important to make time for whatever matters to you. Plan time alone together. Go to a motel overnight without the children. Have someone take the children overnight, leaving the house to you and your spouse alone.

Feeling good about yourself sexually is important in fueling the flame. This requires underlying faith that romantic sex is God's will for yourself and your spouse. Sex is more than having children; it is meeting each other's real needs (1 Cor. 7:3).

Romantic love play is the way sex should be experienced in a Christian marriage. God gave us this capacity for enjoyment; He wants couples to relate in deep communion with one another at this important level.

SEASLEEPING: CAPE COD

Lying in bed with
the evening window
open to the bay
I feel his kinship
with the sea: he's like
the waves who
reach for me as they
accomplish a kind
of breathing—again and
again a push and a pull
to the limits.
    As each
crest and the next
breaks and retreats from
the play of foam, our
inlet is replenished
with a salt wash,
cloudy with sand,
warmed by its brief
excursion,
    leaving me
smooth as a dune, polished,
winking in subdued light,
lapped by a husband
whose every breath
swells, pauses, retreats
with a silver sigh.
    Like
a sandbar I shift under
the weight of an
ocean until the tide
fills our whole bay.
It is then that the wind
flattens, and a skin
of silence settles
like a sheet
over our midnight sleep.

Luci Shaw

Related Articles
Chapter 1: Love as Romance
Chapter 8: Learning to Be Lovers

Mental Fidelity

DAVID R. MAINS

I once attended a small, exclusive conference of mostly successful business executives. In a sharing session each man present was asked to tell in a few sentences what he felt to be one of his greatest successes. After a few minutes of reflection, the reports began.

Soon I was hearing people report on "my first million at age 27" and "control of the company at age 31" and "university department chairman as a result of my monumental research work." All too soon it was my turn.

"As I think about it," I said, not quite as bombastically as the others, "I consider my marriage to be my greatest success. I think that's because it's taken quite a bit of effort to make it what it is, but it has also brought me some of my greatest satisfaction."

That's when I got the distinct impression that the other men were saying to themselves, "Who invited this guy in his funny Sears, Roebuck sportcoat who's refusing to play the game by our rules?" But I was being honest—to me my marriage had become something of which I was proud.

Though no one at the time discussed the topic further, on numerous other occasions people have said to Karen or me, "Someday I hope my marriage can be like yours." Well, if it doesn't sound too bold, so do I—because I find our relationship very satisfying. Good as it is, however, it hasn't just happened.

"As we get married, David, is there a 'secret ingredient' you can share with us during the ceremony that kind of ensures happiness?" The request came from a couple for whom I was tying the knot. I thought about the challenge, discussed the matter with Karen, and decided to say this: *A model marriage involves determining to be faithful even in one's mind.*

There's no question but that infidelity does terrible things to a marriage. I've counseled enough people to know that the new morality produces only pseudo-happiness. I very much believe it's for our own good that Scripture says: "It is God's will that you should be holy; that you should avoid sexual immorality; that each of you should learn to control his own body in a way that is holy and honorable, not in passionate lust like the heathen, who do not know God; and that in this matter no one should wrong his brother or take advantage of him. The Lord will punish men for all such sins, as we have already told you and warned you" (1 Thes. 4:3-6).

So I decided to share with this young couple what I share with you now. Understand that your bodies were meant to be reserved exclusively for each other. Yet for your marriage to rise above the commonplace, you'll need to couple this knowledge with Christ's words in Matthew 5:27-28: "You have heard that it was said, 'Do not commit adultery.' But I tell you that anyone who looks at a woman lustfully has already committed adultery with her in his heart." Thus our Lord makes it clear that unfaithfulness is not just physical; it is mental as well. And model marriages require faithfulness of both body and mind.

Now I'm not just talking about refusing to think impure thoughts regarding someone other than your mate. What I have in mind is the careful channeling of all your romantic feelings to one person alone—your marriage partner. Comparisons, though necessary in the dating process, are to exist no more. Going out of your way to get to know someone better because of a romantic attraction is to be carefully guarded against. Fantasizing about another is taboo! If need be, avoid people of the opposite sex whom you begin to find more attractive than you should. And of course, all obvious impurity is out of bounds.

"Isn't this a bit severe?" you ask. Maybe without the compensation of our absolutely delightful marriage I would think so. But I think you'll find something beautiful beyond anything you dreamed possible in God's plan of giving yourself exclusively and therefore unreservedly to one person only. Through the years, Karen and I have found that the promise of total faithfulness, mental as well as physical, pays rich dividends.

Part of this is because it doesn't take too long before a person begins to feel insecure in a marriage. Why? Because hidden flaws start showing up. Everyone's either sloppy or lazy or selfish or crude or spiritually immature, or inconsiderate or undisciplined or a workaholic or a crybaby or a lousy breadwinner or a crummy bread maker or . . . need I go on? And what a joy it is to know that your mate isn't going to seek to compensate for your deficiencies by finding in a relationship with someone else (however innocent) the several good qualities you lack!

Does this sound difficult? I think the truth is just the opposite. It's the double-standard way of life that's tough, and it doesn't have nearly the benefits of total mental faithfulness. What if I take the marriage vow and add something to it— "I promise to keep myself wholly unto her, except possibly on certain occasions"? What if I say to her, "I love you, Darling, but I also enjoy my dreams of what it might be like to be married to my mystery lover"? Such comments ruin something very beautiful, don't they?

From the very beginning, then, determine not to allow these intrusions. The moment such thoughts appear, refuse to entertain them. Form the habit of immediately saying no! Remember that a good habit is just as hard to break as a bad one.

Some years ago I remember being very mad at Karen for a reason I no longer even recall. I fumed out of the house and got into the car to drive around and mentally nurse my hurts. "I know what I'll do," I thought. "I'll show her. I'll break my pattern and think about another woman. That will be the ultimate insult! Now, who will I think about? No, I can't think about her—she's a Christian. Maybe—no, that wouldn't be right either. Let's see. . . ." You know, as funny as it sounds, I couldn't come up with a name. And it's not that I didn't know anybody. It's just that over time a habit of mental faithfulness had been formed that was proving very difficult to break, and I was glad.

Many couples come to the altar and pledge faithfulness to each other, usually thinking only of their bodies. In today's world, I suppose that much is to be commended. But I believe a model marriage involves determining to be faithful even in one's mind. Thus I can think of no better gift married people could give their mates than the pledge to channel all romantic feelings and thoughts to that one with whom they shared the vows of marriage.

That's our secret.

Related Articles

THE IMPORTANCE OF MONOGAMY

The dream of exclusive, lifelong intimacy seems to be universal. Even the children of promiscuous parents seem to be born with the determination to make the first relationship the last one, to make a commitment "forever." Even promiscuous one-night-stand artists continue to speak the language of exclusiveness: "I never loved anybody so much before!" "You are the first person I ever *really* loved."

The ultimate moral issue in sexual intimacy has nothing to do with pregnancy or with acquiring a disease. The ultimate moral issue centers on the fact that humans cannot squander their emotional resources among multiple partners and survive to establish a healthy, honest, lifelong marriage relationship with the last person in the lineup. The human capacity for lifelong bonding is a nonrenewable and most precious resource.

The lifelong, bonded union we call marriage must be totally honest. This is not to say that each must know absolutely everything about the other's past, present, and future, but marriage partners must not defraud each other emotionally, affectionally, or sexually. Marriage rests on a trusting acceptance of the instinctual dream: the relationship is exclusive and unconditional, and it intentionally closes out any overtures to compromise the exclusive bond.

Studies of couples who agreed to release each other to become involved in sexual adventures with other partners have found that one of two things happened: either the marriages broke apart, or the extramarital sexual activity ended. A typical spouse in a surviving marriage commented, "We found that we needed to spend the extra time with each other, since we were more important to each other than we were to anybody else."

Donald & Robbie Joy

How Premarital Sex Can Affect Your Marriage

DONALD & ROBBIE JOY

Why does the Bible forbid premarital sex? Because sex outside marriage hurts people. One doesn't have to be a theologian or even a Christian to recognize the damage it does; it is self-evident.

Here are some effects of premarital sex that show up consistently:

1. *Humans seem to be programmed to sense that the first sexual partner ought to be the lifelong, exclusive partner.* Typically the first love takes on an indelible character. The loss of that partner is grieved by both males and females, but researchers have learned that males grieve longer. The grief is often tinged with guilt—a feeling of personal

responsibility for having committed a crime against oneself and others. Thus a man and woman who become "one flesh" without first protecting their union publicly and legally are, at best, indifferent and negligent; at worst they are exploitative.

2. *Premarital genital contact with multiple partners blunts a person's capacity for forming a deep, permanent relationship.* If marriage follows a series of sexual partners, marital fidelity is less likely to occur, because the person's ability to bond with someone else has been damaged. A person who has been damaged by multiple sexual relationships is likely to continue a pattern of promiscuity after marriage, even though it leads to an increasingly lower view of his or her own value as well as those of other people.

3. *People who begin sexual intimacy before marriage tend to divorce sexual pleasure from responsibility.* They usually assume that sex is primarily recreational, most enjoyable when it occurs with no consequences and no strings attached. This attitude undercuts the enormous power of sexual pleasure to serve as a natural, God-given tranquilizer to sustain a couple through the trials, drudgery, and agonies of parenthood, breadwinning, and general life stresses. Instead of seeing sexual pleasure as a rejuvenating payoff in the midst of pain, they find sex hard to enjoy unless it represents escape from responsibilities. It is not uncommon for "recreational sex" types to quickly lose their sexual capaci-

ty as the realities of establishing a household increase their responsibilities. On the other hand, couples who take full responsibility for their sexuality tend to find that their sexual motivation holds up well under the demands of home and family.

4. *If a premarital sexual union leaves one partner with the long-term effects of a healthy bonding relationship, that "ghost" can haunt future relationships and marriages for the rest of the person's life.* Unless the person works through his or her grief, the older bond will remain present and will compete with any new bonds the person tries to establish.

The possibilities of beginning an unplanned pregnancy or of contracting a sexually transmitted disease are frequently cited as reasons to avoid premarital sex. These are serious considerations, but they are not the most important reason. The ultimate moral tragedy of premarital genital contact is that two personalities have opened and joined at their very core with no public and legal guarantees that they will never have to be separated, whether by negligence, parental interference, or sheer inability to cope with the host of responsibilities the intimacy sets loose. Such careless bonding sets the stage for heartbreak.

Related Articles
Chapter 3: Sex Before Marriage: Why Say No?
Chapter 8: What to Do When You've Already Messed Things Up

What to Do When You've Already Messed Things Up

LaVONNE NEFF

When Christians talk about moral choices, they tend to give serious warnings—especially when those choices are in some way related to sex. Premarital sex, adultery, abortion, divorce, and even sterilization are condemned for being anti-life and selfish, eroders of trust, and producers of unending guilt.

There is truth in these warnings. God does not forbid certain behaviors simply because He likes to say no. He knows far more than we do about cause and effect, and He knows what actions will make us miserable, sick, and evil. Because He loves us, He protects us by warning us against those actions.

There's no getting around it—bad choices produce disastrous results. And yet all of us have made bad choices, and all of us have to face their consequences.

What will my wrong choices mean for me? What if I was not a virgin when I married? What if I have had an affair? What if I have been involved in pornography, homosexuality, or some other distortion of sex? What if I have had an abortion, have produced a child I could not care for properly, or have refused to produce children I should have had? What if I have used sex as a weapon instead of as a loving form of communication with my spouse? Am I condemned to eternal remorse and undying guilt? Is my life ruined?

No, not if I am a Christian.

It is important to understand something about Christianity. Although it teaches moral behavior and condemns immorality, it is not primarily a religion of morals. The Bible never tells us we are saved because we are good. Instead, Scripture affirms what observation reveals: we are all sinners from birth. Every one of us was raised by parents who in their intimate lives fell short of God's ideal. Every one of us has made moral choices—sexual choices—that have resulted in pain and regret. And, though it is hard for us to face, every one of our children will also make choices that are at least unwise and perhaps immoral. As sinners in a sinful world, we humans seem bent on destroying our own happiness.

But God does not leave us in sin and despair. Rather, He offers us hope.

Christianity is, above all else, a religion of new beginnings. The Christian faith began early one Easter morning, when all reason for hope seemed lost. Jesus Christ was dead, and His followers were in hiding. But to the terror of the Roman guards and the disbelief even of Jesus' own disciples, He rose from the dead. He walked out of the tomb fully alive, full of power, immortal.

Jesus and His followers then gave the world a nearly unbelievable message: the Man who conquered death has also conquered sin. No matter how dead we are in sins, no matter how we have tried to ruin our lives, He can raise us up and give us new life in Him. "We were therefore buried with Him through baptism into death in order that, just as Christ was raised from the dead through the glory of the Father, we too may live a new life" (Rom. 6:4; read the whole chapter about freedom from sin through Christ).

This means that even if my bad choices have made my life unhappy, I have hope. I can recognize that my unhappiness is the direct result of my sin. I can confess my sin to Jesus, who promises to forgive me (see 1 John 1:9). And then—good news!—I can turn my life over to Him, and He will make it beautiful again.

What was Jesus' mission on earth?—"to bind up the brokenhearted, to proclaim freedom for the captives and release for the prisoners . . . to comfort all who mourn, and provide for those who grieve in Zion—to bestow on them a crown of beauty instead of ashes, the oil of gladness instead of mourning, and a garment of praise instead of a spirit of despair" (Isa. 61:1-3).

Jesus never says, "Your suffering is your own fault, and you might as well learn to enjoy it." Instead He says, "Come to Me, all you who are weary and burdened, and I will give you rest" (Matt. 11:28).

The Bible never says, "Christ will save your soul, but you've ruined your chances for happiness in this life." Instead it says, "If anyone is in Christ, he is a new creation; the old has gone, the new has come!" (2 Cor. 5:17)

What does this mean for me? I can't call an aborted baby back to life or cancel a child that should not have been conceived. I can't revive a broken first marriage or become a virgin again. I can't restore fertility that was damaged by surgery or by a sexually transmitted disease. I have to live with the consequences of my choices—*but I don't have to be ruined by them.*

I can become a loving parent and raise my children for the Lord, even if I did not intend to conceive them. I can work toward making my marriage strong and loving, a reflection of Christ's love for His church (see Eph. 5:21-33), even if I have sinned against this spouse

THE BIBLE ON SEX AND MARRIAGE

God created sex for various reasons. One reason, of course, was procreation—having children. Many people think that's where it stops.

But another reason is so that husband and wife might become one. In Genesis 2:24, we read, "They will become one flesh," and in Ephesians 5 Paul describes God's overall program for marriage, a relationship between husband and wife in which bonding has occurred.

Bonding means that the couple is joined together spiritually, emotionally, and psychologically as well as physically. Sex promotes bonding. It helps two people feel one with each other. That is why when a couple in a dating relationship has sex, it gets more difficult to break up than if sex had never been involved. God designed sex that way, to strengthen the union between marriage partners.

In 1 Corinthians 7:2-5, Paul advises husbands and wives to meet each other's sexual needs on a regular basis. This is not so that they may have more children, but so that they will avoid temptation and strengthen their own union.

According to Scripture, sex in marriage is wonderful, healthy, and fulfilling. It is not just for procreation—it is also for recreation and the sharing of love.

Josh McDowell

or a previous one. If, because of my own choices, I have no children or spouse, I can consecrate myself to "feeding God's lambs," the needy people to whom He directs me.

God has promised to "hurl all our iniquities into the depths of the sea" (Micah 7:19) and to "remember [our] sins no more" (Jer. 31:34). He wants to look at us where we are now, and to help us live our present lives to His glory. If He doesn't want to dwell on our past mistakes, do we have any right to do so? Shouldn't we imitate Him by asking, "How can I live for Christ with what I have?"

Guilt and regret can be an important signal that I need to confess my sins to Jesus. But if I have confessed them and He has forgiven them, then guilt and regret aren't necessary anymore. In fact, they are likely to keep me from putting on the "crown of beauty" God promises. If, though I have received God's forgiveness, my inner voice says, "Why did I . . ." or "I wish I hadn't . . ." or "How could I have . . ." I need to turn it off, *firmly.* I do not need to be tied to my past. I am living in the present, and a wonderful future lies ahead of me. God

has forgiven me, and now He wants me to get on with life, making the very best of what I've got.

The overwhelming message in Scripture is *God's grace*—His willingness to take us where we are and turn us into His own beautiful creations. If, in the process of making us like Him, He has to pick us up over and over again, thanks be to God, He will do just that. In the words of the Apostle Paul:

"What, then, shall we say in response to this? If God is for us, who can be against us? . . . Who will bring any charge against those whom God has chosen? . . . Who shall separate us from the love of Christ? . . . I am convinced that neither death nor life, neither angels nor demons, neither the present nor the future, nor any powers, neither height nor depth, nor anything else in all creation, will be able to separate us from the love of God that is in Christ Jesus our Lord" (Rom. 8:31-39).

God wants to take your life where it is right now and make it beautiful. He'll do it, if you ask Him.

Related Articles
Chapter 15: Bringing Love Back to Life
Chapter 16: Restoring a Broken Marriage

Learning to Be Lovers

EARL & SANDY WILSON

Most husbands are surprised to learn that their wives like affection more than sex. Yes, there is a difference. In fact, they often communicate two entirely different messages. Affection says, "I want to make you feel good by showing you how much I love you." Sex often says, "I want you to make me feel good." When sex and affection are properly blended in a well-adjusted marriage, the message is this: "We are crazy about each other,

and we like to share those feelings when we 'make like' and when we 'make love.'"

We use the terms *make like* and *make love* because they are both important elements of sexual adjustment. Couples need to spend time kissing, hugging, tenderly talking, and doing things for each other. These activities are the basic elements of sexual adjustment. They need to take place daily.

"Making like" keeps the excitement alive and helps prepare the couple mentally and physically for making love.

We believe that healthy sexual adjustment involves three key attitudes and three key behaviors.

Attitude 1. Our bodies belong to each other and are intended as God's gift to each other for sexual pleasure. (First Corinthians 7:3-5 may be the most important sex manual ever written.) Sexual pleasure is for both husband and wife. Each should work to ensure the pleasure of the other.

Attitude 2. Good sex and selfishness don't go together. Both husband and wife need to give all they can give rather than try to take all they can take. Sexual pleasure is a gift to be given to your spouse, not an experience to be gained at the other person's expense.

Attitude 3. Sexual adjustment is a process, not a performance. Modern sexual technology is disgusting. It has produced frigid women and impotent men. Husbands and wives are afraid to enjoy each other for fear they won't do it right. We believe that a couple should devote themselves to the process of learning to be lovers rather than expecting to know how to do it perfectly even before they get married. For example, with very few exceptions, simultaneous mutual orgasm is a myth, and striving for it rather than having fun together may be a disaster. What myths might *you* be vainly pursuing?

Now for the active part. What behaviors are necessary for a good sex life?

Behavior 1. Keep your romance alive. Communicate love and excitement all day long, not just when you want to have sex. Good sex is a combination of anticipation and tenderness. Communicate to each other your excitement and willingness as regularly as possible and in as many ways as possible. Suggestive notes and telephone calls may help keep your level of desire compatible.

SONG OF SONGS
7:10-13

I belong to my lover, and his desire is for me. Come, my lover, let us go to the countryside, let us spend the night in the villages. Let us go early to the vineyards to see if the vines have budded, if their blossoms have opened, and if the pomegranates are in bloom—and there I will give you my love. The mandrakes send out their fragrance, and at our door is every delicacy, both new and old, that I have stored up for you, my lover.

Behavior 2. Spend plenty of time in physical togetherness even when sexual intercourse is not the objective. Before marriage you were probably often aroused sexually, and now you wonder what has happened. Think about how you acted then as compared to now. You spent hours talking, kissing, hugging, and touching. You still need that now. To become responsive, wives often need romantic foreplay without the threat of rushing too quickly to sexual intercourse. Men need to learn to enjoy "making like" in order to make their sexual experience richer.

Behavior 3. Take time for each other, and make that time a priority. You can have sex in 1 to 10 minutes, but making love deserves plenty of time. Savor each other's bodies. Allow the normal arousal process to take place, especially for the wife. Most men make the mistake of doing what arouses them too soon and too fast without considering the time needed by the wife. Last, take time to wind down together after orgasm has occurred. Some of the most precious moments are those when you hold each other and remember just how good it is to be so close to each other.

Finally, an underlying process must occur if optimal sexual adjustment is to occur—communication. Talk to each other. Tell your mate what you enjoy. Tell him or her what you appreciate. Tell him or her kindly what isn't helpful. Good sex requires good and constant communication. It isn't doing what comes naturally. You will need to talk to each other and enjoy the intimacy of communication just as much as the physical pleasure of sexual intercourse.

Related Articles
Chapter 4: Cultivating Romance
Chapter 8: How to Obtain and Maintain Sexual Intimacy
Chapter 8: Sexual Stages in Marriage

Sexual Stages in Marriage

CHARLES M. SELL

Sex in marriage isn't necessarily like the flight of an eagle, starting with a great leap and then steadily soaring into newer and greater heights. Nor is it always like a baby learning to walk, clumsily stumbling along through numerous failed attempts before finally achieving a stable stride. The place and pleasure of sex in marriage have some ups and downs. In part, these highs and lows are tied to the adult life stages.

• *Young adulthood (ages 18-39).* Young marrieds will be learning the art of lovemaking. This includes discovering good and creative sex technique. A marriage manual or two will help them understand their own bodies and sexual responses and will show them how to give as well as receive pleasure. Reading aloud a marriage manual together is a good way to make it easier to talk about sex. Patience is called for. It sometimes takes time to lose inhibitions and develop open passion, especially for women, who tend to become most sexually responsive in their 30s.

Though research tells us most couples have happy honeymoons and easy sexual adjustment, some do have problems. The husband may not be able to keep from climaxing too soon or may be unable to perform intercourse; the wife may feel little or nothing during intercourse or may not have an orgasm. The couple should be careful so that an initial problem does not grow into a major one. A downward spiral could occur: a temporary problem leads to disappointment, the disappointment leads to even more difficulty, which sets the stage for further "failure." What was a temporary problem of adjustment can turn into a major difficulty this way. If the couple can't solve the problem in a few months with the help of a sex manual, they should see a counselor for help.

Another task for the young adult is the cultivation of romance and intimacy along with physical sex. This may be especially difficult for men, who tend to get caught up in the physical passion of sex and separate that from personal closeness. And even a very romantic person can change after he marries. This occurs because after marriage he sees himself in a different role. A man, for example, may think that romantic walks and talks are for boyfriends and girlfriends, but not for husbands and wives—who already have plenty of time together running the household and watching TV. He may suddenly stop taking his wife out on dates now that they are married. He is the same person, but

246

now perceives his role differently. The result is that the couple has sex, but little romance and intimacy.

A leading expert on adult development, Erik Erikson, said that learning intimacy is the young adult's major developmental task. Being more complex, the art of interpersonal intimacy takes longer to master than the techniques for exciting physical sex. Couples need to be patient with one another through the many years it will require for them to achieve an open, honest, close companionship. "Intimacy is always difficult," writes one expert. "If it isn't difficult, it isn't intimacy."

Couples learn that many things affect their sex life: overwork, fatigue, sickness. One of the first major adjustments may come when the wife gets pregnant. At first the pregnancy may make sex even more thrilling and intimate. The couple no longer has to worry about using birth control, and the wife may be even more desirable to her husband during the early months. Of course, some physical problems with pregnancy, including the wife's increasing girth, may demand new forms of patience and understanding. Emotional issues related to pregnancy may also cause temporary changes in the couple's relationship. Because so much of her energy is concentrated on her womb's occupant, a wife may have little left to support her husband. He might feel neglected or unloved or feel that his wife resents him.

After the baby takes his first breath, the couple's sex life faces another adjustment. Being a parent may change a person's attitude toward lovemaking. A man, for example, may think he is now making love to a mother. Since mothers are not considered sex symbols, this thought could dampen his ardor with his wife if he's not careful.

The presence of children in the home does not permit the kind of romantic, sensual life the couple could have alone. With children comes an increased need

GETTING OFF TO A GOOD SEXUAL START

Engaged couples dream about the honeymoon—they picture the perfect sexual experience, just like the ones they see on TV or in movies. But the media gives an unrealistic picture. It is more realistic for the honeymooners to expect that they will feel uncomfortable, vulnerable, pressure to perform, pressure to live up to expectations, concern over their own misconceptions, and maybe even fear.

So as you plan your honeymoon, realize that good sex takes time. The first sexual experience needs to be taken slowly, with tenderness and understanding, and with sensitivity toward each other. This is not the time for criticism, attacks, foolish and hurtful comments, or tense conversations.

In addition, as you plan the honeymoon, plan other activities for your getaway, realizing that you're developing your friendship and your marriage, not just your sex life. Don't get overtired or sunburned; think about where you will be in relation to privacy and distractions.

And above all, remember that as you grow to know and love each other more deeply over the years, your sexual relationship will deepen and become more satisfying.

YFC Editors

for privacy, especially for wives, who are easily distracted by the sound of a child in the next room or the fear that he may barge through the door. The couple should be sure to make time to be alone and to continue their relationship as lovers. They should be careful of calling each other "Mom" and "Dad" or of thinking of one another only in those terms. A lock on the bedroom door can do a lot for the couple's sex life.

• *Midlife (ages 40-60).* Midlife is mostly a positive sexual time for couples. Studies show that marital satisfaction takes a leap when the nest begins to empty. Second honeymoons do happen, sparked by increased privacy, less worry about children, and more intimate time together. During midlife, a man and woman tend to become more alike in their attitude toward sex, making it richer for both of them. Men who once prized the physical part of sex begin to place high value on the intimate personal relationship. And women who as young adults valued intimacy start to take greater delight in the physical pleasures of the bedroom. There is a happy meeting of bodies and minds.

Relatively few women have any sexual problems related to menopause. The midlife transition becomes a real crisis for only a minority of men, some of whose general dissatisfaction with life may make them less interested in sex or even unable to perform sexually. Answers to these problems are available through a trip or two to a physician and/or counselor.

• *Older adults (over 60).* Sex continues to play a major part in the couple's relationship after retirement. Often it plays an even greater part than before since there is more leisure, less distraction, and more togetherness. Expressions of affection may be needed more than ever. Fables about sex being a strain on the heart or fears that sex in old age is unnatural should be laid aside. As one doctor put it, "Most people can and should expect to have sex long after they no longer wish to ride bicycles." There is no time clock in the body that turns off sexual feelings. Besides exploring new and creative ways of expressing their sensual love, older people will discover all kinds of meaning in their sexual relationship.

There *are* some changes. Older people have sex less frequently than younger people. But because all physical and mental reactions slow down in old age, sexual episodes tend to last longer than they did earlier. This can lead to greater satisfaction. Other major changes might include a man's losing some of the stiffness of his erection or a woman's having less vaginal secretion and elasticity. The greatest sexual adjustments will be related to bouts with illness: heart disease, arthritis, diabetes, etc. Symptoms from some diseases or the medicine taken for them may diminish the sex drive or hinder performance. The ill person may have to help his partner reach climax in ways other than intercourse, and the well partner will need to trust God for patience and strength to handle times of abstinence.

Related Articles
Chapter 1: Love as Romance
Chapter 8: How to Obtain and Maintain Sexual Intimacy

248

Male/Female Attitudes Toward Sex

INGRID TROBISCH

For a man, the sexual act is something that happens within a limited time. His physical desire is quickly aroused and just as quickly satisfied. He does not need a long preparation. In a relatively short time he reaches climax, and after that he can turn immediately to other things and interests. His curve of pleasure goes up steeply, and when climax is reached, it returns almost instantly to zero.

For a woman, sex is quite different. She needs much more time. Her curve of pleasure rises gently and gradually. She experiences climax not as one point, but more like a plateau. From this plateau she descends slowly and reluctantly.

One of my African sisters, Ernestine Banyolak, used the following comparison to illustrate the different time element for man and woman in the act of love: a man's experience is like a fire of dry leaves. It is easily kindled, flaring up suddenly and dying down just as quickly. A woman's experience, on the other hand, is like a fire of glowing charcoal. Her husband has to blow on these coals with loving patience. Once the blaze is burning brightly, it will keep on glowing and radiating warmth for a long time.

A man is aroused by what he sees; a woman, by what she hears. The greatest erogenous zone of a woman's body is her heart. It is the words she hears from her husband that reach her heart and "open up" her body. For her, the sexual act is not an event with a definite beginning and end. Rather, all that she does is enclosed in this atomosphere of love.

Her thinking and feeling are centered on her husband even if she is working, preparing a meal, cleaning the house, doing the laundry, or shopping. She cannot separate her body from her soul. That which she feels inside is the same as that which she expresses outwardly.

Sexual desire and longing for love, for her, are one. They permeate her whole being. Perhaps that is why, when her sexual longing is fulfilled, she has almost supernatural strength. Peace and fulfillment give her a contagious and radiant joy for life.

If the husband has learned to wait for his wife; if there is a certain restfulness, gentleness, even playfulness when they unite physically, there will be deeper fulfillment for both. A new realm of experience opens up also for the husband. With every moment he is able to prolong the sexual union, his self-confidence grows. If he has learned to find rest inside the body of his wife, he feels sheltered, like a child reposing on his mother's lap and encircled by her arms. This can help him relax in his innermost being and can give him new strength.

He needs the strength that this kind of union can provide, since he is so often attacked from outside where more is demanded from him than he is able to give. And the wife who tends to lose herself in her subjective feelings will experience, in her husband's ability to master himself and wait for her, a strong, fatherly hand to whom she can entrust herself. She is able to let herself go completely, because she knows he will safely lead her through the turmoil of her emotions.

I have often thought that since a man's sexual organs are external, perhaps he is more vulnerable when it comes to sexual performance. Premature ejaculation or failure to have an erection can be for him a far greater threat than what a woman experiences if she fails to have a climax. It is the wife who gives her husband confidence in his ability to love and thus helps him love himself as a man, just as he helps her love herself as a woman.

In many ways it is easier for a man to be satisfied sexually. He's thirsty, he takes a drink of water, and then his thirst is quenched. A woman is thirsty too, but in the moment she is ready to take a drink, the glass may fall and break into a thousand pieces through a cross word or a disappointment. If this happens, she is left with her thirst. What should she do then? Look ahead. God is greater than our hearts (1 John 3:20), and He has promised to wipe away every tear (Rev. 21:4). There are times when we may need to give up the ripe fruit of love into His hands, letting Him use it to bear fruit for others.

When the Lights Are Out, My Husband Wants to Do the Strangest Things

EARL & SANDY WILSON

This is not an article about kinky sex. It is more than that. We want to help you better understand yourself and your spouse sexually. Is oral sex OK for the Christian? What about tying each other up or dressing so that you look like your spouse's sexual fantasy? Should you ever do a striptease for your mate? What about anal sex?

To help determine what is right and wrong in these areas, we believe there are four questions that need to be answered.

1. *Does the Bible directly prohibit the activity?* With the possible exception of anal sex, which may be referred to in Romans 1:26-27, none of the activities listed above are specifically mentioned in Scripture. Maybe that is because they are products of our sex-crazy world. It is hard to know for sure what is meant by the phrases "shameful lusts," "unnatural relations," and "indecent acts," all used in this passage. Ask the Holy Spirit to show you whether your pet sexual activity would be excluded by these or other verses.

2. *Is there a medical reason for avoiding the activity?* The potential for damage to rectal tissue may rule out anal sex. You could also argue that any form of sexual activity involving physical constraints or whipping should be avoided. Oral sex and the other activities cited would not be ruled out on medical grounds alone.

3. *Will engaging in the activity bring the couple closer together emotionally?* The answer to this question will be yes only if both parties are in fa-

250

vor of trying it. Too often the desires of one are forced on the other, resulting in more distance rather than closeness. Each partner must respect the other and be sensitive to his or her comfort level. No sexual activity apart from regular intercourse should be engaged in unless the couple can enjoy it together. This does not mean that the more sensitive partner should not be willing to experiment sexually. Scripture says that a married couple's bodies belong to each other (1 Cor. 7:4). We believe this opens the door for a wide range of sexual activity if each partner respects the feelings of the other.

4. *Will engaging in the activity result in conformity to Christ or conformity to the standard of the world?* Have we been indoctrinated by our pornographic society to believe that only kinky sex can make us happy? If so, we are in bad trouble. Regular sexual union is God's standard. Other activities may not be wrong if both partners agree, but if they become such an obsession that we think about them all the time, they are wrong for us. Read 1 Corinthians 6:12 carefully: " 'Everything is permissi-ble for me'— but not everything is beneficial. 'Everything is permissible for me'—but I will not be mastered by anything."

Finally, let us conclude with what we consider a basic principle of healthy sexual involvement: we are to savor each other and each other's bodies—not the bodies of someone else. Sexual fantasy can lead to anonymous sex, even with your mate. God does not intend you to think of anyone but your mate when you are making love. Avoid any activities that lead you in the wrong direction. Learn to give pleasure to and receive pleasure from your mate in any ways that pass the test of the four questions above, but avoid at all costs any sexual fantasies that lead you away from Christ or your mate. Fantasy is no substitute for a rich love life with the life partner God has given you. Sex is very personal. Keep it that way—just between you and your mate.

Related Articles
Chapter 8: Learning to Be Lovers
Chapter 8: Male/Female Attitudes Toward Sex

Common Sexual Problems and What to Do About Them

ED WHEAT, M.D.

Only a few years ago a discussion of common sexual problems would have focused almost entirely on medical dysfunctions such as impotence. But the emphasis has changed. Today most Christian couples are well aware of the blessings and pleasures the Lord has designed for them in the one-flesh relationship of marriage. As a result, they are eager to experience every good thing; their expectations are high. If their sexual relationship falls short of total fulfillment, they consider it a problem to be solved, and they search for the solution. Not for them the silent endurance and trial-and-error methods of their parents and grandparents! I consider this a positive development, for we know that satis-

DIFFERING DESIRES

What should you do if you want sex more (or less) often than your partner?

It is helpful to realize that this is a normal problem. Many married couples find that one desires sex more often than the other. This could be due to several factors—differing work schedules, differing types of work (one spouse does hard physical labor all day and truly is too tired), or differing expectations for how often married couples should have sex. It is important to realize that the media bombards us with sexual pressure—pressure that gives us an unrealistic idea of the frequency of sex and the "way it should be done."

As spouses deal with their differences in this area, they need to remember to be sensitive to each other's needs and feelings. They should ask themselves: (1) What is it I really want from my spouse? (2) Are my expectations too high? (3) Am I taking this too personally? (4) Can I talk about this with my spouse?

Of course, talking about the frequency of intercourse is the first step toward reaching a solution satisfactory to both husband and wife. Spouses need to acknowledge their feelings, find out if there is truly a deeper problem, or if they just need to work out a scheduled time to be together. Both need to realize that as a married couple, they have rights in love to each other's bodies—thus they should neither withhold sex nor demand it (see 1 Cor. 7:1-5). Because they love each other, they need to be sensitive to the other person's needs and regard his or her desires.

It is also possible that this issue is symptomatic of deeper problems. The root problem may be something that needs to be dealt with in counseling. If this is the case, understanding and encouragement are key.

YFC Editors

fying sexual intimacy has a remarkable power to renew, refresh, and sustain a marriage.

In the hundreds of couples I see from all over the world, one basic problem usually exists: for varied reasons they have been unable to please one another sexually. In most cases, this results in a frustrated wife who seldom or never reaches sexual release and an equally unhappy husband who does not know what to do about it. In some cases, both reach release, but neither enjoys it very much. Before we discuss some reasons for this problem and offer solutions, we need to understand these principles:

1. Every sexual problem is a couple problem. It takes two to find the solution together, so avoid placing blame on one another.

2. Every sexual problem has a solution that can lead to pleasure and satisfaction for both partners. Don't give up!

3. The solutions always require additional knowledge and the application of that knowledge so that there is a change in behavior and attitude. This includes accurate medical information, a clear understanding of biblical teachings on the total relationship of husband and wife, and an ever-growing personal knowledge of your own mate.

4. Always remember that your daily behavior toward one another will color and actually determine the extent and depth of pleasure you experience when

you come together sexually.

5. Let your attitudes toward sex be shaped by what God says about it in the Bible. As I wrote in *Intended for Pleasure* (Revell, 1981), know that "you have God's permission to enjoy sex within your marriage. He invented sex; He thought it up to begin with. You can learn to enjoy it, and, husband, you can develop a thrilling, happy marriage with 'the wife of your youth.' If your marriage has been a civil-war battlefield or a dreary wasteland, instead of a lovers' trysting place, all that can change. . . . God has a perfect plan for marriage which we may choose to step into at any time, and the mistakes of the past can be dealt with and left behind."

Now let's consider some of the most common reasons for an inability to please one another sexually, along with some suggested remedies:

1. *A problem with the mechanics of bringing about the wife's sexual release.* God designed the wife so that persistent and intensifying stimulation along the shaft of the clitoris for 20 minutes or so is necessary to bring about orgasm. Many times the couple simply needs to learn exactly where, how, and for how long. Begin with a careful study of *Intended for Pleasure,* which gives all the information you need. But see a concerned physician or sex therapist if additional help is required.

2. *An absence of positive, loving communication as to what is sexually pleasing and a failure to demonstrate a desire to meet one another's needs.* Great lovers do not just "do what comes naturally." They study their partner and become sensitive to his or her wishes, implied or stated. They learn how to impart maximum pleasure to their mate. Since each individual is quite different, you need to become an expert on what brings pleasure (and displeasure) to your own partner. Let one another know what you enjoy, but keep your communication positive and loving. Courtesy

and tact are characteristics of the true lover.

3. *Not enough time in foreplay to bring about the wife's arousal.* This time also enhances the husband's pleasurable sensations during ejaculation. The pleasure of sex is not just the fleeting moment of orgasm; it is the thrilling physical and emotional closeness of the entire experience. Take more time with the preliminaries; focus on pleasure, not performance.

4. *A lack of cuddling and snuggling and daily intimacy when not engaged in sex.* It is essential to build the feelings of love in your daily life, and to learn to relate always as lovers. One of the best ways to do this is by affectionate, non-sexual touching. Focus on your partner. Treat him or her as the most prized and honored person in your life. Unkindness, inconsideration, rudeness, or a critical spirit will smother any feeling of being loved and desired and is sure to sabotage sexual pleasure. For important information on how to build and enhance your total love life, see my book *Love Life for Every Married Couple* (Zondervan, 1980).

5. *Repressed anger, resentment, or bitterness in the marriage.* Sexual intercourse is either a joyful affirmation of two people's life together, or it is a revelation of defects in their relationship. Your sexual relationship will tend to reflect your emotional standing. This can and must be dealt with biblically through the process of resolving, forgiving, and "forgetting what lies behind." Often a biblical counselor can help a couple struggling with this problem.

6. *A lack of trust; insecurity in the marriage.* Even one episode of infidelity can poison the sense of trust and security which is so essential for a fulfilling sexual relationship. God designed sex to be enjoyed by one man and one woman within the permanent shelter of total commitment to each other in marriage. There must be an acknowledgment and

forsaking of sin; a biblical restoration; and the slow rebuilding of love and trust. Never tell your mate details of a sexual experience with someone else, however. Do not put this burden on your partner, for details are hard to forget!

7. *A lack of creativity in lovemaking.* Stirring the imagination is an important key to evoking a sexual response. Be creative, but be very sensitive to what turns your partner on . . . or off. Keep in mind that simple exhaustion because of hard work, a demanding schedule, small children, or too much social life can diminish sexual interest. Creativity will do little good if one or both are too tired to enjoy it.

Specific physical problems cannot be discussed in this brief article, so please refer to *Intended for Pleasure* for answers to your questions not answered here. Whether the difficulty be impotence or premature ejaculation or a health problem or disability, there is always a way—either to correct the problem or to learn how to bring each other sexual pleasure even under unusual conditions.

The true joy of sex includes the following elements, and if these are present you will gain the benefits of fulfilling sex: (1) an assurance of being accepted and desired; (2) the well-being that comes from intimate physical and emotional closeness; (3) the sensuous delights of loving sexual and nonsexual caresses; and (4) the wonderful feeling of oneness and of belonging to each other. The greatest turn-on is seeing your mate respond to you and your lovemaking with pleasure.

Related Articles
Chapter 1: Love as Romance
Chapter 8: Rekindling the Flame of Romantic Sex
Chapter 8: Male/Female Attitudes Toward Sex

Selfishness in Sex

CAROLE MAYHALL
(with Jack's help)

She was a wise woman. A godly woman. A woman who did not speak casually. Yet her statement shocked me.

"I am coming to believe," she mused, "that almost all problems in sex are due to selfishness."

In the days that followed, I turned that statement around and around, trying to find holes in its surface. Then I put it away to bring out every time I heard someone lamenting about his or her sex life. My conclusion, after a great many years of listening and interacting on this subject with couples of every age, is that the statement is true.

A woman and I walked along the lake, bright sunlight splashing off the water in chuckles and ripples, but she wasn't noticing. Jack and I had spent the last two hours presenting the physical aspect of marriage to a church group. We had talked about the fact that many of us have so many negative ideas about sex that we have to let God renew our minds until we see sex as God intended it— wholesome and beautiful. Our bodies are created for each other's pleasure, and that is right and good. We had mentioned that some wives are afraid of undressing in the same room as their husbands, but God has said we belong to each other—we are one—and we need to pray for God's mind on this. Shortly after this session, this woman asked me to take a walk with her.

Her head down, her voice low, she said tearfully, "I know I'm supposed to let God renew my mind until I feel and think as God feels and thinks, and I want to do that. But right now I don't feel good about my body. I think it's ugly. Yet my husband insists on making love in broad daylight, and I can't respond. What can I do?"

In a quaint old restaurant in a small European hotel, a wife leaned across the table and said softly, "I don't know what to do. When we make love, my husband insists on being—being—well, very *verbal*. He wants to talk all the time. I want to be quiet and just enjoy the feelings, and his talking turns me off. What should I do?"

In another country and another year, a wife sat on a hard wooden chair in a motel room, her sweet face torn with concern. "I want to please him. I really do. But I need more time when we make love. I need to have a couple of hours to talk things through, to prepare, to build up to lovemaking. But often in our busy schedule there isn't time to do that, and he wants to make love in a few minutes. It's hard to respond, and I find myself resenting it."

A man called our hotel room to tell Jack, "My wife has hated sex the whole 18 years we've been married, but it has gotten worse lately. We haven't made love in months, and I don't know how much more I can stand. She refuses to see a counselor."

Look closely at these problems and what do you see? Each one is really a matter of selfishness. One or both partners desire to *get* more than to *give*. One or both want things their own way rather than the other's way.

Selfishness in sex is often a two-way street. For example, the wife who dreaded making love in broad daylight needed to pray for God's view about her body, for it was made to please her husband. But the renewing of a mind isn't done in a day. It may take weeks or months. In the meantime, her husband must unselfishly understand her feelings and yield to her desire for softer light—black-out drapes over the window, perhaps, or more times of making love in the evening.

Compromise is a necessary ingredient in any good marriage. What a simple matter it is to say, "Honey, I enjoy sex more when I can concentrate on the feelings rather than on words. I know you enjoy it more when you express how you are feeling. Could we enjoy silence or soft music together one time, and then the next I'll really work on being more verbal?"

Or, "Sweetheart, I enjoy our lovemaking more fully when we have several hours to talk and enjoy each other beforehand, but I know there isn't always time to do that. Let's set aside Tuesday evenings for a longer time together and then, if I know we'll have that one evening to really explore our feelings and talk together, I think I'll be able to respond to your needs more readily when there isn't much time."

The husband whose wife hated sex had, of course, a much more difficult problem, but it too can be traced to selfishness. The wife was too proud to get counsel which both of them desperately needed, and pride is an ugly form of selfishness. Fortunately, she eventually agreed to get help, but the previous 18 years had eroded much of their happiness.

As couples, we need to talk over our preferences in lovemaking, and, because we constantly change, we should do this often. We must know what amount of dress or undress is preferred; where to touch and to what degree; what lighting, mood, music, and setting are preferred; the length of time needed to arouse. Once we know such things, we must adjust and work together until a solution satisfying to both is discovered.

It has been said that a wife must look

on sex, in part, as an opportunity to be a blessing to her husband. A husband must look on it that way as well. Pray separately for wisdom as to how to express your needs. Then pray together and explore ideas that will meet both your needs and your desires. If we have *agape* love—Christ's giving love—then we will look for ways to give pleasure,

not just take pleasure, in the physical relationship. May our lovemaking be unselfish, a true *giving* love that reflects the sacrificial love of Christ as He gives to His bride, the church.

Related Articles
   Chapter 8: Learning to Be Lovers
   Chapter 8: Common Sexual Problems and What to Do About Them

How Those Who Have Been Abused Can Handle Marital Sex

RICHARD A. MEIER

One out of every 20 women has a history of sexual abuse by her father, other relative, or boyfriend. Whether this abuse stopped at fondling or proceeded to actual penetration, it is likely to affect her adult attitude toward sex, especially if the abuse came from her father. A common result is low self-esteem and general distrust of the opposite sex.

Let's look at a counseling scenario. You have come to my office because you feel cold, insecure, anxious, and unable to enjoy sex in marriage. In the course of our conversation you tell me your father abused you several times during your early childhood. You wonder if this could be causing your sexual difficulty today.

The answer certainly is yes. And knowing the probable cause of your problems, we can begin to put together an action plan that will help correct them.

The first step I would suggest is to *be sure you have worked through the normal emotions connected to this kind of trauma.* Very often leftover anger and guilt from the past remain with a person for many years after the abuse

has taken place. Consider having a heart-to-heart talk with your mother. If you suspect she is unaware of the abuse, consider informing her. Of course, you need to carefully weigh the effect this information may have on the relationship between your mother and your father. But if the abuse continued over any length of time, it is possible that she knew what was going on or at least suspected it, even if she said nothing about it. If she had some culpability in not protecting you from your father, then confronting her with the issue and verbalizing it in an appropriate Christian manner is in order. Beyond that point, if at all possible, it would be good to have her prayers and support as you consider confronting your father.

Next, *confront your father.* You can prepare yourself to do this by writing a letter to him, expressing your anger over the way he abused you as a child. Describe the emotions you felt as this frightening experience took place. Lay responsibility at his feet for your embarrassment, fear, and shame. It is important for you to finally forgive him. This does not mean you accept what he did, but that you are bringing the issue to a close, committing it to God, and giving up the right to hurt back the one who hurt you. This letter will help you compose your thoughts and know what to say when you confront him. If you simply cannot bring yourself to talk to him, then the last resort is to give this letter to him to read in your presence. Even if your father is deceased, it is important to write such a letter to him as if he were still alive. This will help you get in touch with your justifiable feelings of anger. Express them, and then choose to forgive. You will have a great sense of relief once you have taken this step.

Once you have worked through your feelings of anger against your father, you need to *deal with your guilt feelings.* Usually a small girl who has been abused blames herself for what happened. At the very least, she feels guilty for not having told somebody about it. That guilt must be handled by realizing the beautiful truths of the Gospel of Jesus Christ. Christ died for our sins and paid the price for our guilt. When we trust Him as Saviour, He blots out our sins and transfers our guilt to the cross. From that moment, our guilt is paid for in God's sight. God sees us as cleansed from our sins. Don't let the devil impose false guilt on you by hanging the memory of your abuse over your head and telling you you must be a bad person as a result of it. If you are God's child, you are a good person. The "old man" of your former life was crucified with Christ and is no longer part of your history. You are clean and righteous in your position before God through your identification with Christ (see Rom. 6:6; 2 Cor. 5:21).

Next, *learn where your feelings come from.* Feelings are based on beliefs, and not all our beliefs are rational. The past is gone, but our beliefs about the past link the past to the present. Let me illustrate how this works. I recently talked with a man who admitted he was

HOW TO CHANGE A DAMAGING BELIEF

One way to help you erase an old tape of the past and replace it with the truth of today is by making a "stop card." Use both sides of a 3 x 5 index card. Write the misbelief on one side and the truth on the other. After the misbelief, write STOP! in bold letters. Here is what a stop card might look like:

MISBELIEF
Sexual closeness to my husband threatens my security as a woman.
S T O P !

TRUTH
Although at times I may feel terrified, sexual closeness to my husband is God's will for me. Because of this, I choose to look to God as my source of security as a woman and to risk yielding myself to His will. I choose to relax and let myself go as I enjoy closeness, pleasure, and release.

Now meditate on this card 10 minutes each day for at least 30 days. Read the "stop" side first. When you come to the word *stop,* scream it internally, thus emotionally unseating the old tape and gradually replacing it with the truth.

Richard Meier

afraid of riding a motorcycle. When he was young, he said, one of his best friends was seriously injured while riding one, and at that time he began to believe all motorcycles were unsafe. His behavior today reflects his belief. He could learn to ride a motorcycle and would probably be as safe as anyone else carefully riding one. But to do so would cause him a great deal of fear and anxiety. His behavior is in line with his belief; because he hangs on to his childhood belief that motorcycles are unsafe, he will not risk riding one.

If you are going to overcome your negative feelings about married sex, you need to discover what your experience of abuse caused you to believe about yourself and about men in general. Probably you have concluded that emotional closeness to a man is not safe, that your personal security is threatened if you allow yourself to be vulnerable to a man. You learned this in order to protect yourself from your father, and this belief system still controls your feelings toward other men, including your husband, unless you vigorously challenge it. You have blocked emotional intimacy to your husband by transferring your beliefs about your father to your husband, even though you know your husband is not like your father. In order to change your feelings toward your husband, then, you need to change your misbelief.

If I were your counselor, I would help you *understand the meaning of security*. Security is knowing you are unconditionally loved, accepted, and cared for. A child learns—or does not learn—security from her parents. Now, as an adult, you can learn that as a believer in Jesus Christ your real needs are met in your relationship to Him. No man can threaten your security. You can claim many promises from God's Word such as Romans 8:31, 38-39; 1 Peter 5:7; and Matthew 6:33-34.

Since you are secure in your relationship to Christ, you can risk doing God's will, which includes being vulnerable and relating sexually to your husband. You can trust God to meet your needs and keep you safe as you obey His will. If you really believe God cares for you and is protecting you as His child, you can risk going against your automatic feelings of insecurity. Knowing you are secure no matter how you feel, you can obey God in the difficult areas.

You don't want to deny your feelings of anxiety and fearfulness, but you also do not want to let them become your masters. You know where they come from—memories of the past. The feelings are not related to truth in the present. Therefore, you can risk obeying God despite your feelings of anxiety. You can take little steps into the very face of your fears, believing you are secure in Christ. Use a "stop card," described in the accompanying sidebar, to begin to change the fears themselves.

It is time to take a behavioral step. *Choose to act on the truth you now believe.* Initiate closeness with your husband. Prepare yourself by thinking the "truth" thought of your stop card. Choose to act on the basis of faith rather than feeling. Slowly the anxiety feelings will be desensitized.

It is important for you and your husband to have good communication, especially before sexual intimacy. You need plenty of time then to express your feelings and talk about personal issues. You also need positive, uplifting physical experiences—touching, hugging, caressing, back rubs, body massages, and so forth, depending on your desires. This helps move you gradually toward sex while encouraging feelings of safety. While this is going on, express your positive feelings of pleasure and love. If old fears crowd in, counter them by meditating on the memorized truth side of your stop card.

An additional step might be to take about 10 minutes every day to sit down, relax, and *meditate on 5 positive traits about your husband.* Imagine warm feelings of being with him. Picture romantic vacations with just the two of you on some remote beach or in a hideaway cabin. Condition your mind to think about sex in a safe, biblical manner. Vigorously challenge any negative thought you might have about him or about healthy marital sex.

Expect to have occasional relapses. Remember, your feelings are the results of your beliefs. It is easy to have memory lapses and go back to old feelings, old conclusions, old hurts that you experienced in childhood. When this happens, relax. Understand where you have come from, but give yourself and God credit for where you are today. Get back in touch with your thoughts. Correct them and bring them back into obedience to Christ. Don't let the devil have the victory.

But *be patient with yourself.* It is faith, your desire to grow, and your determination not to quit that will make the difference in the days and years ahead.

Related Articles
Chapter 8: Learning to Be Lovers
Chapter 15: Bringing Love Back to Life

An Introduction to Natural Family Planning

INGRID TROBISCH

Natural Family Planning (NFP) is based on the simple biological fact that women are infertile most of the time during the reproductive years of their lives. This knowledge, together with planned abstinence, can be used either to achieve or avoid conception. It is not to be confused with mechanical or chemical contraceptive methods. Rather it is a way of life, based on the couple's knowledge of the wife's fertile and infertile days in her cycle.

My late husband and I had the privilege of teaching family-life seminars throughout the world. We taught many couples facing their responsibility of parenting about this way of life, giving them the information they needed so that their decisions—whether to achieve or avoid pregnancy—could be based on awareness of the natural fertility cycle. Here is some of the information we shared with them:

Conception can occur on only a few days of the menstrual cycle. Most of the days of the cycle are infertile because the narrow canal leading through the cervix (the neck of the uterus) is closed, and therefore upward sperm migration is impossible. For that simple reason, it is only when the following changes have occurred that conception is possible: (1) the narrow canal in the cervix has become wider, and (2) increased secretion of a thin, watery fluid (mucus) from the widened cervix makes it possible for sperm to travel upward in the uterus. In the absence of this mucus the sperm die within a few hours in the vagina.

Therefore the fertile time of each cycle is a combination of the duration of sperm life and that of ovum life. In the favorable vaginal environment caused by the cervical mucus, sperm life is considered to be 72 hours, while ovum life after ovulation is estimated to be a maximum of 24 hours. Because the menstrual cycle differs from woman to woman and often from cycle to cycle, the probable number of fertile days must be figured out on an individual basis.

The cycle is divided into three parts:

259

1. Preovulation infertility marked by the so-called dry days
2. The fertile time, or the wet days
3. Postovulation infertility

Dr. Josef Roetzer, one of the world's specialists in NFP, often says, "Chemical or mechanical contraceptive methods are 100 percent effective only during the infertile days of the cycle." And then, of course, they are unnecessary. Dr. Roetzer's method involves pinpointing the time of fertility through recording basal body temperature and through learning to recognize symptoms of fertile and infertile days. His Golden Rule: wait for three consecutive elevated readings to occur *after* the peak day of mucus to determine the infertile time.

Some people fear that NFP is too complicated. In our teaching of NFP, however, we found that it worked very well for African couples. It was reliable. It did not require money for equipment or prescriptions, and no doctor needed to supervise its use. It coped with the Africans' aversion to artificial methods. It was even applicable to an illiterate population.

After I had given a lecture in Zimbabwe on NFP, a Lutheran bishop's wife told me, "You are the first white woman I have heard talking about these secrets. I was taught about dry days and wet days by the older women in our tribe before I got married. After 25 years of marriage and three planned children, I can verify all that you say."

NFP is taught most effectively by couples who have learned and practiced it themselves. I have had the joy of talking to hundreds of these teacher-couples throughout the world and participating in their international congresses. In Canada, the Serena movement has taught more than 100,000 couples since their beginnings in 1965 and at present has more than 500 active teacher-couples. In the States, the Couple to Couple League (P.O. Box 11084, 3621 Glenmore Avenue, Cincinnati, Ohio

45211) currently has more than 800 teacher-couples. By the way, NFP does not mean Not For Protestants!

In a brochure entitled "A Physician's Reference to Natural Family Planning," the marital benefits to couples practicing NFP are described as follows: "When a mutually interested couple practices NFP, it is commonplace for that couple to enjoy an improvement in their marital relationship. The reasons given by couples vary: increased communication, absence of the feeling of being used, increased mutual respect, relief from sexual satiation and/or boredom, freedom from worry about medical side-effects of other methods, peace of conscience, and others. Whereas teachers of NFP formerly tended to apologize for the abstinence involved, many now realize that abstinence with the consequent necessity of developing non-genital forms of expressing marital love and affection is one of the big advantages of NFP. From informal surveys among couples practicing NFP, the divorce rate appears to be only a minor fraction of the rate in the general population."

NFP is a reliable and long-awaited way of achieving or avoiding conception without the use of potentially harmful artificial contraceptives. But it is far more than that. It represents an invitation to marriage partners to deepen their spiritual union by cooperating in the observance of the fertility cycle.

We dedicated our book *An Experience of Love: Understanding Natural Family Planning* to "couples who have the courage to take the high road of love that the book describes." We believe that periods of fasting followed by celebrations and feasts keep life from becoming monotonous. To learn to enjoy the sacrament of the present moment is a great art.

May I share this personal testimony of a couple who are NFP users:

"What shall we say after 10 years of marriage? NFP has given us a way of life which has made our love grow. The periodic abstinence is possible only out of love and makes love deepen at the same time. The self-awareness and self-acceptance serve the developing of the personality. Fantastic, to be able to call a child into being when the right moment has come! We are convinced God has put a meaning into human sexuality that lets us stand in awe before the greatness of the human being. Even if we do not feel this awe all the time, we believe it is profoundly true. NFP helps us to practice day by day our respect before the miracle of the creation of the human being."

Related Articles

Chapter 8: Can Contraception Be Challenged?
Chapter 8: The Christian Case for Birth Control
Chapter 8: Thoughts on Sterilization

Can Contraception Be Challenged?

LARRY & NORDIS CHRISTENSON

When we were married in 1951, it never occurred to us to question the practice of contraception. It seemed to be the standard procedure for Protestant couples starting out in marriage. We certainly planned to have children, but first we'd get established.

We understood that Catholics looked at the question a bit differently, but that was just their religious idiosyncrasy.

We encountered no major problems, yet we did not feel that our use of contraceptives did much to enhance our sexual relationship either. We had once talked with another couple who said that contraceptives had improved their sexual relationship by taking away the fear of pregnancy, but this was not our experience. With us they always seemed like an unwelcome, yet somehow necessary, intruder. After 12 years of marriage, we decided we would no longer use any contraceptive devices.

Our initial reaction against contraception was essentially aesthetic: it brought an unwelcome sense of intrusion into our relationship. In that regard, we were more than rewarded by our decision. It led us into a study and practice of Natural Family Planning which brought with it a deeper appreciation of God's gift of sexuality in marriage.

We once visited a young couple in Germany who asked Larry what he thought about "the pill." The wife had previously lived with us for a year as an exchange student. They had one child, and it was clear that they were not yet ready for another one.

Larry told them that when he first heard about birth control pills (this was before we had made our own decision not to use contraceptives), some kind of alarm went off inside him. He knew nothing about the medical or physiological aspects of the pill at that time. His questions were essentially theological and philosophical.

The normal function of medication is to heal a sickness or correct an imbalance in the body. This is not the case with the birth control pill: it is designed to suppress a natural biological function, ovulation. The question is, what else might it do as well?

How intricately has God put us

261

together as human beings? The Bible says that we are "fearfully and wonderfully made" (Ps. 139:14, KJV). What else, besides the release of an egg, might God have linked to a woman's monthly cycle? What physical, emotional, psychological, or spiritual side effects might be involved? Are we reaching into the human makeup like a ham-handed electronics fixer who tries to modify some wiring and ends up scrambling a whole circuit board? These were the kinds of questions Larry shared with this couple.

Nordis shared some similar thoughts when an engaged girl wrote and asked for her views on contraception: "What are we really saying to ourselves when we prepare for this most intimate act by donning contraceptive machinery or by negating the act chemically? Can we treat ourselves like machines, closing off an undesirable valve and expecting the rest of the machine to operate smoothly? As persons we are a profound union of many components which are subtly interrelated and interdependent. We are much more than a biological machine" (quoted in their book, *The Christian Couple*, Bethany House, 1977, p. 75).

Questions of aesthetics, of an enhanced sexual relationship, even of theology and philosophy, might reasonably be shelved under the category of private taste or opinion. But the use of birth control pills (and of the intrauterine device or IUD, for a similar reason) raises a more serious issue, a question of morality.

Many laypeople do not know what the medical community has known for a long time, namely, that birth control pills not only can act as contraceptives, but can and do act as abortifacients. This means that when the pill does not successfully suppress ovulation, it can cause a fertilized egg to abort. Since no pill on the market suppresses ovulation in all women all the time, this means that the use of the pill may be linked with the possibility that a woman may, quite unknowingly, be partner to an abortion.

The way antifertility drugs induce abortion is explained by Dr. Alfred Gilman as follows: "It is abundantly clear from animal experiments that the endometrium [the mucous membrane lining the uterus] must be just in the right stage of development under estrogen and progesterone for nidation [implantation] to take place. It seems unlikely that implantation would be possible in the altered endometrium developed under the influence of most of the suppressants [oral contraceptives]" (Gilman, et al., *The Pharmacological Basis of Therapeutics,* 7th ed., Macmillan, 1985, pp. 1432-33).

In other words, the pill produces a change in the lining of the uterus that obstructs the implantation of a fertilized egg. The unborn child, just a few hours old, finds himself or herself without a home. He or she dies unknown by any but God—shut out not by cruel and wicked parents, but by those who have not even known what they were doing. Surely the prayer of Jesus applies, "Father, forgive them, for they know not what they do."

Of course, other contraceptives are available that prevent conception from taking place and therefore do not involve the same kind of moral questions we have raised in regard to the pill. Not every couple will come to the same decision that we did. We believe, however, that husbands and wives should become as fully informed as possible about human sexuality and the gift God has given them in their sexual relationship. This was the essence of what Nordis shared with the young woman who wrote her:

"I know that it is possible for a woman to be perfectly secure and at ease in using a natural method of family planning if she obtains good instruction and gives herself time to gain experience. I have had this experience myself and have talked with many other experienced women. If a young woman takes the time and effort to learn the meaning of the different signs of fertility (ideally she should begin to do this several months before marriage), it will serve her well until the menopause.

"The natural methods involve no risk to a woman's health. They enhance her understanding and appreciation of her bodily functions and allow her to live in harmony with her womanhood. They treat fertility as a precious gift of God, to be loved, respected, understood, and wisely used.

"We recommend that couples once again accept the entirety of the marriage act and the full truth of their relationship: that they either limit their family's size through periodic abstinence based on fertility awareness or else adopt a lifestyle compatible with a larger family. In other words, let us take responsibility for our actions—or not act" (*The Christian Couple*, pp. 85, 88).

Related Articles
Chapter 8: An Introduction to Natural Family Planning
Chapter 8: The Christian Case for Birth Control
Chapter 8: Thoughts on Sterilization

NATURAL FAMILY PLANNING AND SEXUAL ENJOYMENT

All natural family planning methods depend on one common denominator: periodic abstinence; that is, not having intercourse on the days of the month when a women is most likely to get pregnant. Periodic abstinence need not detract from a couple's enjoyment of the sexual relationship. It may actually enhance it. After the time of separation, the relationship is refreshed.

A key factor in Natural Family Planning is the couple's, and particularly the husband's, agreement to order their sexual relationship in this way. A husband who grouses that he can't have sex because it's "family quiet week" puts an unfair burden on his wife. The implication is that she is arbitrarily imposing this abstinence on him. Faced with the choice between denying her husband and getting pregnant, many wives will risk pregnancy.

When a couple agrees to practice Natural Family Planning, the wife's primary responsibility is to learn how to determine her time of ovulation and to inform her husband. The husband's responsibility is then to take the lead in initiating other ways of expressing love and affection. Family quiet week should not be a matter of gritting your teeth until next Tuesday. It is an opportunity to allow your relationship to deepen and expand as love invents new ways to express affection and care.

The surest way to enhance the enjoyment of food is not to continually concoct new and exotic dishes, but to stop eating for a while, as anyone who practices periodic fasting will tell you. You sit down to a meal of soup and salad after a fast, and every mouthful is a sheer delight. The practice of periodic sexual abstinence has the same effect. "It's a new honeymoon every month," one husband said to us.

Larry & Nordis Christenson

The Christian Case for Birth Control

JOHN K. TESTERMAN, M.D.

Nowhere does the Bible teach specifically about birth control. However, we are not left without guidance in this important area, because our views on birth control will flow naturally from our understanding of the nature and purpose of human sexuality. On this subject a number of important inferences can be drawn from both God's general revelation in nature and special revelation in Scripture.

The Book of Genesis teaches that the world, as it came from the hand of the Creator, was "very good" (1:31). The human body and its God-created capacity for sexual expression in marriage are included in this benediction. However, Christians have not always consistently held to the positive view of the body and sexuality developed in Genesis. The reason has to do with outside influences on the Christian church in its early centuries. Certain pagan philosophers taught that the body, its appetites, functions, and even material existence itself, were inherently evil. These Gnostic teachers naturally held a very low opinion of sex. I am alluding to these teachings here only to make the point that the aura of "dirtiness" that still surrounds the subject of sexuality in some Christian quarters is of pagan, not biblical, origin.

If we study this human body that God created in His image and pronounced "good," we find that for conception to occur, it is not biologically necessary that the woman experience orgasm or climax. Yet God created the woman's body with such a capacity, and an organ, the clitoris, which has no other bio-logical function than sexual pleasure.

If we look at the created order and compare human sexuality to sexual behavior in other species, some striking differences emerge. Animal copulation is a series of automatic reflexes, involving mainly the lower centers of the brain. Human sexuality is incredibly more complex, involving higher brain functions. Animal copulation is reproductive sex. Human sexuality involves intimacy.

We also find that the human female is the only female that experiences sexual climax, that possesses permanent mammary glands, and that is sexually receptive outside the fertile period. Among the nonhuman species, the female is receptive only when she is fertile, which may occur as seldom as a yearly mating season, or even once in a lifetime. In human beings, however, sexual activity is not confined to the fertile period of about two days per month, but occurs throughout the month and even past menopause, when no conception is possible. In marked contrast to other species, then, most human sexual intercourse occurs when conception is impossible.

Why were we created with sexual capabilities far beyond what is necessary to reproduce the species? Scripture teaches that sex is not only for reproduction (Gen. 1:31), but also for the emotional and spiritual bonding of husband and wife (Eph. 5:31). This theme is developed in the Song of Solomon, and the Apostle Paul compares the sexually bonded marriage relationship to the relationship between Christ and the

264

church.

The research of Desmond Morris, Donald Joy, and others has confirmed that sexual intercourse plays an important role in building and maintaining the emotional bond between husband and wife. Yet throughout many of the fertile years of our lives, it would be unwise or even irresponsible to produce children.

"Be fruitful and multiply" is the only biblical command that has generally been obeyed. Babies are easily produced by unskilled laborers who enjoy their work. In simpler days, numerous children were an economic asset in a largely agricultural society, and extended family were present to help with their care. In addition, many children died before reaching maturity. Today, too many offspring can produce financial, physical, and emotional exhaustion in the parents, and Grandma lives in a condo in California.

According to the doctrine of stewardship, we are accountable to God for the prudent use of our talents and resources, and for the welfare of our children. Responsible couples will try not to bring children into the world that they are not prepared to support financially, emotionally, and spiritually. Some means of controlling the timing, spacing, and number of children is then necessary for the good of the children, as well as for the parents and society. Yet it is desirable for marital bonding purposes that intercourse continue throughout the marriage. If sex ought to continue, yet reproduction be stopped, some method is needed for uncoupling copulation from conception.

Contraception involves some means of preventing sperm from meeting an egg. These means fall into two classes: preventing an egg from being produced (the pill), or preventing sperm from reaching the egg by interposing a barrier of spermicide, latex, time (the rhythm method), or tissue (sterilization).

Some Christians consider the rhythm method, or "natural" family planning, in which intercourse is avoided during the fertile portion of the woman's menstrual cycle, to be a morally superior form of birth control. However, if the New Testament teaches us anything about morality, it teaches that motive is important. It is the intent of the person that counts.

Now the intent of the couple using condoms is to have intercourse without causing conception. The intent of the couple using the rhythm method is to have intercourse without causing conception. Both the motive and the end result are the same in the two cases. In the second case, a time barrier to sperm is substituted for a latex barrier. I would suggest that time is not morally superior to latex as a sperm barrier.

I would also take issue with those who say that sterilization of the man by vasectomy or the woman by tubal ligation is a morally repugnant form of birth control. Sterilization erects a tissue barrier rather than a latex or time barrier to the passage of sperm. It differs from other barrier methods mainly in that the barrier is usually permanent, and that it requires a higher level of technological intervention. Permanency does not necessarily represent an ethical difficulty. The decision to have a child, once put into action, is just as permanent. Having a baby or having a tubal ligation are both irreversible actions, with equally permanent consequences.

Some object to sterilization (and possibly the birth control pill as well) because it involves a higher degree of intervention. Now if technological intervention in the body is sinful, all of us who have ever benefited from a surgical operation, immunizations, or modern medicine have something of which to repent. But in this day of the "back-to-nature" movement, it is understandable that those of us who like to can our own organically grown vegetables may prefer the more do-it-yourself forms of birth control purely as a matter of taste. This preference, however, should not be elevated to a moral imperative.

The best method of birth control will differ at different times in the marriage. A young couple in college or early in their career-building phase will need a highly effective method, as a pregnancy at this time could cause great economic hardship and strain the still developing marriage bond. Unless there is a specific medical reason not to use it, the birth control pill is quite safe at this age. During the couple's childbearing phase, a moderately efficacious method, such as rhythm, condoms, the diaphragm, the sponge, or spermicidal agents are usually adequate for spacing children.

After the couple have had all the children they want or can provide for, they will again need a highly effective form of contraception. Unfortunately, as age increases, the options in birth control decrease. The safety of the pill diminishes with age. The rhythm method requires two highly disciplined people willing to consistently devote the required effort over a period of possibly 15 to 20 years with no mistakes. This would exclude many couples. The combination of spermicidal foam and condoms can be fairly efficacious if used diligently, but after many years their use can get pretty tedious, and many women find spermicides irritating to the mucous membranes. Then the temptation arises to take chances. All of us know at least one couple who was surprised by an unwanted pregnancy after 40.

By default, sterilization becomes the best option for many couples at this time of life. Due to unpredictables such as drunk drivers and divorce, I counsel couples not to consider this usually irreversible step unless they are sure that they would never consider having any more children.

The method of birth control selected should be the safest practical one having the degree of effectiveness needed to meet the family planning needs of the married couple at their stage in life. For this purpose, the couple can choose with a clear conscience from a number of morally acceptable methods.

Related Articles
Chapter 8: An Introduction to Natural Family Planning
Chapter 8: Can Contraception Be Challenged?
Chapter 8: Thoughts on Sterilization

Thoughts on Sterilization

INGRID TROBISCH

A young wife wrote to us: "My husband and I have two children, and we are expecting our third in a few months. We have discussed the possibility of a tubal sterilization and both agree that we just do not want me to go through with this major surgery. However, my husband is not adverse to the idea of a vasectomy. In fact he feels, as do many of our friends, that it is about time for husbands to begin sharing some responsibility for birth control with their wives. As I have always had extremely difficult pregnancies—both physically and emotionally—and a vasectomy does not bother my husband, why not let him go ahead with this minor operation?"

This is only one of many letters we have received describing a situation filled with contradictory arguments and emotions. To many people, sterilization offers a tempting solution. It seems like a clear, simple, and unproblematic way to be rid of the fertility dilemma.

Nevertheless, the wife may hear a voice within, warning her. Filled with second thoughts and doubts, her conscience begins to bother her. She senses that something is not quite right. Her maternal instinct tells her that, at a very deep level, something is wrong with this "solution" and will stay wrong for the rest of her life.

Many women pay little attention to this inner voice, or they even suppress it. They listen to what their friends or their husbands say, or they consult their reason instead of obeying their feeling for what is right. They go ahead and have themselves sterilized. But the inner voice often surfaces anew and makes itself heard after sterilization has taken place.

There is seldom a chance to return. So it happens that some women, even years after the operation, are overcome by a profound sense of guilt, sadness, and depression. The best of rational arguments cannot help them.

The husband of such a woman stands beside her, helpless to do anything for his depressed wife. Too late, he finds out that instead of a final solution, he has an endless problem on his hands. No pat answer is available. What is done cannot be undone. Whatever went wrong cannot be made right now.

Is it any better for the husband who decides to have a vasectomy? He too often hears that voice deep within, whispering that something is indeed terribly wrong. While the choice may have been made for legitimate reasons, the outcome may create far greater problems, both physical and psychological.

As creatures of God, we are called by Him to acknowledge and live with our fertility in a responsible manner. We are different from every other creature, because God made us accountable to Himself (see Gen. 1:26-27). We have a responsibility to nature as well. It is disobedience to God, and unworthy of us as human beings, simply to allow ourselves to be driven to and fro, come what may. A sense of responsibility for our fertility demands that we not leave the origin of new human life to chance.

There are several ways of living with one's fertility, however, and sterilization is not the best one. Sterilization involves mutilation of the body itself rather than temporary suppression or nonuse of a bodily function. Because in most cases it involves an irreversible intervention in the life process, the sterilization decision is difficult to justify. It needs more compelling arguments than any other means of avoiding conception.

There is no doubt that sometimes a decision must be made that includes the loss of fertility. We no longer live in paradise. There is a rift in God's good world that extends to every realm of life, including our fertility. And so, let it be said openly, God's good gift of fertility may become a 'burden and misery. Sometimes weighty medical reasons allow no alternative but to separate marriage and procreation from each other, though in God's creative plan, they belong together. Such cases will be few and far between, however, and can be handled personally in consultation with a conscientious physician. In recent years society has misused what was once intended as a solution for only extreme cases.

Walter Trobisch wrote: "Sterilization for convenience is disobedience to the Creator. It is an intentional rupture of the intimate union of marriage and fertility, and as such will not go unpunished. . . . The precious trust we have received in our capacity to reproduce is not something that we may thoughtlessly dismiss. A shortsighted decision in favor of sterilization can be costly in terms of the anxiety and sorrow that may result from it.

"Many—particularly young couples under 30—have little vision or ability to foresee the future. They do not really grasp what it means, never again to be able to have the child they may one day desire. Sterilization represents a sort of Damocles' sword always hanging over both the husband and wife. Nothing dare happen to any of the children, now that the parents are sterilized.

"Besides this anxiety, there is the sorrow that overcomes a man and woman when they begin to realize that something has been irrecoverably lost. Even if they don't admit it, they feel unconsciously that they are no longer whole and healthy. Our reproductive capacity should not be a handicap to be gotten rid of as quickly as possible. It is rather a precious value that no one should give up without a great deal of thought.

"Sometimes what appears to be quite reasonable on the surface is, in the end, unwholesome. What Paul wrote to the community at Corinth can be applied to the question of sterilization: 'All things are lawful for me, but not all things are helpful' (1 Cor. 6:12, RSV), and a few verses later, 'Do you not know that your body is a temple of the Holy Spirit within you, which you have from God? You are not your own; you were bought with a price. So glorify God in your body' (v. 19)."

Fertility can be a problem and a burden. But that is simply part of what it means to be human in a fallen creation. Technology cannot heal this burden or brokenness. There is no formula by which the world can pick itself up by its own bootstraps from its fallen condition. There is only one Person who can heal the rift in creation. It is He by whom the apostle says we were bought at a great price: Jesus Christ. He does not simply remove the burden from us; He promises to carry us, complete with our burdens.

Once pragmatic and utilitarian categories lose their grip on our thinking and living, the burden of fertility can become a joyful gift. We begin to praise God in our bodies. We have seen how healing can radiate to the whole of creation through children whose conception was seen at first as a burden.

Let us not forget that when God became man, He came as a child conceived unexpectedly.

Related Articles

What your mate thinks about your communication style may be more important than what you think, because he or she is the one you're trying to communicate with. Ask your mate to check the statements that apply to you. Then you check the ones that apply to him or her.

Are you surprised by the results? If you don't like them, don't get discouraged—or angry. Instead, read the articles in this chapter about communication and think of ways to strengthen your own communication skills.

Husband	Wife	
————	————	thinks things through before talking
————	————	talks things through until conclusion is reached
————	————	speaks when information must be communicated
————	————	speaks to gain understanding of self and others
————	————	enjoys sitting around and talking with people
————	————	easily expresses personal feelings
————	————	prefers not to talk about personal feelings
————	————	likes to give all the details
————	————	likes to get to the point
————	————	affirms
————	————	criticizes
————	————	encourages
————	————	nags
————	————	asks directly for what is wanted
————	————	hints or hopes for what is wanted
————	————	talks more, listens less
————	————	listens more, talks less
————	————	will argue until resolution is reached
————	————	wants peace at any price
————	————	will talk about anything
————	————	refuses to discuss some topics
————	————	listens intently
————	————	interrupts
————	————	gives praise
————	————	is sarcastic
————	————	tries to see others' viewpoint
————	————	likes to state own viewpoint
————	————	ignores person who is talking
————	————	monopolizes conversation
————	————	is willing to apologize
————	————	has to be right
————	————	makes requests
————	————	gives orders

COMMUNICATION

Good marriages and poor marriages have one thing in common—communication. Happy unions and troubled ones face exactly the same problems; the differences lie in the ability to communicate. Either communication is free and open, or it is choked. Nothing is as easy as talking; but nothing is as difficult as transparent communication.

Difficult, but completely do-able. Communication is a developmental skill; it gets better as it is cultivated. Look at the components: talking, listening, understanding, and desire (the driveshaft of the first three).

There is an idiocy abroad that if you live together, eat, sleep, and store your stuff under the same roof, you will grow together. Expert research seems to dismantle this fallacy. The secret is not where you live, but how. We communicate both verbally and nonverbally, and the messages must be congruent, not conflicting, with actions. Look at these statistics:

Communication by words alone—7 percent

By tone of voice—38 percent

By facial expression (body language)—55 percent

Communication is not what you say, but what your partner understands by what you say. That makes the difference.

Howard & Jeanne Hendricks

Blocks to Communication

DEAN MERRILL

"**I** can think of no person to whom one talks less than his wife."— Socrates

"The less we have to say to each other, the better I'm gonna like it."—J.R. Ewing to his wife, Sue Ellen.

Why is it that what once flowed so automatically ends up slowing to a trickle? How can the same two people who, during engagement, ran up astronomical phone bills now go weeks without sharing the inner regions of their lives?

In the beginning, the Lord God created His world part by part, and Genesis pronounces the same refrain after each one: "It was good." When God created the first human being, the Scripture even exudes, "It was *very* good" (Gen. 1:31).

Then came a jarring change. Something showed up in Creation that made God wince. "It is *not* good," He announced (Gen. 2:18). What was it?

Aloneness.

God immediately did something

about that. He made woman, thereby bringing about the possibility of marriage, companionship, togetherness.

We all need communication. Feedback. Interaction. Especially if we believe in marriage as a partnership of souls, not just an economic or sexual alliance.

What trips us up? What maneuvers us into the not-good state of aloneness? Here are five common stumbling blocks:

1. *The rat race.* Too many urgent (but not necessarily important) things to tend to. Too many appointments, obligations, requirements on our time. Too much "stuff" on our calendars. Things that have to be done, or so we think. Work really does expand to fill the time available, as Parkinson's Law notes. Work of all kinds. Paid work, but unpaid work too.

In such a state, most husbands and wives still communicate such matters as, "Don't forget your mother's birthday next week." "The front right tire has a thump in it." "Can you pick up Suzanne at 6:30?" "We're almost out of charcoal for the grill." The particulars get handled (usually).

Meanwhile, the fun topics, the "what ifs," get forgotten. And the "heavies" get postponed indefinitely.

2. *Kids.* Not intentionally, you understand. Kids don't plot to squeeze out adult communication.

It is rather a case of the squeakiest axle getting the grease. Kids let their needs be known right away, and conscientious parents rush to respond. After all, it's pretty hard to ignore a fourth-grader who's stumped on long division, a preschooler with a bloody knee, a sophomore whose friends are gossiping about her.

But when do moms and dads get *their* needs met? When do they gain the inner fortitude and composure to handle the hundreds of external challenges? After all, parenting lasts only a couple of decades, while marriage is for a lifetime. If children are at the hub of the commu-

OPENING UP BLOCKED COMMUNICATION CHANNELS

"Luis," men frequently say to me, "my wife and I aren't experiencing oneness in our marriage. In fact, sometimes I feel we don't even know each other. Often we disagree or just go our separate ways. What should we do?"

I counsel these men: "Gather your wife in your arms by your bedside. Open up your Bible, kneel together, read a passage, and talk about what it says. See what God's Word has to say about your situation, and then share prayer requests and talk to God about them together."

I challenged an engineer to do this. Later he told me, "I want to tell you, Luis, my wife and I love each other like we have never loved each other before."

A medical doctor also accepted my challenge, and then wrote to tell me: "My wife and I have been living together for 25 years, but we haven't been happy. We hardly talk to each other. Our older son is an alcoholic. Our daughter is rebellious. Our younger boy is uncontrollable. Until I heard you, nobody had ever suggested to me that I should open up the Bible, kneel together with my wife, embrace her, ask forgiveness, and pray together. I did what you said, and I want to tell you that love is coming back into our home."

Luis Palau

nication circle, what happens when they grow up and move away?

3. *The media, especially TV.* If it is true, as some research studies claim, that American husbands and wives communicate with each other an average of 27.5 minutes a week, that means many of us know more about Cliff and Claire Huxtable's marriage than about our own.

Two people sitting in the same room watching the same show are not really communicating, in the sense of engaging each other's minds. They are merely absorbing a distant medium simultaneously. Meanwhile the evening ticks away, and soon it's time for sleep.

TV watching *can* be a joint experience, if the viewers talk to each other about what they've seen, what it means, how it spawns a fresh idea about this or that. But how often does that happen?

4. *Fatigue.* I've occasionally talked with audiences about body metabolism and the difference between "morning people" and "night people," and then asked a curious question:

"How many of you are married to someone the opposite of yourself?"

A forest of hands always goes up. Those of us who hit the day with vigor at 6 A.M. and run out of steam about 8:30 at night are very different from those who get cranking about noon and can work productively till 2 in the morning. In a marriage of opposites, late-night pil-

low talk is doomed. It takes creativity and determination to find a time when *both* spouses can interact effectively.

5. *Fear of conflict.* Not many husbands and wives *enjoy* arguing. So whenever a sticky matter needs attention, the natural thing is to put it off, hope it will blow over, go do something different that's positive instead of negative. Why stir up a hornets' nest if you can avoid it?

Of course, in many cases the hornets need to be evicted before someone gets hurt. Not all problems resolve themselves. They must be tackled with honest, serious communication.

The blockage of communication in a marriage does not trigger an instant crisis. It's not a bombshell like, say, adultery. It is rather like the slow, steady buildup of cholesterol in the arteries, reducing the flow of nourishment to the limbs and organs and brain—a process that takes its toll only after long years. But it can be lethal.

How do we prevent this blockage? Other articles in this chapter spell out the steps in detail. They show the way to build the kind of communicating marriage that makes both God and us say, "It is good."

Related Articles
Chapter 9: Communication That Energizes
Chapter 12: Beware of Overscheduling!

Communication That Energizes

NORM WAKEFIELD

During a family-life seminar I asked participants to tell how they had experienced love. A middle-aged lady told that she had done some small act of kindness for her husband. He called her

from work and asked, "Were you the one who did that?" Somewhat embarrassed, she admitted she was. When her husband came home from work he drew a large heart on the refrigerator door and wrote, "John loves Mary." Then they discovered that the marking pen had indelible ink! Years later, the heart is still on the refrigerator door, and Mary's face was aglow as she told us about it.

What a delight to hear persons express admiration for their spouses! How often it brings a smile and inner warmth to the person being encouraged. How it strengthens the person and the relationship!

Scripture expresses the power of positive communication in Ephesians 4:29 (NASB): "Let no unwholesome word proceed from your mouth, but only such a word as is good for edification according to the need of the moment, that it may give grace to those who hear." For many years this verse has challenged me to practice positive communication toward my family members. In meditating on it, I have discovered four helpful insights that guide me. I want to apply them to the marriage relationship.

I avoid negative communication because it tears down my partner. "No unwholesome word," Paul says. The word *unwholesome* originally referred to spoiled fish, decayed matter, or rotten fruit. What we say to each other can have the scent of death in it. It can undermine a person's self-confidence, weaken the courage to try again, or erode areas of strength. Soon he begins to question his ability or worth and hesitates when he should be moving forward. If such undermining continues, the spouse begins to draw back.

What is negative, unwholesome communication? I call it *Style 2 communication.* Style 2 actions include criticism, demands, sarcasm, put-down jokes, and rejection. They attack the person, pulling him down or tearing him apart. Some marriage relationships never get off the ground because the basic style of communication used by one or both persons is negative, destructive, "rotten."

Style 2 communication sounds like

CHECKLIST FOR A CRITICAL SPIRIT

Many spouses who have a critical spirit don't even know it. Their reactions toward their spouse have become habit, and they treat him or her far worse than they would even think of treating their friends. Do you consistently do any of the following:
• Notice and keep record of every wrong done, every birthday missed, every promise forgotten
• Collect "ammunition" for the next argument, no matter what the argument may be about
• Serve as an expert on your spouse's flaws, always willing to tell whoever will listen about them
• Forgive reluctantly or not at all
• Act judgmental and self-righteous, assuming the problem is elsewhere

This doesn't mean that you should close your eyes to problems and your own needs—you need to be able to talk to your spouse about problems, expectations, and hurts. As the person closest to your mate, you are the one most able to help him or her see who they are, how they come across, where they could use some improvement. But all must be done in the cushion of your commitment and love to each other. Don't allow a critical spirit to ruin your communication and your marriage.

YFC Editors

274

this:

"That was a stupid thing to do. Don't you know any better?"

"You eat like a pig. Didn't your mother teach you any manners?"

"You don't know what you're talking about. Any fool knows that's not true."

"Hah! You, ski? You can't stand on a wet floor."

Thankfully the verse provides another option. It points me in a better direction. *Positive communication is vital because it strengthens the person and strengthens the marriage.* I call this *Style 1 communication.* Style 1 includes words of affirmation, encouragement, support, intimacy, and admiration. The power of Style 1 is that it builds up the person. It affirms worth, reinforces strength, and offers support where growth is needed. It includes statements such as these:

"I admire how skilled you are at. . . ."

"How can I help correct the problem?"

"I appreciate all the work you put into preparing meals."

"That's going to be difficult for you, but I'll be standing with you as you face it."

The starting point for positive communication is with our inner attitudes. If I am committed to speak kind, compassionate, thoughtful words to my partner, my attitude sets in motion a positive process that will reinforce itself. Even when my spouse is having an upsetting day, my words of "blessing" will keep our communication from deteriorating. My commitment to extend kindness when the other person is upset is basic to Style 1. "When we are cursed, we bless . . . when we are slandered, we answer kindly" (1 Cor. 4:12-13).

Ephesians 4:29 gives me a third practical insight into effective communication. *The positive communicator discovers the response that is appropriate for the situation.* Our words should be "according to the need of the moment."

This challenges me to become more discerning, to perceive my spouse's need, and to frame a response in harmony with that need.

Imagine that, arriving home from work, you sense that your wife has had an exhausting day with your two preschoolers. What words (and actions) would be appropriate? What would strengthen your spouse? Certainly not "We all have tough days; don't be a griper" (I hear Style 2 there). But the following responses would probably encourage and strengthen her: "It must have been an exhausting day. What could I do to relieve the pressure?" Or, "This makes me realize how much you give to our children. I appreciate the sacrifice you make."

There is a fourth insight in our verse. *The positive communicator is a source of God's life-changing grace.* "It may give grace to those who hear," says Paul. Think about it—our words can be an important means whereby God passes on His gracious love to others. Our loving Father can use them to tell others of His compassion, support, and affirmation. We can be the channels.

This idea, when it first dawned on me, created excitement within me. I realized that the Lord can use the simplest statements to enrich others' lives. Words of kindness communicate God's kindness; words of encouragement express His encouragement; words of affirmation witness to an affirming God. This realization has caused me to reevaluate my attitude toward what I say. It has given a healthy "sacredness" to my words. Whatever else I do, I want my mouth to be a channel of God's grace.

Since discovering the amazing potency of Ephesians 4:29, I have more closely monitored my words to my wife, Winnie. I have also listened with interest to husbands and wives speaking to each other. Style 1 communication is consistently matched with healthy, growing marriages. It is used by couples who smile at each other, enjoy each other's company, and tell others how wonderful their spouse is. By contrast, Style 2 communication is usually found where marriages are unsatisfying, floundering, or in their last stages of existence. When I am around Style 2 marriages, I feel uncomfortable. I want to flee the negativism.

Our communication has great potential to energize or destroy others. James reminds us that it can be a channel of God's grace or a "restless evil, full of deadly poison" (James 3:3-12). Every day we are either building others up or tearing them down. All of us would be wise to evaluate what is coming from our mouths. Let's determine to be those who speak life, not death.

Related Articles
Chapter 1: Love as Respect
Chapter 9: How to Affirm Your Spouse

How to Affirm Your Spouse

CHARLES M. SELL

A middle-aged woman struck the same impression on my wife as she did on me. Later, Ginger and I shared notes on what a mature, charming person we had just met. She was one of God's beautiful people, we both agreed. When we met her husband later that evening he came across as a high-caliber Christian too. That's when we thought of what we once heard a prominent marriage expert say: "Through the years of a relationship, a husband plays a major part in turning his wife into a beautiful being."

Husbands and wives can build up each other through affirmation. It comes in many forms: it means saying when you approve and agree, stating your appreciation, showing you believe in your spouse, supporting during a difficult time, giving credit and praise. When we do these things, we build our mates' confidence and make them feel good about themselves and about life. In a sense, we are the most important mirror our partners have; they will tend to see themselves as we see them. Positive reflections will create a positive self-image.

Affirmation is not the same as flattery. Our aim is to build up, not puff up. Flattery is insincere; affirmation is honest. Flattery is manipulative. People flatter others for their own selfish benefit, to get something out of someone. Affirmation, by contrast, is for the partner's benefit.

The Bible encourages us to praise and honor others. Of the faithful wife and mother it says, "Her children arise and call her blessed; her husband also, and he praises her" (Prov. 31:28). Peter tells husbands to grant their wives honor (1 Peter 3:7). To be more affirming, try some of the following suggestions:

1. *Resist the urge to be negative.* Sometimes marriage turns our sweet remarks into sour ones. "You can tell when the honeymoon is over," someone has said. "They go from saying, 'You're so wonderful' to 'The problem with you is. . . .'" There are some standard ways of putting people down:

- Question what they do or say. "That's not correct." "Where did you get that idea?"
- Reject whatever they suggest. "That will never work."
- Contradict them and argue with them.

After a while the person begins to feel his or her comments, suggestions, and ideas are worthless to you. If you are that person's lover, he or she may begin to feel worthless.

2. *Affirm in nonverbal ways.* You can make your spouse feel good about himself or herself without even speaking. A hug at the right time sends a bundle of positive messages. An enthusiastic nod or an excited reaction are powerful forms of approval.

3. *Put a touch of creativity in your words of praise.* Write a love letter once in a while, especially when it's not expected. Carefully select special greeting cards. Scribble a note of appreciation on the bedroom mirror. On some holidays, send a long note or create your own greeting card in place of a commercial one. Express your feelings. Good lovers not only feel emotional toward their partners, they talk about their emotions. If you aren't very good at choosing words to say, watch for quotations from your reading that state how you feel. Memorize statements to include in your love notes.

4. *Affirm your spouse publicly or indirectly.* A husband can tell his wife's mother how much he appreciates her daughter. When his wife later hears it from her mother, the message will be amplified. Speak positively of each other in public. If given any public honor or acclaim, be sure to share the credit with your partner.

5. *Search for positive things in all areas of your partner's life.* In the Song of Songs, the lovers constantly affirm each other for their masculine and feminine charms. "How beautiful you are, my

---

WHAT REALLY MATTERS TO YOUR SPOUSE?

Being a great husband or wife is an art. It is something you learn, and like most things, how fast and how well you learn it depends on the amount of thought, time, and effort you put into it.

Make sure you put your best efforts into the things that really matter most to your mate. I have a neighbor whose husband takes her out to dinner every Saturday. But she has told me, as she has often told him, that what she would really like is for him to occasionally offer to pick up her mother and bring her to their home for dinner with the family. *He* likes to go out to dinner, and perhaps he knows that lots of women like to do that, but he has not bothered to learn what would really please his wife.

In my own marriage, I learned long ago that my husband appreciates the time and effort I put into helping him with the letters and articles he writes or ideas he wants to discuss more than he does any time I spend decorating (or even cleaning!) our house. Yet I have a good friend whose husband is simply delighted to have a beautiful setting to which to come home each evening. She pleases him by fixing fresh flowers, frequently rearranging the furniture, and making their home a lovely place. Each of us has learned a different way of showing love for her own special person.

It's easy to do what *you* think your spouse *should* appreciate. The challenge is to figure out what he or she really wants, and the fun is to learn how to provide whatever it is better than anyone else possibly could!

Margaret Campolo

darling! Oh, how beautiful!" (4:1) Don't shy away from telling your spouse what his or her body means to you. Though you may not like everything about it, constantly mention what thrills you. "My lover is radiant and ruddy, outstanding among ten thousand" (5:10). Affirm each other's character traits and spiritual strengths: "How great to have a husband who prays for me." Even affirm those things so easily taken for granted: "You are such a good provider." "You are so faithful at keeping the house nice." And offer praise for efforts, not just achievements: "I know how hard you worked on that project."

Because affirmation doesn't come easy for most of us, we have to be deliberate in giving it. Charlie Shedd advises a husband to write down 30 qualities he greatly respects about his wife. The first day of the month he should repeatedly mention the first one to her. The second day, he should find times to affirm her for the second, and so on until the month is over. Then he should write down four more things, mentioning the first during the first week of the next month, the second the second week, and so on. After that he should keep watching for more and more of the positive traits. This is sound advice. Practicing affirmation takes hard work, but it brings rich rewards.

Related Articles
Chapter 1: Love as Honoring Each Other
Chapter 4: Encouragement: That Vital Element
Chapter 9: Reflecting Each Other

The Language of Appreciation

JUDSON SWIHART

The famous psychologist William James noted that possibly the deepest human need is the need to feel appreciated. It seems to me that in marriage, then, couples need to learn how to effectively express their appreciation to each other. In many marriages this does not occur at a level the couple would really like. In marriage counseling we frequently find husbands and wives saying they simply do not feel valued or appreciated by their spouse.

Being able to communicate appreciation to your spouse may be the most important task of marriage. How can a person learn to do this?

To communicate appreciation, it is important to understand what forms of communication your husband or wife can hear. Love speaks many languages, and marriage partners do not necessarily speak the same one. If the husband spoke French and his wife spoke German, and he tried to tell her in French that he appreciated her, she might smile but would receive little impact from his communication because she could not understand it. Likewise, husbands and wives must learn to communicate appreciation in a way that is meaningful to each other. This means taking the time and effort to learn the language the spouse can hear. Otherwise, no matter how much love the husband has for his wife, it may never be communicated.

Let me describe for you eight different ways of expressing appreciation—the eight languages of love.

1. *Meeting material needs.* Some people feel especially appreciated when their spouse does something special for them. Maybe he stops on his way home from work to buy flowers for his wife, or maybe she gets him that new tackle for

MESSAGES THAT ARE OFF LIMITS

Communication is an art, and as we communicate daily with our spouses, those we love so dearly, we ought to be honing that art to perfection. Thus, some types of messages need to be off limits, phrases such as:

- "You never . . ."
- "You always . . ."
- "Why can't you be more like . . ."
- "I don't know why I married you."
- "I hate you!"
- "You're lucky I'm so understanding."
- "Won't you ever learn?"
- "Won't you ever change?"

Communication with our spouses needs to be honest and straightforward, but that doesn't give license to hurl insults and painful jabs. Try these words instead:

- "When this happens, I feel . . ." By saying this, you're taking responsibility for your feelings, not attacking his or her actions, although you're bringing them up as a problem.
- Use "I" instead of "you" as much as possible. Talk about how you feel, not about how your spouse should change.
- Try using "we," even if you know you aren't part of the problem. This shows you're sharing the responsibility and are willing to work out a solution together.

Consider loving ways to say what you want to say. And realize that many of those little irritations and problems that are driving you crazy are probably the very personality traits that drew you to him or her in the first place. Thank the Lord for his or her good qualities and for what you saw, and can still see if you try, through the eyes of love.

YFC Editors

---

his fishing equipment. In addition to buying gifts, this form of expressing appreciation can include loving actions. He takes the time to wash the car because she would really like that, or she picks up his suit from the laundry.

2. *Helping.* A friend of mine told me that when he really wants to express appreciation to his wife, he goes out and helps her weed her flower garden. Although he couldn't care less about all those weeds, she lights up like a Christmas tree when he helps her. This way of expressing appreciation may sometimes get blocked by role expectations, but for many people it can be an effective approach.

3. *Spending time.* We live in a hectic society in which time has become a precious commodity. Still, we all have 24 hours a day to spend on something. By choosing to spend it with the wife or the husband, the person communicates the high value he or she places on the spouse.

4. *Meeting emotional needs.* Partners either share some of their own feelings, or they take the time and effort to seek to understand their spouse's feelings. By looking at some deep emotion-

al issues together, two people become better known to each other and their relationship grows stronger. The willingness to be vulnerable and open oneself or to seek to understand the other partner is certainly a way to express appreciation.

5. *Saying words.* Many wives are waiting to hear "I love you," while their husbands are saying, "I never tell my wife I love her in words; it's actions that really count." Yet we know the importance of words: "Listen closely to my words," we read in Proverbs, ". . . for they are life to those who find them and health to a man's whole body" (4:20, 22). I encourage husbands and wives to ask themselves, "Are words important to my spouse?" If so, then words are the language in which appreciation needs to be communicated.

6. *Touching.* Sometimes a warm hug or an arm around the shoulder can say "I value you" or "I love you" better than any other language of appreciation.

7. *Being on the same side.* The husband communicates to the wife or the wife to the husband that they are on the same team, that a partnership exists between them. They are like two countries allied with each other. They express concern for each other's well-being; they care about each other and protect each other.

8. *Bringing out the best.* One partner helps the other develop some gift or ability or interest. This says, "I recognize that you're distinct from me, and I want to help you be the best you can be."

Expressing appreciation is vitally important, but it is effective only if the partner hears and understands your message. From these eight ways of communicating appreciation—eight languages of love—you can find at least one that your partner knows. As the Apostle Paul reminds us, "There are all sorts of languages in the world, yet none of them is without meaning. If then I do not grasp the meaning of what someone

GETTING THINGS STRAIGHT

Research indicates that only 7 percent of what we hear from our spouses involves words, 38 percent involves tone of voice, and the remaining 55 percent is made up of various nonverbal forms of communication. The verbal part of communication is far from simple; it involves at least eight steps:

1. What husband intends to say to wife
2. What husband actually says to wife
3. What wife hears
4. What wife says to herself about what she has heard
5. What wife intends to say back to husband
6. What wife actually says to husband
7. What husband hears
8. What husband says to himself about what he hears

Obviously, communication can get fouled up anywhere along the eight steps, and it often does. It takes a lot of patience, understanding, and good humor for men and women to get anything straight between them.

Jim Smith

is saying, I am a foreigner to the speaker, and he is a foreigner to me" (1 Cor. 14:10-11). Husbands and wives should make every effort to learn to speak the language of appreciation that the other understands.

Related Articles

The Importance of Talking Straight

EARNIE LARSEN

Whether you want your marriage to go from good to better, from fair to good, or from terrible to salvageable, one element is of primary importance: *talking straight.*

Through my own married life and over 20 years' clinical experience, I am constantly reminded of the fundamental importance of this skill. Relationships fail when trust fails, and trust starts to erode when people do not talk straight.

Talking straight is more than just not lying. Married couples are "crooked" when they don't ask for what they need, even if they hide such behavior under the banner of virtue. They are crooked when they are not honest about their feelings. They are crooked when they minimize important words, acts, or events.

Each of these three forms of crookedness initiates the process of dwindling trust, and each is common in married relationships.

Not asking for what we need. So very many of us, when we need a hug, can't ask for it. We may need some time off, or we may long to hear a compliment, yet we refrain from ever letting our partners know what is going on inside us. We may need our mates to come home for dinner on time or to get off the phone when we are trying to talk to them, but rather than say so we suffer in silence. Soon we start to simmer, then to boil, and finally we boil over. All the while, trust is vanishing.

Being dishonest with our feelings. Not many people are mind readers. If we don't tell our partners how we are feel-ing, how will they ever know? And if they don't know, how can they possibly respond appropriately? And how prone are we to punish them for failing to respond to a feeling of ours that we never told them about?

If our feelings are hurt, we should say so. If we are feeling blue, we need to be honest about it. If we are feeling marvelous and want to go out on the town, let's be honest with that feeling too. When we share our feelings, we are not forcing our partners to respond. All we are doing is refusing to play hide-and-seek with them.

Minimizing. A lot of neurotic religiosity that passes for virtue is merely minimizing. It is not talking straight to say "I don't care" when we really do, or "It doesn't matter" when it does, or "Anything you want is fine with me" when it isn't. We may have been trained to think that suffering in silence is a noble virtue, and sometimes it can be. But in the run-of-the-mill events of marriage, minimizing events that really matter is not a virtue. It certainly is not of God.

In my personal life as well as with thousands of couples clinically I have seen brilliant lights go on as one says, "I never knew that. Why didn't you tell me?"

Why didn't you tell me it hurt your feelings when I talked about how good a cook my mother was? I didn't have to do that—and besides, I like your cooking even better.

Why didn't you tell me my admiration for the neighbor's new car made you question your ability as a provider? I could have told you how satisfied I am with the way you care for us.

Why didn't you tell me how much you liked Valentines? Over all these years I could have gotten you a thousand of them.

Why didn't you tell me you like getting a hug when you come home from work? I thought you considered hugs a bore. If I had known, I would have left armprints all over you.

Why didn't you tell me . . . ? Year after year can vanish into history, never to return, and with each passing year immense human treasure can disappear. Opportunities can be lost and relationships can stop growing, all because we didn't know. No one told us.

Wherever you are on the continuum of bad to good marriages, there can be no moving forward without straight talk—directly asking for what we need, honestly sharing our feelings, courageously owning what is important to us. Let it be said at the end of our journey that we didn't cheat ourselves or our partner of any lovely experience just because we didn't know.

Timing: When to Say It

MARGARET DAVIDSON CAMPOLO

Most people who are happily married have learned a great deal about when *not* to say things. They know that often *when* something is said is every bit as important as *what* is said.

During our years as young parents, Tony had to learn that when he came home to find me exhausted and overwhelmed by two young children who always had more energy than I did, this was not the time to share his insights about how I might better organize my schedule. However wise and well-meant his words, at such times my weary mind could hear only criticism, and my response would be to become defensive and angry.

But if Tony was occasionally guilty of bad timing, I raised it to a fine art form in our early years together.

"You should have allowed more time," I would chide as the hour for the meeting came and went while we searched for a church in an unfamiliar town.

"I want to plan our schedule for next month," would be my greeting as he collapsed into a chair at 11 P.M. following a hard day's work.

"How about if we have some friends over for dinner this Saturday?" I would call after him as he hurried to class after a quick perusal of his notes over lunch.

Such statements invariably brought angry or irritable responses from him, and usually quick tears from me. What I had said always seemed so reasonable. It took me much longer than it should have to realize that my problem was timing. And timing is a problem with which I still struggle, because I am the kind of person who likes to take care of things right when I think of them. And this, like most traits, has a negative side as well as a positive one.

For Tony and me, a special area of concern is the demands other people make on our time. This is a place where

282

I am often guilty of bad timing. When people give me messages for Tony, I tend to err in the direction of trying to get them what they want, even though my first duty should be to consider how my husband feels. Is he tired or overloaded with details? Is this a time when he has chosen to rest rather than to work? Sometimes when I realize how bad my timing has been, I wonder how I could have been so insensitive.

But I am improving! Working on a marriage for a long time does teach you some things about timing. You learn to ask yourself, "When would be a good time to talk about this?" Or, better yet, you learn to ask your spouse that same question. And you learn that sometimes it is a matter of waiting for and recognizing the right time before you say anything at all.

In every marriage there are things that are better never said. Into this category fall those statements that we utter only to make ourselves feel better, such as "I knew that would never work," or "My mother is so much easier to get along with than yours." Such words often seem to burn within us, to goad us into speaking them. That is the time to beware, to pray to the Lord for the strength to throw them away unspoken. Each time you do that, it makes the next victory easier.

Sometimes a question, an idea, or even a criticism *ought* to be expressed, but the Lord knows you don't have the right words to do it just yet. If you ask Him, He will help you to wait for the right time to say it in the best possible way.

The Bible has much to say about the trouble into which our tongues can get us (James 3) and wisely counsels us

THINK BEFORE YOU SPEAK

The "open-and-honest" school of communication has given us a half-truth about human relationships. Its advocates tell us to "let it all hang out" in our communication with each other, to say what we think. But the other half of the truth is that we should think before we speak.

As James tells us, "Everyone should be quick to listen, slow to speak, and slow to become angry" (James 1:19). Instead of simply obeying the fight responses created by our adrenal glands, we are commanded to process such responses through the higher cortical areas of the brain. These enable us to consider our partner's best interests, our own integrity, and the long-range health of our marriage before we open our mouths.

Wayne Oates

that there is a time to keep silent as well as a time to speak (Ecc. 3:7). "Look out for that car!" falls into the category of things that must be said immediately, but most of the words that make up the conversations of a marriage will come out better after some thought and prayer.

Related Article
Chapter 4: Learning to Be Considerate

283

Reflecting Each Other

MARGARET DAVIDSON CAMPOLO

Remember how much you enjoyed looking terrible in the funny mirrors at amusement parks when you were a child? It was fun because you knew you really did not look like that. You could always find a real mirror and be sure you were you.

In marriage, each partner becomes the mirror for the other. Social scientists tell us that our self-concepts are largely determined by what we think the people who matter most to us think of us. Often a problem in a bad marriage is that one or both of the mirrors is working like those old amusement park mirrors. A spouse begins to reflect ugly things, and the other one feels that his or her best self isn't there anymore.

Mirrors reflect in simple ways; people are far more complicated. We choose what we reflect, and what we choose has much to do with what the other person becomes. One of the most exciting things about being married is helping your partner become his or her best self by reflecting with love.

I was at first incredulous, then amused, and finally quite touched by the fact that my husband can receive a standing ovation from several thousand people following a message, and still need to ask me on the way home, "But how was it really? What did you think?" Husbands and wives have an awesome power to build each other up or to tear each other down.

Most of the time the same thing can be said either negatively or positively. For some reason we seem to be more aware of this when dealing with our children than when dealing with our mates. It is easy to see children as little people in the process of "becoming," but our spouses are "becoming" too. Be alert for good traits you can encourage by reflecting with praise.

Every marriage has its bad days, its bad weeks, and sometimes even its bad years. It is then that being a good reflector becomes most difficult or, to put it positively, requires the most talent and the most prayer. There are dark times when you will not be able to find anything positive about your spouse without the Lord's help. Prayer can draw away the poisonous thoughts before they come out in the wrong words, and it can also empower you to notice the good things you ought to be reflecting.

Remember how wonderful you felt about each other the day you got married? The way you reflected each other then had a great deal to do with how you felt. Many affairs get started, not because the third party is more attractive or suitable than the spouse who is cast aside, but because the wandering partner has found a new mirror and likes the way he or she looks in it.

Positive reflecting will make your spouse feel good about himself/herself and about you, but it will also change the way *you* feel. As you look for the positive and overlook the negative, you will become happier about your marriage and the person you married. *This will happen even if your spouse does not change at all!*

All of this is fine for a good marriage, you say, but what about when your spouse is a really rotten person? How do you keep on loving and reflecting positively then? A long time ago my husband explained to me that Jesus was able to love the unlovable people He met because He truly understood even the worst of them. In a difficult marriage, as in the difficult times of a good marriage, ask God for understanding and the ability to do what is humanly impossible. Jesus is our model. And in reflecting our marriage partners positively we are following His example.

Related Articles
Chapter 4: Encouragement: That Vital Element
Chapter 9: How to Affirm Your Spouse

Making Your Communication Work

ANDRE & FAY BUSTANOBY

Do you want to see a great improvement in your marital communication? Try following these three suggestions:

1. *Break the bad habit of communicating to coerce.* To make communication in marriage work, we must break a bad habit that most of us don't even realize we have: communicating to *convince* our spouses of our point of view or *persuade* them to give first place to our wants and wishes. We engage in verbal arm-twisting to get them to give up their point of view. We verbally bludgeon them into giving us what we want.

But communication in marriage should not be primarily to coerce. It should be first and foremost to achieve understanding. Your husband or wife has a point of view and some very strong feelings about it. Do you understand what he or she thinks? Do you care that he or she feels that way?

2. *Be willing to talk about any bitterness that keeps you from caring about your spouse's feelings.* Often we don't care, and we don't want to understand. Sometimes this uncaring attitude is due to a root of bitterness that lies beneath the surface in an otherwise tranquil marriage.

Before you can begin to talk about the many problems you need to solve—how to spend money, when to redecorate the house, where to go to church, or how to discipline the kids—you must talk about the number-one issue: why you don't listen to each other with understanding and caring ears. There may be a root of bitterness poisoning your communication.

You may be timid about opening up the issue of your spouse's uncaring attitude. Because prior attempts always generated more heat than light, you're reluctant to try again. You prefer to play it safe and not talk about how you really feel. Don't shy away from the truth! Your marriage is likely to die of terminal superficiality.

3. *Observe the fundamental rules for good communication when you talk to each other.* Here are some tips to make communication more effective:

● When you speak, use the word *I* instead of *you.* For example, instead of saying, "You never talk to me," say this: "Honey, when I try to talk about problems between us and I don't get any response, I feel frustrated and wonder what I'm doing wrong." Your spouse probably is more willing to talk about your bad feelings than about his or her bad behavior!

● When your spouse speaks, listen actively. Respond in such a way as to let him or her know you are hearing and understanding. For example, nod your head and say, "I see." Or if you don't see, say, "I don't understand what you mean by. . . ." Just be sure your questions are legitimate—that you really want to know how your spouse thinks and feels. "When did I ever do that?" is not a legitimate question. You really don't want to know the answer, and if you get one, you'll probably argue the point.

• Don't be in a hurry to correct facts. Whether or not you think your spouse should see the situation the way he does, this is his perception of the matter, and his feelings are based on that perception. He doesn't need to be corrected. He needs to know you understand how he sees the situation and how he feels about it; he needs to know you care. When we hurry to correct the facts, we give the impression that we're more interested in being right than in empathizing with the other person's pain.

Once your spouse is assured that you understand and care about how he feels, he will be more open to hearing your perception of the facts and how you feel. We don't need to agree on the facts in order to communicate in marriage, but we must understand and care about each other's perceptions and feelings.

• Don't defend yourself, even if you are unjustly accused. When we defend ourselves, we are not communicating for understanding. If your spouse accuses you of something that is not true, reply, "No wonder you are angry [or whatever the emotion is] with me. I would be angry too!" Permit him to talk out his feelings, and empathize with those feelings.

1 CORINTHIANS 13:1

If I speak in the tongues of men and of angels, but have not love, I am only a resounding gong or a clanging cymbal.

Once he is convinced that you understand, he is likely to want to hear and understand your side of the story.

These three suggestions and four tips are fundamental to good communication, but they are only a beginning. You may wish to check your bookstore or library for books on communication in marriage that will teach you much more about effectively talking with your spouse.

Remember that the evidence of a successful marriage is not the absence of problems, but the constructive way we talk about them.

Related Articles
Chapter 4: Learning to Be Considerate
Chapter 9: Blocks to Communication

COMMUNICATION COUNSEL

Here are some tips to help you and your spouse communicate:

C—Commit yourself to listening to your spouse every day.

O—Observe each other's unspoken needs.

M—Make regular appointments to spend time together and talk.

M—Mend your arguments before you go to bed.

U—Utilize the opportunities to let your actions speak louder than words.

N—Notice the positive things your spouse does, and say thanks.

I—Initiate conversation by asking feeling-oriented questions.

C—Care about your spouse's opinions, even if they differ from yours.

A—Admit to your spouse when you're wrong.

T—Touch each other when you listen or talk.

E—Expect the best of your spouse.

Byron Emmert

Perspective: Seeing What Your Spouse Sees

NORM WAKEFIELD

Several years ago I conducted training seminars for teachers of preschoolers. To help them better understand the world of the young child I gave them the following assignment: walk through your classroom on your knees. As you do, ask yourself, "How does the room look from this perspective? How is it different from my adult view? What does a child see—and not see—in this room that is different from what an adult sees or doesn't see?"

More recently I was speaking to the faculties of two elementary schools. I asked them to write down three ways the classroom was different for the students than for them, the teachers. After I had finished my seminar, a significant number of teachers indicated they had never considered the students' perspective of the classroom. They assumed the student was viewing it as they were. As they began to see the difference in perspective, they could better see why students behave as they do—they are not paid to be there; they often feel incompetent; they feel much peer pressure, and so on.

A fundamental error most of us make in relationships is to assume that others view life as we do. This error leads us to misperceptions, false judgments, breakdown in communication, and weakening relationships. This does not have to happen if we are open to learning a new dimension of relating to others.

Let me make a few observations about perspective.

First, each person's experiences are personal. No one else can fully comprehend how that person sees and how he feels about what he is experiencing. For example, I have a 17-year-old daughter who is a high-school junior, and I realize that relationships are important to her. But I'm not likely to take time to think through how she perceives and feels as she relates to her classmates, as she feels their acceptance or rejection, as she experiences pressure to conform, and so forth. I am more likely to make assumptions that are superficial—and often judgmental.

Second, each person develops personal meaning and values from his experiences. Thus he interprets life from the composite of all his insights, interpretations, and perceptions. Life will look different for him than for me—often radically different! *But I tend to assume that he sees life as I see it.* As I relate to this person, I often act as if he has the same view, the same perspective, that I have.

What does all this mean to me as a husband, or to you as a wife? What implications can we discover?

I have found that I can enrich my relationship with my wife, Winnie, if I build and maintain a strong *perspective-taking skill*. In fact, I would say without reservation that developing this skill has significantly enhanced my relations with all family members. Yet as I interact with people in communication seminars, I find few who know how to use it effectively.

Perspective-taking means asking myself two questions:

1. What does this situation, problem,

287

or event look or feel like from Winnie's perspective?

2. How is her perception different from mine?

After I ask myself these questions, I do three things:

I am alert to observe. I thoughtfully look at circumstances, problems, and situations to see how they might appear to her. I watch her reactions to events to see if she may experience them differently than I do. For example, I have found that Winnie's reaction to sports events is radically different from mine. She is enthusiastic, joyful, celebrative. She jumps, cheers, waves her arms. It matters little to her which team scores the touchdown. I, on the other hand, am stoic and controlled but uptight if "my" team falls behind. I'd rather watch the event at home on television in privacy.

As I've watched my wife, I've learned to appreciate her perspective. I don't belittle it, because I have come to value her zest for life, her playful spirit.

I am careful to listen. By perceptive listening, I discover how the world looks to Winnie. I try to hear the emotions that underlie her messages. I try to discern if her emotional response is different from mine and what this may tell me about her. I explore the things left unsaid, and I ask questions to discover what life looks like to her, how she perceives this situation.

None of this is done with the intent to manipulate, coerce, or intimidate my wife. My goal is to know her, to appreciate her perspective, to build a bridge between us that will help me understand life through her eyes.

I think about what I see and hear. And I think about what life is like (1) when you are a woman; (2) when many of your tasks are routine and boring; (3) when people often praise your husband more than you; (4) when people expect you to be different because you're a pastor's wife.

The discipline of thinking about an-

other person's point of view can be very productive, especially when I really want to be loving, supportive, and affirming. It is vital when problems arise and I need to realize how the other individual feels and thinks, or when I need to demonstrate that I'm concerned about what she has at stake in the outcome of a decision we are making.

I have said that perspective-taking is a skill. Like all skills, it has to be learned, and it requires practice.

An effective way to practice is to jot down your spouse's name. Then begin to list ways life is different for him or her. Stretch your thinking to consider emotions, values, pressures, interests, needs, and other factors you might overlook. This stimulating exercise will strengthen your awareness of your partner's perspective. You'll begin to appreciate some of the issues he or she has to contend with.

Another way to expand awareness is to imagine situations other people are in. Here are some examples. What is it like to (1) daily enter a classroom where you're failing the subject? (2) have 24-hour care of two energetic preschoolers? (3) fail to meet your sales quota for two months? (4) be a single parent, work full time, and care for three young children?

I'm grateful I discovered this insight that helps me relate to others in an empathetic, supportive manner. It has enriched my relationships with others in significant ways. It has helped me see behind the scenes into their lives and to be more thoughtful and compassionate. That is why I encourage you to develop the skill of perspective-taking. You'll find others grateful for your considerate understanding of them. They will thank God for your love.

Related Articles

NAG, NAG, NAG

Nagging—it happens even in good marriages. We should not be overly alarmed when nagging by either partner happens occasionally, but we must always be alert to the fact that nagging can ruin a marriage like the constant drip of water can wear down even the hardest rock.

Words of wisdom to the nagger: don't think that your nagging is going to help your spouse work harder, do better, or complete the tasks you want done. Nagging only hurts your relationship. So, ask why you feel so strongly about whatever you're harping on. Are you trying to keep control over your spouse? Are you trying to make your spouse feel guilty? You may think not, but be totally honest. Then consider alternatives to nagging.

Start by lowering your expectations and prioritizing your list of tasks at hand. You may find that some things that seem so important really aren't. Try to see your requests from your spouse's perspective. And then have a set time each day or every few days to discuss priorities. You could explain that you really want the grass mowed this week because company is coming Saturday night. Making sure your spouse understands the reasons for your concerns will help make sure you're both working toward the same goals.

Words of wisdom to the "naggee": your response to nagging can make all the difference. First, ask "What is the real message behind the nagging? Is there some truth to it?" Had you made a promise to do something and then forgotten about it? If so, an apology is in order and, if possible, the promise kept. Are you being lax in certain responsibilities? Are you being a true servant to your spouse?

Then follow through on the preceding principles for communicating priorities. With a little work and sharing, you can turn off the dripping faucet of nagging before it wears you both down completely.

YFC Editors

Speak Your Partner's Language

H. NORMAN WRIGHT

When a couple marries, two different cultures come together. You are foreigners to each other, each with your own set of values, beliefs, language, and style of talking.

For example, in many marriages one person tends to give a lot of details while the partner sends "telegrams," keeping communication as brief as possible. We could call the first person an *amplifier* and the second, a *condenser*. There is nothing wrong with either style, but frustration can arise when the two kinds of communicators must talk with each other. The amplifier is frustrated because the partner never gives enough information. The condenser is frustrated because he wants a concise answer. As one condenser commented to me, "When I ask my partner for the time of day, that's all I want. I don't want to hear how the watch was made!"

For a relationship to blossom, each partner must learn the other's language. And each must be willing to use the other's language without demanding that the other person become just like him or her.

If you are an amplifier talking with a condenser, shorten what you are going to say and put it in your partner's style. If you are a condenser talking with an amplifier, elaborate. If you usually give a one-line response, give several lines. Use the descriptive adjectives your partner likes.

Though exceptions exist, often men are the condensers and women the amplifiers. Part of this is cultural conditioning and part is because of the way men and women use (or don't use) both sides of the brain. But we can all learn and adapt to another person's style if we so desire.

When people communicate, they process their information in different ways. Some people are *visual:* they think by generating visual images in their minds, and they see the sentences they speak.

Others are *auditory:* they think best by talking to themselves or hearing sounds, and they respond best to what they hear.

Still others are *feeling oriented:* they have a heightened sense of touch, emotion, or intuition, and they respond on the basis of their feelings.

Each of us has a dominant mode of perception. Though we all use all three modes, one is better developed in us than the others. But it is possible to learn to function and communicate in the other modes as well. What are you like? Are you primarily a visual, auditory,

---

IDEAS AND FEELINGS

We've made it a rule: answer an idea with an idea, but a feeling with a feeling. It's as disconcerting to share a thoughtful idea and get an emotional response as it is to share an emotion and get an idea thrown back at you. We learned this rule one night after we had gone to bed. Here is what happened. Wife told husband about an apprehension she had. Husband, wishing to go to sleep, said she shouldn't feel that way. This only made her feel more that way. So she tried again. This time husband told her how she ought to feel. We both began to laugh because it was such a silly impasse.

We drew a diagram of what was happening. Wife was asking for such a simple thing: *understanding.* As soon as husband let her know that he understood how she felt, he moved emotionally close to her. Then she could accept the solutions he offered. Understanding is more important than solutions for our personal closeness, we discovered that night. And it's been true every day and night since.

Keith & Gladys Hunt

---

or feeling person? What about your spouse? Are you aware of your differences and similarities? Can you communicate, or do you pass each other like ships in the night?

An easy way to understand the way you and your spouse communicate is to pay attention to the words, images, and phrases you both use. What do these phrases say to you?

☐ I see what you are saying.

☐ That looks like a good idea. Show me more.

☐ I would like to know your point of view.

The above phrases reflect a visual bias. The person thinks and speaks on the basis of strong visual pictures. Other people see vague pictures, and some see no pictures at all.

☐ Boy, that sounds great to me.

☐ Tell me that again.

☐ That's coming through loud and clear.

☐ Let's hear that again.

These phrases come from a person who is basically auditory. Sounds are of primary importance to him.

☐ I sense you are upset with me.

☐ This car has a good feel.

☐ My instincts say this is the right thing to do.

These phrases come from a person who responds in a feeling mode.

Perhaps you have been in a group where a new idea has been shared. If at that time you had been aware of these three methods of responding, you might have heard, "That idea feels right," "It looks OK to me," and "That sounds like a good idea." They all mean the same thing, but they are presented in three different ways.

What does this have to do with husband-wife communication? Just this: if you learn to use your spouse's style of speaking, he or she will listen to you. It may take you awhile to become skillful at it, but the work will pay off. Too often we expect our spouses to cater to us and do it our way. But if we are willing to take the initiative and move into their world first, we establish a common ground for communication.

At times you may feel that your spouse is resisting a suggestion you are making. Perhaps you have failed to communicate in a way he or she can understand. If you ask a question and do not receive a satisfactory response, switch to another way of asking the question. "How does this sound to you?" No response. "Does this look all right to you?" No response. "How do you feel about this issue?" A response!

A wife asks her husband to complete a chore. He says, "Write it down," or, "Make me a list." If in the future she writes a note and hands it to him as she tells him what she wants him to do, she may get a quicker response.

I have found these principles essential in communicating with my clients in the counseling office. As I listen, I try to discover their perceptual mode so I can enter into their world with them. I also listen to their tone of voice and the phrases they use. I study their nonverbal forms of communication, such as posture and facial expression. I have learned that if I communicate as they do at first, eventually they are willing to listen and move in the direction I would like them to move.

In the same way, you can learn your spouse's language. Once you are able to communicate with your spouse in his or her mode, your spouse may be willing to move into your world. If you learn to see, hear, and feel as your spouse sees, hears, and feels, communication is bound to improve.

Related Articles
Chapter 6: Valuing the Differences Between Men and Women
Chapter 9: Why Men and Women Have Trouble Communicating With Each Other

Being Able to Laugh

JERRY & MARY WHITE

Jerry arrived home after a hectic day. He had to dress hurriedly for a dinner that evening. Mary could sense his preoccupation and tension. Searching for a way to lighten his mood, she slipped on his old combat boots, left over from early days in the military. They were easily hidden under her long skirt. He didn't notice them until they were in the car and she casually crossed her legs, exposing the boots. Shouting with laughter, he had to pull the car to the side of the road to collect himself. The tension was broken.

Laughter lightens any relationship. Between husband and wife, it beautifully balances the work needed to build a lasting and enjoyable marriage.

Laughter reflects an overflow of joy, a positive attitude, and a healthy outlook. We're not speaking here of foolishness or giddiness, but of genuine mutual enjoyment and response to life. God has provided both laughter and tears for emotional outlets. A balanced expression of both helps any relationship.

We want to laugh together, not only during light and happy times, but also in the middle of difficulties. Spontaneous laughter can defuse many arguments, cover personal offenses, and dispel hostility. When we can deliberately laugh together during points of stress, we know our relationship is deepening.

Throughout Jerry's working career, he has had to travel a good deal. Sometimes the time away from his family becomes tedious, and he leaves home with reluctance. On one trip he unpacked his suitcase and found a card from Mary tucked into his shaving bag, which read, "Remember, no matter where you go—there you are!" The laughter resulting from this card made him feel closer to home and gave him enthusiasm to face the day.

Of course there are times when pain is so deep that laughter is inappropriate. But if we realize that eventually laughter and joy will return, we feel a measure of hope. We have often heard someone say, "He'll laugh about this someday," and it's true. We do laugh again someday, no matter how deep the pain now.

Healthy laughter begins with a willingness to laugh at ourselves. If we take ourselves so seriously that we can't laugh at a personal mistake or silly error, we will open ourselves to lots of unnecessary hassle, even pain, in marriage.

When we loosen up and laugh at our own shortcomings and failures, we can learn to laugh *with* our partner—but never *at* him or her. Laughing *at* a spouse creates tension and resentment instead of defusing it. Laughing at the weaknesses or mistakes of a partner wounds his or her self-esteem and leads to bitterness.

Has laughter been missing from your marriage? To make it an integral part, you may need to structure opportunities at first. What type of humor does your partner like? Slapstick? Intellectual? Satire? Whimsy? Puns? Irony? The ridiculous? Look for ways to inject that type of humor into everyday situations.

Clip cartoons and comics for one another that might offer a comic ending to an argument or a bright way to start the day. Finding a cartoon taped to the mirror in the morning can remind a spouse that his loved one is thinking of him. A humorous greeting card can draw couples together and help them reflect on some joyous aspect of their relationship. Watch a funny television program together, or see a movie. Read aloud to one another from humorous plays, books, and articles.

It helps to include children in the process of bringing more laughter into your family life. Children seem to take a special delight in humor, passing through various stages of appreciation as they grow. When our children were young, we would occasionally announce "joke night" for the dinner table. Every family member would bring a few jokes or rid-dles to the table. Simple, yes, but some of our favorite inside family sayings and jokes evolved during that time.

Medical science is beginning to recognize the value of laughter and humor in physical healing. Laughter brings the same restoration to a strained marriage relationship. It creates a healthy, healing atmosphere. Laughter isn't a panacea for a failing marriage, but it gives a joyful boost to a growing relationship.

Related Articles
Chapter 1: Love as Friendship
Chapter 4: Making Your Spouse Your Best Friend

GIVE, GIVE, GIVE

For years, I have heard that when there is a marriage problem, it always has two sides. However, as I looked toward my own marriage, now almost 20 years ago, the thought crossed my mind several times, "I wonder if those two-sided conflicts will come up in Sandy's and my relationship?" To prepare for what I heard was inevitable, I asked a dear friend, Bible teacher, and radio personality to give me the best marriage counseling possible.

About a month before our marriage, Kelly invited me into his office. With pen in hand, I entered, ready to take notes on what I anticipated would be a one- or two-hour session of wisdom and instruction.

"Rolly," Kelly said, "what you must learn to do is this: give and give and give and give and give . . . and give some more."

Well, I came to the meeting with high expectations of what information and help would be shared. I got it, but it was packaged much differently than I had expected.

The principle Kelly taught me that day—or rather, in those five minutes—turns out to be perfect in several ways:

☐ When one gives, it is consistent with Christ's example of how He dealt with relationships while on earth.
☐ When you are busy giving, you are not expecting any return.
☐ By applying the giving principle, I've found that Sandy's and my relationship grows and grows—even after 20 years, 8 homes, 7 states, 5 jobs, 2 kids, and youth ministry as a profession.

We don't give to get any more than we serve to be served or love to be loved. We give, serve, and love because Jesus Christ lived that way.

Yes, marriage conflicts are always two-sided. However, they are more often "no-sided" when giving is in full gear. Marriage has now consumed approximately half of my years on earth. I love it, I love Sandy, and I love Christ, the One who gave and gave and keeps on giving.

Rolly Richert

How to Listen

JIM SMITH

A sage once said that the Lord gave us two ears and one mouth, and that ratio ought to tell us something. But listening is more than just not talking, and several things need to be said up front about it.

First, listening takes lots of energy. Sometimes we want to listen, but we are just too tired. We don't have the physical resources. Better to admit that to your spouse than to fall asleep in the middle of a conversation and then try to explain yourself.

Second, opposites attract, and often morning people marry night people. Morning people like to talk before breakfast. Night people aren't even Christian until after 10 A.M. Night people like to talk after midnight, but morning people shut down at 10 P.M. It takes real effort to coordinate schedules so both husband and wife have the energy and willingness to listen to each other.

Third, listening is threatening. The more I have invested in the relationship, the more threatened I may be by what I hear. Since listening is a potentially dangerous activity, it makes sense to learn how to do it well. Here are some tips:

The most important question you can ask yourself when someone starts to talk to you is this: "What does this person want me to do with this information?" The answer helps you create a *listening stance.* As a counselor and a husband, I choose among several basic listening stances when people wish to talk to me.

The first I call the *hold-the-bucket* stance. Sometimes people simply need to vomit up their hurt, frustration, pain, anger, and rage, and they need someone to listen with mercy and integrity.

They aren't asking me to fix it—only to take them seriously and listen. This kind of listening may be what's implied in the biblical injunction: "Carry each other's burdens, and in this way you will fulfill the law of Christ" (Gal. 6:2).

Some days when my wife comes home from her business, she needs to ventilate her feelings to someone who will hear and understand and sympathize. If I know that's what she needs, I can just hold the bucket. I'm even trained to do that without getting any on me. However, if I mistakenly think she wants me to fix things—which I know I can't—I may turn off the listening switch and retreat to a safe place inside my head where I won't feel inadequate. My lights are on, but I'm not at home!

Realize that holding the bucket is perfectly OK. You don't need to run and hide; you don't have to jump in and fix things. In fact, your spouse may not even want you to try. Just listening may be all that is needed.

The second listening stance might be called the *mirror.* I listen and then I try to say back what I have heard, only in a different way so the other person can hear it in a different frame of reference. When we hear our own words mirrored back to us, we often get a fresh perspective that leads to new insights. Jan and I often try to mirror each other in order to get a better look at what is going on in our thinking processes.

Third is a *male/female perspective* stance. Often women want to know how a man sees things. I often need a female's perspective, so I ask my wife how a woman would think about something. Being male, there is no way I could know this without asking.

Fourth is a *counseling* stance. This is where, as a second or third party with less emotional involvement in an issue, I bring a detached viewpoint to those who are too close to the forest to see the trees. Admittedly, this is not an easy stance to maintain in marriage, because I am usually emotionally involved in any issue that affects my spouse.

The fifth is a *spiritual* stance. Because I am a pastoral counselor, people often wish to know what I understand to be God's viewpoint or what Scripture has to say on a given issue. As a spiritual leader in my home, I sometimes take this stance.

It is important to understand that each stance requires a different focus as I listen. If I assume the wrong stance, I will not listen in a creative way and my wife will not feel she has been heard—as, in reality, she has not.

A counselor spends many hours responding with little more than "Hmmm. Is that right? Interesting! Hmmmm." At the end of these sessions, people often say, "You don't know how much help you have been!" Actually, I have offered no direct help at all. All I have done is try to listen with integrity. But think about it—isn't listening to another person, really listening, one of the greatest compliments you can pay that person?

The Art of Listening

H. NORMAN WRIGHT

The best communicators in marriage do not rely on their mouths. Instead they rely on their eyes and their ears. Outstanding communicators are those who listen, and you listen as much with your eyes as with your ears (or you should).

My son, Matthew, taught me to listen with my eyes. I had no other option. Even today, as he nears the age of 20, my profoundly mentally retarded boy still knows just a few words, and even those have little or no meaning. But he is also a tremendous gift from God, because his presence has changed our lives. We have learned so much from him.

When Matthew lived at home, he couldn't communicate his needs. He would grab our hands and place them on his head or rub his head against us to show us that something was wrong. We learned to read his body movements and his eyes to detect any type of seizure activity. In time, I found I had also begun to listen to my clients with my eyes and hear what they could not put into words. I was becoming a total listener!

You can learn to listen. Yes, listening is a skill to be learned. Your mind and ears can be taught to hear more clearly; your eyes can be taught to see more clearly. Our pattern for listening is very simple and clear in Scripture: "He who answers before listening—that is his folly and his shame" (Prov. 18:13). "Let every man be quick to hear (a ready listener)" (James 1:19, AMP).

Listeners have influence. Are you aware that the listener, not the speaker, controls the conversation? Most of us operate under the assumption that the more we talk, the more we influence the listener. If both people in a conversation believe this, the talking escalates and becomes more intense, which is quite sad. The words fly through the air with nowhere to land, and deafness prevails!

Why do you listen to your partner? There are four good reasons to do so:
1. To understand
2. To enjoy
3. To learn something
4. To give help or comfort

There are many pseudolisteners who masquerade as the real product, but anyone who has not listened for the aforementioned reasons does not really listen.

Would you like to improve your listening skills? Let me share a few general hints on how to polish them and overcome hindrances to listening.

1. *Listen in an active manner.* Be alive when you listen: no one wants to talk to a corpse. Pay attention to the other person's language. Notice how he talks. If he asks questions or gives feedback in an abbreviated form, do the same. If he gives detail and elaborates with descriptive words, do the same.

When you actively listen, you do three things: paraphrase, clarify, and give feedback. Paraphrasing means stating in your own words what you believe the other person said. This helps you understand what he means. It also lets him correct you if you are mistaken. Clarifying often accompanies paraphrasing. It is very simple: you just ask questions until you fully understand what the other person means. Feedback is sharing your own thoughts and feelings in a nonjudgmental way. Your feedback helps the other person understand the effect of his communication. During feedback apply this biblical principle that builds vital relationships: "A word fitly spoken and in due season is like apples of gold in a setting of silver" (Prov. 25:11, AMP).

2. *Listen with empathy.* This means both caring and seeing the situation from the other person's perspective. You may not like or agree with what is being

---

DEALING WITH YOUR IRRITABILITY

1. Give up your secret belief that the world should be perfect.

2. Think of three blessings for which you are truly grateful.

3. Remind yourself that God created the person who irritates you, and this person is responsible to Him, not to you.

4. Remember the last time you did something that irritated someone else, and forgive yourself.

5. Ask yourself, "Is this problem going to seem important next week?"

6. Take a break. Maybe you're just tired.

7. Read a psalm, and pray for God's perspective.

YFC Editors

---

said, but as you listen, you realize that if you were experiencing what he is experiencing, if you were standing where he is standing, you would probably feel the same way. Romans 12:15 tells us to weep with those who weep and rejoice with those who rejoice. That is what empathy is all about.

3. *Listen with openness.* Selective listening, defensive listening, and filtered listening are not open listening. Listening with openness means discovering how the other person's point of view makes sense to you. How do you do this? Someone has suggested that you listen as though you were an anthropologist and the other person were from another planet. His customs, beliefs, and way of thinking are different from yours, and you are trying to understand them. This means you must listen to all that is being shared, without judgment.

4. *Listen with awareness.* Be aware

of what the other person says and how it compares with the facts. Be aware of whether or not the message of the other person is consistent.

If you have listened actively, empathetically, and openly and still don't understand the other person's point of view, you don't have to attack. One of the best ways to respond is by asking a question so you can gather more information from which to evaluate what was said. "Could you tell me a bit more?" "Could you give me a specific example?" "What would you like me to do differently?"

Or you might say, "Thank you for letting me know your perspective. I'll think about it." Or, "That's interesting. I hadn't considered it in that light." Or, "What you're saying may have some truth in it.

Tell me more." These statements can have a disarming effect on the other person as well as give you more information.

When you listen to your spouse, you send your partner the message that you believe he or she has something worthwhile to say, that he or she has value. Listening is an act of love and caring. It helps us venture into the life of another person. If you are a good listener, more people will invite you to be a guest in their lives, and the people whose lives already touch yours—such as your spouse—will begin to reveal themselves to you on a deeper level.

Related Articles
Chapter 9: Blocks to Communication
Chapter 9: How to Listen

TO MY DEAR AND LOVING HUSBAND (17TH CENTURY)

If ever two were one, then surely we.
If ever man were loved by wife, then thee;
If ever wife was happy in a man,
Compare with me, ye women, if you can.
I prize thy love more than whole mines of gold
Or all the riches that the East doth hold.
My love is such that rivers cannot quench,
Nor ought but love from thee, give recompense.
Thy love is such I can no way repay.
The heavens reward thee manifold, I pray.
Then while we live, in love let's so persever
That when we live no more, we may live ever.

Anne Bradstreet

Nonverbal Communication: What It Can Say

JOSH McDOWELL

Nonverbal communication is more powerful than verbal communication. As the proverb says, "Actions speak louder than words." If you say "I love you," but your behavior doesn't back that up, then your actions cancel your words and make them void.

Love as a statement is insignificant unless it is placed in a context of loving action. This is why, when love is described in the Bible, it is always described by what it does. "Dear children, let us not love with words or tongue but with actions and in truth" (1 John 3:18). When we say to our mate, "I love you," our nonverbal communication—that is, our actions—interpret our words.

The other day Dottie was feeling bad because our daughter was at camp and had had a hard first day. I said to her, "Honey, it's going to be OK," but this didn't seem to help much. So I got up, walked over to her, and gave her a big hug. Then I sat down and wrote our daughter a letter. My actions—offering physical comfort and then doing something about the situation—said more to my wife than my words.

It's a good idea for a married person to ask himself or herself, "Are my actions backing up what I have expressed verbally?" Take 1 Corinthians 13:4-7 and substitute your name for the word love. Add your spouse's name, and see how your nonverbal communication measures up.

- [ ] Is Josh patient with Dottie?
- [ ] Is Josh kind to Dottie?
- [ ] Or is Josh envious, boastful, and proud?
- [ ] Is Josh rude to Dottie?
- [ ] Is Josh selfish, or does he serve Dottie?
- [ ] Is Josh often angry with Dottie?
- [ ] Does he hold grudges against Dottie?
- [ ] Is Josh truthful with Dottie?
- [ ] Does Josh protect Dottie?
- [ ] Does Josh trust Dottie?
- [ ] Does Josh hope for the best for Dottie?
- [ ] Does Josh persevere in loving actions, even when they are difficult?

When I check myself by Scripture, I learn a lot about myself. The Holy Spirit convicts me of where I need to improve. And love grows as I put it in the context of action.

Related Articles
Chapter 1: Love Is the Gift of a Caring Self
Chapter 4: The Love Exchange

Why Men and Women Have Trouble Communicating With Each Other

JIM SMITH

Communication between any two human beings is an enormously difficult task. When one happens to be female and the other male, it gets even trickier.

Genesis states that in the beginning, God made us different—male and female. Whether by divine design or by socialization, we certainly tend to communicate differently. The following differences are not universally true, of course, but even casual observation would confirm the general tendencies:

1. *Men talk in generalities; women talk in specifics.* Next time you're at a mixed party, listen to men talk and then listen to women talk. Or listen to a man tell about his last out-of-town trip: "Caught a plane in Chicago, stayed in the Hilton, went to a bunch of meetings, and came home." His wife starts getting angry; she wants detail. "What was the flight attendant wearing? What did the taxicab driver say between O'Hare and the hotel? What did you have for breakfast? What color was your bedspread?" In other words, give me detail! A man just can't understand how anyone could be so interested in so many little details.

Think about that last argument you had. Hubby is going out the door, and you have a 45-second discussion about an issue. By the time he is out the driveway, he has totally forgotten it. But she spends the day rehashing, mulling, stewing over it. At 6 he is met at the door by his wife, who says, "We need to talk!" He says, "About what?" He has completely forgotten about the argument, but she needs to talk it out in detail. As women talk things out in detail, somewhere along the line they let go of them—but if they do not get the chance to talk, they file their resentments away. You can be sure they will be brought up at a later date.

2. *Men tend to be in touch with their thoughts first and then their feelings; women tend to be in touch with their feelings first and then their thoughts.* When a wife asks her husband how he feels about something, he often tells her what he is thinking about it. Likewise, when a husband asks his wife what she thinks about something, she will often tell him how she feels. If a man wants to get to his wife's thoughts on an issue, he must first listen to her feelings; if a wife wishes to get to her husband's feelings, she will need to let him air his thoughts first. If we confuse thoughts and feelings, we can get pretty confused!

3. *Men and women have some characteristic bad habits in communication.* Women, for example, have a tremendous need to fix things. Hubby brings home a problem from work and wants to share it with his wife (a rare event). "We hired a new secretary today, and boy is she a loser! She can't type, she can't spell, she handles the phone in a horrible way, she doesn't know how to file, and to top it all off, she isn't even cute!" Wife responds, "Why don't you

299

fire her?" Husband inwardly translates her answer to mean: "Well, turkey, anyone with a lick of sense knows how to fix that." Husband makes a mental note not to risk sharing a work problem with wife again.

Men have an equally bad habit: they tend to cover over emotions with rationality. The wife is sharing her feelings with her husband, and he says, "Well, when you get yourself together, we'll sit down and discuss this in a logical manner." The wife ends up thinking her feelings have been completely discounted, so next time she just stuffs them inside rather than risk getting put down again.

4. *Men and women have very different ideas on how evenings should be spent.* Men tend to feel they have earned the right to come home to their castle, draw up the drawbridge, and let the alligators swim in the moat. Having done battle all day, they wish to retreat and do something in which no additional demands are placed upon them—read the newspaper, putter around in the garage, or sit in a stupor and watch some mindless TV program.

Women, even those with their own careers, like to take time to share from their day's work, to get emotionally close to their husbands. But men hear their wives' plea for conversation as an additional demand, and often they further withdraw into silence, leaving their wives feeling isolated and unappreciated. A vicious circle begins. The more hubby withdraws into silence, the more his wife escalates her demands to share and confide. And the more she demands, the less he says.

5. *Men and women approach sex from different perspectives.* Men tend to be physically oriented, while women tend to be relationally oriented. A husband and wife have had a fight and both are tired of fighting. He figures that having sex would be a great way to make up. She wants to make up before they come together sexually. She says, "How

can you even think of sex when we're not even speaking?" He replies, "Well, couldn't we just do it silently?" And another fight begins.

Do men and women have different communication styles? You bet—and this can be very confusing when husbands and wives are trying to communicate their needs and wishes. But just as

300

it is possible to learn to understand a foreign language, it is also possible to learn to understand your spouse. Next time you get your signals crossed, stop and ask yourself, "Are we looking at things differently because one of us is a man and the other a woman?" If this is the case, it may take only a little reflection to figure out why your spouse is acting in that impossible way. If you can then get him or her to understand why *you* are behaving the way you are, you will have come a long way. You might even start understanding each other!

Related Articles
Chapter 6: Valuing the Differences Between Men and Women
Chapter 8: Male/Female Attitudes Toward Sex
Chapter 9: Speak Your Partner's Language

But What Can We Talk About?

ALICE FRYLING

Sometimes couples don't spend time talking together because they don't know what to talk about. The following questions are discussion starters. Use them in any order. Pick one to fit the moment. Use them again and again. There is no expiration date. Your answers and discussion will change over the years.

Have fun with the questions. Listen to each other. Enjoy each other.

☐ What are five things I do that say to you "I love you"?

☐ What do you wish I did (that I don't do often) to say "I love you"?

☐ What activity that we did together last week did you enjoy most?

☐ What are two things you hope will happen in our relationship in the next year?

☐ What do you like to talk about the most? People—who? Things—what? Places—where? Ideas—what?

☐ How can I help you this week?

☐ What do you find to be the most difficult aspect of making plans with me?

☐ What things have we done together that have been the most fun?

☐ What is one of your most treasured memories from ages 1-10? 10-20? 20-30? After that?

☐ How would you like me to pray for you this week?

☐ What does forgiveness mean to you? In what ways have you forgiven me this week?

☐ What are some things I do that make you laugh?

☐ How do you hear God speaking to you?

☐ If someone gave you $1,000 tonight, what would you do with it?

☐ If someone gave you a week's vacation, what would you do with it?

☐ What is something you really like about my mother? About my father?

☐ What is something you really like about your mother? About your father?

☐ What do you remember as one of your greatest successes? What do you remember as one of your greatest failures?

☐ What do you like best about our children?

☐ What is one dream you had about having your own marriage and family that hasn't been fulfilled yet?

☐ Is our physical relationship what you hoped it would be? Why? Why not?

☐ What is the best gift anyone ever gave you? What gift have I given you that you liked the most?

- List 10 adjectives that describe yourself. List 10 adjectives that describe me.
- What do you think is the most important thing I do in an average day?
- What is the hardest feeling for you to express? How can I help you express it?
- What do you think is the hardest feeling for me to express? Would you like me to express that feeling?
- What is something that you enjoy about your days, but don't talk about much?
- When did you first know you loved me?

Related Articles

WHAT SHOULD WE TALK ABOUT?

We need to communicate about everything that is important to either party—not to both parties, but to either one. Whatever is important to my wife, I need to be willing to discuss; whatever is important to me, I need to be willing to share.

Josh McDowell

The Stumbling Block of Uncommunicated Expectations

NETA JACKSON

This year Dave and I celebrated our 20th wedding anniversary. We threw a party and invited all our friends and relatives, then sneaked away for a weekend alone to reflect on 20 years of married life.

"What a long way we've come!" I thought. Of course, compared to both sets of our parents, who have recently celebrated golden wedding anniversaries, we also have a long way to go. But in looking back I realized that one of the biggest hurdles we've had to face and overcome is the problem of *uncommunicated expectations.*

Idealism was the first stumbling block. As a young bride I thought a caring and sensitive husband would anticipate my needs and desires and take the initiative to meet them without my having to say

a thing. So we ended up having interactions like this:

ME: (coming home from work at the end of the day) Boy, am I tired. (That's what I said. What I meant was, "I sure would like help making supper.")

HIM: Yeah, I had a rough day too. Why don't we just relax tonight in front of the TV?

ME: (suddenly irritated because he didn't catch the hook) Can't. I have to wash the floor tonight.

HIM: (incredulous) Tonight? You just said you were tired! It looks fine to me. Let's relax tonight—there's a good movie on at 8.

ME: Forget it! I've got to start supper.

Which I did, feeling not only tired but also unappreciated, overworked, and saddled with an insensitive husband. I

302

also washed the floor that night, sighing now and then. He ignored me. That made me mad.

Sometimes my inner expectations took the form of little tests. "I wish," I'd think to myself, "Dave would offer to give me a back rub from time to time, not because I ask, but just because he knows I'd enjoy it and he wants to do something nice for me." If too many days went by without that offer, I'd start feeling unloved.

Unfortunately a pattern of erratic communication was being set up, and it got worse. Intellectually, I supported Dave's desire to be a writer; emotionally, I wanted him to get a job and bring in money. His enjoyment of TV clashed with my image of how he should like to spend his spare time. And with the consciousness raising of the women's movement, I began to have some new expectations of him—largely uncommunicated. When I did discuss them, my words or tone of voice conveyed disapproval, frustration, or blame. Dave would end up feeling attacked and would usually back off, leaving us both defensive.

But over the years we've both been learning some principles to help deal with uncommunicated expectations:

1. *Make needs or wishes known,* instead of expecting the partner to know automatically what they are. I was surprised at how much pride is involved in this.

2. *Don't test the other's love.* This is game playing at its worst and totally unfair to the other person. When tempted to feel sorry for myself, I ask, "Am I looking for ways to show my husband that *he* is loved?"

3. *State needs simply; don't generalize or add blame.* "Could you help peel these carrots? I'm running behind schedule," not "Why don't you ever help with supper?"

4. *Think ahead to problematic or recurring situations and agree ahead of*

time on mutual expectations. Does "leaving early" on the family vacation mean 5:30 A.M. or 8 A.M.? Who puts which kids to bed which nights? "Why don't I make breakfast while you make school lunches?"

5. *Don't have expectations for things not agreed on ahead of time.* When I make a request, I should accept no as an answer.

6. *Be specific if something is bothering you.* Don't make vague comments that give hidden messages, leaving others feeling uncomfortable and defensive. "I wish people would pick up after themselves around here!" is not likely to get results.

7. *Timing is important.* Right in the middle of an upsetting situation is not the time to unload feelings. Deal with the immediate situation in a simple way;

later talk about expectations for the future.

8. *When personal tastes differ, be willing to agree to disagree, compromise, or take turns.* Dave and I sometimes like to do different things with our leisure time, so we take turns making plans for our night out. The important thing is that we like being together!

9. *Remember that love is forgiveness.* This principle undergirds all the others. Knowing that neither one of us hurts the other intentionally helps take away the hurt and the urge to blame when one fails to live up to the other's expectations. Rather than expecting perfection, we are not surprised by our human weaknesses and mistakes. Just as we live daily in God's forgiveness, we must be willing to allow each other to live in the assurance of our own forgiving love.

Related Articles
Chapter 9: Making Your Communication Work
Chapter 9: Speak Your Partner's Language

An Appeal to Husbands

WESLEY & ELAINE WILLIS

Some time ago a friend of ours stunned us with the announcement that he was divorcing his wife. Wes numbly recalled the ministries the two men had shared together. Both he and his wife gave every indication of a deep commitment to Jesus Christ, and they had served in a variety of leadership positions in their church. Yet now they were getting divorced.

While we're painfully aware of the growing divorce rate, we are always shocked to see Christian couples break up. We puzzle over how two people who are committed to God and who have pledged their commitment to each other can turn their backs on those pledges.

In our friend's case, the explanation was disarmingly simple. "I don't love her any more. I am not happy with my wife, and since God wants me to be happy, it is His will that I divorce her." Such an obvious distortion of God's will would seem easy to correct, but hours of counsel, prayer, and even tears did nothing to dissuade him. He proceeded with the divorce, confident that he was justified in his actions.

Of course, nothing like that could happen to us. Or could it? It doesn't take too much perception to notice husbands and wives in our solidly evangelical churches who are growing apart at a frightening rate. We see husbands who act as though they are enduring their wives. They demean them and strip them of dignity and self-confidence. Oh, not deliberately (although we sometimes see that too), but in subtle ways.

Perhaps the cruelest blow of all is to ignore your wife. Ignoring a person says, "You are not important enough for me to argue with. You are a nonperson." A husband may not intend to project such an attitude. He may sincerely love and value his wife. But ignoring a wife unintentionally destroys a relationship just as effectively as doing so on purpose.

The world pushes us toward such an attitude. Most of us face financial pressures. That may mean overtime or a second job. We are constantly reminded of our need for recreation, and many a man is drawn away from his wife to pursue leisure-time activities. Men deeply involved in Christian service may get so involved in it that they neglect their wives. Many pastors fall into this trap. Yet Paul clearly says that one qualification for church leadership is the ability to maintain proper relationships at home (1 Tim. 3; Titus 1). A husband who ignores his wife in order to serve God is contributing to the destruction of his family. The result may be just as disastrous as if he had committed adultery.

In many cases, adultery comes as a result of a man's failure to build a continuing relationship with his wife. God has created men and women with a deep need to communicate. We are not complete when we are isolated and wrapped up in ourselves. What many men don't realize is that when significant communication and relationships are not nurtured at home, they will often be formed outside the home.

We think that was the problem in our friend's case. He did not communicate with his wife. Instead, he began sharing and building a relationship with another woman. We're sure it began innocently, but the result was tragic. He soon found he was emotionally attracted to the second woman, and later he was physically attracted as well. He violated a basic element in building a marriage that lasts— consistent communication. Love and acceptance are an outgrowth of this communication.

This concept is clearly taught in the biblical account of Eve's creation. Genesis 2:18 records that Adam's aloneness was not good. Adam was in an ideal environment. He could communicate every day with God. And yet God observed that it was not good for Adam to dwell alone. Adam needed a human being with whom to communicate, someone to whom he could reach out.

God provided a solution to Adam's problem. He created Eve. God said, "I will make a helper suitable for him" (Gen. 2:18). A "helpmeet" is one who can meet a man face to face and answer back to him. God did not make a slave or a beautiful but stupid companion. He provided a person with whom Adam could have face-to-face communication. Even before creating the sexual relationship and children, God ordained communication as a key element in marriage.

But many men, even Christian men, bring into marriage the macho American image of manhood. We idolize the rugged pioneer who was strong and independent. Many men feel guilty if they display normal human emotions or if they are interested in the things their wives enjoy. These men nevertheless have been created by God with a need to communicate regularly and deeply with their wives about those things that concern them.

In a recent study of Christian families, wives indicated that their greatest desire was for their husbands to pray with them. Along with this was a strong desire for their husbands to talk to them. We suspect that most of us fail to communicate at all levels. When a husband and wife don't talk together about things in general, they find it extremely uncomfortable to suddenly try to pray together. Perhaps a lack of spiritual sharing reflects a lack of sharing in general.

Lack of communication frequently destroys a marriage. If the need for communication is not met within the family relationship, it will be met outside. And communication inevitably leads to deeper and deeper involvement. Many men, even spiritual leaders, have found themselves deeply involved with women other than their wives because they failed to recognize the inevitable consequences of meaningful communication.

Related Articles
Chapter 2: Characteristics of a Mature Marriage
Chapter 9: Communication That Energizes

Most married persons have disagreements and conflicts. Please indicate below the extent of agreement or disagreement between you and your partner for each area of potential conflict. You may wish to ask your partner if he or she agrees or disagrees with your assessment!

Usually agree	*Sometimes disagree*	*Usually disagree*	
——	——	——	family finances
——	——	——	recreation
——	——	——	religion
——	——	——	demonstration of affection
——	——	——	friends
——	——	——	sexual relations
——	——	——	correct or proper behavior
——	——	——	philosophy of life
——	——	——	ways of dealing with parents/in-laws
——	——	——	aims, goals, and values
——	——	——	amount of time spent together
——	——	——	major decisions
——	——	——	household tasks
——	——	——	leisure-time activities
——	——	——	career decisions
——	——	——	prayer and Bible study together
——	——	——	child-rearing procedures
——	——	——	where to live

There are many good, constructive ways to handle conflict. This chapter describes some of them. But there are also negative, damaging ways. Do you ever react to disagreement in any of the following ways?

—— clam up		—— withhold sex
—— yell		—— get depressed
—— kick the dog		—— drive like a maniac
—— sulk		—— swear
—— throw things		—— withdraw
—— hurt people physically		—— get sick
—— become sarcastic		—— storm out of the house
—— plot revenge		—— slam doors
—— do things you later regret		—— threaten
—— push your feelings away		—— preach
—— say hurtful things		—— give in to something wrong
—— break promises		—— deny your anger

[The quiz is adapted from *Communication and Conflict Resolution in Marriage*, by H. Norman Wright, David C. Cook, 1977. Used by permission.]

10

CONFLICTS

Some may label them "irreconcilable differences," but the very barriers that seem insurmountable may provide the greatest potential for the growing edges of marital solidarity. Dissimilar personalities (in contrast to similar ones) breed possibilities for conflict, but they also provide opportunity for growth and enrichment. Several myths need exploding:

MYTH 1. Good marriages do not have problems. Good and poor marriages face exactly the same sets of problems. The difference comes in the ability to find and act out a workable system for conflict resolution. Love is not the absence of conflict; conflict is not the absence of love.

MYTH 2. Conflict is destructive to a good marriage. In his book, *Cherishable Love and Marriage,* David Augsburger answers this misconception: "Marital happiness is won through conflict. . . . But only through conflict that is termed creative through understanding. Creative conflict can be the force that breaks through to emotional intimacy."

Couples are often like cold porcupines trying to get warm by moving closer together! The greater the intimacy, the greater the conflict potential. Superficial marriages are the product of superficial relationships.

MYTH 3. Quality marriages happen to a fortunate few. Good marriages are cultivated; poor marriages are caused. The grave of a dying relationship is dug by little digs. Our only options: grow or dry up.

Whereas morbidity marriages lack initiative and investment, live ones are mutually nourished. Marriage cannot exist in a status quo.

Howard & Jeanne Hendricks

How Can We Handle Disagreements?

KENN & BETTY GANGEL

We live in a society in which everybody seems to be clamoring for "rights." There are civil rights and women's rights, the right to be gay and the right to be free of censorship, the right to a job and the right to an education, and of course, the epitome of them all, the right to be happy.

The Bible, however, doesn't talk much about rights. It focuses on responsibilities. And one of those major responsibilities offers us a key word in handling all disagreements, including those between husbands and wives. That word is *submit.*

Godly husbands and wives *submit to*

God's Word. We're foolish to think God will bless our efforts at marital harmony if we either ignore or overtly disobey what He has told us about family life. Couples who study the Bible together, pray together, and voluntarily place themselves under the authority of the Heavenly Father will not only be able to handle disagreements, they'll discover fewer of them appearing to disturb family waters.

Godly couples *submit to one another.* The well-known family passage in Ephesians 5 is clearly introduced by verse 21, which says, "Submit to one another out of reverence for Christ." The mutual submission of believers ought to begin at home. Voluntary submission of husbands and wives has nothing to do with the equality or status of any member of the family—it is the practice of a biblical lifestyle that ought to characterize every Christian. When disagreements turn into quarrels it is usually because both husband and wife are determined to have their own way.

C-L-A-S-P

Proverbs 15:1 offers good advice for solving arguments: "A gentle answer turns away wrath, but a harsh word stirs up anger."

Too many arguments begin and end with "harsh words." But we Christians are called to give "gentle answers." How can we do that when an argument is either imminent or escalating? Try the *CLASP* method.

C—Calm down. When you are attacked verbally, when your spouse is angry or is trying to start an argument, don't say anything right away. Try to calm down first.

L—Lower your voice. Don't yell at your spouse; speak in a soft, gentle voice. The words you say will probably be more "gentle" too.

A—Acknowledge your spouse's request. This is especially important when you feel like your own interests aren't being considered and you don't even want to hear what your spouse is saying. It is better to say, "You want me to get out and mow the lawn," or "You want me to cook better meals for dinner"; and then add, "Why is that so important to you right now?" Then listen for the reason.

S—State your request. This is explaining your side. Your mate may want the lawn mowed because company is coming Saturday, so your side could be, "I want the yard to look nice too, but I'm really tired tonight." Or the husband who wants better dinners may feel that meals should be the way his mother made them. Your side is to say, "I grew up differently."

P—Propose a solution. You don't want to stop at the preceding step; you want to acknowledge both needs and find a workable solution. Say, "I will be sure to mow the lawn right after work tomorrow night so it will look good for Saturday." Or, "I'd be glad to cook a full-fledged dinner one night a week. Maybe you could get your mom to send some of her favorite recipes."

CLASP the opportunities to diffuse as many arguments as possible by giving gentle answers that turn away anger.

YFC Editors

"But," you say, "I *am* right." That doesn't make a bit of difference. We're talking about handling disagreements, not winning arguments. Suppose that while driving your compact car within the speed limit on the outside lane of an interstate highway, you see an 18-wheeler coming straight at you, obviously in the wrong lane. You may be in the right, but if I were you I'd submit and head for the shoulder—fast.

Godly couples *submit to their commitment to marriage.* How often we have used Larry Christenson's great line: "It is not the love that sustains the marriage, but the marriage that sustains the love." In our day couples want a divorce when their love runs out. They may be committed to personal happiness and pleasure, but certainly not to the marriage vows. Marriages work because God blesses the commitment of His children to the promises they have made to each other and to Him "in the presence of these witnesses." When disagreements come, we enter the discussion on the assumption that we *can* work things out because we love each other and are committed to spending our lives together.

Godly couples *submit to the wise advice of trusted friends.* The Book of Proverbs reminds us that there is wisdom in a multitude of counselors. At a church we attended while living in Florida some years ago, the elders were always available for counsel to any member of the congregation. They would often gather as a group with people who requested their services to discuss problems and pray for God's wisdom in the solutions. Sometimes disagreements might not be solvable just between husband and wife. A higher level of humility requires us on those occasions to seek the help of others—pastor, elders or deacons, friends, parents, or perhaps even grown children. Swallowing one's personal pride is a major first step in handling marital misunderstandings.

Godly couples *submit to counseling.* Not always, because it's not always necessary. In fact, if we consistently practiced the first three steps mentioned, the fourth would be rare and the fifth virtually never necessary. But when it is necessary, for God's sake and the sake of the family, let's do it! Obviously, Christian counseling that has its roots in biblical answers is the only safe road to travel.

Secular psychologists talk about "fair fighting" in marriage. They recommend setting certain rules for argument to which both parties can adhere, thereby creating a "fair fight." We believe God doesn't want fighting at all. Conflict, which is doubtlessly inevitable, need not deteriorate into a squabble or quarrel. Christian husbands and wives handle their disagreements by following the patterns of God's Word and by humble submission so ideally patterned by the Lord Jesus Himself.

Related Articles

Fighting Fair

GARY D. BENNETT

Conflict in marriage is both normal and necessary. When two people come together from different backgrounds—with different values, opposing views on money matters, preconceived notions about marriage and sex, their own personal goals, and so forth—conflict is inevitable. As someone once said, "If two people agree on everything, one of them is not needed."

Don't be afraid to fight. It's expected and OK if it's done constructively and fairly. Couples need not feel devastated by fighting; instead they can use fighting as a tool to reach deeper communication.

Fighting gets its bad name because many people don't fight fairly. Here are some evidences of not fighting fair:

☐ Not listening to one another

☐ Giving up on each other; no longer caring; no longer willing to share and talk things out

☐ Not being honest; lying; telling half-truths to protect oneself

☐ Not being open; refusing to talk about subjects because of past pain or present feelings

☐ Losing confidence in the relationship; not trusting spouse's judgment, abilities, intelligence, ability to learn and change; relying on friends or parents more than spouse

☐ Losing ability to plan, work, and play together; never wanting to be alone with each other except for sex or sleep

☐ Doubting each other; not fully trusting each other because of previous hurts

☐ Frequently escaping through avoidance, sleep, TV, hobbies, work, clubs, silence, and so on

☐ Bickering and nagging; rudeness; name calling; crudeness about the other's relatives

If you or your spouse have experienced any of the preceding symptoms, it's a good indicator that someone has not been fighting fair. Nevertheless, the two of you together can begin making changes that will preserve your relationship during future conflict.

Basic Rules for Fighting Fair

1. You must be willing to change *yourself*, not your spouse. You cannot make another person change. You can encourage and try to motivate, but you have control only over yourself, and even then imperfectly. So work at seeing how you've contributed to the problem, and change that.

2. If possible, choose a good time and place to fight, preferably away from the children. Avoid using your bedroom for fights; keep it for rest, relaxation, and recreation (make love, not war, in your bedroom).

3. Set a time limit to avoid interminable fighting. Allow only a given amount of your precious time to fight about a given problem.

4. Agree on a specific "beef" and stick to it. Leave out the past, and don't get sidetracked on incidental issues. Work together to resolve one problem at a time.

5. Keep your focus. Concentrate on dealing with the real problem and not just the symptoms.

6. Do your best not to bicker and nag. No low blows, name calling, or bringing up material you know will hurt your spouse.

7. Listen carefully. Don't be thinking about what you're going to say next, but pay attention to what your spouse is saying. Don't presume you know what your spouse thinks, feels, or is going to say. Wait to hear.

8. Respect your spouse's feelings. Feelings are neither right nor wrong; they merely are. Your spouse has a right to his or her own feelings, even if they differ from yours. Revealing feelings is risky; it makes a person vulnerable to being hurt. Don't use intimate knowledge of your spouse's feelings as a weapon to hurt him or her.

9. At the end of the pre-set time, try to reach a conclusion—even if it's to postpone the fight to another time. Or simply agree to disagree.

10. Forgive readily when it's all over. Don't leave the fight with resentment, anger, or an "I'll get even" attitude. Settle your feelings together before ending the session. You may not be able to forget the issue, but forgiving each other and then sharing in prayer and seeking God's wisdom can be a tremendous sealer of love. "Do not let the sun go down while you are still angry" (Eph. 3:26).

Results of Fighting Fair

Perhaps one of the biggest bonuses of fighting fair with your spouse is the con-

UNFAIR FIGHTING

Unfair fighting only hurts. What kinds of attitudes or actions are unfair in a fight?

1. *Cold war.* You refuse to discuss not only the problem but virtually give your spouse the silent treatment.

2. *Withdrawal.* You internalize the problem because you don't want to argue, only to have it surface later, perhaps even in an unrelated argument or frustration.

3. *Justice collecting.* This is when that internalized problem comes out and you try to get justice for it right now, rather than at the time it occurred.

4. *Bringing up past problems.* Once an argument is over and forgiveness given and accepted, it should be forgotten. Unfortunately, too many spouses hold onto those "sins" and bring them up again and again.

5. *Name calling.* Using words that hurt can cause a wound that may never completely heal.

6. *"Hitting" the person where he or she is most vulnerable.* You point out character flaws, physical flaws, painful facts (laid off from a job, had a miscarriage), or other personal information that you had trusted each other with.

7. *Smokescreening.* This is dealing with the smoke rather than the fire, the facade of the problem rather than its root. Resorting to such behavior means the problem will keep cropping up, never to be resolved until both of you become honest with yourselves and each other.

When arguments happen, and they will, don't allow unfair tactics to make the fight an unhealthy and even damaging experience. Arguments need to lead to solving the problem and deepening the relationship—not tearing it apart.

YFC Editors

fidence you will gain in one another and in your marriage. Having confidence that you can work out difficulties, and that your love can withstand trials and fights, will build security.

Fighting fair also allows strong feelings to be aired and intimate revelations to be shared. And if you never betray your spouse's confidences, always keeping each other's innermost thoughts and feelings sacred, your trust in each other will deepen.

Finally, to fight fair with your spouse is to open clogged lines of communication and to afford yourselves the opportunity to grow and change. If you want to let your spouse know that you care, appreciate, accept, respect, and cherish him or her, then fight fair!

Related Articles
Chapter 9: Making Your Communication Work
Chapter 10: All

How to Have a Successful Argument

RANDY & THERESE CIRNER

Do Christian couples really have disagreements? Arguments, even? Aren't Christians supposed to live happily ever after once they give their lives to the Lord Jesus?

Actually, we've never met a couple who never disagrees or argues. As far as we know, such a state of wedded bliss exists solely in some people's imaginations.

In our own 18 years of marriage, we have certainly disagreed with one another, and in serving other married couples through counseling and marriage retreats, we have found that every Christian couple we have met has disagreements. In fact, the more intimate the relationship, the more opportunities there are for disagreement.

Why do couples disagree?

Just because husbands are men and wives are women is grounds enough for disagreement.

Expectations within a marriage may be different. Our role models—our mothers and fathers—are often very dif-

ferent. What did our parents show us about how to be husbands and wives?

Sinfulness is another major reason. We are not totally redeemed, and the flesh wars within us. Selfishness, anger, and irresponsibility in one or both of the partners may cause a multitude of disagreements.

Our different temperaments set the stage for clashes. Each of us goes into marriage with our own particular set of strengths and weaknesses.

Fatigue and stress also contribute: job pressures, the physical strain of bearing and raising children, financial strains.

Relatives are an age-old problem (note the ever-popular mother-in-law jokes). And the list could go on forever. A whole range of circumstances and provocations can provide us with many opportunities to disagree with one another.

Discouraged? We hope not. We've found that the Lord has some very specific ways to handle disagreements and arguments.

The first and most important principle we've learned is to practice preventive medicine. We've found that by setting aside a specific time each week—yes, each week—to talk about the details of our separate lives, we prevent a number of disagreements from ever happening. *Good communication is the best preventive medicine.*

The more we talk to one another outside of a crisis situation, the more likely we can prevent crises from developing. If, over a cup of coffee on Saturday morning, we talk about how we're raising the children, we may be able to prevent tensions later in the week when Johnny misbehaves at the dinner table, and Dad handles it one way and Mom, another.

We cannot stress enough how important it is for husbands and wives to talk to each other *weekly* about the details of their lives: who needs the car when, what next week's schedule is going to be, what they're expecting to do on the weekend (it helps to discover, several days in advance, that husband expects to watch the football playoffs while wife is expecting him to finish painting the living room). Such details make up our very human lives; loving God does not excuse us from the good communication that husbands and wives need to have.

Does this mean, then, that good communication can prevent all arguments and disagreements? We wish that were true, but unfortunately it is not. There is no way we can anticipate every set of circumstances that might create tension in the future. Besides, no matter how much we talk about them, there are some things we're just not going to agree about. Where shall we spend our vacation? How often should your mother come to visit? How do we spend the $25 left over at the end of the month? Do we send our kids to private or public schools? We also need to take into account our sinful natures. We're going to

---

EPHESIANS 4:26-27

"In your anger do not sin": Do not let the sun go down while you are still angry, and do not give the devil a foothold.

---

get angry sometimes—whether justly or not; we're going to say things we don't mean; words we wish we had never spoken are going to pass our lips.

Of course Christian husbands and wives are going to have arguments and disagreements. How then should we handle them?

1. If an argument begins, the partner who first realizes things have gotten out of hand should immediately take steps to change them. This is a very difficult step. It requires discipline and dedication to working things out, usually just when you are tempted to dig in your heels.

2. After you regain control of the situation, evaluate what happened. Discuss the dynamics, what caused each person to react strongly or wrongly.

3. Discuss the issue that began the argument, if there is one. Sometimes there is not; the husband and wife are merely reacting to pressure. Often, however, there is a specific issue that needs to be discussed when the heat is off.

4. Pray together. Bring what has just happened to the Lord. Ask God's grace and blessing to be present to both of you and to heal whatever hurt you have caused each other.

5. Do not fail to express some sort of affection for one another after the argument is over.

It is not easy to stop an argument from becoming destructive and turn it into a growth experience, but this is undeniably the Christian approach. Read, for example, Paul's description of Christian relationships in Colossians 3:12-14: "As God's chosen people, holy and dearly loved, clothe yourselves with compassion, kindness, humility, gentleness, and patience. Bear with each other and forgive whatever grievances you may have against one another. Forgive as the Lord forgave you. And over all these virtues put on love, which binds them all together in perfect unity."

This is how to have a successful argument—not successful because you win it, but successful because you have won victory in the Lord over the impulses of the flesh.

Related Articles

Handling Conflict— Good Ways and Bad

KRISTINE TOMASIK

There's probably no tougher challenge in marriage than handling conflict, and we all have to do it. It may be conflict over the tube of toothpaste—do you roll it or do you squeeze it? Or it may be more serious—do I take the job transfer to Washington, D.C., or do we stay in Chicago?

Of course, conflict is not just about external factors. It's also about inner needs and wants. Mature handling of conflict involves the ability to satisfy to some degree both one's own needs *and* one's partner's needs, not either/or.

People try to handle conflict in five basic ways: forcing, running, passively pleasing, compromising, and negotiating.

Forcing. Imagine someone with arms crossed, jaw set, and feet planted firmly. That's the forcing stance. "We'll do it my way. Period!" Forcers certainly meet their own needs, but they do it at others' expense.

Sounds pretty immature? You bet. But which of us hasn't at some point backed our opponent into a corner and "bulldogged?" We tend to try to force our own way especially when we're scared, when the stakes are high, or, believe it or not, when we don't know how to say

what we really want. We may be insisting that we want X when what we really want is Y—but we don't know how to express that or are afraid to do so.

Running. Many people find conflict so unpleasant that they just run away from it. People who've been taught that it's wrong to fight, or who are invested in maintaining a "Mr. Nice Guy" or "Miss Sweetness and Light" image, tend to run from conflict.

Ironically, running from conflict is just as bad as forcing your own way. It doesn't even have the advantage that forcing does, of meeting your own needs. And it certainly does nothing to solve the conflict.

In fact, running may even escalate conflict as the other person grows more and more frustrated and begins chasing after the one who's running. "Hey! Stop! Come back—we've got a conflict here that we've got to solve."

Passively pleasing. These are yesmen or yes-women. In an effort to keep conflict to a minimum, they say, "Yeah, sure, OK, OK. I'll do whatever you want." Of course, they sacrifice their own needs and wants.

Passively pleasing has a high price tag, even though it seems to preserve the external appearance of peace. It sends its costly bills in the form of depression, loss of energy, and internalized rage. Ultimately, it doesn't even work. In fact, it can destroy the relationship when passive pleasers get completely fed up with not getting what they want and either blow up or run away.

In our society, women traditionally have been trained and encouraged to be passive pleasers. Women also suffer from depression more than men do. There seems to be a connection. Women especially need to learn that their needs and wants are OK, and that it's OK to express them.

Compromising. This is a tit-for-tat approach to resolving conflict. "You scratch my back and I'll scratch yours." It's a trade-off, trade-even.

Though compromise may be somewhat mechanical, it's a step in the right direction. At least both partners are expressing—and getting—some of what they want. Compromise is often useful as a quick, easy, middle-ground solution. In the long haul, however, it's not always the best way of resolving conflict. It leaves too many unmet or half-met needs dangling—needs that will continue to grow, sores that will continue to fester.

Negotiating. Negotiating is the ideal way to work through conflict in any long-term, high-value relationship such as marriage. Negotiating takes time. It demands work. It requires risk. Negotiating calls for maturity.

Negotiating involves the ability of both partners to take turns saying what they need and then together creating a third alternative. The first three ways of handling conflict seek an either/or solution to the problem, "either my way or your way." Compromise seeks a quickie trade-off. Only negotiating seeks a mutually satisfying solution.

Negotiating is a dialogue, a dialectic. If we were to diagram it, we'd see a line zigzagging back and forth between the

OVERCOMING A CRITICAL SPIRIT

Sometimes a critical spirit develops when one partner tries to take too much responsibility for the other.

I am responsible to be loving to my wife, to communicate with her, to be patient, to meet as many of her physical and emotional needs as I can. But she has her own mind, her own decisions to make, and her own life to lead. I am not responsible to live her life for her.

If I am fulfilling my responsibilities to my wife, then it's her responsibility—not mine—for what takes place in her life. And now that I understand the limits of my responsibility, I am much less likely to criticize her for the decisions she makes.

Josh McDowell

two people.

To negotiate, both partners must be able to:

1. Know what they want and believe they are entitled to have it

2. Express what they want

3. Hear what the other person wants and not be threatened by it

4. Think creatively in order to forge acceptable need-meeting solutions for both partners

Real negotiating takes practice. Some people are fortunate in having grown up in families where they got to practice negotiating with their parents. They've been developing the skill since childhood. Others, not so lucky, must learn the skill as adults. The good news is that negotiating *is* a learned skill, and we can all get better at it.

A final thought. Though negotiating is

the ideal way to handle conflict, the other four ways can have their uses. At times, and depending on one's partner's usual style, it's necessary to insist on one's own way. Sometimes a tit-for-tat compromise saves everyone's time and energy over a minor conflict. At times we all feel the need just to say, "Oh, all right"—and passively please. And at other times, the opposition may be so immovable that giving up on the conflict may well be the mature choice, rather than beating one's head against a brick wall.

But in the long haul, the marriage that works works on negotiating. In large conflicts and small, both partners get their needs met. They also get the equally important privilege of meeting their partner's needs. And in the process, they learn to know each other better and better.

Related Articles
Chapter 9: Making Your Communication Work
Chapter 10: All

SPICE

"Despite the Queen's and Prince Phillip's many differences (he's not keen on corgis or horse-racing, he's impatient and controversial, she can be stubborn, prim, and dictatorial) the marriage is a good one."
—*Good Housekeeping*

Sentimentalists, purists, and some
preachers, advocate marital absolutes—
stability, a clear hierarchy for
decision, a predictable union,
unflawed as a blank page. No wonder
it ends up flat. A truer wedding's
grounded in paradox, answers the pull
of the particular, grapples a score
of rugged issues. Like horned toads
in Eden, incongruities add surprise
to a complacent landscape.

Thank heaven you're romantic and
irascible, I'm opinionated in my
impulsiveness. Thank God we can
lean together in our failing—a rusty
trellis propping a thorned rose.

Luci Shaw

From *Postcard from the Shore.* Used by permission.

Using Conflict to Understand Each Other

JACK MAYHALL

I couldn't believe it! In four sentences we had violated three of our very own rules of good communication.

After two weeks of intensive ministry, we had seven days to explore Scotland. But the lock on the rear door of the station wagon we rented had jammed, and we spent two days throwing our suitcases and paraphernalia over the backseat. By the third day I couldn't stand it anymore, and we stopped to get it fixed at a small garage. While I looked over the mechanic's shoulder, Carole walked across the street to wander among the gravestones and ruins of a beautiful ancient abbey.

As she came back across the street, I was unloading all our things in order to rearrange them in proper order.

"Why are you doing that now?" she questioned.

"Because I want to load it *right,*" was my very firm reply.

"Well, don't get mad at me."

"But you always argue with me!"

Miffed, Carole walked away to gaze at a nearby river until the luggage was finally arranged to my satisfaction. Then we drove away from the village in cool silence.

Five minutes later, Carole started to chuckle, and I soon joined in. We were laughing at ourselves because of the dumb things we'd said. We apologized and quickly forgave each other—something that 20 years ago would have taken the whole day to do.

Now, most couples stop right there. They have forgiven each other and all is at peace between them. But we feel if you do that, you have passed up one of the greatest opportunities to understand one another that life affords.

Conflict can be *used* profitably and constructively. Admittedly, it takes a little practice and a lot of patience. It takes stepping back and viewing the situation objectively (hard for subjective people like Carole, but not impossible). It may take several tries before anger or tears will not stifle discussion. But it can be one of the most valuable tools you have in marriage to learn not only what to avoid next time, but also how to understand one another this time.

In 20 minutes, we were talking about our four-sentence conversation. Right off the bat we recognized that Carole's *why* question was threatening. Her *why* question, which was really not a question but a statement ("How dumb to arrange suitcases when the sun is shining and a ruined abbey is across the street"), caused me to feel defensive and get a bit irritated.

My *always* statement was explosive. Besides, it wasn't true. We really do try not to use the words *always* and *never* in our communication.

But as we discussed the incident, we realized the main thing we had forgotten was how different we are. Carole has known for years that I tend to be a perfectionist. As such, I couldn't leave those suitcases and that gear thrown helter-skelter in the backseat one minute longer than necessary. But for a moment, she forgot.

On the other hand, Carole was eager to get started. The haphazard suitcases

317

didn't bother her one bit—what was uppermost on her mind was to get going. We had all of Scotland ahead of us!

In talking about the incident, each came to understand the other's point of view and accept it. This made it easier to forgive the other violations (the *why* question and the *always* statement) as well. And I trust we will understand and accept each other's personality the next time my organized nature momentarily interrupts Carole's desire to get going.

The ability to resolve conflict is essential to a good marriage. Beyond that, the ability to *use* conflict for better understanding is vital for two people to complete and enjoy one another as God would have them do.

In order to use conflict in a positive manner, some suggestions may help:

1. *Define the conflict.* Do both know what the issue is? Has it been defined to the other's satisfaction?

2. *Has each party clearly stated what he or she wants or needs?* My desire on the sunny morning in Scotland was to straighten out the luggage before I went crazy. Carole's was to get going as soon as the lock was fixed.

3. *Search until you get to the reasons for the words or actions.* Generally, neither person's actions are wrong. They are merely different from what the other person would have done.

4. *Keep short accounts.* Forgive quickly and then come back and discuss the conflict within 24 hours while it is still on your minds. If tension develops again, back off for a few hours—but keep coming back to it.

5. *Ask God for His help.* "If any of you lacks wisdom," James counsels, "he should ask God . . . and it will be given to him" (James 1:5). God made us, knows exactly what makes us tick, and can give us insight into ourselves and our spouses. So pray about it separately and together. Ask God for the ability to keep your sense of humor, especially the ability to laugh at yourself. We

ANGER

Families are a little like Mount Everest. They make us angry because they're there. "Marriage and family living generate in normal people more anger than people experience in any other social situation," says marriage counselor David Mace. . . .

One of the reasons we feel angrier with loved ones or friends is because we feel safer and more secure in their company. We have a pretty good idea of how they will respond to us. But there are other reasons:

☐ Close contact provides more opportunities for anger to develop.

☐ Irritations can become cumulative.

☐ We are inclined to try to get loved ones to change, and we get angry when they don't.

☐ Loved ones are inclined to try to get us to change, and we get angry when they try.

Gayle Rosellini & Mark Worden

[Excerpted from *Of Course You're Angry*, Harper/Hazelden, 1985, p. 12.]

are all very funny people, you know!

Using conflict to truly understand your spouse takes maturity and self-control, commodities scarce in many of us. But as our roots go down deep into the soil of God's marvelous love, the Spirit of the living God will mature us, give us wisdom, and grant us the patience to use conflict to understand one another. And to understand is to love.

CELEBRATING CONFLICT

Communication, a two-dimensional art
So hard I cannot master it!
Yet it is the only way across the
   impasse of killing silence.
We, at twenty-two, celebrated
So easily the myriad of things
We held in common.
And were amazed
That after we had made our promise
We saw so very differently.
Marriages at first can only see
The easy and the alike.
And they move only dangerously
And far too slowly
To celebrate the differences
That often have destroyed
   fledgling naive vows
Before they can be celebrated.
In young love we agreed
There were so many things
We held in common and wasn't it nice
that we could communicate?
Didn't you like Wordsworth?
Didn't I like plays that ended
With lingering implications?
Didn't we like novels
Filled with subtle symbols?
Each common love became
a pier in our alikeness.
So we liked and prized as one flannel
   pajamas in the winter, and corduroy
   house shoes for cold floors,
Leonard Bernstein for evenings
when "regrouping" was important,
and vanilla cocoa because
Nebraska winters usually need a
   little help.
And what we didn't love as one,
We derogated as one.
We both enjoyed a warm animosity
for Agatha Christie and oyster soup
and cable television.
Now we need to argue more, it
   seems.
Fatigue and boredom are twin
   killers

Of old disagreements.
Conflict invited because
Marriage always makes us honest.
And now we do get tired,
And it's hard to feel alike
When we are tired.
We are too sleepy now
to keep awake till the twenty-eight-
   commercial end
of our all-time favorite movie,
even if it does have lingering
implications we once agreed
we both admired.
Now our conflicts make us
Wonder why we didn't take more time.
And Wordsworth, whom we both
   declared we loved so much,
We really didn't love so much.
We both preferred McKuen, even
   though we
seem less literary for the choice.
And truthfully we both liked tea
Much better than the sticky taste
   of cocoa.
Leather house shoes
are friendlier than corduroy,
And oyster soup is better than
   we said.
Let's argue if we must
And I suppose we must
But squeeze the toothpaste
Any way you like and I'll say it is
But the Jure Divino
Of being you, the you
The world would lose
If we never argued
Or called on our uniqueness
To take its stand for meaning.
Our vision then will all be clear!
We've grown till differences are
   blessings,
And conflicts bring us close
And keep us talking,
Reassuring us we are not alone in life.

Calvin Miller

Managing Your Anger

RICHARD A. MEIER

Anger is a vigorous emotional reaction. It is not always bad; in fact, it can be very constructive. The Bible says, "Be angry, and yet do not sin" (Eph. 4:26, NASB). It is what we do with our anger that makes it bad or good.

We can have good anger when our God-given rights or convictions are threatened or violated. Jesus was angry when the Pharisees criticized Him for healing a man on the Sabbath Day. They wished to keep Him from acting on His conviction that "the Sabbath was made for man, not man for the Sabbath" (Mark 2:27).

When were you angry last? What right or conviction was being violated or threatened? What did you do with your anger? We can sin with our anger when we take either extreme: blow up or clam up.

To blow up is to mix good anger with a vengeance motive, which is forbidden by God. This vengeance takes the form of physical abuse (actual attack, slamming doors, driving recklessly) or verbal abuse (put-downs, name-calling, yelling, temper outbursts, threats, or sarcasm). Blowing up means taking the whip in hand and paying back the offender. When we do this, we want to hurt him as he hurt us.

The other extreme is clamming up. Here we say nothing about our angry feelings, but we continue to hold a grudge. This pent-up energy turns into bitterness. It affects our health; it turns into depression and can lead to suicidal thoughts; it grieves the Lord and blocks our fellowship with Him. Holding a grudge, like blowing up, is motivated by a desire for vengeance.

Another kind of bad anger occurs when we react to the violation, not of a right or conviction, but of a selfish or perfectionistic demand. This kind of anger is not valid. It needs to be put away by confessing it to God and realizing that it reflects more on our own immaturity than on some misconduct in the life of another.

When feelings of anger come over us, it is best not to express any on-the-spot words or actions. Stop! Think: is the anger valid? If so, then deal with it scripturally. If not, then let it go. Give it up to God. Thank Him for giving you the wisdom to tell the difference. The Bible says we should be "slow to become angry" (James 1:19). Stop and think of what is going on before you react.

Now let's look at three things we can do with anger so that it will have a positive effect in our lives:

1. *Verbalize your angry feelings.* The Word teaches us to confront our offender, if possible, or else we are as guilty as he is (Lev. 19:17). Turn your anger into words. Tell the person what you *feel.* Do not attack him, but confess your own feelings, using an "I feel" message rather than a "you" or "why" message.

Sometimes when the offender cannot be confronted constructively or is not present, it is helpful to write out your feelings in a letter you can either send him or throw away. Writing is a good way to verbalize your feelings and drain them of their hostile energy. David did this in some of the psalms. He even wrote an angry letter to God (Ps. 13). Have you ever been angry with God? Share your feelings with Him. You will

IS YOUR MARRIAGE A BATTLEGROUND?

Many marriages could easily be compared to battlegrounds. Some couples are involved in guerrilla warfare in which the assault is daily nitpicking and nagging—dropping a few shells whenever possible. Others are often in full-scale assault—charging in with both barrels blazing, ready with loads of ammunition gathered over many days. Still others try to ambush each other by coming from the blind side with unexpected hits, barbs, and angry words.

A better picture for marriage is binding arbitration—working together in a common effort toward a common goal.

YFC Editors

then be able to think more clearly about His mercy and love that are at work behind the scene.

2. *Let God be the one to get even.* "It is Mine to avenge; I will repay," God says (Deut. 32:35). Sometimes forgiving someone, especially someone who isn't sorry, makes you wonder, "Don't I count? Should I just pretend that it didn't happen?" Yes, you count; and no, you shouldn't pretend it didn't happen. Instead, turn the matter over to the highest power in the universe, God Himself. He promises to deal with the person in the best possible way. In a prayer say, "Dear Lord, I give up any personal right to get even with this person. I turn him over to You. I know You will do the right thing."

3. *Forgive the offender.* What is forgiveness? It is choosing not to bring up the verbalized issues again—either to the offender in the form of further accusations, or to others in the form of gossip, or to oneself in the form of holding a grudge. These issues are dead. I can remember them, but I will not brood over the past. If I begin to dwell on the past, I will stop thinking negative thoughts and replace them with positive thoughts about the good things in my life at present.

If the person who has offended me has repented, I will look for ways to rebuild the friendship. If he hasn't, I will still treat him with dignity, even if my feelings send me contrary messages for a while.

I will choose to be loyal to my faith and stand by my choice to forgive. The hurts may come back from time to time for many months, but I will not act on my feelings at those moments. I will reaffirm my choice to forgive, even if I have to do it every day for a long time. My feelings will eventually catch up with my faith, and my hurts will heal in time.

In summary, we should verbalize our feelings of anger, commit the offender to God, and personally forgive. Can you do it? Will you do it?

Related Articles
Chapter 9: Making Your Communication Work
Chapter 10: All

Gentle Anger

JUDITH C. LECHMAN

We don't often think of gentleness as an essential ingredient in a successful Christian marriage. The other eight fruits of the Spirit listed by the Apostle Paul in his letter to the Galatians sound so obviously necessary for developing strong, healthy marriages. We instinctively know that love, joy, patience, kindness, goodness, faithfulness, and self-control must be woven into the fabric of a God-centered relationship. But when we think of gentleness in marriage, our first response is to hold this spiritual fruit in low esteem.

We equate being gentle with being weak and lacking courage. In our mind's eye, we see the gentle person as unreasonably sweet, passive, powerless, timid. Gentleness doesn't appear to be a virtue that will help strengthen our marriage, open our communication, or lessen the tensions and strains that are part of daily intimacy.

Yet, when we look at the biblical roots of gentleness, we discover that it means something far removed from this negative image of bland sweetness, powerless passivity, and timidity. In using the Greek *praotēs* for gentleness, Paul chose a word that fairly overflows with meanings. Plato considered *praotēs* the cement of civilized society. Aristotle defined it as the mean between being too angry and never becoming angry. To Paul, the gentle person was one who expressed anger for the right reason and duration and in the right way.

In other places in the New Testament, *praotēs* is mentioned as the characteristic needed to exercise discipline (Gal. 6:1), face opposition (2 Tim. 2:25), and become open to learning (James 1:21).

The Bible paints a complex portrait of gentle people. They are courteous, courageous, teachable, and disciplined. They are also capable of displaying great yet controlled firestorms of indignation, kindled by the wrongs and sufferings of others.

I feel that of all the aspects of gentleness, the unselfish, controlled anger of *praotēs* is the one we most need to develop and practice. For our relationships to grow strong and flourish in Christ, it is essential that we find and walk that narrow, gentle path between becoming too angry with our spouses and never acknowledging our anger.

To gain such balance, we turn to the Greek language once again, this time to the adjective for *gentle—praus*. Initially this word was used to describe an animal that had been tamed and brought under control. With time it has grown to include all those who practice the control over thoughts, emotions, actions, and speech that Christ alone can give. Our anger is the product of our inner nature. When our inner nature is Spirit-controlled, we will not slip from a healthy, Christlike expression of anger into its sinful use.

We tend to lump together as sinful anger everything from rage, hostility, seething bitterness, and resentment to physical violence, force, irritation, and frustration. Yet several of these angry reactions may have nothing to do with sin. Rather than condemn all such responses as wrong, we need to examine our anger in light of the definition of *praus*.

1. *Is our anger measured?* We need to use the inner strength Christ has given us to control our passion and curb

HOW TO START AN ARGUMENT

Here are some tips to help you and your spouse get into an argument:

A– Act like there's something wrong, but insist there isn't.

R– Rely on your emotions all the time.

G– Get defensive whenever your spouse makes a suggestion or expresses an opinion.

U– Use every opportunity to get your own way.

M– Misinterpret your spouse's actions/words and read into them.

E– Expect the worst of your spouse.

N– Neglect your spouse's personal and emotional needs.

T– Tell your spouse anything that puts him/her down and nothing that builds him/her up.

Byron Emmert

our desire to hurt our spouse. Anger shouldn't govern us; we are to govern our anger instead. Gentle anger isn't a blind response; with the help of the Holy Spirit working actively within us, we restrain our anger. We begin to achieve this by obeying the biblical command to "be quick to listen, slow to speak, and slow to become angry" (James 1:19).

2. *Is our anger temperate?* Even in the heat of the moment, we need to consider calmly how we should respond to our angry feelings in accordance with God's law. We must learn how to express the proper amount of anger in the proper way by making our angry words and actions harmonize with God's Word rather than violate it. When our anger becomes moderate, we find that we have cleansed ourselves of the desire to harm our marriage partners, to damage their self-esteem, or to sow seeds of bitterness and destruction in the relationship.

3. *Is our anger wise?* To become legitimately gentle, our anger must be filtered through the Christlike quality of wisdom. We work at growing in wisdom by being willing to study Scripture and learn what God demands of us in our marriages. Though we may be blessed with common sense, we shouldn't confuse this gift with the soundness of judgment that comes with the struggle to obey God's standards in our marital relationship. Such holy wisdom helps us better understand the overt and subterranean sources of our anger and the gentle ways we may harness it.

4. *Is our anger constructive?* Violence is the expression of negative, uncontrolled anger. Based on fear, it is filled with unreasonable hatred. There is no way we can embrace violence in thought or deed and remain gentle. By contrast, gentle anger springs from a God-centered desire within us to oppose sinful behavior, point out evil, and express God's will as fully as we know it. And we best express constructive anger in our marriages when we practice reaching out to our spouses in our angry moments free of hatred or fear.

When truly Spirit-controlled, gentle anger in our marital relationships can become a force for change. We can learn to confront evil and correct our shortcomings and those of our spouses with truthful, wise, temperate, measured, and constructive thoughts and actions. As we progress toward greater maturity, our marriages will also move that much closer to embodying the fruit of the Spirit called gentleness.

Related Articles

Settling Disagreements By Dividing Responsibility

PATRICIA GUNDRY

We have been taught traditionally that, when the husband and wife do not agree, the husband is to make the decision. But there is another way of settling disagreements, more in harmony with the biblical principle of mutual submission as presented in Ephesians 5:21.

1. *First of all, the couple divides up areas of responsibility according to ability and interest.* That is, each takes certain areas as his or her responsibility—not necessarily to *do* everything that needs doing in that area, but to make sure it gets done properly.

These areas are distributed more or less equally between the two. They are divided along lines of expertise and interest, not necessarily according to traditional sex roles. For example, the husband may be in charge of food preparation if he is a good cook and enjoys it while the wife isn't and doesn't.

It is important to share in decisions about the children, of course, but even here there are several possible ways to divide the responsibility. One parent can be in charge of decisions during the week and the other one on the weekend. One can make decisions during the day and the other during the evening. Each parent can have one week on and one week off.

2. *All minor decisions are handled by the person into whose area of responsibility they fall.* That person does not have to consult the other one unless he or she wants to; he or she just goes ahead and takes care of it.

3. *All major decisions are made together and not acted on until both*

partners can agree on the action to take. It is a major decision if either one thinks it is.

4. *In cases of emergency, a natural leader will emerge.* For example, in most families one parent will instinctively grab a wet washcloth and scoop up the child who has just gashed his chin, stop the bleeding, and soothe the child. Meanwhile, the other parent may still be staring in alarm.

5. *In some instances one partner will have an obviously larger stake in the outcome of the decision.* When this is the case, the one with more at stake has the larger share in making the decision. His or her opinion needs to carry more weight. And if it comes down to having to make a decision before all the differences can be worked out, the partner who will be affected the most makes the final decision.

These ground rules will cover just about every possible disagreement you are apt to have. They are fair and efficient ways to run the family machine. Bear in mind that they are only guidelines for you to use in creating your own division of labor and responsibility. Adapt and adjust them freely to suit your own needs and inclinations.

When they first hear of it, some people doubt that this way of deciding will work. They say, "Well, what if we just *can't* agree?" That is the beauty of this approach: then you do nothing. You will be surprised at how living with the undecided question, "What color shall we paint the bathroom?" motivates you to find a compromise color. When you

324

both get tired enough of the color it is, you will find one you can agree on.

This method of deciding is better than letting the husband always make the final decision, because it protects the relationship.

Couples who have lived harmoniously together for a long time often work out a division of labor and responsibility much as I have outlined, but because it has happened gradually, they are unaware of it. Eventually a decision is needed that does not fall into their naturally evolved division of responsibility. And because they have been taught that the husband must decide in such a case, he is forced to make the final decision alone.

This puts him in a most difficult position. He may feel uncomfortable and inadequate to make the decision. He may also feel guilty about lording it over his wife. The wife will quite possibly resent the decision and him for making it, as well as feeling guilty for her resentment. As a result, the two of them are pulled farther apart and the relationship is damaged.

By contrast, a couple who decides not to decide until they can agree are ultimately brought closer together. They must work together to come up with a solution they can both live with comfortably, and this strengthens their relationship.

Related Articles
Chapter 7: Equal Persons, Unique Roles
Chapter 10: All

Who Makes the Decisions?

NORM WAKEFIELD

Last October I conducted the wedding of my daughter, Amy, and my son-in-law, Mike. As well as affirming their marriage I wanted to challenge them to build their relationship on a biblical foundation. One vital scriptural principle I believed they needed to grasp is found in Colossians 3:15: "Let the peace of Christ rule in your hearts, since as members of one body you were called to peace."

Amy and Mike will face problems. They will have disagreements, if for no other reason than the fact that they see issues from different perspectives. We all have our own point of view, and we differ on our approach to values, problems, and issues. Thus it is important for Amy and Mike to have an effective way to solve problems they will encounter and still respect each other's viewpoints.

Some people believe that issues should be settled by one-man rule. One person takes charge of the relationship and determines how problems should be solved; the other person complies without resistance. Other people talk about "democratic" marriages: "We talk issues over and have equal say on solutions." But with only two people voting,

By the way, the word *rule* in this verse actually means "to be the umpire or arbitrator." When two sports teams disagree, the players and coaches do not determine the outcome; umpires decide. We often observe arguing, but the umpire's call stands. In similar fashion, God intends Jesus Christ to be the umpire who tells family members how to proceed when differences are encountered and problems need to be solved.

When Christ is genuinely installed as family arbitrator, a delightful change occurs in problem-solving situations. The husband and wife are never put in a win/lose situation. Instead they are on equal ground, together seeking the Lord's best solution. Rather than being divided by the problem, the couple stands united, facing it. Rather than competing with each other, they bring their total resources together to attack the problem, not each other.

This scriptural approach deals with strong-willed, dominant individuals who overpower others. Powerful personalities must bend to Christ's authority. This approach also protects the insecure person who habitually gives in to his insecurities and to the other person. This approach provides a context in which both individuals can discuss problems and issues openly with the confidence that Jesus Christ is genuinely concerned for their well-being and involved in leading them to an effective, mutually satisfactory solution.

Third, I observe that the peace of Christ rules "in my heart." For this approach to problem-solving to work, an internal reorganization has to begin within me. Internally I relinquish control—no more ruling or manipulating my partner. I have to decide if Christ is really going to become the ruling Person in our marriage. I have to decide whether or not I will take the time to pray about issues and wait for direction to be given. I also have to decide whether I really believe Christ will guide us in decisions such as

many issues can end up in a draw!

Colossians 3:15 reveals a clear and definite means for effective problem-solving in marriage. It indicates who is to take responsibility for decision-making. Let's look carefully at this verse and notice what it teaches.

First, it indicates that God's goal for interpersonal relationships is *peace*—a word that is mentioned twice. We were called to peace. Our loving Father wants us to enjoy tranquil, harmonious relationships with each other, so He designed a process which will accomplish that goal. Personally I find great comfort in knowing that God has established an effective means for Winnie and me to deal with problems.

Second, I observe that God's method to achieve this goal is to make Christ the decision maker in our marriage. This is neither one-man rule nor democracy; we both submit to the Lord of peace and invite Him to guide us in the problem-solving process.

purchasing an automobile, finding a church to attend, choosing where to go on vacation, or sharing household tasks.

Allowing Christ to be the "umpire" in our decisions is basic to maturity. It is one of God's primary means to motivate us to seek His ways, His wisdom, His honor. It is a clear, practical indication of our commitment to seek our spouse's well-being. It reveals whether I have entered this relationship for what I can get out of it or for what I can give to another person. It indicates the genuineness of my humility.

You may be thinking, "This sounds too idealistic, too mystical. Does it really work?" I assure you it not only works, it also enriches a marriage and gives it an environment of peace. It creates a setting in which Jesus Christ can truly bless a home.

Let me describe how this process might work. You and your spouse face a problem. Your first response is to bring it to the Lord together in prayer. You say, in effect, "Lord, we are facing this dilemma. We believe You know how it can be best resolved. We seek Your guidance."

Having prayed in this spirit, you begin to discuss the facts and emotions involved. Each person speaks openly and listens compassionately, unafraid of being exploited or overpowered by the other. Where appropriate, you investigate Scripture together to gain insight. You talk with people you respect to enlarge your understanding. You continue praying together, *expecting the Lord to give insight, open doors, or touch your emotions.* You have nothing to defend, no position to protect.

In this process you can anticipate Christ's leadership to manifest itself in some way. No one can predict exactly the form it will take. But you can be assured He will fulfill His promise to "instruct you and teach you in the way you should go"; He will "counsel you and watch over you" (Ps. 32:8). You will also discover that approaching problems in this way unites you as husband and wife and draws you closer to Christ.

Two weeks ago I traveled to the city where Amy and Mike live and spent a day with them in their apartment. During the conversation it became apparent that they had encountered typical marriage problems related to finances, church, friendship, expectations, and so on. I also noted that the spirit of Colossians 3:15 prevailed. They were following this effective principle to gain God's perspective and His resources.

I came home with a spirit of thankfulness.

Related Articles

The Course of Severe Marital Conflict

WAYNE E. OATES

When married couples are in conflict with each other, they move through observable stages from one level of severity to the next. Understanding the phases can help you think more objectively about conflict between you and your mate. It can help you diagnose the seriousness of your conflict. It can also help you know what kinds of help you need for each other and from outsiders to slow down the conflict, arrest the damages, and reverse the process.

Let me describe the course of severe marital conflict:

Stage One: Normal Adjustment. All couples have friction during the first two years of marriage over several adjustments. They have to work out a mutually satisfying routine of work, sleep, social activities, and frequency and form of sexual relations. They need to agree about how to be involved in the rituals of each other's parental families at major holidays and family rituals. They must learn the subtleties of each other's nonverbal behaviors and ways of communicating feelings. They have to come to terms with their desires to change each other. And they must make explicit the unspoken and previous unconscious assumptions about marriage that they brought to their union.

Usually these adjustments can be hammered out between the husband and wife. It can be extremely helpful to be part of a group of other couples who are interested in building a lasting relationship with each other; ask your pastor to help you form such a group. These adjustments, however, are not auto-matic. Many people live together many years and are still chronically unhappy over issues that should have been settled during the first two years of marriage.

Stage Two: The Violation of the Covenant of Trust. Breaches of a couple's basic covenant of trust and respect occur when either feels the other has betrayed him or her. This can happen in many ways: catching the partner in an act of deception, discovery of secrets about the other that should have been revealed before marriage, unfaithfulness with a member of the same or opposite sex, physical and even verbal abuse. Whatever the cause, the marriage is thrown into crisis and the worth of the relationship is questioned.

Stage Three: Isolated Misunderstanding. The spouses withdraw from each other emotionally. They may be civil to each other, but they cease to be intimate either verbally or sexually. Severe isolation sets in, though people outside the family may not realize that a problem exists.

Stage Four: Social Involvement. The strain of isolation becomes too great for one spouse or both to bear, and outside help is sought. This may come from a parent, a sibling, an associate at work, a friend, or a trained counselor. Often, however, one spouse or both get involved with a person of the opposite sex. Initial contacts may be innocent, but soon they begin seeing each other secretly and an affair is in the making.

Stage Five: Separation. Sometimes a couple will decide to separate while they

WHY CAN'T WE AGREE?

The brand-new house was our first—and our first chance to decorate it together. But it wasn't long before we realized that the decorating itself was going to be a major cause of contention. Jim wanted all the walls painted; Kathe wanted to wallpaper. Jim wanted to decorate in geometric designs; Kathe consistently chose flowers and soft country patterns. And no matter how much we talked, we couldn't agree.

Then Jim thought of something. He asked Kathe how her home always looked when she was growing up. Her answer: it was wallpapered with floral designs. Jim's home had painted walls and anything decorative was geometric and modern. When we realized that our tastes (and our argument) was based not on absolutes but simply on how the homes we grew up in always looked, then we were ready to compromise.

When you and your spouse find yourselves unable to agree, think about how you were raised, how your mom or dad always acted, what you came to expect. You may discover that many of your expectations are carryovers. When you see that happening, you can then work with your spouse for an agreeable compromise.

Jim & Kathe Galvin

are in counseling so that they will not do more damage to each other's spirits. More often, separations are unplanned. In a rage, one partner will move out or throw the other one out, and the two of them take up separate residences. A therapeutic separation can enable a couple to devote themselves to prayer and self-examination, and if the separation is not too long, it can provide an opening for the counsel of the Holy Spirit (see 1 Cor. 7:5). A chaotic separation is much less likely to have positive results.

Stage Six: Legal Action. At this point the couple begins talking about the kind of divorce they want, how the property should be divided, and how child custody will be arranged. Even at this stage of marriage conflict, all hope is not necessarily lost. The stages can be reversed. If you are considering divorce, consider what Scripture has to say about it. Ask your pastor to study Mark 10:2-12, Matthew 19:3-12, John 4:7-29, John 8:1-11, and 1 Corinthians 7:1-17 with you.

Stage Seven: Post-Divorce Bereavement. Many couples who divorce have the illusion that they will never see each other again. Rarely does this happen. Though no longer married to each other, the two of them may still have many things to work out, particularly if they have children. In addition, each will go through a time of grief and bereavement, no matter how much the divorce was desired. If you were recently divorced, beware of hastening into another marriage. Continue seeking a counselor's guidance. Give yourself time to heal.

Perhaps you are troubled by conflict in your marriage—chronic, smoldering problems, or an acute eruption of hostility. What should you do to keep from sliding downhill to separation and divorce? First, don't threaten divorce. To do so is to draw a gun on your marriage. Second, don't take your problems to willing listeners of the opposite sex. If you are already involved in an unwise or immoral liaison, break it off immediately. Third, talk with a trusted counselor who is trained in marriage and family therapy. Your pastor may be such a person, or he may want to refer you to a person who works full-time as a marriage and family counselor. A husband and wife who sincerely want to restore their relationship can usually do so, with the Lord's help and a lot of hard work. Conflict can become chronic and marriages can self-destruct, or healing and reconciliation can occur. A mature, committed couple can do a great deal toward promoting healing.

Related Articles
Chapter 15: Bringing Love Back to Life
Chapter 15: Stages of Divorce
Chapter 16: How Do We Know If We Need Professional Help?

HELP! I'M A FOOTBALL WIDOW!

"My husband works all week, comes home, and sits in his easy chair and watches football all weekend! Is it too much to ask that he spend some time talking with me and playing with the kids (not to mention doing some work around the house)?"

The sports widow has several options as she responds to her husband's addiction to the game:

1. She can give in and give up by resigning herself to a lonely fate of never seeing her husband.

2. She can fight it head-on by nagging him, drawing battle lines, offering ultimatums, even stooping to insults or attacks to try to shock him into understanding her plight.

3. She can decide to discover why her husband likes the sport so much. She can learn the rules, get interested in the game, ask questions; in short, she can share his enjoyment and make watching football something they can do together. (This is a good option, but she still may feel frustrated about work left undone and kids who need some fathering.)

4. Beyond learning to enjoy the game, she can negotiate a workable solution—a compromise—that allows him to enjoy his games, yet allows her needs (and the kids' needs) to be met. For example, she may talk to him about saving Sundays for family activities if he watches sports on Saturdays. Or maybe he could decide to pick the one big game he wants to watch and do needed jobs around the house before that game comes on.

5. She can create a new solution by solving the problem in a creative way that meets everyone's needs. She could get some tickets to the big home game and make the outing a family activity. Dad gets to see the game live, the kids and Mom get time with Dad.

These options are ordered from least preferable to most preferable. The ideal solution is not always attainable or even practical. But the point is to try to work backward from 5 to 4 to 3, not going any lower. Remember that the relationship is most important. Communicate with your husband, and be willing to work toward a mutually favorable solution.

YFC Editors

Forgiveness: The Secret of a Great Marriage

EVELYN CHRISTENSON

It has been said that a good marriage is made up not of two good lovers, but of two good forgivers.

Today there are multiple books, TV programs, and seminars on how to be a better lover, but I find all that teaching in vain if I do not forgive my husband of anything I am holding against him. No matter how much training and trying, there is no way to have real love in our marriage if one or both of us are seething inside because of some past hurtful deed.

Forgiving is hard to do because it is necessary only when we really have been hurt. But God in His Word doesn't give us a choice. In Colossians 3:13 Paul says, "Bear with each other and forgive whatever grievances you may have against one another. Forgive as the Lord forgave you."

It is easy for me to accept the traditional explanation of this verse—that I should forgive my husband *because* the Lord forgave me. Knowing that I am a sinner never has been a problem for me. I can obediently agree that because Christ forgave me, I should forgive my spouse also. And I can discipline myself to do it. But that word *as*—"Forgive *as* the Lord forgave you"—means much more than just "because." It also means "in the same way that," "just like," and "to the extent that."

In the same way that Jesus forgave me? You mean unconditionally? Not holding it to the offender's account after forgiving? Not compiling ugly statistics of evil to cherish deep inside? Since there is no perfect mate, we all do and

say things—sometimes big things, sometimes little—that are hurtful. When I'm wounded by my spouse, I frequently find myself grumbling, "God certainly expects a lot, telling me to forgive my husband unconditionally—the same way He forgave me."

Just like Jesus forgave me? Even when I'm innocent, as Christ was when I sinned against Him, I must forgive? God says yes. Of course, no marriage partner is ever completely without sin as Christ was, and in the little everyday hurts both are offenders. In the big, serious grievings, however, there is usually one erring spouse and one desperately trying to keep the marriage alive. "O Lord," my heart has cried when I felt I was not at fault, "that seems unfair!"

To the extent that Jesus forgave me, I must forgive? No matter how huge the sin my spouse has committed? Whatever the sum total of what he did? As many times as needed? "That's how I forgave you," God gently reminds me when I want to resist obeying that command.

I've wondered many times why God put such harsh commands in the Bible. But He had very good reasons for requiring us to forgive.

First, forgiveness is His method of keeping Satan from getting a toehold in our marriages. In 2 Corinthians 2:7-11 we have God's three-word formula for thwarting Satan's devastating attempt to break up Christian relationships, including marriages. *Forgive . . . comfort . . . love*—"in order that Satan might not outwit us." Satan's onslaught against

331

Christian marriages these days is relentless. But God has the answer. I've seen thousands of breaking marriages, even those already in the divorce courts, come back together in my prayer seminars as we have studied and practiced these three words. As long as both partners consistently practice them, God has a marvelous marriage in store for them.

These three words—*forgive, comfort, love*—also are God's test to see whether we are obedient in *all* things (2 Cor. 2:9). It is easy to obey when I'm asked to teach a Sunday School class, do another seminar, even feed the poor. But it is much harder to obey God's orders to forgive when my husband has said or done something that hurts me. However, God expects us to obey all His commands, including forgiving everyone who hurts us—which of course includes our mates.

In His model prayer, Jesus taught us to ask God to forgive us our sins only as we have forgiven those who have sinned against us (Matt. 6:12). Complete reconciliation to God is not possible unless I too am willing to forgive. No matter how much I ask God to forgive the things I do wrong in my marriage, Jesus said if I don't forgive my mate, God doesn't forgive me either. And what a miserable marriage partner I am when I am not forgiven—struggling in my own power to be a good wife, but with a broken relationship with my Lord who alone can give me all those attributes I need to be a good marriage partner.

One of the greatest reasons God insists that we forgive is what not forgiving will do to us. God knows that when we refuse to forgive, we are damaged emotionally and physically. Our mates may be completely unaware of having hurt us, while we are being eaten from within by our unforgiving attitude. And the venom churning in the pit of our stomachs spews out into every facet of our lives.

A bitter young wife and mother, hardly able to function adequately in any area of life, attended one of my recent retreats. Devastated and angry, she shared with me how her husband had had a sexual affair with her very beautiful little sister, who was only fourteen years old at the time. The wife had been in counseling for four years about it. She told me that whenever a counselor asked, "When can you forgive your husband?" she shot back, "Never!"

But on the second day of the retreat a breathless, beaming, transformed young woman caught up with me in the hall. She was exploding with excitement as she said, "This afternoon when you told us to admit a need to our prayer partner, all I said to her was that I needed to forgive someone. I didn't even tell her who. But as she prayed for me, I suddenly had the desire and ability from

APOLOGIES

When should I apologize to my spouse?
Only when I know I'm wrong? What about when I know I'm right?
Only when I've hurt him or her? What if he/she deserved it?
Only when I don't feel like fighting anymore? What if I'm winning?
Only when I want him or her to quit nagging?
When should you apologize to your spouse?
How about now?

YFC Editors

God to forgive my husband. And I did!" Her eyes danced as she bubbled, "Oh, Mrs. Chris, I can't wait to get home to tell him!"

Forgiveness—God's prescription for a great marriage!

Related Articles
Chapter 1: Love as Mercy
Chapter 10: Tender Acceptance and Total Forgiveness

Tender Acceptance and Total Forgiveness

BOB ARNOLD

According to the romantic novel, *Love Story,* "Love means never having to say you're sorry." In the real world, however, love means constantly having to say you're sorry. Even more important, it means constantly forgiving others for injustices they have done to you. This is what it means to imitate Jesus Christ in our marriages. His message is tender acceptance and total forgiveness.

The first way to imitate our Lord is by accepting others for who they are. We should encourage them to be the unique persons God has created them to be.

The greatest mistake we can make is assuming we can change people after marriage. Basically, people change very little. They especially will not change through negative criticism and excessive badgering. The most effective way to bring about change in others is to accept them for who they are.

Mature marriages result when couples begin letting each other be themselves. Marriages grow when couples stop trying to change each other and begin accepting and tolerating each other. When we do this, we begin to discover the beauty in our marriage partner. As we accept him or her, we also begin to understand the unique way God has matched us.

My wife, Jeanne, continues to wonder why God put us together: we seemingly have so many opposite characteristics. Yet time and again I find that our opposite traits tend to balance each other out. Where one of us has a weakness, the other has a strength.

Many times the things we don't like in each other are the very things we need to change in ourselves. Blinded by our own personality and gifts, we often project our characteristics on others and expect them to be just like us—only without the faults.

If we learn to look beyond ourselves, we begin to understand and appreciate the beauty of God's unique creation in others. God created each of us different from everyone else. If we want to imitate Him, we need to respect and appreciate those differences.

But what about areas in which a spouse is obviously sinful, selfish, or in error? The second way we can imitate Christ is by offering total forgiveness. Jesus said we should forgive 70-times-7 times.

Marriage is a place where we quickly learn about each other's sinfulness. You may have heard a preacher talk about utter depravity. In marriage we discover that this idea is a reality.

A good indication that we are growing

333

in Christ is that we are willing to offer forgiveness over and over again. Jesus said, "Blessed are the merciful, for they will be shown mercy" (Matt. 5:7). When you realize the multitude of sins Jesus has forgiven you, you should be willing to forgive others for just as many.

If we do not offer forgiveness to our spouse, our life and our marriage will become full of bitterness and anger. Regular forgiveness, by contrast, brings back joy.

The 19th-century Scottish author and preacher George MacDonald said that unwillingness to forgive is a greater sin than murder. With murder, the deed is done and complete; unforgiveness destroys for a lifetime.

Deep-rooted problems in marriage are often the result of years of being unwilling to forgive others where they have offended us. Sometimes the offenses are very minor, but eventually they mount up and produce overwhelming bitterness.

If you are not experiencing joy in your marriage, it may be because you are

HOW TO APOLOGIZE

When you apologize, don't say:
  "Even though it wasn't my fault, I'll take the blame."
  "I guess we were both wrong."
  "I'm sorry you got upset."
  "I'm sorry I did that, but . . ."
Instead, try:
  "I was wrong. Will you forgive me?"

YFC Editors

harboring anger and bitterness in your heart against your spouse. There may be offenses you are unwilling to forgive.

Do you want joy to return to your marriage? Tenderly accept, and totally forgive!

Related Articles
Chapter 1: Love as Grace
Chapter 10: Forgiveness: The Secret of a Great Marriage

"I'M SORRY!"

One of the first lessons I learned in our marriage was the necessity of saying, "I'm sorry." My wife, Christy, is much better at it than me. In fact, it seems that whenever we had a disagreement, she would be the first to apologize. Due to my delicate male ego, I would let her.

After one of our "discussions," Christy decided that it was my turn to say "I'm sorry." Since I wasn't used to apologizing, I thought nothing of the stony silence that existed between us for the next hour. However, I caught her nonverbal message after awhile: "Either you apologize, or face the consequences." As a newlywed, it didn't take me long to figure out what those consequences might be!

But I was feeling stubborn that evening and thought maybe I could outwait her. I was wrong. There was no way she was going to apologize first. She had made up her mind, and the next move was up to me.

I knew I should do my part; Christy was a very forgiving person. And after all, wasn't I the head of our home? Wasn't I the one who was supposed to be showing the way? Wasn't I to love Christy as Christ loved His church?

Finally, I dropped to my knees. Not to pray, although I probably should have. I dropped to my knees so I could crawl across the living room and beg Christy's forgiveness. It was a well-calculated move, and it brought the desired result: laughter. For all her determination, she couldn't stay mad when she saw her penitent husband crawling on the floor.

When I finally reached her, we collapsed in each other's arms, almost simultaneously saying, "I'm sorry!" The ice had been broken, and we could return to the joys of our relationship.

Since that time, I've said "I'm sorry" many times. Sometimes I've added flowers or a gift. I doubt I'll ever be as quick to forgive as Christy, but I'll never forget the lesson I learned that night. Love means you always have to say "I'm sorry."

J. D. Holt

A husband and wife who live together in perfect harmony may be shocked at what happens when their family grows larger. Maybe they have a child— or several. Maybe an aging parent moves in, or a sister or brother, a foster child, an exchange student, another relative or friend. Suddenly they don't see things eye to eye anymore.

Take this quiz with your mate and see where you differ. Then talk about your attitudes, trying to understand each other's viewpoint—especially if you're expecting a child or one of your mothers already has her bags packed!

Mark the relative importance to you of each item on the list. If, for example, you think regular meals with the whole family together are extremely important, circle 5. If you think they are not important at all, circle 1. Or, if your valuing of family meals is somewhere in the middle, circle 2, 3, or 4 depending on your strength of feeling.

1 2 3 4 5   having regular meals with the whole family together
1 2 3 4 5   having family traditions
1 2 3 4 5   spending holidays at my relatives' home
1 2 3 4 5   spending holidays at my spouse's relatives' home
1 2 3 4 5   spending holidays at home, inviting relatives in
1 2 3 4 5   spending holidays at home with just the immediate family
1 2 3 4 5   taking vacations with the whole family
1 2 3 4 5   helping relatives in need
1 2 3 4 5   taking in aging parents
1 2 3 4 5   opening our home to people in need
1 2 3 4 5   putting husband-wife relationship above parent-child
              relationship
1 2 3 4 5   spending regular time alone with each child
1 2 3 4 5   having children
1 2 3 4 5   living close to extended family
1 2 3 4 5   spending time with grandchildren
1 2 3 4 5   financing children's college education
1 2 3 4 5   financing grandchildren's college education
1 2 3 4 5   financing big wedding for children
1 2 3 4 5   giving children down payment for first mortgage
1 2 3 4 5   attending children's school activities
1 2 3 4 5   educating children at home
1 2 3 4 5   teaching children about God
1 2 3 4 5   being good friends with children
1 2 3 4 5   disciplining children firmly
1 2 3 4 5   having well-defined family rules
1 2 3 4 5   accepting money from relatives
1 2 3 4 5   involving children in out-of-school learning activities
1 2 3 4 5   maintaining warm relationship with teens
1 2 3 4 5   moving wherever schools are best
1 2 3 4 5   sending children to Christian schools

CHILDREN
AND OTHERS

Parenthood is a career that often imposes itself without prior regard to the competence of those on whom it lands. Perhaps the reason many fail in child rearing is that they insist on ownership rather than stewardship. We call children "ours," whereas the real know-how comes exclusively from the rightful Master, God.

Children are eager, open, and teachable. Yet they arrive frighteningly unfortified. From the beginning, therefore, God taught His people to train and to protect the young generation. For example, Psalm 127 was sung regularly en route to the temple at feast times. Three epithets in this psalm describe children:

"Sons are a heritage from the Lord" (v. 3). The word *heritage* carries the meaning of an allotment or a commission. The sense is that children bring something to the parent—and a proper response is assumed.

"Children [are] a reward from Him" (v. 3). The presence of children in the home is a sign of God's favor. They are cause for thanksgiving and worship.

"Like arrows in the hands of a warrior are sons" (v. 4). Children are to be seen as a convincing answer with a cutting edge, a weapon against a hostile world. They are to be launched toward a given target.

An assignment, a reward, an arrow. Each child has these possibilities under the loving care and direction of truly wise parents.

Howard & Jeanne Hendricks

Let Your Children See You Love Your Mate

ZIG ZIGLAR

When my son was 15, I asked him what he would say to people if they asked him what he liked best about his dad. He paused only a moment before responding, "The thing I like best about my dad is that he loves my mom."

"Why do you say that, Son?" I naturally asked.

"Well, Dad," he answered, "as long as you love Mom I know you'll treat her right, and as long as you treat her right I know we'll always be a family, and I'll never have to choose between living with you or living with Mom." I had no way of knowing it at the time, but that very day one of his close friends had been given that choice.

How do you communicate to your

children that you and your mate are in love? A number of actions can show them your love:

1. *Let your children see you united as a team.* My friend Fred Smith, who is truly one of the wisest men I've ever known, tells of a man who came home one evening to discover his wife in tears because their two children, about 8 and 10 years of age, were being sassy and belligerent.

Fred says the man reached down, caught each child by the back of the collar, and bumped their heads together—hard enough so they knew they had just met a solid object, but not hard enough to do any damage. They were shocked, of course. The man looked at both of them and said, "Don't harass your mother. She was my wife before you came along, and she's going to be my wife long after you have gone, and I won't stand for any of this."

Here's the message: let the kids know you and your mate work together. Children are more secure knowing that Mom and Dad love each other than knowing Mom and Dad love them. Interestingly, when Mom and Dad truly love each other, they will also love their offspring, and this love will manifest itself in a thousand ways.

2. *Let your children see you showing each other little courtesies.* The kindnesses, such as opening doors and holding the chair for your wife as she is seated. The way you introduce one another—"This is *my* wife," or "This is *my* husband." The affection you display for each other, remembering that husband and wife should never let their children see any display of affection in which the children cannot participate. The "welcome home" kiss, the hug you give each other as you pass in the hallway or den, the holding of hands as you are seated at the table, the snuggling together when you're listening to music or watching television, the 101 little things that communicate to the children

DOES OUR MARITAL LOVE AFFECT OUR CHILDREN?

I remember a dinner conversation that taught me more than most books I've read or sermons I've heard.

"Do you boys think Mommy and Daddy love you?" I asked.

Tyler gave me his two-year-old's grin, which obviously meant yes, while his four-year-old brother rolled his eyes and replied, "Uh-huh."

"How do you know, Benji?"

"Because you always give us hugs and kisses."

I really wasn't trying to take this conversation anywhere in particular, but I like to quiz my kids.

"Benji, what if, for some reason, Mommy and I couldn't hug you or kiss you. Would you still know that we love you?"

"Uh-huh."

"How?"

"Because you're always telling me that you love me."

Smart kid, I thought. I may as well push him a little and ask a bonus question.

"Benji, what if, for some reason, we couldn't hug you or kiss you and we couldn't tell you that we love you. Would you still know that we love you?"

Now I could see those little wheels turning in his head. He paused, looked at my wife, and then right into my eyes.

"Uh-huh."

"You would? How?"

"Because, Daddy, when I see you and Mommy loving each other, then I know you love me too."

Byron Emmert

that Mom and Dad love each other. Incidentally, these little acts are an absolute necessity if love is to flourish and the marriage remain vibrant.

3. *Let your children hear you talk about each other respectfully.* Always build each other up. This does not mean parents cannot be in error—we often are! But when a parent makes a serious mistake with a child, the mate should wait to discuss the situation until the two adults are alone. In most cases, the one in error is aware of the fact; if he or she is not, the other parent can gently and lovingly point out that the situation might have been handled differently. The offending parent should then go to the child and ask forgiveness (this is a sure sign of maturity). In no way does this weaken the parent in the eyes of the child. As a matter of fact, it strengthens him or her and reinforces the love between them. And all this can be accomplished without weakening either mate's position with the child by openly opposing what was said or done.

4. *Let your children hear your love in your voice.* It is not so much what is said as the way it is said that makes the big difference. When husbands and wives in ordinary conversation are gentle and kind with each other, children pick up the strong feelings of love and respect Mom and Dad have for each other. This loving example not only gives their children security, it also prepares the kids for the day they have mates of their own.

By doing these things, husbands and wives are practicing Ephesians 4:32: "Be kind and compassionate to one another, forgiving each other, just as in Christ God forgave you."

Related Articles
Chapter 11: The Most Important Thing You Can Do for Your Child
Chapter 11: Parenting as a Team Activity

The Most Important Thing You Can Do for Your Child

JANETTE OKE

For my husband and me the days of actively raising children are in the past. We still have a part in our children's lives, but the training years are behind us. Now our position is one of love and support, prayerfully urging them on to all that God has for them.

The years with children in our home were good years, although in honesty I would have to admit that we made mistakes. A number of things, though, I would not change if I were starting over. Important things. The very things I feel have helped to produce four God-fearing, worthwhile, sensitive, beautiful adults from the four tiny babies God placed in our home.

The most important thing we can do for our children is to build a good marriage relationship. There is nothing that gives a child more security, a greater sense of love, and a more solid base from which to face the world than having two parents who genuinely love and respect one another. Contrast that to the home with bickering, tension, sparring, battles, and side-taking. A child from that kind of situation is defensive, embittered, withdrawn or outwardly combative, lacking in self-esteem and torment-

WHAT DO YOUR CHILDREN LEARN ABOUT MARRIAGE BY WATCHING YOU?

The only way we learn about marriage is by experiencing it—and the first marriage we experience is that of our parents. Ever since their birth, your children have been taking lessons from you and your spouse. What have they been learning?

1. *How a man treats a woman.* Does he open doors, hold chairs, bring flowers? Does he help with housework, consider her needs, speak to her respectfully? Or does he insist on his own way, treat her roughly, spend little time with her?

2. *How a woman treats a man.* Does she make him comfortable, listen to him, express her appreciation? Does she respect him, stand by him, pamper him a little? Or does she nag him, put him down, treat him coldly?

3. *How a couple relates to each other.* Do they act like rivals, master and slave, strangers? Or like lovers, companions, partners?

4. *How a couple relates to others*—their own parents, their children, their friends, the needy.

By watching your marriage, your children are forming opinions about what they want—and don't want—in their own. They are also forming habits that will be very hard to break: they are learning to act like you.

What are you teaching your children about marriage?

YFC Editors

ed by fear and guilt.

Love one another. Don't be afraid to show it. It is good for the children to see open affection between their parents. I'm not talking about things that should be kept to the privacy of the bedroom, but rather caring, respecting, and honoring one another. Embraces and kisses are OK too. Form a circle and take the children in. I remember so many times when our children were small and my husband and I were giving each other a hug. They would cry, "Me too! Me too!" and crawl into the circle of our arms to get in on the embrace.

There should be caring touches among all family members. I fear that in our great desire to combat the negative touching so prevalent in modern society, we are in danger of becoming rigid and restrictive and losing the necessary and beautiful communication of proper touch. We need touching. Christ used touch over and over in His ministry to hurting people. As Christians, we must not let the world rob us of that right.

Share. Enjoy sharing things with one another, and include the children in the sharing times. There are so many things that can be shared. Not only the good times, the games and walks and talks and teasing, but also the bad times, the difficulties, the heartaches. Share the responsibilities of teacher interviews, the excitement of the school play, the hard task of enforcing the "grounding" rule, the privilege of prayer time—all of life, with one another and with your children.

Create family traditions. They needn't be elaborate or complicated. What is important is that the family have some things that are uniquely their own. Traditions are the things memories are made of—something special about Sunday breakfast, a certain decoration or procedure that is part of each Christmas, a birthday remembrance that is just your family's. Anything that your children can identify as *your own* will unify you.

Be united. Show your children that

you are a team. Make them happy that they are loved and protected by that team. Let them see you pray together. Stand together in decision-making.

If your marriage relationship is close and loving, your children will not need to weather storms of controversy. I know there are times when one is caught off guard and responds too quickly to a situation. Do not let those times be the norm. As much as humanly possible, do your disagreeing in private. It is difficult for children to handle conflict between parents. Something that seems minor to you might seem like a major confrontation to them, and can fill them with fear concerning the family unit and the future.

If you truly love and respect one another, you will not put each other down, especially not in front of your children. Some people make a game of seeing who can outdo the other in ridicule or criticism. Don't tease by exchanging insults—it can become such a habit that you're hardly aware you're doing it. But other people notice, and certainly your listening children do. Not only does it undermine their opinion of the individual slammed; it also lowers their opinion of the slammer. In addition, they may follow the parent's example and pick up the slamming habit. If you love one another, by contrast, you will seek to build each other up in everyone's eyes.

In a good relationship, you will never talk behind your spouse's back in a critical or derogatory fashion. Even children can understand the deceitfulness of backstabbing, and it is particularly upsetting if the person attacked is someone they love. Love for your partner will prevent you from resorting to such tactics or creating a power struggle for the children's love and support. Attempting to win a child to your side in order to give yourself a feeling of power over your spouse is deadly. It will probably lose you the very thing you set out to gain. There are no winners in such a contest. All parties lose in love and respect.

A good marriage relationship takes time. It takes prayer. It takes commitment. It takes unselfishness and love and respect. But it is more than worth it, not only to the husband and wife, but also to the children.

Related Articles
Chapter 1: Love as Respect
Chapter 11: Let Your Children See You Love Your Mate

Should We Have Children?

GARY D. BENNETT

One of God's most precious gifts to mankind is the gift of bringing new human life into the world. He has bestowed upon us the blessed privilege of fashioning offspring like ourselves and in His image.

That does not mean, of course, that everyone should have children—or even that everyone can. Not all reasons for reproducing are good ones. It is very important to know your own motivations regarding parenthood, because these can make a tremendous difference in your parenting attitudes and actions.

First of all, don't have children in the hope of saving a shaky marriage, because children will probably shake your marriage completely loose. Professionals have been pointing out for years the ways in which children test the strength of a marriage. They can put strain on a marriage in two ways: (1) they consume a great deal of time and energy from both parents, especially during the early childhood years; (2) their presence tends to reactivate past unresolved problems the husband and wife may have had with their own parents or siblings (and all of us have had some). On the other hand, when a marriage is basically sound, children can strengthen the bonds between husband and wife and add new dimensions to the marriage relationship.

Don't have children to fulfill your own unaccomplished goals or as an ego boost. It's natural for parents to identify to some extent with their children. They are elated by their children's successes and saddened by their failures. This is fine, as long as we recognize that those successes and failures belong to our children and not to us. Having parents who try to live through them is very counterproductive for children.

Neither should you have children because you are bored or need something to make you feel worthwhile. All women and men have to resolve their need for fulfilling work, but having children in order to keep busy is not a valid motivation. Children are not toys or recreational equipment. They are demanding, time consuming, emotionally draining, and physically taxing. Indeed, they are usually more responsibility than ever anticipated. That is not to say that children are more of a burden than a blessing. They can enrich our lives in countless ways, if we have them for the right reasons.

There are numerous good reasons for becoming parents. No one reason is absolutely perfect, and no motivation is ever 100 percent pure. Here are two basic principles that should guide your thinking:

First, consider becoming parents if you and your spouse strongly desire to extend your love to the point of blending and creating an offshoot of your two selves. In Genesis 1:28 God commanded the first human couple to "be fruitful and increase in number."

Second, become parents if your love for children is so overpowering that it demands concrete expression in a child of your own, whether by birth or adoption.

There is no absolutely perfect time to have children. If you wait until you think you're financially ready or emotionally fit or until everything seems perfect, you may wait forever. Timing of conception may or may not seem right, but every child is a gift of God and not an accident or coincidence. God indicates in Psalm 139:13-16 that every child conceived is formed by Him to be born at a given point in history.

Still, certain things must be discussed by a husband and wife who are thinking about having children.

- [ ] What are your long-range marriage goals?
- [ ] Do either of you have career aspirations? If so, can you meet them with children, or will they have to be adjusted or discarded?
- [ ] How large a family do you and your spouse want? What do the two of you think the Lord may want?
- [ ] Will having children drastically change your standard of living? If so, in what ways?
- [ ] What other effects will children have on your marriage?
- [ ] Have you discussed and determined a philosophy of parenting, disciplinary practices, the spiritual development of your children, and so on?

These are only a few issues you must face when becoming parents. Fortunately, most of us have nine months to prepare to give birth and usually even longer to prepare to adopt. We need this time to get ready emotionally, mentally, and spiritually.

When we become parents, we do not cease to be people with lives of our own;

we still possess needs that cannot be totally satisfied simply by having and rearing children. As marriage partners, always remember that you started together before children and that, God willing, you will finish together after children. Enjoy your children, but don't lose sight of your partnership.

Related Articles
Chapter 2: The Couple With Small Children
Chapter 11: How Children Affect a Marriage

AND BABY MAKES THREE

What can the husband and wife expect when the new baby arrives? Seldom does a couple realize the impact of the first child on every aspect of their lives. Your relationship will change—it becomes less flexible, less spontaneous, and at times more strained. Time for sex needs to be adjusted, even scheduled. Your sleep patterns change. Your roles change. You are no longer just husband and wife; you are also mother and father, with all the implications and responsibilities those roles carry.

The social life becomes less flexible—suddenly it takes 45 minutes to get out the door, and you may find you'd just rather have people over than try to get out. And when your friends have kids of their own, getting together becomes even more complicated.

Your budget is suddenly affected—the little one costs more than his or her size might lead you to believe. You may need a larger apartment or that first house. You'll empty your wallet for furniture, clothing, doctor visits, shots, not to mention diapers, food, bottles, formula, toys, etc. You need a car seat, paraphernalia to carry, and if the little one stays home, a baby-sitter to schedule, pick up, pay, and take home.

You'll find that it feels strange to have another person in your happy family of two, and that demands a major adjustment. But from the instant the child arrives, you can't imagine your family without him or her. You have gained another opportunity to love, and an awesome and God-given responsibility to nurture and train—and God promises to help and guide you.

YFC Editors

What Does the Bible Say About Children?

JUDITH ALLEN SHELLY

Children are a blessing from the Lord. In Old Testament times they were needed for survival. Not only did they carry on the family name, even at a young age they did their share of the family work. When parents grew too old to work, their children supported them entirely.

Childless couples sometimes turned to extreme measures. Sarah told Abraham to have children by her maid when God seemed slow in keeping His promise of heirs (Gen. 16:2)—the first recorded case of a surrogate mother. Rachel's childlessness caused serious friction in her marriage to Jacob, so she turned to the same desperate plan. After that she tried quack medicine, bargaining her sister, Leah, out of her son's mandrake roots (Gen. 30:1-24). Hannah went into deep depression over her childlessness. She wept, refused to eat, and prayed desperately for years. Finally she made a deal with God, agreeing to give her first son to Him (1 Sam. 1).

We live in a radically different culture from that of Sarah, Rachel, and Hannah. Children are no longer necessary for financial security—in fact, they are very expensive to maintain—but the intense desire for children continues to nag at most couples. Even career-oriented women who thought they did not want children earlier in life may suddenly change their minds by their mid-30s. Most people seem to sense instinctively that children "are a heritage from the Lord" (Ps. 127:3). However, in saying that, let me clearly emphasize that they are not the only sign of His blessing. He blesses some people equally with other gifts.

Children are a serious responsibility. Scripture commands parents to diligently teach their children the Word of God (Deut. 6:6-7), to train them in the way they should go (Prov. 22:6), to discipline them appropriately (Heb. 12:7-11), and never to cause them to sin (Matt. 18:6). Parenting requires a deep commitment to put children before career, social involvement, or personal pleasure. Many parents are able to continue other pursuits, but they must nonetheless constantly evaluate how outside activities affect their children.

My own work schedule, church and community involvement, and relationship with my husband are continually adapting as the children grow and their needs change. Whenever they become unusually fussy or rebellious I have to pull back and reevaluate. Am I spending enough time with them? Is it quality time? Am I really listening to them? Parents are crucial in shaping a child's understanding of God. If children cannot trust their parents to be consistent, to love them unconditionally, to hear them when they cry out, to be faithfully present, then they will have great difficulty trusting their Heavenly Father. Shaping the faith of our children is an awesome responsibility and a tremendous privilege.

The Christian family is a model of relationships within the family of God (Eph. 5:21–6:4; 1 Tim. 3:1-13). My husband, Jim, and I never realized how important that model was until we adopted children of our own. Not only have we

THE ISSUE OF ABORTION

The legal right to abortion on demand is certainly one of the most shameful decisions ever upheld in our country. Wrapped in so many emotions, circumstances, and fears, it has become tolerated, chosen, and even recommended by friends, parents, spouses, boyfriends, and doctors across the country.

When abortion is chosen as an option for an unmarried pregnant couple, it is merely for the sake of convenience, no matter what emotions and circumstances surround it.

But what about the married couple—are they ever faced with the decision whether or not to abort? Some are. At my first pregnancy checkup, my doctor highly recommended genetic counseling and amniocentesis because my husband's younger brother has Down's syndrome. I refused.

But suppose I decided to have amniocentesis, and suppose I discovered that I'm carrying a baby with some defect (and believe it or not, for some married couples the "defect" can be that the baby is the "wrong" sex!). If that were so, I could choose to have an abortion. And why might I decide to do that? Well, what would our friends think if we had a retarded or handicapped baby? Maybe we wouldn't want the extra work and care such a child would need. Perhaps we'd even feel it would be better for the baby! All those excuses center around quality of life. In our society, the philosophy is: if it's not high-quality and perfect, get rid of it—we don't want it.

Instead, I choose not to know. And yes, like any expectant mother, I hope and pray our baby is perfect. I know I'd have the right to kill a less-than-perfect child, but I choose to waive that right because of my responsibility to a higher Power who already has planned this child's life. And besides, I personally couldn't do it. I have my husband's complete support. We are ready to accept and raise this child, no matter what.

You and your husband may be faced with the abortion issue when pregnancy occurs. How will you decide? What will you do? Talk it through and honestly share your feelings and concerns. Talk about the possibility of having a handicapped or retarded child and how you both would deal with it.

The choice, and the responsibility for that choice, are yours.

Linda Taylor

---

learned a great deal about God's love and faithfulness through caring for them, we have also discovered that other people are watching.

Several years ago Jim and I were speakers at a summer conference. It was the first time since our daughter, Janell, arrived, that we had attempted to minister in a camp setting as a family. We were both feeling frustrated: it seemed as if so much time was spent taking care of our family needs that we didn't have enough time to spend with other people. Then, as we were packing to leave, a young woman pulled me aside to say, "I want to thank you for coming. You have taught me so much just by being here. My home life was terrible when I was growing up. I never knew what it was like to be loved by my

AND ANOTHER BABY MAKES FOUR

Many people wonder about the impact of the second child. The first child causes major upheaval in the weeks following birth, but many parents find that adjustment at last comes once they have developed a system. Then comes child #2.

Child #2 means both Mom and Dad are busy when they try a simple act like going to McDonald's for lunch. Suddenly twice as much paraphernalia is needed and, if the children are both very young and active, you need two carseats, two sets of everything, two sets of hands to just stay ahead of them. Mom finds herself unable to really relax during the day with at least one child always on the move (unless both kids take naps at the same time). One child may precipitate a problem with the other; sibling rivalry is inevitable. The house may not seem big enough for all of you.

But the same miraculous thing happens as with the first child—you can't imagine the family without him or her. And the adjustment can be made smoothly if both spouses are willing to share the load; if the working spouse can baby-sit now and then to allow the other some time away; if they commit themselves to regular dates alone. Let the children become an addition to your marriage, not a substitution for it. You both need to commit yourselves to deepening your marriage. After all, the kids will leave one day, but you'll be together the rest of your lives.

YFC Editors

parents. I have struggled to understand what it means to be loved by God the Father and to be adopted by Him. Seeing the way you and Jim love and enjoy Janell has helped me accept God's love for me."

Children are a constant reminder of God's grace. Only a parent can fully identify with God's grief in Hosea 11:1-4: "When Israel was a child, I loved him . . . but the more I called Israel, the further they went from me. . . . It was I who taught Ephraim to walk, taking them by the arms; but they did not realize it was I who healed them. I led them with cords of human kindness, with ties of love . . . and bent down to feed them."

As we parents try to instill our children with godly values it is painful to have to discipline them and harder still to see them go astray. Through it all we are forced to develop patience and grow in our understanding of what it means to forgive. Yet that doesn't begin to match the mercy the Lord has for us (Ps. 103:11-14).

Jesus tells us, "Unless you change and become like little children, you will never enter the kingdom of heaven" (Matt. 18:3). Every parent knows that children are not perfect. Our home usually rings with the sound of "Me first!" and "How come I didn't get one if Jonny did?" or "Mommy, Janell took my book!" Adults usually learn to cover and control their selfishness, but children are blatant examples of original sin. However, outbursts of anger and selfishness are quickly followed by a "Mommy, I love you" and a desire to make things right again. That kind of total dependence on our Heavenly Father is what Jesus wants us to learn. Most adults are extremely uncomfortable about being dependent on anyone, even God. Perhaps that is why God said through the Prophet Isaiah that in the coming kingdom "a little child will lead them" (Isa. 11:6).

Proverbs 31:28 tells us of the good

wife: "Her children arise and call her blessed." Parenthood has great perks. When children show they are learning the lessons of faith you hope to teach them, when they imitate your good points and ignore your faults, the blessing seems to overflow. For instance, four-year-old Janell has become my special encourager. In the morning she comes into my bedroom as soon as she sees me stir, hands me my Bible, and says, "Mommy, it's time for your quiet time." Then she crawls in bed beside me and says, "Let's pray for your staff workers."

On one occasion I overheard a conversation between Janell and Jonathan, three, as they were sitting in a tent in his bedroom. Jonathan was sobbing quietly because he had been sent to his room for acting like a bully. Janell was carefully explaining to him, "Now you know Jesus, and you know He loves you. Well, Jesus is God, so you don't have to worry, because that means God loves you and He always will." In times like this I know we are truly blessed. For God has promised that our children are an ongoing channel of His blessing, not only in our immediate families, but reaching out to the whole world (Gen. 17:4-8; Acts 2:39). Our children are God's messengers to future generations.

How Children Affect a Marriage

KEVIN LEMAN

The advent of children destroys many of the dreams young men and women have as they enter marriage. When I did a survey on women and stress, I learned that the number-one stress in a woman's life is her children. When the children come, a couple's lifestyle changes completely. The young mom who just 12 months ago walked down the flower-strewn aisle can experience resentment, rage, anger, and a feeling of being smothered and trapped. That's why it is a good idea for young couples to wait and have a family after they have had a good chance to adjust to one another.

But even parents who waited four or five years to start a family can be amazed at the changes children bring, even in the way husband and wife relate to one another. That is why this is the best advice I could ever give a couple who is bringing home a new little bundle of responsibility and joy: within the first weeks of that child's life, leave the child at home and go out for an evening by yourselves.

This does the child a wonderful favor because it does your marriage a favor. We Americans do well at putting our children first; I try to encourage couples to put their marriage first instead. I would like for my children to be able to say I've modeled marriage well for them.

Going out for an evening right from the start also sets a pattern that will be tremendously helpful to the young mother who stays at home with the ankle-biter battalion. One child will drain a mom of her energy. She has to plan her day around that child, and she has to take naps just to survive. But if just a few months into being a mother she discovers she's pregnant again, then life gets really interesting. With two or more children underfoot, fatigue and exhaustion become a way of life.

347

Children are so dependent on us, and mothers go out of their way to meet their children's every need. Every whimper, every coo is going to get some kind of reaction from Mom. Mothers have to get good at protecting themselves, at showing their children they cannot dominate every moment of Mommy's life.

Fathers can be a big help. They have to realize that parenthood is not woman's work; a man's place also is in the home. Men can pitch in and take care of the kids so their wives can do a few things they want to do. It's true, though, that most husbands don't understand why their wives get so tired.

When my three older children were young, my wife went to an all-day seminar. I told her not to worry about it; I assured her I'd take care of the kids. I wanted to be a good husband and practice what I preached!

She came home about 10 minutes to 5. As she came through the door, I said, "You're home! How many days have you been gone?"

She said, "What are you talking about?" Then she walked into the family room, looked around, and said, "What happened?"

"Don't give me the what-happened bit," I said. "I picked this room up three times today. There were little kids in here I don't even know. It was a zoo."

I learned that day about the challenge and a half mothers face all the time. And if the mother works outside the home—as 56 percent of women with children under 18 do—the challenge is even greater. My surveys have indicated that even though the wife pulls her weight and then some outside the home, guess who prepares dinner and tucks the children in bed. I call it the Banana Peel Syndrome: throw a banana peel on the floor and stand back and watch. The husband will step over it. The kids will play with it. Somehow everyone thinks it's Mom's job to pick it up.

A man checks out no later than 7:45 in the evening after dinner. A woman doesn't check out until she hits the bed, exhausted. Then Harry really helps when he says, "Marge, do you want to fool around?" She looks at him strangely and says, "Do I look like I want to fool around? Good night." And she pulls the covers over her head.

It isn't just babies that cause stress. Kids of all ages are good at it. Young children have high dependency needs, and they cause a great deal of fatigue. Once they start school, Mom begins to feel like she's finally getting a little time to herself, unless she goes back to work at that time. Then more worries come when the kids hit junior high and notice the opposite sex. Peer pressure begins to create a different kind of child, it seems. And of course the adolescent years—I call them the Hormone Years—are tough, because parents realize all the temptations that are out there for kids.

At every stage, the fundamental principle of child rearing is love—and an important part of love is discipline. If discipline is missing, all your love is simply turning your children into selfish little takers. They will take from your energy, from your patience, and even from your marriage. And disciplining kids starts with disciplining yourselves as parents.

That brings me back to my first piece of advice: during the child's earliest weeks, discipline yourselves to leave the baby at home—with Grandpa and Grandma, or with a Ph.D. in pediatric nursing, if necessary—and go out together as a couple. This will give your relationship the boost that it really needs at that point, and it will show little Buford even at his young age that Mommy and Daddy aren't always going to be there, and that he is not the king of the household.

We Americans always feel as if we have an unlimited supply of everything, but we don't have an unlimited supply of energy. Children take up an enormous amount of what we have, and they make it that much easier for us to wear down and short out.

We start with dreams of what marriage is supposed to be like—a kind, considerate husband who brings flowers and sends cute little notes; an energetic, sexy wife who looks good and smells nice. In reality, he's out in the corporate world trying to climb the ladder of success, and she's home cleaning up messes and talking baby talk all day. About two years into marriage, a lot of people think their princes and princesses have turned into frogs. With some self-discipline and planning, though, you can keep your marriage alive in spite of the stresses of bringing up children. You just have to remember to put your mate first.

Related Articles
Chapter 2: The Couple With Small Children
Chapter 9: Perspective: Seeing What Your Spouse Sees

THE IMPACT OF THE THIRD AND FOURTH CHILDREN

The addition of a third child carries with it a whole new set of situations. For the most part, the parents are already used to the mobility problem, the financial adjustments, the housing adjustments, the time and rest adjustments. But for the first time, the parents are outnumbered; the compact car doesn't hold everyone comfortably; the square kitchen table doesn't fit anymore; the family won't even fit into a booth at a restaurant. As the kids get older, parents find themselves chauffeuring children here and there for activities, so that just organizing and scheduling three children can be a major accomplishment.

But there are pluses too. Hand-me-downs work now because at least two of the kids will be the same sex. There is some companionship among the children. If there is a large enough age difference, the older children can help take care of the younger ones.

With four children, the already full and hectic schedule is affected even more, but life never gets boring.

It is vitally important, no matter how many children you have—but especially with three or four—to plan ahead financially as much as possible. College tuition and wedding costs can hit suddenly and overwhelm the unprepared family. Even the daily expenses of clothing for growing children need careful planning and budgeting.

One father of four said it was hard to be fair—it was hard for he and his wife to remember what they did with the others at what age. For example, when did allowances start and raise? When did each child get the first bike? What special activities were done with which child at which age? Of course, he added that if he didn't remember, the children did!

YFC Editors

How Teenagers Affect
a Marriage

JIM & SALLY CONWAY

Study after study shows that teenagers in the family have a negative influence on the husband-wife relationship. The many physical, emotional, and social changes taking place as the teen moves from being a child to being a young adult are sometimes difficult to integrate and accept. The parents may receive a lot of static, not so much because the teen is upset with them, but because the teen is experiencing too much pressure from too many things to integrate all at once. The teen's process of completing important tasks to become mature may put a strain on the marriage. *Maturity equals intimacy, identity, and independence.*

The teen needs to learn how to be *intimate,* that is, how to give love and receive love. Frequently the model he or she is seeing in the parents' love life is that of a business relationship rather than an intimate caring for each other. The teen innately rejects the parents' sterile way of relating to each other and looks for a different kind of intimacy.

Sometimes that search for intimacy, without much experience or understanding of what love means, may lead the teen into some adventures of sexual promiscuity. Christian parents are naturally shocked by this distortion, but they frequently fail to realize that the distortion could have been minimized if a truly loving model of intimacy and mutuality had been present in the parents' marriage for the teen to observe.

A second task that the teen needs to be working on is *identity* or self-understanding. He or she needs to ask many

questions:
- [ ] Who am I?
- [ ] What are the gifts God has given me, and how do I use those in the world?
- [ ] What are my values?
- [ ] What is my personal relationship to God?
- [ ] How do I respond to people in need or to those who are different from me?
- [ ] What is it that marks me as a unique person?

Freewheeling, casual discussions with parents and peers speed up this important development.

The teenager also needs to be developing *independence*—being able to be responsible for himself or herself, to make independent decisions, to be accountable to a boss and to other significant persons. This transition from the dependent role of child to the independent role of young adult is like walking through a minefield in the dark. One day the teen will act dependent and want parental assistance; the next day, over the very same issue, the teen will view the parent's suggestions or assistance as an outlandish intrusion into his or her personal life.

Each of these important developmental aspects of the teen's life interfaces with the others. The push for independence affects the understanding of identity and the expressions of intimacy. Intimacy and self-identity also affect independence.

The development of each of these three "I's" can make the teen's and the parents' lives more hectic, or they can

changes. Obviously, rejection or suppression will be counterproductive.

THE IMPORTANCE OF OUR FAMILY HOMES

I'm very thankful for the homes in which Walter and I grew up.

My mother was optimistic. She didn't complain, and she was ready to tackle almost any new project with vitality.

My father made table talk a tradition in our home. In the evenings, he sat with us around the supper table reading, teaching, and somehow creating a family altar at table.

Walter's parents taught him how to play, how to have a great time with games and vacations. His mother was a master pedagogue. She said that if a child is going to learn anything at all, that child must be happy. Her first rule was to have a happy atmosphere in her classroom or in her home.

Our parents' homes were precious gifts to us. They helped us build our own home and strengthen the homes of people we ministered to.

Ingrid Trobisch

Two Changing Generations

At the same time that the teenager is experiencing rapid developmental change, the husband and wife are experiencing their own pressures. The husband probably is deeply committed to his career and may be viewing these years as the last years to really make it big in his job. He may feel that all this teenage tension is putting an unnecessary drain on him when he wants to focus his energies on his career. He may be going through his own intense struggles due to his midlife transition.

At the same time, massive changes may be taking place in the wife. She may feel unneeded by the teen and her husband. Her mothering career is coming to an end, and her husband seems preoccupied with his achievements. She may have a strong urge to go back to school, pursue her own career, or fulfill the dreams God gave her earlier.

In addition, midlife is reported as the least satisfying era in marriage. This is a high-risk time for divorce, and the divorce danger extends for a long time— approximately from ages 35 to 55.

The sad reality is that the teenager, the husband, and the wife may all feel exploited and misunderstood. They each may be wishing that the others would act differently so that their personal life would be easier. They each are using up their internal energy to resolve their own problems and have little energy to share in understanding each other.

Coupled with the tensions produced as each of the players in this family drama continues his or her rapid changes are the demands for the largest house, the most cars, and the greatest child-raising expense of any time during the marriage.

A teenager does affect a marriage negatively, but it is not the teenager's fault. It is just the reality that the teen as

cause stability. For example, as the teen feels more comfortable with his or her own identity, he or she tends to be less arrogant in the push for independence or less radical in the expression of intimacy. The key is to begin moving the child toward growth in these three areas before the onslaught of rapid development in the teen years.

Parents react to the teenager's developmental process in very different ways. Some parents understand what is going on and encourage this growth, while others reject the teenager and the growth process or try to suppress

well as the husband and wife are all going through changes.

Focusing from Negative to Positive

Turning your teenagers' effect on your marriage from a weakness to a strength can be accomplished in the following ways:

1. Help teens wrestle with their personal development. Don't stifle the process; instead, be their coach. Help them think through all the *why* questions of life. Encourage them to be reflective and to ask, for example, "Why don't I drink or use drugs?" If their answer is, "My parents told me not to," they and you are in big trouble. The reasons have to come from inside them, not from your commands.

They must develop an independence that fits with their identity. Give teens increasing responsibilities and privileges that fit with their gifts and abilities. Affirm them frequently. The energy you spend in helping your teens become whole people will also have a direct bearing on a more peaceful husband-and-wife relationship.

2. Remember, stress in midlife marriage is not basically the fault of teenagers' development. The marital trouble is more related to the breakdown of intimacy between the husband and wife. The solution is not to project the blame onto your teenagers but to focus on your mate and your marriage relationship.

Spend the necessary time to know your mate. This is not the same person you married years ago. Your mate has changed and has different needs, values, and goals. Get to know this new person, and then do your very best to help your mate achieve what he or she wants in life. Help your mate be the person God created him or her to be.

It will be only a few more years until your nest is totally empty. Then it will be just the two of you. Prepare now. Reestablish intimacy. Rekindle the fires so that the two of you have the emotional strength from a nourishing marriage to help your teenagers become all they need to be. Rebuilding intimacy now will also give you marital satisfaction and pleasure for years to come.

3. Realize that teens aren't all negative for the marriage relationship. Our daughters became true peers with us during their teen years. The earlier years of friendship, sharing, and casual discussions paid off. Each daughter had a fairly strong grip on her own personal development and was able to help strengthen us. They were concerned for our spiritual and emotional health, and they frequently encouraged us to take time off and to go on dates together. During both of our midlife crises, our daughters gave us encouragement and perspective.

Related Articles
Chapter 2: The Second Decade of Marriage
Chapter 2: Marriage and Midlife

Disagreements About Discipline

DEAN MERRILL

Did your parents believe in spanking? When your father became dead serious, did his voice get louder or softer? What about your mother?

Did you get paid for doing certain chores, or were they just expected as part of family obligation?

Did your parents set a minimum age

for dating, or did they wait to see how mature you were?

When you got in trouble, how long did it take for the "storm to blow over"? A day? A week? Five minutes?

The answers to these and a hundred other questions have shaped your approach to child discipline far more than you realize. By and large, you raise kids the way you were raised. So do we all. We may have consciously decided *not* to follow our parents' lead in one area or another, but such changes are the exception rather than the rule. Our general inclination is to repeat history. After all, *we* turned out pretty good, didn't we?

The trouble is this: your husband or wife didn't grow up in the same home you did. He or she brings to this marriage a different set of assumptions about the best way to raise kids. Who's right?

This question is more than just academic, because good parenting absolutely demands a united front. Kids are quick to notice discrepancies between Mom's way and Dad's way, Mom's rule and Dad's rule—and exploit them to the hilt. They find the cracks and borderlines, playing one parent against the other to their personal advantage. No wonder God designed marriage as a union of minds and hearts; He knew parenting would prove to be the acid test.

I once interviewed a father and mother who, try as they might, could not seem to come up with a common strategy for handling their headstrong son. He began smoking in junior high and then got into drugs; the week after he turned 16, he was picked up by the police. The worse his behavior became, the more the parents seemed to polarize: Mom wanting to protect her son, support him if at all possible, try to talk him into straightening up; Dad deciding it was time to wash his hands of the mess and let the School of Hard Knocks bear down on the boy.

UNITED DISCIPLINE

If there is harmony between husband and wife, they can stand together in discipline. It seems easier for parents just to let things slide, to let a child go unchallenged, than to make and enforce rules. But I can't think of anything parents could do to children more heartless than failing to discipline.

What a difficult situation for them to deal with all through life! How can they do well in school? How can they succeed on the job? What possible hope do they have for a good marriage? How can they adjust to letting God lead in their lives? So much depends on our learning how to accept and handle discipline when we are children. Then when we reach adulthood we know how to discipline ourselves. But in the family, if our discipline is to be consistent, it must have the full support of both husband and wife.

Janette Oke

They never did resolve their disagreement. As a result, the son kept getting mixed signals. His rebellion raged on until, at age 19, only a near-fatal construction accident brought him to his senses and back to the Lord.

Meanwhile, something worse had happened: the father found someone to agree with his disciplinary philosophy, a younger woman at work who said, "You're right—he's not a kid anymore. He's almost a grown man. Consequences have to take their toll." From this sliver grew a plank that split the marriage, spreading pain in all directions and also costing the father his career.

I came away from those interviews deeply saddened—and impressed as

353

never before with the importance of singlemindedness in discipline. There cannot be two policies under the same roof; Mom and Dad must speak with one mind. The children must know that when they've heard from one parent, they've heard from the other as well, and it won't do any good to ask again—they'll just get the same answer.

How do we come to consensus? Here are some steps:

1. *Set a clear goal of the kind of son or daughter you'd like your child to be at age 18.* What will the "finished product" look like? Make a list of your most desired qualities: initiative, kindness, honesty, thoroughness, punctuality, responsiveness to God, etc.

2. *Study how other successful Christian parents have done it.* Read the accounts of people all the way from Susannah Wesley to those in modern times, noticing what made their parenting efforts turn out as they did.

3. *Pray aloud together about your disciplinary tactics.* God is certainly as interested as the two of you are in raising a well-adjusted child. "If any of you lacks wisdom, he should ask God, who gives generously to all without finding fault, and it will be given to him" (James 1:5). Sometimes, after days of fruitless, solitary mind wracking, a solution pops up during these prayer times.

4. *Make the necessary time to confer privately.* This is often late at night, later than you'd wish. But make the time anyway. Work out your plan for handling sloppy rooms, backtalk, sibling squabbles, and all the rest. Be prepared!

5. *Refuse to be trapped by a child.* Don't accept, "But Mom said . . ." if it doesn't sound like something Mom would say. Not every question has to be answered right now. There's no sin in saying, "I'll get back to you about that," and then consulting with your spouse before issuing a response.

Kids deserve a steady hand on the controls of their lives. Otherwise, how will they become good parents themselves in 20 years?

Related Articles

Parenting as a Team Activity

KENN & BETTY GANGEL

In a recent survey of adolescents, researchers discovered that half of seventh-graders and two-thirds of ninth-graders reported cheating during the past year. Eighty-eight percent of the nation's ninth-graders claimed they lie to their parents, and 40 percent of high-school seniors said they get drunk on a regular basis.

Is the Christian home really different? In times like these, can two ordinary people work hard enough at parenting so that God will reward their efforts with righteous, obedient, and loving children? God will bless us, but not because we work hard. Rather, God's grace and blessing accompany our commitment to do things His way.

Let's try a simple metaphor. For the past two weeks, as we write these words, Dad has been playing in a two-on-two basketball league with our son as teammate. Basketball is always a team sport, and the importance of working as a team is heightened significantly in two-on-two. The two players may be very dif-

CHILDREN ARE PEOPLE TOO

Parents try to treat children like children, too often thinking of them as immature and unable to handle any responsibility. But it is far better to treat them in a manner consistent with their age and maturity. That means giving them the freedom to act their age. Let them be children while they're children, but train them to be the kind of children you want to live with—polite, responsible, patient, loving.

Don't talk down or at them and then expect them to act maturely. Rather, talk across. Involve the children in the process of building the family by allowing them to participate in any decision-making appropriate to their age—decisions about family rules, family chores, and spending family money, for example.

YFC Editors

ferent in height, positioning on the court, and ability, but they count equally in the game's outcome and the team's success. In many ways, effective teamwork on the basketball court is like the effective teamwork of husband and wife as they put together the "home team" for the game of life. To be an effective team player, remember the following:

Practice your game. Our league plays only one game a week, but both father and son bring to that game years of background in basketball that must be augmented by some regular practice commitment during the week. Team parenting likewise requires constant practice. Crises requiring parental wisdom are usually few and far between, but regular attention to our children's needs keeps us in shape and ready to respond in the big moments. Both team members need this kind of practice; one cannot delegate all the daily responsibilities to the other and then expect to step in and perform wonderfully when the grandstands are full.

Prioritize your participation. What if at one of our Monday-night games one team member just didn't show up? Busy schedules and legitimate excuses notwithstanding, the team would lose by default. Christian moms and dads often prioritize their team participation at personal sacrifice, but in no other way can the team learn to play together—and win. A recent survey shows middle-class fathers spend an average of 37 seconds a day talking with their children! A man with such a dismal record obviously has not made parenting a priority.

Plan ahead. In sports we call this a *game plan*. Even in our little amateur basketball league we have to agree on shared duties. Who will guard which player on the other team? Who'll play outside, and who'll be under the basket? What signals will we use? Every mom and dad needs a game plan. As Dolores Curran has reminded us, a healthy family exhibits a sense of shared responsibility.

Play according to the house rules. All basketball rules are not the same. They vary from high school to college and from college to professional play. Since our league plays on a racquetball court, the rules are very different.

Here the metaphor breaks down, because on a basketball court a referee enforces the rules. In a family, by contrast, the team polices itself and team members have to consistently observe whatever rules have been mutually agreed upon. If bedtime comes at 8:30, Dad doesn't regularly ask if Billy can stay up another hour while Mom pleads that he needs his sleep and has been tired and cranky of late. Of course there are exceptions, but in general the family team works better together when everyone knows and keeps the rules.

Pull together on court. Every once in a while we face teams who start quarreling during the game. One player blames the other for sloppy defense or too much shooting. Quickly their unity dissipates and with it, the quality of play. Parenting is like that. Yes, there will be disagreements as to what should be done with and for the children, but wise parents never quarrel "on court." If the plan is effective and we play according to the rules, all that's needed is a locker-room debriefing to decide what changes we'll make next time.

Praise your partner. It doesn't take much—"You really had your shot going tonight" or "I've never seen you so tough on defense" express appreciation for the privilege of being involved in joint team effort. And just as criticism between team members needs to be done in private, praise is wisely offered in public. What a model for a 10-year-old boy to see Dad complimenting Mom's dinner, her hairstyle, or a new piece of art she has just painted! What a biblical posture to be constantly uplifting and affirming one's lifetime partner and team member in the family!

Related Articles

How Infertility Affects Marriage

LYNDA RUTLEDGE STEPHENSON

"**S**o, when are you two going to have a baby?"

Today, one out of almost every five couples of childbearing age will face some sort of infertility problem. Over half of these couples will eventually have a child; the rest will not. But whether these couples have a child, adopt, or decide to live without children, the life crisis forced upon them by infertility is inherently also a marriage crisis.

The social pressure is intense, especially within the Christian community where raising children is somehow deemed the only natural thing to do. And slowly, questions like the preceding one turn from mildly annoying to very irritating to absolutely maddening. Yet the questions from "out there" only fuel the questions "in here."

Infertility is a force in marriage like no other. It is not so much an outer force as an inner one that nibbles away at areas hard to talk about: your individual self-image, your sexuality, your ways of responding to crisis—every area of your marriage from the inside out.

One woman said, "I feel a deep and profound sense of failure as a woman." Another woman had the erroneous idea that her husband's low sperm count, a very basic infertility problem, must reflect a lack of interest in her. Painful questions form in your minds: What kind of man am I if I don't have offspring? What kind of woman can I be if I never bear a child?

And the effect infertility has on a couple's sexual relationship is positively criminal. The medical workup intrudes so much that sometimes it seems as if there are three in the bedroom each

356

night—the wife, the husband, and the doctor.

Though a husband and wife may want to cope with this crisis through a united front, it just may not be possible at first. Because so many deeply personal issues are involved, the wife will more than likely find that she is coping in different ways than her spouse, and vice versa. That can begin a drift apart. The resulting scenario usually goes something like this:

He copes by keeping it to himself and focusing on her; she copes by expressing over and over how awful and unfair and frustrating everything is. She pushes more and more; he retreats more and more. He feels overwhelmed by her need because he is powerless to take away the pain; she feels abandoned when she needs him the most. The scene goes on night after night.

Some men may not feel the crisis as personally as their wives. Possible infertility is harder on women because of our culture's female role conditioning. A man's "life image" usually includes parenting along with many other things; a woman's often puts parenting in first place and includes the other things only afterward. But a woman cannot assume from her husband's silence that he isn't hurting too. Often a man will hold his feelings in, trying to be strong for his wife. He believes his emotions would only make her feel worse, when in actuality they would probably fill her with a sense of communion, of shared pain.

After months of this sort of tension, even a marriage made in heaven will feel the strain. Indirect channeling of anger can surface. Little things—a broken dish, a muddy floor—may cause you to blow up at each other when it's really infertility causing the anger.

The issue is so, so personal. Psychiatrist Miriam Mazor says, "Infertility makes couples take a harder look at each other. . . . They begin to assess the marriage at a stage when other couples are too busy with child care to do so." The marriage, then, must stand the glare of that spotlight and keep standing the glare for the duration of the infertility crisis, however long that turns out to be. How can a couple do that?

There's only one answer: communication.

That, of course, is easier said than done. But it must be done. Here are some suggestions:

1. *Begin by incorporating the "20-minute rule" into your discussions.* Set a timer, and then let the wife talk for 20 minutes about how she feels. At the end of 20 minutes, she has to stop. For many women, this means much less talking—and less is more in this instance. Surprisingly, when the wife talks less, the husband usually talks more. One good idea is for the wife to ask her husband, "What's it like for you?"

2. *Share how you feel about the medical encroachment on your intimate relationship.* Consider ways to separate "work sex," the times you are forced to make love for your infertility workup, and "play sex," the times you make love because you love one another.

3. *Stop and ask yourselves why you want to parent.* Yes, a child is of value. But isn't your marriage partner of much more value? A marriage is first and last a relationship of two, a nurturing of each other, a sacred union—if we believe our marriage vows. To think a child is needed for a healthy marriage is to miss the value of the marriage bond.

Infertility is a shared problem. Keeping your marriage healthy through this crisis may mean communicating in a new way, deeper than ever before. It may mean looking painfully deep into yourself, into your long-held beliefs about yourself, your marriage, and your priorities. It may mean listening painfully to the one you hold dearest. But the united front is possible. And surviving the emotional, mental, and physical stress of infertility can forge a marital bond that can face anything—and survive.

Related Articles
Chapter 9: Perspective: Seeing What Your Spouse Sees
Chapter 14: Helping Your Mate During a Time of Suffering

Childless By Choice

KRISTINE TOMASIK

The choice to be childless is not made lightly. It involves soul-searching by both husband and wife, usually over some years. What motivates this choice, and how does it affect a couple's life?

Deciding to pursue other life goals may be one of the biggest factors in the choice not to have children.

"I just never saw myself as having children," said Linnea, who comes from a big family. "I always saw myself as a doctor instead. I know what motherhood demands, and I didn't feel I could do both. The biggest reason I chose not to have children is because I felt called to do something else with my life."

Age is another factor.

"My wife and I feel we're just too old now to have children," said Todd. "The children would be teenagers when we are in our 50s. That would be too much!"

Some people feel unable to cope with the demands of children. "Whenever I'm around small children, I feel trapped," said Mary. "I feel as if I would simply be unable to give them the caring they constantly need."

For some, physical factors or extenuating circumstances help swing this most difficult of choices one way or the other. "I recently learned from my doctor that if I became pregnant, I would almost certainly miscarry again," said Mary. "It's hard, but that information helps me make the decision I've been wavering over for years: not to have children."

Other couples name other reasons—the need to care for parents or other relatives, reasonable expectation of producing a baby with a genetic defect, chronic or life-threatening disease, financial problems.

The choice to be childless is certainly one that a couple should make together. The decision process could involve comparing notes with both parents and non-parents to see the pros and cons from different points of view, spending time together baby-sitting other people's children, talking about your own personal feelings, and praying about the choice.

For some couples, the choice is clear from the outset of their marriage. "When we got married Ellen and I both knew we didn't want to have children," said Mark. "After a couple of years, we took permanent measures. That doesn't mean we don't both still wonder sometimes. But our confidence lies in the fact that we did indeed *choose*. We did not drift into childlessness."

For others, the choice is long and slow and agonizing. "We played Russian roulette with birth control for quite a while," recalled Linnea. "I wanted to give God a chance. Nothing happened, but my doctor was quite amazed that I didn't get pregnant."

However the choice is made, there are

some things it does *not* mean.

Choosing to be childless does not mean a couple is selfish. Many who take this route do so precisely so they can serve God and humanity better. "We want to use our time and energy to fully develop the talents of writing and teaching that God has given us," said Ellen.

Choosing to be childless does not mean a couple is "out of God's will." "There are many callings," said Linnea. "It is not every woman's calling to have children, though sometimes the church seems to think so. I'm hurt when people think my calling to serve God through being a physician is less valuable than their calling to serve Him through raising children."

Choosing to be childless does not mean the couple dislikes children. In fact, some couples choose not to have children of their own precisely so they can do more for other people's children. "We are loony about kids," said Mark, who together with Ellen teaches grade-schoolers and writes children's books. "But we are able to give as much as we do to our work and our kids because we know we can come home and be grown-ups. If we had children at home, we'd lack a vital refueling time."

How does choosing to be childless affect a couple's lives? What special problems do childless couples face?

"Holidays can be difficult," said Mary. "My parents are still living, and I enjoy visiting them, but sometimes it's hard to see everyone at holidays and think about the ideal of the generations continuing. Some of my happiest holidays are when I go out into the 'highways and byways' and invite people in who have no other place to go."

Linnea agreed. "I get a sense of family from knowing that I belong to the family of God, and the family of humanity," she said.

"I see my kindred in larger terms, and my offspring in those I nurture," said Ellen.

Old age is another consideration. "I know I may be lonely in my old age without children," said Linnea. "But then again, maybe not. One of the happiest old people I know is Dr. I. He never had a wife, let alone any children. He's in a nursing home, and he's nearly blind. But he's such a rich man! He loves people, and he shows them that he cares. His friends are friends for years and years. No, I don't think he's lonely.

"I knew an older woman, now deceased, who was also a very happy person without children," continued Linnea. "She lived with her sister. They both just loved their nieces and nephews.

"I think if you truly love God and try to follow Him, you're going to be satisfied no matter whether you choose the typical way of family or not," Linnea concluded. "I don't think this kind of satisfaction comes from having children. Nor can I expect it from my career. Real satisfaction comes from God."

Related Article

Chapter 2: Family of Two

Being In Step as a Stepparent

GARY D. BENNETT

Raising children is one of the most demanding jobs that any adult ever assumes. And the job of being a stepparent makes the responsibility even more difficult and frustrating. How can you stay in step as a stepparent and still preserve both your sanity and your marriage?

The answer lies in relationships—the depth of relationship you develop with your new spouse, and the personal relationship you cultivate with each of your stepchildren.

Upon Entering the Family

A problem that always comes up is what the children should call their stepparent. The very young child is almost always going to parrot whatever everyone else calls you, but the older child is caught in a dilemma. On the one hand, he doesn't want to call you the same name he calls his real parents, yet he may be the only one in the family not calling you Mom or Dad.

Adolescents may feel OK using first names if you are comfortable with such an arrangement. Some families have the children refer to the stepparent as Mother or Father and to their biological parents by the customary Mom and Dad. Other families have used a combination of title and stepparent's first name, such as Mom Susan or Dad Tom. Nevertheless, it's certainly good to discuss the matter with each other and the children so that everyone can agree on something that's both easy and comfortable.

Don't be surprised if, after you enter the family, the children drag out all their worst behaviors and perhaps some surprising new behaviors to see how much they can get away with. They may test the limits to see what the rules really are in this new family. Remember, this is normal and the natural way all children learn; so don't panic and feel that "he's worse than he was before."

Of course, during such a transition, it's imperative that you and your spouse keep talking. Don't allow the children to drive a wedge between the two of you. Present a united front. Agree on a set of realistic limits, state your rules, then follow through with the consequences of disobedience. With no consistent boundaries, children will keep on testing everything until each knows what his or her new role is and what is expected by this new family.

One of the best ways to help children accept the remarriage is to understand what they may be feeling. It's important to remember that separation, whether through divorce or death, represents a significant loss, especially to the child. Sadness, anger, guilt, and ambivalence are always present to some degree. When you help the children to acknowledge and identify their various feelings, they are quicker to accept the remarriage and strengthen the new family.

Supporting the Old, Developing the New

According to the Stepfamily Association of America, one of every five children belongs to a stepfamily. Stepfamilies are the fastest growing social phenomenon in our country today. Thirteen hundred new stepfamilies form daily, and often at the expense and devastation of the former family.

Stepparents and spouses must be

supportive of the "old" family members. Encouraging the children to talk about earlier childhood experiences, keeping pictures of "old family" events, and speaking respectfully of the other biological parent are some of the best ways to ensure the children's acceptance and adjustment to the remarriage and new family. Providing the children with memories of their past and helping keep those memories alive will also enable them to develop a wholesome sense of self.

Former relatives will react to the remarriage in various ways, but don't overlook the importance of including them in the children's new family life too. Whether it be grandparents, a favorite uncle, or a special cousin, each will add something worthwhile to the children's emerging sense of identity. Since significant relationships usually override legal status anyway, refusing to allow stepchildren contact with former relatives may backfire and cause you and your spouse more frustration than necessary.

We Are Family

All children need to belong and deserve a sense of security. Strive to give that protection to the children by creating an atmosphere of long-term commitment. Positive affirmations such as "We are family, and we will make it!" can go far in building confidence and unity.

As previously mentioned, the responsibility of stepparenting is a demanding and difficult task, but it's also one which can be extremely fulfilling and rewarding. As a stepparent, always be honest with yourself, your spouse, and the children. Be realistic, positive, and prepared to have your feelings hurt along the way. At times, it may feel like a thankless job, but focus on the big picture. Someday you and your spouse will be grandparents: today you are helping raise the future parents of your grandchildren. Doing your best now will pay great dividends later!

Building a Relationship With Your Stepchild

GARY D. BENNETT

A stepparent should begin initiating positive interactions with a stepchild as soon as they begin life together. Social interactions, not routine care, are the most important part of stepparenting. The more social interactions a stepchild has with you, the more strongly attached he becomes. If you happen to get off on the wrong foot in your relationship, don't give up. The following are good ways to build and promote a healthy relationship between you and your stepchild:

1. *Accept your stepchild as he is.* God made each of us with little differences that make us interesting. Appreciate your stepchild for the person he is without forcing him into your mold.

2. *Cultivate a love for him and make it known.* Tell your stepchild you love him, then show it. Most children need to see love in action as much as they need to hear it.

361

3. *Show affection.* Hugs, kisses, and physical closeness can break down barriers.

4. *Show genuine interest in his activities.* Support your stepchild's outside interests by providing transportation, or being an adult sponsor for one of his activities.

5. *Display interest in your stepchild's school performance.* Help him with homework when he needs it, but don't expect him to ask for help. Be careful not to nag.

6. *Trust your stepchild.* Show interest in and acceptance of his friends.

7. *Give your stepchild a place of importance.* Make him an integral part of the family unit by giving him a voice in family decisions and responsibilities in the home.

8. *Help your stepchild meet the expectations of his biological parent (your spouse).*

9. *Let your stepchild in on your own family jokes or sayings.*

10. *Read together; play games together.* Being together and doing things of common interest is a tremendous aid in building the relationship.

11. *Go shopping together and on special outings.* If the remarriage involves mixing sets of kids, take them out together sometimes and separately sometimes. Taking turns can be fun. You won't be so tired and each child can have a little special time alone with you.

12. *Teach your stepchild a new life skill.* Teach him how to cook, bake, change spark plugs, repair a door. Involve him with you as you carry out the normal tasks of maintaining a home.

13. *Be affectionately firm and con-*

PSALM 128:1-6

Blessed are all who fear the Lord, who walk in His ways. You will eat the fruit of your labor; blessings and prosperity will be yours. Your wife will be like a fruitful vine within your house; your sons will be like olive shoots around your table. Thus is the man blessed who fears the Lord. May the Lord bless you from Zion all the days of your life; may you see the prosperity of Jerusalem, and may you live to see your children's children. Peace be upon Israel.

---

sistent in discipline. It's extremely important that you and your spouse agree on discipline matters. Your stepchild generally will respond positively if he has understandable reasons for the expected behavior, and if you discipline fairly and lovingly.

14. *Minister to your stepchild.* Focus on his spiritual needs, questions, and emerging beliefs. Read Bible stories together, pray together, worship together. Cultivate his spiritual growth.

Remember too that shared laughter and tears are powerful bonding tools. Allowing yourself to be vulnerable will strengthen your relationship with your stepchild.

Related Articles
Chapter 3: Second Marriages: Two Important Issues
Chapter 11: Being In Step as a Stepparent

362

Creating New Christmas Traditions

PATRICIA GUNDRY

One problem with marriage is that we are making something completely new out of something completely old. We are thrilled with our new relationship. But our families of origin—our mothers and fathers, aunts and uncles, grandparents, and all those who came before them—are also a part of our marriage. They give us, among other contributions, tradition.

We feel things are right when we do what tradition has taught us line upon line, precept upon precept, experience upon experience. It doesn't feel right to do it the way the other spouse's family did it. That's not Christmas! That's new and uncomfortable and *not right.*

Just as we have taken the raw materials of two people and made a new relationship, though, we can take the raw materials of our separate traditions and make a new one that will be unique to our new family. But this probably won't happen automatically for most of us. For some people—those who live close enough to both families to be present at their gatherings and those whose family-of-origin's ways are compatible or complementary—blending traditions will be smooth and automatic. They won't need any help.

But you do need it—or you think you might need it later—or you wouldn't be reading this. You want to know how to solve the Christmas Problem.

We can learn a great deal here from those brave people who have created blended families; that is, because of death, divorce, or other reasons they have combined parts of two different families into one new one. These families find inevitably that they must start from scratch, assuming nothing.

They find that unless everything is spelled out specifically and forthrightly decided upon, anything and everything will cause conflict. Families do things differently. They give different meanings to the same things. And if you assume anything, it will turn out to be wrong.

Successfully blended families begin at the beginning and invent the family. They say, "We have here a man and a woman and a certain number of children. Here is who is going to do the dishes, and when they are to do them. Here is how you will know we want you to do this or that. Here is what will happen if you do not."

Only by meticulously creating a new set of requirements and expectations and carefully making them specific can the newly blended family live well together. To borrow from them their techniques for solving the Christmas Problem, you will need to create your own Christmas tradition for your own new family, from scratch.

This may not be easy, just as it isn't easy for blended families. It will take some trial and adjustment, experimenting with possible ways to do it. But if you approach Christmas from this perspective you can create a combination of elements from your homes of origin and/or an entirely new set of traditions that you set in motion yourselves.

Our families of origin are rich with useful information for us, and we are wise to retain it and use it appropriately and well. At Christmas, I often tell my family about my Grandma Dicy's Christmas behavior. When she arose Christmas morning she would say, "Christmas gift!" to whomever she met first. In fact, she would say it to several people if they did not say it to her first. Whoever said it first, she told us, was supposed to receive a gift. I don't remember ever hearing it said to her first or remembering to do so myself, nor did I ever see anyone give her a gift in response to her greeting. But she took great joy in this tradition from her childhood, even though her present family did not observe the custom by handing over a gift.

So while we may not choose to take part in some traditions and observations, we can incorporate them into our own observance by telling about them or by adapting them in some way.

If you want Christmas to be satisfying in spite of the wide difference between your traditions, invent your own Christmas. Make it the way you want it to be—together.

Related Articles

How to Develop a Pattern of Family Traditions

KENN & BETTY GANGEL

What reminds you of your childhood years? It might be a distinct smell, the taste of a certain food, or hearing a familiar song. Kenn grew up in a large Eastern city, so the hustle and bustle of an urban street or the sound of children playing in a vacant lot remind him of his early years.

Betty grew up on a Midwestern farm. When she hears the sounds of animals or smells the newly mown hay, her mind is drawn back to those years in her life.

Developing family traditions is, as Edith Schaeffer says, "building a museum of memories." Simply defined, traditions are the handing down of information, beliefs, and customs from one generation to another.

One thing we know for sure—couples who have cultivated traditions to practice regularly and then pass on to their children and grandchildren usually experience a close, secure feeling of togetherness. But how do we go about doing it? Start with special days such as birthdays and holidays. Carry on some traditions

that you knew as a child, and then begin to add new ones of your own.

A couple years ago we taught a family class for young seminary wives. They shared with us some of the traditions which were a part of their families. Birthdays were a natural beginning place. Here are some ideas the women in the class suggested:

The birthday person becomes the focus of all kinds of special treatment. He or she gets to choose the menu at home or a meal at some favorite restaurant. It usually includes a decorated cake, a tape recording of the day's activities, a birthday banner, a special plate, a notice in the local newspaper (if you live in a small town), pictures or slides of previous birthdays, and, of course, gifts.

Christmas is also a time filled with traditions. Make an effort to carry on certain family recipes, special ways to exchange gifts, or strategies to reach out to unsaved neighbors. There are so many things that can be included in the celebration of this wonderful time of the year; you may need to be selective so that you do not become overly busy. Remember you want the holiday activities to be an enjoyment for everyone.

Develop at least one tradition that reaches out to others. Deliver an anonymous present to a needy person's front porch on Christmas Eve; plan a Christmas program; go caroling for your neighbors; prepare extra Christmas goodies or a handmade gift for unexpected callers; or write a letter expressing appreciation to your pastor or Sunday School teacher.

Then, of course, you need to think up traditions of your own. Some things we did included trimming the tree on Thanksgiving weekend, making or buying a special new tree ornament each year, setting aside a day to make cookies, singing carols before opening our gifts, and taking an annual trip to Ohio to spend Christmas Eve with grandparents, aunts, uncles, and cousins.

Many family traditions just happen. All of a sudden you realize you've started doing something in a certain way, and it feels strange to do it any other way.

Our summer trips came about this way. When our children were still quite young, Kenn was doing considerable traveling for ministry. So when he was asked to teach at summer Bible conferences or camps, we decided to accept only if the entire family could also attend. That decision began a tradition of summer travel that took us all over North America and to 11 countries during the next 15 years.

Now married and establishing their own homes, our children still love to see the slides as we relive our summer adventures. Just the mention of a lake, a mountain, a city, or even a particular food will draw us back together to savor that precious moment again.

Some traditions do not just happen; they must be planned. Perhaps you have decided you, as husband and wife, need a regular weekly time together, so you

WHEN ADULT CHILDREN MOVE BACK IN

Few parents will turn away a needy child, even if that "child" is 30 years old. But when an adult child moves back home for longer than a week, problems inevitably develop.

- Who pays for the added expenses?
- Do house rules still apply?
- How is the housework divided up?
- Are friends welcome?
- How can all the adults in the family find the privacy they need?
- When does the adult child plan to move out again?

If one of your adult children moves back in, you can be sure you will have problems to face and solve, just as you did when you had that child in the first place. Remember that your relationship with your spouse takes precedence over your relationship with your child, especially now that your child is an adult. Stand together, and as a couple you can help your child through his or her time of crisis.

YFC Editors

set aside Friday evening, Saturday morning, or perhaps Sunday afternoon. Do something as a couple that you both enjoy, whether it's a game of tennis or a trip to the pizza restaurant. The key is the sameness and regularity of this special time together.

One couple has a "joy jar." Each person watches for some thoughtful deed performed by the other. He or she writes it down on a piece of paper and puts it in the "joy jar." At the end of the week, these are read. What a beautiful way to give compliments and praise!

Your special time might be just an evening of popcorn and games, a walk to the park, a bike ride, a trip to the mall, or reading in front of the fireplace.

Whatever your status—newly married, parents of young children, parents of teens, entering the empty-nest era, nearing retirement; whether you are a couple with no children, a single parent, or grandparents—develop a pattern of family traditions. When the people dear to us are gone or far away, happy memories still remain.

Related Articles

Enriching Your Marriage Through Grandparenting

JOHN GILLIES

As the years of marriage pass by and the anniversaries become silver, then golden, the relationship between wife and husband needs special nourishment. Retirement is not always fulfilling. One wife has said that retirement, for her, means "twice as much husband and half as much income." The nest is empty and, sometimes, so are our lives.

This is precisely the time when grandparenting can become a wonderful gift for us, as well as for our grandchildren.

My wife and I have found it to be so, though we were a bit slow in recognizing the possibility.

After our children married and moved away, Carolyn and I spent 10 years caring for our aging parents. One day we paused in our caregiving to remember that our children now had children of their own. Our grandchildren were growing and maturing, and we were missing a happy opportunity. Busy and sometimes overwhelmed in caring for our parents, we were overlooking the needs of the new generation. That had to change.

Of course, this wasn't a matter of our taking charge. Our sons and daughters wouldn't—and shouldn't—allow that to happen! Nevertheless, we knew we could help our children provide the stability and guidelines their children craved. We knew we could share ourselves.

We began to share by inviting our grandchildren into our home. Usually these are only overnight events, but they are important to both grandparent and grandchild. Each gets to know the other around a meal, while playing a game, or just chatting in front of a fire. Such occasions comfortably bridge the generation gap.

We've learned we must not do all the talking; we need to listen, without judging. We want to get to know these children—what they think, what motivates them, what troubles them, what excites them.

Still, we have the responsibility of sharing. We can tell what we have learned and felt and experienced. That's always better than preaching, especially if we reminisce with humor. Eric

Severeid says older people help youngsters, who haven't read much history or lived very long, reach back into the past. Also we can help them reach out, because we who are older have experienced so much more through our reading and travel. We can help them learn about their cultural, religious, and family heritage. We can demonstrate acceptable manners. We can help them experience the joy of making (not buying!) gifts for others. We can witness to our faith.

All this can be done quietly, without fanfare, without intimidation, within an environment that often only grandparents may be able to provide in today's fractured and frenetic society.

Gift-giving to grandchildren can become creative. We don't have to give that famous-label shirt this youngster thinks he can't possibly live without. Instead, we can give a good book, introduce him to stamp collecting or some other long-lasting hobby, or share a contemporary recording that sings about the Good News rather than despair.

We can also give gifts that last a lifetime. Grandparents may be the only persons who will give a child a never-to-be-forgotten experience in a summer camp, where one's inner strength is tested and one's need for a loving and enabling God is perceived. Happy is the grandparent who can share adventures with a grandchild, walking a nature trail, exploring a museum, or sitting together in church.

If grandchildren live far away, then grandparents will have to plan for visits. They can go themselves, or they can arrange for grandchildren to visit them. And if the grandchildren are simply too far away, geographically or emotionally, then we can still practice the art of grandparenting as surrogate grandparents. There are dozens of love-starved children around us who might yet thrive if we helped fill their void.

Reaching out is the perfect antidote for loneliness and will help a husband and wife recapture a sense of meaning and purpose for their lives. Reaching out to one's grandchildren and great-grandchildren can renew us, and them.

Carolyn and I are closer to each other as we play with our grandchildren and pray for them. With the psalmist we also petition: "So even to old age and gray hairs, O God, do not forsake [us], till [we] proclaim Thy might to all the generations to come" (Ps. 71:18, RSV).

Related Article
Chapter 2: Making the Later Years Even Better

AGING PARENTS

Husbands and wives would be wise to think about the fact that their parents are aging and may, at some point, need various levels of assistance from their children. Each spouse needs to face the possibilities that could arise and discuss the consequences as a couple *beforehand*. For example, is one spouse against the idea of grandparents moving in? How would you handle special-care needs? Remember this: although we must be willing to help our parents, we don't want to destroy our marriage in the process.

In addition to communication between spouses, communication among siblings is equally vital. If the need arises, can Mom and Dad live with one while the others chip in financially?

And, although difficult, it would be wise for siblings to talk about the future with their parents. Have wills been prepared? What kind of insurance coverage do Mom and Dad have, etc.?

YFC Editors

YOUR MOTHER, YOURSELF

Most of marriage's great promises I
Made to you—
And yet you were the daughter of
the very woman
Who became my mother too.
How I wish I might have made my
understanding fuller . . .
My promises more wide.
Did I forget that your mother was
as dear
to you as mine was to me?
Did I forget that those two hyphens
between in and law
were only my petty ways to spell
her name?
Did I need to try her need to be the
way she was
with all my pseudo-elite standards?
Was it right to force her to watch
Olivier do Lear
and resent her fondness for old
Lucille Ball reruns?
Did I need to isolate your loyalty in
petty quarrels of ego
to make you choose between your
mother and myself?
Only at last did I come to see her
as the
giver . . . a great giver. She gave
me
what I prize the most in life—you.
You were her gift of excellence
that she gave gloriously to me.
Now I see that it was the way
she gave the gift that was so
glorious.
I remember now her sewing on
your wedding dress.
She would present you in the
church—
the only church that you and she
had ever known—
to all her friends.

She would stitch each tiny pearl in
the lace
as if its glistening small importance said,
"She is mine. With God's help I
made her
before God bade me give her up.
Once God's gift to me, now my gift
to Him.
He, her unsure cavalier, must
take her to his home.
He, her groom, is the receiver of
my gift.
He has no idea how I feel in the
giving.
God help the years to teach us
both."
And so the years did teach, and
being
taught I know, now, how special
is the word that blessed my
life: mother-in-law.
The matchless pledge of Ruth 1—
the "entreat me not to leave thee"
pledge—
was made by a daughter-in-law to a
mother-in-law.
I read it, now, and
Wonder that I came
Too late to know its wisdom.
And of your mother, my in-law,
Does she wait, as Hebrews 11 says,
Among the cloud of witnesses
Who gave their gifts and joined
God?
I hold even yet
The gift she gave me
Back three decades past.
It's new each morning,
Better filled with meaning
Than it was that simple
Day in May she gave it.

Calvin Miller

Getting Along With In-laws

WESLEY & ELAINE WILLIS

Someone once observed that Adam and Eve got along as well as they did because neither had any in-laws to worry about. While it's true that they had no in-laws, it's also true that they had problems anyway.

Many feel that talk of in-law problems constitutes a self-fulfilling prophecy. We hear jokes, dire warnings, and counsel on how to deal with situations that we fear will arise. Is it any wonder there are conflicts with in-laws?

Quite the opposite, many of us can testify to the important role that in-laws have played in our marriages. In the Willis family, we are keenly aware of the strategic role parents have played in our lives. And now that we are married with teenage children of our own, parents continue making contributions to our family.

But the fact remains that some families have relationship problems with in-laws. All the jokes, warnings, and advice persist because of such situations. We know that where there is smoke, there's fire (except on a camping trip). So how do we minimize the problems and build meaningful relationships with parents as we establish our own families?

1. *Expect no problems.* Though it may seem unrealistic, we should seek a relationship without problems. And while this may not always be our actual experience, a positive attitude helps. Several days ago we were talking with Kevin, our 16-year-old, about how he shoots soccer goals. When he takes a shot, he always expects to score. And while he doesn't always succeed, he has the right attitude. If he approaches the ball thinking to himself, "I know I'll miss; I'm sure the ball will go over the goal," his chances of scoring will be greatly reduced.

The same is true in relationships. We should always look for the best and expect no problems. For if we begin negatively, we often will find that our expectation becomes a self-fulfilling prophecy. As the story goes: a man moving to a new city asked a longtime resident what the people were like. The resident inquired, "What were they like in your old town?" The newcomer replied that they were hostile, aloof, and unkind. "That's the same kind you'll find here," the resident predicted. Another newcomer asked the oldtimer the same question and received the same question in return. The newcomer answered that in his old town, people were open, friendly, and kind. The resident said, "That's the same kind you'll find here."

2. *Build your own new family traditions.* Often in-law problems arise if the newlyweds adopt the traditions of one family to the exclusion of those of the other. The result is that one set of parents feels rejected, and so they competitively try to regain what they see as a loss of influence. By personalizing new traditions, we can draw on the best from each family.

New traditions are especially important at holiday times. Over the years, one Willis tradition is spending Christmas holidays with relatives. Even though it has meant traveling many miles, we and our boys have deeply appreciated the times we have spent together. We made sure, however, that we spent roughly equal time with both sets of relatives. In that way we were able to establish new

369

traditions while not implying rejection of either family.

3. *Value your spouse's family.* There is no such thing as a self-made man or woman: all of us have received input from many sources. God has used all our previous relationships and experiences to bring us to where we are today. And while many things may have happened to us that were negative in themselves, even those have played a strategic part in helping us become who and what we are.

Recognize that your spouse's parents were part of God's plan. Though they certainly did not do everything perfectly, nevertheless God worked through them. Appreciate them for bringing your spouse into the world; for time, energy, and money invested in child rearing; and especially for being part of God's sovereign plan. Value their strategic contribution to your life through your spouse.

4. *Respect in-laws as individuals.* For some reason we often expect far more from relatives than we ever would from friends. We permit friends to have their little idiosyncrasies, their own preferences and independent opinions. But when in-laws register any differences or foibles, we often become irritated and intolerant.

This respect includes recognizing that in-laws have needs and feelings too. Some needs include communication and a sense of being valued. In the Willis family, Elaine is much better at recognizing and meeting those needs. Wes does not do too well at remembering special occasions and does even worse at phoning and writing letters. In other families, the roles may be reversed. But however it is handled, we must plan regular and meaningful ways to show that we value and respect our in-laws, even if sometimes they act in what we might think are bizarre ways.

5. *Keep visits short.* Recently Wes was talking to parents who moved to a town near where their son and his family lived. They told him that a great benefit was being able to enjoy the grandchildren in small doses. When they lived far away, the son's family came occasionally for extended visits. This ran the grandparents ragged, exhausted the parents, and stressed out the children. Ben Franklin's advice could be paraphrased, "Fish and grandchildren begin to smell after three days."

6. *Seek parents' wisdom.* In-laws want to be valued and respected. Most of them know you need to make decisions for yourself. But they will feel less obligated to give unsolicited advice if you periodically consult them about your plans.

Shortly after we were married, we asked Elaine's parents for advice on a decision we had to make. They later told us that whether or not we took their advice was irrelevant: they deeply appreciated the fact that we respected them enough to include their opinion as part of our input. It only makes sense to draw on the wisdom and insight of mature relatives. And God has instructed us to seek wise counsel.

When we ask for counsel, we should communicate that we value good suggestions but still have to make our own decisions. After we have secured wise input from various sources, our decision will be the best one possible.

It *is* possible to get along well with in-laws. As a matter of fact, many of us can testify to appreciating and loving them deeply. And even though you would never guess it to hear many of the jokes, parents have made—and will continue to make—significant contributions to the lives of countless families.

Related Articles
Chapter 3: Before You Say, "I Do"
Chapter 11: How to Develop a Pattern of Family Traditions

PARENTS MOVING IN

Deciding to bring grandparents into the family circle is a major decision that needs to be discussed and agreed on by both husband and wife. Many will say that it is the only option—of course Mom and Dad should move in. But it would be unfair to push that decision on a spouse who is unsure how the system will work out, or who may feel that the marriage is being sacrificed for the family.

Before such a step is taken, both husband and wife (and children too) need to talk through the special needs, the extra responsibilities, and potential conflicts. If it is a family decision, it can be an extremely positive experience.

Talk with the grandparent(s) beforehand and try to head off any major conflicts before they occur. If the grandparents are able, bring them in as part of the family, responsible for certain jobs around the house—this will make them feel both needed and less of a burden. If they are immobile or unable to do certain tasks, they will probably be willing to help with homework or just be a listening ear when the children come home from school. Grandparents have years of wisdom and guidance that they can give to children, sometimes more effectively than parents can. Children gain the wonderful opportunity to get to know their grandparents, an opportunity many of today's children don't have.

But, just as in adding a child to the family, the husband and wife need to be sensitive to each other's needs and be sure to take time to be together away from the kids and Mom and Dad. They need to agree to keep an openness that allows communication of problems before problems become out of hand.

YFC Editors

Embracing the Extended Family
V. GILBERT & ARLISLE BEERS

If a plumber or electrician needs extensive training to do his job well, why not a husband? If a nurse must have educational preparation to do her job well, why not a wife? We may smile at the idea of a course called Husband 101 or Wife 102 (although there are sociology courses in marriage), but in a sense we have all taken a course in marriage relationships. As children we observed our parents and their peers, and though we may not have consciously formulated a philosophy of husband-wife relationships from them, subconsciously we did.

But this is becoming more and more difficult in our era of broken marriages. The once "ideal" role models are becoming rare. The traditional family is

371

changing, almost before our eyes. And many of us are finding that our parents cannot give us all the help we need as we manage families of our own.

When we were children, we thought *family* meant a mother, father, boy, girl (perhaps several boys and girls), dog, cat, and maybe a goldfish. It meant a house with a mortgage, a station wagon with wood-grain paneling, and a life insurance policy or two. Father was the wage earner; mother stayed home to take care of the children and clean the house. Our parents expected to present a reasonably exemplary model of husband-wife relationships because they knew their children were watching and listening.

But the stereotype is gone, even in Christian homes. There is no traditional family anymore; a family today may be managed by a single parent or by two parents who are wage earners; and the wife may be better trained and more successful, earning more than the husband. The roles for husbands and wives, even in successful Christian homes, are likely to be different from those of our parents.

In this time of rapid changes, we may want to follow some of our parents' patterns but not others. It is unreasonable to expect most children to want to duplicate their parents' husband-wife relationships in every detail. At best there are gaps in the modeling process, gaps that others must fill. Sometimes children cannot see certain qualities because of circumstances. For example, a father may want to be helpful, but his job may take him away from the home where the children could observe his helpfulness. Or the cares generated by a tight budget during the children's growing-up years might choke out a fun-loving spirit in one or both parents.

Furthermore, parents are seen at some distance because they are parents—disciplinarians as well as a loving couple. As children grow up, they may see the disciplinarian role more than the loving husband-wife role. The children themselves will not become disciplinarians until their own children come along.

To develop our own philosophy of the husband-wife relationship, we may need to reach out beyond our parents to other role models and counselors. The extended family has always been important for this kind of input. Uncles, aunts, grandparents, and in-laws have always been a rich source of counseling and role modeling for those who are yet to become husbands and wives.

The heartbeat of extended-family role modeling is the relationships that go one step beyond parenting. A grandparent is one step beyond *vertically,* a parent's parent; while an aunt or uncle is one step beyond *horizontally,* a parent's peer.

Grandparents have a special relationship with their child's child. Even grandparents have a difficult time explaining it. Being a grandparent is a privilege with less responsibility than being a parent. The grandparent can offer guidance without having to give parental discipline. The grandchildren, in return, often think that Grandpa and Grandma can do no wrong. This matures into the conviction that they will do no harm. Children whose grandparents have been married long and happily have a rich heritage as they go into their own marriages.

Aunts and uncles have special opportunities to counsel their nieces and nephews and model the Christian graces for them. By observing the marriages of their parents' siblings, young people learn more about family living than they could ever pick up from books. Fortunate is the young person who has committed Christian aunts and uncles to help present in word or action what it means to live for Christ!

In-laws offer still other opportunities for learning about husband-wife relationships. They are especially valuable to the young spouse who is trying to figure out why his or her partner is acting a particular way! Arlie and I could never understand or appreciate mother-in-law jokes, because we both enjoyed delightful relationships with our mothers- and fathers-in-law. We obviously did not care to duplicate all facets of the relationships we observed in one another's parents, but we gained new perspectives on our own relationship that we would not have learned from observing our own parents alone.

Even friends can be part of the extended family that helps a young couple prepare for marriage—friends of your parents or parents of your friends can provide role models that will help you see what marriage can be like.

Embrace the extended family wherever you find exemplary role models—grandparents, uncles, aunts, in-laws, friends. Your Husband 101 or Wife 102 course will be significantly enriched by what you observe and hear from these important people.

And for those of you who are grandparents, uncles, aunts, in-laws, or friends, here is a ministry that will reap great dividends. How rewarding to know we have had a part in the process of establishing a permanent, Christian husband-wife relationship between two young people we love! That kind of ministry will surely please the Lord as well.

Related Article
Chapter 11: Getting Along With In-laws

What Friends Contribute to Your Marriage

BOB & CINNY HICKS

No man is an island, and neither is a marriage. Unfortunately, with the loss of the extended family, many couples are dying for the lack of friends. At a time when couples have never had more opportunities and discretionary income, many live isolated lives. In our ministry, we constantly hear couples expressing their simple need for friends.

George Eliot said it clearly: "Oh, the comfort, the inexpressible comfort of feeling safe with a person; having neither to weigh thoughts nor measure words but to pour them all out just as it is, chaff and grain together, knowing that a faithful hand will take and sift them, keeping what is worth keeping and then with the breath of kindness blow the rest away" (quoted in Alan Loy McGinnis,

The Friendship Factor, Augsburg, 1979, p. 36).

In our overstressed, nomadic society, every couple needs mutual friends to lend support, give accountability, offer perspective, and add fun and variety to life.

Good friends lend support to one's marriage. In the past there has always been a supportive network of family, community peers, and friends. However, today most couples live a great distance from family and the close friends of their youth. Consequently when questions about parenting or how to fix a faucet arise, each couple must face them very much alone, without personal help.

Support means coming alongside and sharing the load with someone. This is a basic biblical concept (Gal. 6:2). At times the couple is the object of this support, and at other times, the giver. We received support from many friends when the Lord unexpectedly made it possible for us to take a month-long trip to the Holy Land. Two couples took over the care of our three children during this time with only one day's notice. We left with full confidence that our children would be fine.

During our pastorate in Hawaii, many of our Navy wives were left for six months while their husbands were out on sea duty. One mother who had become a close friend to Cinny found it very frightening to be home alone at night. On many occasions either Cinny or another friend would spend the night with her. This support was necessary for the survival of her family, and it was very much appreciated by her absent husband.

Good friends contribute accountability to a marriage. Cain's question still confronts us today—are we our brother's keeper? (Gen. 4:9) The whole Bible teaches that we are indeed responsible for the welfare of others (see, for example, the Parable of the Good Samaritan in Luke 10:29-37). This argues for a relational accountability. Every couple needs someone who loves them enough to confront their weaknesses, faults, and sins in a caring way.

Many today intentionally strive for accountable relationships. We feel, however, that the best accountability grows out of a mutual love-trust relationship. It is earned, not demanded. It is difficult to hold friends accountable, because we fear rejection, misunderstanding, and loss of friendship. Anytime one confronts a friend, the relationship is put in jeopardy. But Proverbs 27:5-6 declares that the wounds of a friend, painful though they may be, are faithful, for they grow out of a love willing to risk misunderstanding and rejection for the sake of another's well-being.

Good friends contribute perspective to a marriage. The longer one is married, the more one tends to become hardened and inflexible. As Howard Hendricks has said, "Hardening of the viewpoint is far more devastating than hardening of the arteries."

One's viewpoint is naturally enlarged through friends. From various friends Bob has learned about plumbing, computers, foreign policy, military tactics, and how to dress for success. Through love and appreciation, a close friend has enabled Cinny to be aware of personal strengths that for years she had disregarded. As one writer put it, "Our opinion of people depends less upon what we see in them, than upon what they make us see in ourselves" (*The Friendship Factor,* p. 40).

Whether the issue is finding God's will, seeing the specialness of our spouse, or selecting wallpaper, friends provide the fresh perspective. The writer of Proverbs might see them as the precious and pleasant riches that fill one's home with needed understanding and wisdom. "By wisdom a house is built, and through understanding it is established; through knowledge its rooms are filled with rare and beautiful treasures" (Prov. 24:3-4).

Good friends contribute fun and variety. Couples tend to get into a rut—a shallow grave—and become uninteresting through the years. Shared interests, sports, and other fun times provide a spontaneous context for friendships between couples and others to develop. It enables us to come out of ourselves, lighten up, and laugh. As a couple, we had never played tennis together. Some good friends brought this skill into our life. We began playing a couple of times a week in doubles matches. This was fun, and it also brought a new dimension to our marriage. Seeing your spouse run around in cute tennis clothes is most appealing!

Through other close friends we have

broadened our experiences by sharing vocational interests and problems. We would probably never have seen how a television news program is run if a friend had not brought us into her world of newscasting. We might never have seen the birth of a new stage play without an actor friend and his wife who allowed us to be part of their creativity and struggles in the world of the theater. As a result of the experiences friends have brought into our lives, we are far more interesting to ourselves and to each other.

Friends contribute freshness, stimulation, and vitality to marriage. We need to break down the barriers of busyness, fear of rejection, isolation, and whatever else may separate us from the exciting world of friendship. Our friends are one of our greatest shared gifts. Throughout the years, they have brought us unforgettable moments of love. Through their support, our mutual accountability, their perspective, and the catharsis they have brought through shared laughter and tears, we are better people, better marriage partners, better Christians. Our cup runneth over!

Related Articles
Chapter 11: Embracing the Extended Family
Chapter 16: How Friends Can Help

Feel as if you have less time than you used to? Make an inventory of all the things you do in a typical week.

You have 168 hours to use. Are you satisfied with the way you use them? What could you cut out or trim down so that you have more time for the more important activities—time with your spouse, for example, or time for private devotions?

Activity	Hours spent per week HUSBAND	WIFE
Getting ready for the day	——	——
Commuting	——	——
Working (for money)	——	——
Housework	——	——
Yard work	——	——
Errands	——	——
Child care	——	——
Chauffeuring	——	——
Meal preparation	——	——
Meal cleanup	——	——
Eating lunch	——	——
Eating dinner	——	——
Talking on phone	——	——
Watching TV	——	——
Shopping	——	——
Reading	——	——
Paying bills	——	——
Church	——	——
Devotions	——	——
Recreation	——	——
Couple time	——	——
_____	——	——
_____	——	——
_____	——	——
_____	——	——
_____	——	——
_____	——	——
_____	——	——
_____	——	——
_____	——	——
_____	——	——

MANAGING TIME

The experimental biologist, Hudson Hoagland, concluded that there is some kind of chemical pacemaker in the brain, which allows us to sense the passage of time. Time is wedded to our material world, and we measure it by change. Since change is perceived differently by men and women, married couples often discover that usage of time becomes a matter of dissension and disagreement.

"A woman," says Dr. Arthur C. Custance, Christian physicist, "is timing life, not by the even spacing of the minutes or the hours in the way a man times his, but in cycles which are longer and not nearly so precise." He describes her sense of time as "event oriented."

Whereas all other basic resources of natural life vary, time is a constant, the one thing we all have in common. We can neither get more of it, nor store it away.

Two biblical references reveal God's purpose in giving us time. Moses prayed, "Teach us to number our days aright, that we may gain a heart of wisdom" (Ps. 90:12). Paul advised believers to make the most of every opportunity "because the days are evil" (Eph. 5:16). A proper view of time is the framework for a productive lifestyle. God tells us that when we understand how many, and what kind, of days we have, we will be able to use them wisely.

Howard & Jeanne Hendricks

How Much Time Should We Spend Together?

JUDITH ALLEN SHELLY

Marriage is a special relationship. In the words of the Apostle Paul: "We [Christians] are members of [Christ's] body. 'For this reason a man will leave his father and mother and be united to his wife, and the two will become one flesh.' This is a profound mystery—but I am talking about Christ and the church" (Eph. 5:30-32).

Most of us have observed committed Christians who were once active in the church and eager for fellowship, but gradually fell away from involvement. Perhaps the pressures of school and community events kept them from participating in weekday activities at church. Then late-night commitments on Saturdays made it hard to get up on Sunday morning, so they stopped coming to Sunday School. Eventually they were missing Sunday worship more often than not. They still claimed to love the Lord, but their priorities were shaped by the demands of the world rather than by their relationship to God. The same pattern can develop in a marriage before we realize what is happening.

Sheila and Ray love each other passionately, but see each other only on weekends. They each hold high-powered jobs in cities 400 miles apart. After four years of commuting, they are beginning to realize that they do not really know each other. Most of their hopes, dreams, and thoughts are centered in their jobs and their separate circles of friends. Their marriage has been an exciting weekend diversion, but the hassles of commuting are making their relationship wear thin.

Connie and Andrew are young and struggling to get started on their own. Connie became pregnant before they felt they were able to afford a child, so after the baby was born they both decided to continue working full time, on separate shifts, in order to save money for a house. They seldom see each other awake, and when they do, they are exhausted.

Marie and Jeff are the parents of three teenagers. The children are involved in sports, band, choir, youth group, and showing dogs and horses. Most of the parents' free time is taken up with driving to special events, which are often double scheduled. Marie serves on several church committees, teaches Sunday School, and is active in community organizations. Jeff is a volunteer fireman and serves on the church board. The family seldom has a meal together. Marie and Jeff almost never make time to sit down and talk with one another alone. Life is too busy.

All of these people would say that they love their spouses deeply. None of them could identify any major disagreements between them. However, each of these marriages is in trouble. Though all three couples are legally married, none of the basic ingredients of a marriage listed by Paul in Ephesians—leaving, being united, becoming one flesh—is present in their relationships.

Paul, quoting Genesis 2:24, spoke of *leaving* father and mother. In other words, a couple is to forsake former primary allegiances for one another. In our society, that primary allegiance may not be to our parents. It is more likely to a career, or a sense of independence, or even a set idea of what must be achieved in order to be successful (for example, education, money, prestige). If we are to be faithful to God's requirements for a healthy marriage, anything (aside from our relationship with God) which prevents us from putting our spouses first needs to be left at the altar when we say our marriage vows.

Being united is more than obtaining a marriage certificate or even living in the same house. It involves functioning together as a unit. By working together, a married couple should be able to accomplish more than the combination of both spouses working independently. Though at times this may require couples to be temporarily apart from one another, unity can develop only through spending quality time together. Part of the quality is quantity: unless couples spend adequate time working, praying, worshiping, dreaming, and talking together, they never get to the final goal in marriage—becoming one flesh.

Becoming one flesh is expressed in the sexual relationship, but it encompasses one's whole personality. Sex, even in marriage, without a total giving over of oneself to the spouse, becomes an empty symbol. It can also become a duty, a weapon, or a game. We are sexually attracted to someone who accepts us unconditionally, hears us when we hurt, shares our joys and triumphs, and sticks with us when everyone else seems to turn away. *Becoming* implies a process, and a process takes time. Becoming one flesh takes a lifetime of shared thoughts, hopes, fears, joys, and struggles.

When Jim and I were first married, he made it clear that he did not want me to go away overnight without him. I worked for a Christian organization that expects its staff members to travel, so I had to do a bit of negotiating between Jim's desires and my supervisor's expectations. Both tried to be understanding, and we came to a reasonable compromise: I continued to travel to a few staff conferences and task forces, and Jim went with me to a number of conferences and camps.

Not everyone was as understanding as my supervisor. Several friends and colleagues complained that Jim and I spent too much time together. They told us we should develop more separate interests and activities. Several of those who voiced their opinions the loudest are now divorced.

True sharing occurs only when two people are together. Invariably when I am away, Jim will face some major crisis at work or at home. Sharing on the phone simply is not the same as being there to support him. If one of us is away at a particularly inspirational conference, it is very difficult to communicate the spiritual growth that took place when it was not a common experience.

Our culture constantly pulls at us to spend time apart. Even the church can separate couples and families from one another unless they carefully plan their time together. Couples with young children may find that all their together time is consumed with child care rather than focusing on one another's needs and concerns. Even good things come between us.

Jim and I have found it necessary to set aside strategic times when being together is a definite priority. We put those times on our calendars and be-

---

ALL WORK AND NO PLAY

All work and no play makes for a dull marriage. Recreation revitalizes a relationship. Going for a walk, having a meal out, sharing a humorous incident from the day's activities, swimming, jogging, playing games with friends—these are all ways to "re-create" a marriage. The sole requirement is for the activity to be one you both enjoy.

David Foster

---

come almost legalistic in sticking to our plans.

First in our priorities is a daily half-hour before bed when we sit down together to talk and pray. We review the events of the day and discuss our thoughts and feelings, then commit them to the Lord.

Worship services are important shared times, even though we cannot sit together except on rare occasions when Jim is not conducting the service. I know that Jim depends on my support and encouragement every Sunday, so I do not volunteer for nursery duty or other activities that might take me out of the worship service.

Every Monday is family day. Monday evening is our special time together as a couple. It is the only time during the week when we know we can relax together with no other demands on us, and it has become sacred.

We also try to have a shared ministry project. Our jobs keep us going in separate directions, though with similar goals, much of the time. My ministry within the church helps to reinforce and support Jim's leadership, but it is not usually something we do together. The project we currently share is cochairing a synod-wide world missions committee in our denomination. It gives us a rare evening out together, making the hour's drive each way to the meetings enjoyable. We share a passionate desire to see churches in our area gain a vision for missions, and we are enjoying seeing that happen as we work together.

Different couples arrange their priorities differently, but the principle remains the same: whatever is most important to you and your spouse should be a shared experience. The sharing needs to be total, including physical presence as well as talking about your thoughts, feelings, hopes, and dreams. Such mutual interdependency is rare in a culture that glorifies rugged individualism. Nevertheless, it is essential. It takes time to leave previous allegiances and forge new ones; it takes time to be united; it takes time to become one flesh. But these are the basic ingredients of marriage.

Related Articles

PRINCIPLES OF TIME MANAGEMENT

1. Before the day begins—either early in the morning or late the night before—make a list of what you plan to do.
2. Assign priorities to your tasks. If the task simply must be done, label it "A." If you could reasonably ignore it or do it another day, label it "C." Label the other tasks "B."
3. Do all the "A" tasks before beginning any "B" tasks. Do all the "B" tasks before beginning any "C" tasks.
4. Beware of time stealers.

YFC Editors

Taking Time for Yourself

KRISTINE TOMASIK

It takes two whole people to make one whole marriage. To be a whole person, we need to spend time on ourselves. While we're single, that can be easier to do. But once we marry and assume the full sphere of adult activities—job, church, friends, community, and family—time for ourselves can evaporate. As a result, we simply don't take time for "me"! In the face of such neglect, "me" can shrivel up and wither away. And that can mean trouble for the marriage, if half the partnership is missing.

It is important to take time for oneself, but it is scary. Accustomed to rushing from one item on our agenda to the next, we are frightened at the idea of just sitting quietly by ourselves. Or perhaps we feel it would be selfish to spend time on just ourselves. But without time alone, personal growth—and marital growth—ceases.

Here are some approaches that have helped many people get to know themselves and gain or regain their sense of self to contribute to the marriage.

Meditation. Have you ever closed your eyes, entered into your silent secret

BENEFITS OF THE FAMILY DINNER TABLE

Taking time to sit down as a family and have dinner together is extremely important for family togetherness—even if it's just husband and wife. It is important to use the time wisely—don't allow the dinner table to be the place to drag out arguments or to punish your children. Instead, let the family dinner time include an exchange of communication and information. Catch up on each other's lives; talk through schedules and head off potential problems. It should be a time when everyone can relax and be themselves, an oasis and buffer against the pressures of daily living. Have fun, laugh together, pray together, have family devotions. Learn to enjoy time just as a family.

YFC Editors

center with God, and just listened in stillness? This is meditation. It is being alone with yourself and with God.

It is not necessary to meditate on anything, though some may use the words of a Psalm to begin. That is because meditation is not the same as thinking. It is *being.*

Having a place to just *be* is very important for meditation. One pastor goes into the church sanctuary for his 5 to 15 minutes of meditation. There, he says, no phones ring. And if anyone sees him, they think twice about interrupting.

Those of us without a ready-made sanctuary need to find one. It's humorous, but I personally have found bathrooms to be wonderful places of sanctu-ary, especially at work. It's possible to slip quietly into a stall, meditate for a brief moment, and return to work quite refreshed. Conference rooms, stairwells, and other out-of-the-way corners can also make great office sanctuaries.

Just as important as having a *place* of sanctuary is having a *time* for meditation. Are there a few minutes during your day when time naturally seems to slow a bit? Perhaps it's after the kids leave for school. Maybe it's just after morning coffee break at the office, when people are still slowly drifting back to their desks. Or maybe it's during that midafternoon lull.

Nothing is as essential to personal growth as meditation. It should become as regular as breathing. As you meditate in God's presence, what is important for you will begin to emerge. Your life will begin to come into focus.

Journaling. As you grow in your ability to take time for yourself, plan to spend some time writing in a journal.

A journal is *not* a record of the day's events, like a junior-high diary. Instead, it's a conversation with yourself.

You may want to write your journal in dialogue form. Ask yourself how you are feeling about certain events or about how it feels just being you right at that moment. Then answer. You can give the two parts of yourself different names, if you like, to tell them apart.

Many people find that keeping a record of their dreams is a fine way to stimulate personal growth. Others find that writing out their conversations with God is very useful. You will find your own journaling styles as you experiment.

Exploring. As you become more advanced in your ability to take time for yourself, try this: take a half day or an evening just for yourself. You don't necessarily have to spend money, although you can if you want to.

Go somewhere other than your home, office, church, or other usual haunts. (Beware of shopping—that may not count.)

Take yourself out to some little place for coffee and dessert. Go to the library to read a book. Set foot in a building you've never been in before. Take in a movie or a play. Go for a walk in the woods or along a river or lakeshore. Have an adventure, all on your own.

This time, don't go with someone else. In drawing him or her out, you might forget yourself. The point is to take yourself seriously enough to get to know yourself. Going by yourself will help you remember you.

Spending time with a mentor. A final way to encourage personal growth can't be done alone. But although you don't do it by yourself, you still focus on yourself. Whether you call your helper a mentor, a spiritual director, a pastor, or a therapist, his or her task is to serve as your mirror. He or she does this by listening to you and reflecting your self back to you. Friends, colleagues, and spouses may be mentors of each other.

Why do we need this important other person in order to grow? Too often, our own images of ourselves are skewed. We think we have been generous when instead we may have been cowardly. We think we have not been trying hard enough when in fact we may have been knocking ourselves out. The mentor, by acting as our mirror, gives us information about ourselves that is more objective than what we can come up with on our own. Yes, it may hurt to hear! But it will also heal. It will certainly nudge us toward personal growth.

So take yourself seriously. Spend time with yourself. Talk to yourself. Listen to yourself. You are a wonderful person to get to know, and once you think so, your spouse will too.

SABBATH TIME

Some of us read the Bible selectively. We read, "Whatsoever thy hand findeth to do, do it with all thy might" (Ecc. 9:10, KJV), but we ignore "Remember the Sabbath Day, to keep it holy" (Ex. 20:8, KJV).

God does not think of us as machines. He doesn't judge us mainly in terms of output, productivity, number of tasks completed, as does the world. He thinks of us as persons. He wants to enjoy a personal relationship with us, and He wants us to have strong relationships with each other. And relationships take time—Sabbath time.

Just as we need time to read the Word, we need time to communicate with our spouses. Just as we need time for the Lord's Supper, we need time to "break bread" with our families. Just as we need time to worship, we need time to enjoy our mates.

This needs to be Sabbath time. Time that we set apart, regularly. Time that we refuse to violate by daily work and concerns. Time for growing, experiencing, loving, being together—both with the Lord and with each other.

YFC Editors

Beware of Overscheduling!

GARY & JULIE COLLINS

Almost everybody we know is too busy! Some of us complain about it. Some take pride in it, as if busy-ness is a sign of importance. Too often our marriages and families are harmed because of it.

In our house, overscheduling creeps up on us and suddenly one or both of us feels swamped. There is more to do than time allows and we feel pressured by our own commitments.

At times like this, it is difficult for many couples to relax or to communicate without feeling rushed. How easy it is for us to feel tired, run-down, irritable, and impatient. We may start work on one project, but can't concentrate fully because of the "still-to-do" list that fights for attention. Pushing to finish one project, we let other things slip, including the quality of our work, repairs or routine cleaning at home, time for the kids, time to be with friends, even time for sex. We vow never to let this happen again—but we feel trapped by a schedule that we can't seem to control. It would be comforting if we could blame all of this on somebody else, but often we realize that the problem is of our own making. That awareness creates even more pressure.

To avoid this problem in the future, consider some of the causes of overscheduling:

1. *A failure to think ahead.* Ask one of us to do something next week and the answer often will be no. Ask for a commitment in six months and the answer may be yes because six months seems a long way off. A commitment for the future doesn't create any pressure now, but in six months we may regret our earlier decisions.

To avoid this problem, write everything down. Keep a detailed calendar that lets you see what is ahead. Try to remember routine pressures that aren't on the calendar. We try not to take on extras in December, for example, because we know that Christmas is always a busy time. We try to compare our long-range schedules periodically. This doesn't take long and sometimes one of us will spot a future pressure time that the other doesn't see. Then there is time to juggle schedules—well in advance.

2. *A failure to allow for flexibility.* Can you believe that the last article submitted to the editors of this book is this article on overscheduling? We agreed to write it several months before it was due. Everything was well-scheduled—until some family members had medical problems and one of our parents died. Suddenly the schedule was forgotten as we turned to more demanding issues. During that time everything, including this article, was put aside while we dealt with unexpected family crises. When these settled down, we were faced with too many persisting commitments— commitments that created pressure largely because of our own failure to allow for flexibility.

3. *A failure to say no.* We work with seminary students who learn a lot of Greek and Hebrew words. Regrettably, there is one English word that many of them never learn: *no.*

It is hard to say no when:
● We see a need and know we can fill it.
● We feel pressure (or even manipulation) from people who want our involvement.

• We are made to feel guilty if we say no. (Sometimes our kids, our spouses, our pastors, or others arouse guilt and push us into making commitments that we shouldn't.)

• There is nobody else available to do what we feel pressured to do.

4. *A failure to set priorities.* Romans 12, 1 Corinthians 12, and Ephesians 4 all talk about spiritual gifts that God gives to each of us for building up the church. Neither Julie nor I have a gift (or interest) in administration, so invitations to serve on church boards are turned down. Since neither of us is musical, we don't sing in the choir. Instead we serve where we can use our gifts. This helps set our priorities.

What are the priorities in your life? For one week, keep a record of your time. That may give you a clue to your priorities and use of time.

Next, drop what isn't on your priority list, or what you don't have the time, desire, or abilities to do well. Cutting back on your schedule won't be easy, especially if others pressure you to stay overcommitted.

Then, as a couple, discuss how you would like to be spending your time. Each of you should communicate your own needs as well as discussing goals for your marriage. Ask God to help as you ponder this. What can you do, specifically, to work toward your goals and priorities? One guideline may be helpful: say no if another person can do something as well or better than you. (In our house, a lot of speaking invitations are turned down on that basis.) But nobody else can work on our marriage or build rapport with the kids like we can. For us, these are important priorities.

We also make it a priority to help each other when one of us gets overscheduled. How do you help an overscheduled spouse?

• Remember you are partners together in marriage. Be supportive and interested in your spouse's activities, but don't

protect your spouse from seeing the difficulties that overscheduling causes.

• Don't feel that you can't bother your spouse because he or she is serving the Lord. You are part of God's plan for your spouse and each of you is responsible before the Lord to meet family needs.

• Resist the temptation to become resentful or bitter. That only puts more stress on you and on the marriage. Instead, gently remind your spouse of the family's needs for support and companionship.

• Keep the lines of communication open. Don't nag or keep mentioning previous choices that led to the overscheduling.

- Lovingly pray for your spouse. If possible, help with the overcommitments that cannot be changed. Then help your spouse explore the reasons for continual overscheduling.

By working together and constantly communicating, you and your spouse can avoid the pressures of over-scheduling, and thus have time for the people and activities that are most important.

Related Articles

Vacations for Two

KENT & BARBARA HUGHES

When our family was young we learned a secret about vacations that has worn remarkably well through the years: *you can have a wonderful vacation if you plan for it.*

I was pastoring a small church at the time, and we longed for a vacation. There was only one problem—with 4 children between the ages of 5 and 10, we had very little money. What to do?

Barbara and a friend decided to set up a handcraft "vacation business," from which she deposited her share of the profits in a vacation account. The glorious result was a vacation that exceeded our dreams. The modest business profits plus some careful vacation shopping made it possible to rent the largest bayfront rental property on plush Balboa Island in Newport Beach, California for two golden weeks of building family sandcastles, swimming, boating, and fishing topped off with our own talent show!

Thus we learned early that planning and creativity make all the difference in vacations, and that great vacations do not require a fat wallet or a surplus of time. All that is needed for a memorable vacation is a little forethought and some common sense, whether you are anticipating a long holiday, a weekend away, or a day off.

- **Major Vacations**
Vacations lasting a week or more may include travel at home or abroad. Keep in mind these general principles, which extend to shorter vacations as well.

1. *Assess your needs and expectations.* These will vary greatly. They may include rest and quiet, time together for intimacy, the company of others (perhaps even relatives), diversion (plays, concerts, sightseeing, shopping), intellectual stimulation, recreation (fishing, tennis, surfing, camping). Each partner will probably have several expectations, and yours may not overlap with those of your spouse. For example, the wife may feel she needs time for reading and intimacy, and the husband may want rest and recreation—say, fishing. The answer may be a quiet cabin in the woods where all needs can be leisurely pursued. Each couple has different needs, so communication is vital. Try coming up with a plan that suits the expectations of both of you. You may be surprised with the great ideas that come.

2. *Choose a location.* Do your best to insure that the place you choose for a vacation will meet your needs. A good travel agent can be of immense help. Be very careful about choosing any place that has not been personally seen by you, your agent, or a friend. Then, hav-

ing made your choice, do not expect it will perfectly meet your expectations. Take it as it comes. Never allow your expectations to spoil your vacation. Relax!

3. *Don't overplan.* Our strong recommendation that vacations should be planned must not be taken by some compulsive soul to mean that every vacation detail must be decided in advance. Not at all! Such thinking will earn the forlorn quip, "Are we having fun yet?" Instead, go with the flow. Perhaps you dreamed of fishing, but you're just too tired. Then sleep. Be willing to give up your "rights" in deference to your spouse. Be spontaneous.

4. *Avoid the last-minute rush.* How many vacations have gotten off to a bad start, and even ruined, because of this! The scene is familiar: it's 6:15 P.M., and Harold and Martha are scheduled to depart from the airport at 8:00 for a relaxing vacation. Harold is late getting home, and the boy who is supposed to mow the lawn while they are gone hasn't come for his instructions. Martha is on the phone frantically trying to get someone to feed the dog and water the plants when Harold bursts in the door complaining about the traffic. They will have to drop the keys off at the Jones'. There is no time for Harold to change. Tickets? Where are they? Each thinks the other has them. Racing to the Jones' and then the airport, they fear they will run out of gas. They make it, but the seat selection is limited. Sitting apart on the 747, they remember their responsibilities: the sprinkler is running, the tennis shoes are in the dryer—and who has the camera?

● **Shorter Vacations**

For weekend vacations lasting only two to four days, the travel time factor is of particular importance. We recommend that travel take no more than four hours, or too much of the vacation will be used up behind the wheel. It is helpful to take a map and draw a four-hour radius around your hometown. You may be surprised what falls within it. Within four hours of our town, Wheaton, Illinois, there are four major cities (Chicago, Springfield, Madison, and Milwaukee) plus hundreds of small towns, scores of state and national parks, and innumerable lakes and rivers. All of these are potential short-vacation territory.

Nearly all Americans live within a few hours of a major city. Why consider it for a vacation? Because most of us do not know our cities well. Buy a travel guide or a city magazine and study the riches lying close at hand. Chicago, for example, has over 20 museums and numerous art galleries including the great Art Institute. It also has beaches, shopping, theater, music, exotic yet inexpensive restaurants, festivals, ball parks, and hundreds of other possibilities. What is more, the great hotels offer their best prices on weekends. Not a few wise couples have had memorable mini-vacations at a fraction of the cost of midweek stays—and with virtually no travel costs!

You might want to consider your state capital. Most people live within four hours of their capital, but many never enjoy the special attractions. Capital cities are repositories for historical treasures, and they often take great pride in their public buildings and museums. These can provide hours of relaxation and education for couples wise enough to take advantage of them.

Country towns are also untapped vacation resources. Travel the back roads and you are bound to have repeated surprises. Virtually all states feature publications describing their rural life and giving information on hotels, camping, bed-and-breakfast inns, and seasonal events such as harvest festivals, fairs, flea markets, rodeos, and theatrical productions. Nearby country towns can often provide far more than one couple can possibly cover. For couples who enjoy the outdoors, public parks, wildlife preserves, and fisheries can provide inexpensive vacation enjoyment. Do not be a victim of the "grass is greener in the other state" syndrome. Within a few hours of your home, there are wonders galore!

Christian couples should not overlook the excellent short and long vacation opportunities afforded by many Christian camps. Often the facilities are superb and the costs minimal, especially if you are able to rent a cabin off-season.

All that is needed for a husband and wife to experience some wonderful vacation time together is a little forethought. Plan to have great vacations. As Vance Havner once said, "If we do not follow the Lord's example of coming apart for a while to rest, we may just—come apart!"

Related Articles
Chapter 12: How Much Time Should We Spend Together?
Chapter 12: Take That Extra Honeymoon

THE VACATION BEGINS

The rhythmic taps of my fingers echoed off the dash as I sat in the drive. "Where are those kids?" I grumbled to no one in particular. Everything was packed, and we should have left 10 minutes ago! Finally, after the last bathroom trips and door checks, the girls and Gail piled in. I shifted into reverse, and the vacation trip began.

"With this new speed limit of 65, I should be able to make up some time," I thought, heading toward the interstate highway. All of us were looking forward to this week of relaxation and water sports in the Wisconsin northwoods, and we could hardly wait to get there. "It's too bad the cabin is eight hours away," I said, and everyone agreed.

Pushing the van to the speed limit (and a little beyond, I must admit), I began to think through the trip. "By leaving at 8:30 we will arrive at about 4:30. I'll unlock the doors and turn on the gas and electricity and . . ."

Suddenly my stomach tightened with anxiety as I thought of unlocking the doors. I turned to Gail and asked with a nervous laugh, "You did remember to bring the keys, didn't you?"

When she answered that she thought I had picked them up, I yelled my disbelief and a few other choice comments about incompetence and losing time. Then, at the first available crossing, I swung an illegal U-turn, and began to retrace the half-hour trip to our home.

While I continued to mutter, Gail said quietly, "When does the vacation start? Now, or when we get there?" I wanted to lash back with a clever retort, but she caught me off guard, and I began to think. Gail was right. Just being together, away from the pressures of home and work was our vacation. And I was ruining it for everyone by being tense, hurried, irritable, and angry. Sufficiently chastened, I breathed a sigh of relief, slowed the car a bit, and asked her to pray for our vacation which was beginning "right now."

Every now and then, I remind myself of that lesson as I hurry through traffic, appointments, or meals, pushing to get *there* where the fun or relaxation or rewards supposedly begin. The truth is that each moment is a gift from God—the payoff doesn't come tomorrow or around the next corner; it is now.

Dave Veerman

Take That Extra Honeymoon

V. GILBERT & ARLISLE BEERS

Our first honeymoon was 37 years ago as we write this. Much water has flowed under life's bridge since that time. There have been times when life lifted us above the mountaintops and times when we walked through deep valleys. But in all times we worked together and stayed together and laughed or cried together. And now that we have done our best for our five children, we savor together the fruits of mature life with a rich family relationship.

Looking back over these years, we believe that a special ingredient in our togetherness has been those extra honeymoon times, times when we stepped aside from daily routines and went somewhere special to relax and play together.

Play is not so much escape as recreation, being created anew. Life stagnates when its routines sap it of originality and freshness. Even the best marriages get stale if they become too predictable. Play recharges our batteries, fills our gas tanks, and gives us a tune-up to prepare us for the next stretch.

So the second, third, fourth (and beyond) honeymoons should have a recreative purpose. They can refresh us and renew us. How about a fresh perspective on your job? Or a fresh perspective on your routines? A new look at meeting some tough times or hurts?

An extra honeymoon can give you the time and distance to take a fresh look at yourselves, individually and as a couple. Have I as the husband been helping my wife to be fulfilled as a person? Have I been as loving and kind as I should be to her? Have I as a wife been as supportive as I should? Have I been interested in my husband and his work? To these you can add a hundred new questions that will rejuvenate a tired marriage.

And don't forget to take a quiet look at yourself on these little extra honeymoons. You may not be all you want to be as a husband because you are not all you think you should be as a Christian. You may not be coping too well as a wife or mother because you have not come to terms with certain personal problems or nagging little attitudes that overshadow the happy relationships you want to have.

We recommend that you do not take a businessman's holiday—a honeymoon that throws you back into the things you have set aside. If you are weary of overfilled schedules, don't rush off to another city and fill up your honeymoon time with cluttered activities. It's merely more of the same, and it won't give you time to sort out your priorities as you should. Have you been drained by giving to others, perhaps ministering or teaching or helping? Perhaps you would be helped by spending some time with a mature Christian who could lovingly help recharge your batteries and give you new perspective. We don't normally think of honeymoons with other couples, but there may be something to say for the two of you spending a week with a godly couple who can help you get a fresh new look at life.

Some of us hesitate to spend money for things like this, especially if we think we don't have it. Or we resent taking time for "nothing" when we are so busy. That's a priority problem. Look at that extra honeymoon as an investment in the future, your future together and your

LOVE AS PLAY

For us love as play has always
  been
The time away, the vacation,
The time when there was time.
The glory of discovery
When there was time to discover
The two-week swim in serendipity.
The unexpected fudge shop
In a long parade of T-shirt stores.
Yet no love is ever all discovery, all
  joy!
What happiness is there
that never lets a single aggravation
punctuate its laughter?
Still, I love you most—or show it
  most—away from the routine.
There in distant places
where we have no
single obligation,
there is time.
The hassles of our too-familiar
  world
shove appointments at us
we never would have made
except from guilt and obligation.
But it comes at last—our
  vacation—
we marked it fully out.
We wrote down *Rocky Gorge*
We circled it one year ahead of
  time
inside that mindless square of
  calendar.
A circle of June or August in
ink as crimson as Christmas.
A single square of time
when play could be and love could
  grow.
Next winter when we look at slides
we
made of Rocky Gorge this summer,
we will forget we left

the eight-dollar bottle of shampoo
that we could only buy
in your local beauty shop 1,435
  miles away.
We'll forget we "Egg McMuffined"
  at McDonald's,
bothered by the oldness in the
  coffee,
and that Formica booth
with someone else's
ketchup drying on it.
What of it?
We played together
beyond the phones
and order blanks
of sassy lifestyles
we couldn't thumb
our noses at.
Now we can.
We need life here
at Rocky Gorge.
Making slides
no one will
want to see,
not even us.
For now we
need to be here.
We need to eat those breakfasts
somebody else cooks
and sleep in beds
somebody else makes.
We need to laugh
in nameless streets
in a town we never thought we'd
  visit
because among the T-shirt stores
is an unexpected fudge shop,
and routines need a little help
  sometimes.

Calvin Miller

own mental and spiritual well-being. Good investments pay dividends, and we think you will find these extra honeymoons paying rich dividends in your re-created attitudes and perspectives.

Most of us fill up our appointment books with encounters with strangers, viewing these as trusts that must not be broken. Seldom do we view our times with our mates as such high priorities. We urge you to put each other at the top of your list. Make a special appointment with each other for your honeymoon, and don't let anything come in to rob you of it.

These honeymoons may last a week, or they may be just a lunchtime together. Do you ever set aside an hour or two to play—go on a hike, browse through antique stores, play a game, or whatever you like to do together? Try it sometime.

One final word. Be sure you are doing what you both like to do on these little honeymoons. If the husband likes to fish and the wife hates it, that doesn't count unless you take two honeymoons—one for him and the other for her. We like it better when we both enjoy the same honeymoon.

So take time for those extra honeymoons. We think they are some of the best investments we have made. Thirty-seven years of happy marriage is a convincing argument for them, isn't it?

Related Articles
Chapter 12: How Much Time Should We Spend Together?
Chapter 12: Vacations for Two

Juggling Career and Marriage
TED W. ENGSTROM

When we define career as one's lifework, whether that work is home related or marketplace related or a combination of the two, the demands of keeping both career and marriage in progress at the same time can be arduous. Both husband and wife have the challenge of creatively juggling career and marriage.

How can the Christian husband and wife successfully juggle these two irreducible components of contemporary life? Is it possible to develop and enhance one's marriage and career simultaneously?

One of life's tragedies is that second chances seldom occur. Far too often we wait too long—until sickness, accidents, threatened separation or divorce, or other calamities happen—before making significant decisions or providing for changes to be made. Many die without ever enjoying life's fullness in both marriage and career because they lacked the courage to alter their lifestyle before some circumstance changed it for them.

In their careers, some stay at a job long after its challenge has passed. They remain prisoners to comfortable lifework routines rather than tapping into their God-given creative desires to develop themselves and others and initiating Spirit-breathed changes.

In their marriages, some fail to grasp the biblical view of an exclusive, lifelong relationship of two partners bound together, properly living for each other with Christ at the center. They fail to learn that a married person cannot live as an individual but only as one bound up with the other's life.

Those who neglect taking charge of their careers and their marriages are

390

courting disaster.

Strenuous effort at one's lifework is good; inordinately consuming work for either husband or wife, increasingly common in American culture, is wrong. The vast majority of American couples seem to err in sacrificing marriage for the sake of lifework. But, for the sake of both career and marriage, we must constantly guard against overwork that will deprive us of health, family, and a strong spiritual life. (Often overwork is not the disease itself, but only the symptom of a deeper problem—tension, inadequacy, a need to feel worthwhile.)

One of life's special privileges is spending precious moments with those who love us dearly, particularly our spouses. The ecstatic moments—celebrating an anniversary, sharing the great joy over the birth of a child or grandchild, getting involved in a pet project with one's spouse, listening patiently to the stumbling efforts of a wife or husband expressing intimate feelings—can never be recovered by seeking to cram them all into one fabulous future vacation together. These things are the stuff of daily life, and they can never be relived or replaced.

Many spouses find it extremely difficult to make a commitment to allowing time for these significant events and experiences, yet there is no substitute for them.

For a husband and wife to succeed, they must find avocations and interests which they can enjoy together, away from the work that occupies most of their time. I have found that an excellent marriage demands that each spouse give highest priority to the other over the long haul. If your lifework has been capturing your best and most creative time and energy, stealing those priceless moments you meant to invest with the person you love most on earth, then you have a serious problem of *misplaced priorities.* Your basic values are askew, and sooner or later life will break down

ECCLESIASTES 3:1-8

There is a time for everything, and a season for every activity under heaven: a time to be born and a time to die, a time to plant and a time to uproot, a time to kill and a time to heal, a time to tear down and a time to build, a time to weep and a time to laugh, a time to mourn and a time to dance, a time to scatter stones and a time to gather them, a time to embrace and a time to refrain, a time to search and a time to give up, a time to keep and a time to throw away, a time to tear and a time to mend, a time to be silent and a time to speak, a time to love and a time to hate, a time for war and a time for peace.

for you.

Remember always that your work or ministry or position must never keep you from a growing, intimate life with your spouse. In isolated instances, for short periods of time, the responsibility of marriage may be overridden by some higher obligation of the kingdom of God. But if you fail your spouse, you fail your greatest responsibility, and in large measure you are a failure in life.

It is important to recognize that the priorities we set for ourselves are the result of our value system. Our value system reflects our commitments, and they are measured by what we are actually doing. A Christian, in my judgment, has three broad priorities in his or her value system, and their order is very important.

First is our commitment to God in Christ. This is paramount. A total commitment to Christ takes care of many frustrations as far as time and life pressures are concerned.

Second is our commitment to the

body of Christ. All of us who are Christian are permanently related to each other and belong to each other. Within this second level of commitment, our highest priority is our spouse. Marriage means two lives intimately bound up together. God views each partner as belonging to the other; the two become one. Outside our relationship with Him, marriage is our primary relationship. All others are secondary.

Third is our commitment to Christ's work in the world, the task God gives us as a lifework. Far too often we reverse the order and put this third-place commitment in second place, lifework ahead of marriage.

Perhaps one way to keep marriage a higher priority than our career is to remember that a career is meant to be a noun, not a verb, for a Christian. As a noun, *career* means "occupation" or "lifework." As a verb, it means "to rush headlong, full speed." Are you careering through life, rushing full speed toward some unbalanced, perhaps neurotic goal or dream? If so, your marriage is suffering, and you need to check your priorities from a biblical perspective.

Remember, the life of Jesus was not one of rushing and impatient activity, though it was obviously significant and filled with important accomplishments. He had time for deep, satisfying relationships in the midst of doing the most important lifework that would ever be asked of anyone. If we are to successfully juggle career and marriage, we too must have the priorities He chose and accept the values He has asked us to live by.

Related Articles

Chapter 12: Learning to Be Supportive of a Working Wife

Chapter 12: How Working Spouses Can Make Time for Each Other

MY SPOUSE WON'T STOP WORKING!

Whether it's working around the house or bringing office work home, what do you do when your spouse simply won't stop working?

1. It would be wise to analyze why such behavior occurs. Is he bringing home work from the office because of your subtle comments about needing more money? Is she constantly cleaning because you've made a few snide remarks to friends about the state of the house? Find out if you're part of the problem and take steps to remedy that.

2. If you truly have a workaholic on your hands, you can try to help him/her realize that relaxation is essential to be able to do one's best work. In addition, it is an important facet of education for the children.

3. Prearrange a quitting time, then have a break. Find out what he/she likes to do to relax (don't try to impose what you like to do). If possible, get away from the workplace and be creative. Take a mental *and* physical break.

4. Don't involve yourself in your spouse's obsessive behavior. If she just won't sit down until the house is completely picked up, you won't do any good by trying to help get the job done. Allow her to do it, then kidnap her for a cup of coffee—even pour it and have it ready.

5. If the work is an overhanging task—such as spring cleaning before the grandparents visit—get the whole family involved in helping, then schedule a fun break.

YFC Editors

Learning to Be Supportive of a Working Wife

JOHN GILLIES

Carolyn and I were both employed when we married. Then she became employed at home, raising three children and me.

After our youngest child entered first grade, Carolyn returned to the "marketplace" as a part-time nursery-school teacher. When he was in the fourth grade, she entered the library system as a full-time children's librarian. She's been at it now for more than 20 years.

I've held several jobs during that same period of time. Twice I've worked out of an office at home as a full-time freelance writer. If Carolyn hadn't had her steady job, we certainly couldn't have managed on my income.

Thus we're not novices at being working partners in marriage. There has been lots of learning and adapting, but it hasn't been traumatic.

What have we learned?

Primarily this: that it takes a lot of cooperation and communication to make a partnership work. Schedules require both cooperation and communication. So do housekeeping, money management, and meals.

Scheduling. When our children lived at home, we had to keep an up-to-date calendar listing everybody's commitments. Now that the children are gone, we still keep a master calendar next to the kitchen telephone. It lets each of us know who is traveling, who has a committee meeting or a dentist's appointment, whom we've invited for a meal, who has invited us and when, and those special events we don't want to miss.

We negotiate about vacations and put them on the calendar. We've learned that vacations are vital when both partners work, under separate pressures, and together manage a household. During our decades of caring for our parents we found that even brief weekend respites were essential for our peace of mind and well-being. We opt for vacations *together,* because we cherish that quality time.

This doesn't mean we are always together during our free time. We have our individual interests. Carolyn's is art; mine is music. We're free to pursue those interests, as long as we ensure adequate time together by planning ahead and visually plotting our schedules.

Money. Carolyn has her checking account and I have mine. We have access to each other's account, if there is an emergency. We've agreed that each will pay certain categories of bills. Carolyn handles the mortgage, utilities, and food. I take care of insurance, car expenses, house maintenance, and telephone. We file a joint income tax return.

Meals. Carolyn has always been a good cook, and I've become one. We eat well, nutritiously, and with variety. I've enjoyed unraveling the mysteries of a cookbook, and I feel very strongly that husbands should learn to cook, to know more than how to boil an egg or open a can of soup. A dear friend of ours, dying of cancer, wrote down recipes and taught her husband to cook every one of his favorite dishes. What a gift she left him!

We don't have a lot of time for cooking, so we plan ahead. We alternate between slow cooker, electric wok, and pressure cooker. Occasionally we fall back on frozen dinners of the low-calorie variety. We usually eat a meal at a restaurant or cafeteria once a week. That may change as we review the limits of our retirement incomes, but for the present we enjoy the treat.

Housekeeping. We have our chores, which is the only way we can manage housekeeping without maid service, which we neither want nor can afford. We iron while watching TV. We use a dishwasher after there is a collection of several meals' dishes. Either of us will wash clothes and linens and dry them, in the dryer if it's raining or on the outdoor clothesline if it's sunny and warm. I like to cut the grass, which is a year-round activity in our part of Texas, most of the time. Carolyn tends the garden. We vacuum once a week. Our major chores are finished in two or three hours on Saturdays.

Beyond cooperation. Supporting a working wife involves more than equalizing household duties. It involves *communication.*

I think the most important thing I've learned in our work-partnership in recent years is the need (and the privilege) of listening. Carolyn has been successful in her career and is now a supervisor. She's not mingling with and telling stories to children as much as she used to; she's less involved with the creative side of things. A lot of what she has to do is drudgery and often bureaucratic nonsense. She has to unload some of her frustration onto someone, and I'm that someone. Mostly I listen, asking a question now and then.

The other night it struck me that in this regard our roles have changed. It used to be that I was the one who recounted all the day's horrors to her and she was the one who listened, asked questions that defused my anger, and helped me understand. Having once been pushed upward into management

TIME STEALERS

Do you ever come to the end of a day and wonder where all your time went? Often it goes, a chunk at a time, to *time stealers*:

1. *The telephone.* Refuse to listen to phoned sales pitches. Set a timer and limit your personal phone calls. If the phone interrupts an important task, return the call later.

2. *Newspapers and magazines.* Five minutes of reading headlines can easily turn into an hour of reading articles that don't even interest you. Decide in advance how much time you want to spend reading.

3. *The television.* This is probably the biggest time stealer of all. How much time do you spend in front of the TV set each week? Keep a record—you may be surprised at the tally.

4. *Low-priority tasks.* Many people spend a great deal of time on interesting but relatively unimportant tasks and then wonder why their first-priority tasks don't get done.

5. *Interruptions.* At the end of each day, do you have half a dozen jobs left to finish? Don't be sidetracked by interruptions. Finish one task before beginning another.

6. *Inefficiency.* How many times a day do you make a quick trip into town to do an errand? Group your tasks. Make a batch of phone calls. Run all your errands on one trip. Keep a grocery list so you don't have to run back to the store for the forgotten light bulbs.

YFC Editors

THE NATURE OF WORK

Work is the natural exercise
and function of man.
Work is not primarily
a thing one does to live,
but the thing one lives to do.
It is, or should be,
the full expression
of the worker's faculties,
the thing in which
he finds spiritual, mental,
and bodily satisfaction,
and the medium in which
he offers himself to God.

—Dorothy L. Sayers

MAY 25, 1997

Power for Living

STUART BRISCOE:
Ministering to your working spouse

have a family? How does he get food? The same questions came to mind each morning, and then, as no answers surfaced, my concern grew.

His cameo appearance each morning was all I ever saw of him and then he was gone until the next day—same time, same intersection.

into my unknown friend's morning routine. Friend. I don't know when I began to think of him as my friend. To me he was "friend," but to him I was a merely the driver of another anonymous vehicle in the monstrous intersection he conquered each morning.

Curiously, my friend never appeared in any other part of my life. His cameo appearance each morning was all I ever saw of him and then he was gone until the

Was there anything I could do to help this man, who had so many obvious special needs?

Clearly, I couldn't walk up to this stranger, ask him personal questions, and then figure out how I could help. He didn't even know I existed!

BEEP! BEEP!

"Lord," I prayed aloud, "please bless this man today and send someone along to meet his every need."

For two years I had been allowed this keyhole peek

next day—same time, same intersection. Everything changed, however, one snowy January eve.

I pushed through the doors of our storefront church and felt the warm air hit my face. I pulled off my gloves, unwrapped my scarf, and was immediately drawn into the atmosphere of excitement and expectation that filled every nook and cranny of the room. I greeted others who had traveled from miles around to take part in the revival services and share in the wonderful work God was doing in our small New England church.

The icy roads and sub-zero temperatures had caused me to be a little late and, as I made my way through smiles and hugs to the sanctuary, I could see that the only seats left were in the first row. I hurried to the front of the room and sat down as the strains of the organ began to fill the air.

Between choruses and hymns, people stood up and shared with other members of the congregation about God's provision in their lives. As I turned around to face those behind me, my eyes met a familiar face.

Where have I seen him before? I wondered. *The intersection!* I thought moments later. This was my friend with the special needs.

I watched him from across the church as he listened with interest to the words being shared by others. Moments later, he placed his hands on either side of his seat and, like a child in an oversized chair, shifted his weight forward until his toes touched the floor. He

stood, waiting patiently for the person who was speaking to finish. Then he began.

"I. . . I . . . w-w-wanted. . . to th. . . th. . . thank G-G-God. . ." he stammered.

Lord, his speech! I thought. My stomach churned. I struggled as he worked his way through his barely understandable words of thanks to God. He sat down, and I exhaled.

The service continued, but my mind was filled, not with the words of the sermon, but with the faltering words my friend had shared. His words of praise disclosed that his needs were being met, but I knew his speech impediment must have added another degree of difficulty to his life that I could not comprehend.

At the end of the sermon, our pastor invited members of the congregation to pray at the altar. While many people filed forward to publicly present their needs to God, I closed my eyes and stayed in my seat. Within moments, my prayer was interrupted by a light tap on my shoulder. I opened my eyes.

"W-w-w-will. . . y-y. . . ou p-p-raaa-y w-w-w-ith ... me?" My friend looked into my eyes as if he

knew me. Wit[h] answer, he too[k] me several step[s] knelt down an[d] pray without ev[er] need. Somehow have to.

The prayers s[pilled] mouth along wit[h] my eyes. I have prayed; all I knew were connected that went far bey[ond] standing. I felt as Lord I serve was s me (Acts 12:7), gu

Our prayer tim[e] friend hoisted him He gently squeeze[d] turned, and walke[d]

Winter has passe[d] come and gone. Ea[ch] pull to a stop at the scan the faces of th[e] curb, hoping to cat[ch] my friend. Old habit[s] break. I no longer w him, however. I sim prayer knowing that legions of angels are every need.

President: DAVID MEHLIS ◆ *Managing Editor:* JAMES T. DYET
Senior Editor: JOYCE L. GIBSON ◆ *Editor:* DON ALBAN, JR. ◆ *Editorial Assistant:* MABEL H
Editorial Services: JOAN MORRIS ◆ *Production:* MARILYN DUNN
Art Director: DAN VAN LOON ◆ *Designer:* DESIGN RESOURCE CENTER

POWER FOR LIVING®, a POWER/LINE® paper for adults, is published quarterly in weekly parts
Yearly subscriptions available. Subscription addresses: SP Publications, Inc., Box 632, Glen Ellyn, IL 6c
Box 2000, Paris, ON N3L 3X5 Canada; SP Trust Ltd., Triangle Business Park, Wendover Rd., Stock M
Bucks, HP22 5BL England. ©1996, SP Publications, Inc. All rights reserved. Unless otherwise indicate
articles are owned exclusively by the authors. No part of this publication may be reproduced in any fc
mission. Printed in USA. Photos are for illustrative purposes only and do not represent specific individ

Volume 55, Number 2 ◆ March ◆ April ◆ May 1997

and losing the joy of personal creativity, I know a lot of what she is feeling. And I am listening more.

When married partners are both employed it's nice to be friends and not competitors, to enhance the marriage through cooperation and communication. "In honor preferring one another" (Rom. 12:10, KJV). Loving each other. Affirming each other. Appreciating each other's gifts.

Related Articles
Chapter 1: Love as Teamwork
Chapter 12: How Working Spouses Can Make Time for Each Other

How Working Spouses Can Make Time for Each Other

D. STUART BRISCOE

Once upon a time men and women worked together in the fields, tending their crops, feeding their livestock, raising their kids, and living happily ever after. They were tired out at the end of the day, and after supper they promptly fell asleep.

Then along came the Industrial Revolution, which meant that men went off to the factories where they produced all kinds of bright and shiny things that they then bought and brought home, and the women spent lots of time looking after them. This was so tiring for all concerned that after supper they crawled into bed and fell asleep.

World War II changed all that, because the men went away to fight and the women went into the factories to make things for them to fight with. At the end of the war people decided they needed to have more fun, since life had been so hard, so they got busy having fun, which was hard work, and they all fell exhausted into bed.

Along came Betty Friedan, who persuaded women they could do anything if they put their minds to it (men had always been told this). So women brushed up their skills, typed up their resumes, put up their hair, and took up their careers. At night they came home, met their weary men, and together they fell exhausted into bed.

So you see everything has changed without anything changing at all. Spouses have always had a hard time finding time for each other. But that doesn't make it right.

Jill and I both live busy working lives. I pastor a large church and also travel extensively, while Jill directs the women's ministry, writes, and also travels in every direction. So we identify and sympathize with those of you who have two-career marriages.

We realized we needed to do something about our situation one day when I was preaching in Minneapolis. At the end of the day I returned to my hotel room and was just settling in when I heard the key turn in the lock. To my amazement, Jill was standing there. If I was amazed, she was flabbergasted. "What are you doing here?" we said in unrehearsed unison. "I'm preaching here, what d'you think I'm doing?" we continued.

We discovered that we both had appointments in the same city on the same day, but neither was aware of what the other was doing. The two churches concerned, however, had discovered what we did not know and without telling us had booked us in the same room. That evening we had a good talk and admitted to each other that we needed to communicate far better than we had been doing so far.

We discovered that our lack of communication was the result of a certain lack of interest in what the other was doing. Now, of course, we both would have denied this, but when we examined the situation we needed little help in noting that if neither of us had bothered to ask where the other was going, there was clearly little interest. And that was intolerable.

We discovered something else. We had both become so wrapped up in our independent activities that they had begun to override our mutual commitment to a united life.

Duly chastened by what we had discovered, Jill and I vowed never to slip again into such a state of affairs. Like many vows, this one went quickly down the tube. Good intentions need to be backed up by a modicum of planning.

We both enjoy drama, so we bought season tickets for the Milwaukee Repertory Theatre. We found that, having paid in advance for the tickets, we don't let other activities crowd out our evening together. Every single time we set out for the show one of us will say, "I really don't have time to be going out tonight." But without exception at the end of the evening we say, "I'm glad we took the time." It's a hassle even to have fun when you're both working hard, but the together-fun-times must be written into the schedule.

One day Jill, in frustration, decided that as everybody else in the church seemed to rank ahead of her for my attention, and since they got my attention by making an appointment, the obvious thing for her to do was to make an appointment too. She also made her point, and since that time we actually write ap-

WHO WILL CLEAN THE BATHROOM?

When both spouses hold full-time jobs, the energy expended leaves little left for the mundane tasks of keeping up the house and running the family. But bathrooms do need to be cleaned, furniture continues to collect dust, and children do have to be taken hither and yon. How can it all get done?

The obvious answer is to divide the chores. When both spouses work, neither deserves the fate of cleaning up or playing taxi driver every night. Sit down and work out a compromise (and if you have children, include them because even young children can be given certain responsibilities). First determine the nonnegotiables—the activities that you know have to be done to keep the health inspector away. Next, realize that each of you has pet peeves about certain things in the cleaning realm. List the ones that are most important to each of you; then list the ones that you'd like to have done but aren't life-or-death issues. Be willing to lower your standards a little, especially if one of you is a diehard perfectionist.

Finally, agree on and set up a schedule, take assignments, and share responsibilities.

Then reward yourselves!

YFC Editors

pointments on each other's calendars to ensure time for each other.

My father-in-law was watching television when my brother-in-law went to ask if he could marry Jill's sister. Recognizing the seriousness of the moment, my father-in-law got up from his chair, walked across the room, and carefully turned the volume down a little. This enabled him to give his total attention to the young man without interfering with his primary interest—the boob tube.

He was thoroughly kidded about this for the rest of his life, but I recognize the same tendency in myself. There are times when Jill is so excited about what she has been doing that common courtesy insists that I give her my full attention. The fact that she often has an insatiable desire to share this urgent information just as I'm going to sleep is not without significance. But I've come to realize that even sleep can wait when someone as important as my wife wants to talk and when something as significant as her work needs to be discussed.

We haven't solved everything by any means. Once when we flew together to Brazil we were met at the Sao Paulo airport by two groups of people. One group took Jill to Sierra Negra for a missionary conference while the other group took me to a pastors' conference in Sao Paulo. I felt a little guilty because I knew about the arrangement but had neglected to let Jill know. But we survived—we talked about it, laughed, and went on. And that's exactly what we plan to do as long as we have the strength to do it and each other to do it with.

Some people live in each other's pockets. Others pass like ships in the night. We tend to be more like jets passing in the fog. But we do land, and the times at the airport are special. We wouldn't want it any other way.

Related Articles

Do you and your spouse see eye to eye about money? Fill out this inventory and see. You may not be able to change each other's underlying attitudes, but you can still figure out ways to cooperate in running your household together. What areas do you need to discuss? How are you going to come to agreement?

1. When making a large purchase, I prefer to use (a) a credit card, (b) a check, (c) cash.

2. I am willing to go into debt for the following purchases (mark all that apply): (a) house, (b) car, (c) education, (d) home improvement, (e) vacation, (f) major appliances and furnishings, (g) clothing, (h) anything I want or need, (i) nothing at all.

3. If I put a purchase on a credit card, I pay for it (a) as soon as the bill arrives, (b) within a few months, (c) over as long a time as possible.

4. Income tax should be computed by (a) the husband, (b) the wife, (c) the spouses together, (d) an accountant.

5. Husband and wife should have (a) a joint checking account, (b) separate checking accounts, (c) both joint and separate checking accounts.

6. The family budget should be prepared by (a) the husband, (b) the wife, (c) the spouses together, (d) an accountant.

7. In a time of family financial crisis, the best solution is to (a) cut back expenses, (b) borrow, (c) add income by getting additional work, (d) accept welfare or unemployment payments.

8. When I have money, I like to (a) save it, (b) spend it on myself, (c) spend it on loved ones, (d) give it away, (e) pay bills.

9. Expenses should be recorded (a) in detail, (b) in general categories, (c) not at all.

10. If I really want something but don't have the money for it, I will (a) wait and save, (b) borrow from a friend or family member, (c) go without, (d) use credit, (e) use money budgeted for something else.

11. It is more important to (a) live comfortably now, (b) plan for retirement, (c) support worthy causes.

12. A family should have which of the following types of insurance (mark all that apply): (a) car, (b) house, (c) health, (d) life, (e) disability.

13. I consider these to be necessities (mark all that apply): (a) a pleasant comfortable home, (b) a late-model car, (c) good-quality clothes, (d) restaurant meals, (e) vacations, (f) a private-university education for the children, (g) tasteful furnishings, (h) state-of-the-art electronic equipment, (i) up-to-date household appliances.

14. Debt should not exceed __ percent of a family's gross income.

15. A family should save __ percent of their gross income.

16. A family should give __ percent of their gross income to their church or other worthy causes.

17. For me, a comfortable family income would be $ _____ a year.

MANAGING MONEY

Money is the pivot point of our modern world. No home can escape its subtle clutches, yet its presence breeds covetous temptation. To satisfy our lust for instant indulgence, the concept of credit buying has bloated to a point where presently 80 percent of American people owe more than they own. Only 2 percent are financially self-sustaining.

Money has become a skeleton in the closet of many Christian homes, appearing regularly to harass and haunt married couples. Checkbooks, credit cards, and past-due bills are the feathers that fly in many domestic disputes.

Jesus Christ said more about money than about heaven and hell combined. He knew that money cuts deeply into character; therefore, His teaching highlighted the difference between convenient giving and costly giving. "This poor widow," He said, observing a woman giving two copper coins, "has put more into the treasury than all the others."

The size of the income and output was obviously not the Lord's criteria. Rather, amount is always secondary to attitude and motive. Scripture is full of examples, exhortations, commands, and warnings about money. Greed is everywhere denounced; generosity is everywhere extolled. The reason? God never created a person to be satisfied with things. True wealth is the treasure in heaven. "For where your treasure is, there your heart will be also" (Matt. 6:21).

Howard & Jeanne Hendricks

Five Budgets of a Married Couple

WAYNE E. OATES

When we hear the word *stewardship,* we usually think of giving money—to the church, to a relief organization, to a mission, and so on. But money represents many different things to us. It crystalizes our time, our energy, our relationships, and our aggressive effort. That is why I would like to broaden our understanding of stewardship and apply it to all the things money represents, and not just money itself.

In our lives as husbands and wives, we actually have five budgets, not just one: Money, Time, Energy, Relationships, and Anger. Stewardship of your life together as Christians means carefully managing these five different budgets according to their relationship to each other and in terms of which of them is in least supply and most demand at any given time. Remember this: productive living as husband and wife can move no farther than the particular budget that is in most demand and greatest scarcity at any given time.

1. *Money.* Marriage is more than a romantic adventure. It is an economic covenant as well. Who is going to work at what kind of work for how much money? The answer to this question tends to cause you and your spouse to define who you are and what you are going to mean to each other. It determines whether, when, and where you are going to eat, sleep, and play. It shapes who is dependent on whom and for what reasons. Your support of your church and your community and your definition of luxury turn on the axis of money. Your major temptation is to let money be your god.

2. *Time.* A newly married couple can easily assume that money is their scarcest commodity as they face the economic necessities of setting up housekeeping for the first time. They may assume they have to start off at the same standard of living as their parents, who have spent many years reaching their present level of affluence. Hence their buying habits and easy credit may push them so far into debt that they have to spend large amounts of time working for low amounts of money because of their inexperience at work.

Yet money is not their most pressing need. Time is their scarcest budget—time together to build an adequate routine of eating, sleeping, working, loving, and worshiping. Taking time to be with each other, to learn each other's nonverbal ways of communicating their deepest feelings, is the most pressing budget.

3. *Energy.* Next to time, energy is the most precious budget of married life at any stage. Fatigue is the dry rot of the marriage covenant. With it comes neglect, irritability, and lording it over each

other, because our patience is threadbare.

As a couple becomes parents, child care demands massive outputs of energy. If illness strikes us, energy becomes a premium budget. As we grow older, age can be worn gracefully if we are wise stewards of even more limited energy. Therefore we show our thoughtfulness—the stuff of which love is made—by watching out for and removing energy wasters for ourselves and our spouses.

4. *Relationships.* Scripture admon-

A HOT TOPIC

Finances are usually the hottest topic in marriages. Perhaps the leading cause of disagreements, fights, and sometimes even divorce, money affects a loving relationship in unloving ways. How should the money be spent? Which spouse is better at handling financial matters? What should be your spending and saving priorities? What goals and expectations do you have regarding your standard of living?

Many couples simply respond to financial issues on a trial-and-error basis. A better approach, however, is for you and your spouse to create a plan with both short-range and long-range goals. Once you have done this you will be able to respond to financial concerns without unnecessary stress between the two of you.

Such a plan must be developed together, usually with the Lord's help, and should always be viewed as adaptable. A financial plan is a guide to live by, not a weapon to kill your marriage with.

Gary Bennett

ishes us as husbands and wives to respect and love each other as Christ loved the church and gave Himself for it. Our relationship to each other, then, is our first priority after our relationship to the Lord Jesus Christ. Maintaining this priority demands a day-to-day budgeting of loyalties. Other institutions and other persons compete for first place, but putting them there would damage our marriage. A marriage tends to endure if the partners feel they are in first place in their mate's affections and loyalties. Such a marriage can weather most storms. Even our children should not be allowed to push our marriage relationship into second place. Only the Lord Jesus Christ should take precedence over each other.

5. *Anger.* When we ignore the first four budgets—money, time, energy, and relationships—our spouses begin to build up feelings of injustice, frustration, aggravation, and hurt. These will eventually boil over in bursts of anger. As husbands and wives, we need to be stewards of our anger. Jesus guides us to agree with each other immediately, and not wait until a dispute becomes a court case (Matt. 5:21-26). Paul advises us, "In your anger do not sin: Do not let the sun go down while you are still angry" (Eph. 4:26). Being a good steward of anger means settling differences before going to sleep each night. This calls for being "kind and compassionate to one another, forgiving each other, just as in Christ God forgave you" (v. 32).

As husbands and wives, we are called to be stewards of our money—but our stewardship does not stop there. All five budgets must be in order for us to live productively and happily together.

Related Articles
Chapter 9: Communication That Energizes
Chapter 12: How Much Time Should We Spend Together?
Chapter 13: Determine Financial Priorities

Establish Financial Goals

GEORGE FOOSHEE

To build a complete budget, you simply set up pages for each spending category as shown in the following chart entitled "Our Financial Goals" (p. 402). To help you include in each spending category those expenses you can reasonably expect, study carefully the section called "Notes for Our Financial Goals."

With separate pages for each budget category, your system will allow you to check your spending against your plans or goals each month. Keep track of your spending in each budget category. When you begin to run short in any category, cut back in order to stay within your plan.

NOTES FOR OUR FINANCIAL GOALS

These explanations will guide you in arriving at the amount to designate for each category. If you have a monthly spending estimate, multiply it by 12 for the annual figure. If you have an annual figure, divide it by 12 for the monthly figure. You may need to refer to your checkbook to see what your previous expenditures have been.

1. TITHES AND OFFERINGS. All charitable giving: church, United Way, etc.

2. FEDERAL INCOME TAX. All amounts withheld, plus estimates paid, plus any amounts due with tax return.

OUR FINANCIAL GOALS

	MONTHLY	ANNUALLY
1. Tithes and offerings		
2. Federal income tax		
3. State income tax		
4. Social Security tax		
5. Other taxes (such as city)		
6. Shelter		
7. Food		
8. Clothing		
9. Health		
10. Education		
11. Life insurance		
12. Gifts		
13. Transportation		
14. Personal allowances		
15. Vacations		
16. Savings		
17. Household purchases		
18. Debt reduction		
19. _____		
20. _____		
21. _____		
Totals		

[Chart taken from *You Can Beat the Money Squeeze,* Fleming H. Revell, 1980, by George and Marjean Fooshee.]

3. STATE INCOME TAX. All amounts withheld, plus estimates paid, plus amounts due with tax return.

4. SOCIAL SECURITY TAX. All amounts withheld, plus any amounts due on self-employment income, up to a predetermined limit that changes from year to year. Check the limit and the current percentages with a Social Security office or at your public library.

5. OTHER TAXES. Taxes on your wages such as city income taxes.

6. SHELTER. If you are renting, include rent, heat, lights, telephone, household supplies, appliance repairs, magazine and newspaper subscriptions, other home-related expenses. If you are buying, include house payments, interest, insurance, real estate taxes, repairs and maintenance; include also the other renters' expenses.

7. FOOD. Grocery store items, paper goods, cleaning supplies, pet foods. Include all eating out and carry-out items and school lunches. May also include entertainment.

8. CLOTHING. Purchases, cleaning, repairs. May be divided with separate budget for each family member.

9. HEALTH. Health insurance premiums; medical, dental, and hospital expenses; drug items, medicine, cosmetics.

10. EDUCATION. School tuition and supplies, lessons, college expenses, uniforms, equipment, dues for organizations.

11. LIFE INSURANCE. All premiums whether paid monthly, annually, or quarterly.

12. GIFTS. Birthdays, anniversaries, special occasions, Christmas, weddings,

funerals, office collections.

13. TRANSPORTATION. Gas, oil, repairs, licenses, personal property tax, insurance. Include car payments or an amount set aside to purchase your next car.

14. PERSONAL ALLOWANCES. Set these aside for each family member to spend personally. Include hair care, recreation, baby-sitting, hobbies, and children's allowances.

15. VACATIONS. Trips, camps, weekend outings. Include also trips for weddings, funerals, and family visits.

16. SAVINGS. Amount set aside now for future needs.

17. HOUSEHOLD PURCHASES. Amount set aside for major appliances, furniture, carpeting, and major home maintenance such as roofing and painting.

18. DEBT REDUCTION. Includes all payments on debt not included in other categories. School loans; amounts due relatives, banks, or others.

Related Articles
Chapter 13: Determine Financial Priorities
Chapter 13: A Wise Saver or a Foolish Spender?

SIMPLIFYING YOUR BUDGET

In reality, no family budget is simple. Nevertheless, no matter how much money your family brings in, try to simplify your budget as much as possible—trimming where you can, saving, and spending wisely. The entire family can benefit from such "belt tightening," because they can learn how to budget intelligently.

Talk through family spending priorities. Talk about the fixed expenditures such as mortgage or rent, utilities, and car payments, and discuss ways to trim any "fat." Maybe the heat needs to be turned lower at night; maybe lights need to be turned off when not in use. Obviously you don't want to simplify by getting rid of the car, because then you end up being a nuisance to those you have to borrow from. But talk about the kind of car you need and how much you can afford. Discuss the priority of tithing. Figure your budget on percentages and how much money can go where.

Talk through major purchases as a whole family. When the desire or need for a major item arises, make it a family activity to research prices, consumer reports, sales, etc. Talk about whether the budget can handle such a purchase at the moment and, if you must buy, decide how you will pay.

Save together for special purchases or trips. Family vacations are never cheap; major purchases can be a drain on the budget. If possible, work out a plan to save for those items rather than putting them on credit.

Use the do-it-yourself principle when possible. Can you work on the car yourself? Could you trade time and skills with others? Stay away from your credit cards except for emergencies. There is little that complicates life more than excessive charges on credit cards.

Simplifying your budget is really a matter of wisdom and common sense. And you'll find that you have more to save, give away, and use for unexpected purchases.

YFC Editors

Determine Financial Priorities

DAVE JACKSON

In the early years of our marriage, we avoided debt but lived without a plan. I was the major wage earner, but my wife, Neta, was the one who stretched the money, paid the bills, and balanced the checkbook. At times I resented this. Childishly, I said to myself—and sometimes to my wife—"I earned it, so why can't I spend some of it?" My attitude led to a crisis, out of which I agreed to administer our family finances once we set up a mutual plan. We put a lot of thought and study into that plan, and it has served us well.

God owns all. Our perspective on money is based on our conviction that everything belongs to God and that He allows us to manage a portion as His stewards. That means we are to handle our money as He would. This principle led us to three management priorities:

—We recognize God's ownership by faithful tithing.

—We further His purposes by generous sharing.

—We honor His character by careful management.

Paying what when? Our tithe to our church and gifts to missions are the first checks I write each month—even when there isn't money to pay the other expenses. This practice has the biblical precedent of bringing the "firstfruits" to the Lord, and the Lord has always provided enough to finish out the month.

Another practice we have is not to use credit. We have plastic money, but we use it only for convenience when we know we have the cash to pay the bill without accruing any interest. At this point, the only exception is our house mortgage and financing for our kids' college education.

Budgeting. We decided to keep a budget. Each family member gets a small monthly allowance (yes, even Mom and Dad!) for which no accounting is required. Otherwise, everything is recorded. A petty cash box serves for small expenditures, but since they can add up to hundreds of dollars per month, they are each listed in a notebook. We pay larger bills by check and then transfer all records into the budget book, accounting for every dollar.

In the budget book, we set goal limits. Some categories accumulate from month to month so, for example, there will eventually be money to replace the car. Other categories, like food, do not accumulate.

At first the budget book served only as a record of our spending, but as we adjusted the goal amounts, it became a realistic way to limit some spending and make more conscious decisions about other purchases. One should not be a slave to a budget; it can be adjusted as necessary. But it is freeing to make a large purchase knowing we can afford it because we've saved for it.

All this seems tedious to some people, but the time required is not excessive—about six hours a month for bill paying, record keeping, checkbook balancing, and tax calculations (another reason I'm glad for careful records).

Living more with less. To have more money to give away and to foster the Christian virtue of sharing, we have looked for ways to live more simply without making that a fetish. One method has been to co-own a two-flat with another Christian family in our church. As

404

a result, we have more privacy than most apartment dwellers plus a large yard, garage, and help with maintenance, all for two-thirds what we'd spend on a single-family home. In addition we have the luxury of Christian fellowship and support when we desire it. There are challenging details to such an arrangement—mostly relational—but they can be worked out. Several families in our church are doing it.

Another intentional way to live more on less has been to locate close to others in our church. Relationships are far more important to us than investment values, ideal views, or proximity to one's job (which can unexpectedly change anyway). "Clustering" is quite possible when a vision for its value is upheld in the church. Just six years ago no one from our church lived in our neighborhood. We prayed with the first family that they could be the seed of a cluster. Now there are 15 families within 3 blocks. Clustering lowers transportation costs. Many social contacts, church committee meetings, and kids' play arrangements are within walking distance. Some trips, like regular shopping, can be carpooled. The occasional need for a second car can be met by borrowing. Not only is gas saved, but many families find they don't need two cars anymore.

Another more-with-less practice has been to spend money on experiences rather than things. Because our income is limited, vacation trips together, eating out as a family, going hunting with my son, and other experiences get the nod before replacing our appalling living room rug.

One of the most tangible temporal advantages of our faith is its encouragement to establish priorities. Only where

---

WHAT ARE YOUR REAL FINANCIAL PRIORITIES?

There are only five ways to use the money that comes into your household:
1. Giving
2. Supporting your lifestyle
3. Repaying debts
4. Meeting your tax obligations
5. Accumulating

Most of us would say that our top financial priorities are *giving* and *accumulating.* However, our checkbooks reveal our actual priorities, and these can be very convicting.

Most Americans—including Christians—make supporting their lifestyle their top priority, at least in practice. Their second priority is debt repayment—which is a result of their lifestyle. Third place is paying taxes (one has little choice in the matter). Accumulation is in fourth place, and giving is last of all.

Ronald Blue

---

life presents some absolutes can one organize other concerns accordingly. The challenge remains: have we really organized our whole lives around Christ and His church?

Related Articles
Chapter 13: Establish Financial Goals
Chapter 16: Making Your Dreams Come True

Faith, Finances, and Vocation

JUDITH C. LECHMAN

Several years ago I left the security of a regular paycheck and the job title "Editor" to venture into the financially unstable world of full-time freelance writing, lecturing, and workshop facilitating. Armed with a five-year plan, a support group, a network of valuable contacts, and a healthy dose of faith, I wrote and spoke and taught with a safety net beneath me—my husband's income.

Yet vocation, when it's truly a leading of the Spirit, doesn't adhere to earthly five-year plans. Mine was no exception. Lecturing became less important, as did the writing of short stories and inspirational articles—the lucrative centerpiece of my plan.

As the weeks and months slipped by, I found my work reflecting more and more the difficult changes occurring in my life. The children becoming adults and leaving home, the unexpected death of loved ones, and two major cross-country moves that left me uprooted from family, friends, and my church home—all became sources of pain and spiritual growth.

As if these emotional challenges weren't enough to bear, our family's financial security was shattered almost overnight when my husband lost his job. With our older son starting college that very year, we looked long and hard at our meager bank balance, remaining assets, expenditures, and sources of income. Although by worldly standards a bleak financial picture emerged, we recognized that, paradoxically, the solution rested in the eternal.

Both my husband and I knew how essential it was for our continued spiritual growth to live by faith during this finan-cially troubled period. For the first time we articulated our shared conviction that we needed to remain true to the vocations we had struggled so hard to find and follow. And in faithfully following our vocations, we would find the answers to our financial obligations.

Simply put, vocation has little to do with making a place for ourselves in this world. Instead, it is finding and living fully in that place which has been prepared for us and for which we have been preparing ourselves. Discovering our vocation and remaining faithful to it is a fourfold spiritual process that we repeat again and again on ever deepening and demanding levels.

The first step we take is *learning to be increasingly open to God's reality in every aspect of our daily lives.* Our perspective shifts so that self no longer is the focus of our thoughts and actions. Becoming Other-oriented, we grow in our knowledge of God. Ever so gradually, we realize that God is taking His rightful place in the center of our universe. We know that He is continually in us and around us, ready to occupy our hearts, minds, and lives.

At this point, we enter the second stage by *learning to communicate with this God who is within us.* Through meditation, reading, prayer, study, and other acts of devotion, we strengthen our communion with God. As our relationship with the divine grows, we learn to trust our Lord so that we may be transformed into a more Christlike image.

For such change to happen, we take the third critical step: *discovering the purpose for which we have been creat-*

ed. We learn to surrender our life to the Father and imitate the life of the Son. We listen to the will of Another rather than the insistent voice of self. We are asked to give all rights to God, yet, incredibly, we receive much in return. In surrendering, we soon know a quiet grace and growing sense of spiritual power that frees us to take the last and most demanding step.

Obedience is perhaps the most difficult of the four steps, for it requires us to do what God demands of us unconditionally. Having opened ourselves to God's presence in our lives, deepened our communication with Him, and surrendered self, we now follow where He leads us, *putting our belief into obedient action.*

As we repeat this fourfold process again and again, we discover that transformation has occurred within us. We now live under the aspect of the eternal where our worldly anxieties, worries, and fears are quieted, our pain and grief diminished, and our troubled hearts soothed.

With this changed perspective grounded in the eternal, my husband and I have grown to accept our financial difficulties as an unwanted but necessary lesson in openness, devotion, surrender, and obedience. We have learned to trust the Lord with our pocketbooks as well as with the pursuit of our vocations. We now study the Word of God and pray for insight and guidance in all our fiscal matters, whether about taking

---

ECCLESIASTES 5:10, 18-19

Whoever loves money never has money enough; whoever loves wealth is never satisfied. . . . [But] it is good and proper for a man to eat and drink, and to find satisfaction in his toilsome labor under the sun during the few days of life God has given him—for this is his lot. Moreover, when God gives any man wealth and possessions, and enables him to enjoy them, to accept his lot and be happy in his work—this is a gift of God.

---

on debt to finance our children's education or about ways to simplify our lifestyle.

With our focus firmly fixed on God and the biblical standards He has set for us, we are striving to act as responsible stewards of *His* earth and *His* resources, believing He will provide the necessities for us, His creatures. We no longer expect an abundance of financial rewards for faithfully following our vocations. We realize that living for God and working to accomplish the purpose for which we were created is enough.

Related Articles
Chapter 5: Husbands and Wives With Jesus as Lord
Chapter 5: Can I Trust God for My Spouse?

The Gift of Giving

DEAN MERRILL

I remember the day my wife and I stopped tithing. No, we hadn't departed from the faith, nor were we even rebelling against our upbringing (both of us grew up in pastors' homes and had been diligently taught to give God 10 percent).

We'd been married about three years when we realized tithing had become a duty. It was a bill to pay, along with the bills from the phone company, Shell Oil, and MasterCard. Every two weeks, you wrote out the checks and watched the dollars float away.

"Wait a minute!" we said. "This is no way to present a *gift.*" We got to talking about what a joyous experience a birthday is, or Christmas, with boxes wrapped up in shiny paper and smiles all around. What's inside? The giver knows, but he won't tell. He waits for the climactic moment to present his generosity. Now *that's* giving.

How could we create a similar mood about our gifts to the Lord?

We decided to play a little word game with ourselves. No more tithing; from now on we would give as at Christmastime. We were tired of giving "reluctantly or under compulsion"; we wanted to become cheerful givers (2 Cor. 9:7).

We began setting our offering envelope with the check inside on the kitchen table, along with the salt and pepper, where we could pray over it at Sunday morning breakfast. "Lord, we have something special to give You today, and we hope You like it. It's our way of saying we love You."

Did the dollar amount change under this new approach? No. We established 10 percent as a minimum, and in subsequent years we began bumping up the percentage as the Lord increased our earnings. (One of the small blessings of modern calculators is that they make incremental giving easy to compute.) We steadfastly refused to let ourselves ever begrudge this money.

I honestly believe God would rather have a joyous 5 percent than a reluctant 10 percent. And I *know* He'd much prefer steady, planned giving to hit-or-miss giving. He gives His many blessings to us steadily and consistently, and we can well afford to do the same.

In addition to giving with the proper attitude, here are some other guidelines:

1. *Give God His portion first.* That's the whole point: He is the source of "every good and perfect gift" (James 1:17). To leave Him till last, after the other bills are paid, is backward. If you had to trim your Christmas list, you wouldn't omit those dearest to you, would you? The same principle applies to giving to God.

2. *Make sure God endorses the destination of your gift.* While God's kingdom has many different offices, not everyone who hangs out the Christian shingle deserves God's money. You are responsible for getting those dollars into efforts that please Him.

3. *Let your children know what you're doing.* Don't hide the fact of your giving. While younger ones don't need to know actual amounts, let them see you actually presenting your gifts to the Lord—joyfully.

4. *Guide your children to do the same.* Money they give should come from their pockets, not yours. The exercise of proportionate giving can be started early (besides, it's a good math drill).

408

Any child old enough to spend is old enough to give.

5. *Don't look for "pay-backs."* Just as we all despise the relative who gives a birthday gift and keeps reminding us of it for the next three years, God doesn't appreciate manipulation. To say to God, "Well, here's my offering, and now You owe me one" only sours the relationship. People who, on the basis of tithing, look to God for health, next year's raise, or free trips are engaging in coercion, not love.

It is true that Scripture promises blessing to those who honor the Lord with their assets. "Give, and it will be giv-en to you" is a biblical fact (Luke 6:38). But no one likes to be hounded to fulfill promises he's made. Most parents have faced the irritation of a pouty child whining, "But you *promised!*" It drains all the joy out of doing whatever nice thing the parent had originally intended. The same is true of our Heavenly Father.

To cite one final admonition from Jesus: "Freely you have received, freely give" (Matt. 10:8).

Related Articles
Chapter 13: Determine Financial Priorities
Chapter 13: Train Your Child to Manage Money

Avoid Living One Lump at a Time

GEORGE FOOSHEE

You may have seen the "Ziggy" cartoon in which the well-known loser's little bird says to him, "You've got to learn to plan ahead." Ziggy's prompt response is "It doesn't pay. I believe in living one lump at a time."

In my 30-year experience as a professional bill collector, I have become convinced that most couples live their financial lives one lump at a time. These lumps are labeled *the unexpected.* Your car quits, your mechanic tells you it will cost $350 to get it running, and your checkbook is empty. In early April you find out you owe $740 income taxes, and you don't have the money. Your child visits the dentist and brings home the news that braces are needed. How can you plan for the unexpected and avoid living one lump at a time?

The Bible suggests a method for financial success. Proverbs 24:3-4 (TLB) says: "Any enterprise is built by wise planning, becomes strong through common sense, and profits wonderfully by keeping abreast of the facts." In simple language, a *budget* can be a tool to promote family harmony and help you avoid the lumps and panic that come from a lack of financial planning.

My definition of a budget is "planned spending." A budget is telling your money where you want it to go rather than wondering where it went. Here is an illustration that will explain simply how budgeting works.

Imagine for a moment that the only money you have to spend is for the place where you live. Let's call this spending category *shelter*. By some miracle, food, clothing, transportation, and all other expenses except for shelter are covered.

Assume that you plan to spend $900 a month for all expenses connected with your house, apartment, or condomin-

409

DATE	SOURCE	AMOUNT	BALANCE
1/01	Deposit	$900	$900
1/01	Envelope (for petty cash)	$ 15	$885
1/03	ABC Mortgage Co.	$700	$185
1/03	Local Electric Co.	$ 85	$100
1/10	Wet Water Co.	$ 13	$ 87
1/20	Flame Gas Co.	$ 38	$ 49
1/23	XYZ Telephone Co.	$ 31	$ 18
2/01	Deposit	$900	$918

ium. Also assume that your total spendable income is $900 a month. You deposit the $900 in your checking account, and your check record shows a $900 balance.

As you pay all bills connected with shelter, such as mortgage payment, utility bills, property and personal possession insurance, taxes, and maintenance, subtract the amount of each check from your checkbook balance. At the end of the month, you can see how well you have done.

The next month deposit another $900 and again pay your shelter expenses. As the year goes on, you can see exactly where your money has been spent. Either you will have spent according to your plan, or you will be overdrawn because you spent more than you planned to spend in your shelter account.

A shelter plan in your budget book might look like this at the end of the first month:

You can see from this illustration that a budget has two parts: (1) a plan for your spending and (2) a record of your spending to see how well you have followed your plan. (For ideas on devising a budget, see the article that follows.)

"Joy fills hearts that are planning for good!" (Prov. 12:20, TLB) As you learn to plan for financial lumps and avoid the panicky present, the joy of the Lord will fill your lives.

Related Articles
Chapter 13: Establish Financial Goals
Chapter 13: A Wise Saver or a Foolish Spender?

YOUR BUDGET AND CONCERN FOR THE POOR

It's a well-known fact that the more we make, the more we spend. But many of us want to control our money rather than having it control us, so we can show concern for those less fortunate. Here's how:

1. Designate portions of each paycheck to needs that you know about—relief agencies, church missions, other non-profit organizations.

2. "Adopt" an orphan (overseas, local, etc.) and help support him/her with the money you designate.

3. Have a meal of rice one night a month and donate the money you saved by not eating a full-fledged meal.

4. Organize a potluck dinner at your house and tell your guests that the money that would have been spent by each family eating out will be collected and given to a designated need.

5. Have a garage sale and give away the money collected.

6. Brainstorm ways to anonymously help people in need. Can you help fund the education of a child in the local Christian school? Can you help offset a person's medical expenses? Will a $20 bill help buy groceries this week for the needy family down the street?

7. Open your home and offer hospitality to those in need.

YFC Editors

FINANCIAL STRESSES AND STRAINS

The stress points of our financial system stem from two distinct sets of desires and priorities—Gail's and mine. It is easy, for example, for me to rationalize spending money on a steak dinner or on a family vacation. For Gail, however, that would be wasteful. She would rather buy something for the house or nice clothes for the girls.

Gail is also more conservative than I am regarding investments. Her way of saving money is to use a passbook savings account so we can get it when we need it, though we have compromised on a few less conventional investments over the years.

Then there is the matter of more money. Unfortunately, it seems as though there is never enough. And because we are in Christian work, we aren't getting rich on what I earn. When money is short or paychecks late, the tension builds. Gail is acutely aware of our expenses because she pays the bills; therefore, it is easy for her to become discouraged with our financial shortfalls. At times like these, she pressures me to ask for a raise or to take another job.

We don't make much, but still we can fall into the materialism trap, thinking that we'll be satisfied if only we had a little more. The truth is that most people spend all they have and never have enough. Materialism is insatiable.

Easing these tensions takes much talking, planning, and praying—again and again and again.

Dave & Gail Veerman

The Dilemma of Debt

HOWARD L. DAYTON

Families are drowning in a sea of debt! Individual Americans owe more than three trillion dollars. The average American family spends $400 more than it earns each year. Personal consumer debt increases at the rate of $1,000 per second, and debt has now reached the level that 23 percent of the average American's take-home pay is already committed to pay existing debt, not including the home mortgage!

With all this credit floating around, we are experiencing serious financial difficulties. This year almost 500,000 individuals in our country will file bankruptcy. And most sobering, a recent poll found that 56 percent of all divorces are related to financial tension in the home.

Financial tension is created largely by believing the gospel according to Madison Avenue—buy now and pay later with those *easy* monthly payments. We all know there is nothing easy about those payments. Madison Avenue leaves out one little word—*debt*.

What is debt? The dictionary defines it as "money or property which one person is obligated to pay to another." Examples of debts would be money owed to credit card companies, bank loans, money borrowed from relatives, the home mortgage, and past-due medical bills. Bills that come due, such as the monthly electrical bill, are not debts if they are paid on time.

What does Scripture say about debt? Romans 13:8 flashes a red light: "Keep out of debt and owe no man anything" (AMP). And in Proverbs 22:7 we learn why Scripture speaks so directly about debt: "The rich rule over the poor, and the borrower is servant to the lender." When we are in debt we are in a position of servitude, and the deeper we are in debt, the more we must serve. By legally obligating ourselves to meet our debts, we lose the freedom of deciding where to spend our income.

The Apostle Paul writes, "You were bought at a price; do not become slaves of men" (1 Cor. 7:23). Our Father made the ultimate sacrifice by giving His Son, the Lord Jesus Christ, to die for us. And the Lord now wants His children free to serve Him in whatever way He chooses.

When can we owe money? Scripture is silent as to when we can owe money, so the following is my own opinion. I believe it is permissible to owe money for any of three reasons: to purchase a *house,* to finance a *business,* or to pay for an *education.*

This allowable debt is permissible *only* if the following three criteria are all met:

1. The item purchased must be an appreciating asset or an asset that produces an income.

2. The value of the item must be equal to or more than the amount owed against it.

3. The amount owed should not be so high that repayment puts undue strain on your budget. Even if you meet all three of the criteria, this does not guarantee that you are going to be able to repay the debt. It only improves your chances.

But how can I pay cash for a new car? Seventy percent of the automobiles in our country are financed. The average person keeps a car between three and four years. The average car lasts 10 years. Here is how to escape using cred-

412

WHEN HUSBAND AND WIFE HANDLE MONEY DIFFERENTLY

Before any couple gets married, they should answer the following questions:

1. How was money handled as you were growing up?
2. Who earned the money and who was in charge of the budget?
3. How much came in?
4. How were decisions made on how to spend the money?
5. What was usually done with it (i.e., saving, buying, giving away)?
6. What values determined how money would be spent?
7. Were money problems discussed openly?
8. How were money problems handled?
9. What was the philosophy about debt, borrowing, credit cards, saving?
10. Was money invested? How?
11. Was insurance purchased? On what? How much?
12. How were major purchases decided on?

The differences in how the husband and wife were raised can lead to major problems handling money. If you and your spouse find that your money backgrounds clash, what should you do? First, communicate openly about money and thoroughly understand where the other person is coming from. Second, agree on a workable system for your home. Third, realize that your budget will change in the different phases of marriage (i.e., apartment to house, having kids, job transitions, paychecks added or subtracted).

Money is the largest problem in most marriages. Work it out early so you need not face the struggle.

YFC Editors

it: first, decide in advance to keep your car for at least six years; second, pay off your automobile loan; third—and this is the key—continue paying the monthly car payment, but to yourself into a special savings account. Then when you are ready to replace your car, the savings plus the trade-in should be sufficient to buy the next car without credit. It may not be a new car, but you should be able to purchase a good low-mileage used car free of any debt.

How about the home mortgage? I would like to challenge you to seek Christ and learn what He would have you do with all your debts, including the mortgage. Is it possible that He may

want you to pay off everything you owe including the mortgage? Obviously this can't be done overnight, but it might be something to work toward.

Years ago Bev and I felt the Lord wanted us to pay off everything including our home. We slowly began to make extra payments, and over a period of years we were able to completely satisfy the mortgage. I believe the Lord is calling many to do the same.

What about investment debt? Should you borrow money to make an investment? In my opinion this is permissible, but only if you are not required to personally guarantee the repayment of the debt. The investment for which you borrow should be the sole collateral for the debt.

It is important to limit your potential loss to the money you invested, because of the possibility of difficult financial events over which you have no control. It is painful to lose your investment, but it is much more serious to jeopardize meeting your family's needs by risking all your assets on investment debt.

Protect your freedom! It has been said that the typical American drives on a bond-financed highway in a bank-financed car (fueled by charge card-financed gasoline) to purchase furniture on the installment plan to put in the savings-and-loan-financed home! But this person, even if typical, has sold his own freedom. As Christians, we need to be especially careful to avoid debt so that we can be free to serve the Lord.

Related Articles
Chapter 13: How to Get Out of Debt
Chapter 13: A Wise Saver or a Foolish Spender?

How to Get Out of Debt

HOWARD L. DAYTON

There are nine easy steps for getting out of debt. The steps are easy, but it is still hard work to follow them. The goal is D-Day—Debtless Day, becoming absolutely free of debt.

1. *Pray.* In 2 Kings 4:1-7 a widow was threatened with losing her children to her creditor, and she appealed to Elisha for help. Elisha instructed the widow to borrow many empty jars from her neighbors. The Lord supernaturally multiplied her only possession, a small quantity of oil, until all the jars she could find or borrow were filled. She sold the increased oil and paid her debts to free her children.

The same God that supernaturally provided for the widow is interested in you becoming free from debt. The first and most important step is to pray,

seeking the Lord's help and guidance in your journey toward Debtless Day.

2. *Establish a written budget.* A written budget helps you in three areas. It enables you to plan ahead, helps you analyze your spending pattern, and assists in controlling impulsive spending.

3. *List everything you own.* Then determine whether there is anything you do not really need that might be sold to enable you to get out of debt more quickly.

4. *List what you owe.* Most people do not know precisely what they owe. It must be human nature to think that if I avoid something unpleasant, it might go away. However, it is crucial to list your debts to help you determine your current financial situation. It is also important to list the interest rate your creditors

REPAYMENT SCHEDULE

Month	Monthly Payment	Months Remaining	Balance Due
January	$100	11	$915
February	$100	10	$829
March	$100	9	$741

414

are charging for each debt, because it is usually best to pay off those charging the highest rate of interest first.

5. *Establish a debt repayment schedule for each creditor.* This is very important, because we all need to be encouraged during the struggle to get out of debt. In the example below, I owe the XYZ Company $1,000, with monthly payments of $100 at 18 percent interest, for a period of 12 months. The most important column is the one tracking the balance due. It is encouraging to see that balance steadily reduced.

6. *Consider earning additional income.* Many people hold jobs that simply do not produce enough income to meet their needs, even if they are spending wisely. Earning additional income may be a solution if you can do so without harming your relationship with your family. You may have to be creative in finding ways to involve the whole family in a project that will bring the family together rather than tear it apart.

7. *Accumulate no new debt.* The only way I know to accumulate no new debt is to pay for everything with cash or check at time of purchase. This raises the issue of credit cards. I do not believe credit cards are sinful, but they are dangerous. Americans carry over 700 million of them, and only 30 percent of their charge accounts are paid in full each month. It has been statistically shown that people spend approximately one-third more when they use credit cards rather than cash, probably because they feel they are not really spending money. They are like the shopper who said to a friend, "I like credit cards more than money, because they go so much farther!"

Here's the rule of thumb: if you always pay the entire monthly balance due, you can probably handle your credit cards. If you do not, they are too dangerous for you. In that case, I suggest you perform plastic surgery—any good pair of scissors will do.

8. *Be content with what you have.* Our culture's advertising industry has devised sophisticated methods of inducing the consumer to buy. Frequently the message is intended to create discontent with what we have.

An American company opened a new plant in Central America where labor was plentiful and inexpensive. Everything progressed smoothly until the first paychecks were distributed. The next day, the villagers did not return to work. The manager went to the village chief to determine the cause of the problem, and the chief responded, "Why should we work? We now have everything we need." The plant stood idle until someone came up with the bright idea of sending a Sears catalog to every villager. There has never been an employment problem since.

9. *Do not give up!* This last step is the most difficult of all. It is hard work getting out of debt, but the freedom to be gained is worth the effort.

Related Articles

WHAT DOES DEBT REALLY COST?

It is motivating to visualize the real cost of debt. We will use three standards of measurement: (1) amount of interest paid, (2) what you would have earned if you had invested the interest at 9 percent, and (3) how much money the lender earns at 18 percent. In this illustration we will assume you are spending $2,000 per year for interest.

	Year 5	Year 10	Year 20	Year 30	Year 40
Amount of interest paid:	$10,000	$20,000	$ 40,000	$ 60,000	$ 80,000
What you would have earned at 9 percent:	$11,969	$30,386	$102,320	$ 272,615	$ 675,765
What lender earns at 18 percent:	$14,308	$47,043	$293,256	$1,581,896	$8,326,426

I hope you will understand what bankers have known for a long time—the remarkable impact of compound interest. The lender earns well over 8 million dollars if you pay him $2,000 a year for 40 years and he earns 18 percent on your payment!

Now compare what you paid in interest over 40 years ($80,000) with what you could have accumulated if you had invested the money at 9 percent interest—$675,765! This would yield you a monthly income of $5,068 without invading the principal.

Howard Dayton

A Wise Saver or a Foolish Spender?

GEORGE FOOSHEE

What creature is commended in Scripture for being a saver? If you answered "the ant," you are correct. Twice the Bible mentions the ant's wisdom, illustrated by its practice of saving food in the summer so that there would be something to eat in the winter (see Prov. 6:6-8; 30:24-25).

Saving is also stressed in Genesis 41. In a dream, God revealed to Joseph his plan of saving food during the seven abundant years so that there would be enough to eat during the seven years of famine. I like to refer to such saving in times of plenty as "the Joseph principle."

One of God's money management principles is saving a portion of all we earn and receive. My experience with Christians, however, proves that this is a very difficult biblical principle to follow.

Amazingly, many Christians believe that saving money is not compatible with living by faith. Some refer to such New Testament verses as "We live by faith, not by sight" (2 Cor. 5:7) and "Do not store up for yourselves treasures on earth" (Matt. 6:19), using them to justify their lack of savings. But Jesus is not opposed to saving money. He is simply pointing out that our treasure should not be in things, for they are not permanent. Our focus should be on Him and His kingdom, not on our savings accounts or our worldly wealth. It is possible, of course, to save for the future without making money our first priority. That, in fact, is the Christian approach to saving.

People frequently use excuses for each stage of life as reasons for not saving money. These include the following:

Ages 25-30: I can't save now. I'm just getting started, and my income is low.

Ages 30-40: I can't save now. I have a young family to raise.

Ages 40-50: I can't save now. I have two children in college.

Ages 50-60: I can't save now. My spouse and I want to enjoy life.

Ages 60-65: I can't save enough between now and retirement to make much difference.

Ages 65 and over: I can't save now. I'm living with my son and his wife.

I have never seen a Christian who wanted to be called a fool, and yet the contrast between a wise man and a fool is nowhere presented more clearly than in Proverbs 21:20 (TLB): "The wise man saves for the future, but the foolish man spends whatever he gets."

I identify two kinds of savings: *savings to spend,* and *savings never to spend.*

Savings to spend may seem contradictory. However, almost all successful money managers save money to spend. Such savings are their secret for avoiding the debt trap. They save to spend for major purchases such as the following:

—replacement of items such as washers, dryers, and water heaters;

—major car repairs or a newer car;

—college expenses for the children;

—a dream vacation for the family;

—major home repairs such as a new roof, furnace, or air conditioner.

Very few families can make such expenditures out of current income. Saving to spend is the practical way to be the prudent man mentioned in Proverbs

If you deposit $1,000 each year (that's $2.75 a day), here is what will happen to it:							
End-of-Year Values							
5	10	15	20	25	30	35	40
5% $5,525	$12,578	$21,578	$33,065	$ 47,727	$ 66,439	$ 90,320	$120,800
8% 5,867	14,487	27,152	45,762	73,106	113,283	172,317	259,056
12% 6,353	17,548	37,279	72,052	133,333	241,332	431,663	767,091

22:3 (TLB): "A prudent man foresees the difficulties ahead and prepares for them; the simpleton goes blindly on and suffers the consequences."

Savings never to spend is money in virtually untouchable funds. This money may be intended for some of the following purposes:

—extreme emergencies such as major medical costs, unemployment, or destruction of home or personal possessions;

—retirement income;

—an inheritance for the children.

These savings are usually long-term investments such as the equity in your home, a pension plan at work, or Individual Retirement Accounts. Such funds, invested wisely, should double every 7 to 10 years.

Because of the sale of my small company, we recently had to terminate our 23-year-old profit-sharing trust. Each year, after personnel became eligible, a contribution equal to 15 percent of their annual earnings was set aside tax free in a profit-sharing trust. The earnings and appreciation of the trust added to the fund. At the time of distribution, even though there were only 21 people in the plan, approximately $800,000 was distributed. As I handed out the checks to the participants, I pointed out the number of years they had left until age 65 and showed them that in most cases if they left the fund invested at an 8 percent interest rate, their money would

more than double by then.

Just as tithing should become a habit, so should saving. Each payday, right after making your gift to the Lord, pay yourself, and you'll likely arrive at retirement financially independent.

The Bible warns against trying to get rich quickly, but it counsels us to build wealth slowly. Proverbs 21:5 (TLB) says: "Steady plodding brings prosperity; hasty speculation brings poverty." Wealth can be built on small amounts. For example, it takes only $2.75 a day to end up with $1,000 a year. And $1,000 a year saved over 40 years at an 8 percent compounded interest rate will yield $259,056. At a 12.5 percent interest rate, it will yield a million dollars!

Can you save $2.75 a day? That is about the difference between eating lunch out and carrying a brown bag. It works out to be only $19.25 a week, which the average family could easily spend at one visit to the local pizza parlor. Most folks in financial trouble that I counsel are spending at least $50 a month in long-distance charges; others spend between $20 and $30 a month on cable television. The average American family could save $1,000 a year simply by cutting out needless, undisciplined expenditures.

No matter what stage of life you are in, now is the time to begin the savings habit. Why not turn from being the foolish spender and become a wise man who, like the ant, stores up food for the winter?

Pay yourself first and be a saver. Spend more than your income and be a fool. The choice is yours.

Related Articles
Chapter 13: Establish Financial Goals
Chapter 13: Determine Financial Priorities

Deciding to Buy a Home

RONALD W. BLUE
with LaVONNE NEFF

Buying a house is one of the most significant financial decisions a married couple will ever make. When you add the down payment to the sum of the monthly payments made for up to 30 years, you get a very impressive sum. The location of your house may have a lot to do with what friends you will make, where you will go to church, and where your children will go to school. Thus the decision to buy a house must be made wisely and carefully.

A lot of home buyers base this important decision on intuition alone. There is a better way, however—subjecting your intuition to objective analysis. Here is how it is done:

1. *Make a decision statement.* What decision are you really making? If it's whether to buy the house on Elm Street, you've already narrowed down the field too far. It's better to start at a more basic level: *I must choose a new house* (because I am moving to a new town or because my old house is too small) or even *I must choose a place to live* (and I am open to considering either buying or renting).

There are several issues to consider before rushing into the purchase of a home. When a young person graduates from college, starts in the work force, and begins to accumulate cash, he should resist the urge to jump immediately into home ownership without having an emergency fund and a significant down payment—we recommend at least 20 percent of the house's purchase price. Otherwise he will soon find he must use credit cards to buy the many things he needs to operate the house and keep it going. This can start an unending cycle of debt.

In general, a family must live in a house at least two years to make buying it financially worthwhile. If your vocation requires you to move every few years, renting would probably be just as wise as purchasing. However, because of your family's desires and ministry opportunities, owning may still be more appropriate for you than renting.

Once you are sure you are ready to own a home, move on to the next step.

2. *Examine your criteria.* First, list every factor that is important to you in a house (this is your opportunity to dream!). For example, you might be concerned with location, purchase price, amount of down payment available, amount of monthly payments, school district, style, size, aesthetics, neighborhood, or condition. Get the whole family involved in making this list, and think of all possible criteria for evaluating a house.

Second, prioritize. For each criterion you have listed, assign a priority number between 1 and 5, with 5 being most important to you and 1 least important. For example, if cost and size are both extremely important to you, you would as-

419

GUIDELINES FOR MAJOR PURCHASES

All families face major purchases, be it a refrigerator, a computer, or even a car. But those major purchases can often be the cause of family arguments and overextending the budget to the breaking point. Following are some guidelines to consider as you contemplate a major purchase:

1. Ask the question, "Do we really need it?"

2. Put the item on a list, wait for 30 days, then reevaluate to see if you still "really need it."

3. Consider price and quality. What can you afford? What is the best you can get for what you can afford? Check the consumer reports. Look over the "used" section in the newspaper—see if perhaps a secondhand item would suffice as well as a brand new one.

4. Watch for bargains and sales.

5. Save the money for a major purchase ahead of time rather than buy on credit.

6. Fill in and return the warranty card, then keep it on file.

7. Keep your receipts and guarantees—just in case.

YFC Editors

---

sign each factor a 5. If you don't really care how much money down is required, give that factor a 1. If style is important, but less important than size, you might give it a 4—and so on.

Third, make your criteria specific. For each criterion you have listed, write down the most desirable way that it could be reached. Make your standard so specific that you will clearly see whether an alternative measures up to it. For example, for the location criterion,

the best house for you might be "between Elm Street and the expressway" or "less than 15 minutes from work during rush hour" or "walking distance to schools and to the train station." The cost criterion might be defined as "less than $15,000 down" or "monthly payments under $800." When you have finished, you will have painted a picture of your ideal house. It may not exist, but knowing exactly what you want will help you either get it or find a realistic alternative.

3. *Weigh each house you like against your criteria.* Each time you find a house you like, weigh it against your criteria one by one. For example, check out the house's *location.* If you want to live less than 15 minutes from work and the house is 10 minutes from your office during rush hour, rate it 5 on location. If it's 16 minutes away, give it 4. If it's an hour away and the road is under construction, rate it 1.

Now multiply this number by the priority number you assigned to the location criterion. If location received a priority rating of 3, the closest house would earn 15 points in that category (5 weight points times 3 priority points); the just-over-the-limit house would earn 12 points, and the charming house out in the sticks would earn only 3 points.

Perform this evaluative process for each criterion—size, style, cost, and so on—until you have a total score for the house. Then, each time you look at a house, evaluate it by the same process. The house with the highest score is the one that best meets all your objectives.

4. *Analyze the possible risks.* Although the house with the highest score may appear to be the best one to meet your needs, there may be factors that could prevent it from doing so. Think of the worst thing that could happen with a particular house. For example, if meeting the monthly payments is based on two incomes, what happens if one of you loses your job? Or perhaps new in-

HOMEBUYERS' EXPECTATIONS

I find in my counseling that one of the biggest problems Americans face today is unrealistic expectations. This problem is magnified when we deal with the home purchase decision, because it is probably the most significant financial decision any married couple will make. What should your expectations be, particularly if you are a young couple?

First, unless you have financial help from relatives, expect that owning a home may be out of reach for a long time. The average price of homes has reached a level that makes it difficult for a young couple to afford unless both work or are willing to overextend themselves financially. You can live with this unfortunate situation if you recognize that home ownership is a privilege, not a right. If you think it is a right, you may suffer a high level of frustration while you wait.

Second, expect that purchasing a home will mean making financial sacrifices somewhere else. Anyone entering into a first-time purchase should be well aware of the ancillary costs of home ownership: unexpected costs at time of purchase, increased utility bills, maintenance costs, rising property taxes, and major appliance purchases.

Third, and most important, expect that God can be trusted to meet your needs. He will not necessarily meet your wants and desires, but without question He will meet every legitimate need you have. Everyone needs housing, but not everyone needs a dream house. Many times God will withhold a blessing until it can be given in such a way as to demonstrate His faithfulness, goodness, and trustworthiness.

Ronald Blue

dustry will result in traffic jams between the house and your place of work, pushing your commuting time up to 45 minutes. Or maybe the neighborhood school will close for lack of sufficient students.

Put on your pessimist cap and think creatively. Then ask yourself, "How *serious* is this risk?" If you lose your job, would you lose the house, or would rich Uncle Ernie come to your rescue? Would the extra commuting time drive you crazy, or would you see it as an excellent time to listen to tapes? If the school closes, are you willing to have your children bussed or to send them to private school? If your worst scene would be utterly devastating, rate it high—90 to 100 percent on the calamity scale. If it would annoy you severely but

not ruin your life, give it a moderate rating—50 to 60 percent. If you could overcome it with no damages, rate it low—under 20 percent.

Finally, ask yourself how *probable* the risk is. If the worst possible risk is losing the house because of inability to meet payments, but you're a bona fide Rockefeller, your probability percentage is low. Give it 5 percent on the probability scale. If the foundations have already been laid for those new industries, the risk of their being built is high. Rate it 100 percent if no new roads are being built to accommodate the extra traffic.

Now multiply the calamity scale percentage by the probability scale percentage, and you have a risk factor. If a closed school would be tragic for your family, the calamity factor may be 95 percent. If, however, the school's enrollment has increased by 5 percent for each of the last 10 years, the probability factor is only, say, 10 percent. Thus the risk factor is .95 times .10, or 9½ percent—not very great.

If your best home has a risk factor of 80 percent and your second-best home has a risk factor of only 10 percent, you might seriously want to move house number two to the top of your list.

In summary, evaluate any house you are considering with a long-range perspective. Consider your vocation and your lifestyle desires. Buying a home may be the American dream, but don't rush to the bank with your eyes closed. Use wisdom in deciding whether it's best for you.

Related Articles
Chapter 13: Establish Financial Goals
Chapter 13: A Wise Saver or a Foolish Spender?

What Every Wife Should Know About Family Finances

MARY JANE WORDEN

In our 16 years of marriage Jim and I had established a fairly workable system for handling the family finances, a cooperative effort with a mutually agreed upon goal: try not to spend more money than we make. He collected the paycheck, I wrote the checks to pay the bills, and together we struggled through the agonies of the annual IRS form.

But an unexpected telephone call in the middle of the night changed everything. The emergency room nurse in a small-town hospital called to inform me that my husband was dead on arrival, killed in a head-on collision with a drunk driver. Suddenly I was a 36-year-old widow with 3 children to raise alone.

We all hope never to be faced with this kind of situation. But given the statistics—three out of four women will eventually be widowed—it is prudent to prepare ourselves as adequately as we can.

1. *Know how your family finances work.* Both spouses should be familiar with and competent to handle the everyday finances of the family, including bill paying and record keeping, budgeting, and making routine trips to the bank. Don't allow yourself to be handicapped by ignorance.

2. *Know where important documents are kept.* These are some of the financial issues I had to deal with in those first days after Jim's death:
- Where are the copies of our wills?
- Where is his birth certificate?
- Where is our marriage license?
- Where is the key to the safe deposit box?

I had to track down our various savings and checking accounts, as well as investment information (mutual funds, stock portfolios, pension funds). I strongly recommend that every family maintain an emergency file indicating the locations of all pertinent information.

3. *Plan ahead as a couple.* Since one of you will eventually be left alone, it's important to make as many decisions in advance as you can. Sit down together at least once a year to review decisions and consolidate information (see my related article in Chapter 2,

"Seasons of Marriage").

4. *Educate yourself.* Your local library has books and periodicals that give financial advice geared to the non-wizard. Call your local university for information about evening college classes open to the community. But beware of those taught by hungry investment brokers—remember that taking a class should never obligate you to invest anything more than your time and tuition. Some local banks in larger cities offer seminars especially for women, teaching the basics of planning and budgeting, investments, wills and estates, insurance, and so forth. Costs for such classes, seminars, books, and periodicals are generally tax deductible.

5. *Secure the services of qualified professionals.* If you should find yourself in the agonizing situation of being left alone, you will probably need professional help in four financial areas: (1) a lawyer or tax attorney to close out the estate, apply for insurance and Social Security benefits, and eventually help you prepare a new will; (2) an insurance person to advise you regarding your present and future needs; (3) an accountant to help you prepare your tax return (the first year or two special considerations are given to surviving spouses); and (4) an investment counselor to help you handle your insurance benefits. Overseeing all should be a professional financial planner, who may serve in one of the preceding capacities as well. How much better it is to have these systems already in place before you find yourself in a position of extreme need, lacking the time, energy, and good judgment necessary to make wise choices!

How does one find a competent financial planner? First, ask several trusted friends, particularly those who seem to be managing their financial affairs wisely, for recommendations. Second, arrange appointments with three of them, asking for an initial interview. There

---

WHO'S THE MONEY MANAGER?

Based on my personal experience, I think there's a benefit when husbands accept the task of managing the family finances. This is not because women can't keep books or make wise decisions. Most do a fine job! But for me there has been a distinct connection between managing our finances and accepting full responsibility as the head of our family.

Establishing priorities, creating the budget, and all major decisions are made together with Neta, and Neta is a full partner in our writing business. But in our modern, economically based society, nothing represents overall responsibility for the family's physical welfare more than managing its finances. It is not enough just to "bring home the bacon." I'm also responsible for using it wisely and fairly, protecting us from bill collectors and financial disaster, and leading us in thanks to and trust in God. Also, the long-term priorities and plans that make for financial stability require the creative mental percolation that is possible only by constant immersion in the family's financial facts. I can't lead the family as effectively if I leave financial worries to my wife and must ask her to find out what's happening with our money.

Dave Jackson

---

should be no charge for this investigative appointment. Be aware that certification does not guarantee competence.

In this initial interview ask questions like these:

● What do you do? (What is your area

of expertise—insurance? stocks? mutual funds?)

• How do you do it? (What information would you need from me? How would you process it?)

• What recommendations might you make for me? (Given some idea of your situation, general suggestions could be made. Look for suggestions of diversification—not all mutual funds or utility company stocks.)

• How are you compensated? (Fees? Commissions?) Finally, request the names and telephone numbers of three current clients whom you might call for their view of the services offered.

Trust your intuition as well as the facts gained during these initial interviews. Would you feel comfortable working with this person? Do you sense you can trust him or her? Is the office comfortable? Listen to those inner voices telling you it is disorganized to the point of chaos or, on the other hand, excessively luxurious for your taste.

Take a similar approach in obtaining the services of any of the other professionals; very likely you are already linked up with several of them.

I was relatively unprepared to handle our family finances, but God graciously provided a neighbor-lawyer who was extremely helpful. He handled all the legal and financial details, taking me by the hand (literally, sometimes) and leading me through the maze of details that must be attended to in the case of a spouse's death. He wisely told me not to trust my own judgment in that time of extreme stress, not to make any major decisions hastily. Understanding both my vulnerability and the unhappy fact that there are people who prey on recent widows, he said in strong and convincing words, "There will never be a financial opportunity that can't wait until tomorrow. Always get another opinion before giving your money to anyone."

In rethinking our family's financial goals and why we hold them, I have come to a clearer understanding of stewardship: all of life is a gift to be used for the kingdom. Life may be briefer than we expect, and I don't want to be owned by my things. As one friend said when something dear to her was broken, "Oh well, someday it's all gonna burn."

As children of the King we are all called to be stewards. Become informed—this is one part of your education that shouldn't be neglected. You'll feel better about yourself if you know how to manage the family finances, even if you never need to do it alone.

Related Article
Chapter 2: Be Prepared to Say Good-bye

424

Train Your Child to Manage Money

RONALD & JUDITH BLUE

Research shows that one of the biggest stressors felt by married couples is money, and one of the most frequent arguments is over how to bring up the children. It logically follows, then, that a book on husbands and wives should include a section on teaching children to handle money. If you and your spouse ever disagree in this area, read this article and discuss it together. Perhaps as you teach your children sound financial values, you will also draw closer together in your approach to money management.

Children must be taught four fundamental truths about handling resources. The first is that *God owns everything.* One's perspective on money management is determined by whether he views himself as an owner or a manager. As stewards of the resources owned by God, we have no rights— only responsibilities.

How can you inculcate this principle in your child's life? When discussing family financial decisions, make sure you explain how this truth relates to that particular decision. Pray as a family about specific financial decisions, especially those involving gifts to churches or Christian organizations. Encourage tithing. The percentage isn't as important as the principle: be sure to explain that God owns the whole amount, not just the percentage given back to Him.

The second principle a child must learn is that *there is a trade-off between time/effort and money/rewards.* In other words, "money doesn't grow on trees." We can tell him that all day long, but he must learn for himself that money comes from investing time, energy, and talents in certain worthwhile activities.

To learn this principle, the child must be denied some things. You can teach this by establishing a schedule of household chores for which you pay your child a modest allowance. Require him to earn some of the things he desires. Use the allowance to teach him that the amount of time and efforts he invests affects the amount of money he receives. Otherwise you may raise a child who as an adult will expect to receive whatever he wants without working for it.

The third principle is that *each spending decision has an impact on other spending opportunities.* That is, when you decide to spend money on one item, then the opportunity to spend that money another way is lost forever. In other words, "you can't have everything!"

When your child plans to purchase an item or spend money on an activity, encourage him to evaluate his decision and shop wisely. Sometimes children learn best when you give them a lump sum to purchase something—say, school clothes—and let them learn the consequences of buying expensive designer clothes while forgetting socks and underwear!

Fourth, a child must learn that *it is important to delay gratification.* Today young married couples often experience deep frustration because they feel enti-

425

tled to start out in a fully furnished four-bedroom home in an exclusive subdivision. They struggle because they are not able to begin where their parents left off. Why? Today's world stresses instant gratification. And with the prevalence of credit, many see no reason not to buy whatever they want right now. But over the long term, it's financial suicide to do so.

One way to help your child learn to delay gratification is to encourage him to save for the future with a savings account on which you pay him interest. You may even want to consider matching the amount he saves for one year as a reward for his prudence. But don't make that a habit or he will expect it!

As he saves, remind him that over time a little bit grows to a large amount.

Frequently review with him his savings balance. Have him add on the interest himself so he can see the growth occurring. Delayed gratification is difficult to teach because of its long-term nature, so it is essential to reward your child for goals accomplished along the way.

These four principles—God's ownership of all things, the trade-off between effort and money, the loss of opportunity from spending decisions, and delayed gratification—will help your children become responsible adults, but only if you determine to help them learn these principles while they are young. Take the first steps today, and you won't regret it tomorrow.

Related Articles

HANDLING MONEY

As newlyweds, Gail and I had two incomes and one checkbook. We deposited her teaching check in a savings account and determined to live off mine, knowing that she would have to stop working when we had children. I wrote the checks, paid the bills, and gave Gail cash for food and other expenses.

This system proved to be cumbersome and forced Gail to carry too much cash, so we added another checking account. I still had the "main" one through which we ran all the household expenses, but Gail had her own account into which she would deposit her "spending money," the food allowance, etc.

At the birth of our first child, Gail stopped teaching, and, of course, we lost that source of income. Because I brought in all the money and was also the checkbook handler, Gail soon felt shut out of the financial side of our marriage. Though we would talk things over, she had no control over the income or the expenses. And great was the increase of our tense moments and arguments regarding where the money was going, our spending priorities, and how we could increase our income.

To relieve this tension, we switched the budgeting and bill-paying roles. I brought home the paycheck but gave it to her. She would deposit the check, give me spending money, and pay the bills. This was not threatening to me because I was contributing to our financial situation as the "breadwinner." In fact, it was a relief—I no longer had to spend time worrying over how to stretch the dollars left at the end of the month or to struggle with balancing the checkbook. Though Gail has never enjoyed these pressures, she has become an integral partner in our finances as the "budgeter" and "check-writer." One checkbook works well, with Gail controlling it.

Dave & Gail Veerman

Psychologists have learned that certain events are more likely than others to cause stress. One of the most popular ways of rating stress is by using the Social Readjustment Rating Scale developed by T.H. Holmes and R.H. Rahe in 1967 (*Journal of Psychomatic Research,* vol. 11, Pergamon Press). Which of these events has occurred in your life during the last 12 months? What is your stress score? According to the authors of the SRRS, a score under 150 indicates low stress; 150-199, mild stress; 200-299, moderate stress; 300 or more, major stress.

100 Death of spouse
73 Divorce
65 Marital separation from mate
63 Detention in jail or other institution
63 Death of a close family member
53 Major personal injury or illness
50 Marriage
47 Being fired at work
45 Marital reconciliation with mate
45 Retirement from work
44 Major change in the health or behavior of a family member
40 Pregnancy
39 Sexual difficulties
39 Gaining a new family member (e.g., through birth, adoption, oldster moving in, etc.)
39 Major business readjustment (e.g., merger, reorganization, bankruptcy, etc.)
38 Major change in financial state (e.g., a lot worse off or a lot better off than usual)
37 Death of a close friend
36 Changing to a different line of work
35 Major change in the number of arguments with spouse (e.g., either a lot more or a lot less than usual regarding child rearing, personal habits, etc.)
31 Taking on a mortgage greater than $10,000 (e.g., purchasing a home, business, etc.)
30 Foreclosure on a mortgage or loan
29 Major change in responsibilities at work (e.g., promotion, demotion, lateral transfer)
29 Son or daughter leaving home (e.g., marriage, attending college, etc.)
29 In-law troubles
28 Outstanding personal achievement
26 Wife beginning or ceasing work outside the home
26 Beginning or ceasing formal schooling
25 Major change in living conditions (e.g., building a new home, remodeling, deterioration of home or neighborhood)
24 Revision of personal habits (dress, manners, associations, etc.)
23 Troubles with the boss
20 Major change in working hours or conditions
20 Change in residence
20 Changing to a new school
19 Major change in usual type and/or amount of recreation
19 Major change in church activities (e.g., a lot more or a lot less than usual)
18 Major change in social activities (e.g., clubs, dancing, movies, visiting, etc.)
17 Taking on a mortgage or loan less than $10,000 (e.g., purchasing a car, TV, freezer, etc.)
16 Major change in sleeping habits (a lot more or a lot less sleep, or change in part of day when asleep)
15 Major change in number of family get-togethers (e.g., a lot more or a lot less than usual)
15 Major change in eating habits (a lot more or a lot less food intake, or very different meal hours or surroundings)
13 Vacation
12 Christmas
11 Minor violations of the law (e.g., traffic tickets, jaywalking, disturbing the peace, etc.)

STRESSES
AND CRISES

Someone has quipped, "There are two ways to react to stress—you can be either laid back or laid out." The incessant tensions of living in the "fast lane" force one to fall down as a victim or to somehow convert stress, like noxious fumes, into controlled energy.

Marriages, where both partners hold a piece of our breakneck corporate tiger by the tail, can be jeopardized. Conversely, when two share the stress load with mutual caring concern, more weight can be carried. Nowhere does Scripture promise exemption from stress, but enablement is God's specialty. He will not allow His children to be stretched beyond bearable limits.

But at times, things may seem unbearable. Life is so constructed that crises are inevitable in the course of human existence. When circumstances worsen to a point where radical change is inevitable, marital bonds are often threatened. The survival instinct excludes the spouse and may even blame him/her for the emergency.

What is the biblical response for a husband or a wife when ordinary human solutions seem impotent? In all times of stress and crisis, words are weak; a competent Person is needed, One who has "been there." The Book of Hebrews presents Jesus Christ as the believer's High Priest. He was tempted in every way, just as we are, "yet was without sin" (4:15). Consequently, the Christian may approach His throne of grace with confidence.

Howard & Jeanne Hendricks

Helping Your Mate During a Time of Suffering

DENNIS & BARBARA RAINEY

Suffering takes many forms, and all of them can damage the marriage relationship. In the case of a major catastrophe such as the death of a child or the birth of a handicapped child, 6 out of 10 marriages end in separation or divorce within 5 years. Less severe disasters—loss of work, relational problems in the family—also take their toll. Even daily stresses and pressures can eat away at marriage.

If a husband and wife turn *on* each other rather than *toward* each other, any stress or suffering will hurt them. Rather than attacking your partner, try to build him or her up. Here are some suggestions:

429

1. *Realize that circumstances can erode your mate's self-confidence.* It only takes a phone call, a letter, or a pink slip to reduce a confident, assertive, on-top-of-the-world man or woman to rubble. The more we realize that none of us is as secure as we appear, the better equipped we are to help a suffering person.

2. *Communicate.* The more we keep things bottled up inside, and the more we think our mate wouldn't really want to hear what we're thinking, the more distance is going to separate us. Express what you think, how you feel, what you are afraid of, what you are worried about. Get it all out. Only then will your mate begin to understand what you're experiencing.

3. *Listen.* Even if the suffering seems to affect one partner more than the other, it affects you both. Since both of you are suffering, both need to hear and be heard. Encourage your mate to open up by drawing him or her out. Find out what he or she thinks and feels. Keep a two-way exchange going at all times.

4. *Ask your partner what he or she needs.* Different people need different things at different times. Don't try to second-guess your mate. Ask! Say, "I'm having a hard time knowing exactly what you need. Could you help me by telling me what you need from me? Is it time alone? A listening ear? Solutions? Planning? Prayer?"

5. *Encourage your mate.* Don't try to overprotect your mate or give him or her too much direction, but do try to meet his or her needs. A husband who takes the kids or finds a baby-sitter so his wife can get away is encouraging her. A wife who creates a situation where her husband can have needed time alone is encouraging him.

6. *Turn to your friends.* It is extremely important for a couple to have at least one friendship with another couple where each can identify with the

RESPONDING TO CRISES

A "life crisis" brings different pictures to different people. What may seem like a crisis to one person may be just a cause of stress for another. Nevertheless, if we consider something a "crisis," our response to it parallels the response to grief.

The first stage is *shock/denial.* We refuse to accept the facts and we deny them (i.e., we refuse to have the lump checked because we deny that it could be cancerous).

The second stage of crisis reaction is *anger.* We question why this is happening to us or someone we love and we demand that God give a reason for this unfairness.

Third, *depression* hits as we realize there is nothing to be done and we are truly human and vulnerable.

Stage four is *understanding.* We begin to gain back our perspective, even if we don't truly comprehend all that is happening.

Finally, we hope to reach the stage of *acceptance* in which we can rest in God's sovereignty and continue with life.

As we face a crisis in life, no matter how devastating, it is important that we work through the stages of grief so we are eventually able to accept what is happening. Only then can we move beyond it. Unfortunately, most people stall at the first or second stage, unable to move beyond denial or anger.

YFC Editors

person of the same sex. Especially during times of suffering, such friendships can be a life-or-death matter. In many cases a friend can take the place of a professional counselor. When you talk things over with someone outside the family, you gain new perspective.

7. *Pray for one another.* God will teach you what you need to know; He will help you go through your suffering in His timing. You will experience more of His strength and comfort if you pray—with other people who are involved, but especially together as a couple.

8. *Help bring a sense of purpose to your suffering.* The first question most people ask when they go through a difficult time is, "Why?" We can't usually know why, but we can bring purpose to our suffering by looking at what it can produce in us: character, perseverance, hope, fruitfulness, patience (see John 15:2; Rom. 5:3-5; James 1:3-4). Try as a couple to find out how your suffering can be redeemed.

9. *Give each other freedom.* We do not all take the same path through suffering. Some go through it quickly; some take a long time. Some skim its surface; some plunge into its depths. Let your mate suffer in his or her own way. Offer support, but do not tell your mate how he or she ought to feel or act.

10. *Give each other time.* Whether your suffering stems from an enormous tragedy or a relatively small irritation, it may not resolve itself overnight. Don't expect each other to snap out of it quickly. Communicate that whether it takes two weeks or two years, you will stand by your partner, loving and helping him or her. This can take a lot of pressure off your mate.

Last summer we visited a forest of giant sequoia trees. Many of these enormous trees had been burned. They showed deep scorch marks, but they were still living and growing and putting out new branches. That is because their roots were sunk deep into the earth. Peter tells us to "grow in the grace and knowledge of our Lord and Saviour Jesus Christ" (2 Peter 3:18). To do this, even in times of suffering, we need to sink our roots deep in Christ.

Related Articles

Chapter 4: Encouragement: That Vital Element

Chapter 9: The Art of Listening

Chapter 14: Loyalty to Each Other

Loyalty to Each Other

NETA JACKSON

What does it mean for a husband and wife to be loyal to one another? A number of incidents in our marriage have helped us grapple with the issue of loyalty.

Recently our church was struggling with the question of men's and women's roles in church leadership and in the family. Papers had been presented, and both leaders and laypeople had shared viewpoints and feelings in a series of congregational meetings. My husband, who was chairing the proceedings, had kept himself somewhat detached and neutral in order to give a fair hearing to all sides. At the last scheduled meeting, however, he laid aside his official role and shared some of his personal concerns about the declining role of fathers in society and in the church, and the increasing number of families headed by female single parents. He cited the impact that a high incidence of father-less families was having on the black community—a phenomenon created by racism and a vicious cycle of poverty and welfare, and a concern of black leaders and the black press—and he asked, "What is it we're choosing? Where will be the male role models for our children?"

Well, the mud hit the fan. Single parents were offended. Some women were offended. And the black members in our church were offended. For days afterward, we got calls and notes. One friend in particular seemed unable to forgive my husband, even after they got together to listen to and learn from each other. The particular hurts were dealt with, apologies were given and received—but the relationship went dead. Only a few close friends and the elders understood what he was trying to say and stood with him, feeling that the response was an overreaction.

Where was I in all of this? I too understood Dave's concerns and shared them. But I was hurt and upset by all the flack. I lost sleep. I was afraid of being categorized on the issue, when I saw myself as walking a middle ground, trying to hear and learn from the concerns of both sides.

"Wait a minute!" I thought. "I'm not the one who gave this speech. I probably would have been more diplomatic. How come I'm suffering too? How come relationships are being lost to me too?"

As I struggled with these thoughts and feelings, I struggled with loyalty. The problem wasn't really mine—could I distance myself from it? But if I did, wouldn't I just add to the pain Dave was experiencing from others who distanced themselves? Or should I own the problem, take it on myself out of love for him, bearing his burden as if it were my own? Because we are one flesh, are we not one spirit too? When Dave is honored, am I not honored too? If Dave is rejected or misunderstood, should I not

be willing to be rejected or misunderstood as well?

Don't say, "Of course!" Because it's not easy, especially if mistakes have been made along the way. I was often tempted to think, "If only he hadn't said that," or "If only he had said this a different way."

Loyalty won. Deep down, in spite of the pain, I knew I belonged at his side. I needed to share his pain, not add to it by leaving him to face the situation alone.

When we were first married 20 years ago, we met with a group of professional Christians to talk about urban ministry. Both of us felt young and inexperienced, but we tried to look self-confident. However, when trying to ask a question at one point, I couldn't find the right words to express my thoughts. I stumbled around, leaving an awkward pause. Dave spoke up impatiently, "Come on, spit it out. What are you trying to say?" I was devastated. I had been cut off from my only anchor in that group of intimidating people. I was frozen for the rest of the meeting.

Later I was able to tell him what his response had done to me. He felt terrible; he had spoken out of his own insecurity and desire to make a good impression. He asked my forgiveness, and we both vowed then and there to be loyal to one another in public, no matter what.

After several years of married life, I thought I knew Dave's typical responses to most things. If I felt overwhelmed and he suggested that I give up one of my many responsibilities, I'd think, "Oh, that's what you always say"—and ignore his advice. If a friend or another leader expressed concern that I was overloaded, however, I would take it seriously. This became a bad pattern for several years: if Dave suggested something contrary to my own feeling on the subject, I took it with a grain of salt; if someone else suggested the same thing, I considered it valid.

What was going on here? Ignoring Dave's advice made him feel that I gave more respect and loyalty to others than to my own husband. On the other hand, when I complained about overwork, often what I most wanted was a comforting shoulder and listening ear. We both had to learn what loyalty and respect for one another meant in this situation. I learned that his advice grew out of real concern for me, and that I should take his direction more seriously than anyone else's; he learned that standing by me was sometimes more helpful than offering a solution.

Loyalty. Being there, no matter what. Respecting your partner above all others. Sharing the pain as well as the joy. Never cutting the emotional anchor you both need in order to survive.

Related Articles

FALLING BACK IN LOVE

Loving your mate is important—everyone agrees. From the male side, I might point out that God clearly says, "Husbands, love your wives." God does not add, "but only if she is lovable." You obviously thought she was lovable or you would not have married her to begin with. If you have fallen out of love with her, you can fall back in love by courting her as you did back when you were trying to win her heart.

Logic will not change your emotion, but action will.

Zig Ziglar

How to Survive the Loss of Child

BOB & CINNY HICKS

"Delta Jumbo down." The words echoed through the corridors of the Dallas-Fort Worth airport August 2, 1985. A wind shear had caused Delta Flight 191 to come up short, just north of the runway. The jumbo jet slammed into water tanks, exploded, and instantly killed over a hundred passengers, many of them children. Delta flew their parents to Dallas and housed them at the DFW Hilton. As chaplain for the Texas Air National Guard, I coordinated the ministry to the families for the week following the disaster. From this experience I learned much from courageous couples who wrestled with shock, outrage, and despair.

Losing a child, whether through long degenerative illness or sudden tragedy, is one of the hardest blows a couple ever faces. It attacks all their individual and marital resources. Many don't survive. Others go on but never fully face the reality of what happened. A few become valued mourning partners and learn together to accept the loss, growing closer through their shared grief.

What are some of the things these survivors must learn in order to remain intact through the loss of a child? Although each couple's experience differs, here are a few important insights the healthy survivors learn:

1. *Allow each other to grieve.* As basic as this seems, normal grief reactions are often denied in our culture, frequently by Christians. Most cultures have appropriate rituals in which grief reactions are vented. However, in our fast-paced Western society, many couples do not allow themselves the time necessary to grieve properly. Many researchers have noticed the various stages of grief associated with loss. To resolve grief successfully, the couple needs to work through these stages (denial, anger, depression, bargaining, acceptance) without fixating on any one.

When a couple has lost a child, it is easy for the husband to go back to work or for the wife to quickly throw out the no-longer-needed clothes and appear to have dealt with the loss. In reality, however, they both still have much work to do. Each grieving parent must allow the other the distance required to deal with the loss and come to his or her own final resolution. Couples can in fact inhibit the grief process by forcing each other to "be strong" or "stop crying," or by saying, "Why can't you get your act together? It's been months now since Susy died." This is not a time for platitudes or for playing the macho. Grief is a normal human reaction to the devastating loss of a child. Losing a child, knowing we will never see him or her grow up, challenges our most basic assumptions about the goodness of life. Couples must allow each other time to grieve.

2. *Allow each other to grieve differently.* In a study conducted at Purdue University, Kathleen Gilbert noted that most couples go through the grief process "out of step" with each other. In their methods of both grieving and coping with the child's loss, they are very different. A husband tends to be a problem-solver, trying mostly to resolve his wife's overt grief, while his grief is the more shadowy type that passively lingers and follows his every step. Often this difference becomes a source of acute tension and conflict in a couple's relationship. The wife wants her husband to experience the same emotions at the same time she does. The husband likewise cannot understand why his wife cannot "move on" and bury the hurt the way he does. These differing expectations can become severe stress points for the grieving couple.

When Lazarus died, Mary and Martha, his grieving sisters, expressed their grief differently (John 11:17-29). Martha was more verbal, engaging the Lord with almost hostile emotions. Mary, on the other hand, was more passive and withdrawn, staying at home until the Lord called her. If God has not made two snowflakes alike, why should we think that two human beings working through a tragic loss together should experience it in the same way?

3. *Avoid simplistic answers.* When tragedy strikes, "Job's comforters" sooner or later show up. They are usually well-meaning, but sometimes wrong. In Job's crisis his friends tried to find some reason for his extreme loss of wealth, health, and family, but they did not understand God's ways or Job's experience.

The death of a child undermines a couple's view of life. It strikes at the heart of their assumption that God is a good God, that bad things shouldn't happen to good people. They do not need to be offered a simplistic worldview. Although they ask basic questions, their questions are more likely to be emotional reactions than truly intellectual reflections. It is tempting to respond with intellectual or philosophical wisdom, but this is not what the couple needs at this point. Later in the grief process, cognitive restructuring—especially from a biblical perspective—will play a very important part in resolving the loss. But before then, a couple needs to be insulated from incomplete or erroneous explanations.

In the DFW disaster I heard some pathetic "answers." One minister told a couple who asked, "Why did God allow my child to die?" that God had nothing to do with the crash. This answer may have satisfied them at that time, but its long-term implications are anything but comforting. A biblical view of God would suggest that if God is not in some way involved in everything, then He is not involved in anything. Taking God out of the picture leaves man with no reason or meaning at all. This answer is no answer. Another person told me that God allowed the crash because there was a married businessman on the flight traveling with his mistress. Would God take 136 lives because one man on board was slipping away for a weekend with his secretary? I don't think that's an answer either.

The tendency is either to read into the loss no meaning whatsoever, or to give it more meaning than it deserves. "Job's comforters" are always lurking in hospital hallways or church corridors, offering their simplistic answers to life's most perplexing questions. It is wise for a couple who is grieving for their lost child to avoid these answers. Answers like "God must have known that your child would deny the faith," or "He wanted your baby in heaven because he was so special," or "You know you haven't been walking with the Lord lately" may all be true, but only God knows for sure. If we don't know for sure, it is better to trust the Lord with whatever happened and refuse to accept such simplistic explanations. Job never knew why he suffered!

4. *Pray for a mourning partner.* If a husband and wife bear their grief in different ways and at different times, then with whom do they share it? It is obviously better if the couple can go through the grief process together, being supportive partners throughout. However, this is probably rare. Both husbands and wives need supportive mourning partners who are acquainted with grief and can provide a listening ear and a strong shoulder. A mourning partner is one who stands with us in our grief, accepts us where we are, and moves us along in the grief process. It may be a minister, therapist, or friend.

A nearly forgotten character in Job's story is Elihu (Job 32–37). Elihu plays the role of the mourning partner. He is there all the time, but he does not speak until all the others have exhausted their "answers." When he is ready, he speaks both for God and for Job. As a mourning partner, Elihu is a good friend, listening before talking, reflecting before responding, seeking to understand the situation before providing answers for it. Every couple needs an "Elihu" as a mourning partner.

5. *Be a mourning partner to others.* One of the best ways to cope with and eventually survive the loss of a child is to begin to reach out to others who have suffered the same kind of experience. The Apostle Paul conveys this insight in 2 Corinthians 1:3-4, when he says, "The Father of compassion and the God of all comfort . . . comforts us in all our troubles, so that we can comfort those in any trouble with the comfort we ourselves have received from God."

Losing a child is so devastating it can breed great self-absorption and self-pity. These are natural responses; however, they can become very unhealthy when they dominate a couple. Turning outward and helping others has great therapeutic value.

In the Delta crash, as I worked with couples dealing with the loss of children, I noticed they largely grieved alone. Most stayed in their hotel rooms and came out only to eat. In the Hilton dining room, almost every table was filled with families dealing with loss. But for two days no one ever looked across the room or the aisle to a fellow sufferer. On Sunday night the dynamics changed. We held an ecumenical memorial service in the hotel. We encouraged the families to express their grief, even anger, to God in prayer. At the conclusion of the service the aisles were filled with families embracing each other. For the first time they realized there was grief beyond their own. They began to be mourning partners even before their own mourning was over.

6. *Rediscover the vast purposes of God.* When a couple suffers the loss of a child, a danger is always lurking under their attempts to make life go on as usual. Many couples confess a profound sense of meaninglessness. Even some of the most religious and diligent suddenly find themselves doubting the most basic elements of their faith. The process is not uncommon, and certainly not unnatural. All human suffering is most intolerable when it is inexplicable.

In my experience with family survivors, I have been amazed by the fact that, whether they are religiously committed, agnostic, or atheistic, they all ask the same question: "Why did God allow this to happen?" This almost universal question is a great affirmation that God has made us to be meaningful creatures. We not only desire meaning in what happens, we demand it!

A rational restructuring of the loss must take place for proper healing to take place. Although this is very difficult in the initial phases, it eventually becomes necessary. Since the couple's worldview has been shattered, it must now be rebuilt. The loss must be fitted into a larger view of life. This is where a

EXPECTATIONS

A good friend of ours who lost his six-year-old son in a plane crash once offered us a priceless bit of wisdom:

"Life wouldn't be so hard if we didn't expect it to be so easy."

Dennis & Barbara Rainey

rediscovery of God's vast purposes is necessary. Job did not rest his case with God until God spoke to him (Job 38–41). God still speaks today through His Word. Though we will probably never know what exact purpose God had in taking one of His little ones home, we can trust that He knows what He is doing. There are no meaningless events in His meaningful oversight (Rev. 4:11).

Dr. Julius Segal, psychiatrist to POWs, Holocaust survivors, and more recently the Iranian hostages, wrote, "I have been impressed with the magnificent ability of human beings to rebuild shattered lives, careers, and families, even as they wrestle with the bitterest of memories" (*Winning Life's Toughest Battles,* McGraw, 1986, p. 9). Losing a child is one of the most bitter losses of all, but survival is possible and grief can be conquered. "Thanks be to God who always leads us in triumphal procession in Christ" (2 Cor. 2:14).

Related Articles
Chapter 1: Love as Grace
Chapter 5: Prayer in the Husband-Wife
Relationship

In Sickness and In Health

JOHN ROBERT THROOP

When we exchange wedding vows, we are usually the picture of health. The husband-to-be looks into the face of his bride and sees the radiant glow of vigor and energy. But we are mortal and fragile, and even the young become ill. When this happens, too often we can identify with David in his discouragement: "My friends and companions stand aloof from my plague, and my kinsmen stand afar off" (Ps. 38:11, RSV). Sadly, not only our kinfolk keep their distance. Sometimes our spouses are not there for us either.

Tony and Jean loved the outdoors. Natives of Southern California, they moved to Montana to escape the urban rat race and find some wide open space. About three years after their wedding and their move, Tony began to notice some numbness in his extremities and some slurring of his speech. He was in his mid 20s, and such symptoms should not appear in a man his age. But they do when multiple sclerosis is the cause.

Tony grew weaker very quickly. Suddenly he was dependent on his wife for even the most basic needs. One morning Tony awoke rather late and called for Jean to help him out of bed—but there was no answer. He turned over and found a note on Jean's pillow. It read, "I can't take any more. I'm sorry."

Tony called everywhere he could think to try to locate Jean and find out what had gone wrong, but he couldn't track her down. Now he was not only sick, he was also alone. His mother flew from California, took him home, and put him in a hospital. Within a month Tony got a letter from Jean saying she would not come back to him. He was not the man she married, and she needed him healthy. After a year Tony, exhausted, defeated, and very ill, filed for divorce on the grounds of desertion. Jean never responded.

Cases like Tony's are more frequent than one might imagine. And marriage problems arise not only when a spouse becomes ill, but also when a child is disabled. Sean, a bouncing two-year-old, had eye surgery to correct a congenital defect. The surgery had a 50-50 chance of success, and Sean was on the wrong side of the 50. He will have minimal vision the rest of his life. Sean's father simply could not handle a disabled and dependent child, and he insisted on divorcing his wife. Sean's father is a doctor.

Illness—especially when it is chronic—taxes marriages. Why? For one thing, an illness creates a deep dependence of one spouse on the other. The sick spouse simply can't do the things he or she used to do effortlessly. The relationship changes: now the caregiving and serving goes mostly in one direction, whereas it formerly was mutual.

Sickness also brings out selfishness even in people who are spiritually deep. When you're sick, you must employ all your resources in getting well. The focus is on yourself and your needs. Or if a child is the ill member of the family, all caring goes to that child and the marriage is put on hold. Finally, if your spouse suffers, it may be too much for you to handle emotionally. For men especially, the vulnerability revealed by pain and suffering is nothing short of overwhelming. In our culture, men have been encouraged to keep feelings hid-

IF YOUR SPOUSE IS SERIOUSLY ILL

Here are some things to do if your spouse is seriously ill:

1. *Pray.* When praying for your spouse, pray for healing—but pray also that God will be glorified in your spouse's illness.

2. *Visualize handing over your spouse to God's loving care as you pray that His will be done.* Pray for wisdom to know what practical steps to take. It is essential that you take time to pray on your own as well as with your ill spouse or others.

3. *Become part of a support group.* Join a support group in your community for those who have a family member with the disease. Men especially need to find others who can understand what they are going through. Such support groups can also provide detailed information and tips on care.

4. *Educate yourself about the disease.* For chronic diseases, there is usually a county, state, or city chapter of a national organization working on a cure (e.g., the Multiple Sclerosis Society or the American Cancer Society). If you don't know how to locate the local chapter, call your public library for information.

5. *Do not hesitate to ask your doctor any question about the disease.* If the doctor's response is too fast, ask him or her to slow down. If you don't understand a word, ask for a translation. You need the most accurate and understandable information possible.

6. *Take care of yourself.* Have another family member or caregiver give you a relief shift so you can get out now and then.

John Throop

---

den, and this can be unbearable if part of the "one flesh" is hurting.

The situation is even more complex if the illness is mental, not physical. Jill suffered from acute depression. Because her problems were due to chemical imbalances in the brain, her moods were very hard for her to control. Bob did his best to keep focused on his work, on caring for the two children, and on looking after his wife's needs when she was not hospitalized. The strain and pain was written all over his face. "At least when there's a physical problem, like cancer or heart disease, you have an idea of what life will be like," said Bob. "But in mental illness, I never know what to expect when I get home from work. And I never know what will be expected from me."

As often as there are tragic stories—or perhaps more often, thank God—there are examples of heroic service. Carol nursed her husband, Don, as his health deteriorated over a year. She stood by her husband through thick and thin, and her family surrounded her and Don when he died. Eldon served his wife, Margaret, for 10 years after a massive stroke left her almost completely incapacitated and speechless. Mary and Phil's relationship deepened tremendously during his battle with cancer, as he learned how to communicate lavishly his deepest feelings and faith.

Sickness in a mate challenges both partners' faith. While we profess to love God deeply and say we have committed our lives into His care, we often forget we are mortal and fragile, dust that returns to the earth. When illness strikes, our first reaction is often, "Why has this happened?" Like Job we cry out in dismay, "God has cast me into the mire, and I have become like dust and ashes. I cry to Thee and Thou dost not answer me; I stand, and Thou dost not heed me" (Job 30:19-20, RSV).

Attached at the deepest level to one another, we cannot bear to let our mates truly rely on God's care. There must be something we can do to help. Faithful though we may be, we find it hard to grapple with human mortality. At the very time we must trust the Lord most, we cannot. At the very time we most need God's healing power, we cannot easily pray that His will be done. Perhaps in us, as in Job, only a kernel of faith remains. Sometimes that is just enough to keep us together.

I have come to understand that the vow to be faithful in sickness and in health is there not only to remind us to "hang in there" when the going gets rough, but also to remind us that by God's grace we have health, and equally by His grace we can stay together bearing the burden of illness. It is possible in sickness to grow more deeply in service and humility and to recognize our mutual dependence not only on one another, but also on God. Illness is an opportunity for ministry far more often than merely an occasion for misery.

Related Articles
Introduction: Two Shall Become One
Chapter 14: You, Me, a Wheelchair, and God

Dealing With Depression

GARY & JULIE COLLINS

It isn't easy to be depressed—and neither is it easy living with a depressed partner.

Researchers at the University of Michigan recently studied the effect of depression on marriage. For most couples the stress was intense. Communication deteriorated, the husband and wife tended to avoid discussions of significant topics, family conflict was common, and the couple's social and recreational activities were more limited. When the depression lifted, the husband/wife tension often remained and for about one-sixth of the couples, the strain was so great that divorce followed.

But that doesn't need to happen. We know, because each of us has experienced depression at some time during our marriage. The experience isn't easy, but several things have helped us.

It helps when both husband and wife recognize the symptoms of depression. In addition to the sadness he or she feels, the depressed person often is:
—apathetic
—disinterested in activities that once were pleasurable (including sex)
—withdrawn
—pessimistic
—bogged down with self-condemnation and feelings of worthlessness
—hopeless
—sometimes suicidal

Frequently the depressed person feels so unworthy he or she fears divine rejection. When visitors appear, these symptoms sometimes can be hidden behind a smiling face, but the doldrums return when the couple is alone. Encouraging your mate to "snap out" of the depression rarely does any good. Depressed people often want to rid themselves of the symptoms, but often the despair, exhaustion, fear, immobilizing apathy, hopelessness, and inner desperation remain, despite their desires to change or frequent prayers for divine liberation.

King David, the man after God's own heart, struggled more than once with depression. Psalms 69, 88, 102, and especially 43, record his desperation. Many other Bible figures struggled with depression and so have generations of people since, both believers and nonbelievers. The causes of depression are complex and differ from person to person.

Often depression has a physical cause that may be as simple as a lack of rest and exercise, as common as the monthly premenstrual syndrome in some women, or as serious as biochemical malfunctioning, brain tumors, or glandular disorders. Some research suggests that depression may have a genetic basis that runs in families.

Often the causes are psychological. The loss of a job, status, health, possessions, or valued objects can lead to depression, and so can the loss of significant relationships. The death of a loved one, divorce, or prolonged separations are painful and each can create depression that, in turn, can influence the depressed person's marriage.

Other causes include feelings of helplessness, a tendency to think negative thoughts, sin and guilt in the depressed person's life, and frequently, anger. So often do anger and depression appear together that some counselors suggest the one causes the other. Whenever one of us feels depressed, the first question we ask is, "What has happened to make us angry?" When we get the answer to that question and begin to deal with the anger-producing situation, the depression often begins to go away. But dealing with depression usually isn't that easy.

If the depression persists, it is good to

JEALOUSY— THE GREEN MONSTER

Few things can destroy a relationship as quickly as jealousy. Why? Because at the root of jealousy lies distrust. If you are jealous because your spouse had to work late, you are basically saying, "I don't trust you."

The root of jealousy must be dealt with from the start. Assuming that you have a healthy marriage and you really do trust your spouse, there is no room for jealousy. If such feelings do arise for one reason or another, get them in the open immediately. Don't allow what may have been a simple misunderstanding to boil into a bitter argument because you didn't communicate. Explain your feelings; ask your questions; relieve your mind. And then, believe your spouse and put aside your doubts. Let trust, not jealousy, rule your relationship.

YFC Editors

get a physical examination. Your doctor may prescribe antidepressant drugs to help while you deal with the depression's causes. Counseling can be helpful and often the counselor will recommend that the person change behavior patterns or ways of thinking to resolve the depression. For some, the depression will be brief and gone as suddenly as it came. More often recovery will take time and there will be periods of relapse—each a little shorter and less intense than the one that came before.

How does the spouse handle the strain during this difficult time? Remember that your mate may not be able to communicate his or her desperate needs for your love and acceptance. Try, then, to be patient, supportive, and understanding. Physical contact, such as touching or hugging, is important even if your spouse doesn't show much response. Ask God daily to bring healing to your depressed mate and to give you strength, wisdom, and patience. Try to find a same-sex friend who can keep confidences, who will pray with you and who can help you keep things in perspective while you pick up additional family and other responsibilities.

When a family member is depressed, it is easy to be impatient, critical, frustrated, and sometimes angry. It can be threatening to realize that your spouse is depressed, in part because he or she may be angry with you. Your schedules are likely to be disrupted; concern over the depressed person's condition will be common; social activities will be curtailed; and often there will be the pain of wanting to help but not knowing what to do.

But you *can* pray. And you can stick with the depressed person. Psychiatric research is accumulating to show that the support and love of caring family members will do wonders to aid the counseling process and to bring healing. For us, the awareness that our spouse's love was unwavering—even when the depressed one wasn't easy to love—resulted in a deeper mutual love and commitment. It has helped to remember too that even though we don't understand God's reasons, He often lets depression exist, even in the lives of committed believers.

Always remember, however, that for the Christian there is hope. It may take a while, but things will get better. And God will give us strength while we wait.

Related Articles
Chapter 1: Love as Faithfulness
Chapter 14: In Sickness and In Health

Marriage and the Premenstrual Syndrome

GARY & JULIE COLLINS

Sandie Smith was a British barmaid who fatally stabbed another barmaid during a fight in a pub several years ago. To the surprise of many, the woman was released on probation, under a doctor's care, because she argued that premenstrual tension had made her violent.

There was a time when physicians and many husbands assumed that the premenstrual syndrome (usually abbreviated PMS) was "all in the heads" of the women who complained of monthly symptoms. Slowly, this incorrect attitude is changing.

The symptoms often occur a few days prior to menstruation. Some women also have symptoms at the time of ovulation and still others may be affected from the time of ovulation until the beginning of the menstrual period. While some women have extreme discomfort at every monthly period, others experience symptoms less severe, and over 50 percent of women between 14 and 50 do not have PMS at all. While few become violent, like Sandie Smith, many women experience one or more of 150 to 200 symptoms that range from the mild to the severely debilitating.

The symptoms, familiar to many women and their husbands, may include mood swings, headaches, sinus problems, and other allergic reactions, weight gain, anxiety, dizziness, crying spells, forgetfulness, irritability, clumsiness, feelings of worthlessness or incompetence, cravings for certain foods, abdominal bloating and cramping, panic, depression, poor judgment and coping ability, and even thoughts of suicide. Some women get short-tempered or impatient; others feel they are going crazy. For the husband (and father of teenage girls) who has never experienced these symptoms, the woman's PMS can create confusion, impatience, and frustration. Telling one's wife or daughter to "snap out of it" doesn't help at all and usually creates more tension.

PMS is an organically-based disorder that can last from 2 to 14 days prior to the menstrual period and disappears once the period begins. Despite its prevalence, it has no diagnostic test, and no agreed-upon cause or treatment. The symptoms of PMS are sometimes initiated or aggravated by a pregnancy, reaching the mid-30s, a tubal ligation or hysterectomy, or the onset of menopause.

Experts recommend that women who suspect PMS should keep a daily record of exactly when symptoms occur. Do this for a minimum of three consecutive cycles. Since this is a medical condition, a physician should be consulted for help in handling PMS, but several "home remedies" can be used to reduce symptoms:

• Eliminate or limit caffeine, alcohol, and refined sugar (such as we find in candy bars, baked goods, or many processed foods) from the diet; eat more complex carbohydrates (like those found in fruits and vegetables, as well as poultry and fish).

• Avoid diuretics, tranquilizers, and any medications that contain caffeine.

• Take a multiple vitamin with minerals, some of which are formulated specifically for women with PMS. Take these with meals to prevent stomach upsets.

• Eat five or six small meals a day instead of two or three large ones. This helps keep blood sugar stable.

• Exercise more. Low impact aerobics such as walking, swimming, and bicycling are recommended. Exercise can reduce tension, improve blood circulation, and provide a sense of well-being. Avoid exercise that is more strenuous than you are accustomed to doing.

Marriages are better when wives communicate about their symptoms and when husbands try to understand how PMS affects their wives. Sometimes, for example, women experience a change in sex drive when PMS symptoms are apparent, and the sensitive husband will try to be aware of this. Your doctor can often help you better understand the condition, but in the United States information is also available toll-free if you call PMS Access, 1-800-222-4PMS. (In Wisconsin, call 1-608-833-4PMS.) This organization is a reliable source of information for women and health care professionals. It provides helpful educational materials and a referral list of doctors who specialize in treating PMS.

Some women have criticized the Sandie Smith verdict, fearing that the severe premenstrual symptoms of a few could brand all women as helpless victims of their biology. This isn't true and neither is it valid to assume that PMS sufferers cannot function effectively as wives, mothers, and business/professional people. But the condition is real, and couples who want good marriages cannot ignore the symptoms, especially since they appear regularly. When PMS occurs, it affects more than the women; it affects entire families.

Related Articles
    Chapter 14: In Sickness and In Health
    Chapter 14: Dealing With Depression

Menopause and the Marriage Bond

JIM & SALLY CONWAY

"**S**tudies show that menopause occurs in half the people in every marriage!" We make that statement with tongue in cheek, of course. We all know that women make up half the married population, and that women in their late 40s or early 50s experience menopause (unless it occurred earlier due to surgery).

We know these facts, but do we understand how much the effects of the climacteric touch both people in a midlife marriage? The wife experiences the actual physical and emotional changes, but those changes usually have a dramatic impact on the husband as well.

Some husbands and wives approach the menopausal adjustment years without much thought, as if they don't know it's coming. Others have a stockpile of old wives' tales and myths that nurture fears and misunderstandings. Still others feel that trusting the Lord will ensure smooth sailing, and any hitches are because of a bad attitude. A few are informed and prepared for both the good and the bad. Probably none of us, however, is totally realistic about the changes that both husband and wife experience during the climacteric years—until we have lived through them.

Contrary to what some people think, menopause is not just the cessation of the menstrual cycle. All the complicated mechanisms that have been working together to cause a woman's monthly period also affect other body systems, both physical and emotional.

Among the other changes noticed by many women are hot flashes, variation in the vaginal structure, thinning of the vaginal lining, reduced vaginal lubrication, dryness and loss of elasticity of other tissues, and urinary incontinence. In addition, postmenopausal women have increased chances of heart attack and osteoporosis, a potentially crippling

443

bone affliction.

Closely associated with these symptoms are others that are less measurable but just as real. The nervous sytem is generally more sensitive; emotions are more intense, both up and down; sexual desire may diminish; self-esteem may be at an all-time low; life perception in general may be askew; and depression may become severe. These may happen in spite of a woman's best intentions and her previous healthy adjustment to life.

Just as women's bodies differ, the severity and form of menopausal symptoms vary from woman to woman. Some have an easy transition; others do not. It's cruel to make a woman feel guilty when her climacteric is more difficult than we might think it should be.

I (Sally) had an easy time giving birth to each of our three daughters. Should I chide women who had a harder time in childbirth? Their difficulty wasn't because they didn't have their priorities straight or because of some character flaw. Neither was my easy childbirth because of any special spiritual quality in me. Yet sometimes women with a difficult climacteric phase are made to feel that it's their fault or that they are just wanting attention.

Because menopausal changes touch many aspects of their lives for a number of years, both husband and wife need to be aware that their marriage will be affected. Having an open, secure relationship ahead of time will make it easier for the wife to express her feelings of depression, anxiety, or whatever negative emotions are hitting her.

Sometimes, however, the couple may discover that their marital bonds are not very strong, and the wife's vacillating moods and altered perceptions may severely strain their relationship. If the husband is going through a difficult midlife evaluation at the same time, a real crisis may occur in their marriage. Each one needs the other to be patient and loving,

but neither may have the strength to help the other. If this is the case, it is important to get some professional marriage counseling and to draw on a support group of close friends.

Enlisting medical help for the wife's hormone imbalance and other physical needs is important. She may need to see more than one doctor in order to find one who truly understands the full menopausal experience. The doctor should be able to discuss the advantages and disadvantages of various forms of treatment, including hormone replacement therapy, and should have an empathetic attitude for the emotional changes going on. If he or she implies that "it's all in your head," a different doctor is needed.

Hormone replacement therapy is a wise option for many women. Scares about increased risk of ovarian or uterine cancer because of estrogen treatment have been proven invalid by the latest research, especially if the estrogen is balanced with progesterone as was done naturally by the body before menopause. The doctor can determine if it is advisable in a particular situation. We strongly encourage women to use hormone replacement if at all possible. A woman using estrogen should find that her miserable hot flashes stop, as well as her drastic mood swings. Her tissues will be more elastic, and she will be better protected from heart attack and osteoporosis.

For many a husband, estrogen treatment is cause for celebration as his wife returns to her normal self. One of our friends became a raging, angry dynamo, taking on everyone who crossed her path. Then she began taking estrogen and is once again a sweet-tempered woman. Her elated husband says he goes around singing "An Ode to Estrogen"!

A wife doesn't mean for her emotions to cause marital turmoil, but they do. She may cry buckets of tears over the slightest thing that would have elicited only a sigh before, or she may just feel down or blue for no reason at all.

She may never have expressed much anger previously, but now she may be easily triggered to explode or just feel hostile and bristly toward everyone. She may lose all confidence and hate everything about herself. She may be depressed for days.

At times she can't stand being in crowds; at other times she can't stand being alone. She may be forgetful and think senility has set in early. She may be edgy and jumpy. I (Jim) have grown accustomed to Sally's flinching as we drive in traffic. She is sure those cars are going to sideswipe us! Telling her she's going crazy doesn't help, but gentle reassurance does.

As you can see, it is best if the husband can be objective and understanding. If he scolds, belittles, or ignores his wife, tensions will mount within her and between the two of them.

A wife may have trouble with sexual intercourse because of vaginal dryness or thin, tender membranes. Her sexual desire may be affected by her psychological struggles brought on by bodily changes. Her breasts may become limp and small; her skin may look wrinkly; her other tissues may seem spongy; she may gain weight easily—all this while society is emphasizing "the body beautiful," which is lean, firm, and energetic. If she feels her husband is attracted only to young, curvaceous women, she may feel very threatened and unable to give herself in a mutually satisfying sexual relationship.

The menopausal symptoms can become wedges to force apart the marriage, or they can be one more difficulty the couple faces together, which forges a stronger bond. Together they can see that the wife gets appropriate medical help. Together they can laugh at the symptoms, such as the fiery glow the wife may radiate when they snuggle in bed so that they both have to throw off the covers. Together they can chat about her erratic feelings and assure each other that their relationship is solid.

An interesting phenomenon is that, although her emotions and perceptions may be exaggerated, a kernel of truth probably exists in them. Some inner needs and feelings may be more honestly expressed than ever before, providing new insights for personal and marital growth.

All these changes require that a husband be sensitive and understanding. He needs to keep the big picture in mind so that he doesn't feel threatened or angry if his wife's statements and actions are overmagnified. He, of all people, should be on her side, giving her hope.

Husband and wife will now have sexual freedom without the bother of contraception, the nuisance of the monthly period, or the dread of an unwanted pregnancy. They may find a renewed romance in their lovemaking as they have more spontaneous times together.

If you use the physical and emotional stresses of the climacteric years to understand and love each other more, you will have the joy of knowing that together you have won another battle. You can look forward to many peaceful, productive years to come.

Together you can claim God's promise to be with you through all the stages of life. "Listen to Me . . . you whom I have upheld since you were conceived, and have carried since your birth. Even to your old age and gray hairs . . . I am He who will sustain you. I have made you and I will carry you; I will sustain you and I will rescue you" (Isa. 46:3-4).

Related Articles
Chapter 14: Helping Your Mate During a Time of Suffering
Chapter 14: Loyalty to Each Other

You, Me, a Wheelchair, and God

JONI EARECKSON TADA

Sometimes I wonder how Ken can love me. Don't get me wrong. I don't doubt that he loves me. But once in a while something happens—usually it has to do with my disability—and I feel as if my strong, strapping husband is *stuck* with a wife in a wheelchair.

This is what happened recently: I was reading a book at the kitchen table. Turning pages is not easy for me since I don't have use of my hands. I have to wedge my wrist under a dog-eared page, shrug my shoulder, and then lift my arm to flip a page. On this particular day my arm went into an unexpected spasm in the middle of page turning. The book slid off the table, taking with it a sandwich on a plate and a full glass of orange juice.

What a mess. I sat in utter frustration, unable to do anything about the stains, the soaked sandwich, and the crumpled, sticky book lying in a puddle. "What kind of wife am I?" I thought angrily. "Now Ken will have to clean it and me up . . . after he returns from working in the backyard!"

Finally my husband walked through the back door, stopped when he spotted the accident—and laughed! I guess I did look rather funny. And I was surprised at how I relaxed and warmed under his response.

Now can you understand why I occasionally wonder how my husband is able to love me? The list of things I can't do sometimes seems so long. I can't open the refrigerator door, reach for the frying pan, crack the eggs, or slice the bacon. But if all I did was look at the long list of "can'ts," my marriage would be a pity party.

The neat thing about Ken is that he helps me look at my disability as an asset rather than a liability. We choose to believe that my disability will strengthen our sense of commitment. It will press us to be unified (sometimes whether we want to or not!) as we tackle problems together. After all, it's impossible to ignore the chair—and you try staying angry at someone who smears cold cream on your face.

Because of my disability, we have to be creative and inventive about activities we can actually do together. (Presently we are putting our heads together, figuring out a way for me to use a fishing reel!) We are becoming more intimate, more open, and far more honest than we might be if I were able-bodied.

In order to keep this perspective, we must be watchful. It is my responsibility to do as much as I can for my husband, despite my limitations. I plan menus, go shopping, borrow people's hands to whip up a casserole, organize my housekeeper's time, order my own medical supplies, and even take my own handicap-equipped van to the garage for tune-ups and oil changes. I may not be able to mop a floor, but I can at least wrangle with a mechanic.

That pleases Ken. And it makes it easier for him to tolerate those household routines that are normally termed "women's work." Pushing a vacuum cleaner doesn't threaten his masculinity. He is secure enough to fold laundry. And Ken cooks up a mean sukiyaki!

Although the roles aren't standard, Ken and I are still becoming one in a unique way.

Yet that doesn't make frustrations disappear with a snap of a finger. Sometimes I have felt like resigning not only from marriage, but from life! I struggle with feeling like a burden. "Look at me," I thought to myself as I sat in the middle of my book, sandwich, and orange juice. "How can Ken hang in there with a wife who is so severely disabled?"

But he does hang in there. He loves me willingly. Gladly.

There is Someone else who gladly and willingly loves me. He loves the "me" who is in even more of a mess—not just on the outside, but on the inside where only He can see the ugly stains. Romans 5:8 says, "While we were still sinners, Christ died for us." The Lord Jesus is always doing a clean-up job on me, loving and giving even though I offer Him so little in return.

Ken loves and accepts me in the same way. And marriage reaches its highest goal when husbands and wives see that Christ-reflection in each other.

"Therefore I will boast all the more gladly about my weaknesses," Paul says in 2 Corinthians 12:9. Are you able to say the same about the limitations and frustrations in your marriage? Can you

---

ISAIAH 53:3-5

He was despised and rejected by men, a man of sorrows, and familiar with suffering. Like one from whom men hide their faces He was despised, and we esteemed Him not. Surely He took up our infirmities and carried our sorrows, yet we considered Him stricken by God, smitten by Him, and afflicted. But He was pierced for our transgressions, He was crushed for our iniquities; the punishment that brought us peace was upon Him, and by His wounds we are healed.

---

see these impairments as the very opportunities that allow Christ's love for your spouse to show up best?

If you're ever tempted to wonder, "How can my husband love me?" or perhaps "How can I love my husband?" let those weaknesses, through the grace of God, be your *strength*.

Related Articles
Introduction: Two Shall Become One
Chapter   1: Love as Faithfulness

Dealing With Mental Illness

GARY D. BENNETT

If you're living with a spouse who is having emotional or mental problems, you're not alone. There is hardly a home in America that is not affected, either directly or indirectly, by some form of mental illness. Obviously, some cases are far more serious than others. In our high-tech, fast-paced society, people continue to fray at the edges. Perhaps you are one of the many who suffer in silence watching your spouse come unraveled, and you don't know what to do or how to help.

How to Live With a Mentally Ill Spouse

First of all, *accept your spouse's condition.* Having the right attitude regarding his irrational behaviors, thoughts, and feelings will keep you from becoming perplexed and confused yourself. Accepting his illness will put you more at ease with him. He, of course, will sense this and will respond to you more readily as well.

Be there. No matter how much your spouse reacts to you, or how bizarre or boisterous he becomes, be present when he needs you. Your presence during a time of overwhelming confusion and anxiety is evidence to him of your love. He needs your reassurance.

Don't argue. Whenever we talk with someone we don't understand, it's natural to argue. Your spouse already senses that she is behaving differently than normal, and when you disagree with her, it simply drives her further into isolation and illness. Ignore her baiting words and defeating behaviors. Stay in reality, and help her to remain in reality too. Be direct but understanding.

Help your spouse focus on some-thing other than herself. Emotional and mental problems are often perpetuated by "ingrown eyeballs." Too much introspection or idle thinking time can hinder more than help. So encourage her to get involved in some type of outside activity. Doing so may be a good way to help you both cope. Emotional exhaustion drains us, whereas activity is a cleansing agent for our systems.

Don't sympathize. Helping your spouse justify his self-pity or rationalize his behavior simply sends the message that you are condoning such and that there is no hope for his condition.

Program hope. Usually an emotionally distraught or mentally ill person believes that recovery is impossible. Your spouse's hopelessness and despair may be key obstacles in overcoming the illness. One of the best antidotes is kind encouragement and realistic hope. Give your spouse regular and loving doses of both.

Be careful not to be too cheerful. Proverbs 25:20 says, "Like one who takes away a garment on a cold day, or like vinegar poured on soda, is one who sings songs to a heavy heart." Temper your cheerfulness with sincerity and gentleness. Doing so will enable your spouse to receive and respond to it in the right manner.

Get him to talk. Encourage your spouse to share and express his feelings. This doesn't mean you need to take a counseling role, but having someone listen to what he's thinking or feeling can make a difference. His irrational thoughts and feelings need to be expressed. Simply getting it off his chest can be therapeutic.

Use the Word of God—carefully. Use Scripture to rehearse the promises of God with your spouse, but do so with discretion. Unfortunately, your spouse's mental condition may cause him to blame or be resentful of God. Emphasize God's love and comfort and of course His many promises.

Maintain a source of help for yourself. Help for yourself could come in a variety of forms: a supportive pastor, a close friend (one who can keep confidences and is of the same sex), a favorite activity outside the home, anything that will help give you equilibrium and a reference point. Maintaining your own devotional time with the Lord will prove very helpful too.

When to Seek Help

Those who are mentally ill are like the rest of us: people who are troubled, unhappy, and in need of help. The difference is one of degree. When your spouse shows signs of emotional or mental difficulties, she is sending a message to those around that she needs help. Her bizarre behavior may be her way of dealing with things that are too painful, confusing, demanding, or overwhelming for her to cope with. Seek professional help if your spouse requests or indicates in other ways that she needs help, or whenever you feel you can no longer handle the situation as it remains.

Sometimes a few counseling sessions with a professional may be all that is needed to enable your spouse to handle her own personal anxieties and problems. Sometimes extensive evaluations and treatments may be required, but the first step is to secure the assistance of a competent professional. God, in His wisdom, has permitted social workers, psychologists, and psychiatrists to develop modern treatment techniques to successfully deal with abnormal behavior. Don't hesitate to avail yourself of their services.

Getting Your Spouse to Go

1. Make clear to your spouse your concern and need for him to receive outside help.

2. Convey to your spouse that seeking help doesn't mean she is weak, worthless, or a failure. It's simply a recognition of need, and a step toward a healthier adjustment.

3. Make your spouse aware of the availability of specific resources and services that might be helpful.

4. Share the responsibility for exploring and selecting appropriate services.

5. Unless he is totally "over the edge," allow your spouse to have a voice and vote on where to seek help.

6. Find out as much as possible about how the agency or professional provides services, and discuss together what will happen, how your spouse will be received, what questions will be asked, etc.

7. Help your spouse understand that going to a professional does not give that person control over her life, and that she will retain the right to decide to continue or discontinue using their service.

8. Share the responsibility, but allow your spouse to make and keep the appointments.

9. When possible, accompany your spouse for treatment. Doing so will reinforce your commitment and ongoing love.

What About Hospitalization?

Hospitalization would be the highest level of service for mental illness. Hospitalization occurs upon the referral and recommendation of a trained professional, upon the order of a judge, or on the basis of self-admittance. Hospitalization may be for a short time (three to six months) or for an extended period, and, upon discharge, is usually followed by outpatient services.

Hospitalization provides a period of separation from the home and work environment while receiving treatment services. This period of separation also enables you and the family to work on personal changes that should be made, thus guaranteeing a smoother adjustment when your spouse returns home. Any such changes would be prescribed by the professional staff as you remain intimately involved with your spouse's program of treatment.

Related Articles
Chapter 14: In Sickness and In Health
Chapter 16: When to Go for Counseling

The Affair: An Empty Promise

DWIGHT HERVEY SMALL

From an objective standpoint we can define an *affair* as "a passionate romantic attachment, typically of limited duration, obsessive while it lasts, which may or may not have sexual components but always includes emotional possessiveness." An affair, however, is rarely viewed objectively!

What sets the scene for an affair? In our time, emotionally tinted friendships with the opposite sex are common. Daily interaction between the sexes in the workaday world gives opportunity for people to become personally intimate to whatever degree they desire. The more hours people share together, the more a personal emotional bond tends to develop. And since friendship is natural and desirable, we are not on guard. After all, what's wrong if two fine, compatible people like each other? That's no sin! But before one knows it, an irresistible, emotionally dependent bonding may develop. A trap is set.

Personal needs—loneliness, lack of love or affirmation, misunderstanding, unresolved conflict—leave one reaching out to others, though rarely in a conscious way. Imagination whispers that there is a promising possibility on the other side of the fence; find it and things will change for you. The discovery that your friend shares your needs—perhaps even your dissatisfaction with marriage—can create a powerful bond. And each new disclosure strengthens the bond in ever more intimate fashion.

Whenever men and women enter each other's lives, their separate mysteries begin to unfold to each other. They are taken up into an emotional flow that will carry them to places neither has been before. The man has emotional resources and yearnings never before suspected. The woman has hidden reserves of feeling until now lying dormant. Neither person knows what the other will reveal or, for that matter, what he or she will reveal.

Since all this takes place away from one's marriage partner, a false sense of freedom comes into play—freedom to share feelings, make romantic gestures, say sentimental things, communicate with the eyes and body language. All is discreet, of course, so nobody knows and nobody is hurt. But secret infidelity is forming without the two people being fully aware of it.

There is excitement in disclosure; adventure is in the making. In time, there emerges a sense of "We know and understand each other as no other two do. We really belong together." The two feel "made for each other," and the prospect of deeper sharing is seductive. In ever so subtle ways one's true perception of life and responsibility is overcome, and then prudence along with it.

Progression can be in only one direction. Words lead to light touching, light touching to more sustained and intimate touch. The fuse is lit; it won't take much for the relationship to become sexual. Deceptive games are now just a natural part of things. Even the desperation generated by the risks and suspense of secretly balancing marriage and an affair becomes part of the exhilaration.

Temptation appeals to our natural, God-given desires, but it offers to satisfy them in the wrong way. Even the best things, such as personal affection or the wish to be helpful, are avenues of temptation. It is easy to lower one's guard, to allow things to "just happen." Warning signals are ignored. As a formerly entrapped person said, "I forgot who I was and whose I was!" One blames one's mate for everything wrong in the marriage and credits the other person involved with any present happiness. Thus the affair is rationalized as a good thing, brought on by bad things outside oneself, and beyond one's control.

Sadly, however, the affair does not last. The illusion that one has finally found real love, real passion, real intimacy, real understanding dissipates more quickly than one can imagine. Time, familiarity, and previously concealed realities bring the affair to its inevitable end. In its wake lie regrets, bitterness, and often hopelessness. The affair, so beautiful at first, dies as an empty promise. One sees himself or herself to have been playing the fool.

Once begun, an affair is nearly impossible to stop without causing heartbreak. The only safeguard is to take precautions not to encourage its start. The best precaution is to commit oneself to that

FIDELITY AND FRIENDSHIPS

Fidelity is more than staying out of someone else's bed. It is a positive thing, a matter of the heart, a commitment intended to fortify and sanctify marriage. A faithful partner is committed to maintaining marital integrity in both observable and unobservable behavior.

Fidelity has to do with the integrity of one's thoughts. Tough moral discipline must be accepted. Questions must be asked of any close male-female friendship, no matter how innocent it may seem:

How appropriate are our actions toward each other? Is there anything between us that makes me uneasy, that I would not want my mate to know? Are there emotional elements that I crave? Is there a growing obsession to be together, to share ever more deeply? Am I finding excuses to phone or to find ways of being together? Is this friendship causing me to distance myself from my mate, actually or in my thoughts? Am I playing games? What, if anything, am I putting at risk? Have I really talked with the Lord about this?

An intimate friendship seems innocent alongside a sexual affair, but a purely emotional attachment can do more to threaten marriage than falling into sexual sin. In a friendship one does more than lend his body to passing pleasure; one gives his heart away.

Dwight Hervey Small

positive fidelity of the heart which makes marriage strong. Daily reaffirm your commitment to your spouse. Then be honest with yourself before God.

I Think My Spouse May Be Playing Around

EARL & SANDY WILSON

It is devastating to feel that you are not the only person your spouse is having sex with. Even worse is to feel that your spouse is in love with someone else. Unfortunately these feelings are all too common, even in Christian marriages. Both physical and mental adultery often occur, and lack of self-control in these areas has destroyed many marriages and left scars on countless others. What can you do if you suspect that your spouse is playing around?

First, realize that whether or not adultery is occurring, your suspicions at least tell you something is wrong. A premature accusation, however, may only result in denial, whatever the truth of the matter. You may wish to approach your spouse by sharing your feelings of distance rather than with accusations of infidelity. Let your spouse know your desire to build a stronger relationship. Show your sincerity by moving toward your mate, even if you feel him or her moving away from you. And remember that it is the Holy Spirit who convicts of sin.

Second, if there is evidence of playing around, confront your spouse as kindly but as forcefully as you can. Sometimes it helps to couple verbal confrontation with a note or letter in which you clearly state what you know and ask the person to stop the involvement. If denial occurs or continues, you may wish to enlist the aid of a third party who knows what is going on.

Third, try to get the message across that you want the other relationship to stop so that your relationship can grow once again. If your spouse is receptive, spend more time listening than talking. If he or she can talk to you about the problem, he or she will grow closer to you. If that is not possible, your spouse may turn to the other person and develop more closeness there.

Fourth, don't use guilt to try to motivate your spouse to come back. You may make him or her feel bad, but that won't make love grow again. Tell your spouse how you feel, but don't make statements like, "You are ruining my life," or "How could you do this to the children?" Your spouse may already feel guilty, but if you pile on even more guilt, it is likely that defensiveness and denial, not repentance, will result. Openness and understanding coupled with firmness are often the best healers.

It is not true that your spouse is ruining your life. God has something to say about that. It is also not true that the children will be ruined. What is true is that you, your children, your spouse, and everyone close to you will hurt a lot.

452

That is why God warns against the sin of adultery and tells us to cleave only to our spouse. Sin and suffering always go together.

After you have drawn the line and asked for the involvement to stop, you will go through an extended period of feeling helpless. You cannot make the decision for your spouse; only he or she can do that. Keep listening, talking, and praying. God cares, but He won't browbeat your spouse. You shouldn't either.

There are two more things you need to consider: forgiving your spouse and not blaming yourself. Before you can forgive, you have to assess the damage. If your spouse's attitudes and behavior haven't hurt you deeply, you really have nothing to forgive. Realize all that has been done to you, and then choose not to hold it against him or her. You will need to forgive many times. Don't leave room for the biggest hurt of all—bitterness.

Last, don't blame yourself. It is not your fault. Yes, you probably made some mistakes, but your spouse chose to fool around. Even if you had a perfect body and a great attitude, your spouse might still have taken his or her affections elsewhere. That is the nature of sin: it always wants what it can't have.

Forgive yourself. Learn what you can from the happening, and then step forward with God into the next phase of your life. Our prayer for you and your spouse is that you will be able to build a life together that far exceeds what you had before.

GOD KNOWS BETTER THAN WE DO

Perhaps the hardest thing is to hang in there, to keep on loving when you feel unloved and cast aside. Years ago, during a very bad time for us, I felt that way, and I wanted very much to say, "I don't need you either." Today, while I can remember intellectually how much I hurt, emotionally it is hard to recall. There has been too much good in the years since then.

I know now that in my dark days, Tony was having his own difficult time. Looking back, I can see that my perception of things at that time was all wrong. And yet, feeling as I did, I would have walked out if it had not been for God's rules. Thank God that Christians do not have to trust their own best judgment!

Margaret Campolo

My Spouse Is a Liar

GARY D. BENNETT

How can I build a trusting relationship when I never know when to believe my spouse? Why does my spouse continue to lie when he knows better? How can I help?

Adults lie for several reasons:

Denial: To rid themselves of painful feelings or memories.

Wish fulfillment: To try to make things better.

Fantasy: Daydreams and imagined events become real to them, and they convey these as envisioned.

Reality testing: To find out what is real by testing other people's reactions.

Recognition: To be part of a peer group or to enhance their reputation.

Power: To control others, or to get even.

Negative attention: Preferring to have someone angry at them rather than to be ignored completely.

Developmental: They've been taught to lie as children (i.e., a parent says, "Tell her I'm not at home") and continue similar patterns of behavior as adults.

Self-worth: Coming out of a sense of insecurity, lying may be a mechanism to justify their worth to themselves and others.

To understand these reasons doesn't make lying any more acceptable, of course. Lying, according to Scripture, is still sin and in need of God's gracious forgiveness.

You can help your spouse deal with lying in several ways:

1. Define and discuss the problem with your spouse. Expect denial and resistance, but lovingly persist and bring your spouse to the point of acknowledging that a problem does exist.

2. Let your spouse know, in a way that leaves no doubt of your love, that her lying is the source of your concern.

3. Try to discover together under what circumstances his lying occurs. What sparks it, and what does he receive emotionally from doing it?

4. Ask your spouse if you are doing something to contribute to, encourage, or trigger her lying. Brace yourself and accept any responsibility you may have in the cause.

5. Brainstorm together various ways to help your spouse stop lying. For instance, it may involve devising a signal, to be kept between the two of you, that you can use as a gentle reminder. Once he knows you are on to him, he can shift his answer (or story) toward the truth and save face quietly.

6. Take baby steps in trying to solve a long-standing or habitual problem. Don't try to eliminate all in one sweep. First try to reduce the frequency of lying, then ultimately work toward complete elimination.

7. Have your spouse choose a series of positive and natural rewards to help reinforce her efforts to stop lying. People usually are unable to change their behavior patterns until they find sufficient reason or reward to do so.

8. Be consistent in helping (not harping) and timely in rewarding (not reprimanding). Above all else, don't expect perfection. Support without condoning; confront without condemning.

9. Assure your spouse that your continued love does not depend on abolishing her lying. Your reassurance and forgiveness in the face of failure could be the one catalyst she's always needed.

10. Pray for your spouse. Without the power of prayer undergirding your spouse, he will not be able to effect any real and lasting change in his life. Praying and working together on this sinful habit will help build trust and bonding in your relationship—not overnight, but over time.

Related Articles
Chapter 4: Building Trust
Chapter 9: Making Your Communication Work

MY HUSBAND PREFERS THE TV TO ME!

"When my husband gets home, the first thing he does is turn on the TV—and it doesn't go off until he goes to bed! How can I get him to talk to me?"

As the spouse of the TV-aholic, consider several things:

First, when he (or she) *has* talked to you, what does he hear? If he turns off the TV and turns to you, does he get nagged, torn apart, put down, prodded about everything else he should be doing? Or does he get some true interest in who he is, how he feels, and what he's doing? Maybe the TV is on because he had a hard enough day at work and isn't in the mood to listen to you.

Second, realize that he (or she) may just need to wind down, and give him some space to do that. He has spent the entire day working hard, perhaps dealing with difficult people, crises, or other work-world frustrations. Let him relax as he chooses, without having to either talk about his day or immediately decide how to handle the crises at home.

Third, when you do have a chance to talk, communicate your feelings to him (or her) and try to reach a compromise that will keep you both happy.

Now, for the TV-aholic himself (or herself). Is turning on the TV just a habit? Are you trying to avoid any kind of conversation because of a selfish desire to not hear about things you need to do, concerns your spouse has, constructive criticisms you should work through, crises you wish to avoid? You may deserve time to relax, but you also need to realize that your marriage won't survive well on doses of conversation only during commercials. You may have had a day full of conversation and mental stimulation, but your spouse may not have. He (or she) needs to communicate with you.

Also realize that indiscriminate "tube" watching is poor use of time and detrimental to family life (not to mention that it can turn your mind to jelly). Develop other interests that are both enjoyable and worthwhile, realizing that some of these hobbies should include your spouse and kids.

What kinds of compromise can you reach? As a couple or as a family, check the TV viewing guide each week and pick out the shows that will be worth watching—then set aside some time to enjoy them together with a bowl of popcorn. Allow your spouse to occasionally "veg out" in front of the TV, but set a time limit and then remind him/her when time is up. Neither of you should allow the TV to control your life and/or your marriage.

YFC Editors

Living With a Nonrecovering Alcoholic

EARNIE LARSEN

Understanding is a vital element in any relationship, but it is particularly important when you are living with a nonrecovering alcoholic—that is, an alcoholic who continues to drink. If this is your situation, you need to take a look at five facts that will help you understand what is going on.

1. *Alcoholism is an addiction, and all addictions are forms of insanity.* Yes, insanity is the correct word. This insanity may not lead to incarceration in an asylum, but addicted persons are nevertheless out of touch with reality. To addicted persons, truth is totally concealed under a blanket of delusion and denial. With the car full of dents from their auto accident last night, they will deny they were driving at all or even that there was an accident. *The addicted person does not see reality the way you do.*

2. *One feature of the addicted person's insanity is total self-centeredness and selfishness.* The center of nonrecovering alcoholics' lives is themselves. They are what they care about. Even though they may truly love you or other family members, they are not capable of the kind of caring and giving required for healthy relationships. Again—alcoholism is a form of insanity. Failing to understand this, nonalcoholic spouses may expect alcoholic spouses to respond in honest, fair, loving ways. When this is not forthcoming (and it never is on any consistent basis), nonalcoholic spouses often feel off balance, confused, and quite insane themselves.

3. *Under the weight of their disease and until the process of recovery begins, there are only two main concerns for alcoholics: to obtain their alcohol and to use it.* If they must lie to achieve these ends, they will do so. If you or other family members get in the way of their chemical use, then you or they must be sacrificed. If the job gets in the way, that too must go—although many practicing alcoholics go to great lengths to hold down a job because without it, they would not be able to buy alcohol. Holding down a job, therefore, is *not* proof that someone is not alcoholic.

Alcoholics will go to tragic extremes to fulfill these imperatives of their addiction. Abuse in every shape and form, tragic loss, destroyed children, dashed dreams, and at times very real blood spilled—for alcoholics who have not genuinely recovered, such pain does not seem too high a price to pay.

4. *Nonrecovering alcoholics do not play fair in relationships.* If their spouses are going to preserve their own sanity, they cannot expect the alcoholic to do so. It is no more reasonable to expect fairness from a nonrecovering alcoholic than to expect a crippled person to get up and run. Since frustration is always relative to expectation, when your expectations are unrealistic you will always be the loser.

5. *Practicing alcoholics may very well love.* What they cannot do is participate in loving relationships. This is because of the first four facts listed earlier: they are out of touch with reality, self-centered, desperate to obtain alcohol,

456

and unfair with others.

Once you understand what it means to be addicted to alcohol, it is crucial that you understand your role as the spouse of a nonrecovering alcoholic. Let us look at three areas:

1. *You cannot live with insanity and not be affected.* Just by living in proximity to a using alcoholic, you change. Your judgments become faulty. Your belief in yourself erodes. Your own grip on sanity starts to slip. It is vital to your survival to realize that you also need help.

2. *You must therefore learn to take care of yourself.* There are several ways to do this, but perhaps none is more important than getting involved with a group of people dealing with the same issues—specifically, Al-Anon. There is no substitute for this kind of support and source of wisdom in dealing with the trauma caused by living with a non-recovering alcoholic.

3. *Don't enable.* Lacking support and wisdom, spouses of alcoholics often fall into the trap of enabling. They tend to lie for their mates, make excuses, minimize the damage done by their drinking, and cover for them in any number of other ways. But by not making alcoholics live up to their responsibilities, spouses allow them to drink without paying the price their drinking demands. As long as alcoholics don't have to live up to their responsibilities, they won't. Enabling allows them to have it both ways. Not enabling, however, requires enormous amounts of wisdom and strength. This kind of help comes only through a group such as Al-Anon.

MORE THAN NOT DRINKING

Many alcoholics have managed to stop drinking but still exhibit the same, or nearly the same, attitudes, behaviors, and emotional retardation as when they were drinking. If recovery is seen only as abstinence from alcohol, the spouse of this sober but non-recovering person truly ends up feeling insane!

The alcoholic may well endlessly repeat, "I'm not drinking anymore; what else do you want?" The fact is, it wasn't the drinking that was the main problem but rather the person's behavior and attitudes while he or she was drinking. Merely abstaining from alcohol does not necessarily change the relationship-destroying traits of the alcoholic.

Earnie Larsen

Alcoholics can and do recover. So can spouses of alcoholics—and they do. Some of these relationships can be saved and indeed become things of beauty. But such salvaging takes wisdom and strength—and that demands effort on your part.

Related Articles
Chapter 14: Tough Love
Chapter 14: Alcoholism: The Process of Recovery

Tough Love: An Absolute Necessity for Those Who Live With Alcoholics

EARNIE LARSEN

Love is indeed a many splendored thing. One side of this multifaceted jewel is toughness. Love that is not tough is not love. On the other hand, love that is only tough is not the genuine article either.

By *tough* I do not mean hard, uncaring, or me-first attitudes. Tough love cares deeply and is willing to do whatever is needed for the well-being of the beloved. Tough love does not ask if it is easy or not, if the other person will like it or not, or even if it risks destroying the relationship. The only thing tough love asks is this: is it necessary?

Meet Jan. She loved her husband, Rick, very much, but he was an alcoholic. His drinking progressed until he was drinking not only away from home but also in front of the children, much to their horror and embarrassment.

Jan saw that this was doing terrible damage to the children. Through the help of Al-Anon, she was able to see what was going on and employ the principles of tough love. She loved Rick enough to confront him. Jan told him he simply could not be around the house if he was drinking, whether that drinking started at home or not.

One cold, rainy night Rick stumbled home, banged on the door, and demanded to be let in. Decision time! It was obvious to Jan that Rick was drunk. She knew what her tough love rule was—and so did he. She told him he could not come in.

Of course he was angry. Then sorry. Then sad. In typical alcoholic fashion he pulled out every emotional trick in his bag. He told Jan if she didn't let him in he would lie down right there on the front lawn, get soaked, get pneumonia, and die. Because Jan loved him, she simply told him (with her heart breaking), "Do what you have to do, but I simply can't let you in."

Rick didn't get in. He spent a very cold, wet night. But he didn't catch pneumonia and die.

This story has a happy ending. Now, after 20 years of drinking, Rick is sober. Jan recognizes that Rick deserves the credit for his own recovery, but she is also quick to point out that if she had not been willing to use tough love Rick would probably be dead by now. "If I had let him in that night," she says, "the message would have been very clear— it was OK for him to drink, because there really were no penalties to pay. He could drink and still have a roof over his head and a warm meal in his stomach."

If you are reading this article, I assume it is because there is an alcoholic in your life. People afflicted with the disease of alcoholism tend to be the most persuasive, manipulative, cunning people alive. When anything challenges or threatens their alcohol use, the persuasion begins. How does your alcoholic act?

Many alcoholics are masters at guilt. "It's your fault if I drink. Who wouldn't drink married to someone like you?"

Another favorite tactic is eating humble pie. "You are right; I'm a terrible person. You should leave me and get on with your life. I'll just stay here and die in the gutter."

Anger and rage may then erupt. "Stop acting so stupid or I'll smash your face in and kill the kids." This may or may not be an idle threat, but whatever the case, it is a form of manipulation.

The alcoholic is probably well aware of the best way to "hook" you, to induce you to give in and enable his or her drinking to continue. Tough love does not take the bait. Instead it demands that no matter how vulnerable you feel, no matter how clever the attempted manipulation, you stick to your guns *because* you love the other person. You must hold your alcoholic partner responsible for his or her actions.

People play manipulative games only as long as they work. When alcoholics discover that their old favorites no longer do, they have three choices: find new games; find someone else to play their games on; or recover to the point that games become unnecessary.

Tough love is not easy. It requires the wisdom and undergirding of a strong support system. Most people involved in alcoholic relationships find this in Al-Anon. Tough love is extremely difficult—but it is essential.

Related Articles
Chapter 14: Living With a Nonrecovering Alcoholic
Chapter 14: Alcoholism: The Process of Recovery

Alcoholism: The Process of Recovery

GAYLE ROSELLINI & MARK WORDEN

We're not going to find an angrier person in the world than an alcoholic, unless, of course, we look at the spouse and kids of an alcoholic. And getting sober doesn't make all that anger magically disappear.

Sometimes sobriety makes anger worse, for the family anyway. At least when the alcoholic is drinking, we have something to blame the anger on. The bottle. The booze. The drunkenness. We can hate the *alcohol,* we can detest the *alcoholism,* and somehow still manage to love the alcoholic. Take away the drinking or other drug use and what do we have left? All that anger with nothing to blame it on! And that doesn't feel good.

We end up confused.

Weren't all the awful family problems supposed to stop once Dad got sober? Well, he's sober now, but the house is still filled with tension. He doesn't kick in the door and break the dishes anymore. He doesn't launch into drunken tirades like he used to. He doesn't stay out all night and leave us wakeful and terrified that the phone might ring, with a gentle official voice regretfully informing us Dad was in a fatal accident at 2 A.M.

So, it is better. There's a small sense of trust developing, slowly, almost as if we're cordial strangers. But there's tension in the air, mixed with the memories of all of yesterday's pain. You see, when an alcoholic first sobers up, there isn't much of a change in the family dynamics. The situation—and the anger—in

459

the family is still far from normal, far from healthy.

We're supposed to be happy now, but the pain and anger don't magically disappear. We still have work to do. Sobriety, in and of itself, is no guarantee for happiness. For an alcoholic, it's the starting point, the single most important thing necessary to begin the *process* of recovery.

Remember that. *Recovery is a process.* Sometimes dramatic changes happen in a blinding flash of insight, a sudden and surprising awakening in our minds. Most of the time, it's a slow and painstaking thing, a snail-like crawl to growth, maturity, and happiness.

And the process takes work.

[Excerpted from *Of Course You're Angry*, Harper/Hazelden, 1985, pp. 4-5.]

Related Articles
Chapter 14: Living With a Nonrecovering Alcoholic
Chapter 14: Tough Love

SONNET 29
(17TH CENTURY)

When in disgrace with fortune and men's eyes
I all alone beweep my outcast state,
And trouble deaf heaven with my bootless cries,
And look upon myself and curse my fate,
Wishing me like to one more rich in hope,
Featured like him, like him with friends possessed,
Desiring this man's art, and that man's scope,
With what I most enjoy contented least;
Yet in these thoughts myself almost despising,
Haply I think on thee—and then my state,
Like to the lark at break of day arising
From sullen earth, sings hymns at heaven's gate;
    For thy sweet love remembered, such wealth brings
    That then I scorn to change my state with kings.

William Shakespeare

How Much Abuse Should a Woman Take?

DAVID & CAROLYN ROPER

How much physical and emotional abuse does a Christian woman have to take from her husband? Must she accept beatings in the name of Christian submission? Should she take verbal abuse without rejoinder? Is this what Peter means when he writes that women are to be submissive to their husbands as Christ was to those who reviled and battered Him? (1 Peter 2:21–3:6)

We don't think so, and we don't think that's what the biblical writers mean by submission. In fact, we believe that if a woman does not resist her husband's attempts to humiliate her, she is participating in his sins.

John Calvin once wrote to Antoinette Fumee, a woman being harassed by a cruel husband, that she should endure persecution bravely. She responded, "A number of people think your assertions are thoroughly wretched. They accuse you of being merciless and very severe to those who are afflicted; and they say that it is very easy for you to preach and threaten over there, but that if you were here you would perhaps feel differently."

Women like Antoinette do feel differently, particularly if they've been told by their leaders that women must submit meekly to injustice and suffer silently. The real issue, however, is not how one feels but what Scripture says. Does the Bible present a way to suffer that is more successful than merely taking it? We believe it does.

Since 1 Peter 3:1-6 is the passage most often quoted in defense of passivity, we should try to understand what Peter is saying to us there. The apostle affirms the principle of a husband's headship by instructing women to submit even to their unbelieving husbands. The purpose of such submission is to win their men, if they are to be won at all. The most impelling argument for the truth of the Gospel, Peter argues, is the tranquil, respectful behavior of an unbeliever's wife.

The text is introduced by the phrase, "Wives, *in the same way* be submissive" (italics added), which connects the command to the preceding verses which describe Christ's demeanor when He was abused. The argument is usually made this way: Jesus, like a lamb led to slaughter, did not open His mouth; women in the same way should not open their mouths when their husbands abuse them. But that explanation doesn't take the text seriously. Nothing is said in 2:21-25 about our Lord's suffering in silence. The text's emphasis is not on His silence but rather on the fact that *He did nothing wrong* when He was unjustly treated. His example lies in the fact that "He committed no sin. . . . When they hurled their insults at Him, He did not retaliate; when He suffered, He made no threats" (vv. 22-23).

It's a matter of record that during His trial, Jesus did in fact speak out against injustice (John 18:22-23; see also Acts 23:3 for an example of the Apostle Paul doing the same thing). He was not servile or utterly silent. Therefore we believe that when Peter says women are to submit to injustice "in the same way," he is not saying that women can say nothing. He is asking them to say nothing

461

wrong—that they not revile or threaten their husbands.

We believe that abused women have a redemptive way to proceed that preserves a man's headship and yet deals with the offense. Suffering in silence seems to be no answer at all; it may, in fact, only make things worse. Some men, as Agatha Christie once pointed out, will be as bad as their women will let them be. To allow cruel behavior is to enable it. Therefore, the way to save both the abusing husband and the abused wife is for the woman to speak out against abuse whenever it occurs. It's a matter of redemptive concern.

Of course, how something is done is often just as important as what is done. One must speak from a quiet spirit, which, it's important to note, is not merely a feminine trait. It is an attitude that ought to characterize men under attack as well as women. Both men and women are taught by Scripture to be tranquil, gentle, and strong.

Whatever one says in response to abuse should be said with respect for the person and without malice. As Paul says, "The Lord's servant must not quarrel; instead, he must be kind to everyone, able to teach, not resentful. *Those who oppose him he must gently instruct,* in the hope that God will grant them repentance leading them to a knowledge of the truth" (2 Tim. 2:24-25, italics added). A gentle spirit is significant; for truth to penetrate, it must be coupled with grace. As the proverb puts it, "Pleasant words promote instruction" (Prov. 16:21).

But the truth must be declared. One must hold one's ground. No one—not even a husband—has the right to abuse another human being. His right to leadership does not give him the right to do harm. To abuse one's wife either verbally or physically is wrong; therefore it's proper to put a stop to such treatment. It is very Christian to say to a verbally abusive husband, "It's not right to speak to

FINDING HELP IF YOU HAVE BEEN ABUSED

If you found talking to your pastor unhelpful, if you were not believed, or if you were counseled to
—submit to your husband
—pray harder
—try to get your husband to church
—be a better Christian wife
—lift up the abuse to the Lord
—forgive your abuser and take him back
without dealing with the battering and abuse, then your pastor does not understand what you have been through. Many pastors have no comprehension of your experience and no information about wife abuse. At this point they will not be a helpful resource to you.

Remember that most ministers have not received any training to prepare them to understand your abuse. Although they may care deeply about you and want to help, their lack of knowledge and skill will prevent them from being the support that you need. Do not feel guilty about choosing not to discuss your abuse further with them at this time. God will provide other pastors or counselors who may be more knowledgeable and prepared to help.

Marie Fortune

[Adapted from *Keeping the Faith: Questions and Answers for the Abused Woman,* Harper & Row, 1987, pp. 75-76.]

another person that way." This must be said with dignity and grace—but it must be said.

It's right to put a stop to physical abuse also. Though most women are unable to defend themselves against a male assailant, they can and must resist violence, speaking out against it, walking out if possible, and refusing to stay in a house where they are likely to be hurt. In addition, legal ways exist to maintain one's safety until tempers cool and long-term solutions can be implemented. A woman can invoke the law—what Paul calls "God's servant to do you good" (Rom. 13:4)—by calling the police.

If further help is needed, abused wives may appeal to the elders of their church or other mature men or women for protection and asylum. In extreme cases, a temporary legal separation may be necessary in order to safeguard the family until counseling can be secured. We stress, however, that the goal of that separation is not the dissolution of the marriage but its ultimate healing.

It should be obvious that these principles apply to child abuse as well as to wife abuse. A mother should not permit her children to be physically or verbally abused by her husband any more than she would permit a stranger to abuse them. Those under our care are entitled to protection from harm. It's wrong for

anyone to abuse a child, and it's wrong for anyone to permit it.

What we're saying is that submission does not entail servility or consent to evil and injustice. It is thoroughly Christian to bring such wrong to an end; in fact, it is un-Christian to permit it to continue. Certainly the Bible gives us the right to defend ourselves against assaults, and the mere fact that the assaulter is a family member does not vitiate that right. Jesus' word about turning the other cheek refers to insults for Christ's sake, not assaults by people intent on doing us harm.

We are convinced, then, that a woman has the right and responsibility to protect both herself and her children from verbal and physical attack. At such times, she can and must speak up. The manner in which she speaks is very important. As Peter says, she must do no wrong. She must not retaliate in the same spirit, hurl insults, or make threats, but she must speak up and confront her husband about his evil. It's our experience that when this is done kindly and firmly, it can bring a man to his senses. The alternative is to be responsible to some extent for perpetuating his sin.

Related Articles

CHAPTER **15** *DISCUSSION STARTER*

What are your beliefs about divorce? Where did you learn them? Are they well founded? Evaluate these statements (A=Agree, U=Uncertain, D=Disagree). Then read the articles in this chapter. Are your beliefs biblical? Do you need to change any of them?

A D U The Bible prohibits divorce in all situations.

A D U The Bible sometimes allows divorce, but not remarriage.

A D U The Bible permits divorce when adultery has occurred.

A D U The Bible permits divorce for desertion.

A D U Divorce may be necessary if a spouse is alcoholic.

A D U Divorce may be necesssary if a spouse is abusive.

A D U Divorce may be necessary if a spouse is an unbeliever.

A D U Divorce may be necessary if a spouse is very hard to live with.

A D U Divorce is never necessary.

A D U It is better to divorce than to subject children to living with parents who do not get along.

A D U Parents should stay together for the sake of the children.

A D U After divorce, children should live with the mother.

A D U It is important for children of divorce to maintain a relationship with the absent parent.

A D U Divorce is better than misery.

A D U In a divorce, there is usually a guilty person and an innocent person.

A D U Divorced people should be asked to leave the church fellowship.

A D U Divorced people should not have leadership positions in the church.

DIVORCE

"I hate divorce!" Malachi fairly explodes with exasperation in delivering God's case against Judah's leaders. "The Lord is acting as the witness between you and the wife of your youth, because you have broken faith with her, though she is your partner, the wife of your marriage covenant" (2:14). This accusation, often quoted by evangelicals, does not mean that God hates divorced people. We may be in danger of making divorce an unpardonable sin!

Divorce is the miscarriage of a marriage. No matter how hard some people try, their marriage seems to disintegrate; their hopes and dreams self-destruct. While many observers are clear and convincing about the Bible's teaching concerning divorce, very few are clear and convinced about what to do with divorced people.

Far too few troubled marriages are handled by competent, spiritually astute counselors. Hurting, fearful husbands and wives tend to ignore signs of deterioration; they run from the scene when divorce seems inevitable and hope against hope that "something can be done." What started out as stars in their eyes has become sand; that which began with delight has ended in disillusionment. The pain and guilt cannot be expressed in words.

But good news and real hope are attainable even in our broken society. Jesus Christ heals brokenness for those who come to Him in faith believing.

Howard & Jeanne Hendricks

Overcoming Five Underlying Reasons for Divorce

LUIS PALAU

Mike and Jean have been married five years. They come from good families and belong to a good church, and their friends think they are compatible. What their friends don't know is that Mike and Jean, like so many others, are getting a divorce.

This couple is not unique. One in two marriages now end in divorce, and many divorcing couples are Christians. I believe divorce is the enemy's plan to thwart God's blueprint for happy homes: homes in which beautiful marriages produce strong children and thus strengthen both their churches and their communities.

Satan whispers excuses into the ears of men and women—even Christians—

to persuade them to divorce their spouses. His rationalizations sound convincing to people who are going through difficulties in their life together. Nevertheless, most divorces need never happen.

To protect your own marriage, I encourage you to learn how to identify and overcome five typical underlying reasons for divorce.

1. *Unreasonable expectations.* Ironically, while marriages are failing today in historically unprecedented proportions, our expectations for marriage have never been higher. Couples expect completely unrealistic things from marriage. In a word, they want total fulfillment. They expect marriage to meet all their sexual, emotional, and personal needs and desires. Of course, such expectations eventually lead to disaster.

A woman phoned me during a live call-in television counseling program. She had been married and divorced and had lived with quite a few men, but she had never found the rather idealized fulfillment and satisfaction she was looking for. Finally she realized that many of her so-called lovers had simply used her and discarded her. She told me, "I can't even look at men anymore, I've been hurt by so many." She was only 29 years old. Her problem: expecting some man to come along and completely fulfill her.

In reality, no spouse can totally fulfill our every need, let alone our desires and fantasies and dreams. No husband can give his wife everything she wants, and no wife can do that for her husband. In marriage we help, encourage, and complement each other, but we can't fulfill each other. Sometimes the key to improving our marriages is bringing our expectations down to earth.

2. *Ungodly focus.* As one song says, "Only Jesus can satisfy the soul." If our relationship with Him isn't right, no wonder that we feel unfulfilled and discontent. We may blame our marriages, when in reality our spiritual poverty is the problem.

A marriage is in danger whenever the partners maintain a wrong center of focus. Some focus on their spouses, others devote themselves to their children, and many simply concentrate on themselves. The only truly satisfying focus, however, is Jesus Christ.

Diana left her husband and their three children—then ages six, five, and one—and moved to another city. Her reason is typical: "If I had stayed I would have ended up embittered, telling them all their lives that I stayed just for them. Leaving nearly broke my heart, but in the end I had to put my own needs first."

Such selfishness comes when we fail to acknowledge Jesus as Lord of our lives. He has the power to restore relationships, to heal wounds, to give "a crown of beauty instead of ashes, the oil of gladness instead of mourning, and a garment of praise instead of a spirit of despair" (Isa. 61:3), if we turn to Him and obey Him. We must realign our focus, or attention, and our allegiance toward Him. Only then can we have strong family relationships.

3. *Uncontrolled passions.* As much as we in the Western world pride ourselves on our technological and scientific advances, we are incredibly impulsive. One of our most uncontrolled passions is spending. We have bought into the materialistic philosophy that says, "Get more out of life." So we spend our lives trying to accumulate things, often to the neglect of our marriages.

Another uncontrolled passion is sensualism. We are made callous by the immorality we see in print, on television, and in movies. A little girl sent me this simple letter written in pencil: "Dear Luis Palau: Please will you pray for my daddy because he left me and my mommy. Please ask God to help Daddy realize what he has done wrong leaving me alone." Her dad, believing Satan's lie about sensuality, left his family for a young woman who pleased him more

466

than his wife did. Now this seven-year-old child must suffer for his irresponsibility.

God says, "Above all else, guard your heart, for it is the wellspring of life" (Prov. 4:23). Husbands and fathers, evaluate the material you allow to come before your eyes, and get a grip on your impulsive spending. For your family's sake, guard your heart from uncontrolled passions.

4. *Unforgiving attitudes.* We're all weak. We all fail. Our marriages stand or fall depending on how we respond to our spouses' shortcomings.

Maybe your spouse has hurt you deeply by unreasonable expectations or an ungodly focus or uncontrolled passions. Or maybe your spouse is unforgiving toward you. No matter. Decide in your heart today to "forgive as the Lord forgave you" (Col. 3:13). How has He forgiven us? First, sacrificially—by dying for us on the cross. Second, completely—by washing away all our sins. Third, eternally—by remembering our iniquities no more (Heb. 10:17).

After more than 25 years of marriage, Pat and I still find that practicing forgiveness is a vital key to our relationship. We've had to forgive each other a lot. That doesn't mean we go around all day saying, "Forgive me, forgive me." For us, at least, forgiveness is more an attitude. When I lose my temper, for instance, Pat often tells me by the way she looks and acts that she has forgiven me. Sometimes, of course, I need to actually say, "I realize I've hurt you—will you forgive me?"

5. *Unbiblical presuppositions.* Scripture, interestingly enough, connects marriage and sexual intimacy with the most sacred relationship of all: our spiritual unity with Jesus Christ. Marriage is an incredible metaphor of what it means to be right with God. No wonder Scripture places such a high premium on faithfulness and lifelong commitment within marriage.

Speaking of a married couple, the Bible says, "What God has joined together, let man not separate" (Mark 10:9). One psychologist commented, "In certain circumstances I recommend that couples get divorced because God never put them together in the first place." This is playing games with the Word of God. In God's eyes, when a man and woman join their lives together, they are married until death separates them. The Bible warns, "'I hate divorce,' says the Lord God of Israel" (Mal. 2:16).

Why does God hate divorce? One reason: because of the incredible hurt it causes the spouse, children, family, and friends. Another reason: because if the family suffers, the church and the nation are endangered. Third: because marriage is a divine metaphor of the relationship between Christ and the church. God's plan is for us to enjoy beautiful marriages and happy homes, and thus show forth His glory in a fallen world. But we must follow His blueprint, as revealed in the Bible, or else we may eventually shipwreck our marriages as so many others have done.

I encourage you: whatever state your marriage is in today, commit your life anew to God. Tell Him, "I want to acknowledge You as Lord of my life. I want to follow Your blueprint for marriage. I want to be a truly Christian husband or wife. Lord, I want You to be the center of my life."

God wants to revolutionize your marriage. I challenge you to let Him.

Related Articles

WHY SO MUCH DIVORCE?

Three factors affect whether a marriage will be permanent: the husband's commitment to the marriage, the wife's commitment to the marriage, and society's commitment to the institution of marriage. Where two of those three factors are strong, the marriage is likely to last. If only one is strong, it is likely to break up.

A hundred years ago, most marriages lasted because only one committed person was necessary. Society provided any commitment that might be lacking in the other partner. Popular literature of the late 19th century is full of tales of women who were faithful to men who drank up the family's money, beat their wives and children, and spent weekends in gamblers' dens and whorehouses. These women tended to die in their 30s, but they did not get divorced.

Nowadays an abused partner does not have to live in misery and terror. Society does not frown on her for leaving a dangerous marriage, and the law does not make it difficult for her to do so. By the same token, however, a bored or selfish or irritated partner does not have to stay in his or her marriage either. Society will not ostracize such a person for walking out, and the no-fault law will not even ask for reasons. If one spouse is uncommitted to the union, the other spouse is powerless to make him or her stay.

A hundred years ago, a person had to think carefully before marrying because a bad marriage was a life sentence. Today a person has to think carefully before marrying because an uncommitted marriage will fall apart. In any age, there is just one safe approach: marry someone whose commitment to you is exceeded only by his or her commitment to God.

LaVonne Neff

Why Wait Till Divorce?

BRUCE & MITZIE BARTON

Years ago, in our society, marriages were often formed between people who lived in the same part of town, maybe even in the same block, and many times between families whose parents were good friends. They shared the same spiritual, economic, and political points of view, and the same social values. When they got married, it was a celebration for the "heavenly twins."

Now, years later, our children go off to college and meet potential mates in a broader marriage market. They're from different parts of the country, different political backgrounds, different economic values. Their backgrounds no longer serve as a support to marriage pressures. They get married, often to find out that instead of a dynamic duo, they are more like the "gruesome twosome."

In fact, differences can now be so great that it's a miracle if anyone stays married. When we go to weddings, our reactions have become subdued and reserved. We would prefer to wait for the 25th wedding anniversary to celebrate. Then we feel there is good reason to celebrate, for the partners have proven their commitment. Unfortunately, there seem to be fewer and fewer long-lasting marriages or causes for celebration because of the tremendous pressures on marriages today.

Equally disturbing is how many people want to look into the Bible to find out its position on divorce, adultery, and sin and to see how it might justify their situation. The purpose of the Bible is not to show us how to get out of marriage gracefully and biblically, but how to use God's Word to strengthen and heal our marriages. It's not just the sin of divorce that disturbs us, but the whole chain of "single sins" that occur prior to the divorce to bring it about.

There was an episode on the "Dick Van Dyke" TV series some years ago where Rob and Laura Petrie got so mad at each other they finally decided to get divorced. They drew up a divorce certificate but because they couldn't agree on the grounds for divorce, they could never get everything finalized. When they did resolve their differences, they put the divorce certificate on the wall as a constant reminder that it was within their power to get divorced. All they had to do was fill out the forms. And it served as a reminder of what it took to keep their marriage alive and vital—constant, daily, willful commitment to the process . . . and *that* sparked a renewal in their marriage.

That's just what it takes . . . constant, daily, willful commitment to the process. Otherwise, you can let single sins slowly erode your marriage until suddenly you find yourselves facing the "big sin" of divorce.

What "little sins" can erode a marriage?

1. *It is a sin to ignore your spouse.*
Many people spend their whole lives ignoring their spouse; refusing to develop any common interests; ignoring color, style, fashion, self-improvement, humor, or any of the efforts that make a person interesting; refusing even to communicate. It takes more than commitment to make a marriage work—you need passion. And in order to convey passion, you must be an interesting person, and you must develop a way to show interest in your spouse by reaching out and showing your strong, intense feelings, both physically and verbally.

2. *It's a sin to be preoccupied with your own development.* Many people in the early stages of marriage find that their achievement needs are at war with their intimacy needs. They find it more gratifying and fulfilling to do well in a career or raising the children than to relate to their spouse. They seek personal gratification by doing what they feel they do best. To do so and to neglect the development of your spouse is wrong. You must be equally concerned with the other's growth spiritually, physically, and emotionally. You need to take time to see that your mate develops. Encourage your mate to develop as you work on your own development together.

3. *It's a sin to be closed.* You need communication and intimacy in your marriage. Your marriage cannot survive if you keep all your thoughts to yourself without ever talking or sharing. You must be *willing* to be vulnerable and committed to growing closer to your spouse every day.

4. *It's a sin to be self-justified.* Many marriages fall apart because every time there is a hurt, a wrong, a slight, an omission, or error, one spouse pastes it like a stamp in a coupon book in order to cash it in for one great big adulterous binge, fantasy, vengeful act, affair, or even divorce. You are not to keep count of every wrong, every slight, every hurt—many of these are generated by feelings of inferiority or self-doubt. And they are

469

not excuses or justifications to cash in on your marriage.

5. *It is a sin to wallow in your own hurt.* It's one thing to collect cases where the other person has wronged you; it's another thing to wallow in it, to make yourself the victim in your relationship. There is enough hurt, misunderstanding, and wrong in every marriage for one partner to justify leaving. No human being can meet all the needs of another. Every human being is capable of hurting and hindering another person.

We need not only rid ourselves of the sin of divorce—the sin of seeing divorce as too ready a solution for conflict in marriage—but we also need to rid ourselves of the single sins in marriage that lead to those irreparable situations. Why wait until divorce looms before us?

The Book of Hebrews give clears advice: "Try to stay out of all quarrels and seek to live a clean and holy life, for one who is not holy will not see the Lord. Look after each other so that not one of you will fail to find God's blessings. Watch out that no bitterness takes root among you, for as it springs up it causes deep trouble, hurting many in their spiritual lives" (Heb. 12:14-15, TLB). If men and women took to heart their common Christian responsibility to contribute to a marriage, recognizing the pitfalls and difficulties, perhaps there would be a better chance for it to grow and flourish.

Don't wait until divorce. Work now on recognizing the responsibilities of marriage. Then be willing to recognize, repent of, and overcome the sins that can erode a marriage.

Related Articles

Bringing Love Back to Life

RICHARD A. MEIER

A major reason given for divorce is the loss of emotional intimacy. People communicate this in a variety of ways:

—We are no longer in love.

—We are going through the motions, but our hearts are not in it.

—It seems as if a wall has developed between us.

—The chemistry is gone.

In fact, any couple occasionally senses a loss of the feelings of love. This may last a day or two or even longer. If it lasts more than two weeks, I believe marriage counseling is indicated. But even if it has lasted months and years, the answer is not a divorce. Instead, a husband and wife must develop and nourish that original love.

To do this, we must make sure that the blocks to emotional intimacy are removed.

The first block to look for is any *unresolved anger* that needs to be verbalized, any offenses that need to be forgiven. The anger may be over a specific issue, or it may simply result from an accumulation of little resentments that the individual didn't think were important enough to discuss with his or her spouse. Whether the anger is over one big problem or many tiny ones, it can build a wall and block feelings of love.

Anxiety is another common block that must be removed. It can stem from

470

fear of rejection, fear of pregnancy, fear of loss of control, or many other fears, real or imagined.

Guilt is another potential block. It may have grown out of unresolved issues going back to premarital sex, or it may be based on self-condemning messages about personal worth. Sometimes guilt is connected with past experiences of abuse or rape. It can even be related to excessive weight gain.

Transference is another potential block. If a third party is receiving one spouse's emotional investment, even if there is no physical relationship between them, an emotional affair is going on, and love for the spouse will be blocked.

How can we tear down the blocks and revitalize love? There are two approaches: behavioral and cognitive.

The *behavioral* approach means choosing to give caring behaviors to the spouse, no matter how we feel at the moment. It is based on the principle suggested in Revelation 2:4-5, where the way back to love for the Ephesian church is to "do the things you did at first." We can't directly command our emotions, but we can affect them indirectly by choosing our behavior.

Here is an example of a behavioral approach to tearing down blocks and restoring love: sit down and list the things you would do if you had a strong love for your spouse. (Paul's description in 1 Corinthians 13:4-8 of what love does and doesn't do might inspire you.) Choose four or five of these behaviors, and commit yourself before God to give them to your spouse this week whether

TAKE A GOOD LOOK AT YOURSELF

It's a rare person who hasn't experienced some pain in a relationship. It's also a rare person who pauses for a good look at what's going on. Most people just muddle on, wishing things could get better. If it gets too painful, they end the relationship and look for another one. After observing thousands of pain-filled relationships in my counseling practice, I've come to recognize a few principles:

1. *Who you are with in a relationship says as much about you as it does about the other person.* If you look at your history and say, "I have been in relationships with 17 baby men who want mothers, not partners," what does that say about you? The problem isn't *them;* it's *you.* Babies are everywhere, but what are you doing in relationships with them?

2. *Wherever you go, there you are.* You are sick and tired of crummy relationships in Minneapolis, so you go to Phoenix. What kinds of relationships are you going to have there? The same. You cannot outrun yourself. Wherever you are, you take yourself with you.

3. *If nothing changes, nothing changes.* You can't change anyone else; the only person you have to work on is yourself. And unless you really do some work, nothing will change. If nothing changes, you will continue to suffer pain in your relationships.

In a way, that's good news. You can't change other people or circumstances, but you can change yourself. If you are ready to stop blaming and stop running away, you *can* learn how to have happy relationships. It's hard work, but it's worth it.

Earnie Larsen

you feel like it or not.

The *cognitive* approach brings love back to life by changing the way we think. Make a list of five of your spouse's best qualities. Twice a day, meditate on these qualities for 10 minutes. Vigorously reject negative thoughts about your spouse. Recall his or her characteristics that you have most enjoyed in the past, and anticipate some exciting times you could have in the future. Carry your spouse's picture in your billfold or put it where you can see it as you work, so that you can be reminded of the gift God has given you.

Ideally, behavioral and cognitive approaches work together. A person who chooses to behave as if he cared is likely to begin thinking caring thoughts. A person who meditates on the spouse's strengths is likely to translate those meditations into loving actions. Translate your desire for a happy marriage into risk-taking action. Claim God's love by faith, and go to work on your behavior *and* your thoughts. Ask God to give you His love and release it through you so that you can express it in tangible ways to your spouse.

Related Articles
Chapter 7: What Would You Do If You Loved Her?
Chapter 9: Making Your Communication Work

Coming Apart at the Seams

DAVID VEERMAN

The phone rang, and my associate reached for the receiver. A few moments later he called to the receptionist who was in the supply room, "It's your first husband!"

"It is?" she replied. "How did he know I worked here?"

Ted and I looked at each other in stunned silence. We didn't know she had been married before. What Ted had spoken as a joke had touched reality.

The fact is that our culture overflows with broken relationships and dreams. Whether a result of teenage romance or passion, the idealized plans of college sweethearts, or even the reasoned decision of a confirmed bachelor (and "ette"), ill-fated marriages set sail. Then they flounder and sink.

Why is this? How can two honest, well-intentioned people stand before a church of witnesses and announce undying allegiance ("I will cherish you, no matter what happens!"), and soon thereafter declare the relationship bankrupt and the commitment null and void? Why are so many marriages falling apart these days?

The answer, of course, is not simple nor universal. Many factors lurk beneath surface "incompatibility." There are, for example, the problems of youthful idealism. Romantic love, popularized in song and on the screen, sees only a future life filled with laughter, sexual ecstacy, and happy trails. Very few, if any, couples walk the aisle thinking that their relationship will crumble before the wedding cake is stale. The expectations are as high as their emotions. But marriage takes work—two people deciding to smooth things out when they rub each other wrong. And life has pain and hardships. For youth reared on idealism and pleasure at all costs, this is intolerable. Expecting too much—fulfillment, support, and unending bliss—the marriage becomes a grave disappointment.

Marriages also break under the strain of a pop culture which promotes self-gratification. Take a personal poll of television ads and shows, and you will see that they center around doing what is best for the individual, with little regard for sacrifice. Find personal fulfillment, get your share, have a career, make lots of money, stand for your rights—these messages assault us continually.

But the foundation for marriage is sacrifice—giving oneself to the other. When one partner vomits, the other must clean it up; when the baby cries at 3 A.M., one spouse must lose sleep; when two careers collide, one must give in. Good marriages are not 50-50 propositions; they are 100-100, with each person willing to give everything for the sake of the other.

The subtle tide of materialism also pulls many marriages to the rocks. I don't know who started the rumor that two can live as cheaply as one, but it's a lie. In fact, expenses grow in marriage, and they multiply as children arrive. The person who wants to collect and then spend her paycheck on some new adult toy will not enjoy watching her wallet quickly flatten for miscellaneous household needs. And very soon the career- and money-minded spouse will begin to see the marriage as a weight, keeping him on the lower rungs of the corporate ladder and cramping his style. He will begin to remember and then yearn for the single life where he was free to move, to make money, and to spend.

Couples are also susceptible to other myths of society: that solutions to problems should be quick and easy, that sexual excitement and fulfillment come with a variety of partners, that the "good life" is the only life worth living, that all that matters is now.

Another contributing factor to marriage breakups is the relative ease of divorce. In past generations, a divorce was a scandal, whispered about in the family and neighborhood. Today there are divorce parties and "no fault" split-ups. Divorce is socially acceptable—even Christian leaders are leaving their spouses, remarrying, and resuming their roles. And despite all the evidence to the contrary, the myth persists that children of divorce are doing just fine coping with the loss of Mom and/or Dad. Comedians joke about their multiple marriages, as though failure is a mark of success. Without stigma, red tape, or other barriers, husbands and wives see separation and divorce as very live options.

Whatever the reason, marriage as an enduring institution is in trouble. Of course, a lot go the distance, but so many drop out at the first sign of trouble or pain. Whatever the real reason for the breaking of each sacred relationship, the Bible calls it sin. Marriage is ordained by God, and it is for life.

Don't give in to the pressures of culture or self. Be true to your commitment made at the altar and before God. Stay married and work together to untangle each of life's knots.

Related Articles

Is Adultery Grounds for Divorce?

DONALD & ROBBIE JOY

Growing up evangelical before the *King James Version* slipped out of its place as the only translation, every kid had to be told the meanings of certain words. So we learned that *fornication* means "sex before marriage or instead of marriage," and *adultery* means "sex between a married person and someone who is not his or her spouse."

How, then, could we interpret Jesus' words in Matthew 19:9 on divorce: "I say unto you, 'Whosoever shall put away his wife, except it be for fornication, and shall marry another, committeth adultery' "? How could a married woman commit fornication?

Since, by today's definition of the word, she can't, many interpreters of this text substitute the word *adultery*. Since adultery breaks the marriage bond, they say, it is the only acceptable cause for divorce. But adultery, in Scripture, is punishable by death, not divorce. And *adultery* is not the word used in this text.

The word *fornication* (*porneia* in Greek) had a somewhat different meaning in Scripture from the definition we use today. The idea of fornication included a wide range of behaviors: a demand for instant gratification, a compulsive enslavement to appetite, an addiction to self-satisfaction. This behavior was often, but not always, sexual. In Revelation, the "great whore" is judged for the sin of fornication. When we read the description of Harlot City in Revelation 17–18, it is clear that it was plagued with all sorts of self-indulgent addictions, not just illicit sexual behavior.

In fact, there is not a single text in which premarital sex is the focus when *fornication* is used. Fornicators can be single, married, or divorced, but they have one thing in common—they are out of control, compulsively preoccupied with self-satisfaction. Their addictions almost never show up singly, but in clusters. People who are sexually promiscuous, for example, tend also to be substance abusers or addicted to pornography or masturbation. Fornication is clearly a trap into which a person moves deeper and deeper; it is a profound disturbance in personality. A "fornicating" husband or wife, typically with a whole cluster of compulsive behavior patterns, evidently can even wear out the epoxy glue of the marriage bond and effectively end the marital attachment long before legal steps are taken to end the marriage.

Adultery, or forming a competing bond with another partner, may indeed be the first step into the addictive, fornicating lifestyle. But adultery is often quite different from fornication. An adulterer goes over the edge and allows a friendship to end in sexual intimacy. At this point, sexual intimacy with the original partner is put on hold—healthy people cannot simultaneously carry on sexually with more than one partner. Fornicators, on the other hand, can move freely from one partner to another and may even increase marital sexual activity when outside encounters are in motion.

There is healing for adultery, though it comes at a high price. It requires that the person caught between two loyalties must *choose* to love his or her spouse, regardless of feelings for the new love. This is *agape* love—love with the power of choosing. The adulterer must break the alien bond and set the grieving process in motion so that the adulterous relationship can be permanently laid to rest.

A marriage can survive adultery if the bond is rejuvenated between husband and wife. Recovery from fornication—sexual addiction—is more complicated. The best success involves: (1) writing an entire history of one's sexual addictions; (2) sharing that story with a small, fully trusted accountability group; (3) reporting regularly to that group on continuing battles, including failures; (4) contracting for brief periods of time to control specific sets of behavior and reporting in on schedule; and (5) maintaining such accountability for the rest of one's life. Some churches sponsor confidential recovery groups for people with sexual addictions modeled on Alcoholics Anonymous. (For information on locations of such groups, phone the Golden Valley Health Center in Golden Valley, Minnesota: 612-588-2771.)

Since marriage protects the mysterious and glorious sexual bond that fuses two persons into one whole couple, it is not surprising that any sort of sexual infidelity, whether adultery or fornication, may collapse the marriage. The sexual bond rests on a thousand unspoken assumptions, the first of which is exclusivity. This does not mean, however, that a marriage *must* be dissolved for adultery or even for fornication. Mature people, like God in the Book of Hosea pursuing fornicating Israel, are frequently able to pursue a lover until there is a marvelous coming home.

Related Articles
Chapter 10: Forgiveness: The Secret of a Great Marriage
Chapter 14: The Affair: An Empty Promise
Chapter 14: I Think My Spouse May Be Playing Around

The Bible on Divorce

GARRY FRIESEN

Marriage is a permanent union between a man and a woman that has two aspects. First, it is a public agreement or covenant (Prov. 2:17; Mal. 2:14) that goes into effect when a man leaves his father and mother and is joined to his wife (Gen. 2:24). Second, it is a physical union: "they will become one flesh" (v. 24).

Jesus quoted Genesis 2 when some religious leaders asked Him to comment on divorce, adding, "Therefore what God has joined together, let man not separate" (Matt. 19:6). Contrary to Moses, who allowed divorce if certain procedures were followed, Jesus said, "I tell you that anyone who divorces his wife, except for immorality, and marries another woman commits adultery" (v. 9). Christians have been discussing these words ever since Jesus uttered them. Here are some biblical principles about marriage, divorce, and remarriage:

1. *God expects marriages to be both faithful and permanent.* Note that God's ideal is not permanence no matter what. In fact, according to Old Testament law, the death penalty was to end every marriage where adultery was found (Deut. 22:22). Even if the innocent spouse was ready to forgive and accept the adulterer back, God's law said that the guilty party should die.

Faithful permanence, not just permanence, is God's ideal.

Jewish law required the death penalty for many unlawful sexual acts including adultery (Lev. 20:10), incest (vv. 11-12), homosexual relations (v. 13), and bestiality (vv. 15-16). Divorce was never discussed in such cases, because it was superfluous. Under the law the adulterer died, and the surviving mate was obviously free to marry again. There was never any reason for divorce when sexual sin was involved.

2. *Divorce is lawful when a marriage partner commits adultery.* The question of divorce for sexual sin became important when Israel, under Roman law, was no longer permitted to carry out the death penalty for adultery. What would an upright Jewish husband, living under both Old Testament law and Roman law, do if he found out his wife was an adulterer? "Because Joseph her husband was a righteous man and did not want to expose her to public disgrace, he had in mind to divorce her quietly" (Matt. 1:19).

Righteousness under Mosaic law required Joseph to end a relationship with an adulterous wife—even if she was only a betrothed wife and they had not begun living together yet (see Deut. 22:23-27, where the prescribed penalty is death; under Roman law it became divorce). Joseph's desire not to disgrace Mary moved him to divorce her quietly. "Forgive and forget" was not an option under Mosaic law. Divorce was the expected response to adultery when the death penalty was impossible. Fortunately, Mary was innocent, and the marriage was preserved when God revealed to Joseph that adultery was not the cause of Mary's pregnancy.

3. *For a marriage to end before either partner's death, there must be both adultery and divorce.* Adultery alone is valid grounds for divorce, but of itself does not dissolve the marriage. Neither do divorce proceedings alone

MATTHEW 19:3-9

Some Pharisees came to [Jesus] to test Him. They asked, "Is it lawful for a man to divorce his wife for any and every reason?"

"Haven't you read," He replied, "that at the beginning the Creator 'made them male and female,' and said, 'For this reason a man will leave his father and mother and be united to his wife, and the two will become one flesh'? So they are no longer two but one. Therefore what God has joined together, let man not separate." "Why then," they asked, "did Moses command that a man give his wife a certificate of divorce and send her away?"

Jesus replied, "Moses permitted you to divorce your wives because your hearts were hard. But it was not this way from the beginning. I tell you that anyone who divorces his wife, except for marital unfaithfulness, and marries another woman commits adultery."

dissolve a marriage in God's eyes. Jesus said that people with a divorce certificate but no just cause for divorce (adultery) would commit adultery by remarrying, since their first marriage is still binding (Matt. 19:9). It takes both adultery and divorce to dissolve a marriage.

This understanding of when a marriage ends is consistent with our definition of marriage. Marriage involves union through covenant. This union then is consummated physically when the two become "one flesh." To dissolve the marriage, both the covenant and the one-fleshness must be broken. The covenant is broken by divorce, and the physical union is violated by adultery.

4. *A divorced person can be innocent.* God's own figurative marriage with

Israel did not last permanently without interruption. Because of Israel's continual spiritual adultery, God wrote Israel a certificate of divorce (Isa. 50:1; Jer. 3:8). God's divorce of Israel shows that though He wants every marriage to be faithfully permanent, He recognizes innocent parties in divorce cases. According to His own imagery, God is divorced, but He is certainly innocent.

None of us is perfectly innocent like God. Every married person could be a better spouse. But in divorce proceedings, there can be an innocent spouse— one who did not commit adultery and one who did not seek in any way to dissolve the marriage.

The women in Malachi 2 became divorcees, but God's anger was against their husbands. Toward the mistreated women He showed only compassionate concern. These wives were not perfect, but they were innocent of ending their marriages.

It is possible for a person to have a treacherous spouse who carries out an unlawful divorce and then commits adultery by remarrying. In such a case we should show compassion to the innocent person who has been mistreated and bring our case against the guilty spouse only. It is cruel to mistreat the innocent person further by ostracizing him or her.

5. *An innocent divorced person is free to remarry.* In Old Testament times, adultery meant death for the guilty person, and the survivor was free to remarry. When adultery was not punished by death, then divorce was to end the marriage.

In the age of the church, grace has been added. Nowadays adultery does not automatically bring death. It does not even necessitate divorce—the mistreated spouse now has the option to forgive the sinning spouse and try to maintain the marriage. But as in Old Testament times, if adultery occurs, then divorce is lawful; and if the marriage is ended in God's eyes, then remarriage is lawful.

This understanding makes sense out of complicated situations. A man marries a woman lawfully. He tires of her, however, and divorces her against her will. At this point the marriage is still in effect despite the divorce papers since it has not been dissolved in God's court. Neither is allowed to remarry, and both should seek reconciliation. But what if the man then marries another woman?

His initial act of sexual relations with the new woman is adultery against the first marriage. Now, because adultery has now been added to the divorce, the first marriage is dissolved. The second marriage was entered by adultery, but once entered it becomes a real marriage in God's eyes. God hated the divorce and the adultery that produced the second marriage, but once the second marriage became valid, God wants it to be faithfully permanent.

The first wife is now single and free to remarry. She cannot commit adultery against her first husband, because that marriage is dissolved. The husband now cannot leave his second wife to return to his first wife. His first marriage is dissolved, and his second marriage is recognized by God. To leave his marriage for his former wife would just be committing adultery again—this time against his second wife.

For the faithful Christian, of course, adultery is never an option. If every Christian maintained his or her purity, then every Christian marriage would be permanent, since no marriage can be dissolved unless adultery occurs. And that would fulfill God's ideal—marriages that are both faithful and permanent.

Related Articles
    Chapter 15: Jesus' Teaching on Divorce
    Chapter 15: Believers and Divorce

Jesus' Teaching on Divorce

WESLEY & ELAINE WILLIS

Few questions raise more controversy or stir deeper emotions than the question of divorce. Of course, this is not a controversy unique to our age. The very teachings of Jesus demonstrated how deeply the feelings ran almost 2,000 years ago.

We learn Jesus' views on divorce through His being drawn into the long-standing feud between the two schools of Pharisees—the Schools of Shammai and Hillel. The School of Shammai felt that immorality (adultery) was the only justification for divorce. The School of Hillel took the opposite position. Indeed, they held such a loose view of marriage that a man could divorce his wife for *any* reason—even for as petty an offense as burning a meal.

The accounts of the confrontation, and Jesus' subsequent teaching, are recorded both in Matthew 19:1-12 and in Mark 10:1-12. These two passages have many elements in common. In both passages Jesus clearly taught that from the beginning God intended no divorce. At Creation, God created male and female, and He ordained that they should cling to each other and become one flesh.

A second issue in these passages relates to Moses giving permission for a man to divorce his wife. When the Pharisees questioned why Moses "commanded" divorce (Matt. 19:7), Jesus explained that divorce was not a command, but a concession, a permission (v. 8). Because of hard hearts (we take it this meant that because people insisted on violating God's commands), Moses instructed that divorce be formally recognized.

The issue is not whether Moses or God wanted divorce—neither did—and certainly not that Moses and God disagreed. Moses instructed the people under the direction of God, and therefore we can conclude that Moses' teaching had full authority. The focus of concern here seems to be the rights of the one being divorced. Since it was the husband who divorced his wife, the "certificate of divorce" (Matt. 19:7) was a protection for the wife so that she could not be accused of abandonment or adultery.

A third and certainly the most controversial question relates to the exception clause found only in Matthew (19:9): "except for immorality." While there are several interpretations as to the meaning of these three words, and many variations, let's consider two. One possible interpretation, and probably the most popular, is that Christ stated there was only one valid reason for divorcing a spouse—adultery.

Advocates of this position point out that during Old Testament times, adultery was punishable by death. And so a spouse who had committed adultery, breaking the marriage contract, would have been executed under Mosaic law. But since stoning for adultery was forbidden under Roman rule, divorce was the alternative. Therefore giving a divorce certificate would be merely the formalization of what already had been destroyed.

A second view, and one that we personally support, relates to the Jewish flavor of Matthew's Gospel. Under Jewish custom, the engagement period, which lasted for a year, was as legally binding as marriage itself. However, the marriage could not be consumated until that year had elapsed. During this period, if the wife were found to be unfaithful, the marriage could be annulled through a formal procedure—writing a certificate of divorce.

Since Matthew alone contains the exception clause, there is good reason to believe that it relates to the Jewish emphasis of that Gospel, Jews being the book's intended readers. In that case, the clause "except for immorality" would have little relevance for the question of divorce today. No matter what the circumstances, God's plan still includes the permanency of marriage.

Whether or not we conclude that divorce is permitted for adultery, we must recognize that God intended marriage to be a permanent commitment. Whenever that commitment is broken, the emotional and personal penalties are great. And if, under less-than-ideal conditions, God's permanent marriage law is violated, it should be done in such a way that the one being divorced is protected as much as possible.

Related Articles
Introduction: God's Blueprint for Happy Homes
Chapter 15: The Bible on Divorce

Stages of Divorce

JUDSON SWIHART

Sometimes we think that children are affected by divorce only at the time the divorce occurs. It is important to remember that children are involved in adjustments at various stages of the divorce process.

1. *Pre-divorce.* This is often a time of much tension in the home. Even when parents think they conceal the conflict, children, like little radar screens, are very capable of sensing the tension.

This stage often produces much stress for children, which may manifest itself in many ways. Children may try to divert attention to themselves; they may regress, become more dependent, become rebellious, get ill, or even become caretakers or peacemakers.

During this stage parents need to become attuned to their children's emotional needs in spite of being in their own personal turmoil.

2. *The time of divorce.* During this stage the divorce is announced; one parent has packed and moved out; the logistics of visitations with children are being established; property is being divided; and legal paperwork is being done. During this time there may be much rapid change such as a move to a new location or Mom starting work.

For children this is a time of great emotional upheaval. They struggle to cope with all the crises and uncertainty about what will happen next.

Parents need to keep children as informed as possible about changes, be available to thoroughly answer any questions, stabilize any areas that don't have to be changed, and try to provide other significant people to be available to the children.

3. *Post-divorce.* During this stage there may be some settling from the hectic change, but the children are still adjusting to new rules, new ways of relating, a new lifestyle. Mom may have to go to work, so household chores get assigned. She may establish new rules for running the household since she is a

single parent. Issues kids took to Dad are now negotiated with Mom. Children have to adapt to weekdays with Mom and weekends with Dad, who may operate his household in a very different manner. Parents are trying to decide how they will relate to each other once the divorce is final.

Children need understanding during this time, because there is confusion in the way their world is structured. Giving guidelines with clarity, directness, and gentleness often is helpful as they adapt.

4. *Remarriage.* It is common for parents eventually to remarry. This may be a time when some children have a greater adjustment than they had at the time of divorce. They may have strong feelings about the absent parent's being replaced, conflict of loyalty, loss of hope for parents' reconciliation, changing role structure, new household rules, or resentment of the stepparent's authority.

During this phase parents are often caught up in their new situation, and children's issues are on the perimeter. Children need the opportunity to explore with the parent and stepparent the many issues of living in the reconstructed family.

DANGER SIGNS

Though all marriages experience difficult times, certain signals send up red warning flags that a marriage is in need of professional help (or at least in need of immediate attention from both spouses). These include:

☐ Physical abuse
☐ Verbal abuse
☐ Consistently finding excuses for not being together
☐ Consistent lack of intimacy
☐ Domination by one spouse
☐ Consistently divergent values

In addition, a serious personal or family crisis needs to be flagged as a time for concern and extra care for the marriage.

YFC Editors

Related Articles
Chapter 10: The Course of Severe Marital Conflict
Chapter 15: How Divorce Affects Children

Life During Divorce

GARY D. BENNETT

The divorce experience can mean different things for different people depending on their age, identity in the marriage, personal coping skills, relationship with the Lord, and many other factors. Seldom is anyone adequately prepared. Relationships and feelings change in unexpected ways, and life is complicated by legal complexities, emotional trauma, economic upheavals, the struggle for a new identity and self-worth, and the often confusing influence of family, friends, and children.

If you are going through a divorce, you already know this to be true. If you're considering divorce, prayerfully read on and carefully weigh the price you will have to pay to go through it. Perhaps you and your spouse could invest the same amount of energy and make your marriage work. That would be God's desire, but the choice is up to the two of you.

Although your life is not ending when you're struggling through a divorce, loving life may seem an overwhelming task. We will look at four areas of sometimes painful change: relations with friends, relations with family members, loneliness, and physical health.

Relations with friends. It's important not to underestimate the significance of friendships during a divorce. There will be friends who accept you and friends who won't, or can't. Some friendships will have to be renegotiated; others will end. New friends will be made; some old friends will become distant, especially if the friendship was formed as couples. You will have to learn to recognize expectations of friendship that may no longer fit your needs, to decide who will

be your friends now that you are single, and to rediscover your identity as an individual. You will have to decide what you want in relationships and then learn to be yourself in each of those relationships.

As you go through the divorce experience, you'll find your friends reacting to you in a variety of ways. Some will display feelings of anxiety and surprise. Some may try to become mediators and attempt to repair your marriage. Others may desire a sexual relationship with you. Some will confide that they are disillusioned with their own marriage, while others will show fear that you might be interested in marrying their spouse. Some may play Cupid and try to set up a dating service for you.

When examining each friendship, ask yourself, "Can I be myself in this relationship without being on guard? Will the friendship allow for each other's growth and not insist on keeping things the way they used to be? Does the friendship belittle me or build my self-esteem?" As you examine your friendships, keep in mind that it's impossible for any one relationship to completely satisfy all your needs. Perfection should never be an expectation of friendship.

Relations with family members. The reactions of your parents and children may be difficult to understand while you're going through a divorce. You may feel they have no sympathy for or comprehension of your personal struggles. Yet they are experiencing their own grief over a relationship that has died. Many times they will experience feelings similar to yours—guilt, sadness, anger, and discouragement—usually from an

481

exaggerated sense of responsibility for the situation. Parents have to deal with their disappointment in their own way, so it's hard to expect them to understand all you may be feeling. Needless to say, no one ever prepared them to cope with divorce either!

During a divorce, there is often the temptation to fall back into allowing your parents to take care of you again. Even though it feels good to be cared for, and it is important to feel their caring, you must accept the responsibility for yourself and finish the struggle on your own. You must establish expectations for your own life and future, not merely take on someone else's. If you return to live with your parents, even temporarily, permit them to be responsible for their own feelings while you take responsibility for yourself.

Loneliness. At one time or another, you will feel very lonely. This may touch you during a crisis, in the midst of a crowd, when making a major decision, or when self-pity or despair become overwhelming. Even though loneliness affects everyone to some degree, no one can share the particular anguish that accompanies a divorce. You may try to share your greatest sorrows and joys with another person, but the deepest emotions are really yours alone. Wading through loneliness, sadness, anger, and rejection is a painful but necessary part of transition.

In the death of a relationship, it's necessary to move through the same stages of grief as in the death of human life. To do so enables you to come to grips with the past. As you look back on your marriage, you'll probably discover some circumstances that you couldn't change, others that you should have. Going into the past may be very uncomfortable, but it can also be a way to make friends with yourself, redefine your identity, and rediscover your worthiness. The loneliness that drives you to constructive introspec-

tion, then, can become a therapeutic agent for growth.

Acknowledge your loneliness, and do your best not to surround yourself with people simply because it's painful to be with yourself. Don't keep the radio or TV constantly going so as to flee your own thoughts. Avoid becoming a workaholic or getting overly involved in community activities in order to postpone going home. There is a definite difference between a healthy involvement in life and trying to escape from it. Recognize that everyone feels vulnerable, anxious, and lonely for a while. Allow it to happen, and accept yourself where you are.

Physical health. The stress of divorce can also show up in physical symptoms: backaches, stomach problems, tension, headaches, skin disorders, and so on. Realize that such symptoms are usually a partial reaction to stress. Don't skip meals or short yourself on sleep. Keep your diet and daily routine as structured as possible. Good physical habits will help relieve emotional stress. Of course you should check with your physician if the symptoms persist.

Sometimes we can alleviate physical symptoms of stress by applying 1 Peter 5:7 to our lives. When we are able to completely cast our cares, worries, concerns, and even our divorce upon the Lord, our load becomes lighter. Of course, if you believe God expects you to be perfect, the stress of divorce will heighten your feelings of inadequacy, guilt, anger, and bitterness. Sadly, this happens to many Christians. But a biblical perspective of life with God reveals that He is always willing to help us through situations we judge to be failures—and that includes divorce (see Rom. 8:28-29).

Related Articles
Chapter 10: The Course of Severe Marital Conflict
Chapter 15: Stages of Divorce

Life After Divorce

GARY D. BENNETT

Regardless of the cause for the divorce, every divorced person must start over and restructure his or her life.

If you are divorced, you can't spend the rest of your life majoring on how unfair your divorce, your ex-spouse, or life is. To do this is to hurt only yourself. It blocks both your present effectiveness and your future reestablishment. In order to restructure your life after divorce, begin by admitting your feelings of anxiety; then use them to motivate you to build a new life as a single.

Don't dwell exclusively on the past or project unrealistically into the future, but live one day at a time. In so doing, you'll learn how to appraise who you are, to accept yourself as you are, and to acknowledge what you'd like to become. Since God accepts you where you are, even as He helps you grow, it only makes sense for you to do the same.

If you get caught in living for tomorrow and anticipating what might be, you cheat yourself out of the fullness of today. Planning for future realities is important, but not at the expense of the only authentic time you really have—your present day.

If you dwell intensely on the past, you can be overwhelmed, immobilized, and depressed to the point of uselessness. Do your best to avoid thinking about what could have been. Instead, focus on your strengths, which you may have previously overlooked or underrated, as well as on areas in which you want to grow.

Deal with your feelings realistically. Adjusting to singlehood often brings on feelings of loneliness, failure, rejection, guilt, sadness, anger, and loss. Don't put yourself down when you begin to feel blue. Accept your feelings as a normal part of the adjustment process. Recognize that everyone feels bad sometimes. Allow these feelings to come, but don't interpret them to mean you are a failure.

Build your own identity. If you look for your identity in another person, then singleness may make you feel as if you don't exist. Tell yourself that you do exist and that you are valuable, and go to work building your identity. Once you have faced your feelings and accepted them as part of you, you will be able to decide on new directions, clarify values, update your image of yourself, and begin to meet yourself and others as real individuals.

Remember that you are a social creature. Life after divorce can be a tremendous time for developing your inner resources and creating your own techniques for survival as a single. One important fact of life to keep in mind: you will not survive as an island unto yourself! God has created us social creatures, so avoid isolating yourself. Calling a friend or two during painful times can provide you with additional strength, and knowing someone cares is very therapeutic. Don't overlook or underestimate the support that a caring church can offer. Be involved with a community of believers. Get to know a group of people within a church, and put your time and energy where you can contribute as well as receive.

Don't feel pressured to remarry. Well-meaning friends may pressure you to remarry, but it's vitally important to consider marriage as only an option, not a goal. When forming relationships with other singles, see them as friends only. If you're constantly sizing them up as potential marriage partners, they'll sense that and probably won't stick around very long. Remarriage to ease your conscience, get even, or meet others' expectations generally will turn out disheartening and disappointing. Please don't remarry on the rebound. If and when you remarry, do so for the right reasons. Of course, God's preference would be for you and your original spouse to resolve your differences and remarry each other.

Set limits for your sexuality. Life after divorce does not mean you won't have sexual desires, because you most likely will. You will have to predetermine how you will respond to your sexuality and the limits you will set for yourself. Avoid using your sexuality to get revenge on your ex-spouse, to ease loneliness, to relieve boredom, to raise your self-esteem, or to meet your companionship needs. It will not work in any of those areas. You will have to live with your decisions, so make them wisely. The way you handle your sexual feelings reflects your basic beliefs about yourself and the Lord.

In summary, you can have a good life after divorce by giving yourself plenty of time to completely heal from the wounds of your divorce, establishing your identity as an individual, and living each day fully in and under the Lord's grace. God created you unique, and He gifted you with potential. Begin again in His strength.

Related Articles
Chapter 3: Before You Say, "I Do"
Chapter 3: Second Marriages: Two Important Issues
Chapter 15: Do's and Don'ts in Dealing With An Ex-spouse

AFTER DIVORCE

The in-between is hard,
the mid-air, the limbo
between bank
and bank,
the long leap (legs
flailing, body un-
grounded, askew in space)
the scare
of alien air,
the interval of being
in no place,
having no where.

With love left behind,
an uncertain landing waits.
Suspended,
mind
anticipates,
feels the fall—feet first
on firm sod, or (up-ended,
unbalanced, off-guard)
slipping on a cruel
gravel. Yes.
It is the in-between
that is hard.

Luci Shaw

From *The Sighting.* Used by permission.

How Divorce Affects Children

JUDSON SWIHART

Dr. Albert Solnit of the Yale Child Study Center has noted that divorce is one of the most serious and complex mental crises facing children in the 1980s. Since 1950 the divorce rate in the United States has essentially tripled. Most divorces involve couples with children under the age of 18. Each year approximately 1 million children are affected by divorce. What effects does divorce have on these children? Can children make a good adjustment in spite of their parents' divorce?

A major study conducted by Wallerstein and Kelley indicates that about a third of the children from divorcing families make a fairly good adjustment, another third make a moderate adjustment, and the remaining third struggle constantly with the effects of the divorce. This raises the question: what can be done to help children adjust to divorce?

Part of the stress children feel from divorce arises from conflicting pressures bearing down on them simultaneously. For a time, much in their lives is fairly confused. As the divorce occurs, for example, children may have a great need for time with a parent, while the parent may have a great need to be alone.

Another point of confusion has to do with loyalty. Children want both parents to love them, and the parents want their children to love them—but the parents are not loving each other.

Parents may send mixed messages. A parent may become more authoritarian with the children while at the same time wanting them to be more autonomous. Or the father may say, in effect, "I'm angry at your mother, but don't you be angry at her."

Where previously the children went to different parents with different requests, now they have to go to the same parent for everything.

Children are likely to sense their parents' confusion. A parent may claim to be unafraid, while the children may easily sense the parent's underlying fear. Or the parents may stress the importance of forming good relationships while their own marital relationship is coming apart.

Parents need to be aware of what their children are experiencing. The most common reaction is *guilt:* most children tend to in some way blame themselves for their parents' divorce. They may feel that if they could have behaved better or done more, they somehow could have magically held their parents together. If parents in any way blame the children, this response is magnified. Even when parents reassure the children that the divorce was in no way their fault, many children will continue to blame themselves.

Another common reaction is *insecurity.* Children are afraid of being abandoned. They say to themselves, "What if something happens to Mom? Who will take care of me?"

A third common reaction is *anger* and *depression.* The way these emotions are handled varies somewhat with the children's age. Preschool children may regress to earlier stages or spend a great deal of time whining or seeming not to be able to enjoy anything. Children in the grade-school years may express some of their anger and depression through fears of abandonment, intense sadness, or maybe even a great concern over loyalty issues—if they say they like Dad, will Mom be offended? Teenage children may be more open with their anger. It is not unusual for them to pick a parent to blame for the situation. Often it is not until middle or late adolescence that children are able to see how both parents contributed to the divorce.

What can parents do to help their children adjust to the divorce?

1. Do not put the children in the middle. It's better for children to be kept out of any ongoing conflicts that the parents may be attempting to resolve.

2. Tell the children about the separation openly and honestly.

3. Do not hold the children responsible or make them feel that they in any way contributed to the divorce.

4. Do not use the children for your own emotional support. Parents should rely on other adult friends for encouragement rather than turning to their children.

5. See that the children receive support from other important people in their lives: Sunday School teachers, schoolteachers, grandparents, other relatives, friends.

6. Resolve your personal anger quickly. The longer the parents continue to be angry at each other, the more difficult it is for the children to adjust.

7. If you are the absent parent, stay in contact with your children. Adjustment to divorce is much more difficult when the absent parent ignores or avoids the relationship with them.

8. Move into a new schedule fairly quickly. Some families stay in disarray for an extended period of time. This makes the adjustment even more difficult.

9. Try to keep other aspects of the children's lives stable. It helps if the children can stay in their own house, neighborhood, school, and church. Let them stay close to their friends. Avoid any move if possible. If the mother has not

MAGICAL THINKING

School-aged children of divorced parents often fall prey to "magical" thinking. They may say to themselves, "If I hadn't wished my parent dead, then he [or she] wouldn't have had to leave." "If I had done what I was supposed to, my parents wouldn't have gotten a divorce." "If I had brushed my teeth every night like they told me to, Mom and Dad would still be together."

If not given the opportunity to ask questions or express their feelings, children often will extend their magical thinking into other areas, hoping to get Mom and Dad back together. For example, often children will tell themselves, "If I do what I'm supposed to do—clean my room every day, eat all my vegetables—then maybe Mom or Dad will come back."

Of course, when that doesn't happen the children are even more perplexed and confused. That's why it's so important that children be made to feel no blame for their parents' divorce, and that each parent do his or her best to avoid undermining the other's standing with the children.

Gary Bennett

been employed, it is better for her not to start a new job immediately, if that is possible.

10. Frequently spend individual time with each child. It is best if each parent does this.

11. Allow the children to grieve. Like adults, they need time to work through their sense of loss.

12. As a family, focus on the positive in the future. A renewed sense of hope is

a powerful aid to adjustment.

It is important for those who are concerned about children whose parents are divorcing to tune in to each individual child. Children have different ways of trying to cope with this time of stress. They may become show-offs or bullies; they may isolate themselves or become clinging vines; they may be friendly or grouchy. Adults who look beyond the children's behavior to their feelings can encourage them and help them through this time of adjustment.

Related Articles
Chapter 15: Life During Divorce
Chapter 15: Life After Divorce

Do's and Don'ts When Dealing With an Ex-spouse

ANDRE & FAY BUSTANOBY

If you had no children by your previous marriage, you will have few reasons to deal with your ex. Problems with ex-spouses occur most often when you have children and when either or both of you have remarried.

Children are an enduring link with the ex-spouse. Every time you phone to check on visitation for the weekend, every time you pick up the children at your ex's house, you and your new spouse are reminded that your ex is still a big part of your lives.

The ex can be a problem if bitterness still exists. He or she can try to disrupt your new marriage by being difficult about child visitation or support arrangements. Your new marriage will have enough problems of its own without having an ex making matters more difficult.

But strange as it sounds, the ex can be a bigger problem when your relationship is very cordial. Your new spouse may wonder if you are just being nice to each other because of the children, or if you still have feelings for each other. This can make your new spouse feel very insecure.

To reassure your new spouse of your loyalty and commitment to him or her, observe these guidelines when talking with your ex:

● Be businesslike. When you speak over the phone or in person, treat your ex as if he or she were interviewing for a job. Be polite but formal. Most important, don't allow any feelings of attachment that may still exist to show through.

● Keep phone calls short and to the point. Don't linger over questions about the in-laws or old friends. Your curiosity may be killing you, but if you want tranquil relations with your new spouse, spend as little time as possible in dealing with your ex.

Whether you are the custodial or noncustodial parent, the children force you to deal with your ex over visitation arrangements and the children's activities when visiting. Here are some do's and don'ts that will help you avoid having any more contact with your ex than necessary and will also help prevent rancor over visitation:

● *Don't* argue with your child or your ex over what your ex may have told the child. If the child alleges that your ex said something untrue or unfair, simply

487

say, "Your father [mother] and I see things differently. This is the way I see it." Then go ahead and explain your point of view without attacking your ex or defending yourself. If it's a matter of behavior that you don't permit, say, "When you're here, we do it this way."

• *Don't* try to cut down the child's positive image of the other parent. The other parent may not deserve that positive image, but the child will find this out for himself in due time.

• *Don't* try to persuade the child that you are always right and your ex is always wrong. This will encourage the child to defend the absent parent out of loyalty.

• *Don't* react defensively when your child brings home stories that the other parent is telling about you. Again, simply smile and say, "Your father [mother] and I disagree about this." If the child wants to know your views, tell him—but keep your statement short and to the point.

• *Don't* attempt to get the child to offend the religious, moral, or social values of the other family. If your ex has adopted a religious system foreign to biblical Christianity, let your child know what you believe and why, and help him see the differences between Christianity and the other belief system. At the same time, help the child see that we can disagree without being disagreeable.

• *Don't* use your child as a pawn in a power struggle with your ex. The child has loyalties to both parents, whether justified or not, and those loyalties should be respected. If your ex doesn't deserve the child's loyalty, the child will find out in due time and appreciate your not forcing the issue before he was ready to face it.

• *Do* talk with your ex in a way that minimizes conflict. You can set rules for the child without being testy about it.

• *Do* be aware of any problems the child may have, and involve your new spouse in the solution, particularly when the solution affects your ex-spouse. Family counseling that involves the ex-spouse and the new spouse is helpful, because it recognizes that the new spouse is not just a bystander. He or she is affected by the decisions made about the child.

• *Do* be available to the child on a dependable, reliable basis. When you say you are going to pick up or return the child, do it at the time agreed on. Just because you dislike your ex is no reason to use visitation to make his or her life difficult.

• *Do* show that you have consistent standards of behavior. They may differ from those of your ex, but you don't have to argue over who's right or wrong. Just say to the child, "When you're with me, we do things this way." The child's

TAKE CARE OF YOURSELF

As a single parent who has gone through the trauma of a divorce, you must realize that parenting struggles are normal for your situation. At times you will want to take a break from your role as parent and make time for yourself. You may want to be with friends, attend a party, spend time alone, or perhaps even date.

Be honest with yourself and your children about these matters. Strive to create a balance in your life between restructuring your adult world and meeting your children's needs. This does not imply a lack of love or concern for your children. If you take care of yourself physically and spiritually, you will be better able to care for your children.

Gary Bennett

488

loyalty to the other parent may make him defend behavior he knows is wrong. Don't put the child in the position of doing this by bad-mouthing your ex's behavior.

● *Do* make the visit enjoyable rather than looking at it as a time to impress or persuade the child. Your child catches on quickly to your questionable motives, such as using his visit to get back at your ex.

In dealing with your ex-spouse, keep in mind that your new spouse and your children need to be protected against any ill will that still exists in your relationship with your ex. If you find it difficult to deal with your ex in a constructive manner, you should seek counseling. You may need to deal with feelings of grief, bitterness, or attachment that keep you from dealing constructively with your ex and getting on with your life.

Related Articles

Chapter 15: Life After Divorce
Chapter 15: Fulfilling God's Will in Second Marriages

Fulfilling God's Will in Second Marriages

DWIGHT HERVEY SMALL

Marriage is a sacred covenant between two parties. The model is the indissoluble union of Christ and the church. In reality, however, some marriages deteriorate to the point where they end in divorce despite every effort to save them. All divorce represents failure to meet God's ideal, but His grace is available to all. He meets each situation, not in prohibitive law, but in liberating, renewing grace. He delights in completed families, in the normalizing of life according to His design for wholeness in marital partnership.

For some divorced Christians, remarriage is an opportunity to reverse a former failure and establish an enduring, Christ-centered, God-honoring marriage—a second chance to achieve God's ideal. With the help of past experience and greater maturity, remarrieds can commit themselves to God's best from the very start, knowing fully what they are doing, trusting God to fortify them against repeated failure. Thus remarriage in Christ can be a vital witness that God is indeed a God of grace and new beginnings. Here are some tips:

If you are divorced and considering remarriage, wait until you are fully aware of how you yourself may have contributed to the previous failure. If your actions and attitudes were prominent in bringing about the divorce, a proper penitence and willingness to change are required before you can proceed to an understanding of God's will. Counseling is also recommended so that you might know and accept your rightful responsibility for the breakup. God's desire is not to punish you, but to chasten and prepare you for successful remarriage.

Wisdom dictates that a second marriage has all the possible pitfalls of the first one and perhaps more. You must make the same strong commitment you made during the romantic phase of your first marriage, a commitment to give yourself in love to the success of this marriage. You must resist any thought that since you've chalked up one failed marriage, you can always choose the same course if this doesn't work out. To enter a new marriage with a negative, unbelieving self-estimation is to invite failure from the start.

Your desire to remarry is flawed if you are directed by a sense of present deprivation, or by pressing needs, or possibly by a secret envy of married friends who haven't suffered such a break. You anxiously dream of once more being back in the enfolding circle of those married friends. Or there may be a subconscious desire to remarry quickly to spite your former partner, proving that you are desirable after all. Another subtle tug is the notion that remarriage would conceal the fact of your previous failure. Or perhaps you are having a difficult time financially. Then again, just the awkwardness of being a formerly married single is reason to wish remarriage, though not a sufficient one. All these factors tend to feed a sense of urgency. Such motivations must be searched out and honestly laid before God.

Inasmuch as over half of all second marriages end in divorce, there is a more than even chance of your suffering a repeated failure. What that does to one's self-image, to the perception of friends who had hoped for something better, and to children who innocently think their parent's problem is solved, only to have their hopes dashed, can only be imagined. Thus the grave possibility of a second failure must be carefully weighed.

Children sometimes do not take to the new parent in the house and create a difficult situation; this has brought down many a second marriage. Or the new parent can't really relate to his or her new family. This disappoints the partner who had assumed everything would work out just fine. So every attempt must be made to assure that these relationships are in place before the wedding date is set.

If your former marriage seemed lacking in romantic intensity or continuance, do not fall for the seductive fantasy that this time you will experience a greater passion which will carry you through any of the problems you met in your first marriage. If anything, you should have learned that the heart of a successful relationship is mutual caring, that in time the temporary phase of romantic love must be replaced by committed, caring love.

A person devastated by divorce may feel that everything must somehow be made up through another person. But that lays a heavy burden on a potentially adequate mate. This is not God's intent, nor is it a realistic expectation.

Acknowledge any bitterness and any blaming of your former partner, and relinquish it. If possible, enroll in a Christian marriage course. Learn conflict management techniques, communication skills, and the roles God expects of marriage partners. Take time for emotional recovery, for growth in relationship with God and with the opposite sex. Seek Christian counseling. Look to God for His best for your life now, as a single. Weigh every option carefully in prayer. Commit yourself to His will without setting conditions.

It is sound advice not to think of remarriage until a year after divorce, and not to remarry anyone you have not gone with seriously for at least a year. Be sure you both have a firm commitment to the scriptural model for marriage. When you have sought to honor God in every detail of the process, then you can count on His blessing.

The second time around there is far greater need to ask, "Whom am I seeking to please in this marriage?" You now carry wounds that need to be healed, a self-image you wish to erase, perceptions by others you want renewed. It is easy to move in ways calculated to please yourself and others without first ascertaining whether or not you are pleasing God, but that is your first priority. The assurance of His leading and blessing is something you need more than ever before, inasmuch as your own self-assurance has been weakened. This is of vital importance, whether you see yourself as the victim of the breakup or an active factor in it.

There is a subtle tendency to want a second marriage that will exhibit personal advance beyond the status of the first marriage. You may expect your new husband or wife to offer more than the first one; you may hope that your suffering will lead to a conspicuously more satisfying partnership. But your new mate stands as a unique person. He or she is not to be compared with your former mate, not to be thought of as someone who will meet all your needs in a way your first spouse couldn't. You take this person just as he or she takes you—for who you really are, not an idealized self. You appreciate your new partner for the strengths he or she brings, not for the corrections and improvements he or she might offer.

Consciously ask yourself whether your supreme desire is to find the partner God has for you. This is of first and utmost importance. You are not seeking greater benefits or a person with a superior image—one you can showcase more effectively. Rather, you are seeking a faithful spiritual partner, one united with you in mutual servanthood in Christ. And whatever else comes with the package, why not just leave that with God and believe that He will give you what is right and good!

Related Articles

Believers and Divorce

WESLEY & ELAINE WILLIS

What should be a proper Christian attitude toward divorce? Ideally, all of us wish that it were possible to conclude that Christians should not even have to address the issue. But such an attitude would deny reality. More and more often we hear of Christians getting divorces. And many of them use some highly circuitous reasoning to justify or rationalize their actions.

Let's consider what the Apostle Paul had to say on the topic of divorce, specifically what he taught about Christians and divorce in 1 Corinthians 7. Here are several key principles we found taught in this passage:

1. *A Christian should not initiate a divorce.* In 1 Corinthians 7:10 Paul wrote that a believing wife should not leave her husband, and in verse 11 that a believing husband should not initiate divorce proceedings against his wife. A Christian's objective always should be to maintain the marriage.

2. *Separation is a possibility.* If living together is impossible, separation *is* an option. But in such a case, remarriage to another is not acceptable. First Corinthians 7:11 explains that in the event of a separation, the believer should not remarry since the possibility of reconciliation remains a possibility as long as no subsequent marriage has taken place.

3. *God ministers through Christian mates.* The question of a mixed marriage always creates problems. Paul's exhortation to a Christian married to an unbeliever was to remain married. His

rationale is found in verse 14: the unbeliever sustains a different ("sanctified") relationship to God because of the married partner.

Some have assumed that *to sanctify* means "to make holy." But it doesn't. It means "to set apart" or "to dedicate." What the Holy Spirit communicated through Paul was that an unbelieving spouse and the children of such a relationship are set apart for some special favor from God. By remaining married, the believer can be a source of God's blessing to the unbeliever—even to the extent of the unbeliever coming to Christ through the believer (v. 16).

4. *Paul did not contradict Jesus.* Some have concluded that when Paul wrote, "But to the rest I say this (I, not the Lord)" (v. 12), he was giving a lower level of instruction. In reality, Paul was distinguishing what Jesus had already taught while He was on the earth from the additional revelation now given by Paul. What Paul taught was just as authoritative as Jesus' teaching since he too was directed by the Holy Spirit. The words of Jesus and of Paul *both* have the full authority of God; both should be obeyed.

5. *Marriage was designed by God to last until death.* God's ideal is for the relationship to continue as long as both partners live. Thus the marriage bond should be entered with the intention of remaining married. However, at the death of one partner, the remaining spouse is free to marry (but only to a believer), according to 1 Corinthians 7:39.

6. *Divorce and remarriage can terminate a marriage.* Even though God's ideal in a "mixed" marriage is to maintain the relationship (vv. 10-11), sometimes the unbeliever chooses to depart, in which case the believing partner should not resist (v. 15). Apparently Paul assumes that the unbeliever will remarry and that no possibility of restoring the relationship exists. In that case the Christian partner is free—presumably to remarry if he or she chooses (v. 15).

Obviously we merely have touched the surface of 1 Corinthians 7. Anyone who wishes to understand the biblical teaching on divorce should study this chapter deeply. It provides excellent instruction to all who are married or who would be married.

Marriage is a deep commitment—not one to be taken lightly. But it also can be the deepest and most meaningful relationship that a person can experience here on earth. We both (Elaine and Wes) personally can testify to the beauty of God's plan for husband and wife to become one flesh. And our desire is that every husband and every wife will experience the full, rich communication that only those who are happily married can understand.

Related Articles
Chapter 15: The Bible on Divorce
Chapter 15: Jesus' Teaching on Divorce

WHEN YOUR FRIENDS TURN AWAY

No matter what the cause of the divorce, many divorced people will find themselves "cast out" of their previous friendships and/or their churches—either physically or emotionally. Such a response by friends or churches is shocking and painful. But the divorced person must not become isolated; it is vital that new friendships be discovered. But where can you go?

If your church has turned away from you, don't delay in finding another church that can minister to your needs. Remember too that although your church had problems with your divorce, many of the people in the church may still be willing to support and help you. Perhaps you will want to become involved in a divorce support group at a large church where you can find people who are facing the same struggle and can offer advice and needed friendship. This may be a time to get reacquainted with your extended family. Their love and support can pull you through these difficult times.

Once you've begun to heal, you may again feel like reaching out to other groups for friendships. Follow up on people you've met in the past. Take advantage of friendships at work. Move out and meet people in other areas of interest—enroll in college courses you've wanted to take, renew a hobby by taking a class, get involved in local interest and concern groups.

YFC Editors

When a Fellow Believer Gets a Divorce

LaVONNE NEFF

Several years ago the daughter of one of my mother's friends suddenly left her husband. She took the children, moved to an apartment, and refused to have anything more to do with him. She also refused to tell anyone the reason for her actions. The people in her church were scandalized. Instead of support, what she got from them was condemnation and avoidance.

When my mother told me the story, some new facts had come to light. The young woman still was not talking, but apparently a close friend and confidante had spilled her secret. She left her husband because he beat her—savagely and repeatedly. She was afraid for her life, and she was terrified of what might happen to her children. But she hoped for his restoration, and she did not want to accuse him before their church and the community.

The damage, however, was done. After months of judging and condemning her, the church was unable to show enough contrition to make her feel wel-

493

come again.

It is extremely dangerous to judge fellow Christians, even in matters of marriage and divorce. This is not to say that the church should have no standards. It is right to support lifelong marriage. It is sometimes necessary to separate erring members from fellowship—but never in a spirit of prideful condemnation. Remember Paul's words to the Corinthian church, who at his command had expelled a sexually immoral brother: "Now . . . you ought to forgive and comfort him, so that he will not be overwhelmed by excessive sorrow" (2 Cor. 2:7).

Remember also that, whereas the Corinthian man's sin was open and evident, you may not know all the circumstances of someone else's divorce.

The wife of a friend of mine left him and refused to come back. Eventually they were divorced, in spite of his attempts at reconciliation. He learned during the divorce proceedings that she had moved in with another man for a few weeks. If he would be willing to announce that fact to their congregation, he would be accepted and forgiven. If he still loved his former wife too much to accuse her publicly of a sin for which she may have already repented, he would risk his church membership. What should he do?

Another friend of mine, after eight years of marriage, told her husband to hit the road. Wanting to be a faithful wife, she waited that long before giving up on a man who declared himself gay on their honeymoon and was continually involved in homosexual affairs from that time on. He was heartbroken that she left him; he needed her for a front. The church, not knowing what was really going on, sided with him. The wife was punished for her "heartless" behavior.

Of course there are many unnecessary divorces in this age of loose commitments and desire for instant gratification. But it is often very difficult to know whether a given divorce was the result of selfishness, or whether it became a necessity because of one partner's physical violence, abandonment, or sexual escapades. Many divorcing people do not want to trust the church with all the sordid details. They know the potential for gossip, and they do not think their marriages are anyone else's business. In fact, the people who are too eager to lay the blame on their spouses should perhaps be distrusted the most. The spouse may know the real story, and may be too much of a gentleman or lady to tell it.

Jesus never approved of divorce, but neither did He ever wound the divorced. In His day the divorced woman, not the man, was always seen as the guilty party, but that didn't stop Him from talking with the five-times-divorced woman at the well or from associating with women of loose morals—very likely divorcees driven to support themselves as best they knew how.

The simple fact is that there *will* be divorces among church members. Different churches will deal with these situations differently, according to how they read Scripture and do theology. But no matter what official position your church takes about divorce, keep one thing in mind. Our God is a God of grace and forgiveness. He cares deeply about people. He knows what happens behind each marriage's closed doors, and He will handle the necessary judgment.

What He has given to us, His followers, is a "ministry of reconciliation," a message of hope for the brokenhearted and comfort to those who mourn (2 Cor. 5:17-19; Isa. 61:1-3). Divorced people need friends who will listen, empathize, and support them; friends who will show them love, patience, kindness, and gentleness. You can be such a friend, no matter what your theology of divorce, for "against such things there is no law" (Gal. 5:22-23).

Related Article
Chapter 15: Life After Divorce

494

Do any of these short descriptions fit your marriage?

___ lack of communication	___ sexual difficulties
___ physical abuse	
	___ no time for each other
___ verbal abuse	
___ lack of trust	___ adultery
___ boredom with each other	___ dishonesty
	___ avoidance
___ jealousy	
___ mental or emotional illness	___ fear
	___ anxiety
___ depression	
___ a feeling that things should be better	___ substance abuse
	___ indifference
	___ hostility

If you checked even one item on this list, you need help. In some areas—boredom or indifference, for instance—you may be able to help yourselves through insights and hard work. In other areas, such as mental illness or substance abuse, professional help is advisable. No matter what you checked, congratulations!—you are obviously concerned about your marriage, and that is the first step toward improving it.

Which of these sources of help are available to you? Write down their name(s).

Pastor(s)	_____
Social worker	_____
Psychologist	_____
Psychiatrist	_____
Family counselor	_____
Family member(s)	_____
Friend(s)	_____
Marriage growth group	_____

16

WHERE
TO FIND HELP

Seeking help is not an admission of failure. It is the recognition that resources are available on request. God gives gifts to mankind, and gifted men and women to His body, the church. Competent, trained, experienced, and concerned counselors of godly wisdom are available, even though at times the search is difficult and disappointing.

When we speak of counseling we recognize three major levels on which it takes place: (1) by the professional who is a degreed specialist trained for especially difficult mental/spiritual pathology; (2) by pastors and local church leaders schooled in specific areas of Christian living, such as divorce and other domestic upheavals; (3) by lay peer counselors who are caring Christian friends skilled in the use of biblical guidelines for human relationships.

One other resource is sometimes overlooked. Self-help may be the only therapy required. In the book, *Rekindled,* Pat Williams recounts his private struggle with becoming the husband he understood God required, one who loved his wife as Christ loved the church. In a personal endeavor he allowed God to change him, turning a potential divorce into a vibrant marriage.

All marriages need constant maintenance and repair work; for some, complete renovation is called for. Whatever the cost of restoration, it is miniscule compared to the exhorbitant lifetime piracy of a shattered marriage.

Howard & Jeanne Hendricks

How Do We Know If We Need Professional Help?

ALICE FRYLING

Every parent has struggled with the question of whether Johnny's throat is sore enough to see a doctor, or if Sara's fever is high enough to go to the emergency room. "If it reaches 103.5 before midnight," we say, "then we'll go."

But when is the pain in a marriage great enough to warrant a trip to the doctor? What symptoms of marital discord indicate that it is time to see a counselor? Every marriage has problems. When are the problems too great to solve alone?

Because these questions can become painfully personal at times of marital crisis, I decided to ask three Christian marriage counselors to give their perspectives on how a couple can know if they need professional help. What symptoms of marital stress may indicate that a couple's problems are more than they can solve on their own?

The three therapists I interviewed were consistent in their advice:

1. When there are continued, repeated, unresolved conflicts, the couple should consider getting help. If the same complaint ("You don't care about me." "You never listen to my point of view." "I feel stifled by our relationship.") recurs again and again, this is evidence that the couple is not making headway on their own.

2. If one or both partners is continually depressed, then counseling is in order.

3. If either partner is "acting out" anxiety by an affair, by alcohol or drug abuse, or by verbal, physical, or emotional abuse of family members, then the couple should consider counseling.

These therapists were quick to add, however, that the crisis which leads to counseling may not be the result of relational failures. Any family crisis—the death of a child, a job loss, a severe problem in the extended family—may be too difficult to handle alone. In fact, anything that impairs the growth of the marriage relationship or the growth of the two individuals may be reason to seek counseling. Usually the fact that a couple has considered counseling is a hint that it should be pursued.

What, I asked these counselors, is the advantage of professional counseling? Why can't a couple just work things out on their own or with a friend?

The most obvious reason, they told me, is objectivity. To a greater extent than a friend, who may bring preconceived judgments into the relationship, the counselor can be an impartial mediator. Besides objectivity, there is also the advantage of the counselor's training and experience.

In addition, the counselor will hold you accountable. A good counselor will expect you to make changes as a result of the counseling sessions. The regular times of interaction facilitate this accountability.

And, finally, when a couple goes to a counselor, they are making a statement with their time and money that they really care about their marriage. This invest-

---

WHERE CAN WE GET HELP?

Marriages will run into a variety of problems, some small and some very large. When spouses run into rough water, where can they turn?

1. Check out books that have been recently published on the topic of your particular need, especially those by Christian authors. Many self-help books are available in your local Christian bookstore.

2. Rather than going to a secular therapist for the problem, first try a Christian counselor, family counselor, or doctor. They can help you see to the true root of the problem and guide you toward a solution.

3. For serious problems, the counselor can refer you to a specialist in the area of your need.

This 1-2-3 approach will help you save money, as you may be able to work through the problem yourselves. If the advice of a counselor *is* needed, get good recommendations, check his/her qualifications, and let your initial visit be a trial to see how comfortable you feel. You have taken the first step in realizing your need for help, but you need to be able to trust the help you're receiving.

YFC Editors

ment in itself often provides the impetus necessary to overcome emotional blocks and blind spots.

But what if one partner wants to go for counseling and the other doesn't? The therapists I interviewed said that this is usually not as big a problem as it seems. Sometimes the unwilling spouse is afraid that the other wants to go to a counselor in order to get someone else on his or her side. Or it may be that the unwilling partner is afraid that going for counseling is an admission of failure. It often helps if the spouse who wants to go addresses these fears and makes it clear that he or she is primarily interested in strengthening the marriage, not in placing blame.

If resistance to counseling continues, it may be good to set a goal for certain changes. The couple agrees that they will both go for counseling if there is no evidence of these changes within, for instance, six weeks.

As a last resort, the willing partner may decide to go alone. All three of the therapists said that the counselor may then decide to call the unwilling spouse to alleviate any fears and encourage him or her to come. One counselor said that in her experience, only one spouse in hundreds ultimately refuses to come.

According to these counselors, there is indeed hope for couples in crisis. They have seen marriage after marriage healed when the couple is willing to work hard, to face reality honestly, to pray earnestly, and to believe that God will in fact restore their love relationship.

Related Articles
Chapter 10: The Cause of Severe Marital Conflict
Chapter 16: All

When to Go for Counseling

GARY D. BENNETT

When should you seek professional help for marital or individual problems? These can all indicate the need for professional help:

☐ Having trouble concentrating
☐ Acting anxious
☐ Becoming tearful without apparent cause
☐ Lashing out at your spouse
☐ Unresolved tension
☐ A sense of hopelessness in your marriage
☐ A feeling of shame, fear, guilt, or anger
☐ Long periods of non-communication between each other
☐ A poor sex life or none at all

Or you might wish to seek professional help simply because you desire to experience more joy in your marriage.

It is important to get the help when you need it. It's a sign of strength to seek out such aid when you reach the limits of your own understanding and coping. Often a few counseling sessions will be all that is needed. Of course, it's always best if you and your spouse agree to go together for counseling.

How do you encourage your spouse to take advantage of counseling?

1. Discuss with your spouse your concerns and try to agree that a problem exists. Encourage your spouse to go with you to a professional counselor, at least to find out what help may be available.

2. Convey the attitude that seeking help and using appropriate services are

signs of maturity.

3. Help your spouse understand that seeking help doesn't mean that either one of you is sick or crazy, or that your marriage has failed. It's simply recognizing the need for some temporary assistance from a qualified professional.

4. Point out that going to a counselor will not give the counselor control over your life, and that each of you will retain the right to continue or discontinue using the counselor's services.

5. Share the responsibility for making and keeping appointments. Marital problems are already shared; therefore steps to resolve them should also be shared.

6. If your spouse refuses to participate or quits after starting, continue going with your spouse's knowledge of when each appointment is to occur. This will enable your spouse to join you should there be a change of heart, and it will underscore your own sincerity about making changes and improving your relationship. If your spouse never goes with you, you will at least learn how to cope and adjust in your marriage, making the best of your circumstances.

7. Be honest. One fact is absolutely certain: unless you are honest, no one can effectively help you. If you truly want to improve your marriage relationship, you must be honest with each other, with the counselor, and with God.

As you go to the counselor, keep in mind that your willingness to acknowledge your problem is the first step in solving it and improving your marriage. Constructive change and growth always include a certain amount of discomfort and risk. With God's help, what could be a better investment of time and energy than your own marriage? He desires nothing less for you and your spouse than to experience ultimate joy and blessing in your marital relationship!

WHAT A PASTOR WILL—OR WON'T—DO

When Christians want help with their marriages, most go first to their pastors. What can you realistically expect from a minister?

A listening ear. A minister will listen to your problem and then either counsel you directly or refer you to a professional counselor. He will not spill your secrets!

Spiritual help. A pastor is uniquely equipped to see the spiritual implications of your problem. He can pray with you, offer you biblical counsel, recommend helpful books and seminars, and introduce you to support groups in your church.

Ministers have many responsibilities, however, and cannot be expected to be equally competent in all areas. Unless your pastor is a trained counselor, *don't expect* long-term counseling. *Don't expect* an instant solution. *Don't expect* major psychiatric help. *Don't expect* his support for positions that go against the church's teachings.

YFC Editors

Related Articles

What Is It Like to Go to a Counselor?

ALICE FRYLING

One hurdle a couple faces when they consider counseling is fear of the unknown. What will it be like to go to a counselor? What if I don't like him or her? What if he or she doesn't like me? Won't it be embarrassing to let someone see the problems in our marriage?

In an effort to speak to some of these fears, I asked a couple who has gone for counseling what it was like. I asked them to risk this exposure because I think their experiences will encourage others to follow suit. As it happened, their first attempt to find a good counselor failed. So we see in their story not only the fruits of successful counseling, but also some warning signs of an unsuccessful counseling relationship.

This is the story of Jim and Marge O'Connor (not their real names), told from Jim's point of view:

"All our married years we have been involved in Christian leadership. I am in full-time ministry, and Marge speaks to women's groups and counsels young people. Over the years God has used us to help friends grow spiritually and emotionally. This made it especially painful when we reached a tragic impasse in our own marriage. We seemed to be able to help others, but we could not heal our own relationship.

"This crisis was more difficult than others we had faced because it involved an issue that was very important to both of us. We both had very strong opinions about it. Unfortunately, they weren't the same. Marge could not understand my point of view, and I could not appreciate hers.

"Looking back, we can see that we were dealing with the problem using poor patterns of communication that had been incubating in our marriage for years. At the time we didn't know we had serious communication difficulties. We just couldn't resolve the problem at hand.

"We struggled for months. At first we struggled alone. Then we shared our problem with a few friends. Finally, as we saw the impasse destroying our marriage, we decided we needed professional help. We decided to call a counselor. I'm glad we didn't know at the time that our first attempt to find help would fail.

"I called a counselor recommended by a friend. I went to the first appointment alone. (Now we see that this in itself may have been a mistake.) I went with some apprehension, but also with hope for a breakthrough that would save our marriage. The first interview was spent getting acquainted and laying out the issues. There was nothing to be particularly excited or nervous about.

"When Marge went for her first appointment, her response was more specific. She went with two fears: she was afraid the counselor would not validate her point of view, which he didn't; and she was afraid he would take sides, which he did. She told a friend later, 'When I shared my side of the issue, in tears, I had absolutely no sense that he had any feelings or was hearing me in any sympathetic or empathetic way. He either didn't understand or didn't believe what I was saying. I had the feeling he had already taken sides . . . Jim's. So in-

501

stead of opening up, all my doors and windows closed.'

"From this ominous beginning, things went from bad to worse. Marge and I felt that, even though our counselor was a psychiatrist, he was spiritualizing complex issues and giving simplistic answers. He gave very little feedback and no suggestions for how we could work on the problem between sessions. We began to feel we would be in counseling forever.

"That was when we decided this was not what counseling should be. On the advice of another friend we went to see David Stevens (not his real name), another trained counselor and pastor.

"Our second attempt at counseling was as different from our first attempt as night and day. We went together to the first session. Dr. Stevens listened to us carefully and was able to identify several important issues the first time. He gave us a 20-page survey to work on for the next session. Even though the questions involved familiar biographical data, just working through them was a helpful exercise. Dr. Stevens was able to see and appreciate the strengths and weaknesses of both our points of view. Through his eyes, we were able to see some of our own weaknesses and some of the other's strengths.

"At first it was very hard to have to deal with each issue. (There was more involved, of course, than the immediate problem at hand.) Although we liked David, we didn't like the realities of the problems he was identifying. I didn't always like to do the assignments he gave us. It was not easy to make changes in the way we related to each other.

"But the results were worth going through the pain of a good counseling experience. They were even worth persevering through a bad counseling experience. Our marriage is stronger than ever. In the months since our counseling, we have referred at least 20 individuals to the same counselor. God has used the experience to enrich our own lives and to expand our abilities to help others. We have found that God 'comforts us in all our troubles, so that we can comfort those in any trouble with

---

FINDING A COUNSELOR

Many couples would like to see a counselor, but they have no idea where to turn. Here are some people you can ask for help in finding a counselor:

1. *Friends.* Some of your friends at church, work, or in the community may have gone to counselors at one time or another. If you are comfortable confiding in them, they may have excellent suggestions.

2. *Your pastor.* Some pastors are willing and able to counsel; others are not. Almost all, however, are happy to refer couples to Christian counselors who are competent and caring.

3. *The local ministerial association.* Many churches have counseling ministries. Call the ministerial association or the office of a larger church in your community to learn who does counseling in your community.

4. *Other religious organizations.* Try a parachurch organization—Youth for Christ, Young Life—or a Christian educational institution for recommendations.

5. *Your doctor.* Family physicians often work alongside family therapists.

6. *A public agency.* The county health department or family service agency can provide lists of licensed counselors.

YFC Editors

the comfort we ourselves have received from God' (2 Cor. 1:4)."

I rejoiced with Jim and Marge in their good counseling experience, but I wanted to know more. I asked them to be specific about how it was helpful. "What things did you learn," I asked, "that you couldn't have learned on your own?" Jim identified five things:

"1. Our counselor painted a picture of our marriage that we couldn't see ourselves. He helped us see the stark reality of what was happening. He identified how our behavior was affecting each other. He pointed out the consequences of negative behavior. He reinforced the need for us to make changes in our relationship.

"2. Our counselor exposed the clichés and pat responses we were giving each other. He would ask, 'Jim, do you really mean that?' And he would ask, 'Marge, what did you just hear Jim saying?'

"3. He encouraged us to make a distinction between fact and feeling. We could readily identify what we thought were the facts of the issues. He pushed us to identify how we felt about those facts. Sometimes the feelings gave us more helpful information than the facts.

"4. He gave us concrete homework. One time he had me keep a notebook with me at all times and write down every time I felt something. Since I wasn't used to listening to my feelings, this felt awkward, but it proved very helpful.

"5. He held us accountable. He would remind us that the next time we got together, he expected us to have worked on the issues we had discussed. This helped motivate us, and it helped us see our progress."

Jim's final reflections on their coun-

EXCUSES, EXCUSES!

People make all kinds of excuses to avoid going to a counselor. Here are a few:

- ☐ "We don't have a problem."
- ☐ "Counseling is only for nuts."
- ☐ "My spouse won't go."
- ☐ "My spouse won't let me go."
- ☐ "I can't afford it."
- ☐ "I don't have the time."
- ☐ "I don't know where to go."
- ☐ "My friend went to a counselor and got a divorce."
- ☐ "There's nothing wrong with me."
- ☐ "I don't want someone pointing out my faults."

"Nothing will help anyway." Most of these excuses boil down to *fear*—of the unknown, of change, of failure. Don't let fear stand between you and a happy marriage!

YFC Editors

seling experience concerned its lasting benefits. "We can look back and say that we aren't where we were. We have more hope. Now that we have resolved one difficult problem, we believe we will be able to do it again. We have a sense that we have changed, that we have made progress. We have renewed confidence in ourselves, in our Lord, and in the institution of marriage."

Related Articles
Chapter 9: Making Your Communication Work
Chapter 16: Making the Most of Counseling

Making the Most of Counseling

ALICE FRYLING

The Christian life is a process. We are not now what we shall be. Sometimes this is frustrating. Paul said, "When I want to do good, evil is right there with me" (Rom. 7:21). For many Christian individuals and married couples the tension between "what I am" and "what I want to be" is a source of almost unbearable tension.

Paul cried out, "What a wretched man I am! Who will rescue me from this body of death?" (Rom. 7:24) His answer is, of course, Jesus Christ. But it is not a coincidence that just a few chapters later, Paul describes the many parts of the body of Christ (Rom. 12:6-8). Our deliverance from pain and failure may come not only through solitary communion with Jesus, but also through the gifts He has given to those who make up His body.

I have had the privilege of seeing many, many individuals and couples grow in their faith, find health in their relationships, and reap new joy in their daily lives as they have benefited from the gifts God has given to those who are professional counselors. A good Christian counselor may have the gift of teaching and be able to teach a young client to apply her faith to her emotional needs. Or a counselor may have the gift of admonition, encouraging a client to live according to his beliefs rather than accommodating to the patterns of this world. Or perhaps it is the gift of love that the counselor gives the client. We are all to be loving, but many of us live in environments where love is withheld. A counselor may provide the loving environment a client needs to find emotional healing and spiritual health.

God's good gifts to His people may be given through non-Christian as well as Christian counselors. "Every good and perfect gift is from above" (James 1:17). Just as a non-Christian doctor can be used by the Creator to facilitate physical healing, so God may use a non-Christian counselor to facilitate emotional healing.

But how does a Christian find a good counselor? Certainly not all counselors, Christian or not, are equally helpful. If a married couple decides to look for help, it becomes even more complicated because both husband and wife must respect and get along with the counselor. How can they find someone who will be helpful? What can they do, furthermore, to help the counselor help them? In short, how can a couple in crisis make the most of the counseling experience?

The place to begin looking for a good counselor is with the recommendation of a friend, a pastor, a doctor, or someone you respect and trust. Board certification is one thing to look for, but word of mouth is probably one of the best recommendations a counselor can have.

After you have a name, either through a personal recommendation or from the yellow pages in the phone book, plan to speak with the prospective therapist on the phone before the first appointment. Even a phone conversation will give you a hint as to whether or not you can relate well with him. Ask about his professional certification. Ask what approach he uses. Ask what he believes about marriage. Ask how much experience he has had in counseling. Ask how his spiritual values influence his counseling.

Even after interviewing a counselor by phone, you may find after a session or two of counseling that you just do not fit in with his style of counseling. In that case, have the courage to terminate the relationship and try again with someone else. You are not a failure if you do not like your counselor. The counseling relationship is so unique and so personal that it is very important that both husband and wife feel free and comfortable.

Once you find a counselor you trust and respect, you and your spouse can do several things to help make the counseling sessions more effective:

1. Be as open and honest as possible about where you are emotionally. Sometimes it takes a while to build trust, but as soon as possible let the counselor know what you are experiencing. ("I feel hopeless." "I am having an affair." "I have a drug problem." "I wish I were dead.") The counselor's effectiveness is directly related to your openness.

2. Be willing to experiment with new "ways of being" in the relationship. The purpose of counseling is to bring about changes that will heal the relationship. Be willing to change.

3. Be willing to do the assignments the therapist suggests.

4. Stop pointing at your spouse and start asking, "What do I do to contribute to our problems?"

5. Give honest feedback to the therapist if the counseling is not working.

6. Pray before each session and have a friend pray for you regularly while you are in counseling.

Marriage is not always easy. Growing close in human relationships is a difficult process. Counselors do not provide magical solutions to marital problems. Like a medical doctor, the counselor looks at symptoms and tries to provide the best remedy for the problem. But healing comes from the work of the Creator within us. Our job is to take advantage of every gift He has given us for

CHECKING OUT A COUNSELOR

When you go to a counselor, remember that he or she is working for you. You have the right to hire a counselor who is likely to meet your needs.

Here are some questions you may want to ask a prospective counselor when you are deciding whether to use his or her services, especially if you do not know people who have gone to this person:

1. What kind of counselor is he or she? Psychiatrist? Psychologist? Social worker? Pastor? What does this mean about his or her approach to counseling?

2. What professional degree does he or she hold?

3. What kind of license does he or she hold? (Remember that not all states require licenses; not all licenses are meaningful.)

4. What is this counselor's fee? What percentage will your insurance cover?

5. Can this counselor provide you with references?

6. How does this counselor relate to Christian counselees? If the counselor is not a Christian, will he or she respect your beliefs? If the counselor is a Christian, does he or she integrate beliefs with counseling?

YFC Editors

facilitating this healing and to pray that He will restore us.

Related Article
Chapter 16: What Is It Like to Go to a Counselor?

If Your Marriage Is Shaky and Your Spouse Doesn't Want Help

GARY D. CHAPMAN

This article is dedicated to those individuals who have asked their spouses to talk with the pastor, go for counseling, attend a seminar, read a book, or take some other avenue of marital growth, and the spouse has refused. Where do you go from there?

Let's acknowledge from the very first that you cannot force your spouse to do anything. You cannot change your spouse. You say, "I know that, but I want him/her to change himself/herself." Such a statement is based on the assumption that the real problem in this relationship is with the behavior of the spouse. If the spouse would change, then the marriage would improve.

Let me ask, "What do you want your spouse to change?" Here are typical answers given by wives:

- [ ] I want him to spend more time with me.
- [ ] I wish he would be more considerate of my needs.
- [ ] I wish he would help me more around the house.
- [ ] I wish he would get a steady job.
- [ ] I wish he would be more romantic.

The husband typically responds:

- [ ] I wish she would be more responsive sexually.
- [ ] I wish she would give me some attention instead of spending all her time with the children.
- [ ] I wish she would recognize I have needs too.
- [ ] I wish she would not complain about the money.

Jesus indicated that this is the wrong way to try to improve a marriage relationship. Listen to this paraphrase of His words: "Judge not, that you be not judged. Why do you concentrate on the speck that is in your husband's eye, but do not notice the beam in your own eye? Or how can you say to your wife, 'Let me pull the speck out of your eye,' and do not observe that there is a beam in your own eye? You hypocrite, first cast the beam out of your own eye, and then you can see clearly to cast the speck out of your mate's eye" (based on Matt. 7:1-5).

Notice carefully: Jesus did not say, "There is nothing wrong with your spouse." In fact, He indicates that there is a problem—the speck. Your spouse is not perfect. He or she needs to change, but that is not the place to begin.

It is amazing what can happen when you apply Jesus' words to your marriage. The question to ask is this: "Lord, what is wrong with me? Where am I failing my spouse? What am I doing and saying that I should not? What am I failing to do and say that I should? In what way am I failing to meet his or her needs? In what way am I failing to express love (both romantic and tough)? If you can discern the beam in your own eye and remove it, then you will be far more productive in helping your spouse deal with his or her failures.

Find a quiet place and ask God to show you where you are failing your spouse. You may find it helpful to use David's prayer recorded in Psalm 139:23-24: "Search me, O God, and know my heart; test me and know my anxious thoughts. See if there is any of-

506

fensive way in me, and lead me in the way everlasting." Make a list of the things that God brings to mind. Then one by one confess these things to God and accept His forgiveness. Now ask God to fill you with His Holy Spirit and let you be His channel for expressing His love to your spouse.

Some evening when your spouse seems to be in a calm mood, ask for a few minutes to share something with him or her. Tell your spouse what you have done, and read the list of things God brought to your mind. Let your spouse know that you know these are not *all* your failures, but these are the ones that come to your mind. Tell him or her that you want to ask forgiveness. Tell him or her that you genuinely want to become a better wife or husband and that once a week for the next few months, you would like to ask for a suggestion as to how you can improve: something you can stop doing or saying or start doing or saying that will make you a better spouse.

Over the next several months, follow through by asking, "What suggestion do you have for me this week?" Seek to change in order to please your spouse. Ask God to transform you and make you the best possible spouse for your husband or wife.

Establish a daily quiet time with God in which you read a chapter from the Bible, marking at least one idea and talking to God about it. Philippians is a good book to begin with; then read some other New Testament books. Proverbs is also an excellent book to read for suggestions on living a positive life.

I emphasize your relationship with God because you will soon tire of this approach to marital growth unless you have His help. By nature, all of us love when we are loved. If our spouses express love, kindness, thoughtfulness, and tenderness, we feel warmly toward them even without God's help. But if

they are cold, rejecting, hateful, and harsh, we need supernatural power to keep on loving. God has this love and has been expressing it through the years (Rom. 5:8). He will keep pouring it into your heart (Rom. 5:5) and let you be His representative for loving your spouse.

After several months of this approach, if your spouse does not begin to open up and discuss the marriage and reach out for help, you may want to ask, "George, how do you think I'm doing as a wife?" If he responds positively, express appreciation and affirm that you are serious in your commitment to growth. Tell him you hope he will continue to see the difference.

Then say, "You know what would make me happy?" Give him one suggestion that you would like him to follow. Make your request specific and simple. Chances are good he will do it. If so, express appreciation and let him know how much it means to you. If not, don't give up. Go on with your new approach and ask again in a few weeks.

I cannot guarantee that your spouse will reciprocate and return your love in a few weeks, but I can guarantee that this is the best approach, because it is based on Jesus' words. It is far more likely to be productive than your efforts at pressuring your spouse to change. In the process of changing yourself, you become a more mature Christian and will be able to go on living with God no matter what happens in your marriage. If your spouse leaves, he or she will be foolish. Why would anyone want to leave a spouse dedicated to meeting his or her needs? Such a spouse is hard to find.

As I give this advice, I am fully aware that some will read it who have alcoholic or abusive mates. Others have spouses who are involved in immoral extramarital affairs. It is possible that your mate's behavior is not related to your failures.

The steps I have outlined here are not the only steps in such cases, but I believe they are the beginning steps. If, after you have taken these steps, your mate continues in irresponsible behavior, there is a time to follow our Lord's example when He said to Israel, "O Jerusalem, Jerusalem, thou that killest the prophets, and stonest them which are sent unto thee, how often would I have gathered thy children together, even as a hen gathereth her chickens under her wings, and ye would not! Behold, your house is left unto you desolate" (Matt. 23:37-38, KJV).

Genuine love does not allow irresponsible behavior to continue without results. You might say to your spouse, "I love you too much to sit by while you destroy yourself and me. I cannot believe that is the loving thing for me to do. Therefore, I will leave you to your choices. Unless you choose to change your behavior and work on our marriage, I must leave."

Such an approach should always be done with a therapeutic motive. Your action is designed to stimulate positive action in your spouse. At the same time, you must be ready to face the fact that your spouse may refuse to change. You must then be prepared to follow through with this tough-love approach. I suggest that you seek pastoral and legal counsel before taking such a step.

Related Articles

Helping a Friend Who Is Having Marital Trouble

JIM & SALLY CONWAY

You pick up the phone as it rings. A friend is calling. You sense almost immediately that something is wrong. Your friend seems to want to talk but is embarrassed. You feel you were called because your help was wanted, but it is hard for your friend to reach out and tell you what is wrong.

Eventually you learn there is marital trouble, and there's been a terrible fight. Maybe your friend's mate has left or is having an affair. The question is this—*how can you help?*

1. *Make contact with your friend in crisis.* It's better if you can be face to face. Let your friend know you're really there by focusing your whole attention on him or her. You should face your friend, sit close, and look into his or her face. In those early minutes, reach out and touch your friend's hand or, better yet, give a hug. Focusing on your friend shows that you are there to listen and that you really care.

2. *Focus on your friend, not just on the problem.* Yes, there is a problem. Let's assume your friend's mate has just demanded a divorce. Carefully separate, in your mind, your friend's feelings, struggles, and needs from the divorce problem. Your first focus must be on your friend. In a sense, you're ignoring the divorce problem and concentrating on stabilizing your friend.

3. *Listen.* Your primary reason for listening is not to gather information about the problem but to listen to the person. As the feelings spill out, you'll also pick up information about the problem. But analyzing the problem is not your pri-

mary goal at this stage.

Listening that is helpful will not be judgmental or critical. It is not teaching. It is not exhortation. Most of all, helpful listening is not conversational. Think of yourself as an empty bucket. You are sitting there while your friend pours all his or her feelings into you. Remember, the bucket doesn't respond with Bible verses or great insights. At this stage of helping your friend, you are only listening.

You may need to assist your friend to continue. When your friend stops talking, just sit quietly, reach out, and gently touch him or her. Sometimes people need silence to think through what they want to say or to comprehend what's happening to them. Don't be afraid of silence.

It might also be helpful to take the last idea your friend spoke and rephrase it in the form of a question. For example, your friend may say, "John says we never should have gotten married." You wait a few moments and then quietly you ask, "John feels your marriage was a mistake from the beginning?" A question allows your friend to continue talking.

Remember that the purpose of your listening is to drain off your friend's emotions—to help get the feelings out in the open. It also gives you an opportunity to join in the hurt and to bear the problem with your friend, as we're taught in Galatians 6:2: "Carry each other's burdens, and in this way you will fulfill the law of Christ." Remember that helpful listening is hard work.

4. *Express empathy as you listen.* Empathy comes from two Greek words which mean "to feel with." Empathy is sensing someone else's feelings. You see the situation through your friend's eyes. That doesn't mean you lose your perspective, get depressed, feel anxious, and end up in a crisis too. You, however, are able for a little while to walk in your friend's shoes and feel his or her feelings.

Expressing empathy can be done in many ways, such as by being present with that person, listening, and showing care with your eyes, face, and gentle touch. Empathy means modeling the type of understanding Jesus had for people. Hebrews 4:15 teaches that He is touched with the feelings of our weakness.

5. *Help your friend focus on the problem.* Remember not to push your friend to focus on the problem before you have really ministered to him or her through listening carefully and expressing empathy. You will know when your friend is ready to concentrate on the problem, because a sense of peace will come to him or her. The peace is not because the problem is settled, but from knowing you care and are going to be with him or her through the process to the solution. When that sense of calm comes, you are ready to talk about the problem.

It's important that your friend own his or her problem and the solution. Therefore, be very careful not to give any direct advice. Always ask, "What do you think?" "What are your opinions?" "What are your feelings about this problem?" You are focusing your friend's thinking and feelings on his or her problem. Remember, if you do this too early, your friend will think that you are only problem oriented and that you don't care about him or her as a person.

As your friend begins to talk about the problem, listen for a sense of ownership. For example, if you're trying to help a woman whose husband has just left, in the earlier stages she may deny that it has happened. She may think it's all just a bad dream. She may say her husband is going to change his mind and come back. She may project blame on several different people. As long as she projects blame or denies it has happened, she has not owned the problem.

If there is such projection or denial,

you must continue to listen. Help your friend to speak about the bitter, angry feelings. A time will come when she will finally say or imply, "Well, I guess he really wants to leave—so what am I going to do about it?" Now she has owned the problem. You are ready to help with some answers.

6. *Work on solutions.* Say to your friend, "Let's talk about some of your options. If you could do anything you wanted to do, what would you do? Let's list every possible choice." Your role now is to help your friend get a broad perspective on every possibility.

After you identify all the possible solutions, ask him or her to tell you about each one. "What do you think?" More important, "How do you *feel* about each option?" You are encouraging your friend not only to own the problem but also to own any solutions that will come.

7. *Help your friend think through resources.* Resources can be friends, acquaintances, or skills and abilities. Resources are also within your friend, such as the quality of person he or she is. Resources are found in Scripture, in fellowship with a group of believers, and in knowing God in a personal way. Help your friend think through and list the resources he or she might use.

8. *Set the plan into action.* Help your friend decide on a timetable as well as accountability and responsibility. In other words, who will do what, and when? Which things will be done first, second, and so on? What is the projected date when they will be accomplished?

Helping a friend who is having marital trouble is a large undertaking. But if you do it carefully, not only do you help your friend through this time, but you also may teach your friend how to work

---

THE BEST COUNSELOR FOR YOU

When all is said and done, a most important question is this: *Are you and your spouse comfortable with your counselor?* If you are not, you will resist the kind of help he or she has to offer. If you are, you will look forward to your meetings and will be more likely to follow his or her suggestions.

Remember that in a counseling relationship, you are looking for solutions. You are hiring someone to help you with your needs. If the person makes you uncomfortable, you have no obligation to continue hiring him or her. Analyze your discomfort. Talk it over with your spouse and with the counselor. Then, if necessary, look for a counselor who is more effective or more suited to your particular situation and needs.

YFC Editors

---

through future problems. Now your friend can help someone else.

When burdens are shared between friends, the total load is miraculously lightened. Reach out with both hands— one to God for strength and perspective, the other to your hurting friend who needs your love.

Related Articles

How Friends Can Help

WESLEY & ELAINE WILLIS

It is unfortunate that many families feel that they need to be entirely self-sufficient. True, parents have a responsibility to minister to each other and to their children. But Christians also bear other responsibilities. Jesus taught that we are to be salt and light in the world (Matt. 5:13-14). Paul instructed us to bear one another's burdens (Gal. 6:2). And John reminded us that we are to love each other; if we don't do that, it's an indication that we really do not love God (1 John 3:13-17).

When Mom and Dad foster an "island" mentality, a burden is placed upon family members that they cannot bear. Such an attitude is also selfish. Someone has said, "A family wrapped up in itself makes a very small package."

God has put others in the body of Christ to encourage and support us. Naturally when others are not available, God can meet personal and family needs other ways. But generally He chooses to meet needs through people with whom we have meaningful contact. Consider some of the ways friends can help. They can:

1. *Minister directly.* Some of our sons' best Sunday School teachers are our close personal friends. They see our boys in Sunday School, at informal family gatherings, at school activities, and in various other places around town. These good friends know our sons and what they do. They know their personal interests, skills, and abilities. And when they minister, it is with personal concern and interest.

Husbands and wives also receive direct ministry from friends. The nature of the body of Christ is such that each believer should be using ministry gifts to build up and encourage others—whether by teaching, leading home study groups, showing hospitality, praying, or through some other ministry.

2. *Counsel supportively.* Dr. Gary Collins, professional counselor and professor at Trinity Evangelical Divinity School, has observed that the best counseling is often done by friends and acquaintances. Excellent counsel comes from people who are not trained counselors but who are good listeners. We all benefit from concerned friends who will listen and lovingly encourage us. When we have problems, we should share with our friends and receive help from them.

Support also may take the form of suggestions or advice to your children. It may come when the children ask family friends for help, or perhaps friends just happen to be nearby at a teachable moment. When a friend—an interested adult who shares common values—makes suggestions to your children, that person reinforces your beliefs.

All of us have experienced the gap between what we should do and what we feel like doing. Cultivating a group of trusted friends who can encourage us and keep us accountable is a great resource to our spiritual maturity.

3. *Share common activities.* An increasing problem in our society is the amount of time we spend vegetating in front of the TV. But it doesn't have to be that way. We should plan specific times with friends when we don't watch TV but instead share other activities.

We, for example, have friends who get together regularly for game nights. Another couple is in a book discussion

511

group. The group selects a book to read individually; then they periodically meet to discuss its contents and implications. Some friends exercise or play sports together regularly. We are members of a fellowship/caring group which meets for Bible study, prayer, sharing, and occasional social events. We find that this relationship extends beyond planned times together. When any of us faces personal or family problems, it is to this group that we turn for support.

4. *Serve as good examples.* Husbands and wives, along with their children, need to see the Christian life modeled by others. We should build friendships with those who model the positive qualities we admire. And through our interaction, we also will become models for our friends. None of us is equally strong in all areas of character and service. But through meaningful friendships, weaknesses can be minimized and strengths maximized.

Though some have implied that the mature Christian family should be self-sufficient, this contradicts experience. We all need each other. And when we provide mutual support and encouragement, we are much stronger individually. Together we can glorify God more consistently. "Though one may be overpowered, two can defend themselves. A cord of three strands is not quickly broken" (Ecc. 4:12).

Related Articles
Chapter 11: What Friends Contribute to Your Marriage
Chapter 16: Helping a Friend Who Is Having Marital Trouble

THE CHURCH AS A SOURCE OF HELP

A variety of organizations are ready to help you with your marriage problems. Each has its unique emphasis, but only one "agency" in existence today is capable of meeting all needs. Only through the resources of the church of Jesus Christ can your social, mental, physical, and spiritual needs be fully met. Other agencies concentrate on one or two aspects, but the church, the body of Christ, can address all of them.

The church should be your first source of help for your marriage. If your needs are beyond your pastor's expertise, ask him to refer you to an appropriate community agency and to remain involved in a supportive role. There are many Christian psychiatrists, psychologists, social workers, and family therapists who will assist you with your problems from a biblical perspective.

While you are being helped, the church can provide you with a support group—a caring network of believers who will surround you with emotional and prayer support, often without ever having to know the details of your problems.

Gary Bennett

Turning a Marriage Around

DAVID VEERMAN

With proud steeple thrust heavenward, the church had stood for nearly a century, defying the winds of weather and of change. Its worn and discolored stone walls, oak doors, and stained glass windows were remembrances of days gone by and symbols of permanence in an unsteady world. But the congregation had dwindled to a few hardy souls, and the building was sold.

With steady and relentless grind, the crane raised its ball of destruction and then swung it toward the old walls with deadly force. Again and again it pounded, and soon the church was a pile of rubble. What had taken months to build and had stood for decades had been destroyed in a sum of minutes.

That is the way of life. It is always easier to destroy than to build—demolishing a building, smashing a pumpkin, or crushing a can. And relationships are not immune to this process. Consider the progression between a man and a woman. At first they were strangers. Then they met and were acquaintances. They saw each other again and became friends. With interest sparked, they began to date, at first occasionally and then very often. Love was planted, and it grew—they wanted to be together constantly. Then came the question of marriage, the answer "yes," and the wedding. After the honeymoon, they continued the building process—building their marriage and their home. The process took years.

Yes, it takes time to build a solid relationship and marriage, but consider its destruction. A cross word and an explosive response, a sexual liaison, midlife crisis, verbal or physical abuse, alcohol, financial setbacks, tragedy— each or all of these blows crash into the walls and send the partners tumbling. And what had seemed so solid and sure begins to crumble. The good news is that this destructive process can be stopped. The bad news is that it probably will take time. And, to use another analogy, to turn around a speeding car, first it must be slowed or stopped. Then, after the U-turn, the new course can be navigated.

The first step, therefore, in turning around a marriage headed in the wrong direction is to *stop* going that way. It means radically changing the destructive process.

If, for example, trust has been destroyed through adultery, the injured spouse will find it difficult to forgive, let alone forget. After the affair has ended, this healing will take tears, counseling, renewed vows, and a new pattern of love, commitment, and reliability.

If communication has degenerated to an occasional talk about the kids and a breakfast grunt over the morning paper, both partners will have to learn to talk and listen to each other. And they will have to decide to spend time together, just being, caring, and listening.

If both are aware of the malaise, but neither know the reason, they will have to seek help from a qualified counselor, a special seminar, or a marriage weekend.

Whatever the case, don't give up. Your relationship is not beyond repair—God can do anything. And if both you and your spouse want to change, your chances are very good. Here are some possible steps to take:

☐ Decide to change.

- [ ] Pray together about the situation.
- [ ] Identify the problem.
- [ ] Together decide what you want instead.
- [ ] Seek counseling if necessary.
- [ ] Change the destructive patterns.
- [ ] Forgive each other when there are setbacks.
- [ ] Take it one day at a time.
- [ ] Focus on and build on the good and the positive in your relationship.
- [ ] Be patient.

> ## 2 CORINTHIANS 1:3-4
>
> Praise be to the God and Father of our Lord Jesus Christ, the Father of compassion and the God of all comfort, who comforts us in all our troubles, so that we can comfort those in any trouble with the comfort we ourselves have received from God.

Related Articles

Restoring a Broken Marriage

PAT WILLIAMS

When I was growing up, I set a goal for myself to become a major league baseball player. I played through high school and college, then briefly in the pros with the Philadelphia Phillies. But my dreams never fully came true, and I ended up in the administrative end of baseball. When I became a Christian in February 1968, my life abruptly changed. God did not elect to take me out of pro sports, but to change sports—from baseball to basketball. I had just turned 29 when I came to Chicago as general manager of the Chicago Bulls. I poured my life into the work of rebuilding a team that was almost out of business. As a bachelor, I was happily absorbed in my work and pro sports career. Then I met the lovely woman who was to become my wife.

We were married in October, but work never ceased to be my primary concern. The morning of our wedding, my big problem was that the Bulls needed a forward and back-up center, and I made two trades before I walked down the aisle! I think I probably subconsciously gave a sigh of relief at the altar, almost saying, "That's over with now; I've got that area of my life taken care of. I no longer have the social stigma of being single. Now it's time to get on with the important part of life—building the team."

When we came back from our honeymoon, I poured myself into my work. Most men derive their self-esteem from job and career. Work is at the core of men's existence; it dictates how they feel about themselves and how they react to their partners. And this was true for me. I plunged into various jobs, and then came the ultimate challenge—going to Philadelphia in 1974 to the ashes of a team that had won 9 games and lost 73, the worst record in the history of pro sports. We plunged in, and along came some big players and the club began to come together. From 1976 to 1986, the 76ers had the best record in the NBA during the regular season. We began to draw record crowds and won a championship in 1983. But it all took massive amounts of work with night and day absorption.

At this time, our homefront included a couple of small children, and I began to hear some interesting statements from my wife's lips. She would say with increasing frequency, "We don't really talk anymore. And when we do it's always about the kids and the weather. We don't do anything together." I learned how to deal with this—I would rush some flowers home, get the right candy, quickly arrange a dinner out, and so forth. That would temporarily quiet my wife, so I thought everything was under control. But one day everything came rapidly unraveled in a matter of minutes.

After a hectic Sunday morning and a couple of verbal chops from me, my wife said, without emotion or expression, "I hate our marriage. I've hated it for a long time. I'm not going to leave; I will wash the clothes and feed the kids, but I'm giving up." At that moment, my wife died emotionally in front of me. I didn't understand the seriousness of what had happened, but as the days went on, it was really terrifying. This beautiful, vivacious lady whom I dearly loved could not smile, laugh, cry, or even look at me. I tried everything I could to get her back, but it was futile. She had literally died.

My wife is a great book buyer. She often tried to get me to read parts of various books on family and marriage, but I never paid much attention. I suddenly realized that I desperately needed a book that could give me advice on how to help my wife, how to save our marriage. About nine months earlier, Jill had bought a book and left it on my bedside table, front cover down. For nine months it stayed there, untouched. Late one night I was unable to sleep and I reached over and picked up the book.

MARRIAGE MEANS HARD WORK

Christa, an Austrian friend, said to me, "I learned from my parents the clear message that marriage is built on faithfulness. They taught me that living together is hard work. It takes hard work to survive. But they never once thought of an alternative—of leaving each other. Now when I have hard work in my marriage, I think of all the things my parents went through. I'm glad I have their example."

Ingrid Trobisch

The cover said, *Love Life for Every Married Couple—How to Fall in Love, How to Stay in Love, How to Rekindle Your Love.* The book was written by a Christian doctor in Arkansas named Ed Wheat. I started reading, and every page was like water to a parched man in the desert.

Dr. Wheat wrote that God designed every Christian marriage to be the best that the world has ever seen. The fact that a whole lot of them aren't is not God's fault, but our own. He wrote that every marriage needs to apply the BEST formula, and when there are serious problems, this can be especially helpful, even if only one partner wants to save the marriage. Jill was in no state to do anything, so in our case the burden fell on my shoulders. And suddenly, the only thing that mattered to me was our marriage, turning our home into what God wanted it to be. So I learned the BEST applications—the blocks to be used in rebuilding a marriage.

The letter B stands for *blessing.* How do you bless your mate? By speaking well of him or her both publicly and privately, and responding with good words in every situation. It can also mean learning when to be silent. There were many times when I would say that one extra statement that was so unneeded and would mar our relationship for hours.

Another part of blessing includes doing kind things for your spouse. Men, in particular, need to remember to bless by showing thankfulness and appreciation *verbally*. And you bless by praying for your partner's good. It dawned on me that I prayed for missionaries around the world, for Bible studies, for people's salvation—but I was not praying for my wife through her day. I put a little note by my phone that simply says, "Have you prayed for Jill today?"

Dr. Wheat stressed that I should do these kind things without expecting a response. He was right—I didn't get any response from Jill at first. It took a while for her to trust me, and through all of this, she was emotionless and unresponsive.

The next building block is the letter E, for *edifying,* which means "to build up." In our marriage, Jill needed verbal praise and compliments from me. I've heard it said that there's only one way to compliment your wife, and that is *frequently.* A little cut here and a little dig there, and you've torn down your spouse instead of building him or her up. Women suffer from lack of self-esteem more than men. In one study, 50 percent of the women selected low self-esteem as their number-one problem; 80 percent of them ranked it in the top five of all their problems.

I encourage men to remember that their wives may get all kinds of self-esteem from their church groups, workplaces, or friends, but if they don't get it from their husbands every day in the home, they feel empty. My wife needed edification from me if we were going to have the kind of marriage God wanted us to have.

The third building block, the letter S, is *sharing.* Sharing your time and activities, sharing interests and concerns, sharing ideas and innermost thoughts, sharing your spiritual walk, sharing family objectives, sharing goals and dreams, sharing hobbies, in short, sharing your lives. It's really giving of yourself, listening to your mate, developing a sensitive awareness between you. I'm convinced that sharing is the glue that holds people together in a marriage. I realized, in the crisis point of our marriage, that I had better learn to share with my wife.

The final building block is vital. Dr. Wheat says that no matter how accomplished you become at blessing and edifying and sharing, these really don't matter unless you become highly skilled in the letter T. When I read this, I almost dropped the book. T stands for *touching.* A tender touch tells us that we are cared for. It calms fear; it soothes pain; it brings comfort; it gives emotional security. This physical contact is essential.

There are three accepted ways in our society for men to touch. One is the handshake; two is contact sports; three is sex. But the most important area is not promoted at all—nonsexual touching. Jill longed for me just to hold her hand, and she loved when I did it in public. I had a difficult time with that (it probably goes back to my high school days where the football team would tease mercilessly if I was seen holding hands with a girl!). I realized that, in this area, I had my work cut out for me. But I started to do it.

I can report to you authoritatively that in the next few months, Jill became the most blessed, edified, shared with, and nonsexually touched woman in America. I wish I could report to you that in a matter of days the whole situation was resolved, but it wasn't. It took months for Jill to trust me, commit herself, and respond. It was a struggle, but it was worth it because, as the months went on, I suddenly realized I was very much in love with my wife. I got on the phone and called Dr. Wheat to thank him for his book and to ask him if the intense love for my wife, the almost teenage hysteria I felt for her, would end. He told me that if we continued to apply the BEST principles, which are biblical principles, every day of our lives, the intense romantic feeling would increase and intensify for the rest of our marriage. And he was right!

God wants to take our marriages and make them the best the world has seen. As we apply His principles of blessing, edifying, sharing, and touching in our relationships, and especially in marriage, He can rebuild a broken marriage, or make a good marriage the best it can be.

Related Articles
Chapter 15: Bringing Love Back to Life
Chapter 16: Turning a Marriage Around

Making Your Dreams Come True

DALE HANSON BOURKE

A few years ago my friend Ann and her husband Chuck moved into a "handyman's special" house that looked as if it were on the verge of being condemned. The first time I visited Ann I was horrified by the condition of the house; I wondered how anyone could make it habitable. Six years later, the house is truly breathtaking.

How did Ann and Chuck do it? Their house wasn't transformed overnight. It took hard work, determination—and planning. They set their sights on a goal, took time to understand the costs, and then went after it. And they achieved what most people would have thought impossible.

Marriages, like houses, sometimes need work. Some need only a facelift—a little paint here, a little plaster there. Others need complete restoration from the foundation up. Whatever the shape of your marriage now, you and your spouse, working together, can turn it into the kind of marriage you've always dreamed of. To do this, you need a plan.

A plan is a way of taking those dreams that have become goals and turning them into accomplishments. A plan gives you a road map to trace, an agenda to follow, an instruction manual to implement. It's what keeps you going when you want to give up and what keeps you on track when you're tempted to go a different direction. A plan puts dreams into action.

Whatever your marriage goals—improved communication, better sex, a shared spiritual life—you can follow this method of organizing your thinking and directing your energies:

1. *Establish your priorities.* Unless you're unusually gifted and disciplined, you probably won't be able to concentrate on more than three to five goals at any given time. Look through your goals and prioritize them. Decide together which are the most important ones to pursue; then list them in order on a sheet of paper.

2. *Be specific.* If it's your long-term goal to have a happy marriage, try to envision exactly what you mean by that. Talk to your partner about what you consider the key ingredients in a happy marriage. Look at other marriages and discover what you like and don't like about them. Does a happy marriage

517

mean spending more time together? Going away for romantic weekends each year? Never fighting? If you don't have a clear picture of your target, you will become frustrated.

3. *Brainstorm.* For every goal you establish, there are any number of routes by which to achieve it. By spending time brainstorming about the ways to achieve your goal, you explore the various routes and consider your options. I find it helpful to brainstorm on paper, listing all the possible ways I might achieve a particular goal.

4. *Gather information.* The information-gathering stage is a time to shift through the alternative paths and begin to make decisions about the course you'll want to take. It's a time to research and evaluate options in terms of cost, time, and energy commitment.

5. *Prioritize.* After gathering information, you're ready to list your options in order of priority. If you were improving your house, you might not decide to paint all of the interior, but to start with the most visible room or the room whose paint is in the worst condition. Similarly, you may want to work on your marriage one "room" at a time.

6. *Develop a plan.* For each goal you have decided to pursue, establish a written plan. Take a piece of paper and write down your goal in clear, precise language. Then look at your calendar and decide on an exact date by which you hope to achieve your goal. If this is difficult to determine, you may need to break down your long-term goal into several shorter-term projects, or you may wish to set a date by which you will evaluate your progress toward your goal.

The priorities you listed under step 5 become the backbone of your written plan. List them in order beneath your target date.

7. *Commit yourself.* In order to achieve your goals, you will have to make trade-offs. You may have to miss the football game in order to paint the house, and you will have to find time to build up your marriage. It won't be easy, but your goals are worth the price you have to pay. An excellent way to commit yourself to improving your marriage is to pray about it with your spouse. God can give you the power to realize your dreams and help you be all you can be. By asking Him for the strength to achieve your goals, you are also affirming that you can "do all things through Christ" (see Phil. 4:13).

8. *Reinforce your commitment.* Every morning when you wake up, review your goals and mentally reaffirm them. Write them down on a 3-by-5 card to carry in your purse or briefcase. Whenever you have a minute, while waiting for an appointment or standing in line at the checkout counter, reread your goals and commit yourself to them. Remind yourself of the rewards that lie ahead.

9. *Learn from your failures.* Just because you've committed yourself to a goal doesn't mean you'll never succumb to temptation. But don't let a small setback convince you to abandon your goal altogether. If you offend your spouse or miss an important target date, you don't have to give up the whole project.

Don't condemn yourself for failure. You'll only convince yourself that you will never live up to the goal you've established. Instead, face up to it, remind yourself of what you've done right so far, and put it in perspective: "I have two months to reach my goal, and I can still do it if I go back to my plan and stick with it." Then review your reasons for establishing the goal, and envision yourself succeeding once again.

10. *Reward yourself.* Plan something special for yourself and your spouse when you reach a goal—perhaps a nice dinner out, a short excursion, or a purchase you've both been wanting. Every time you're tempted by a momentary diversion that will slow your progress toward your ultimate goal, concentrate on

the reward—not only the immediate one, but the long-term joy of a consistently strong and loving relationship.

INDEX